Contemporary Authors

Autobiography Series

ISSN 0748-0636

Contemporary Authors

Autobiography Series

Joyce Nakamura
Editor

volume **15**

Gale Research Inc. · DETROIT · LONDON

While every effort has been made to ensure the reliability of the information presented in this publication, Gale Research Inc. does not guarantee the accuracy of the data contained herein. Gale accepts no payment for listing; and inclusion in the publication of any organization, agency, institution, publication, service, or individual does not imply endorsement of the editors or publisher. Errors brought to the attention of the publisher and verified to the satisfaction of the publisher will be corrected in future editions.

This book is printed on acid-free paper that meets the minimum requirements of American National Standard for Information Sciences—Permanence Paper for Printed Library Materials, ANSI Z39.48–1984. ∞™

Copyright © 1992
Gale Research Inc.
835 Penobscot Bldg.
Detroit, MI 48226-4094

Library of Congress Catalog Card Number 84-647879
ISBN 0-8103-5348-2
ISSN-0748-0636

Printed in the United States of America

Published simultaneously in the United Kingdom
by Gale Research International Limited
(An affiliated company of Gale Research Inc.)

Contents

Preface

Each volume in the *Contemporary Authors Autobiography Series (CAAS)* presents an original collection of autobiographical essays written especially for the series by noted writers. *CAAS* has grown out of Gale's long-standing interest in author biography, bibliography, and criticism, as well as its successful publications in those areas, like the *Dictionary of Literary Biography, Contemporary Literary Criticism, Something about the Author,* and particularly the bio-bibliographical series *Contemporary Authors (CA),* to which this Autobiography Series is a companion.

As a result of their ongoing communication with authors in compiling *CA* and other books, Gale editors recognized that these writers frequently had more to say than the format of existing Gale publications could accommodate. Inviting authors to write about themselves at essay-length was an inevitable next step. Added to that was the fact that the collected autobiographies of current writers were virtually nonexistent. *CAAS* serves to fill this significant information gap.

Purpose

CA Autobiography Series is designed to be a meeting place for writers and readers--a place where writers can present themselves, on their own terms, to their audience; and a place where general readers, students of contemporary literature, teachers and librarians, even aspiring writers can become better acquainted with familiar authors and make the first acquaintance of others. Here is an opportunity for writers who may never write a full-length autobiography to let their readers know how they see themselves and their work, what carefully laid plans or turns of luck brought them to this time and place. Even for those authors who have already published full-length autobiographies there is the opportunity in *CAAS* to bring their readers "up to date" or perhaps to take a different approach in the essay format. Singly, the essays in this series can illuminate the reader's understanding of a writer's work; collectively, they are lessons in the creative process and in the discovery of its roots.

CAAS makes no attempt to give a comprehensive overview of authors and their works. That outlook is already well represented in biographies, reviews, and critiques published in a wide variety of sources. Instead, *CAAS* complements that perspective and presents what no other ongoing reference source does: the view of contemporary writers that is shaped by their own choice of materials and their own manner of storytelling.

Scope

Like its parent series, *Contemporary Authors,* the *CA Autobiography Series* sets out to meet the needs and interests of a wide range of readers. Each volume provides about twenty essays by writers in all genres whose work is being read today. We consider it extraordinary that twenty busy authors from throughout the world are able to interrupt their existing writing, teaching, speaking, traveling, and other schedules to converge on a given deadline for any one volume. So it is not always possible that all genres can be equally and uniformly represented from volume to volume, although we strive to include writers working in a variety of categories, including fiction, nonfiction, and poetry. As only a few writers specialize in a single area, the breadth of writings by authors in this volume also encompasses drama, translation, and criticism as well as work for movies, television, radio, newspapers, and journals.

Format

Authors who contribute to *CAAS* are invited to write a "mini-autobiography" of approximately 10,000 words. In order to give the writer's imagination free rein, we suggest no guidelines or pattern for the essay. We only ask that each writer tell his or her story in the manner and to the extent that feels most natural and appropriate. In addition, writers are asked to supply a selection of personal photographs showing themselves at various ages, as well as important people and special moments in their lives. Barring unfortunate circumstances like the loss or destruction of early photographs, our contributors have responded generously, sharing with us some of their most treasured mementoes. The result is a special blend of text and photographs that will intrigue even browsers.

A bibliography appears at the end of each essay, listing the author's book-length works in chronological order of publication. Each entry in the bibliography includes the publication information for the book's first printing in the United States, and if an earlier printing has occurred elsewhere, that information is provided as well. The bibliographies in this volume were compiled by members of the *CAAS* editorial staff from their research and the lists of writings that were provided by many of the authors. Each of the bibliographies was submitted to the author for review.

A cumulative index appears in each volume and cites all the essayists in the series as well as the subjects presented in the essays: personal names, titles of works, geographical names, schools of writing, etc. The index format is designed to make these cumulating references as helpful and easy to use as possible. For every reference that appears *in more than one essay*, the name of the essayist is given before the volume and page number(s). For example, W. H. Auden is mentioned by a number of essayists in the series. The entry in the index allows the user to identify the essay writers by name:

> Auden, W.H.
> Allen **6:**18, 24
> Ashby **6:**36, 39
> Bowles **1:**86
> Burroway **6:**90
> Fuller **10:**120, 123
> Hall **7:**58, 61
> Hazo **11:**148, 150
> Howes **3:**143
> Jennings **5:**110
> etc.

For references that appear *in only one essay*, the volume and page number(s) are given but the name of the essayist is omitted. For example:

> Stieglitz, Alfred **1:**104, 109, 110

CAAS is something more than the sum of its individual essays. At many points the essays touch common ground, and from these intersections emerge new patterns of information and impressions. The index, despite its pedestrian appearance, is an important guide to these interconnections.

Looking Ahead

Each essay in the series has a special character and point of view that sets it apart from its companions. A small sampler of anecdotes and musings from the essays in this volume hint at the unique perspective of these life stories.

Claribel Alegría, explaining her precocious reaction to reading Dostoyevski: "I should also say that I was—am I still?—a scandalous liar and mythmaker. When I was twelve, I got hold of one of Dostoyevski's short novels, *Nietoshka Niezvanova*, which my mother did not want me to read at so early an age. I read it clandestinely, and it impressed me so that I came down with fever. I was Nietoshka, naturally, and with tears in my eyes, I recounted to my classmates how my father got drunk every night and beat my mother. 'How can that be?' they exclaimed. 'Everyone says that Dr. Alegría is such a good man.' 'That's what you think,' I replied. 'At night he becomes a different person.' 'How awful!' they exclaimed, and their eyes filled with tears. I was happy whenever that happened. As a result, my father began losing clients and couldn't understand why until I finally confessed what I'd done and had to go around apologizing to all my classmates. I had only wanted to prove to myself that I was capable of making them feel what I had felt when I read the novel."

Willis Barnstone, stimulated by the imagery of the waters off Greece: "At first daybreak I woke as we were rounding a turbulent Peloponnesos. That turbulence I could see through our water level porthole. I climbed in the half-light to a place on the portside deck, and looked with amazement at the water a few feet below. The color and texture were like no water or liquid I had seen. Its uniqueness made me struggle to find a comparison as a way of identifying it. Only through metaphor, by likeness, by indexing, does the mind leap to the next meaningful perception. Finally, the image made sense. The water was like the inside of a purple grape. It had the pulpy thickness, the soft glow, the sweetness. Its brine must have been only an illusory surface attribute, for under it all the water was grape. Then I realized that others were forced into the same simile. There was the first writer we record in the West, Homer, and he anciently called it the 'wineblue sea.'"

Abelardo B. Delgado, reaffirming his manhood: "Most of what I recall from those twelve years in Mexico is often reinforced by what my mother tells me. Other memories are a bit obscure. I may change them at times to suit me. My mom wanted to have a little girl but had to settle for me. She actually would dress me up as a little girl. This made me very angry. It must have been then when I developed my mean look. My grandmother used to tell me of a time she took me to the molino to grind some corn. Some of the women there began to comment about what a nice-looking little girl I was. She tells me that in anger I raised my skirt and showed all of them my tiny manhood proof. I was a boy regardless of how my mother decided to dress me."

Harrison E. Salisbury, sharing a wistful memory of his father's: "My father told me of going to the Dakotas when he was a boy with his father. In those days the buffalo hunters rode the ranges. The buffalo hides were stacked at the prairie stations of the Great Northern and the Burlington lines like cordwood. Thousands and thousands of them. My father had seen the buffalo on the prairie. There was no sight like it in the world. The great herds stretched to the horizon. They moved slowly over the rich prairie, grazing as they went. And there was no cloud of dust as they passed because the prairie was so rich, so thick, the turf so heavy that the buffalo passed by and did not tear it. Now they were gone. My father was saddened and puzzled by this. 'I don't know how it happened,' he said. But the great herds were gone."

Thomas Savage, characterizing life in a small town: "The Boone name could not overshadow the fact that she'd been born a Johnson, and of this she was reminded over and over when she met her brother on the street. He walked a good deal on the street. She wished he would not so much. She often crossed to the other side, wondering if this maneuver had been noticed, if someone must think her heartless, a woman who would cross over to the other side to avoid a brother. Or she turned her face away to look into the window of the City Drug Company at rubber goods displayed there, articles to correct or alleviate some common physical difficulty. But surely Sid, that was his name, as he passed would have recognized her by her shape, so familiar he was with that, so his not pausing to speak to her as she looked in at the rubber goods meant that he knew she did not wish to acknowledge his presence on the street, and he'd have to take that thought home to his little house with the one bedroom built long ago by one who like Sid despaired of having children or even a guest. A little house close by that of Miss Pegram in a lost part of town where nothing much ever turned out right."

Lloyd Van Brunt, on the bitter lessons learned during childhood days spent in an orphanage: "Speaking of the middle class, its children quickly learn that compliments and flattery grease the wagon wheels of daily life. Working-class children learn insults, the kind that hurt, about one's mother and father, uncles and cousins, or lack of them. At the children's home we clawed at one another's self-esteem until the only way of not feeling bad was to make someone else feel worse, reduce him to bawling. The best candidates were the new and usually younger boys who had not yet formed a skein of hate and contempt to protect their emotional wounds—a newly dead mother, a convict father who never wrote, blood kin that never visited on the last Sunday of the month, 'visiting day.' A normal initiation was for an eight-year-old to be pushed and prodded across the playground by a dozen or so older boys, who would chant insanely over and over, 'Your mother's dead / Your father's a Red / You wet the bed / You little shithead.' Wretched rhyme. Welcome to our world, kid, welcome to our world."

These brief examples only suggest what lies ahead in this volume. The essays will speak differently to different readers; but they are certain to speak best, and most eloquently, for themselves.

Authors Forthcoming in *CAAS*

Bella Akhmadulina
Russian poet, translator, and short-story writer

Mulk Raj Anand
Indian novelist, nonfiction writer, and critic

Ed Bullins
American playwright

Rick De Marinis
American novelist and short-story writer

Paul Engle
American poet and educator

Philip José Farmer
American science-fiction writer

Calvin Forbes
American poet

Charles Gordone
American playwright, actor, and director

Daniel Halpern
American poet and editor

Michael S. Harper
American poet

Wilson Harris
Guyanan novelist, poet, and nonfiction writer

Rolando Hinojosa
Mexican American novelist

John Hollander
American poet

James D. Houston
American fiction and nonfiction writer

Jeanne Wakatsuki Houston
Japanese-American fiction and nonfiction writer

Hugh Kenner
Canadian literary critic of major modern authors

Joanne Kyger
American poet

Walter Laqueur
German-born historian, journalist, and novelist

Seymour Mayne
Canadian poet

Leonard Michaels
American short-story writer, editor, and novelist

Bharati Mukherjee
Canadian novelist and short-story writer

Harry Mark Petrakis
American novelist and screenwriter

Alastair Reid
Scottish poet, essayist, and translator

Ernesto Sábato
Argentinean novelist and essayist

Antonis Samarakis
Greek novelist and short-story writer

James Still
American poet, novelist, and short-story writer

Anne Waldman
American poet

Acknowledgments

We wish to acknowledge our special gratitude to each of the authors in this volume. They all have been most kind and cooperative in contributing not only their talents but their enthusiasm and encouragement to this project.

Grateful acknowledgment is also made to those publishers, photographers, and artists whose works appear with these authors' essays.

Photographs/Art

Russell Banks: p. 44, Marion Ettlinger.

Willis Barnstone: p. 47, Bruce W. Buchanan.

Germaine Brée: p. 127, Linda Weaver.

Elizabeth Brewster: p. 149, Jeff Gammon; p. 150, Perry Studio, courtesy of the National Archives of Canada/PA181520; p. 152, courtesy of the National Archives of Canada/PA181512; p. 155, The Harvey Studios; p. 157, courtesy of the National Archives of Canada/PA181515; p. 158, Mary Pacey, courtesy of the National Archives of Canada/PA181514.

Abelardo B. Delgado: p. 173, Daniel Salazar; p. 173, José Andow.

Sam Hamill: p. 215, © 1988 Fritz Dent

Jim Wayne Miller: p. 288, Morehead (KY) State University; p. 291, courtesy of *The Iron Mountain Review*, Emory & Henry College.

James Crerar Reaney: p. 295, Grant Black/*Windsor Daily Star*; p. 303, Matuska; p. 306, Michael Lambeth; p. 307, Arjim Walter.

Harrison E. Salisbury: pp. 317, 320, 322, with permission of *New York Times* Pictures; p. 325, with permission of Curtis Brown Limited; p. 326, Charles Osgood/*Chicago Tribune*.

Francis Sparshott: p. 359, John Robert Colombo.

Lloyd Van Brunt: p. 365, Layle Silbert; p. 376, Oliver N. Simonsen; p. 378, Kathy Morris; p. 382, Martha Tabor/Impact Visuals.

Contemporary Authors
Autobiography Series

Claribel Alegría

1924-

(Translated from the Spanish by Darwin J. Flakoll)

Claribel Alegría, age seven years old, and her pony, 1931

I was five years old in 1929 when my father, mother, younger brother, and I boarded a ship in La Libertad, El Salvador, and sailed to Puerto Corinto, Nicaragua. My father was Nicaraguan, and we were travelling to visit his mother, whom we hadn't seen since we had to leave hurriedly for El Salvador in 1925.

I remember the voyage clearly. We made friends with the sailors, who took us below decks to the engine room, where the glare of the boilers and the clanking machinery fascinated and terrified us. One day my brother and I remained in the cabin while our parents ate lunch. We climbed to the top bunk to watch the sea through the porthole.

"Look," I told him. "The mermaids live down there, and if we can get this window open, you can dive in, and a mermaid will invite you to her palace, and then you can come back for me."

He gazed at me thoughtfully.

"Come on, help me," I urged him. I was still struggling to unscrew the brass wingnut securing the porthole when my parents walked in. My brother informed them of our prospective adventure, and that was the last time they left us locked in the stateroom.

My grandmother was terribly old. She dressed in blouses and long skirts, and she wore dark glasses because one of her eyes was missing. Every evening she would recite passages from the Bible to us. She knew the Gospels by heart and many passages from the Old Testament. It was she who taught me to love the Bible.

There was a globe-trotting uncle who told us ghost stories after dinner, and another with large green eyes who knew how to talk through the earth with a distant friend. One afternoon he demonstrated his gift for us on the patio. When he knelt and knocked on the earth with his knuckles, his friend would sense the vibrations and put his ear to a certain tree. My uncle lay down, put his lips to the ground and delivered his message. Then he jumped up, put his ear to the huge araucaria pine and listened to his friend's reply.

My favorite cousin in Estelí was René, who was a year older than I. He was blonde with dark black eyes, a natural storyteller, and I fell in love with him instantly. I relate René's brief history in *Luisa in Realityland*.

I was born of a Salvadoran mother in Estelí, Nicaragua, under the sign of Taurus and, in the Chinese lunar horoscope, the sign of the rat. The U.S. Marines were occupying Nicaragua during those years, and my father—a staunch Liberal from Las Segovias—who had fought along with Benjamín Zeledón against the first wave of yanqui invaders as a boy, detested them. The sentiment was reciprocal, and it was not long after the newlywed couple arrived when the Marine contingent occupying Estelí commenced deliberately baiting and provoking him. My mother often told me in later years how, when I was eight months old and she was carrying me in her arms in front of our house, a bullet whistled over her head and lodged in the adobe wall. A group of Marines in the central plaza across the street guffawed and jeered at her. Their objective was to terrify her, and it worked. A few days later my parents returned to El Salvador, where I lived until I was eighteen.

When we returned to El Salvador from that second voyage in 1929, I entered school. There were two possibilities: I could attend either the Asunción nun's school where my mother and my aunts had been educated (it was my great-grandfather who brought the Belgian nuns to Santa Ana) or my uncle Ricardo's school, which had just opened. I unhesitatingly chose my uncle's school, even though all my friends attended Asunción, and my parents accepted my decision.

My mother was an avid reader, and we had a well-stocked library, principally in French. My maternal grandfather had studied medicine in Paris, and my mother at Asunción, where she learned to write in French better than in Spanish. Leading Salvadoran intellectuals frequented the house: Salarrué, Alberto Guerra Trigueros, Serafín Quiteño, Claudia Lars, and occasional foreigners. That was how I met José Vasconcelos.

"You're going to meet a giant," my father announced proudly. I was six years old at the time, and I was already dictating poems to my mother: puerile verses about the stars or dedicated to my dolls. When Vasconcelos arrived at the house, I couldn't conceal my disappointment; he was shorter than my father.

"They told me you were a giant," I reproached him as he bent down to kiss me on the forehead. He laughed, and from that moment on we were friends: a friendship that endured until his death in 1958. It was he who prologued my first book of poems, *Anillo de Silencio*.

Sometime later, that enigmatic personage, Wilf, arrived in Santa Ana. He made such a deep impression on me that I also write about him in *Luisa in Realityland*.

Ricardo's school was named José Ingenieros in honor of the renowned Argentine philosopher. It was very progressive for its time.

On her father's shoulder, 1925

"Don't send your daughter there," my mother's friends warned her. "All of Ricardo's teachers are Communists."

Ricardo, don Chico Luarca, and the other teachers took pains from the first grade on to teach us our own regional mythology, history, and geography. That was their "unforgivable sin." We also had a school choir where I first learned that I am tone deaf. The music teacher singled me out for special attention during the first week of classes but finally shook her head and gave up. She told me to form the words with my lips like all the rest, but not to utter a sound. I underwent a similar experience with dance lessons. My mother placed me in a ballet class directed by an aging Russian ballerina. After the first month, the teacher came to her and informed her she was wasting her money.

I was not yet eight years old when the massacre of 1932 took place. Don Chico Luarca explained to us the reasons behind the peasant uprising. He pointed out the inequality of classes in El Salvador: all the wealth of the country was in the hands of a few families and, except for a minuscule middle class, the rest of the nation lived in squalor.

A few years later, don Chico was expelled from the country as a Communist. I tell of all this in the novel *Ashes of Izalco*, which I wrote in collaboration with my husband, Darwin Flakoll. As I write this, I realize that all my books reflect my own biography. They were birthed from memories, particularly those of my early years. In one way or another, all my writing is stamped with reminiscence and nostalgia.

I should also say that I was—am I still?—a scandalous liar and mythmaker. When I was twelve, I got hold of one of Dostoyevski's short novels, *Nietoshka Niezvanova*, which my mother did not want me to read at so early an age. I read it clandestinely, and it impressed me so that I came down with fever. I was Nietoshka, naturally, and with tears in my eyes, I recounted to my classmates how my father got drunk every night and beat my mother.

"How can that be?" they exclaimed. "Everyone says that Dr. Alegría is such a good man."

"That's what you think," I replied. "At night he becomes a different person."

"How awful!" they exclaimed, and their eyes filled with tears. I was happy whenever that happened.

As a result, my father began losing clients and couldn't understand why until I finally confessed what I'd done and had to go around apologizing to all my classmates. I had only wanted to prove to myself that I was capable of making them feel what I had felt when I read the novel.

With her mother, 1958

The Mesón Versalles was located across the street from my house, next to the National Guard fortress. A *mesón* is a Central American tenement: a hollow square of squalid single rooms built around a central patio with two outhouses, a communal wash basin, and a single tap of running water to service all the residents. Each room was occupied by an entire family, and the patio swarmed with naked children whose swollen bellies attested to malnutrition and parasite infestation. It was from seeing how those children lived that I began to understand the cruel reality in which the majority of my countrymen were immersed. That knowledge opened in me a deep psychic wound that has never healed.

There were authors and composers who played a decisive role in my adolescence: Beethoven, for example; Juan Ramón Jiménez's *Platero y Yo*; Rainer Maria Rilke's *Letter to a Young Poet*. I remember one night when I was fourteen and began reading *Letter to a Young Poet*. I couldn't put the book down until I had finished it. Afterward, I moved through the silent house like a sleepwalker, sat on the patio step, and gazed up at the stars. I had just realized that I was meant to be a poet: that this *was* my destiny, cost what it may, or I should never find happiness.

To be a poetess in El Salvador was not easy in those days. Women as well as men looked upon them as either crazed or pedantic. I begged my mother not to tell anyone I wrote. My girlfriends would mock me, and no boy would ever invite me to a dance. To gather strength, I began investigating the lives of the poetesses I most admired: Santa Teresa, Sor Juana Inez de la Cruz, Gabriela Mistral, Delmira Agustini, Alfonsina Storni, Juana de Ibarboru, and, of course, Claudia Lars, who was virtually a neighbor.

Claudia, whose true name was Carmen Brannon, was the tempestuous daughter of an Irishman and a Salvadoran mother. A classmate of my mother's, she methodically flouted middle-class prejudices. Her Irish streak ran deep, and, in both her personal life and her writing career, she always did exactly as she pleased. I owe a great debt to Claudia and to all the great poetesses who came before. Without their examples, I should never have dared become a writer.

My mother was the one who gave me the most encouragement. Others who were in on the secret were my father, my grandfather, Salarrué, Alberto Guerra Trigueros, and Serafín Quiteño. Every afternoon when my father left home to make his calls, I locked myself into his clinic and remained there, reading or writing, until dinnertime. It was the only spot in the big house where I could be alone, the only nook that I could call my own for a few hours. My single companion was a lanky skeleton who stared down at me from empty sockets and occasionally swayed in the breeze from the open window.

I finished secondary school before my sixteenth birthday and pleaded with my father to send me abroad to study. The Santa Ana atmosphere had grown stifling. Dad was a good and generous man, but let's face it, like the vast majority of his generation, he was a thoroughgoing *machista*.

"Leave Santa Ana?" he replied incredulously. "Never! A girl's place is beside her mother, learning from her until it's time to get married."

Next, I told him I wanted to study medicine at the University of San Salvador. This horrified him into another flat rejection.

"I was a student there," was his only attempt at self-justification, "and I won't have you exposed to the obscene jokes medical students play on each other with anatomical scraps. No. You're going to have a piano professor, you'll perfect your French, and you'll learn to cook and crochet."

I went off to weep hysterically. I detested sewing and had no talent for the piano. But despite my sulking fits and my mother's intercession on my behalf, I had no choice but to bow to his will.

I began studying piano with a handsome professor, some twenty years my senior. Bored with finger exercises and my own musical ineptitude, I began flirting with him, knowing he was married. The classes progressed from timid hand-holding to furtive kisses. After a few months, my mother suspected something was afoot, and she being my only confidant, I confessed everything. That freed me from further piano lessons.

As for sewing, I convinced the lady who taught a group of us that the classes would be much more entertaining if she undertook my crocheting while I read romantic novels to the entire group. Every time I brought a new doily home, my father praised me fulsomely, my mother eyed me suspiciously, and I felt my cheeks go red.

It was a trying period, but I read a great deal, particularly French and Russian authors. Dad encouraged me to read Latin American writers: Rubén Darío, Romulo Gallegos, José Hernández, Pablo Neruda, Miguel Angel Asturias, and others. When I first dipped into Neruda I was swept away by his hypnotic rhythm and flow of imagery. I put the book down reluctantly and vowed not to read him again until I was much older, knowing that if I did so I would become just another of his many imitators. I was so dazzled, however, that I told my girlfriends Neruda had dedicated the seventeenth of his *Twenty Love Poems* to me (as you've already learned, I'm a dreadful liar).

"How could he?" they scoffed. "Neruda has never even been here in Santa Ana."

"Oh yes he has," I replied. "He stayed at our house, but he was travelling incognito."

Years later, at a writer's conference in Concepción, Chile, I confessed my adolescent fib to Neruda himself. He laughed and said, "All right, Claribel, I'll dedicate that one to you, but I must say you should have made a more appropriate choice."

The first lines of Poem No. 17 read:

> *Me gustas cuando callas*
> *porque estás como ausente . . .*
>
> (I love you when you're quiet
> because it's as though you're absent . . .)

I also wrote quite a bit during that time. Don Chico Luarca was living in exile in Costa Rica, and I sent him some of my poems. He had them published in *Repertorio Americano*, the best cultural supplement in Central America, edited by don Joaquín García Monge, a man of great talent and generosity who was always attentive to young writers. I was thrilled to see my poems published in a full-page spread, complete with photograph. My parents were also delighted, and there was no danger that any of my friends would find out, because *Repertorio Americano* didn't circulate in Santa Ana.

I kept on dreaming of travelling, of studying at a university. My mother was my accomplice in urging my father to let me go, but he would have none of it.

When my brother graduated from high school, Dad announced that he would attend university in the United States. I entreated him to let me go with my brother, but he was adamant. I swore I'd become a nun and then jump over the wall after I'd taken vows, that I'd marry the first man who proposed to me and then get a quickie divorce (divorce was scandalous in those days), but he refused to budge.

One afternoon, when my brother's travel arrangements were being made, Dad found me weeping and asked me why.

"I've been praying for you to die and leave me free," I told him. "I'm crying because I love you very much, and I'll be sorry when you're dead."

He didn't say a word, but five days later at lunchtime he handed me my passport and airline ticket and told me I would be travelling with my brother.

It was Vasconcelos who, through a friend, arranged my entrance into a girls' finishing school in Hammond, Louisiana, near New Orleans. Mother accompanied me, and we stopped off in Mexico City to give our thanks to Vasconcelos. I'd brought some of my poems along, and I asked him to read them.

"With pleasure," he told me, "but I'm no poet. I'll take you to meet our greatest poet, Alfonso Reyes."

The following day we visited Alfonso Reyes in his huge library, and I was all atremble. Reyes was another diminutive giant, roly-poly, with an intelligent twinkle in his eye. He was extremely kind and put me at ease from the first moment. We chatted—or rather, the two of them chatted—for about an hour, and he promised to read my poems. As we departed, Reyes said with a mischievous grin, "Well, Pepe, I see you still have a fondness for Salvadoran volcanos."

I had no inkling that he was referring to Consuelo Suncín, a smoldering Salvadoran friend of my mother's who was a former mistress of Vasconcelos and who eventually ended up in Paris as the widow of Saint-Exupéry. Seizing my chance to participate in the conversation, I gushed: "Vasconcelos is absolutely right. I love them too, and particularly Izalco, which is always in eruption."

The two of them looked at each other, disconcerted, and afterwards Vasconcelos had the good grace not to clarify matters. His relationship with me, I should add, was always purely paternal.

We arrived at Hammond and were enchanted by the green, rolling pastures surrounding it, by the wide, tree-lined avenues, by the friendliness of its people. Not a soul spoke Spanish, and my mother, who knew a bit of English, served as my interpreter. She remained with me for two weeks and left me well installed and especially recommended to Mrs. Himmler, the dormitory housemother. Her departure wrenched me; for the first time in my life I was on my own. But I couldn't wait to start learning English, to begin my studies in a new language. Despite having graduated in El Salvador, I re-enrolled in the senior year of high school because I couldn't enter university without a knowledge of English.

My roommate was a kindly redhead named Leonelle, who served as my ambulatory dictionary and thesaurus, helped me with my homework at night and answered my myriad questions. After three months of hearing only English, I understood and spoke quite a bit, though with a marked accent I haven't lost to this day.

One day we had a picnic by the riverside and invited students from the boys' school nearby. A boy named Gary came over to sit beside me, and we started talking. Suddenly he said:

"I'd like to fuck you."

"You'd like to what?"

"Fuck you."

"How do you spell it?" I asked.

"Forget it," he said, and he got up and walked away.

That night in the dormitory I asked Leonelle what the word meant, and she was horrified. She said it was a dirty, vulgar word and where had I heard it? I explained, and she went dashing out to tell all the other girls. They were scandalized and on the verge of forming a lynch mob to tar and feather Gary. From then on, they all felt sisterly and overprotective toward me.

I missed my parents a great deal, and I particularly missed not having a private place where I could write. I spoke to Mrs. Himmler about it, and after due consideration she gave me the key to an empty classroom where, every afternoon from five to six, I secluded myself to work on my poetry. I finally had "a room of my own."

After six months I spoke English fairly well. I read a lot and understood prose much better than poetry. I read books that I already knew in Spanish: *Tom Sawyer, Huckleberry Finn, Robinson Crusoe.* A bit later I read Shakespeare. Despite the fact that I was already familiar with a good translation of some of his works, reading him in English was a revelation. Many of the subtleties of his language still escaped me, of course, but the music of his lines bewitched me. Translating poetry, I believe, is the most difficult of literary tasks. However good the translation, something ineffable—the aroma, let's say—is inevitably lost in the sea change between languages.

When I finished the school year in Hammond, Vasconcelos's friends found me a most respectable boarding house in New Orleans, where I spent the summer of 1944. I had won a scholarship to Loyola University, and I attended the summer session there as a freshman.

Prior to that, before leaving Hammond, I learned that Juan Ramón Jiménez and his wife, Zenobia, were living in the United States. In a fit of adolescent enthusiasm, I wrote him a fan letter. I was overwhelmed when I received his reply: a beautiful postcard with the reproduction of a Chinese painting. His handwriting in pencil was almost impossible to decipher: it resembled Arabic calligraphy more than Spanish. He told me he had read some of my poems in *Repertorio* and would like to meet me. Why didn't I come to Washington?

I sent him some of my new poems and we continued corresponding intermittently. Juan Ramón kept insisting that I come to Washington. He saw that

I lacked craftsmanship, and he offered to help me. I replied, saying I would love to go if it were possible, but I had a scholarship in New Orleans, and my father couldn't afford the full burden of all my university expenses.

By the end of the summer term, Juan Ramón had found me a part-time job as secretary to Concha Romero James at the Pan-American Union and had reserved for me a spot at the International Student House in Washington. My father wrote, telling me I was crazy to abandon a four-year university scholarship and warning that he couldn't send me a penny more than my normal sixty dollars a month for room and board.

In September 1944, I got off the train in Washington. Juan Ramón and Zenobia were awaiting me at Union Station and took me to their tasteful apartment at Dorchester House for tea, after which they deposited me at the International Student House. The day after my arrival in Washington, I registered at George Washington University and signed up for courses leading to a B.A. degree in Philosophy and Letters. A few days later I started working in the mornings at the Pan-American Union: a routine that soon revealed to me I would never become an efficient secretary; I was much too distracted.

Once again I found myself without a room of my own. During my three years at International House, I shared my room with girls from all over the world: an intense and fascinating education in comparative anthropology which was to serve me well in my subsequent wanderings.

Twice a week in the afternoon, I went to Dorchester House for my tutorial sessions with Juan Ramón. He plunged me into the Spanish classics, from the *mester de juglaría* to the writers of his own time. One afternoon he asked me if I had ever written a *décima*.

"No," I replied petulantly, "I'm only interested in free verse."

His eyebrows shot up, and then he smiled patiently.

"Free verse is the most difficult poetic form," he told me. "You must begin with *romances* and *silvas* and then work your way through *décimas* and sonnets before venturing into free verse."

From then on, each time I came to his class, besides commenting on the book I was currently reading, I had to bring him a new poem. He was an implacable schoolmaster. For two years he never told me he liked a poem of mine. Instead, he would point out: "This line is a vulgarity," or "That image is a cliché." Often I would return home in tears, asking myself if I really had the stuff of which poets are made.

On weekends, Juan Ramón and Zenobia would take me to visit art museums. He taught me how to absorb myself in a painting and had me spend hours listening to classical music in his apartment.

"All the arts are interrelated," he would tell me, "and you must learn how to 'see' and how to 'listen.'"

Finally, one day in early 1947, the miracle occurred. When I entered their apartment, the two of them smiled at me in a special way.

"We have a surprise for you," Juan Ramón greeted me. Zenobia scurried off to her room and returned with a folder in her hands.

"This is your first book," Juan Ramón said as he handed it to me.

I had to sit down.

I opened the folder, and there they were: more than fifty poems, chosen and corrected by Juan Ramón and typed by Zenobia.

I was ecstatic as I pored through them to see which ones he had selected.

"Now you'll have to find a publisher," he told me.

That same week I sent a copy of the manuscript to Vasconcelos, who not only bullied Editorial Botas in Mexico into publishing it, but also volunteered to write the prologue himself. The book, *Anillo de Silencio* (Ring of silence), came out in 1948.

Besides my reading list of Spanish authors, Juan Ramón recommended to me authors in English. Through him, I discovered Emily Dickinson, who remains one of my favorite poets of all time. I read so much of her work that some years after *Anillo de Silencio* was published, I was assailed by the doubt that one of its poems might be an unconscious plagiary of a poem of hers. I couldn't rest until I obtained a copy of her complete works and went through it, page by page. Luckily, it wasn't a case of plagiarism, but it was evident how much she had affected my writing. Needless to say, my book also reflected a powerful Juan Ramónian influence.

It was through Juan Ramón that I met Ezra Pound. After having me read his poems and explaining to me in a furious outburst the reason for Pound's incarceration, he took me to the St. Elizabeth's Mental Hospital one afternoon. I was deeply moved when I met the man. Pound received me with great sweetness and asked me to come back and visit him. I never did, though, because of a foolish timidity of which I later repented.

The year 1947 was magical. Besides the miracle of my book, I met the man to whom I am still married: Darwin J. Flakoll.

Bud, as everyone calls him, had been a navy officer aboard destroyers during World War II. He was a newspaperman in Washington and was studying for his M.A. degree at George Washington University. We were married three months after our first date, and despite the differences in our ethnic and family backgrounds and religious upbringing we were convinced that we were meant for each other. Besides, we were both writers, and that forged a bond that has withstood the test of time.

We were married in December 1947, and we found a one-bedroom apartment, in those days of severe housing shortages, on the strength of my being a war bride with a quaint Latin American accent. I went on the local radio to explain our problem, and before the program ended, we had offers of six different apartments. We chose a brand-new one in Arlington, Virginia.

Bud knew no Spanish, but started learning with me. In a short time he was able to read the language, and since then he has been my most ferocious critic—shades of Juan Ramón! By that time, I was working on a new book of poems which took me two years to

finish and which I should never have published. It was entitled—please don't laugh—*Suite of Love, Anguish, and Solitude*. As the title, so the book: filled with abstractions and commonplaces. Bud never liked those poems, but I, with wounded vanity, told him he still didn't really understand Spanish. We hardly ever saw Juan Ramón and Zenobia. They moved to Maryland and later to Puerto Rico.

In 1948 I received my B.A. degree and graduated in cap and bulging gown inasmuch as I was pregnant with our first daughter, Maya.

Walt Whitman was one of my favorite poets at that time, and still is. I was also impressed by Robinson Jeffers, whom I discovered by accident, and by Virginia Woolf.

With my new obligations as housekeeper and then as mother, and still with no room of my own, it was more and more difficult to write. Despite my being very much in love with Bud and adoring my daughter, my new life began to weigh on me. We lived in the countryside and almost never went out because baby-sitters were too expensive. I suppose we were poor, though I never thought about it in that

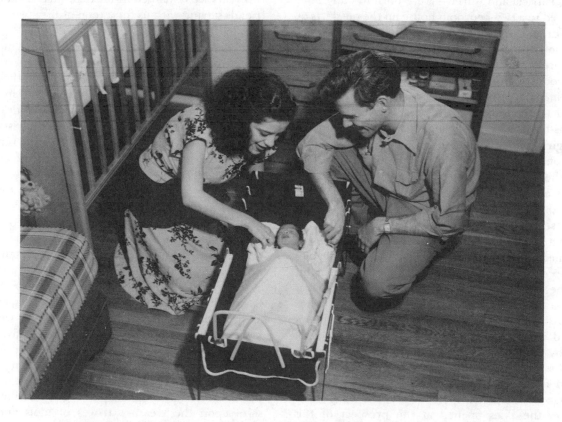

With husband, Darwin J. Flakoll, and daughter Maya, nine days old, 1948

light. Bud had a steady job as assistant editor of a news bulletin on collective bargaining contracts, but his salary was low, and he used to tell me that his chief ambition in life was to have twenty-five dollars in the bank at the end of the month. With a baby to raise and the apartment to care for, I had stopped working, but I still had no sense of the value of money. One day, on a rare shopping expedition in downtown Washington, I found a silver serving spoon that exactly matched the pattern of the dinner service we had received as a wedding present. I wrote a check for eighteen dollars to pay for it and took it home exultantly. When I showed it to Bud, he clapped his forehead and groaned. The purchase left us with $4.53 in our bank account. As of that moment, I had a new obligation thrust upon me; Bud turned his entire salary over to me, and I became family treasurer and accountant.

We had no automobile and no close friends nearby. The neighbors were pleasant, but we shared no common interests. To top things off, I became pregnant again when Maya was six months old. Some months later, X-rays disclosed that I was carrying twins. I had a hysterical outburst of laughter and tears but eventually faced up to the prospect of being a household slavey the rest of my life. Before the twins—Patricia and Karen—were born in mid-1950, we moved to a two-bedroom house on the outskirts of Alexandria, Virginia. Bud had switched to a better-paying job as assistant manager of a small Washington news bureau servicing newspapers in the western part of the country, but our identical twins gobbled up the extra income. After the first several months, I learned that raising twins is only one and one half times as hard as having a single baby. We placed the three girls in the second bedroom, with Patsy and Karen sharing a single crib so they could entertain each other. We christened that room "the tiger cage" because of the overpowering ammoniacal fumes that wafted through the open doorway. Twice a week the diaper service truck stopped at the front door to deliver a cotton bale of fresh diapers and haul away the soiled ones. I remember that the three babies used up one thousand diapers per month. At night, after they were asleep and the bottles and nipples had been washed, boiled, and filled with formula, I was able to finish a book of children's stories for them. Entitled *Tres cuentos,* it was eventually published in 1958 by the Salvadoran Ministry of Culture.

When the twins were ten months old, Bud was offered a job as managing editor of the English-language newspaper in Mexico City, the *Daily News.* For me, the skies opened at the prospect of this fortuitous change. After eight years abroad, I was yearning to return to my cultural roots, to immerse myself in my own language once again. I had often been urged to try writing in English, but I was unable to do so. Had I been writing stories or novels at that time, I might have made the effort. But, for me, poetry could only be composed in Spanish: a visceral, atavistic instinct I still retain. During the last few years I had realized with growing horror that I was losing my grip on my own language, that reading books in Spanish was not nearly enough to compensate for the lack of conversational exchange.

Exile, be it voluntary or forced, has its positive and negative aspects. On the one hand, you learn to view your country and compatriots from a different perspective, which undoubtedly enriches you. On the other hand, particularly if you are a writer, you begin to feel that the subtleties of your own tongue are escaping you, that your usage of it is becoming rusty and it is no longer growing and flowing in you.

In 1951 we moved to Mexico after a short stay in El Salvador, which I had not visited for two years. We rented a house in Colonia Nueva Anzures where, for the first time, I had a maid to do the housework and cooking and another to take care of the children. Furthermore, we had an extra bedroom that I could call my own—at least on a part-time basis. During the two years we remained in Mexico, we had family and friends staying with us for a total of fifty-two weeks. I counted them.

For me, Mexico was a rebirth. Within a month or two of our arrival we had forged new friendships, many of which were to last a lifetime, as in the case of Augusto (Tito) Monterroso, the Guatemalan writer, who was then—and still is—living in political exile.

Juan José Arreola and Juan Rulfo visited the house almost daily and loaned me recently published titles that I devoured voraciously. Juan José and Bud got involved in an endless chess tournament and built increasingly sophisticated model airplanes that they tested and flew on the dry lakebed of Texcoco. Juan Rulfo brought us his as yet unpublished stories, seeking our opinions. Bud and I immediately saw that we were in the presence of a master storyteller, and Rulfo, ever humble and unsure of himself, was happy at our encouragement. He was working for the Goodrich Tire Company during that period, engaged in preparing a tourist guide to Mexico, which he knew, archaeologically and architectonically, as few others we have met. We accompanied him on many weekends to search for clay figurines, pottery shards, and obsidian knives. From him we learned to follow the ox teams during spring plowing at Teotihuacán to seize upon the treasure troves of idols and copal incense burners turned up in the fresh furrows.

*The author with writers Juan Rulfo and
Augusto Monterroso, Mexico, 1952*

On Sundays, we frequently lunched at Vasconcelos's rambling hacienda in Coyoacán, and he would scold me because all my friends were "pinkos." By then, Vasconcelos had become disillusioned with Mexican leftists and had veered sharply to the right, where he remained until his death.

In Mexico I wrote *Vigilias* (Vigils), a book composed largely of sonnets. There is one long poem, "Sunday monologue," in which, for the first time, I hit upon my own poetic voice. The book came out a few weeks before we left Mexico, with a cover drawing by Elvira Gascón, an excellent Spanish artist and wife of the painter Roberto Balbuena. Our friends gave a dinner to celebrate the occasion, complete with *mariachis* and *corridos* from the Mexican Revolution.

I see now that I have overlooked one important moment in my past. A day before I left for the United States in 1943, my father announced that he had a surprise for my younger sister and me. He led us into the living room and pulled away a Manila scarf to reveal a shiny new Steinway baby grand piano.

"This is your working instrument," he told my sister, who, at the age of twelve was already revealing an extraordinary musical talent. "And this," he took from his pocket a small, elongated case, "is yours." Inside, resting on a satin lining, was a gold-pointed Parker fountain pen that I have to this day. How fantastic! I thought. It would be horrible to carry a piano around on your back for the rest of your life. From that day on, whenever I write a poem or jot down ideas in my "seed book," I use the fountain pen my father gave me.

My seed book is a series of spiral notebooks (Bud gave me the first one) in which I write thoughts, dreams, phrases or lines of poetry that have impressed me. Frequently, glancing through it, a poem occurs to me, and I draft the first several versions in its pages. My current seed book accompanies me wherever I go. I long ago learned that poetry is my own particular way of bringing order into the chaos of the madhouse world that surrounds me.

While still in Mexico, Bud and I conceived the idea of preparing an anthology of the young Latin American writers and poets who were laying the groundwork for what was to become known a few years later as the Latin American literary "boom." During our two-year stay we had familiarized ourselves with the work of many fascinating writers who were completely unknown in the English-speaking world. Besides, so many of our friends were winning Guggenheim grants or Rockefeller fellowships that it seemed like a piece of cake to get in on the gold rush. We wrote a project proposal, specifying Chile as our base of operations so we could acquaint ourselves with the work of new writers in the Andean countries and the Cono Sur. We returned to the United States, filled with enthusiasm and apprehension, to present the project personally to several cultural foundations, but we were still flabbergasted when, a few months later, our proposal was accepted by the Catherwood Foundation in Pennsylvania.

We arrived in Santiago, Chile, in the latter part of 1953, and our son, Erik, was born there in January 1954. We remained in Chile, except for occasional side trips, for nearly three years, during which time we read hundreds of books and manuscripts that we received from all over Latin America from authors who were under the age of forty. Existing anthologies covered the previous generations.

The anthology, entitled *New Voices of Hispanic America*, was published by Beacon Press in 1962. Leafing through it today, some thirty-five years after we finished the manuscript, we feel gratified that in a certain sense we "discovered" for the English-speaking audience many of today's best-known Latin

Alegría with her three daughters, Patricia, Maya, and Karen, 1964

American authors who at that time were little known even within their own national boundaries: Ernesto Cardenal, Juan Rulfo, Augusto Monterroso, Augusto Roa Bastos, Cintio Vitier, Rosario Castellanos, Mario Benedetti, Julio Cortázar, Ernesto Mejía Sanchez, Octavio Paz, José Donoso, and Nicanor Parra. We also translated and included an early story by Gabriel García Marquéz, but the editors pruned it out, claiming it was too long and unbalanced the selection.

In Chile, besides working on the anthology, I wrote a new book of poems, *Acuario*, that differs greatly from the previous ones. There is more humor in it, for one thing, and I began to pay more attention to what was happening around me, rather than gazing at my own navel and my interior, subjective states. It was published by the Editorial Universitaria and it was the first of my books that received favorable reviews and had a good sale.

While we were in Chile, Tito Monterroso arrived there, once again in exile following the CIA coup that overthrew the government of Jacobo Arbenz in Guatemala. The two of us often talked of our desire to visit Europe. One day, as we were strolling along

Ahumada, I saw a sign that read "Passage to Marseilles."

"Just a minute," I told Tito and went running to the sales booth. "How much is the passage to Marseilles?" I asked the saleslady.

"Sixteen hundred pesos," she replied.

It seemed incredibly cheap, since at that time the Chilean peso stood at eight hundred to the dollar. But, ever cautious, I countered:

"Is that a round-trip passage or only one way?"

"Claribel," Tito touched my arm patiently, "this is a movie theatre, not a travel agency."

That was when Tito started compiling his "Dictionary of Claribelisms," which, thanks be, he never decided to publish.

After nearly three years in Chile, we finished the anthology and returned to the United States, leaving behind many friends in the literary community, including Manuel Rojas, González Vera, Pepé Donoso, and Enrique Lihn.

Bud, who was at loose ends after this long interruption of his journalistic career, submitted his application for appointment to the Foreign Service

Reserve and, after a lengthy delay for security checks, was accepted. We spent another year and a half in Washington while he was breaking in on his new job, until he was finally appointed second secretary at the U.S. Embassy in Montevideo, Uruguay.

Those were difficult years that put our marriage on trial. Poetry, once again, enabled me to survive. Poetry and friends, such as Idea Vilariño, Zoraida, Mario Benedetti. We were in Montevideo for two years, and I wrote another volume of poems, *Huésped de mi tiempo* (Guest of my time), that was published in Argentina by Américalee. I feel that three or four poems in that volume are worth rescuing.

By this time, writing had become a compulsive act, and at times, when I found I had nothing to say or when I finished a book and was sure I would never be able to write another, I sank into a depressive crisis and weighed Bud and the children down with my neurotic behavior until another poem took possession of me and broke my writer's block. The daily routine of writing, which sometimes included Saturdays and Sundays, has never been slavery for me, but rather sanctuary. Through reading and writing, I have made invisible friends across the centuries. The wonderful thing is that as the years go by I have met many of my favorite writers of this time in the flesh, and I have come to the conclusion that in this life there are no coincidences. I have also learned that before publishing a new poem I must leave it in quarantine for at least six months or later I'll be sorry.

After two years in Uruguay, we were posted to Argentina where I wrote *Vía Unica* (One-way traffic), which was published by Editorial Alfa in Montevideo. In it are nostalgic poems for my lost childhood, which has always been a central component of my poetry, as are love and death. Lately, these elements have become more and more interwoven.

For many years I was a voluntary expatriate. I missed my homeland and wrote about it. But to realize that one cannot return is a hard blow to assimilate, a dash of ice water on the soul. I was unable to return to El Salvador when my mother was dying, even though we were living in Nicaragua, only forty minutes away by air.

We were still in Montevideo when Cuba was liberated. It was an event that filled us with jubilation. I had sincerely believed until then that no Latin American country, and particularly no Central American republic, would ever be able to free itself and regain its sovereignty. I believed that Somoza, Martínez, Carías and others of their ilk would hold power eternally because the United States wanted it that way, as well as the local oligarchies and armed forces. The Cuban revolution astonished us. Previously, I had taken little interest in politics, but now I began reading about current events, talking to friends who were better informed than I, began to realize that it was possible for a small country to escape the fate of a banana republic. Some of the poems in *Vía Unica* reflect this new attitude on my part.

Two years later, when we were ending our stay in Buenos Aires, the Bay of Pigs invasion took place. All of us who considered ourselves friends of Cuba were first indignant and a few days later exhilarated at Goliath's humiliating defeat.

Revolutionary Cuba was, from the outset, an oasis for Latin American artists. Casa de las Américas began inviting us to cultural events, published our books, organized Latin American art exhibits. Cuba brought us in contact with each other and forged a tacit brotherhood between us. Previously, it had been difficult for a Colombian author to become acquainted with a Chilean writer, but the Cuban revolution changed all that.

At the end of 1962, Bud's contract with the Department of State expired and, rather than renew-

With her son, Erik, 1976

ing it, he chose to return to newspapering. Instead of buying a round-trip ticket to Marseilles, we purchased one-way tickets to Paris, where we were to live for nearly four years. I began rereading the books I had devoured during adolescence: *Madame Bovary, Le Rouge et le Noir,* the works of Jules Verne.

There were many Latin American writers living in Paris at that time, among them Julio Cortázar, Carlos Fuentes, Saul Yurkievich, Mario Benedetti, Mario Vargas Llosa. They gathered in our apartment frequently to engage in animated discussions about what was happening in Latin America.

I had long been obsessed by the peasant massacre in El Salvador in 1932 and frequently recounted my memories of it in these reunions. One day Carlos Fuentes asked why I didn't write a historical novel about this event. Little was known about it because the dictator, Martínez, had performed a cultural lobotomy on the Salvadoran people by ordering the destruction of all newspaper files concerning the peasant uprising and its bloody aftermath. I resisted the idea, objecting that I was a poet who had never written so much as a short story. Then Bud suggested that we should write the novel together.

Holding her first grandchild, Jamie, 1971

Enthused, we sat down to plan the structure and sketch the personages we needed to tell the story. The main plot was to be a love story, with Bud writing the male protagonist's story while I wrote the feminine part. It wasn't easy, and we were soon figuratively throwing crockery at each other. Bud wrote in English while I translated his drafts, and vice versa. Each of us revised the other's output, adding and cutting and growing increasingly frustrated. Several times we were on the point of abandoning the project until we finally realized it was our own egos that stood in the way. We learned to be more humble and accept each other's suggestions, which contributed to enriching the novel. In the end, Bud wrote a good deal of the feminine personage's part, and I much of the male lead's story. Today we find it amusing because we can't remember who wrote which part.

The novel took two years to write. We finished it in 1964, and it was a finalist in the Biblioteca Breve competition in Barcelona. Publication was delayed for two years by Spanish censorship. Ten years later it was published in El Salvador when General Molina, one of the rotating dictators of my country, decided to leave office with a liberal image. He ordered the Ministry of Education to start publishing works by Salvadoran writers, and *Cenizas* was one of those included. It soon became a secondary-school text and has gone through numerous editions since then.

Apart from *Cenizas*, I wrote relatively little in Paris. The streets captivated me, as did the museums, churches, markets, and sidewalk cafés. Julio Cortázar gave me a guide book, *Le Conaissance de vieux Paris*, and I carried this with me to virtually every arrondissement in the city. Paris is the city I know best.

In 1966, we decided to move to Mallorca and devote full time to writing. We found two apartments near the beach in Palma Nova to house our sprawling family (my mother lived with us after my father's death in 1965) while we looked for permanent quarters.

In 1968 Maya and Erik discovered Deyá and took us there. The village fascinated us, and we bought and remodelled a stone house some three hundred years old. It had long since been christened Ca'n Blau Vell, which in the Mallorquin dialect means "the old blue house."

My Deyá years were productive. *Pagaré a Cobrar* (Installment payments) was published by Ocnos in 1973. *Sobrevivo* (I survive) won the Casa de las Américas poetry prize in 1978. I never published "Raíces" (Roots) separately because I chopped it up to include in an anthology *Suma y Sigue* (Add and carry), published by Visór in 1981.

In Nicaragua with author Julio Cortázar, 1982

I also wrote three short novels in Deyá: *El Detén* (The talisman), published by Lumen in 1977, *Albúm Familiar* (Family album), published by EDUCA in Costa Rica in 1984 and by Lumen in Barcelona, and *Pueblo de Dios y de Mandinga* (Village of God and the Devil), published in Mexico by Editorial ERA and by Lumen in Spain. The latter is about the magical quality of Deyá, and its principal personage is Robert Graves, who moved to Deyá in the 1920s and who convinced me that I am a hamadryad.

I wrote *Luisa in Realityland* as well while in Deyá, at the urging of Julio Cortázar and his second wife, Carol Dunlap, to whom I had related many anecdotes of my childhood.

What else? Oh, yes. Bud and I did an anthology of Robert Graves's poems in Spanish, and another anthology, *Nuevas Voces de Norteamérica* (New voices of North America), a collection of poems by young U.S. poets. These were published by Lumen and Plaza y Janés respectively.

The years streamed by, our children got married, my mother returned to El Salvador, and in July 1979 the Sandinista revolution came to power in Nicaragua.

On July 17, Anastasio Somoza II and his son (El Chigüín) fled Nicaragua for Homestead Air Force Base, Miami, in a Lear jet, taking with them the coffins of Anastasio Somoza I and his eldest son, Luís. On the same day, at the same hour, Julio Cortázar and Carol were winging from Paris to Mallorca to visit us. We broke the news to them when they arrived at Ca'n Blau Vell, and we spent the rest of the afternoon and evening toasting the event with champagne. Bud and I informed them of our recent decision to travel to Nicaragua and gather data for a book about the Sandinista revolution. The two of them were enthused and promised to visit us there as soon as we were established.

We settled our affairs, closed up Ca'n Blau Vell, and arrived in Managua in early September to immerse ourselves in the chaotic, colorful uproar of the new revolution. Julio and Carol arrived in early November and were immediately enamored of what was taking place in Nicaragua. Julio became a staunch defender of the Sandinistas, and they, for their part, welcomed him and Carol with open arms each time they returned. Months after his death, I was in the Huembes market, which he loved to visit, and I found a vegetable vendor reading one of his books.

We were in Nicaragua for six months, gathering historical data and interviewing the commandants and the *compas* and *compitas* who had achieved the victory after nearly twenty years of struggle against the Somoza dynasty. We returned to Deyá to write our account, *Nicaragua: La revolución sandinista*, which was published by Editorial ERA in 1982.

As we returned from Nicaragua in March 1980, we stopped off in Paris to visit the twins and their offspring, and I was invited to give a poetry reading at the Sorbonne. The night before, Roberto Armijo, Salvadoran writer and good friend, phoned me to announce the assassination of Monsignor Oscar Arnulfo Romero, Archbishop of San Salvador, who had been shot in the back by a member of the death squad while saying mass in a hospital chapel.

Bud and I stayed up all night preparing a paper about Romero's heroic struggle on behalf of the dispossessed—the direct cause of his murder—and the next day I read our denunciation instead of my poems.

Archbishop Romero's assassination marked a crossroad in my life. The death squads had eliminated El Salvador's "voice of the voiceless," and not only I, but many other Salvadoran writers, felt we must do something, however minimal, to compensate for this enormous loss. That was how my "political career" began, though I am no politician. I began speaking

Claribel Alegría and Darwin J. Flakoll, 1972

out to denounce the government-sponsored terrorism that afflicted my country—and still does—and thus I became a political exile. A cousin of mine who was then Minister of Defense—General Eugenio Vides Casanova—sent word to me that he would consider it a personal affront if I were to return, and that he could not assume responsibility for my safety. As they say in Spanish: I don't need a house to fall on me to get the message. Some months later I received a letter under the letterhead of the Women's Auxiliary of ARENA, the death squad party, telling me I was crazy, you could see it in my eyes, and why didn't I stop going around mouthing stupidities. They told me I was old and senile and not worth killing but I should be careful of my children because vengeance would be wreaked on them. Naturally, the letter was unsigned.

With respect to my poetry, I have always written poems under obsession's spur, and what was happening in El Salvador, throughout Latin America, obsessed me. The poems I began to write then are not political, as some have said. To me, they are love poems to my people, to my America. I have never sat

down to write a poem denouncing something. Speeches, pamphlets, and newspaper articles serve for that. But if a situation or event moves me, that emotion can sometimes be translated into poetry, just as love or death or a tranquil evening can be so translated.

Over the next several years, besides writing the Nicaragua book, Bud and I collaborated on a number of historical/testimonial books: *La encrucijada salvadoreña* (Salvadoran crossroads), *No me agarran viva* (They won't take me alive: the story of Comandante Eugenia's life and death), and *Para romper el silencio* (To break the silence: the history of El Salvador's political prisoners). The first was published by Editorial Cidob in Barcelona and the latter two by ERA in Mexico. The material for these books, and the people who could tell the stories, were all in Nicaragua, and after shuttling between Managua and Deyá several times, we decided in 1983 to make our principal residence in Nicaragua, coming back to Deyá occasionally for vacations from the hullabaloo of the U.S.-sponsored Contra invasion and the subsequent civil war in the country.

To get back to my writing, more recently the Catholic University Press in El Salvador published another short novel of mine, *Despierta mi bien despierta* (Awake, my love, awake), and I have published poems, always more poems, in Nicaragua, the United States, England, and France.

As I write these lines, I am sitting in Ca'n Blau Vell, Deyá, working on another testimonial book with Bud: the story of the escape of forty-eight political prisoners from Canto Grande, the maximum-security detention center in Lima, Perú, through a 345-meter tunnel that was dug from a safehouse outside the prison to an exact point inside the walls. We travelled to Perú to interview some twenty of the escapees (in another safehouse, naturally), the youngsters who dug the tunnel, the technician who supervised the job, the doctor-safehouse keeper who played housemother to the diggers, and Victor Polay Campos, head of the Movimiento Revolucionario Túpac Amaru, who himself escaped with the rest of the prisoners.

I am also finishing another book of poems, which I think will be called "Fugas" (Fugues) and which, naturally, will be my best book to date. And in my seed book, I see I have projects that will keep me out of mischief for the next five years.

BIBLIOGRAPHY

Poetry:

Anillo de Silencio (title means "Ring of silence"; also see below), Botas (Mexico), 1948.

Suite of Love, Anguish, and Solitude, Brigadas Líricas (Argentina), 1951.

Vigilias (title means "Vigils"; also see below), Ediciones Poesía de América (Mexico), 1953.

Acuario (also see below), Editorial Universitaria (Santiago, Chile), 1955.

Huésped de mi tiempo (title means "Guest of my time"; also see below), Américalee (Buenos Aires, Argentina), 1961.

Vía Unica (title means "One-way traffic"; includes "Auto de fé" and "Comunicación a larga distancia"; also see below), Editorial Alfa (Montevideo), 1965.

Aprendizaje (includes selections from *Anillo de silencio, Vigilias, Acuario, Huésped de mi tiempo,* and *Vía Unica*), Universitaria (El Salvador), 1970.

Pagaré a Cobrar y otros poemas (title means "Installment payments") Ocnos (Barcelona), 1973.

Sobrevivo (title means "I survive"), Casa de las Américas (Cuba), 1978.

Suma y Sigue (anthology; title means "Add and carry"), Visór (Madrid), 1981.

Flores del volcán / Flowers from the Volcano (anthology; parallel text in English and Spanish), translated by Carolyn Forché, University of Pittsburgh Press, 1982.

Poesía viva (anthology), Blackrose Press (London), 1983.

Mujer del río / Woman of the River (parallel text in English and Spanish), translated by Flakoll, University of Pittsburgh Press, 1989.

Yeste Poema-río, Editorial Nueva Nicaragua (Managua), 1989.

Fiction:

Tres cuentos (children's stories; illustrated by Agustín Blancovaras), Ministerio de Cultura (El Salvador), 1958.

(With Flakoll) *Cenizas de Izalco* (novel), Seix Barral (Barcelona, Spain), 1966, translation by Flakoll published as *Ashes of Izalco,* Curbstone Press, 1989.

El Detén (novella; title means "The talisman"), Lumen, 1977.

Albúm Familiar (title means "Family album"), Editorial Universitaria Centroamericana (San Jose, Costa Rica), 1984.

Pueblo de Dios y de Mandinga: Con el asesoriamiento científico de Slim (title means "Village of God and the Devil"; also see below), Ediciones Era (Mexico), 1985.

Despierta mi bien despierta (title means "Awake, my love, awake"), UCA Editores (San Salvador, El Salvador), 1986.

Pueblo de Dios y de Mandinga (contains *El Detén, Albúm Familiar,* and *Pueblo de Dios y de Mandinga;* also see below), Lumen (Barcelona), 1986.

Luisa en el país de la realidad / Luisa in Realityland (parallel text in English and Spanish), translated by husband, Darwin J. Flakoll, Curbstone Press, 1987.

Editor:

(And translator with Flakoll) *New Voices of Hispanic America,* Beacon Press, 1962.

(With Flakoll) *Nuevas Voces de Norteamérica* (parallel text in English and Spanish), Plaza y Janés (Barcelona), 1981.

(And translator with Flakoll) *On the Front Line: Guerilla Poetry of El Salvador,* Curbstone, 1989.

Other:

(Translator with Flakoll) Mario Benedetti, editor, *Unstill Life: An Introduction to the Spanish Poetry of Latin America,* Harcourt, 1970.

(With Flakoll) *La encrucijada salvadoreña* (historical essays; title means "Salvadoran crossroads"), Editorial Cidob (Barcelona), 1980.

(With Flakoll) *Cien poemas de Robert Graves* (anthology), Lumen, 1981.

(With Flakoll) *Nicaragua: La revolución sandinista; Una crónica política, 1855–1979* (history), Ediciones Era, 1982.

(With Flakoll) *No me agarran viva: La mujer salvadoreña en lucha* (title means "They won't take me alive"), Ediciones Era, 1983.

(Contributor) Doris Meyer, editor, *Lives on the Line: The Testimony of Contemporary Latin American Authors,* University of California Press, 1988.

(With Flakoll) *Para romper el silencio* (a history of El Salvador's political prisoners; title means "To break the silence"), Ediciones Era, 1984.

John Allman

1935-

Why would a young woman whose father had deserted her family *not* marry a young man whose father had deserted his? She was Helen—in her youth known as Ellen—Burghard, the third child (an earlier child, Arthur, had died in infancy) of May Bracken and Charles Burghard, a man whose occupation was listed as "Driver" on Helen's New York City 1912 birth certificate. At the time, May was all of twenty years old. Helen's older sister, Adelaide, would blossom early and marry Joe Gerardi, a high school graduate, a precise, small man who ran his own auto repair business. Her brother Charley would forever mourn the death of their mother in his early thirties, when he worked two jobs in state mental institutions and bought a small house in Central Islip and raised five children with his wife, Josie. Helen's other sibling, an infant named Alice, disappeared while in the care of a neighbor. Whether Alice was given to the neighbor to raise as her own, or abandoned by May Bracken Burghard, or sold, or died—an adjustable fact, though It began the curse that followed the name Alice, since Helen Burghard Allman's second child, given that name, died shortly after birth, and Helen's third child, given that name again, would lose her talent and mind to schizophrenia.

The poverty of Helen's life was in her own recounting often lyrical and amusing, though the turn in her eye was not, and the operation she could never bring herself to describe, when they repositioned her eye, would engender a shudder in her small body. Her favorite expression became, "I'll spare you the gory details." And there were the months she spent at a place called St. Joseph's, a home for children with tuberculosis, where she'd been placed because of heart trouble—that proved to be a functional murmur later passed on to her oldest child, John, and then to his daughter, Jennifer. For May Burghard, it must have been a relief to have (another) child off her hands, since her husband was god-knows-where. But for Helen, it was a place that no one visited, where a nun taught her the rudiments of piano (she thought of her father's unpleasant French-Canadian mother, a piano teacher), where death and religion arranged themselves as metaphysical routine.

John Allman, age eight, first communion, 1943

Of the man she married there would be so little to praise, once his dark good looks and the vulnerable inwardness of his gaze succumbed to anger and male camaraderie and drink. In photographs, there was always a latent sorrow in his eyes and the downward slope of his mouth. Perhaps he thought he'd been destined for other things. As if his mother, Gertrude Prince (born Mary Gertrude Prince Hoggard, 1889, in Newcastle-upon-Tyne, England), coming to the USA as dancer, juggler, singer in vaudeville when she was barely nineteen, had ceded to him her dream of

*Maternal grandmother, May Bracken Burghard,
age sixty*

in school plays because he had a good memory and a way of projecting his voice—something that nullified shame at being so thin—the son on whom a mother would place the man's mantle prematurely, so that for years he believed, bitterly, that she'd used him as a surrogate for his father—until understanding in his middle age that he had also been a substitute for her, with his younger siblings. His notions of manhood early combined with performance and surrogacy, in a climate of noise, bravado, offended dignities, alcoholism, hard work (with no ethos of success), and led the boy into such a web of contrarieties that he learned to postpone emotional reactions to events, to nearly suspend the activities of self. A habit that often simulated coldness in him, a rationalizing demeanor, apprehended by others as patience. Indifference. As if in his nature an Irish quickness and urgency negotiated perpetually with German intelligence, English decorum. Though what he laid off to his father's father was usually something lighthearted, artistic, loose. His father's mother had been labeled as the drinker (of port, her face flushed, how many wet, reeking kisses he remembered) and carried the

recognition and applause—though the Irish tenor, John Allman (known as Jack, additionally as King), who knocked her up, might once have held his dark son in his arms to tease a tune out of him, unsuccessfully, in the air of Ninth Avenue, above the noise of traffic.

The family of this King Allman came from Waterbury, Connecticut, though on his marriage certificate he is listed as born in New York, around 1885. In his show-biz studio photos, he's short, inclined to softness, blue-eyed, blandly smiling, blond, a timorousness and distance in his expression that will surface two generations later in the first-communion photo of his oldest grandson. That grandson would peek into the wooden keepsake box in his father's dresser drawer and pore over the yellowed gossip-column clippings from the *News,* in which King Allman was cited as having been seen in such-and-such a place with so-and-so. It might have been this simple rendering of his family name in print that propelled the grandson into a writing career. Or an extraversion permutated from his paternal grandparents' stock, evident when he won the longish parts

*Mother, Helen Burghard Allman (left), with her
sister Adelaide Burghard Gerardi, 1930s*

schizophrenic gene that would complete the fates of all the Alices.

John King Allman was an only child. The family papers—what was left of them, in a family heedless of its origins, almost contemptuous of documents—show that John ran away to join the circus at the age of twelve, around the time his father had left the family. His mother had tried to get him in a movie as a child actor, but when he bit his young leading lady he ended a career he had no interest in. Little is known about his childhood, except that later he came to detest his father and would have nothing to do with him when his own family grew apace. There was talk that King Allman played a white piano and sang at a club in Brooklyn. There was the girlfriend who showed up in 1958 at the double funeral of Gertrude and her son—mother and son having died an hour apart, in separate hospitals—as if to confirm the death of her lover's first choice, King himself having died the year before.

Like his wife-to-be, John King Allman left school after the eighth grade. During Prohibition, he drove trucks for bootleggers (for the rest of his life, he would be a truck driver), and married Helen Burghard just when that era ended. Their marriage must once have had humor and passion, but went wrong by the time Helen was having her second child, in 1937, when she fled to her mother's apartment. May Bracken Burghard insisted that her daughter leave and take parturition with her (Helen had begun to give birth in the kitchen). Their marriage punctuated by children, perpetual debt, John's erratic paychecks—his duodenal ulcer and drinking cost him many days each year—John and Helen survived their troubled togetherness (she never quite ceased trying to leave him; she never quite found a haven for herself and the children, John, Alice, Daniel, Steven), until a cerebral hemorrhage ended his work life, and for most purposes, life itself, when he was forty-two.

*

August 1987, in a letter from the author, accompanying the finished manuscript of *Curve Away from Stillness,* sent to Peter Glassgold at New Directions: "I wanted to be inside the mind and inside the natural universe at the same time, to represent the heroic effort implicit in the cognitive act: *to know* the same as *to be.* And from the state of knowing, to assert . . . the ambition of organic life: to persist, to grow, to learn, . . . to retain identity while participating in the universal—whether that last process terminates in nirvana, in the great consolidation of

Paternal grandparents, John "King" Allman and Gertrude Prince Allman, about 1912

Father, John King Allman, age twenty, 1932

In-laws, John and Emma Jorge (formerly Jurjevich), with Emma's mother, Viktorija Zgomba, about 1969

being, or in . . . theories about how the world works and what it is, and what we are, is . . . one of the great choices we make in the shadow-border at the edge of knowing. I think the poems cling tenaciously to *this* life." "*Curve Away from Stillness* . . . is the summation of my life-long belief in reason and the power of the mind to choose a work and a way of being. This book is my philosophical platform, articulated through speculation, with many lacunae . . . to fall through. In choosing love—in 'Chemistry' and 'Biology'—I represent the only goodness I understand. In exploring the nature of reality and the solar system—in 'Principles' and 'Planets'—I attempt a world in which evil can be only a part. Perhaps I am not ready yet to write my *Fleurs du Mal.*"

At fifty-two, the writer was bearing the bloom of what had begun as ink drawings of science experiments in high school. Order, clarity, predictability, himself etched almost incidentally (in the letter accompanying *Scenarios for a Mixed Landscape*, sent to Peter Glassgold in November 1985: "I hope to capture in one linguistic form an awesome secret of Nature and the equally impressive action of the human mind—as if the poem were nothing more or less than the reflexive action of Nature occurring within me as in a convenient and transient medium"), so that the acne-scarred boy he was, working at his uncle's Esso gas station in Manhattan on weekends, at home surrounded by siblings he felt too responsible

for, that boy would become a floating presence, a non-Einsteinean and etheric self, the medium not of light or gravity waves but of familial voices.

On June 22, 1940, Eileen Jurjevich was born in Mount Vernon, New York, to Emma Zgomba Jurjevich and John Jurjevich. Emma's parents had both immigrated from Yugoslavia around the turn of the century—though there was, strictly speaking, no such country at that time. Matthias Zgomba, from Kamenica, and his wife, Viktorija Baršić, from Sremska Mitrovica on the Sava (you could see Serbia on the other side of the bridge, she used to say), were both Croats, and their only child, Emma, had as her first language Croatian. Matthias was a difficult man, raised to believe he was princely, but finding no opportunities of that order in the USA. His wife, Viktorija, of lesser education, and beautiful in her youth, joined him in work as a domestic, she being a superlative cook. Eventually, he would become a shipping clerk, though once his daughter married, he seemed to stop working altogether, infuriating his son-in-law by suggesting that he, Matthias, manage the money brought home by others. According to Emma, and to John Jurjevich, Matthias had a mean streak that he turned against his wife. And drinking made it worse. But Viktorija found work for herself, perhaps peaking in her career when she cooked for Luchow's, on Fourteenth Street.

More important for our story is the job she took in a small bakery in the Chelsea district of Manhattan. One of the partners in the business was from Omišalj, a small village on the island of Krk, off the coast of northern Croatia. He was tall, thin, with blazing and abundant red hair. Born Ivo to Kate Kraljić Jurjević and Nikola Jurjević, he was known in the USA as John, and was famous for his good nature and hard work. Having arrived in New York in 1921, knowing no English, he developed a peculiar accent that years later his youngest son-in-law, John Allman, would characterize as partly Brooklynese, Eastern European, and Yiddish. He said "goil" and "woik" and "dat don bodder me." But like many of the men from his island, he smiled frequently, laughed aloud midsentence for no apparent reason, and when the young Emma came to visit her mother, Viktorija Zgomba, he would tease her that the only reason she asked him for the time was to see if he had a watch at the end of the chain tucked in his pocket.

John and Emma married in 1928. She had recently graduated from New York University, had been friendly with a literary crowd in the Village, had written some poetry herself, and no one outside the Croatian circle of family and friends could fathom why she married a man with only a sixth-grade education whose English would never be very good. She would tell her youngest daughter that she had chosen a man whose genetic constitution was sound, a good man with family values, a simple man (once, while driving with the author to a lunch of buffalo burgers in Dutchess County, John said, "If you can't get along wit me, there's something wrong witchoo"), a hard-working man, who didn't drink. She had chosen him almost with eugenics in mind. At the same time, he would be a man who understood taking her parents to live with them from the moment there was a Mr. and Mrs. Jurjevich (Emma nicknamed him "Mr. Googelwich").

John, after Emma's death in 1987, told his daughter, Eileen, and her husband, that he had saved Emma from a terrible family situation—implying abuse and instability, because of Matthias. John saw himself as a savior. But he was in love with this bright, witty young woman, so well-spoken, so educated, a woman who would always manage their home, and all things bureaucratic, while he worked nights as a cake baker. Not that Emma didn't work. But after working to foreclose failed mortgages during the Depression, or at insurance claims adjustment, and after perhaps feeling that she was losing control of her children and household to her mother, she gave up working and devoted herself to their home life.

Sometime after Eileen—the third and last daughter (no boys having been born into the family line for several generations)—was born, the family changed its name to Jorge. It was Eileen Jorge who married John Ronald Allman on August 18, 1962.

On Emma's Loss of Hearing

That small artery to the small bones,
eighty years of blood: tiny hammers
that tap a heard voice, the soughing trees,
an inhabited code you awaken to,
smiling, the pink coverlet drawn to your chin.

    A hiss. An emptiness
like the inside of a fruit: dark,
your husband's mouth opening and closing,

           collapsed flower,
the way stars implode, after momentary redness,
drawn into themselves, your husband's words gone
    back
down, swallowed.

There, he must have said, "there,"
pointing to his left ear, then at yours,
as if diaphanous demons had flitted across,
their mosquito-songs what you feel entering your
    blood,
and what taking out, what silence.

Splash of water. Thermostat's "click."
A storm door thumping when you feel the blast
of cold air. Vibrations through your shoes.
A truck going past. The smell of diesel exhaust.

A chickadee's at the feeder,
snatching sunflower seeds;
now he's on the birch branch,
pecking one between his feet.
You can feel him on the back of your hand,
and your husband tapping you,
until you turn, learning the shape of his lips.

"Emma."

In 1943, Helen Allman decided to move the family to Astoria, Queens, an area already discovered by her sister Adelaide, who had moved into a long, railroad-style apartment over Merkel's Pork Store on Broadway, two blocks from the El. Helen was in her fourth pregnancy, the superintendent of a small apartment house on Forty-fifth Street, off Ninth Avenue, while she also worked late afternoons running an elevator at the Astor Hotel. Alice was almost four years old. John Ronald, the oldest (having been named Ronald at birth, when Helen, in a fit of pique with her husband, named her firstborn after Ronald Colman, but restored the John/Jack tradition by the time of the infant's baptism), had already cut his wrist one morning, trying to drill an extra hole in his new belt—using the huge, French carving knife—before going off to class in a public school on Forty-seventh Street (his third school in almost as many years), and John, the father, was drinking plenty and involved with a bad crowd. Queens was the New World. Astoria a greenness on the other side of the river, where Helen's mother, May Burghard—a large, permissive, inactive woman always scanning the want ads for a job—would for a brief time have an apartment near the El, serving tea with condensed milk and sugar and buttered white bread that became the oldest grandson's dominant memory of her.

May was called Big Nana. Gertrude Prince Allman was Little Nana, and after the family moved into an apartment at 41-11 Twenty-eighth Avenue, she often visited, with her black, beretlike hat fastened to her thinning hair with a long pin, her English jaw narrow and protruding, her purse full of loose change for the children, and a bottle of vitamins, red One-a-Days she popped into their mouths. The bottle of port she stashed in the laundry sink in the kitchen, under the enamel lid. She said *tom-ah-toes*, ate all the fat on pork chops, sucked the marrow from bones, and squashed roaches on the wall with her thumb. She lacked the aura of kindness and humor that was May, Big Nana's, but was more caring—bringing the children with her and her lover, Charley Rooney, whenever they rented rooms in Coney Island or Rockaway (the same Charley who, red-faced, his white hair stiff with amazement, would propose to Helen Allman after the double funeral for Gertrude and her son, John King, on the very day, in fact, when John Ronald met his mother's father for the first and only time, hearing tall tales about World War I, while the old man angled for what he could get from his daughter's insurance benefits—of which there were none). Little Nana had the children over for visits in her three-room flat on Forty-seventh Street in Manhattan. John Ronald remembered living there with his parents years before, during some crisis or other. That living room with its camphorous odor after the huge door separating it from the kitchen slid open—a darkness more than light filtering through the back window, a dust-free statue of the Virgin Mary under bell-shaped glass, a row of white ivory elephants, trunks holding tails in tandem, and three monkeys, neither speaking, hearing, nor seeing evil, hands clasped over the appropriate areas—all these figures in the sensory myths of continuous love.

*

A sunny day in June 1991 and I am renovating the small bathroom that adjoins my study in the basement of our house on Frances Drive. I've stripped the rotted paneling from cinder-block walls, painted everything a vivid gold—the result of mixing gallons of leftover paints—and I'm staring into the toilet tank, where years of rust and lime deposits have permanently fouled the flow and shutoff mechanism. Eileen says there seems some connection between my obsession to redo this bathroom and the writing of my autobiography. The study itself I built in 1979, a year after we moved into this, our very first house, which is attached by a bricked-in breezeway to a smaller house now inhabited only by Eileen's widower father. We have two-and-a-half acres and think of it all as the family compound. This is our good-luck place, bought in the year Eileen was tenured at Lehman College—having placed her book, *Player-King and Adversary: Two Faces of Play in Shakespeare*, with Louisiana State University Press. In fall of that year, 1978, Princeton University Press accepted my book, *Walking Four Ways in the Wind*, poems written mostly between 1972–76.

I am replacing the guts of the toilet tank, installing a flow mechanism of the latest type (a cuplike collar rides up and down the phallic shaft), couplings, rubber tubing. I'm applying black silicone sealer wherever I believe water will seep between old porcelain and squeezed-down vinyl washers. My fingertips are gooey as cormorants caught in the oil slick of the terrorized Persian Gulf. I am caught up in this labor having learned from boyhood that a man works with his hands, the heft of tools passed on from my father, and later from my uncle Joe Gerardi, in whose gas station I worked for two years weekends and summers until I was thrown out of high school in 1952 for nonattendance and found work as a mail clerk for Pepsi-Cola in Long Island City.

This is the rhythm I enjoy and why I understand Robinson Jeffers working on poems, then on his stones. And I think, suddenly, how odd and wonderful it is that this evening three of my poet friends, Dan Masterson, Billy Collins, and Robert Phillips are coming for dinner, that I will be yakking and laughing with them and touring the grounds I have just mowed with my Sears garden tractor, pointing out the thicket of raspberries that began as ten naked sticks in 1978, and stopping to admire my father-in-law's vegetable garden that is neat and precise as the little village of Omišalj from which he immigrated in 1920 and where we visited in 1990—walking with him among the casually bountiful fig trees, looking from the steep cliff of the town into the clear Adriatic blue, the ancient stone houses behind us, he, born Ivo Jurjević in 1903, Americanized as John Jorge, saying, after a seventy-year absence from his birthplace,

"You know, Jack, it's a nice place to visit, but you don't want to live here." And I realize that after thirteen years of living next door and working together, I have become the son of this stooped man whose Titian red hair has thinned and turned white, his laughter and quick and practical intelligence as natural to me as the sunlight pouring down.

I had almost forgotten that morning in April 1955, when I half-carried my father to the bathroom because suddenly he couldn't walk, his speech slurring, a numbness pervading the right side of his body, when he sat on the toilet and beat his head with his fist, gnashing his teeth until the stroke that was emptying his mind deprived him even of his anger.

*

"Eileen and I lived on Douglas Street, a residential area on the other side of James Street, and we loved it—dropping our daughter off at nursery school, going to classes, settling into ourselves." This in a letter to the poet Dick Allen on 2 November 1987, about living in Syracuse, being in graduate school, writing, learning to teach—this place where we arrived in late January 1964, nearly midnight, the snow beginning to coat our belongings that we'd moved out of the rented U-Haul onto the street, as passing students stopped to browse like scavengers. The writer Paul Hastings Wilson, my friend, and my brother Dan, who'd driven with us in a rented Chevy all the way from the Bronx, helping with the sofa bed and the books that we lugged three stories into the dormer apartment, its dark green bedroom with jagged, abstract mural. Jennifer, four months old, small enough to tuck into her folding seat under the dashboard, near the heater, had slept most of the way. Eileen and I stood in the falling snow, wondering what we'd done.

"There are really two pasts in that time [same letter to Dick Allen]: one that I just described; and the other belonging to Vietnam, the terrible anger and confusion, the constant threat that everything one had worked for could be piled on the floor and burned with the draft cards. I mean, one's whole life. One's belief in literature. One's belief in the logos, in work, in making a family. Who didn't hate those bastards in Washington? But who could trust the people screaming in the streets? I wish I could remember it as a time in which I had done something good."

A reviewer once mentioned that John Allman had studied with Delmore Schwartz. It's true that he took a course in literary aesthetics with Schwartz in

1964, Allman's second semester at Syracuse, where he had been accepted into the creative writing program thanks to the recommendation of Leonard Lief, the teacher of Shakespeare that Eileen and he both had studied with, and who later became the first president of Lehman College. It was in Syracuse that Allman met Jay Meek and they read each other's poems. He'd visit Jay at his apartment on Beech Street, or Jay would dine with the Allmans in their place on Douglas Street, and there'd be talk of poets, poems, careers, how to do, not to do. Thanks to Jay, Allman saw the film *In A Dark Time* about Theodore Roethke, and was drawn back into poetry after a long time believing he should be writing short stories. Roethke's "I proclaim once more a condition of joy" swept him back into image and language. It helped, too, when Robert Graves delivered a reading and talk around that time. Even with the phony baloney of swirling his cape and posing with young girls, he was inspiring. And other poets came to read, notably, David Wagoner, who had just accepted Allman's poem "The Reminiscence" for *Poetry Northwest* and who would be the most important editor for him until

Future wife, Eileen Jorge, with her sisters, Diana and Joan Jorge, about 1947

Brother Daniel Allman, Venice, 1987

he worked with Peter Glassgold at New Directions. And there were W. D. Snodgrass, Donald Justice, James Dickey, Allen Ginsberg. Aside from Jay and Eileen [once or twice, Donald Dike], and by mail, Paul Hastings Wilson, the only other person he showed poems to was Philip Booth, who gave of his time and wisdom in ways that remain forever important.

"Mostly, I tried to keep my head. To patch together students who thought they could march around the block and change the world in nothing flat. I remember a student yelling at me that the *D* he received on his essay on some Shakespearean sonnets would get him drafted. I was condemning him to death. Later, I taught for four years at the women's college, Cazenovia College, and was there in 1970 when all the campuses exploded. Cazenovia didn't— but we opened up everything to talk and anger . . . [I must have been doing something 'good,' since members of the American Legion threatened to punch me out if I ever entered the local bar] I don't remember it as heroic but as nasty . . . But, god, I sat behind Ginsberg after introducing him at Syra-

cuse, sat behind him, on the floor, on the stage, while he read all of the 'Wichita Vortex Sutra,' and I thought, this is a great poem, and only a poem that Ginsberg could have written. But everything I tried to write about the war was rhetorical and second-hand. I hated the falseness of my work and I hated having to write about the war . . . How does any poetry relate to politics (if war is ultimate politics)?

"These things torment me, because I look at the homeless and unemployed, and wonder what poetry has to do with them or they with poetry. It's stupid to believe that all art must be postponed until all the people are secure. It's decadent, surely, to believe that all art is *pour* art, but in some ways I know that is true. And I suppose I believe in perpetuating the thin line of being, the single vivid nerve that connects all human consciousness from age to age, while trying to be honest in my politics and humane in my ethics."

Widow

It happens in ways I never expect,
like hailstones in summer. Going
uphill on the bike, I snap the chain.
In the tub, shaving my legs, I cut

my throat on my ankle. I sweat nightly,
pull back the blankets, see my
husband just lying down in the mirror.
I burn my hand on the iron
I test with spit: the children tumble
in from the yard with a dead bird.
I pretend, alone. I cook
for pale guests seen only at 10 p.m.
They forget to wipe their mouths,
chattering like starlings. I bang
the table and they disappear, black
coffee spilled on the white tablecloth.
I've given up smoking, I try push-ups;
for lungs and double chin, I stand on
my head: watching the late news,
the bombs falling up the sky, the men
ascending in their bloody uniforms.

"Political forms do indeed enable us to perpetuate anything, but that there are two worlds we live in all the time is the secret tension of our work. I don't mind paradox or contrariety or Jung's enantiodromia that converts one thing into its opposite—it's when I feel forced to destroy the both/and tensile strength of mind in favor of an either/or mode that is not so much philosophical as political. And however much I would like politics to be a thoughtful and moral event, I know it's the world of action and force. And that's the world that brings art to its knees—unless one has enough countervailing aesthetic that is both sincere and powerful. I believe that is what I'm seeking at the moment; a kind of see-through bulwark, like Picasso's painting on glass, that will contain social pressure but allow personal expression and vision, vision, for god's sake."

Several weeks after he sent this letter, the writer received a phone call—it was the Saturday after Thanksgiving—from Ed Sanders, a down-on-his-luck friend of the youngest Allman brother, Steven, who lived in a welfare hotel on Fourteenth Street. He was to the point. Steven had passed away—to use Ed's expression—in his arms, outside a pharmacy. It was described as a mysterious happening. As if Steven had been struck down by something genetic, invaded by a lethal clot. As if after freeing himself from nineteen years of alcoholism, his drug addiction was incidental. Steven's homelessness and inability to hold a job had become an inability to get a job because he looked so scarred, talked too loud, flew so easily off the handle, with that nonetheless endearing grin, a slight astigmatism in one eye unfitting him for delicate tasks, a hitch in his walk uncannily like his father's, the timbre of his voice likewise, so that his two brothers often experienced not so much Steven as a haunting—this youngest child, born after his father had been too drunk to drive his forty-year-old pregnant wife to the hospital (a task fulfilled by the oldest son)—who had lived for years with a sister dazed by psychiatric medications, a mother who ministered to her breakdowns, two women joined body and mind in symbiotic illness—this thirty-four-year-old man with a boy's mischievousness and adult fury, this man whose two brothers would bring money and clothes to him during the year and at Christmas, not knowing what else could matter to someone so demonically driven—he was finally at rest.

At the morgue in Queens General Hospital, where Dan and John identified the body, they learned that Steven had taken an overdose, a fact his friend had tried to conceal. They stared through the glass panel at their brother, the white cloth around his head from the autopsy's trepanning, and wept, as they had done in 1979, in this same odorous, unclean anteroom, when they viewed the slack-jawed face of their sister, who had consumed all her medications at once.

*

Brother Steven Allman, at twelve, about 1965

[In a letter to James Laughlin, 11 June 1991, about writing this autobiography] "It's like cleaning out an attic. Scraping sludge from a pump. Falling out of a tree. I'm trying not to rebirth myself entirely— something I notice many poets do. . . . They cancel out their mothers and give birth to themselves. I suppose we all do that, in poems or elsewhere. It's when we first breathe our *chosen* time. What's an umbilical but guilt? The tie backward to oblivion. But this going backwards or crabwise is something the mind is too good at. The soupy un-whatness that images evaporate from, I know that, I know the sluggishness of morning and the weird, the *wyrd,* that taints the first fragrance of June—and I want to speak in the present, the now, the all, the only that ever flows. What have I to do with memory?"

D ark, she was dark. As a young woman, her jaw became more prominent and the Englishness of her physical heritage prevailed over what had been in her childhood something exotic and nearly Latin. Her olive skin. Her quickness. Glittering brown eyes. According to her brother Dan, their grandmother, Little Nana, though born in Northumberland, was partly of Spanish stock—derived from a woman somewhere in the past, thought to be somewhat mad. But one could just as easily say Alice's darkness was simply from the north of England or was Norman in origin (the name Allman originally being Allemand, the French word for German, the family's history lost in the fog of a long pilgrimage from Germany through France to Ireland and England to the United States). In childhood, she was close to her older brother who was blond and fair, and for a time they shared a double bed, in which she would awaken him with the trophy of a caught mouse, the trap's steel spring flipped over on its neck, its black eyes like bits of embedded obsidian. Of all the children, she was the most visibly artistic—drawing with conspicuous talent, and eventually being placed, through competitive city-wide tests, in the High School of Industrial Art and Design—though she would leave that school for Bryant High School in Astoria and a General Diploma, a fact that her older brother used to seize upon as the first sign of her withdrawal from her talents, the shrinkage of her native aggressiveness, the conversion of her laughter into tremulous phobias. But in those teenage years, she hated the daily trip by subway from Astoria into Manhattan. When she was sixteen, her home life was complicated by a semi-invalid father who ranted and raged over his lost capacities, who returned regularly to Goldwater Memorial Hospital on Welfare Island (now Roosevelt Island, a tranquil, suburban village of condo-style buildings—with no evidence of the dank and gothic City Hospital, its long wards filled with the poor and dying, where Alice's father had first been taken, hours after he'd been left on a stretcher in the emergency room of a private hospital that refused to

admit him because he had no health insurance. Years later, Alice's older brother, remembering the trips to Welfare Island, the trolley that stopped midway in the Queensboro Bridge, the elevator that took passengers down the shaft of the bridge column, the little bus that took visitors to the hospital, where he brought his father a brown paper bag filled with cigarettes and chewing gum—Alice's brother was almost pleased to learn that this had once been Blackwell's Island, with a prison that housed Emma Goldman). Nor could anyone measure the effects of being the only female child, with three brothers, a father who had little interest in her even in his healthy years, a mother who had shaped herself to crisis and male anger. Alice's desire to be done with school and out in the world, on her own, was outright health. It was not what her older brother once interpreted as timidity in art. At art. In fact, Alice took a small basement apartment in the two-family house where her mother and brothers lived—the family having tried a devastating stint renting a house in Central Islip, Long Island, after the father died, but moving back to Astoria when neither Alice nor her mother could tolerate their jobs as nurse's aides in the psychiatric hospital, nor the isolation from friends—the oldest son hitchhiking into New York City, where he took night classes at Hunter College. Alice seemed on her way. But in the midst of a dispute with her mother, one in which her mother threatened to move out and leave her truly on her own, with no mother upstairs ready to be used, Alice had the first of her breakdowns. Or separations. Or disalignments. Or reconfiguring journeys into illness. The family was completely mystified by the psychologist—who had been treating Alice for what seemed an understandable neurosis, given the family moils, and himself, it appears, having also slept with her—when he declared in the waiting room of Elmhurst General Hospital that Alice was beyond the reach of conventional treatment. He talked of drugs. Electric shock. The older brother was later told by a psychiatrist that Alice relied heavily upon him—a fact he rejected, since he had recently married, and felt that a family power scenario was emerging, with Alice the prime manipulator—an interpretation he would never quite relinquish, even among the talk of schizophrenia, genetics, even when he argued with a psychiatrist in the halls of Creedmoor thirteen years later, refusing to sign his sister out if that meant he was legally responsible for her return.

For sixteen years, the myths and facts of mental illness wove the family into gestures and postures sometimes as ritual and fixed as those in tapestries. From scene to scene, one could trace a continuity implicit in the drinking problem passed from Little

Sister Alice Allman, age twenty, about 1959

under the stars, under the wide, harsh
moonlight that kept her awake
night after night: so little gray
in such a dark sea, but finely shaded
and lighter than the air
in a tin container. I risk my skin,
though she is separated, at last,
from the rotten twine that unraveled
in her blood, knotting her brain,
closing the tiny apertures in the root
of speech. A dirge flows easily
from a battered end. The boat rocks
and hesitates and heaves on the scope
of a hand: whatever grip we move in.
I'm tilting on openness. I have something to say

about dark and fair: sister, inheritor
of someone else's anger, a crossed fate handed on;
and me, lucky, unmusical, thin as a paper clip,
keeping together. Why read catalogues,
while she dissolves toward Europe, returning
a life that almost ended on edges of glass?
The sleeping sand would absorb her history
in words. Let the sea love her,
who drowned on the second story,
where hands at the window made the arabesques
of the rhythmic dead. Her life was filled.
The body pours out. This is not herself,
though the soul crumples like paper
thrown from a boat, though voice becomes the
    bending
of underwater weed. Earth has a grief, trembling.
In the vacuum and total dark between the mineral
bodies of Space, a single ash whirls.

Nana to her son, the frayed genetic thread likewise transferred, the history of unspoken narcissism that battled incestuous nearness, as if separating from each other was more threatening to mother and children than a father's rage or a world's indifference. Alice's assertive intelligence, the fineness of her delineating hands, her love of animals, the too-early use of psychiatric drugs that caused numbness and small strokes in her face, the voluptuousness of her youth, all lost in rigidifying documents and reports.

*

"Do the lives of others take their places in us, where they remain until spoken for? I feel that. The gauzy drift of their faces and voices, they can't any longer be those people we once knew. But more than psychic imprint or cartoon, more than the shredded events of a mind's small aerial bombardments" [letter to James Laughlin, 11 June 1991].

The Scattering

Leaving now the hired help, the niches and
    enclosures,
I give her ashes to the long tide

I'm sitting in my white Jetta, watching a woman in green pants suit making her way in the faculty parking lot against a sudden wind and dust storm that sweeps across the oval reservoir. The afternoon darkens, the whirl of dust is like rain but none has fallen. It resembles light from a grayish yellow filter, confused and repelled, a vortex, and I look toward Sedgwick Avenue for signs of a twister, until I realize the woman being blinded, jacket and pants pinned to her body then twisted to one side like fabric in a wind tunnel, as she accelerates against several gravities, her hair swept back—in Chagall's painting, a woman flying over a shtetl (this very moment an off-duty policeman driving north on the Taconic is crushed by a falling tree)—I realize that I'm staring at Eileen. I try to sound my horn, squeezing and pounding the black cushioned middle of the steering wheel. Without the ignition on, everything is dead. I'm shouting through the closed window, digging into my pocket for the key, Eileen almost completely stalled in a particulate cloud of debris. I roll down the window, my eyes blinking, invaded by soot. I jam the key in, I lean on the horn, I'm sounding the two syllables of her name, one like a breathing in, the second expelled toward her where my voice enters the maelstrom and she hears me. She sees me.

Two people died in that storm. But why I did not recognize Eileen, in the Lehman College parking lot, in the north Bronx, opposite the campus where we had met in 1961, I could easily attribute to the pants suit that I had not before seen her in. Or to having just sat in the rock garden, near Gillet Hall, looking down on the plaque for Dean John W. Wieler, under the yew—this man who had restored twenty-one credits of course work I almost lost because of "excessive absence," even though I had earned an *A* in each course—and I recalled his booming voice, when he would hail one of us in Shuster Hall. Or I was remembering the ancient Greek I studied in Gillet, where I scraped through Plato's *Apologia*. Or that I'd just received a letter from my friend, David Zane Mairowitz, whom I'd first met here, who was now living in Avignon. Or that this college—once Hunter College in the Bronx, where Eileen has been teaching since 1970, and from which she and I received our first degrees, and where I finished my last year while we lived in our first apartment on Rochambeau Avenue—is the hub of Fortuna's wheel on which my life turned from low to high, this gift of education from the working generations before us.

And the failure of my Jetta's horn was a reminder of that. And of a five-story walk-up apartment on Sixth Street in Manhattan, near Avenue C, where the light poured in higher than the plane tree in a dusty Eden of greened yard between buildings, though it was the middle of the night when I wrote tight little lyric poems, rolling back and forth on my wheeled chair that had the people underneath begging the super—a woman blind in one eye—to stop me from moving furniture about, while they slept. I was working the night shift as a part-time temporary substitute clerk at the Church Street Station of the post office.

If a writer cannot make a living from his or her writing, how should it be done? At the end of one year, in the late fifties, I counted thirteen W-2 forms. I had worked at everything from mopping floors as a night porter in a bank to selling grape drinks for the Golub Brothers at the Mark Hellinger Theater. That year, I was reading Dostoevsky and Zen Buddhism and sharing an apartment in the Bronx with Stephen Grosso. He and I would talk about Henry Miller—I never dreamt I'd be published by New Directions—and Stephen would work on his stories (and religious manias), while I labored at something I called "The Chronicle of a Very Young Man." But I yearned for something more consistent, to be free of money

worries, to settle into the flow of what I deemed a writer's work.

In those years, I changed residence every six months. A furnished room on Fifty-eighth Street, next to the Henry Hudson Hotel, a closet of a room in which I could touch both walls by extending my arms. The risers of the metal stairs that led to the front door read, "For Men Only." Or the room in a brownstone on Seventy-first Street, off Central Park West: double sliding doors with frosted glass, gilt mouldings, a defunct fireplace, high ceiling—once the drawing room or parlor. Back less than a month from living in California—in North Hollywood, then Culver City, working for an engineering firm, treating a new substance called Teflon, using lab skills I'd learned in the Product Control Lab at Pepsi-Cola—I was now working two jobs, while attending evening classes at Hunter College (I'd been unmatriculated by Brooklyn College, the first college I attended, having completed only one semester in four or five attempts).

I'd soon find myself sharing an apartment with Derek Verner in the Bronx, around 157th Street and Park Avenue, near the railroad tracks. He needed it for a place to bring his girlfriends to, while I posted signs over his room, "Abandon All Hope Ye Who Enter Here." I began to study German, and considered teaching that language my career. I'd sit up late, writing poems about the moon. Or I'd let the cadences of "Lycidas"—that my English teacher said was the touchstone for poets—seep into me and I'd produce archaic strophes that seemed melodic exercises for an instrument. What mixture of death and longing, what coolness of streetlights and sooty winds, the noise of the New York Central in my ears, while I imagined twitching my mantle in the dawn.

I seemed miles from the hospital bed I'd occupied in Bellevue, when in March 1957, working day and night, trying to finish another semester at Brooklyn College—having changed my interest from medicine to psychology (influenced by readings in Carl Jung)—I experienced severe chest pains while handing out coats from the checkroom at the Mark Hellinger Theater. My left lung had collapsed. The despair I felt, waiting for X rays in the emergency room at Bellevue, where George Kirschenbaum, uncle to the Golub Brothers, had taken me, was as low as hopes had been high. This was the third time one of my lungs had collapsed. Twice before, my right lung had partially collapsed—once, while I was taking a history final in night high school, and once again while I was working at a perfume plant, pushing around giant drums of patchouli, my father home and recovering from his first stroke. But this was the first time my left lung had been affected. It was no wonder I took to the work of D. H. Lawrence, who, combined with Dostoevksy, had shown me a path away from science. Lying in the open ward at Bellevue—another semester at Brooklyn washed away, the old men around me gargling up foul matter, myself too weak and out of breath to get to the marble-slab bathroom, having spent two months for the same thing at Queens General Hospital in 1955—I lost all belief in the future. And my lung would not re-expand. Not until they removed me to the chest ward, where a vacuum device was inserted in my chest, and the lung adhered to the pleural wall. While recuperating among men who had lost part or all of a lung, their chests caved in where ribs had been removed (Mann called it "re-sectioned" in *The Magic Mountain),* a long, thin rubber tube—"the red devil"—inserted into their tracheas to induce coughing, visitors leaning over them and bleating like distressed sheep, all of us patients drifting and loquacious in the mists of Demoral—I couldn't imagine what more could happen, until my mother visited and described how Little Nana had been found sitting on her stoop on Forty-seventh Street in a state of total neglect. Perhaps what the doctors then called schizophrenia would now be called Alzheimer's. Whatever it was, Gertrude Prince Allman was removed to the State Hospital in Central Islip, where she would die on the same day as her son in September 1958.

It came as quite a surprise to me, therefore, when a young Chinese intern leaned over me in the ward I was moved to, days after the vacuum tube had been removed, and informed me that my life expectancy was normal. No signs of physical disease. How could this be? My lungs were the reason I had been rejected when I tried to enlist in the army at the age of nineteen, and twice more when the army tried to induct me in the grim arenas of Whitehall Street. "Psycho-neurosis severe" is what one of the preinduction files read.

I concluded there was nothing wrong that the will could not fix. That in the matter of who one was or wanted to be, the primary guilt was in being unfaithful to oneself. That any decision about one's present and future was as sound as the degree of other guilts absorbed into it. That when I rose from another hospital bed, in Los Angeles County Hospital, the pain mysteriously gone from my chest, I would never again substitute the shadow of disease for a palpable life.

*

1976. I write a statement for an interview on local cable TV in Rockland County, in which my colleague Ann Fey will ask me about writing poetry: "A poem is any verbal construct (for the printed page or voice) that illuminates the ordinary, or treats the extraordinary as habitual and present—and it does this primarily through the use of image and rhythm (and patterns of sound). The better . . . poems tend to link the physical and non-physical worlds—or the material and . . . spiritual or dream worlds we all live in simultaneously, though we rarely see or are aware of that simultaneity. The poem opens the door between those worlds . . . a door that sometimes opens in dreams, and when we walk through, we enter a world that cannot be explained by the usual coordinates of time and space: we are at once walking and flying, at once in the present and the past, and exotic odors from the future enter us, confound us with images, with feelings. . . . we can understand how dreams were once viewed as prophecies." One wants "to choose the vehicle and language that

Daughter, Jennifer Allman, 1986

liberate one's own imagination—that release at once the personal and the a-personal feelings—that bind the personal to the communal self."

I was nearly finished with the collection of poems that became *Walking Four Ways in the Wind* and that two years later David Wagoner would accept for the Princeton Series of Contemporary Poets. (About this book, Helen Carr would say in the *Times Literary Supplement,* 25 April 1980, it "contains a whole range of New York voices, personas, memories . . . it seems that for Allman . . . geography is a means of understanding the ways of others, which he does . . . with novelistic specificity.") I had also taken a leap into material that would occupy me for six years, having that April written "Dostoevsky at Semyonov Square," conceiving of a project I wanted to completely occupy my time. I was moving from family-oriented poems to narratives. I was concerned with how the power of the State imposed upon the power of the person, and I read biographies by the score, seeking the experiential moments in which an individual and history could be expressed in the personal idiom of character. A single voice filled my mind and for years dominated every poem—so much that in the end I began to doubt whether I was working with historical personages or just using them as facades for a sustained meditation on survival. (No one could know that "George Sand at Palaiseau" and "Bruno Bettelheim at Dachau" were about my sister's death in 1979, or that grief over my mother's death in 1980 was encoded in "Marcel Proust Leaving Princesse Soutzo's Room at the Ritz" and "Antonin Artaud in the Land of the Tarahumaras.") We had moved to our second apartment in Yonkers, in a two-family house. I was tenured at Rockland Community College. In a year's time Eileen's book would be accepted by Louisiana State University Press. I would soon receive the Helen Bullis Award from *Poetry Northwest.* We were doing well, but I felt that I was in some way the cultural repository of feelings and images that would be lost, that my poems had been defined too much by personal material, that I wanted to fashion a voice from the combined consciousness of many men and women. I sought, too, the heroic, an unfashionable largeness of motive, a sense of humans caught up in destiny—something pervasively tragic in how individuals strove against the State. I was moving from family history to history. And though I was able to publish almost all of these poems individually— and one of them, "Marcus Garvey Arrested at the 125th Street Station," received a Pushcart Award in 1983, and later some of them would be in a packet that received a National Endowment for the Arts award in 1984—the book-length manuscript received

no welcome at any publishing house until I submitted it to New Directions, and James Laughlin said in his note of 24 February 1984 (by which time we had moved to Somers): "I like your 'historical epiphanies' (my term) *very* much. Even when Pound scrambles it up, I think history is a great subject for poetry. . . . I suppose some people won't like your 'metric,' but I think it works. And useful to me to examine it because I'm involved in a long poem (memory poem) about my life with Pound which, perforce, to work in his utterance, has to be pretty prosey."

I titled the collection *Clio's Children,* added a second paragraph (which I now regret) to the "Preface," and New Directions published it in 1985.

How could I do anything, if each morning Eileen did not sit opposite me at table, her eyes shining with belief? If we were not each other's best friend and lover?

World without You

If this were a dream, I'd be halfway up
the Golden Chain, my ankles twisted in its links,
   angels fluttering their robes, and below
me, calloused hands of brutes, detached from wrists,
   furred and holding on. If this were a dream,
I'd break free and fall once more into the river, a depth
   of 20 feet, I'd watch the hippos cropping weeds,

I'd swim through their massive jaws. If this were a dream,
   the glossy bodies dancing in silt, the algaed
faces of lovers and suicides kissing past with closed
   eyes, I'd comb my fingers through their hair,
I'd let go sorrow like a cinder block, I'd rise to the last
   inch and film of water, to see the blue outline
of your face delicate as scrimshaw. If this were a dream,

   let loose from the river's mouth, I'd thrash
into the sea, and speak to dolphins in the helium-squeak
   of aquanauts, pronouncing your name, which even
here is flammable and quick. Bursting through the nets
   of Portuguese fishermen, limpidly finned, human
and other, quite nearly feathered, I'd fly out of this dream
                    to find you.

*

I am eating oatmeal at a small table in a truck stop in Troutville, Virginia. Opposite me, eating his oatmeal, is my father-in-law, and next to me, eating her oatmeal, is Eileen. We are like the three bears seeking what is just right, as huge, abdominous truckers lean over their food at the horseshoe-shaped counter, stools creaking and swaying beneath them. They all wear sneakers or stained walking shoes with molded soles and cushioned heel guards. The worn-looking married couple, in their late fifties, at the table to my right, are consuming pancakes, eggs, bacon, buttered toast, home fries. I know that's what I'd like to be eating. My oatmeal is cool and lumpy. But I am doing what is right. I watch them light cigarettes. I watch my father-in-law, age eighty-eight, hold his spoon so that one can draw a straight line from it, along his wrist, to the elbow. His arm swivels from the shoulder, partly from arthritis, partly from a learned economy of motion. He rarely talks when eating. It's serious business. But not for the men at the counter. The T-shirted white man with his back to us is a dairy farmer, stomach heaved over his belt, his feet coyly hugging the slender post of the stool. He is talking with a raised spoon like a preacher, inciting to laughter the lean, muscular black man next to him and the young white man with a droopy face and two black men opposite, one in glasses who has just been drumming his fingers impatiently. I can't comprehend what they're saying. Vowels long and

Wife, Eileen Allman, 1991

twisted, the cackle and whoop of their joy blurring nuance, two of them slapping the formica surface ringed from coffee cups, their eyes bright, their need to entertain each other a function of the silence they endure on the road. I realize that thirty years ago they would not all be at the same counter. That my father-in-law's silence at meals is part of an organic rhythm that occasionally shapes itself into conventional gestures, like the time he wept into a towel when his wife died, when he wailed openly and publicly, but never again. And though we are taking him to visit his oldest daughter, Joan, in Keowee Key, South Carolina, though he must sit in the back of the car for nearly two days, he moves in his bent-backed way without restraint, without any sense of coercion in the life about him. It is how I would like to be.

And I remember the squinched-up face of Henry Larom, his mustache trapped between upper lip and nose, sparse gray hair erect as in a crew cut, glasses reflecting light as he scans my resume and himpphs and humpphs, then points to a framed newspaper article on the wall that describes his career as a journalist and writer of children's westerns. I am not clear who is interviewing whom. It is June 1971. I am exhausted from teaching at Cazenovia College, trying to write, trying to maneuver through the war, the invasion of Cambodia, the killings at Kent State, everything political soured by the deaths of Martin Luther King, Jr., and Robert Kennedy. Nixon is about to impose a freeze on prices and wages. Eileen is trying to finish her dissertation. We are living apart and trying to get it together, trying to get unstuck, too, from the calls that persist from my mother about my sister's breakdowns, my brother Steven's alcohol and drug use. Henry Larom chews the end of his cigar—I never remember him with a whole one— and squints at me as he talks about himself. I know he is sizing me up, while he fills the room with jabber and smoke. This is Rockland Community College—a place I have learned of through a colleague at Cazenovia, Lionel Sharp.

By August, I am hired. And I begin my friendship with the poet Dan Masterson, who will read practically every word I write for the next twenty years, who will counsel and befriend me, in whose office I will sit semester after semester, blowing off steam, soliloquizing, shaping poems.

*

1991. I toil (a favorite word of an old teacher, Leo Gurko) in a basement study built to sequester myself from cats who kept jumping onto desk and

John and Eileen Allman, with dogs Lucy and "Big Girl," 1991

manuscripts—a study since become elaborate with book shelves and computer and dehumidifier. Jennifer is back from several years in Munich, now studying to become a teacher of English as a second language. Eileen is working with contemporary critical theory and Jacobean Drama.

It is summer. Eileen and I walk each morning with Lucy—a dog of mixed breed, long-haired and low, like a Border collie, with the floppy ears, brow and black nose of a retriever—found abandoned on Goulden Avenue. A dog Eileen brought home.

"I've done something terrible. I've brought home a puppy."

"A puppy?"

"She's in the car. I'm afraid she's ugly."

I look at the knot in the tail of our aging Siamese cat, Jake, and the frost-damaged ears of Molly, rescued as a kitten racing across a busy street in Mount Vernon.

"Since when have we had requirements?"

BIBLIOGRAPHY

Poetry:

Walking Four Ways in the Wind, Princeton University Press, 1979.

Clio's Children, New Directions, 1985.

Scenarios for a Mixed Landscape, New Directions, 1986.

Curve Away from Stillness, New Directions, 1989.

Contributor:

Helen Plotz, editor, *Saturday's Children: Poems of Work,* Greenwillow, 1982.

Bill Henderson, editor, *Pushcart Prize VIII: Best of the Small Presses,* Pushcart, 1983.

Anthology of American Verse and Yearbook of American Poetry, Monitor Book, 1985.

James Laughlin et al., editors, *New Directions in Prose and Poetry, 54,* New Directions, 1990.

After the Story, Maisonneuve Press, 1992.

Contributor to literary journals, including *Agni Review; Atlantic;* "The Tip" (short story), *Epoch,* spring 1968; *Massachusetts Review;* "Motherless Creation: Motifs in Science Fiction" (essay), *North Dakota Quarterly,* spring 1990; and *Poetry.*

Russell Banks

1940-

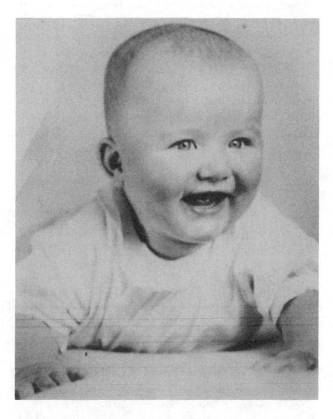

Russell Banks, about six months old

Show us an arc of the curve,
and a good mathematician will find out the whole figure.
—Emerson

A vague chill fills me on this occasion, a superstition, perhaps, that, to honor, makes me stammer and want to lie. I find it hard to believe that I've come this far—that I've turned up alive and more or less coherent at the age of fifty-one. Yet, year after year, like the proverbial bad penny, I do keep on turning up, and the very persistence of the fact continues to astonish me, although I've certainly done little else but try to keep on turning up. It's as if one actually loved someone, all the while never quite believing in one's capacity for love; or as if one were loved, never having believed that one was

loveable. First comes pure delight, and then an awareness of being surprised, and then this present wariness sets in—superstition. A tentative, testing refusal of the inescapable fact. You bite the penny.

But why such a stubborn sense of my own fragility, when by all acounts, even by most of my own, I am a healthy, hearty, and, to a nearly exceeding degree, a resilient fellow? Why, indeed? A question with an obvious answer, gently, almost accidentally, occasioned here—for one turns instantly, naturally, to childhood, to first impressions of the shades that surrounded one then. And yet—suspicious again—what one calls common sense and memory operate as effectively in ferreting out the truth (as it were) of one's childhood as in mythologizing it. One recreates his past in order to meet the needs of his present, and does it far more easily than, for the same reasons, one manipulates the future. And does both by means of common sense and memory. The first, one's educated intelligence, provides the principles of organization, the form and motive for the inquiry; and the second, what one can recall of his experiences, provides the data. And away we go. Anywhere, as Baudelaire says, so long as it's out of this world.

For example, in the early 1960s, when I first began foreign travel, I applied for a passport and discovered that I needed a copy of my birth certificate, which I did not have in my possession. I had no memory of having even seen it (although I must have possessed it once, for I had a social security number). My family was disorderly and mistrusted documentation, however—a residual mistrust of officialdom, perhaps, a suspicion borne of guilt, feelings of inadequacy, and fear of entrapment. People with chaotic lives filled with cut corners, evasion, and compromise are disinclined to collect proof of anything, even birth.

My mother had always told me that I had been born in the Newton-Wellesley Hospital in Newton, Massachusetts. I knew the date, of course, March 28, 1940—one didn't need documentary proof for that: it was tribal knowledge, fixed to the turn of the year, my personal place on the calendar. It was like the color of my eyes: everyone in the family said they were blue, and thus they were; and then, when I looked in the mirror, I saw what blue looked like and discovered a particle of my larger participation in the world of color and of language. They also report, and early snapshots confirm, that I was not an attractive baby, unusually long and skinny, big-headed and bald until I was eighteen months old, when photographs first show me with crossed eyes, caused, according to my mother, by whooping cough. You wouldn't stop coughing, you *couldn't,* and your eyes got crossed then, she reports.

I wrote to the Records Department of the Newton-Wellesley Hospital and asked for a copy of my birth certificate. We have no record of your birth, came the reply. I called my mother, who in those years was living with my teenaged sister, Linda, and the youngest of her four children, my brother Chris, in Santa Ana, California. My other brother, Steve, was in Vietnam. Where was I born? I asked her. In the Newton-Wellesley Hospital, she insisted. We lived in Newton then, your father and I, right after we lived in Watertown, but it was Newton until you were six months old, when we moved to Arlington, and

"My mother, Florence Taylor Banks, about nineteen years old"

then when Steve was born and you were two, we moved to Reading. That was before the year we lived in San Diego, when your father worked in the naval shipyard, and then of course we came back east and settled in New Hampshire, when the war ended, and Linda was born in the first house in Barnstead, the little Cape next to your father's parents' house, Grandpa and Grandma Banks's farm. You remember.

The litany of our early moves always made me dizzy with self-pity and anger, partially because in fact I had little memory of them myself and could not trust my mother's account, but also because I knew the moves had gone on—six months in one apartment or house, a year in another, often just down the road or in the next town, ten different schools before I graduated high school—all the way to the end of our family life, which I mark (although naturally the others do not) from the winter I took myself out of the family and at the age of eighteen hitchhiked to Florida, ostensibly to join Castro, the good father, and got stalled and then installed in St. Petersburg, married a girl and fathered a child, and began there my own series of compulsive relocations.

I did eventually obtain a copy of my birth certificate. I wrote to the City of Newton Bureau of Records and learned that I had indeed been born on March 28, 1940, but in the Newton Hospital, not the more prestigious (at least in my mother's mind) Newton-Wellesley Hospital. She had wanted her first child to have been born in the neighborhood of Wellesley, an upper-class suburb of Boston, and so, by God, he was. It was almost endearing. A request to the Newton Hospital brought me the official documentation and with it an old, all-too-familiar anger for yet again having been forced to penetrate one of my mother's delusions.

She had not lied to me; I don't think my mother ever deliberately lies. She merely projects her needs and desires onto the world and reports back, more or less accurately, what she sees there. She is, and always was, a truthful but somewhat deluded and self-absorbed person, some would say a narcissistic person, and for that reason has always been a lonely, unreliable witness and, for me, an especially dangerous witness to events that I myself have no memory of—like the events of my early childhood.

My father, on the other hand, was a liar. He was interested in seduction, however, not fantasies. He lied consciously, almost perversely, like a bored nihilist, but he rarely drew me in and thus was not so dangerous to me. I think I stopped believing his stories and promises before I was ten, certainly before I was twelve, when he packed his tools and clothes and left the family forever, prefiguring, possibly determining, my own departure six years later. In my mid-thirties, however, when my father was in steady-state alcoholic decline and aging fast, we became guarded friends, he out of a last-ditch need for familial support and I out of pity and filial loyalty, I suppose, and he told a lie that I believed. Foolishly, I had asked him a simple question, how I got my first name. My middle name, Earl, is easily explained: it's his first name. But there were no other Russells in the family. It's not an odd name, but it's not all that common, either, and I wondered what the name, before I came to inhabit it, had meant in 1940 to the handsome, twenty-three-year-old plumber and his beautiful, twenty-five-year-old bride. He worked then for his father, who was also a plumber but had his own truck and worked for himself—Elbourne N. Banks, Plumbing and Heating Co. My mother's father, Ernest Taylor, was a Waltham clockmaker with a small shop on Moody Street. The Depression had kicked both families out of the bottom of the middle class into grinding hard times, although the clockmaker, who had avoided debt, seemed to have survived it better than did the plumber: the clock-maker kept his house, half of which he rented out, and his shop; the plumber went under, sold the house he'd built in Waltham, bought a run-down farm cheap in Barnstead, New Hampshire, moved his family north, and became a traveling man, working where the jobs were and coming home only on weekends. It was a pattern my father would later find irresistible.

But in the late 1930s, Florence Taylor and Earl Banks, high school sweethearts, were good-looking kids from Waltham, Massachusetts, with reckless, high-falluting fancies. They were slick dancers, sharp dressers, and had easily excited senses of humor. They smoked cigarettes and drank a lot and danced to swing bands at the Totem Ball Ballroom in Norumbega Park. Strangers liked them instantly. What a swell couple. My father was a superb clarinet-ist who could do perfect, hour-long imitations of Benny Goodman and Artie Shaw. He was prodigious-ly intelligent and had a photographic memory that amazed people and got him out of high school at the age of sixteen. And my mother—everyone said it—was a charmer. The two of them were clearly gifted.

Your father had wanted to become a doctor, my mother told me, but the Depression . . . well, that meant he had to go to work right away, to help his family. He was the only boy, she explained. She, with her twin sister, Frances, was the youngest of four daughters and one son, Preston, an invalided mathe-

"My father, Earl Banks, at about twenty-four"

matics and chess prodigy who had died of rheumatic fever in his adolescence. After graduation from high school my mother went to work as a sales clerk at Grover Cronin's Department Store. When she was nineteen, her mother, Lillian, died suddenly—anoth-er complicated story hidden behind elaborately shift-ing curtains of delusion and family reticence: the simplest version is that she died after surgery for removal of a pork-chop bone caught in her throat. Lillian Derry, from New Brunswick, was my Grandfa-ther Taylor's second wife and his second cousin as well: she had come south from Canada to keep house for him when Mary, his daughter by his first mar-riage, a brilliant girl and the only Taylor or Banks to go to college until my generation came along, left her father's home for Boston University. He married his housekeeper-cousin, and she quickly bore him four children, and twenty-two years later, when Lillian died, Mary, by now an unmarried high school teacher of Latin and French, returned to her father's house and took care of him, and it, again. But where had *her* mother, Grace Smith, the first wife, gone? She hadn't died. There had been a divorce, apparently, with the two-year-old child remaining with the father, which was certainly unusual. I ask my mother and her twin sister, Frances, seventy-seven-year-old born-again Christian widows, what happened to Grandpa Taylor's first wife, for now that woman's daughter, Mary, their half sister, my favorite aunt on my mother's side, is dead. But they don't seem to know. All they know is that, after their mother died, Mary cruelly displaced them in their father's affections, and to this day they resent her for it, especially my mother. There are vague stories of my mother's having been ill during this period—fainting spells, a brief stay in a sanatorium, asthma, possibly even TB, she claims—which are told to account for her not graduating high school until she was nineteen, a year after my father, who was younger and had skipped grades.

Here's the lie my father told me when I asked him how I got my name. He told me about his great-uncle, Russell, a man I'd never heard of before. We were sitting in the kitchen of his house in Contoocook, New Hampshire; it was a snowy mid-morning, probably a Sunday, because that was when I usually dropped by to visit; he was in pajamas and bathrobe, drinking Bloody Marys. His fourth and last wife, Ginnie, was washing glasses from the night before at the sink. The original Russell, he said, was a fiddler, a hermit, a man who lived in a hut up on Cape Breton Island. And he loved me, my father said. I was a boy then, and we were living in Halifax down in Nova Scotia, and I guess I was a lot of trouble, because every summer my mother and father sent me away to live with Uncle Russell. But we had a great time, he and I. He played the fiddle, and I played the clarinet.

I was flattered by the story and, breaking my rule, believed it. Sometime later, after my father had died in 1979, of what the doctors called "massive alcoholic trauma to the liver," I asked his younger sisters, Edna and Jeannie, about their Canadian great-uncle, Russell, the hermit-fiddler from Cape Breton Isle. My father's side of the family had moved down to the States from Canada when my father was thirteen; his parents and three sisters, especially Edna, had kept the family connections to the old country intact, and all the Banks's spoke with great affection, nostalgia, and sentimental vagueness of their previous life as Canadians. Outside his house in Contoocook, my father had flown two flags, the Stars and Stripes and the Maple Leaf, and for years every summer he drove his pickup truck to New Brunswick alone and fished and drank and returned seeming oddly rejuvenated. The man may have been a compulsive seducer, but actually he loved solitude. Today we would say that he was clinically depressed, and an alcoholic to boot.

My father's mother's ancestors—Musgraves, Gordons, Daleys—were Scottish and Anglo-Irish, mostly seafarers, eighteenth- and nineteenth-century wanderers, recent and somewhat tentative arrivals in the New World. The Banks side of the family was descended from Revolutionary War loyalists, and, according to my aunt Edna, who did the research, they were direct descendents of John and Priscilla Alden. We are a Mayflower Family, she was proud to say. True or not, gravestones in York, Maine, and Waltham, Massachusetts, establish that the Banks's were indeed Bay Colonists from the early seventeenth century. In the late 1920s, when they decided it was finally safe to move back down to the United States, where the Twenties were roaring, they returned to Waltham, the same town they had left in 1776, to discover that, while they were gone, the branch that had remained behind had become illustrious—generals and politicians, industrialists, philanthropists. The Loyalist branch, unfortunately, had become Canadian small farmers, carpenters, plumbers.

There was no Great-Uncle Russell, of course. And I still do not know why I bear his name. I guess your father just liked the name, my mother tells me. Which should be sufficient. But it's not. There is a veil, a shifting, gauzy veil, that hangs between my remembered life and the life that precedes it, between me and the older members of my family, between the man I have become and his origins, and I can't brush it aside and enter there. How did my eyes come to be crossed? I remember sudden flashes of physical pain from those first years, and loud noises. What do they signify? The rooms and yards of my early years mingle and merge like half-remembered dreams. There's a terrible discontinuity, a lack of sequence, back there, which frightens me and resists all my attempts at linkage.

Those stories my mother tells with such relish, of my running away from home at the ages of two and three, of her finding me at play in a graveyard miles from home with a busy highway between me and the play-yard I had left—what was I running away from? Where was she, that I could wander so far? When we lived in San Diego, she says, Earl and I went to a party in the neighborhood and left you, who were four, and Steve, who must have been barely two then, alone and asleep in your beds, and late at night here you came straight into the party, leading Steve by the hand, looking for us. Lord knows, she exclaims, how you found us!

She enjoys telling these stories, because she believes they show how independent and unpredictable I was as a child, which confirms her view of me as an adult. Of course, they also confirm my view of her

(Left to right) Russell at five; brother, Stephen, at three; and a cousin, Neil Palmer

and my father as parents. But I *was* always running away from home. When I was five or six, my favorite book was *Toby Tyler,* the story of the boy who ran off and joined the circus. When I was nine, I packed a knapsack and rode away on my bike from our apartment in Concord, New Hampshire, and got picked up by the police out by the airport and claimed that I was going to my grandparents' house in Barnstead, twenty miles away, when in fact I was headed for the Concord Airport, hoping to stow away on a flight to . . . where? Why, so early, was I fleeing my family and home, abandoning the known thing for the unknown? Was there more actual safety, a better chance for stability and control, in the unknown?

My parents fought constantly; they drank too much; they were violent, especially my father. I remember that. They were like hysterical children,

stuck in a permanent tantrum. Everyone cried and shouted a lot. There was never enough money, and they were always packing up and moving out of an old place, where things had gone wrong, into a new, where everything would improve. We were living in Wakefield, Massachusetts, and I was twelve, Steve was ten, Linda was six, and our baby brother, Chris, was barely one, when, at last, after a half-dozen previous tries, my father finally left for good. My mother divorced him, and although the physical violence and the drunkenness ended, the financial insecurity was worse. We kept on crying, and we still moved from house to apartment to tenement, Wakefield to Newton and back to Wakefield again. When I was sixteen, I and another boy, Dario Morelli, whose mother had died the year before and whose father had immediately remarried a much younger woman, stole a car and disappeared from our homes for two whole months. I may well have been in flight, but this time it was at the moral cost of consciously abandoning my poor distraught mother and my two younger brothers and sister—this from the boy who had been charged by his father four years earlier with the obligation to be "the man of the house." It was a ferociously angry act, but desperate. Morelli and I fled west on Route 66, ran out of money in Amarillo, Texas, where we lived in the YMCA and worked at a White Tower restaurant, until we had enough money to move on to Pasadena, California. There, Morelli, a Catholic, went to confession, told the priest what we had done, got us turned in to our parents, and nearly ended my lifelong flirtation with the certainties of Catholicism.

By then, however, when I was sixteen, I had acquired a rudimentary narrative for my life, for one remembered episode seems to have led to another, and looking back now I can tease out rough, morphological correspondences between them, can divine on occasion more than merely efficient causes and effects, and can actually decipher many of the lesser meanings. The form of the story was clear by then. But the first causes are lost to me. There are mysteries back there; and wrapped inside them must lie the crucial explanations for why and how I became the man I am today. There is the mystery of the strange disappearance of my grandfather Ernest Taylor's first wife, Grace Smith. There are my mother's fainting spells and her stay in a "sanatorium," and her mother, Lillian's, sudden death. Why are there so many old pictures of my short, moustachio'd grandfather around and none of his two wives? My mother insists that she has always felt guilty that the night her mother died she stayed out late on a date and, even though she knew her mother had been taken to the hospital, stayed over with a friend and didn't come home until the next morning. Otherwise, however, she and her sisters rarely speak of their mother. They praise her sweet passivity, they call her a saint, but clearly they loved their dour, preoccupied father more. Why? What really happened that night? I asked her who had she been on her date with, and she said, Your father, I suppose.

There is the mystery of my grandfather Elbourne Banks's orphaned childhood. No one can tell me about his parents, except their names, Adoniram and Nettie, and dates. Nettie died a year and a half after my grandfather was born. Adoniram remarried shortly after, soon fathered a second child, and lived another forty-four years; but the little boy who became my grandfather, Elbourne Banks, was raised by an aunt and uncle, who are nameless. When he was sixteen, my grandfather left their home to follow the reapers west, a six-months-long job that started in Nova Scotia in spring and ended in British Columbia in the fall; after that, evidently, he was on his own. My father's mother, Mary Jeanette Musgrave, seems in family lore to have had no past worth mentioning before her coming down to the States, yet I remem-

ber her as a handsome, bright, and kindly woman with a slightly bawdy sense of humor, a large personality with no past to explain it.

It seems that for the last three generations, at least, everyone on both sides of my family has tried to ignore the mysteries, to dismiss them as meaningless, or to erase the past altogether—except, of course, for my aunt Edna, my father's sister, whose idea of the past was the linkage of our name to the Mayflower and Plymouth Colony, to a Civil War general and U.S. Senator from Massachusetts, and in Canada, by marriage, to Lord Henry Musgrave and Lady Nancy Gordon. On my mother's side, the exception was her half sister, the Latin teacher, Aunt Mary, or Mimi, as we called her, whose idea of the family's past was its link to Richard Taylor who came to Plymouth Colony in 1630 and settled the next year in Yarmouth, giving his name to Richard Rock, which is marked today with a plaque, to the Edward Taylor who wrote poetry in Connecticut in the eighteenth century, to the Dudley Buck who wrote nineteenth-century hymns. It's a typically American telling of family history, I suppose, to leap over the recent generations of hoi polloi to the distantly related nobility.

Russell, age nine; Stephen, age seven; and Linda, age three

I must also, in a more significant way, except, along with those two aunts, my surviving siblings—my brother Steve and my sister, Linda, and my half sister as well, Kathy Nutter, daughter of my father's second marriage. In fact, their sense of the shared family past is increasingly like my own. They care as much as I about the mysteries in our grandparents' lives. After all, those are the people who may have affected us most, who may be our true psychological, if not strictly genetic, origins. When one's parents, like ours, have not succeeded in determining and trying to understand their own origins and have instead shrouded them in mystery, fantasy, and white lie, when one's parents are in effect the pure and largely unconscious products of their own painful childhoods, then one must examine the lives and personalities of one's grandparents. Neurosis is inherently conservative, and often the most powerfully coercive and corrosive influences on our psyches and myths of ourselves descend, not from our parents, but from our grandparents. It's sometimes as if our living parents were little more than the visible tools employed by our grandparents to carve and shape us long after their deaths. As if Ernest and Lillian Taylor on one side and Elbourne and Mary Banks on the other had merely used their attractive and gifted children, Florence and Earl, to get to the grandchildren, to Russell, Steve, Linda, and Chris, and to Kathy Nutter, too. Not wholly, of course, but enough to make it relatively easy for me to forgive Florence and Earl, who no doubt had even more mysteries to penetrate than we, for they, in their turn, appear to have had no connection whatsoever to *their* grandparents. Standing against the centuries stretching back from their parents' adult lives to the mists of colonial New England and aristocratic Britain, all the way back to the time of pre-Edenic gods, Florence and Earl Banks are like poor Cain and Abel, with no one but themselves having actually lived a purely human childhood. Everyone but them was, like Adam, a lifelong adult. Not a fate to envy. If you can't imagine your parents as children, if, as Florence and Earl did, you must think of them as Adam and Eve and view everything else before their time as inpenetrable mystery, then it's unlikely you'll be able to imagine yourself as an adult. Even when you grow up. Even when you marry and have four children of your own.

I have recently been remembering my father in blackface imitating Al Jolson in blackface from the movie *The Jazz Singer.* He was performing as a prominent member of an amateur minstrel show at the town hall in Barnstead, New Hampshire, in 1947 or possibly 1948. The show was a big hit and played that summer in town halls and fairgrounds all over the state. My father had the best voice in the line and the most theatrical presence, and he ended the show with a version of "Mammy" that got standing ovations every time he performed it. He had genuine tears in his eyes when he sang, "I'd walk a million miles for one of your smiles," and his voice broke brilliantly at the final chorus, crying, "Mam-mee! Mam-mee!" and everyone in the audience, especially the males among us, realized how much we loved our mothers. As for me (who probably needed no reminding), I realized in addition how much I loved my *father,* the white man in blackface wringing his hands and singing his heart out on the stage. Oddly, it was as intimate, as personal, and as unthreatening, as he got, or so it seemed to me, for I could see from my front-row seat that he did indeed love his Mammy, loved her desperately, the way I loved mine, and that, like a little boy, like *me,* he was willing to walk a million miles for a smile from her, a smile she never gave him—although she gladly smiled at everyone else. Of course, that was as close as he came to asking for it—up on a stage pretending to be a white movie actor pretending to be a black man. Thrice removed. Poor man, poor boy; poor woman, poor daughter. My heart broke for him then, it goes on breaking for him now. For her as well.

A memory from the same period: my mother's father, the taciturn clockmaker, came north to visit us in our shabby little Cape farmhouse in Barnstead. The house had recently gotten electricity and partial plumbing installed. It was Grandpa Taylor's first visit, an event much anticipated, much discussed, as the date for his arrival neared. Until now, we had seen him only in Waltham at his house on Brown Street, a duplex one block from the old Waltham Watch Factory, when we traveled south for Thanksgiving or Christmas, and he would descend from his room upstairs to take his place at the head of the table, lead the prayers, and carve the turkey. He was a small man with a highly developed sense of his own significance, at least at home among his daughters, their husbands, and children.

The night before he was scheduled to arrive in Barnstead, I remember my mother and father gathering up all the liquor in the house, all the empty, half-full and full bottles—there seem to have been quite a few, my memory is of a filled carton—and removing them from the house. Then my brother Steve and I were instructed to say nothing about drinking, nothing about whiskey and beer, when Grandpa Taylor came to visit. He was to think that our heavy-drinking parents, a man and a woman in their early thirties, parents of three small children, were teetotalers, that our home was alcohol-free. My mother and father suddenly seemed like children to me. And if they were children, then what was I? They were both clearly frightened of this man, though he seemed to me not especially frightening—just old and uninvolved. I doubted he liked me, and that night decided not to like him—in defense of my parents, perhaps, but also because, as I saw it, he had turned us all into liars.

He arrived, and Steve and I kept our promise not to say a word about beer or whiskey, but the morning of the second day, when I left the house for the schoolbus, I saw his large, lovely, gold pocket watch on the table by the sofa, and as I passed out of the room, I slipped it into my jacket. At school, I proudly showed it off to my friends, claiming that my grandfather had made it himself and had given it to me.

Of course, by the time I returned home that afternoon, the watch had been missed, and after a lengthy, harsh interrogation, I broke down and confessed to having stolen it. I don't remember the specifics, but my punishment, I know, was severe and

Maternal grandfather, Ernest Taylor, the clockmaker

lasted until after Grandpa Taylor left. I do remember, however, the peculiar pleasure that colored my mother's and father's loud denunciation of my crime, the relief with which they shouted at me, and the righteous clarity with which my father whacked my backside with his belt. And, for the first time, I had no sense that their violence was driven by anger at *me.* It was something that originated elsewhere and had come to me only by accident. It was ritual. And while this insight, which quickly took up permanent residence in my understanding, may well have preserved me against an ongoing, crippling sense of guilt and unworthiness, it also made me feel invisible, a boy of no true, ultimate account for good or bad, possibly a person without reality. I could laugh while being punished. I could pretend to be sorry.

Luckily, it was during these years, between the ages of seven and nine, that I began to move outside the family for a reliable, lasting sense of my own reality. I remember discovering, being told and then shown, thanks to my early teachers, that I had intelligence and talent. In the two-room Barnstead School, Mrs. Cotton taught grades one through four, and Mrs. Alden taught grades five through eight. And when we moved to Concord, there was Mrs. Dougherty, my fourth-grade teacher, who let me spend the entire year making an enormous plaster-of-paris model of Brazil that was the wonder of the school and was exhibited in the main corridor. Those first teachers, who must have truly loved children, were stern, no-nonsense, middle-aged ladies—at least that is how I remember them—and they thought that I was unusually intelligent, a clever, talented boy who learned his reading, writing, and arithmetic quickly, and in various ways they let me know of my gifts, advancing me through the classes as rapidly as my abilities would allow.

Coming right along behind me was my brother, Steve, discovering, as was I, that we were not utterly and irrecoverably defined by our family life, by the unhappy children who were our parents. We were *not* invisible, after all. Being boys, we, of course, were generally encouraged to seek and seize the terms of our reality, of our worth and meaning, outside the family; our younger sister, Linda, sadly, was not, and though it has taken her until now, as she enters college in her mid-forties, to obtain that simple, just, and necessary prerogative, it's all the more heroic for its late-coming.

If there is a theme to this essay, I suppose it's how the writer came to be the person capable of living the life he now leads. And although, all too typically in the youth of anyone who ends up an artist,

Brother Christopher at about seventeen

there were in my adolescent and early adult years numerous, perhaps hundreds, of crucial turnings and forks in the path, crises and obstacles to overcome, fears and insecurities to endure and eventually face down, nevertheless, from the time I was sixteen, when I stole a car with my pal Dario Morelli and ran off to California, I believe that I was capable of becoming, and possibly even obliged to become, the man I have turned out to be.

I have been lucky, of course. I have been blessed, often undeservedly, by the love and intelligence of several good women, by the faithful companionship of many men my age met along the way, and by the friendship, example, and encouragement of a few tender-hearted older men. (There's no point in naming them here; they know who they are.) I have fathered four daughters whose existence in the world has given me the continuing occasion to elaborate and refine, to bring to its fullest expression, my own capacity for love. And now, in the middle of the middle years of my life, unexpectedly there has come a woman, Chase Twichell, whom I name in order to honor and whom I can only call the love of my life.

I have been lucky in love, then.

And lucky in what did not happen to me, as well. For I did not die drunk in a car crash, as might have easily happened dozens of times in my youth. I was not stabbed or shot in a barroom brawl in Lakeland,

Florida, or Keene, New Hampshire, on those all-too-frequent nights when I was compulsively displacing myself with residual rage from the violence of my childhood. I did not, like my brother Steve, escape home and family by enlisting in the military, ending up in Vietnam in the middle sixties, returning weakened, confused, and haunted for years afterwards. And, except for my having been lucky, an accident like the one that ended my brother Chris's life at seventeen might as easily have ended mine, for he, like me at sixteen, had started to hit the road, when he hitched a ride on a freight train from Los Angeles to San Francisco that was wrecked in a mud-slide outside Santa Barbara and burned. He was a tall, burly, good-looking boy who was bright and musically gifted, who wanted from life what I, eleven years older, seemed to have gotten—a loving wife, children, a rudimentary education, the daily practice of an art. His body was never found.

The luck it takes to have survived a turbulent life into middle age is, of course, treasured and, finally, if one has sufficient wisdom, even cultivated; but in the determination of the particular shape of my adult life, I was especially lucky to have inherited certain talents. My father had a good hand: he could draw what he felt like drawing, which, by the time he was in his thirties, due to his grim acceptance of his trade, was only what was necessary for his work—plumbing and wiring diagrams, floor plans: detailed maps of his labor. He also had a good ear: he had perfect pitch and, until alcohol dulled his brain and thickened his fingers, he played several instruments well enough to memorize and imitate the improvisations of the best jazz clarinetists and soprano saxophonists of his youth. Later, in his forties and fifties, when he moved back to New Hampshire, he played in Masonic marching bands and then, only occasionally, late at night, alone. And, finally, not at all. Silence. My father's youngest sister, Frances, whom we called Aunt Jeannie, could also draw well, and I remember her amusing and amazing us with quick, accurate sketches of flowers, trees, the house across the road. Grandma Banks was said to have been talented in her youth—she was supposed to have written religious poems and stories (which have disappeared)—and as an elderly woman she made beautiful hooked rugs that regularly won blue ribbons at the state fair.

On my mother's side of the family, there was, of course, the distant linkage to Dudley Buck, the composer, and the spidery thin strand to Edward Taylor, the poet; but there were artistic and intellectual gifts that, if more modest, were nonetheless somewhat closer to hand. My mother's older sister, Eleanor, now in her eighties, was a fine classical

Earl and Florence Banks, New Year's Eve, 1950

pianist, and although (according to my mother) she sacrificed what would have been a significant musical career when she married young and had the first of her five children, she has been for her entire adult life the organist for her large and musically demanding church. Aunt Mimi, the French and Latin teacher, unmarried and childless, wrote children's stories, many of which she published in magazines like *Jack and Jill*. She was a reflective woman and until she died kept two photographs on her bedside table, one of her beloved father Ernest, the clockmaker, and one of Albert Einstein, whose face, now that I think of it, resembled her father's more than slightly. Grandpa Taylor himself must have been a man of many talents. Born in 1866 (his father, James, had been a drummer boy in the Civil War), he was apprenticed to a clockmaker at fourteen and thus had little formal schooling, but taught himself French and German well enough to read the European texts on timepieces. He was apparently a skilled lens grinder, famous locally for his custodial relation to Admiral Peary's telescopes and chronometers, which the Admiral himself annually carried down from his home in Maine to my grandfather's shop in Waltham. It amused and, in a perverse way, pleased me when, in recent years, it came out that, due to instrument error, Peary may well have missed the North Pole by a few miles. The saboteur in me prefers to think of my grandfather as having been completely responsible for a world-famous explorer's historical blunder, rather than having been only marginally responsible for the great man's huge success.

In the genetic lottery that distributes a family's talents, I came up luckier than most, mainly because early on I could draw well enough to amaze adults and win their praise. From my first years at school, people assumed that I would become an artist, a visual artist, just as, if I had demonstrated prodigious musical ability, they would have predicted a musical career. It was a foregone conclusion that my talent would someday astound the wider world, just as it then amazed the family. How one actually became an artist was only vaguely understood, however, for there was seen to be little difference between Rembrandt and Norman Rockwell, except that Rembrandt, though certainly as famous an artist as Rockwell, was dead and no one in the family had seen his pictures.

For me, drawing and painting were superior types of play—the process, not the pictures themselves, took me out of my everyday reality, which, by and large, was both threatening and depressing. That the pictures elicited the praise and admiration of adults was at first merely a bonus, but gradually it became an end in itself, so that, by the time I was a teenager, the praise and admiration had become crucial to my sense of worth. Consequently, it soon became impossible to lose myself in the process, impossible to *play*. Fortunately, by this time I had discovered books—the world of novels, stories, poems—again, thanks to middle-aged female teachers who themselves loved literature, women not unlike my aunt Mimi, perhaps. And I had discovered the Wakefield Public Library, where, to my astonished delight, there were thousands of books, enough to last a lifetime. By junior high school, then, for the necessary pleasure and safety of play, I had gone over from art to literature, leaving my ability to draw in the strict service of my ego needs.

In no way did I think of myself as a potential writer of books, however—to do so would have impinged upon my obsessive use of books for an alternative reality, for fantasy and escape. Luckily, no one in my family viewed my reading as something to be praised. It didn't so much amaze and please them that I consumed half-a-dozen books a week as it made them downright anxious. Thus I was freed to read on without self-consciousness, with no other end than to finish one book so as to move to the next; I read for the sheer, simple, utterly necessary pleasure of it.

In the 1950s, generally, and especially in insecure lower-middle-class families like mine, it was not "normal" for a healthy boy to read as much as I did. It was slightly effeminate perhaps, was suspect, even subversive. So, to affirm my masculinity, to reassure my elders (and myself as well) that I was socially "normal," and to obtain the high regard of girls, if not their terrifying, much-desired sexual favors, I pitched myself into sports—football, ice hockey, and track. A medium-sized boy with no special athletic gifts and only average eye-hand coordination could participate successfully in these particular sports if he were reckless enough with his body, had a strong desire to express himself through physical violence, and had a high pain threshold. Consequently, I made myself into a 170-pound interior-lineman in football, a belligerent, slow-skating defenseman in hockey, and a middling middle-distance runner in track—the kind of kid who "guts it out," good enough to make the varsity teams, but never singled out for having been crucial to victory.

I remember this period of my life as having been dominated, however, not by sports or girls, or even by books, which I used mainly as a recreational drug, and certainly not by school, although I was a good, if distracted, student, a flashy "quiz kid" and winner of spelling bees, but by crushing financial worries. My mother worked as a clerk in an electronics company in Wakefield, and from the age of fourteen I worked after school and weekends in local stores, and my brother Steve had paper routes; and though we all contributed our bit to the family coffer, we were always behind in our rent, fending off bill collectors, scheming ways to cut costs without further humiliating ourselves. My mother was frightened and frantic, and sometimes she came home early from work because of having had a "spell," as she called them, and I feared that she would soon be fired. I remember sitting up late with her at the kitchen table, going over the budget, finding an extra dollar here, another there, to make the rent, and then, by the end of the month, coming up short yet again. We moved three or four times, each time to a cheaper, more crowded apartment, sharing bedrooms and closets, feeling increasingly, in the affluent mid-1950s, like abject failures at life. My father, we heard through the family grapevine, had remarried, and was living in Connecticut. There was no other contact with him, no help, no comfort. It was hard, during this period, not to hate him.

Sometime during the winter of 1955–56, before I turned sixteen, I visited Phillips Andover Academy in Andover, Massachusetts, with my pal, Dario Morelli, who was a few months older than I and already had his driver's license. I had never seen a prep school before, and while Morelli smoked contraband cigarettes in a dorm room with his friend, the dentist's son we had come to visit, I wandered alone down the elm-lined paths and into the huge ivy-covered library,

passing self-possessed boys who seemed, if not to own the world, about to inherit it. And for the first time I saw how I myself wanted to feel. Entitled. Free. Empowered by my gifts, not frustrated or embarrassed by them.

I turned into the admissions office, obtained an application for admission and a catalogue and financial-aid form, and made an appointment for an interview the following week. It was a fantasy, certainly, but I was, for the first time in my life, making a concerted attempt to convert my fantasy into reality, I would lift myself up by my own bootstraps, would surround myself not by my peers, for I had no consistent idea of who they were, but by people who were instead like the person I wanted to become. I had identified a shape for my life that I could project out in front of me and could aspire to, and for all the years that followed, that projection, the movement it created in my life, would operate dialectically against its opposite, negative impulse, providing me with a zigzag pattern, perhaps, a life of advance-and-retreat, of achievement and self-sabotage, of commitment and betrayal, but also at the same time providing me with

"*As left guard for Wakefield High School football team,*" about 1957

The author today

great, optimistic energy, and, needless to say, more than enough occasions for self-examination.

A week later on a snowy morning I skipped school and took the bus from Wakefield out to Andover for my interview, wearing a striped tie and borrowed tweed jacket, Morelli's probably, and chinos and penny loafers, which was what I had noticed the Andover boys wearing, and in a steam-heated eighteenth-century drawing room made my case to an evidently intrigued admissions officer. I would need a full scholarship, of course, but there were such scholarships available, he assured me, if I were sufficiently deserving, which was to say, if I proved sufficiently exceptional. I understood that. To bring me up to the academic level of the young men whom I wished to make my peers, I might have to repeat my sophomore year, he warned, but to me that seemed more like an opportunity to excel than compensation for a suburban public school education, more advantage than disadvantage. I spent the entire afternoon alone in a classroom taking achievement and aptitude tests, and rode the bus home in the dark to our apartment on, ironically enough, Yale Avenue in

Wakefield, and said nothing of my adventure to my mother or, for that matter, to anyone else, not even Morelli.

The wait began. One month passed, and then I turned sixteen and got my driver's license. I thought about my Andover fantasy now and then, but it had quickly begun to fade; I felt foolish when I thought of it—a vain and deluded boy setting himself up for rejection. One morning the first week of April, I met Morelli at Finnegan's Drug Store on the way to school, and he was red-eyed from weeping. He hated his life—his mother had died the year before, his father had remarried a young Italian woman who spoke no English, and Morelli wanted to run away from home, family, school—the hell with all of them. He was a sad, bitterly angry, confused boy, with no one but me, it seemed, to turn to.

And who was I?

I said, Let's go. Let's start our lives over somewhere else. And so we did. We gathered up a few clothes and what little cash we could lay our hands on (I think I had a savings account with a few hundred dollars stashed away for the eventual purchase of a used car, a fund my mother was constantly trying to invade for what she regarded, rightly, I'm afraid, as emergencies), and we hot-wired and stole Morelli's father's 1955 Oldsmobile 88. An hour later, radio blasting, we roared out of town, headed west, as straight and fast as possible, two unhappy boys gone to the land of new beginnings.

There's not a great deal more to say. The die seems to have been cast. That morning in April 1956, I became the person I needed to be in order to turn into the man I am today. By late May, we were back in Wakefield, defeated, but only temporarily. Morelli's father, to punish him, sent him off to St. John's Prep, a Catholic boys' school in Danvers, Massachusetts. I have seen him only once since then, twenty years later. He was working as a bartender in an Italian restaurant out on Route 1 in Saugus, and one night, driving north from Boston to New Hampshire, where I was living at the time, I had stopped in by accident for a bite to eat. My third book, *Hamilton Stark*, had just been published by Houghton Mifflin, and I was returning late from a publication party. Morelli and I exchanged addresses and pretended to be delighted to see one another again, but we were both pained by the meeting, and I never went back to the restaurant.

No one punished me. Although I had abandoned and terrorized my mother and brothers and sister, just as my father a few years before had done to us all, there really was no punishment to suit the crime, for we all loved one another, and I suppose my mother knew it. I certainly did. Sometime during my two-month absence, the letter of acceptance and the offer of a full scholarship from Phillips Andover had arrived, but everything, of course, was conditional on my successfully completing all my remaining sophomore courses at Wakefield High School. That was not impossible, and, in fact, in the few remaining weeks of the term, I did manage, out of sheer perversity, to complete my schoolwork and even to get myself onto the honor roll. But the deadline for my response to the offer from Andover had long since passed. I was stuck with who I was.

BIBLIOGRAPHY

Novels:

Family Life, Avon, 1975.

Hamilton Stark, Houghton, 1978.

The Book of Jamaica, Houghton, 1980.

The Relation of My Imprisonment, Sun & Moon Press, 1984.

Continental Drift, Harper, 1985.

Affliction, HarperCollins, 1989.

The Sweet Hereafter, HarperCollins, 1991.

Short stories:

Searching for Survivors, Fiction Collective, 1975.

The New World, University of Illinois Press, 1978.

Trailerpark, Houghton, 1981.

Success Stories, Harper, 1986.

Poetry:

(With William Matthews and Newton Smith) *15 Poems,* Lillabulero Press, 1967.

30/6, The Quest, 1969.

Waiting to Freeze, Lillabulero Press, 1969.

Snow: Meditations of a Cautious Man in Winter, Granite, 1974.

Also co-editor of Lillabulero.

Willis Barnstone

1927-

FROM HAWTHORNE'S GLOOM TO A WHITEWASHED ISLAND

Beginning in Maine

One's origin is never experienced. It is learned. Then one spends a life experiencing that learning, which is half information, speculation, and a third half favored myth. I was born in Maine and so have always felt smugly like a Maineiac, not a New Yorker, although my mother went home to Maine only for my birth and returned to New York after a week or a year. I have no memory of those first days in Maine but have the information, which is enough to engender nostalgic roots.

As I look back into the ignorance of my background, I think of orange wing seeds on brick sidewalks and huge chestnut trees on a lawn around a four-story Victorian mansion dominating Laurel Avenue in Auburn. There my grandparents Lempert lived and I visited them in summers in the early mid-thirties whose memory is a few images floating in and out of darknesses. After boisterous New York, once in Maine I was careful to be almost silent since my grandmother was nervous with Parkinson's disease. Her hands and face shook pitifully and any loud voice upset her. She stayed mainly in the kitchen, cooking hot dumpling soups, stewing meats and potatoes in chicken fat, making applecake desserts, or sat for hours on a chair by the potbelly cast-iron stove, opening its doors and dropping wood into it. At times she would walk trembling into the den where I hung out, never too quiet on my own.

"'Don't upset Bubbie with all your noise," my mother or older sister inevitably warned me.

Bubbie had nice black-and-white speckled dresses and she'd come to kiss me, brushing my face with her cheeks and her lips that defined a flower-bed mustache of soft white hair. She had been stunningly attractive, everyone said, a twin, like my mother, though their doubles had not survived. I'd feel all her years quiver as she pressed me against her freshly pressed cottons.

Before Maine there was the European Pale and a Jewish shtetl in what is today Poland or Lithuania

Willis Barnstone under a portrait of Jorge Luis Borges, noted Argentine author and poet, whose writings and personality were a major influence upon the author

(then Russia), near Vilna, from which my grandfather emigrated in 1881 to come to America. Hyman Lempert, who had attended the Yeshiva in Europe my mother proudly said, had led a horse and wagon around New England to sell his junk metal. The peddler was an early recycling ecologist. Eventually, he seems to have dabbled in real estate, at least enough to leave an inheritance for some of his descendants' living and schooling. Hyman was a short, good-looking man with silver hair, adored by my mother, perhaps stingy, who was given to long feuds with two of his four children over religion and money, which resulted in years of silences and resentments.

I have few clear memories of the grandparents— they died in the mid-thirties. I do remember Hyman, whom I called Zeda, davening in the early morning by the beautiful stair banisters, with small, black phylactery boxes on his forehead and a leather strap wrapped around his left forearm. He was chanting and rocking as later I would see the pale Orthodox Jews chanting and rocking in Jerusalem. To me he was good and tolerant, since I was an unpredictable scamp, climbing, running, not offensive but in a constant fervor of shy eagerness.

My brother, Howard, who was to become an architect, was almost five years older than my six years. One day Howard constructed a small club-house out of old scraps of wood. The next morning I discovered a pile of fresh lumber in the garage, delivered a few hours earlier. I wished to emulate my brother. No one was around and I took a saw, hammer, and nails and sawed and hammered for hours, trying to make an upright room. Nothing

"My mother, Dora Lempert (left), and her twin sister, Jane Lempert"

stood up and what I created was mangled deconstruction. When the family came back around noon, I waited nervously for their approval. Zeda stared at the mess and laughed. All he said was "Billy!" No one rebuked me but the drama of my folly must have been strong, since in the haze of unfocused memories I still have a clear picture of the chaotic house I built which even a small cat couldn't enter.

My father's family is more obscure, since I never met any of the early main figures. How many were there? Their names? The closest to a real-life encounter occurred one Sunday morning in Manhattan, in our apartment facing the Drive. I overheard a racket coming out of my parents' bedroom. My unknown grandfather was on the phone. "I need some money."

"'You never gave me anything but your belt!'" my father was screaming into the phone.

My father's father as well as a cousin to my mother, the old man had been a tailor in Boston. He had come to America in the nineteenth century as Bornstein, meaning (like Bernstein) "amberstone," which is also the meaning the unabridged Webster's gives for "barnstone." His son William Anglicized the name so that by the time I took it up, my name, which in Europe would have been Velvel Bornstein, had fully altered its ethnic glow to become a spanking, odd, New Englandish "Willis Barnstone." It was a name, together with my face, made for "passing."

Peddler and Tailor

My grandfathers come to me in an old film:
peddler and tailor gone to the New World.
In the Old World the image blurs, unknown.
My bones, nose? I must be a bit like them.
Old photos say, look, here you were with a
black hat, white beard, dark faith in the one God.
But they stood dully in the light that day
in Lutz. They were despised. It wasn't odd
a century ago to flee. They wandered here
in steerage, climbing seven flights, and sat
in safety in their tenements. I hear
a plane, a wasp groaning under the sun.
Below I'm undespised and free: the son
peddling a soul and warning no black hat.

But if there is any saturated color in the myths I have lived by, it is from the Boston tailor, his wife, and his black mistress. It began with my father's birth, an event that would determine his early life. My recounting of the birth happened soon after my fiftieth birthday, the evening I began a trilogy of sonnets under the general title *The Secret Reader.* The first book, *Gas Lamp, 1893,* begins with a poem carrying the title "Gas Lamp, 1893" when it appeared in the *Times Literary Supplement:*

Gas Lamp, 1893

In brownstone Boston down on old Milk Street,
up two dark flights, near the gas lamp, the tailor
waits glumly for the midwife. August heat
has worn the woman out. Amid the squalor
she looks around the bed, clutching a cape
she brought from London as a child. It's dawn
and dirty. The dark tailor wants to escape
to his cramped shop. The woman's sheets are drawn
below her waist. She isn't hollering now.
Her eyes are dark and still; blood on her thumbs.
Her name is Sarah. No. I'm guessing. How,
untold, am I to know? Hot day has worn
into the room. The midwife finally comes.
Grandmother bleeds to death. My father's born.

That life in Boston led my father as a boy to go into the world on his own, living by his wits in the tradition of Spanish *picaro* scamps from Europe's first realistic, episodic novels. Who knows why the algebra of chance led him, when he was over fifty, to marry a very young Mexican who at the age of seven was already selling ties on the streets of Mexico City? Although Matilde Franco worked as a child in the streets, she did so for her family and did not leave home at an early age. In fact she shared her bed with her mother until her marriage and only then left it to share sheets with my father from the North. But Mexico was near the end of Father's life. The turn-of-the-century Boston was another scene, one of his turbulent childhood:

Grandfather

Born over there in mist, not even God
or Germans have a record of the house
nor village outside Vilna. Here, the old
poor tyrant snips a cloth, stitches a blouse
or shirt, and finds a black woman to live
with when his wife is dead. His smart son sells
papers in Boston subways, won't forgive
the tyrant fool for whipping him. The smells
of steam and cooking mix with yellow cheeses
when suddenly the wrathful tailor seizes
a belt and flogs his son for rotten grades!
Last drama. Twelve years old, my father leaves
his home and school for good. The tailor fades
from all of us forever, stitching sleeves.

After my father left home, he worked in the subways selling newspapers; he sold papers himself and also distributed them to other boys working for him. There were no laws in those days against minors entering saloons and so his way of finding a good lunch was to go into a bar, sit down by the workers, and order a nickel beer. The beer came with all the cold cuts and sandwiches you could eat. Dad ignored the beer but ate enough sidedishes to carry him through the afternoon and sometimes the evening. At some point in his late adolescence he moved to Maine where he had relatives.

"'I was a wild one in Maine,'" he told me proudly. "The French and Irish kids attacked me but I never ran away from a street fight. I stood there as they rushed me and threw them to either side." With the same French kids (most of Lewiston was French-Canadian) he liked to walk across the railroad bridge over the Androscoggin River, especially if a train was passing by. Then they would hang from the wooden track ties and, if it was a good place, drop into the roaring river between the boulders.

In Auburn he met and married his second cousin Dora Lempert. There is a romantic picture of the young couple, lying on the grass, a high rich grass before a forest, both looking up toward the camera. Although they are on the ground, they are handsomely dressed and groomed, confident of their success to take on the world. They are holding up their radiant faces with very strong fists. Dora and her sister Jane were two beauties in those twin cities of Auburn and Lewiston. I was once told that they could not appear at a public dance because they were Jews. My sister, however, threw cold water on that story, saying it was probably our grandfather's ploy for keeping his daughters away from Christian suitors.

Before settling permanently in Auburn (the twin city with Lewiston, separated by the Androscoggin River), my father, Robert, worked for an older brother in Boston—I think his name was William. William Vincent Barnstone had a jewelry store, and apparently the collaboration did not go well. All these assumptions derive from vaguely overheard remarks. In this instance my own name was a clue to their bad relationship. When I was born my mother wished to name me after her father's brother, whose name was Velvel ("little wolf"), usually translated from Yiddish into English as William. But since the older William B. was still alive, I could not be given that name, for Jews, like American stamps, cannot bear the name of a living soul. I suspect that the Orthodox law was obeyed by my unorthodox mother because she didn't care for William anyway and so had a good reason to come upon the unusual name of Willis. I've always been grateful for that uncommon name. Among other things it is a fine Buddhist description of an egoless thing on the earth: a "will-less barn stone."

In the early twenties Father opened an elegant jewelry store on Lisbon Street in Lewiston in an art deco building. His eye was like a magnifying glass. He saw into the interior of precious stones and knew their inner colors and qualities. He always had good taste and an instinct for design. Later, in New York he imported a Swiss watch which he named Pierre Grange (Stone Barn). The designs he chose for them turned the cases and movements into miniature Bauhaus buildings, with some imaginative Corbusier lines to give measured curves and angles. When he and the family moved to New York in the late twenties, he established a firm for importing Swiss watches. The '29 stockmarket crash wiped him out. He lost three-quarters of a million dollars. When facing bankruptcy, to save the jewelry store in Lewiston, he transferred ownership to Dora and Dora's brother Joe Lempert. The store was saved for the next fifty years but its ownership remained a source of controversy and anger.

When I was born, youngest of the three children, Mother and Father were having domestic problems. So they brought Lucy Thibodeau down from Auburn to be my nurse and live with us. A beautiful brunette, slim and bosomy, in a black kerchief. My sister, Beatrice, once observed to me, "Lucy took possession of you like a tigress. It was unnatural, but Mother had her hands full and accepted it." As for my feelings, Lucy was my first great love, we were engaged, and we stayed that way even after the first five years of my life when Lucy left to work for another family, the Lanes. We were living in the seventies on Riverside Drive, and I scarcely remember the apartment. My sister, twelve years older, was still with us and Lucy had her own room. But I remember Lucy clearly, even without pictures to conjure up and create realities. In fact my first distinct recollection in life is being held in her arms outside the hospital—perhaps I was two—on the landing just outside the hospital door, at the top of a stairway leading to the street. I'm looking up at the cement gray sky, and she is comforting me after the removal of my tonsils, promising lots of ice cream. More darkly I recall entering the corridors of that hospital and being taken to a room where they gave me gas and put me under.

After Lucy left, I was down. "He's almost six, too old to have a nurse," Mother said. But Lucy was employed at the Belnord on Eighty-sixth and Broadway, only a few blocks from our new apartment facing the park and the Hudson River on Ninetieth and Riverside. I visited her, even though I was an outsider in that bright modern apartment. When I got too excited, she calmed me down, and warned, "Billy, you've got to be good now. I'm not *your* nurse any more."

"Yes, you are."

I knew I was lying but what she said hurt my feelings. Worst was when she married Jimmy the doorman and had her own child—who was palsied and never learned to walk. I lost her for a while, because Lucy kept moving around the city. Then things changed as did our friendship. A few years ago I wrote a novel *A Swan Over Manhattan*, drawn in part from childhood, and Lucy enters it, undisguised, and most of the details are not invented:

> But you move again, and I lose track as I start grammar school. All I know for sure is how good when Jimmy dumps you (I'm over nine) and we fix it for me to come daily to your place for lunch between classes. You're back in the city, a block from school. When I get to your building, I shout up at the third-floor window, "Lucy!" I run up the tenement stairs to the smell of potato soup. I kiss a French beauty and we talk like old times.

Eventually, I did grow up and Lucy did disappear. She was the first non-family woman I loved. In those first five years in the same house and the next five of rendezvous visits, I can't say how Lucy formed and changed me, but I suspect the effect was profound.

> You have a smile, a sexy film star's look, with white teeth and warm full lips. But the look, with all that northern light in it, is all your own. And what's more, you're built like a sexbomb. Most of all, no one talks as we do together. And even when I was a real shrimp and a slimy brat, you never spanked me. No matter what my folks say about how you managed in your own things, I don't see a pin of sadness in you. I assume it will always be like this—after all we made a pact—but you move out of the city, and I never see you again. My lover fades, but only the way a photograph yellows in a drawer, someplace under other important papers.

New York City has neighborhoods and kids stick to them and act out their afterschool activities. Twice, I got held up by toughs: once with ice picks at twilight on Ninety-third and West End, the second time with knives at night on my way home from my scoutmaster's house down in the seventies where I had passed a test in semaphore. On Ninety-third I had just said good-bye to my chum Eliot and was daydreaming about women's legs, between their legs, when suddenly three ice picks were against my ribs. The Price gang. Brothers. They'd been in a reformatory.

"'Empty your pockets or we'll stick you," one guy said.

I jammed a nickel into the lining of my knickers and they got nothing, but I was like stone, unbreathing, so scared I felt like a pickle with their spikes inside. Just a few months later, down in the seventies, in the shadow near the brick building some toughs were waiting. As I came near—no one else around—they moved away from the wall and blocked my way. This time three high school kids pushed knives against my stomach.

"'Gimme your change or we'll cut you up," the biggest fellow snarled. Then he stuck me.

I didn't say anything but did the same thing as in the last stickup—jammed a quarter into my lining. I felt a glow after leaving the scoutmaster's place but it hadn't helped. Yet they got nothing and didn't even slug me. They left empty-handed. All they did was draw a little blood and tear my clothing with their knives. But I felt punched somewhere inside my chest. Let's put it this way: I wasn't shaking but was shrunken and pretty stiff. My shirttail was soggy with the muck from that first blade that cut me when the gang first pressed against my body.

Just to feel safer I changed plans for getting back. Instead of sticking to quiet West End Avenue, I went one block out of my way to walk home by Broadway where there was a lot of light, where plenty of people went in and out of delicatessens, buying the next morning's papers outside the subway. I bought a bag of hot chestnuts with part of my salvaged quarter. The chestnut seller, a Greek, was standing next to a woman with a metal cigar box, asking for money to fight the fascists in the Spanish Civil War. On her high-breasted black sweater, she wore a white sign showing a photograph of the bombed city of Guernica, with dead people in the street. I looked close at the sign between her tits. A beautiful woman. And noble ideas. Maybe it was the gang and their knives, but that woman was fire to me.

Each season had its games and every kid was into them. In the fall we set our marble boxes out in the gutter and shot at the square holes to pick up some winnings; in the park we played football (I broke my front tooth when I got nailed catching a pass and fell right on a stone in the grass); when snow filled the big gully we greased our sleds with butter and dragged them to the park and froze on the slope until it got dark; in the fall and spring we played stoopball and stickball on Eighty-ninth or Eighty-eighth streets. Stickball was our street baseball, the sport for little bambinos.

"My mother and father, Dora and Robert Barnstone, in Maine," about 1920

The Babe, the great Bambino, lived in the same wide building as I did, a gray-orange whale lying slightly curved along the Drive that goes up westside Manhattan to the George Washington Bridge. Poor Babe. All we tenants heard about him (as if he were a charity case) was that he was a Catholic orphan boy who grew up to pitch, hit sixty homers in a season, and once, when he felt like it, pointed to a place high in the stands and boomed one up there. Ruth also made it his off-hours practice to visit sick children in hospitals. For one sick boy, Johnny Sylvester, who the papers said was near death, he even promised to hit a special home run, and the next afternoon in the Series he smacked three goners. Yet despite all the charity work and mastery behind the plate, he had, they say with a grin, a softness for women and drink. Even when you're famous—and have a national candy bar named after you—you can't win.

Babe Ruth lived on the other side of the court inside the whale. His brother-in-law jumped from the eighteenth story into the handball area where we played unless we made too much noise and tenants got angry and threw us out. I heard the thump of the body at night when I was in bed. Like a steamer trunk had fallen out of the window. I wondered who had to clean up the bloody splash. The same doorman, Joe, who slapped me for not being nice to retarded Jerry (it wasn't true), took me to the Babe's for the photo that came out on the front page of the *Daily News.* That's when the Babe gave me a baseball diploma, saying on it, ACADEMY OF SPORT, World's Fair, 1938.

Sunday afternoons at home we heard Father Coughlin and Hitler live, shrieking on the radio. They were both ranting against Roosevelt and Jews. Hitler was screaming in German all the way from Berlin. Why did we listen? "We have to know them," Dad said, "even if it makes us vomit." Everyone in the building hated Hitler, including the Babe who said so over the slow thundering speakers at Yankee Stadium.

When the men who work here, elevatormen and doormen, went out on strike, the new fellows kept billy clubs behind the entrance doors. The scabs were very friendly—big, reasonable men, with out-of-town accents. I liked the scabs as much as Ruddy and Joe outside on the sidewalk in the wind, picketing, the guys we brought corn-beef sandwiches to and hot coffee. I heard Ruddy got hit trying to bust in. They almost broke his head.

It was funny for men to ride me up the elevator. I was just a kid and they were doing it for me as if I were a grownup with my own money to pay rent and give Christmas tips. I always ran downstairs. Leaping as many steps as I could, my hand on the railing, trying to float. They slowed me down as I raced across the marble lobby floor to the front entry, and outside into the North Pole wind and gully in Riverside Park.

But often I spent the afternoon sitting in a corner of the elevator, going up and down in the tired coffin. When no one else was riding, they let me close the accordion brass gate. I did it like a grown elevatorman. One afternoon I was sitting in the corner on the floor when the Babe walked in. The Professor of Swat was a little drunk. He wasn't too young, but this big bulk had a kindly iron smile. Ruddy, who was back on the job, looked at me, winked, and said, "Go to it, buddy." I jumped up and grabbed the brass controller stick that made the cage slide up and down, and we descended safely toward the lobby. George Herman Ruth stood staring at the floor numbers slipping by. Lucky, I leveled the car on the first try, and snappily pulled open the folding gate. As the Babe wobbled out, he mumbled, "Clean hit, kid."

At home, it was Mother, Father, and Howard. Beatrice was away and had her own life. Mother was always gentle with me. Beautiful but far on her own mountain. We were trusting and she was sometimes affectionate, but we conversed like strangers from two generations. She worried about me—that I might turn out like Father. I adored her, almost as much as I did Father who told me secrets and was a fellow conspirator. He was a man of enthusiasm, really a dreamer, sometimes about me, and I got caught up in it. He gave me belief that nothing was impossible. Only he wasn't there much for us to talk. My brother and I had an early wrestling relationship. I got up in the morning and we'd wrestle. I came home, and we went at it. It was sport, fun, and real conflict. Howard and Dad had a strange conflict, fighting over Mother, which increased over the years. After my father's death, he became her surrogate husband.

One morning I heard my father and mother arguing. I think it was the sore point of ownership of the store in Lewiston. Father was screaming, "You Goddamn bitch, you, you Goddamn bitch you." He went for the door and I tried to keep him from leaving. "Don't go." But he left. About a year later, he was in bad shape and came in occasionally to see Mother through a special entrance facing the Drive that went down along the boiler room. None of the tenants could know he had come. He'd stay until dawn and I would accompany him down the metal stairs and up to the Drive and the few cars outside coming and disappearing in half light.

Billy Barnstone (left) and Mitchell Rosenheim with Babe Ruth as Professor of Swat, preparing to hand out Academy of Sport diplomas at the World's Fair, 1938

Father had lost everything, and when I was thirteen I spent some wonderful months with him—I didn't go to the expensive camp in Maine that summer. We had a room at the Graystone Hotel on upper Broadway, and I accompanied him downtown as he went from jewelry store to jewelry store, selling what watches and straps he had left in his satchel. We made just enough money to pay for meals and the hotel, but he was feeling optimistic—and I was too. When his business would collapse he went through a manic phase to hide it all and then a depression. He was coming out of depression and it was one of the happiest periods of my life. By the next summer, he sold diamonds and pearls rather than watches as he moved from city to city, from coast to coast, and with his good eye and charm he was driving a Buick convertible.

Meanwhile, I had finished a year at Stuyvesant High School, a school for students "gifted" in science. I was disappointed when the School of Music and Arts turned me down. I drew a railroad engine with a pencil, which was the main component of the entry examination, and it didn't make it. So I took the science test for Stuyvesant and passed. The standards were very high in this New York public school, but Howard thought I should get out of the city and he wisely selected the George School, a coed Quaker boarding school in Pennsylvania, which I entered when I was fourteen. The divorce and need for a change was the main reason for sending me out of the city. It would help me when applying for college. Not least was the thought that my Maine speech was being overcome by a New York accent and that was unacceptable to Howard and Mother who were concerned with social proprieties.

I loved every aspect of the George School where I learned about women, dirty jokes, pranks, peace, civil rights, and meditation, and also studied Latin and the regular curriculum. It was January 1943 when I went to the George School, and unfortunately I rushed through. The word used then was I was "accelerating." Everyone was telling me, "You better have some college behind you, before the Army grabs you." I expected to be drafted at the end of 1945 when I would turn eighteen. So I enrolled in extra courses and took advanced Latin. After the first year with the Quakers, Dad suggested I meet him in Boise, Idaho, and spend the summer together.

I took the train from Philadelphia to Boise— three days on a train crammed with soldiers and sailors—many of them sleeping overhead on the luggage racks. We set off from Boise, going through Reno down to San Francisco where we spent a few weeks at the Saint Regis and ate fish at Bernstein's; then we drove up the redwood coast to Seattle, and down through desert America to Colorado, Texas, and Mexico. Sometimes we drove through the night. Once at midnight a deer leapt into a headlight, struck us, and disappeared just as quickly. In Colorado he taught me to drive. At dawn in Amarillo, Texas, we saw air force cadets marching in rank through the street, singing "Off we go into the wild blue yonder."

When we reached the border, Dad was called into the custom man's booth by a very stern-looking gentleman. I was worried. A few minutes later Dad came out smiling.

"What happened?"

"That fellow said almost nothing. Just sat mum till I threw a few dollars on the table. Then he was happy and said 'Welcome to Mexico.' You must understand that these officials make next to nothing. So they hit us when they can. It's a mess, awful, don't you think?"

"It's sad."

We took our white car through the harsh desert that smelled of cactus and millenia, climbed up through the rain forests of the Pan American highway where we often picked up entire Indian families to take them to the next village, then sloped down through the astonishing colonial stone cities of Querétaro and Guanajuato near Mexico City. After reaching the capital, we kept going south to Tasco, the silver city, and dropped a hundred miles into Zapata country. In that Nahuatl-speaking region, each house had a portrait of their revolutionary hero Emiliano Zapata who, like Madero, was gunned down. In the southernmost village we were given a

room in a small inn. It was late afternoon and the *patrón* closed the door behind us without putting on the light or opening the shutters. "Duck!" I screamed. The room was swarming with bats. We rushed for the windows, tore open the shutters, and the circling creatures darted out into the darkness. Within minutes, the full moon kindly came up over a mountain and walked in through the window used by the departing bats. In all that lunar luminosity, I slept safely, with no desire to pull the sheet over my head.

In Mexico City Dad showed me this great ancient city of the Americas. My favorite street was Avenida de Francisco I. Madero, a street with jewels and precious silver shops, brightly lighted behind steel window cages. Madero Street led to the Zócalo, the huge sixteenth-century plaza, with its cathedral (built on the foundation of a major Aztec temple), the grand palace of the parliament, and other old administrative buildings. On the Zócalo was also the Monte de Piedad (Mount of Piety or National Pawn Shop) where Father bought jewels and silver pieces which he was later to reproduce and manufacture in Colorado. He also introduced me to two sisters, Matilde and Maria Batista. The four of us went out on a double date, which was also the very first date of my life. As the evening came to a close and we were taking the women home, I sat in the backseat with Marti, necking with her. She was about two or three years older than me. She gave me a red handkerchief with a guitar painted on it that I lost on the Pullman going north. A year later when I went to visit Dad in his new home in Colorado Springs, Marti was his wife and she was expecting.

After three terms with the Quakers, I went to Phillips Academy at Exeter for the summer term to finish high school at the "accelerated" rate. So at sixteen I found myself a freshman, back in Maine, at Bowdoin College. That fall I began to smoke a pipe and wear tweedy jackets, which made me feel older and more dignified, yet it hardly worked to make me less eager and immature. I came to Bowdoin with many lessons from George School, not the least being an awareness of the American Friends Service Committee. As a result of the Friends' connection, I went twice to Mexico to dig privies in Indian villages in their work camps. That was the beginning of my Spanish language world, and the beginning of a life of wandering.

Bowdoin was a disappointment after George School. I was sorry I was there. College meant fraternity bigotry, a silly, big-man-on-campus anti-intellectual atmosphere, and, above all, the lack of idealism that had dominated the Quaker school. For all the pranks, George School had an ethos of idealism, whereas Bowdoin was a microcosm of urbane prejudices and the frailties of a rich small college. Everyone was in fraternities with the exception of twenty-two students who lived in one wing of Longfellow dormitory. Of these, twenty were Jewish, one black, one a nonconformist tumbler. I did continue with sports, diving for the swimming team and winning my Bowdoin letter. In a year of minimum competition, with most potential students in military uniform, at sixteen I came in fifth at MIT in the competitions for the New England College Championships.

Slowly I saw more. After all, there were professors, with their own dignity, knowledge, and wisdom, and so the George School faded. My calculus teacher, Professor Holmes, relished the eighteenth-century English novel, the courses I took in philosophy altered everything for me, and I had a few crucial friends who made Bowdoin the eventual place of despair and illumination. When I took my first step as a writer, two older students, a Dane and a Czech, were there to help me make the step permanent. While I was busy fencing with Bowdoin, I heard from Dad. It had been a while.

Father had fallen low again.

His silver empire was in trouble. He made it grow too quickly and couldn't control it, and did extravagant things to prove to himself that he was invulnerable. When he called, he asked me to come to New York, and I went down to the city immediately. I was finishing my sophomore year. We talked the night away, from bed to bed, long after we put the lights out. I tried to raise his spirits. I had almost become his father. Then I returned to Maine to take my finals. A few days later, Dad called again. "Come down to New York. I need you."

"Give me a few days till I finish my exams. Just a few days and I'll be with you."

I was almost annoyed, but I promised to come. We talked a while, and then click. Then I didn't hear from him. He left New York. He went to Mexico City and saw Marti. Then flew to Colorado Springs. The afternoon after I did get through the semester, there was a message to call Colorado. I called and spoke to one of Dad's assistants. He told me that my father had climbed to the eighth floor of the building, went onto the roof, folded his light topcoat and put his hat on top of the coat. Then he leapt into the May air. The funeral would be in three days.

I saw Mother in New York. She was weeping and saying, "Why did he do it?" Indignantly, as if he had pulled another terrible stunt. But that was a facade. She was heartbroken. I took the plane and met Marti.

She was three months pregnant. My younger half brother Ronald, a little more than a year old, was in Mexico City. When we passed by the open coffin, I did not let her look at it. I didn't want to remember, or have Marti remember, Father dead. Years later I felt the same about my mother. It was too unfair to them to have their whole lives recalled and reduced to a few moments at the end. Father had given me voyage. I would never stop dreaming of him—in China, in Tibet, wherever he would show up to talk and give me half information about where he was. He is with me even now.

Father on Glass Wings

From Colorado spring, death on the phone
told me you jumped. An angel with your stone
arms dizzy on glass wings. * But you don't land.
Childhood. We're selling watch straps, store to store,
sharing a shabby Graystone room. The floor
is spread with schoolbooks. As you take my hand
we ride downstairs for papers: SNEAK JAP PLANES
SMASH PEARL HARBOR! I've got Latin to do
but we walk Broadway. * Dropping through the blue
air (I'm in Brunswick in the tedious rains),
you shattered in the gutter. * You'd be gray
by now, I guess, and coming up the stairs
is my young son I love the same old way.
He can't see you. I won't see his gray hairs.

Fishing for Light in Vera Cruz

After the suicide and two years at Bowdoin, I decided to go to Mexico for a year. I was a junior in college, only eighteen, in need of a change. George School was coed and I was beginning to be less shy and perhaps more natural with women. Bowdoin was all male and socially the Dark Ages. In compensation there were blind dates from other colleges (I had one dreary one in two years) and the famous Bowdoin fraternity house parties, where drunken masturbating Bowdoin men were supposed to turn into happy, drunken copulators. As for the wild house parties, I was not in that favored company. Hawthorne, Longfellow, Admiral Peary were asleep. Mexico was calling. I had been there once with my father and then between semesters at George School when I went to Miacatlán, an Indian village near the volcanoes where the American Friends Service Committee had a small work camp.

Now I went to Yautepec, a bigger village with a jukebox in the main square, pastel-colored houses, and many privies to be dug. On Saturday evenings there was a dance in the small city of Cualtla, and the women at the Friends' camp a few miles away came to join us. A male singer sang standard songs in Spanish, but his speciality was "Kees me wonce and kees me twice, and kees me wonce again, it's been a loong, loong time." I liked best the tropical rhythms of the *huapango* from coastal Vera Cruz and danced through the night.

In mid-September, my five companions in the camp were in their cots, recovering from yellow jaundice. Somehow it spared me. And I went into backyards of the poorest campesinos and dug their privies. A few days after I got to Yautepec our numbers were increased by the arrival of two Spanish students who, like myself, were to be there for two months. Paco and Tomás were orphans from the Spanish Civil War, living in an orphanage in Mexico City. In 1939, right after the Spanish Civil War, Mexico, which never recognized the Franco regime, took in some five hundred Spanish refugee orphans, sending them first to the province of Morelia, west of the capital. Now, seven years later, they were living in scattered buildings in Mexico City. I spent all my time with Tomás and Paco, and when our brief but glorious experience in the ditches and cantinas was over, I went with my Spanish friends to the capital, where they managed to get me into one of the orphanages.

I slept on the floor of a soccer-playing chemistry student. Hugo and I made up a funny Spanglish. When we woke in the mornings, before putting on his silver-rimmed glasses Hugo would say to me, *"Bueno, Guillermo, vamos a getearnos up."* (Okay, Willis, let's get up.) Each day we left the house very early, since my stay as a guest was still a secret to the director. A week later, however, Hugo found me an official place on the roof of the other male orphanage in the city, sharing a small white room with Tomás Garcia Borrás, my pal from Yautepec. Tomás, a Catalan, was also in chemistry, and smart, lusty, and obscene. He always wanted to *gatear,* meaning "to look for cats," slang for "maids." "En la cama todas son iguales." In bed they're all alike, he'd say. By agreement we spoke English one day, Spanish the next, and he taught me Catalan popular songs. I was never hungry at the orphanage, but neither was I deliriously well fed. One afternoon Paco took me to the elegant apartment of a French lady who was his friend. An attractive woman in her late thirties, who had had polio as a child, Terése waddled boldly around the living room in her steel braces. I thought I was in love with her after five minutes. She put on Offenbach's *Gaieté Parisienne* and served us dish after dish of the main course, and then plate after plate of pastries. Both Paco and I ate with no embarrassment, yielding to Terése's insistence that we keep eating, and I think my love increased with each bite.

I got my cot on the roof and my share of cold beans and potato tortillas in exchange for teaching English to the fellows. Soon I had five outside people of different ages and background whom I was teaching English to: a fifteen-year-old girl from a wealthy family on the Lomas de Chapultepec, an energetic lawyer, a serious bureaucrat in his forties, and an elderly secretary who was cultivated and always gave me wonderful desserts.

The youngest of my students was Peter Bach, a young Swiss who had been admitted to George School and needed tutoring in English. At his house Peter's father, an economist, talked to me at length about Leon Trotsky. At the outbreak of World War I, Bach had been Trotsky's friend and advisor in Zurich. When Trotsky settled in Mexican exile in 1936, Bach joined him there. Ramón Mercader, a Catalan, worked his way into Trotsky's entourage and one afternoon, while Trotsky was looking at his library, Mercader buried his alpenstock in his scalp. Later, a list of other dangerous Trotskyites marked for assassination was found in the Stalin agent's room, and among them was Mr. Bach.

With these students I enjoyed each lesson and felt part of Mexican life. It gave me enough money to enroll in two literature courses at the Autonomous National University of Mexico and take an outstanding course in Spanish phonetics at Mexico City College. The latter was offered by a Spanish refugee intellectual. It was my first acquaintance with a body of writers and intellectuals who were to shape my life.

One very lonely Sunday morning, Juan, a tall, extremely morose Spaniard at the orphanage, said, *"Guillermo, vamos a la corrida. Lucha Manolete."* (Willis, let's go to the bullfight. Manolete's fighting.) Manolete, the grave, gentleman matador, who looked like Picasso's drawing of Quixote, was on the posters for that afternoon. I don't know why—because of some passivity in a year of venture—I declined. It was not the slaughter itself, which in later years would alone have dissuaded me. In a few years Manolete, the most acclaimed figure in tauromachy, was gored in a provincial Spanish bullring near Jaén. Under very primitive medical conditions, he died a few hours later. He and Federico García Lorca's friend, Ignacio Sánchez Mejías, the literary matador to whom Lorca wrote his extraordinary elegy "Llanto por Ignacio Sánchez Mejías," were the two failed bullfighters in the twentieth century. Manolete was the essential Spanish tragic figure, sacrificed to the ritual of an anachronistic, savage game. Sánchez Mejías died as a result of a series of miscalculations when the older man returned foolishly to the ring. The bullfighter-scholar had lectured at the 1927 tricentennial conference on Luis de Góngora, the baroque Spanish poet whose work inspired a generation of modern poets. Lorca's elegy on Sánchez Mejias is often taken as a mirror reflecting and presaging the poet's own violent death in 1936.

But no Manolete. I hung around the orphanage and finally reached Margaret, an older Canadian woman with whom I went to restaurants and on dates, and took the bus to her apartment. Margaret was a good, romantic friend. Although she was only thirty-two, she had the languid beauty of an expatriate who had seen perhaps too much. We were moments of innocence. She thought me too young for her to have sex with—which she conveyed to me as we lay near each other on her bed—but she introduced the notion of love making, urging me to know that world and that light with someone else, and I was hotly in agreement. Margaret was a passage. We had a secret, candid understanding of affection, and never lost it during the year in Mexico.

The orphanage locked its gate at 10:00 P.M., and unless I could climb over the iron fence and get someone to unlock the door, after ten I had to spend the night elsewhere. My private classes kept me beyond that hour, so several evenings a week I went to crummy restaurants on San Juan Deletrán Street and read Thomas Wolfe, John Dos Passos, and D. H. Lawrence novels through the night. Prostitutes argued with their companions in neighboring booths. Outside, in the cold winter of the city there were inevitably piles of children in the street, sleeping in bundles to keep themselves warm, "the forgotten ones" *(los olvidados)*, as Buñuel called them in his documentary film.

Sometimes I went to the place of George Ballou, a friend who had a room in a typical downtown residential building which had three or four stories of rooms around a patio, with stairways going up each side to the interior tile walkway around the patio on each floor, giving the rooms an extra place outdoors and animated a social life among the occupants. George's desk was filled with manuscripts of sunlight (as he described them) about his trips to Jalisco and his extra bed held cages with the small animals he had picked up. His talent was as a naturalist and he handled animals with savvy, traveling from country to country, through customs, carrying small snakes and rats in his pockets. His first publications were in naturalist journals. A year earlier he had convinced the Smithsonian to send him to Central America and he lived in the jungle for some months, sleeping in a hammock, catching, taming, and writing about small beasts. He glorified these adventures by wearing a Spanish beret over his shaven head, which he said he had shaved to be more comfortable and keep away jungle diseases and pests.

"George, can you put me up again tonight?"

"Sure. Over the stairway."

"You son-of-a-bitch, why can't you move your zoo and let me sleep on the other bed?"

It was useless. The little beasts were tranquil in their home on the cot. So I hung up the jungle hammock and went to sleep, but took it down very early, soon after dawn, so that the tenants wouldn't have to walk under me.

George had interesting connections in the art world, usually made through his mother, Jenny. He showed me pictures of an American black dancer, Jimba, a tall, plump, sensual woman, whom he later introduced me to. In the publicity photographs the dancer was sitting or standing naked, except for an African cloth around her waist. Jimba didn't have a girly-shot look but rather a glare of artistic meditation with religious overtones. George said she also posed for the painter Diego Rivera, who was much in the news because of his mural in the dining room of the Reforma Hotel, which contained a declaration in large letters: DIOS NO EXISTE (God does not exist) that incited a series of angry blotchings out of the word NO. When Margaret and I ate supper and danced at the Reforma dining room, the letters were again restored to read DIOS NO EXISTE.

If I didn't go to a restaurant or George's, I spent the night at Marti's. After Father died, Marti left Colorado and moved back to Mexico City. She had little money and lived with her mother, Rebeca, a Sephardic Jew from Istanbul, and my infant brother, Ronald, in a very old barrio behind the cathedral. Soon she would buy a stunning white suit and become an interior decorator, the first step on her way to great wealth and several marriages. Now she was pregnant with my second half brother, who would be born six months after our father's death. In January she flew to Nuevo Laredo, crossed the border into Texas to give birth to Robert Barnstone, and flew back to Mexico City. She was only twenty or twenty-one. Dad left her some debts, nothing else. But she said he had lifted her forever from her past and given her a knowledge of business that made her liberated. In reality she had a genius and a constancy for business, which Dad never had, and within a few years she was a millionaire, with diverse properties, theaters, a furniture factory, and department store. She also was given to philosophy and religion, flew to Spain to study the works of José Ortega y Gasset with his disciple Julián Marias, and spent time in Asia in pursuit of Tibetan Buddhism.

Barnstone digging privies in Mexico with the American Friends Service Committee, 1946

Now she was poor, young, and filled with plans. Even then Marti was a candid mixture of self-educated, dreamy student of religions and implacable businesswoman. Since I had little money, I often sold my blood to a clinic near the orphanage and once, when I was very broke, I managed to sell it to two clinics in the same day. I got about ten dollars out of that blood-letting, which could easily carry me through the week. I had come to return some pesos Marti had lent me. "Here's the money I owe you."

"Thanks, Billy."

I reached into my side pocket, but found that someone on the jammed bus had got there first. He stole my blood. I don't know whether Marti believed me. Though her face changed with disappointment, she said nothing. (I sold more blood and soon got her the money.) Marti and her mother slept in the bedroom. I regularly slept on a mat on the floor between her brother Sam, who was a captain in the Mexican army, and the Indian maid. A captain in Mexico in those days made a miserable salary, and so the officer chose Marti's floor when he was on leave; but the army was his career. Sam wore dark sun-

glasses, even at night, which gave him a certain allure, though once, years later at a party, his older sister, Luisa, screamed at him to take off his Mafia shades.

At Mexico City College I met a young American woman in the phonetics class. We became good friends. By this time I had moved from the orphanage to a Mexican boarding house where the food was much better and where we even had a cook who liked to hide hot chiles in my mashed potatoes to see me holler. I call my new friend Katherine, although her name has eluded me for years. Katherine was twenty-four (I had just turned nineteen) and, she told me, a virgin, a condition she would be happy to change. I went to her apartment after class and we had a fine supper on the balcony. The night was good and at one moment we must have looked so happy there that some men got out of their car below and shouted up to us "*A la cama, a la cama!*" (To bed, to bed!) We did lie down on the bed and made plans about mutually changing our innocence. We would take a bus to Vera Cruz, the seaport on the coast to the west of Mexico City and spend some days there.

The bus descended from the high capital and crossed the great plain of Puebla which Cortés marched over on his way to his conquest of Tenochtitlán and the Aztec empire. Those plains were filled with ancient building stones and the three hundred sixty-five chapels at Cholula that Spaniards built on the ruins of destroyed Indian temples. We descended through lush mountains of flowers to fast plains of sugarcane to reach the tropical coast. In the afternoon the sun over the coastal area didn't seem to move. It hung in the sky like a grapefruit of fire, and everything under it was touched by its still energy until it finally relented and descended into the ocean.

In Vera Cruz we found a room in a private house. White pajama costumes were still normal dress. A perfect fabric for the climate. That evening there was a dance in the city square. We bought masks, a green and a silver one, and behind our masks we were lost in dance. The *huapango* guitar and the horn and drums casually lifted the street and it floated for a few hours on incandescent light and tequila. We came down to walk back through the streets to our rented room:

Tropical White Pajamas

In Mexico in a poor village near
the live volcano with its summer snow
and smoking heart, the Quakers settled here
and I dug privies in the mornings. Oh!
one evening in the streets of Vera Cruz
I danced, wore a green mask, we heard the wild

huapango song, big stars cooked us. Those loose
tropical white pajamas and the mild
faces of Indian friends soothed us. We went
back to our room, our bed, took off our clothes,
both innocent as Eve. The patrón laughed
at us, smirking. Dawn found our bodies bent
for the surprise and birth of light! Who knows
your name? We fished through white night on our
     raft.

When summer came I left the rich year in
Mexico to attend Middlebury College where I
enrolled in the French School. One course was in the
Spanish School where I was also allowed to take my
lunch. I learned to speak French very quickly in their
saturation program. The heart of the summer, however, was my own immersion into everything Spanish.
I attended lectures by Pedro Salinas, one of the major
poets from that extraordinary Generation of '27.
Years later I translated his book *My Voice Because of
You* (La voz a ti debida), a sequence of seventy love
poems. As with all books of poems I translated, the
activity became my instructor for knowing the poet
and for absorbing lessons into my own work. Like all
writers, I have learned and stolen constantly from
reading—but never as much as I learn and steal from
translating.

I spent time with Salinas's daughter Solita and
her husband Juan Marichal. But my closest friend was
Jaime Salinas, Pedro's son, who became a friend for
life. And then there was Edouette Quillivic, an
instructor in French from the Midi, who the next year
in France invited me to her house for some good days
in Carpentras. That summer I spent with Jaime and
Edouette.

It was a summer of poets. One evening Jorge
Guillén and Luis Cernuda came to visit Pedro Salinas.
I was to see Guillén often in later years and spend a
week at Salinas's house. But this was my one glimpse
of Luis Cernuda, who had been a year at Mount
Holyoke and was about to return to Mexico where he
passed the later years of his exile. When I shook the
hand of this shy, arrogant poet, whose work has only
grown in importance since his relatively early death,
he was wearing a white sport jacket. I see him now
shining elegantly among his fellow poets.

In the evenings we tended to walk for hours in
the Vermont hills. Sometimes we would walk almost
to dawn. I spoke Spanish to Jaime, French to
Edouette. Our common language was French which
Jaime, born in Algeria, knew natively. At about four
in the morning the moon, like a yellow buffoon,
suddenly rose over the hills, dimming the stars. I
stared at it so long Edouette asked me whether I was
having a mystical fit. Jaime, given to dramatic state-

ments, was complaining about the role of being the
son of a famous poet. He claimed not to have read his
father's books, yet at the same time said his father
read him each new poem as he wrote it. I countered
with something to cheer him up when he came out
with, *"Willis, en tu caso es distinto, porque tú eres
poeta."* (Willis, in your case it's different, because
you're a poet.)

"What are you saying! I've never written a poem
in my life—or even thought of writing anything."

But Jaime was almost right. Poetry was less than
a year away.

After Middlebury I was back in New York
before returning to Bowdoin. My friend from Mexico, George Ballou, called to invite me to supper at the
Santa Lucia Hotel to meet two Greek women, one of
whom had arrived that afternoon by liner from
Europe.

"Yes, of course." I knew the place, a small
Spanish hotel in the village. Aliki Tzalopoulou was on
her way from Athens to Mount Holyoke, her sister
Helle was beginning her senior year at Wellesley
College.

Aliki had had an intercontinental affair with
George's father, Harold Ballou, while he was in
Greece, working with the United Nations Relief
Organization. Now to complete the web, George was
there at the hotel with his mother, Jenny Ballou, a
novelist, usually estranged from Harold, to meet
Aliki, Helle, and me. Two Greek women. What to
make of it? If he had said two Slovenians or Bulgarians, I wouldn't have known more. Jenny played the
part of a 1920s expatriate Bohemian. She had lived in
Paris, was in Spain during the Civil War (George was
born in Madrid); her novel *Spanish Olives* was the
second winner in the annual Houghton-Mifflin novel
awards—the initial prize went to Robert Penn Warren. Extravagant, whimsical, Jenny froze George into
a loose image of herself, and he was to spend his life
arduously and agonizingly trying to write and publish
that first best-seller. But in September 1947 in
Greenwich Village, we were all filled with enthusiastic
presence and a sense of fully happy futurity.

After the two contenders for wayward Harold
met, exchanged understated putdowns, we all settled
into slaphappy conversation. When we had eaten,
George said, "I've got Jenny's car. Let's take a spin
over to New Jersey and explore the countryside. I feel
crazy tonight."

"Yes, you seem yourself," I said.

So George and I, Aliki and Helle, spun our way
across the George Washington in search of wild
nature. Fifteen or twenty miles into that frontier of

oil storage tanks, factories, and dim shopping villages, we hit the open road. On finding a rolling meadow, with ponds and odd clumps of trees, we got out. George had his accordion with him and we danced under the stars, George playing, singing at the top of his lungs, and hopping around. He sang in all tongues, including songs in Russian, a language he made up spontaneously. It hardly mattered when we realized that our bit of wild nature was a private golf course. Finally, we drove back to the city.

It was too late for the women to show at the place in Brooklyn where they had been invited for a few days; at about three-thirty I was in a phone booth, calling my mother who was not quite awake. "Mom, I want to put up two Greek girls I met a few hours ago."

"You what?" Somehow, the idea was not appealing to her, so we found a room for them at the Saint Moritz Hotel on Central Park South, not far from the Parc Van Dome where Mother and I were living. When they woke up, the women left for Brooklyn and I took the subway out to see them. It was still a sunny afternoon when I reached their place. Helle was playing Chopin études on the upright piano—a romantic sequel to the night in the country. Aliki was pouring out European charm in her heroic style. The sun was all over the living room, dodging the lace curtains. The high-spirited women were a team, smiting me with Greek magic, ouzo, and fruit preserves swimming in syrup served in a glass cup.

In the fall I was at Bowdoin, studying mainly philosophy courses, though my official major was French. Because my graduating mark in a Victorian novel course at Exeter was *D-*, I had, despite an *A* in freshman English, avoided all courses in English literature. However, a close friend, William Cappellari, urged me to come with him to audit a seminar in recent American poetry. I went with much excitement to a discussion of the poems in Robert Lowell's *Lord Weary's Castle,* but after class, Professor Cleveland, old and distinguished, took me aside quietly. "I have to ask you not to come to any more classes."

I began to read poetry very seriously on my own.

This was my last year as an undergraduate, since by putting two summer terms together I would graduate in August of 1948. My roommate during the last darknesses at Bowdoin was Bret Bare, a philosophy major. Bret was born in New Haven, the illegitimate son of a housemaid at the Taft Hotel and a Yale undergraduate. He was in a Protestant missionary family and spent his childhood in India.

"The minister never even adopted me. He kept me on as a foster child, living with his real children. So much for good religion."

Bret was often bitter—more often quiet and gentle, and though articulate when he wanted to be, he spoke little; when he did speak it was as if he were leaving some protected camp for a while. He looked like a dark, young Abraham Lincoln. Bret went through World War II as an infantryman, unwounded, but when it was over he discovered he was epileptic. Often in the middle of the night in our freezing bedroom, he would have a heaving, groaning attack. It was like some horrible sexual trip. Usually he didn't wake until the next morning, but he felt dry, worn, as if every bone in his body had cracked open. We lived in a dormitory named Hawthorne and perhaps lived in his room, that is, the writer who was Longfellow's classmate in the class of 1825. We had endless discussions about our philosophers. Although I envied the notion of being brought up in India, Bret was sullen and depressive about his past. Yet when in that cloud of darkness he felt happiness he broke up like a big child and giggled. Before the semester was over he found that he liked to paint and that a picture offered him a particular vision. An idea, an abstraction, a conceptual ordering of perceptions could not satisfy him any longer.

Bowdoin, 1948

Hawthorne had this yellowed room. So we share
the morning gloom of alcoholics or
nocturnal masturbators, north and nowhere,
too isolated for a date or whore.
Were you a grind like me? A dreamer slob
and weird? I sleep, the window open to
the black Maine snow, hearing my roommate throb
and scream, an epileptic getting through
another siege. He's a philosopher;
I'm lost. But he was born a bastard, he
says bitterly; my origins I shirk
from. Worst (or best?) I doubt there is a me
concocting words in terrifying blur
within. Dream, Hawthorne. Words no longer work.

The year was strange. I sought in the philosophers answers, and was disappointed when I found systems, each one plausible but in contradiction to every other. Had I read Jorge Luis Borges at the time, I might have believed that there were no absolutes, no keys to the universe, no flawless algebras for language or thought. And so the paradoxical quest, the necessary journey. Heraclitus the Obscure, as Borges called the ancient relativist, told the truth about truth's absence.

I kept a diary. I became increasingly introspective. I read many novels and was self-inspective of each reaction. Finally, I began to doubt everything—language, consciousness, and any truth. I spoke about this to a blind professor of philosophy. "What can I do? I want to get out of this."

"Go see a movie."

"I did, but it didn't work. I couldn't keep my mind on the screen. I couldn't see the film."

I cannot yet verbalize what I discovered that year, but I know it perfectly well. I found the mind disappear, words disappear, found the absolute blankness, noncenter of thought, the emptiness of my head, which filled up only when I stopped inspecting. And so the mind became an area of fearful detachment, almost a nightmare of nonbeing and death, with none of the colorful vision that the mystics make of such an arid night of detachment. Finally, I accepted that only by not examining thought, by not testing, questioning, by letting the arbitrary, mechanical, learned process of thinking go on by itself, could I carry on. By *not* looking for a true picture of consciousness, for the core of being, could I escape into the pragmatic acceptance that keeps everyone working, walking, and managing in the world. More formally, I read Spinoza and books by Henri Bergson and felt in complete accord with the Plotinian notion of the illusions of ordinary life, its appearances, its arbitrary attributes. Beyond that was yearning, but no finalities. When I dropped down inside myself, the winter got blacker and blacker.

How and Why I Became a Mime

Only twenty I saw darkness inside
for one year. No. I lost my eyes and came
to desolate hell, the hill of suicide
of thought. Words lost their act. I felt no flame,
a continent from eyes or passion. Who
was making talk? What polar icecap in
my scalp was me? From looking in, I knew
the secret hoax. Then, rocketing to the skin
I tumbled backward, lost from the dead eye
looking at me. Icepicks of light! But no
bottom or circus cannon to fly me out.
Talking, the good actor, I wriggled dry.
Am I now? Only twenty years or so
from dark, I mime the gray angel of doubt.

From the dark night of the mind, there was an escape: to be away from the geography of Brunswick, Maine. To leave the gray angel of doubt it was best to leave the place where the demon lived. Then I could forget the mind under mind where I was stuck, where nothing worked.

I began to go on weekends to Wellesley College to see Helle Tzalopoulou. In the first months I had a crush on Aliki, whom I hardly saw at all, except for one quick trip to Holyoke. When I went down to Wellesley, outside Boston, I hitched, and had the habit of not wearing more than a sportcoat—no sweater or undershirt underneath, no matter how cold the weather. I had the notion that if one didn't give into the cold the body would adjust. As I waited, sometimes for thirty or forty minutes in the snow or rain for a ride, I didn't seem to mind; and while I often reached Wellesley more as an icicle than hot oatmeal, I never got sick from that experiment in mind reforming matter. Helle laughed about how I would arrive with my jacket wide open, my shirt soaked, my body frozen.

Helle the Pou Tzalóping down the stairs. That's the title her smart literary friends who liked Winnie and the Jabberwocky invented for Helle Tzalopoulou, Greek English major. In 1945, the German occupation and war scarcely over, she came from Greece on the *Big Foot Wallace,* a slow cargo ship, armed with a scholarship to study at Wellesley. Helle was born in Istanbul (where Helle fell off the golden fleece and drowned in the Hellespont). Her mother came from a Phanariot Greek family, her father was an Epirote doctor who went to Turkey with the Red Cross during that brief period in 1921 when, for the first time since 1453, Constantinope was again Constantinople. A few years after the "Catastrophe," the 1921–1922 war between Greece and Turkey, the family left for Athens where Helle grew up. After the occupation, Helle's mother had the dressmaker sew sheets and blankets together to make clothes for her daughter's trip to America. When she got to Wellesley and saw what the students were wearing she bought a skirt and a blouse and threw the Greek "bed clothes" away.

We had fine times. I was intrigued by her foreignness, which included a good knowledge of *Paradise Lost* and the English Victorian novel. And we grew closer. I liked being at Wellesley, its Rockefeller Gothic buildings, its lake well designed and placed with Chinese care in the ample grass and wooded grounds, and all the brightness in the air of smart, alluring students. I met a stunningly attractive couple: an Israeli student at Wellesley and her Palestinian fiancé from MIT. One evening at supper in Tower Court I couldn't make up my mind what to order. When the waitress groaned at my slowness, I resorted to Helle's Milton with "They also serve who only stand and wait" to which the insulted student shot back my comeuppance: "They also wait who only stand and serve."

After a weekend at Tower Court, Bowdoin was drab. Little grace, no etiquette, which was perhaps a plus. And there was an intensity, at least in my circle of central European friends. We laughed a lot, despite the sometime gravity of our vision. The Stalinists had just taken over Czechoslovakia. One evening Slava Klima, who was the deepest of my very deep young buddies, was on the dorm payphone, talking, really shouting because of a bad connection, to his fiancée in Prague. He was asking her to leave, if she could, so they could get married. She couldn't or wouldn't leave Prague. He never saw her again, nor did he marry. Slava was my confidant. I was weary of my otherness. Though Slava had no easy answer, when a way came he helped make it real. Something finally did happen to free me of the obsession of introspection and doubt—and that something returned me to the visibly tangible and gave me a profession.

Christopher Isherwood wrote a short novel, *Prater Violet,* about an Austrian filmmaker. He followed the art and personal life of the director. (Later, Isherwood wrote me that the book was not really fiction and then recounted the postnovel life of his filmmaker friend.) At one memorable moment the director wakes in the morning and decides to write a poem. It is perfectly natural. In others hands the poem and the activity would have been sentimental. Not in this instance. I remember the words as something like, "Sun at my window in the morning. Bird, you wake me with your singing. Keep singing. You make me happy."

About two o'clock one morning I awakened and wrote a poem. It was a love poem. I went back to sleep. Some twenty or thirty minutes later, I woke up again and wrote a second poem, and went back to sleep. The next morning I showed these lyrics to Slava, and to Olaf Hanson, a Dane. Also to a Frenchman whose name I can't recall. To my surprise, they took my first attempt at poetry seriously. Slava mentioned Rilke and Valéry and mumbled something about these poems being in a similar vein. I was overwhelmed by the association. I wrote poems the rest of the week. With no fuss or doubt or even sense of discovery I was a poet, only a poet and, like the post office downtown or night and day and the sun in the sky, I never thereafter questioned that poetry was there and my central identity. It came as a gift, unexpected. It was the luckiest night of my life.

*Resignation to the Luck of Waking
Out of the Night to Scribble a First Poem
and Having a Czech Friend to Read it*

At two A.M. in Maine, an aching night
of winter in the yellow dorm, I woke
and heard my roommate heaving, groan and bite
his epileptic tongue as if he broke
every bone in his corpse. I got up and
floated next door, sat down and wrote eight lines.
That night of moon breasts in my dirty hand
slipped into ink and I was born. The mines
exploded in the clouds. Don't worry. Though
I'm broke, can't sleep, and bumming like my son
slammed by a Boston court, we're all the same.
Groping, I stick a pen against the sun
and stain its yellow heart. Maine is to blame
for breeding me. Fail? Die? I still say no.

Twenty years old, last year in college, and only then the first poems. Wasn't that very late to become a poet? I read poetry and thought about it. In contrast to philosophy, poetry gave the particular, what Rilke in *Sonnets to Orpheus* called the *fühlbaren fernen* (touchable distances). Philosophy left me with words and abstractions but nothing to touch. Though words—even the words of poetry—were only the names of things, inadequate semantic approximations, they were closer, as close as the mind could come, to seizing the things. Words were representations, signs, and in poems they came out as metaphors, symbols, but of course they were not the thing itself. Not even a mirror of it. Painting—at least mimetic painting—pretended to mirrors. It was not good enough to say a mountain, even a blue mountain. Sometimes the mountain was a whale, or a whale a mountain, or, as I was to discover in Patmos, the small islands in the port of the island (that gave John the Theologian the Book of Revelation) lay like seven whales, precious to an ancient author of Patmos and Ephesos who counted them and saw horsemen and cities and churches as extensions of numbers.

I began to read all the poetry, old and contemporary, I could find. In the beginning I looked too hard, as if each line should, as in philosophy, yield the truth of the universe. It was not so in philosophy nor in poetry. I was eager to study all poetry texts, but felt inadequate to judge them. For years I felt I could write better than I could judge other poems. As it turned out, I felt comfortable with my own work. Not cocky. But in the beginning I kept only a small portion. I had to go through all the styles, invent all the forms, discover and discard all the cliches that every writer comes upon. Over the years the proportion I preserved increased. (Now, I still come to each poem with surprise. Yet, right or wrong, my judgment is more secure, and I rarely discard. I work over something until it is right. The few times I do discard I feel good. I'm always glad to be free of bad writing—really elated. Absurd as it seems, to throw away a flawed poem feels almost as good as having written a good one.

By spring I had a collection. The only professor I showed the poems to was Robert Peter Tristam Coffin, a bard who used to recite his poems regularly at the chapel. Coffin was a sentimental Frost, but much closer to Yeats as a holy man, as a shaman of the arts. Yeats had come to Bowdoin a decade and a half earlier to receive an honorary doctorate at a time he was floating in his own oracular tower. Before a banquet in his honor he announced that he would be glad to speak to anybody, provided that he, Yeats, initiated the conversation. Robert Peter Tristam Coffin was not that elevated. I heard him read at George School. His ballads were haunting, like wind through a gothic window. I disapproved because they were belligerently unmodern. At Bowdoin I heard him often and was half tuned in because of his highly skilled performance of the romantic god poet; and in the end, I tuned out. He had nothing to do with the poets I then admired: the English metaphysicals; Blake's early poems, Baudelaire's late city poems; Williams, Eliot, and Auden; Rilke and Antonio Machado and the Spanish Generation of '27, all of whom I was reading with hunger. I was already reading Wang Wei and Tu Fu in translation, but had not yet turned to the Russians and Sappho and Cavafy—or Saint John of the Cross.

With all that, when I handed the sheaf of poems to Coffin I did so with expectancy. Although I had also heard Robert Frost at George School, Coffin was the first poet I actually spoke to. Some days later he returned my sheaf with the comment that I should read A. E. Housman (1859–1936). Strangely, I had just finished reading through Housman, trying hard to bring the Englishman's delicacy, tame meadows, and understated pain into our century, but it all repelled me. Housman's near contemporaries, the short-lived Gerard Manley Hopkins (1844–1889) and Emily Dickinson (1830–1886) were fiercely there. They never failed.

It was time to change continents. In the summer Helle was gone and I planned to meet her in Europe. She went to Geneva to work as an information officer with the United Nations—under flamboyant Harold Ballou, who regularly stood on his head on his desk before going off to lunch. All for health and meditation. Harold was as eccentric as his son; sadly, however, they mutually despised their common traits. I thought of my father and how lucky I was that

between us there was always love. After graduation I planned first to go to Paris in September. That journey to Europe and North Africa was to last five years.

In This Red Room of Paris Student Days

My berth on the *Queen Elizabeth* was close to the fish. Another few feet down and we could all swim together. On the first evening the cockney steward asked if anyone wished to take a *bath*. We were a Pole, a Yugoslav, a French student, and myself. The old Yugoslav in the berth below, who had just retired on Social Security and was returning to his village to find an eighteen-year-old wife, didn't understand. The Polish electrical engineer tried to explain to him what a *bass* was. Enlightenment came. A *bat,* yes he knew all about it. You fill a tub with water and sit down in it. He had done it many times. The Frenchman and I swallowed our laughter. I was glad for the good company.

On deck I became friends with Norman Rudich, then at Princeton, on his way to Paris for a year to write his dissertation on Flaubert. Norman was legally blind. He had some peripheral vision, but he used no cane. Tall, corpulent, usually leaning a bit against the planet as he turned his face to one side or the other to pick up peripheral information, he swished around everyplace. When he danced, he was a windmill and anyone within range could be bashed by his whirling limbs. Rudich was a political ideologue with an acutely intuitive literary sensibility; those two voices, his Communist rhetoric and his love for Shelley (which ironically he shared with Karl Marx), were in constant conflict and were to tie up his later writing. We took to each other immediately. I became his reader, which began in Paris appropriately with a lusty reading of Rabelais's *Gargantua.*

Norman laughed at me for liking Bergson. Wholly ridiculous. He liked my poems, however, and while he was more formalist than I—it was the times—he helped me immensely in establishing standards and forcing me to look at a poem as one without preknowledge of its meaning and intention. The first knowledge of a writer as self-critic is to know that what is in one's head is not in the reader's head—unless the author puts it there.

Ocean liners are for destinations, for changing city and life. There is the intimacy of the crossing, born of transience, given breath and candor by the solitude of the empty deck at night and the sudden friendships. I was full of aspirations. To wander, to experience, to know, to write. And there are people who open up, who speak candidly and make dogmatic declarations which they would not do were these days not days of passage. Like a vacation romance or adventure, these were buoyant hours separated from ordinary life, implications for future responsibility. After dinner the ship orchestra played in the lounge and we tourist-class passengers had a great time. Passengers from the more sedate, duller second- and first-class sections would invade our lounge to enjoy our fun. In late September the ship was rocking hard on the Atlantic and sometimes when the waters were very rough and tables slid from side to side, I'd rush up alone on deck to stare at the mystery of the endless ocean.

One evening I was dancing with a young Hungarian woman. Between numbers I sat down next to a tough guy from Chicago. "Too bad she's got her mother hanging around," I commented. I meant it too.

"Where you going?" the guy asked.

"France?"

"You should get over to Italy as quickly as you can. Beautiful women. Big tits and tight cunts."

As we neared France, America lost its reality. A ship, especially with its days of incubation from the landed world, fosters cuts with the past and a new life. The closest I ever later experienced to an ocean liner for demarcating and altering realities was a plane trip back from Buenos Aires to New York, where in twelve hours we went from torrid January summer to shivering New York winter. Now, France was everything when I descended from the boat train at the Paris Gare du Nord in the midst of a taxi strike, went to the railroad station café bar, sat on a stool before the wall mirror, chose two hard-boiled eggs that sat in a gold holder on the wooden counter, ordered black coffee spiked with a shot of cognac, and took a room for the night. Next morning I went off to the rue Jacob on the Left Bank for a more permanent hotel and found on unpacking my suitcase that on my first night in Paris the housemaid got my wool trousers:

Rocking on the Queen

Deep in the hold we have no porthole, yet
I gaze, X-raying whales and a green squall.
The pitching of ELIZABETH has set
the tables rolling, banging wall to wall.
I push up to the deck and wait for France.
At twenty I'm a character whom Plato
might keep for lunch—yet the Greek's reasoned
     trance
is not my Bergson dream. I'm a potato-
head says my Marxist pal. Norm's blind and grins
at me—naive. As Europe nears, wet shade

washes my eyes with reverie. I dry
my face. Europe is full of women. Inns
of smart delicious lips. We dock. The maid
at l'Hotel Flore pinches my pants and tie.

My room at the Hotel des Tours on rue Jacob had a red carpet, a sink, was filled with light, and cheap. Fifteen dollars was all I needed to live well for a week. The red-nosed concierge knew one phrase in English, "no monkey business," by which she meant no *ménage a trois* in her respectable hotel. "This is a proper place, only couples."

"Any married ones?"

"Yes, I believe there is a Jewish couple who might even be married."

Next to my room lived two painters, a Czech couple, in a room half the size of mine. The beautiful, sad woman, ironing clothes on her worktable, came directly from Picasso's blue canvases. They were good painters, with their exile experience printed on their grave faces. Within days all my friends were foreign painters and writers—from Greece, South Africa, India. I was enrolled at the Sorbonne in a *certificat* in philosophy and a doctor in letters (like a master's) in French literature.

In the room next to me a young Dutch woman lived. She introduced me to Bernard Citroën, a tall blond Dutch poet who was into every Cartier Latin literary activity. That winter he started an Anglo-French bilingual periodical, *Points,* in which I published my first poem. (I had earlier at Bowdoin published a Letter to the Editor in the *Nation,* protesting the bigotry and racism of the fraternity system at the college, which annoyed many people.) *Points* did remarkably well at the kiosks where disappointed women bought it up in the belief, as the French title implied, that it was a knitting magazine. Citroën, a Jew, survived the war in Holland, hiding for five years in a basement. The Dutch woman worked for KLM (Royal Dutch Airlines) and was always broke and unhappy. I lent her a few dollars. We talked a lot in her place; she lent me a current French novel which I devoured, and although I desired her and it was clearly mutual, I did not act:

Gospel of Fire

In this red room of Paris student days,
under the bulb drooping over the foot
of a wood cot, my novel floods with wordplays
of sex and existential thieves. I put
the window down—a cement patio where
a Dutch blonde rooms, who once looked up at me
with young misery as if she felt the stare
of my desire. I read on. No way to be
with her. On the wall right behind my bed,

wallpaper smiling lewd with its black teeth
begins a Quaker shake. I hear the flow
of a loud mattress, light a match beneath
my hand (I'm smoking pipes), and Heer Van Gogh
watches my fingers flaming on the bed.

Half a day in a train in almost any direction from Paris took you to another language and country. After I was settled at the rue Jacob, I took an overnight train to Geneva to see Helle. Although the Swiss were and remain the world's bankers for crime and political moneys, when I saw how clean and correct Geneva was, when I walked its unthreatening and charming streets, I thought of an un-Swiss incident a few days earlier in Paris.

In those days students were constantly carrying banners down Boulevard Saint-Michel only to be confronted by the police *(les flics)* who flew out of their trucks in their batlike blue capes, raised *batons,* and rushed the protesters. The students screamed *"Cochons, cochons!"* (Pigs, pigs!) and scattered, some scrambling up lampposts before being dragged down by the *flics* and tossed in the paddy wagons. Art Buchwald, writing daily for the *International Herald-Tribune* (that paper is a European privilege like small good bookstores and delicious filter coffee), had just done a column saying that the French police used their clubs on civilians' heads astutely, knowing, as a good French cook knows, that you can't scramble eggs without first cracking the shells.

I was returning home from the Sorbonne, walking by the rue du Prince where Verlaine died drunk on a hotel floor. Then I reached the old plaza of the Théatre de l'Odéon. Right near the theater is a quadrangle monument rising some ten feet; in the Paris dusk rain a student was on top the marble structure, orating to an enthusiastic crowd. The streetlamps and rain made the upturned faces shine as under camera lighting. The young man was denouncing Charles de Gaulle—that "fascist"—for daring to represent France in a flower-laying ceremony at the Tomb of the Unknown Soldier. He yelled, *"Je pisse sur de Gaulle! Je pisse sur de Gaulle!"* (I piss on de Gaulle! I piss on de Gaulle!) His supporters shouted back, *"Pissez, donc!, pissez, donc!"* (Go ahead and piss!), and the hero took out his pecker, raised it with his hand, and let loose a high yellow arc into the scattering and wildly cheering crowd.

As I walked the graceful streets of Geneva, I could not imagine such splendid street theater in this Swiss city.

Helle wanted to live in Paris. She spoke French. She had not yet decided to give up writing and become a painter—a definitive choice she made after

we left Paris. But Paris helped her become a painter, as did Greece and Spain, and her lines and colors have never recovered from that good impact. With little background I was already playing with the notion of studying at the Beaux Arts, since painting and poetry for me were almost interchangeable in the dominance of image (even abstract or surreal), in the act of translating a notion into paint or letters. I stuck to letters, except for a year in Greece when I shifted to the brush. In classical China to be a painter and poet was perfectly normal and often the paintings carried lines of poetry on them—as some Lorca drawings do. The Chinese have a saying about Wang Wei, the Tang Buddhist landscape poet who was also a painter: "Wang's paintings are silent poems, his poems talking paintings." Since Paris I've moved in and out of a passion for paint and ink. Recently, my son Tony and I published a book of Wang Wei's poems in translation, which includes eight dry-brush drawings I did for it.

Now we were spending some days in picturesque Switzerland. We took a day's trip to an impeccably beautiful village some fifty miles away. Walking up the hill to the village square and its Calvinist church was like proving the category of Platonic harmony. Everything quietly right and in place. Later I was to work in Geneva, but my fondest association with the city is vicarious. It is through Borges's dead eyes. In later years the blind Argentine poet, essayist, short-story writer was to be teacher, father, friend, companion, and, as far as my poetry and turn to fiction goes, the person who was always there. Borges went to Geneva as an adolescent in 1914 and remained in the city for nearly seven years. He became a writer in Geneva, learned German there, and his first published work was in French. At the end of his life he returned to Geneva and—as if sixty years had not gone by—he took up again with his first intellectual friend, Maurice Abramowicz. Borges and Maria Kodama, his companion of twenty years, chose an attractive apartment in his favorite neighborhood, La Vieille Ville. There in the summer of 1986, on his deathbed, Borges and Maria were married. Several of Borges's stories are set in Geneva, refer to a double, to another Borges, all favorite topics. Geneva was his other city and it was appropriate to find his double from Cambridge or Buenos Aires sitting on a bench by Lac Léman in his consummately peaceful and resonant city.

Wonderful as Geneva was in those days, with ghosts of Borges waiting on benches and in rooms to be reborn at his late return, Helle and I agreed to meet soon in vibrant Paris. I returned to my hotel late in the evening to get my things and take the night train to France. Near the hotel a woman in her late thirties came up to me, puckered her lips, and mumbled something about making love. I had already lost a second pair of trousers in honest Switzerland to the housemaid (it was a vice, I had learned), and in this land of cows so clean that its milk was not normally pasteurized, the very notion of love for Swiss francs seemed strange. When I hesitated, she looked at me as if I were an idiot.

In Paris I began to write poems again, now with France as the source of images. We took a bus trip along the Bretagne coast and I sat on a rock and wrote some stanzas called "Bretagne Coast." We took another bus south of Paris till we came upon an idylic village called Vert-le-Petit, and "Vert-le-Petit" was the title of a love poem. I wrote about the countryside in France, but I didn't have the sense or ability, like Baudelaire or Blake, to bring the city, to bring Paris, into poems. I was too young. A poem like Rimbaud's early "Sensation" was more what I could do, although I didn't know this at the time and had I been asked I would probably have denied that the city was absent. Yet that year I read Baudelaire constantly as I did for many years, and especially those late poems of pathos about workers, beggars, and the homeless.

Norman had an American friend, Katherine Harper, whose mother was French. By now Helle was settled in Paris, and the four of us, Norm, Kathy, Helle, and I went to the chateau mansion of Kathy's French grandfather for the weekend. Only the caretakers were there, but they prepared wild boar for us which we washed down with local wine. After our country feast on forest and village food, we went crazy and took all the pillows we could find and raced through the corridors of the castle, hurling pillows, screaming threats of murder at each other from behind columns and narrow passages. We were all alone, anachronistically, in this ancient castle with its thick stone walls echoing our American English. We also roamed the countryside that had crisp late-autumnal tastes in the air that I associated with pastoral scenes in Colette's deliciously sensual novels.

In Paris I liked going to Katherine's apartment—she was staying with her French aunt. The family had beautiful Corot paintings on the dining-room walls and even an early Monet. On her American side Katherine's relatives were in publishing. Although I had had no thoughts at all about publishing a collection of poems, Kathy came to my room one afternoon around six, actually a terrible afternoon for other reasons, and announced, "Willis, I think I can get a book of your poems published in New York."

"No!"

"Yes," she grinned.

I was lying in bed with a sprained ankle, but that news somehow prompted me to start jumping up and down on the mattress. Clearly the idea of publication was not irrelevant.

"Stop it, Willis, you'll kill yourself or break the ceiling!"

Nothing at all came of this hint of publication, but the grain of irritant sand was planted in the oyster shell, pearl or no pearl.

I liked my hotel, liked to hear the roving musicians coming down rue Bonaparte to play and sing under our window for francs in newspaper packets that came pouring from the apartments like rain down on the performers; I liked to walk around the corner to the immaculate small plaza, La Place de Furstembourg where Géricault had had his atelier; and especially enjoyed dropping in on the small galleries and bookstores at the far end of Jacob. It was enough to fill my spirit simply to look at those lighted store windows with their tasteful treasures. Yet I still moved to a cheaper hotel a few blocks away, which initiated a series of moves, each one unique. I went from rue Jacob to l'Hotel de Langue d'Oc, to the rue du Cherche-Midi, and finally to rue du Vaugirard, when Helle and I were living together. This Vaugirard hotel room faced the Luxembourg Park and had the implausible name of l'Hotel du Lisbon et Portugal.

One evening a gang of friends decided to go out. We began by going to a Russian nightclub favored by a rich American acquaintance who had been in the Soviet Union and danced a convincing Cossack dance. At a nearby table were a party of Hungarians who were wrapped up with drinking, laughing, and throwing their emptied wineglasses at the wall over the fireplace. As I went to the WC, for some reason the headwaiter stopped me and said confidingly that a famous author was sitting at the next table. I had been reading a streak of Arthur Koestler novels and I recognized the author in the group. He was unmistakable. As I came out of the men's room, he was a few feet in front of me. Without thinking, I said, "Are you Arthur Koestler?"

"No, I am not," and he walked on. I was disappointed.

A few days later I spent some hours with Tristan Tzara, the legendary founder of Dadaism. Tzara amazed me for quite the opposite reasons. Not arrogant in the least, we spent a very long afternoon chatting about modern literature. He was unduly interested in my remarks. More surprising, he insistently took books of his poems and other writings from a briefcase, and complained, "Everyone in the world has forgotten me. No one knows me now."

Later, Borges was to remark that Latin was a language better to have learned and to forget than never to have learned at all. But neither Latin nor Tzara is easily forgotten. It is true, however, that Tzara's name and the historic instant of his revolution are more familiar to readers than his actual work—and that is probably what hurt him in regard to actual readership. Tzara's insecurities made me feel better, more normal. No one is immune from doubt. With all his profession of modesty, even proud Robert Frost at the end of his life was asking a friend whether he, Frost, had ever written anything good.

In my irrepressible eagerness as a writer, to be a writer, I was overly generous in laying my poems before the eyes of bemused friends. Norman had my number and was cruelly funny. He nailed me cold in my habits. He said to our gang that Willis was the only person he knew who, if walking down a dark street of some obscure city in eastern Europe happened to come upon an old white horse standing by a door, he might just edge up to the horse and ask him if he would mind looking at a poem.

After the dancing and broken wineglasses at the Russian taverna, we went to a boîte named VENUS, which had a big sign in the window reading: ON EST NU (One Is Naked). We stayed there briefly. It was between shows but I did dance with one of the topless performers who was polite and discreet. It was midnight, we were hungry, and decided on Pigalle and went in search of a restaurant we could afford. We entered a largely deserted place, took over a long table, and George brought out his guitar and set up his harmonica on a special stand which allowed him to stroke the guitar and blow into the harmonica, and he began to tune up endlessly.

"For Christ's sake, George, stop torturing us. Sing one of your damn Russian songs!"

But George kept tuning up. A clochard from a nearby table sat down with us, saying, *"J'adore la musique."* George was sentimentally impressed, especially when he brought out some papers to prove that he had spent time at Devil's Island. Helle was disbelieving and disgusted. She had seen too much during the occupation to be moved by our guest. The clochard stuck with us, however, and even joined us when at dawn we went to the vast market of Les Halles for onion soup and breakfast. In the twenties, e. e. cummings was still drunk after breakfasting in Les Halles, hired a hack, stood up in the back of the open carriage, and took a leak. A gendarme arrested him on the spot, but not for public exposure—since

urinating in public is, or at least used to be, common—although perhaps not from the back of a fiacre. "What is the charge?" cummings asked.

"Monsieur, vous avez pissé sur la France." (Sir, you have pissed on France.)

When we broke up, I had to go off to the Cité Universitaire to change money. The music lover said he was tired and asked if he could get a few hours sleep in my room. I agreed. At this Helle turned and left. I took the man to the room and he lay down on the cot, and went off to the Cité to find my friends, a Turk and Armenian, who roomed together in one of the dorms. Then rushed back to my room in time to hear the concierge say that the laundryman had just come down from my room with a big bundle of clothing wrapped in a white bag. The bag was my sheets and in them were all my clothes and possessions, except for books. He even got my shoes.

Later I calculated that my daring comrade from Devil's Island also sneaked in some sleep before descending with the laundry.

Although we went to the Bon Marché, bought good linen, and Helle sewed them into passable sheets, I was still kicked out of my room—if for nothing other than my stupidity. I moved two streets away to a room with a little more air but where the sheets were a little short. The room was fresh except when it rained. Since people regularly pissed out the window, after a rain the courtyard stank of urine steaming up. A few nights later, an hour before dawn, the police rapped loud and long on the door.

"Securité. Ouvrez la porte!" (Security police. Open the door!)

Helle was with me. The police were obviously checking identity cards. Unlike Guillaume Apollinaire, who was arrested when his roommate stole the Mona Lisa, we were clean and our papers in order. But I didn't feel like getting up and we ignored the knocking. We lay very still. The knocker went away.

La Rue Jacob, 1948

War was fun for Guillaume Apollinaire,
who sent poem-letters from the trenches, yet
a bombshell came fatally combing his hair,
but Guillaume healed in Paris, a cigarette
like a love ballad in his lips. I spied
life from a hotel room with a red rug,
hot water in the corner sink, and sighed
happy when the street singers used a jug
to catch the hailing francs. The courtyard reeked
with rising fumes of piss when evening rain
fell from the wine-blue clouds. Our sheets were far
too short. Fin de la guerre. Spanish flu creeked
into the poet's brain. We were young, zane-
y like Guillaume! who croaked with La Victoire.

The poets I knew who wrote in French, like many of the painters who painted, were not French. And some foreigners were of the French school but wrote in their own language—like the Conde de Monte Verde, an older Spanish gentleman who had been in Paris since the late twenties, who wrote *poesia pura*, pure poetry, like Valéry. I usually met the count at the Flore where he showed me elegant limited editions of his books, printed in France. He always had his Waterman open and a sheaf of yellow pages filled from top to bottom with his meticulous, miniature script. He kept his little workshop between two cups of expresso. There was my pal Citroën, the Dutchman who was a French surrealist, and then there was George Jaszi Sandor de Nagy-Talavera, Baron de Rakoczy, 87 rue Notre-Dame-des Champs, as his business card revealed.

George Jaszi was striking—straight blond hair, actor's face, midnight blue eyes—but despite the titles, frivolity, and pomp, he was a very friendly, insecure, young Hungarian exile in postwar Paris. George was not embarrassed to show me his poems, which were blatant imitations of Verlaine, exquisite, musical, and I thought hopeless. "La musique avant tout," he would say. One evening George Jaszi asked me to come at nine o'clock to the back room of the Deux-Magots which his own Society for the Return of Music to Poetry had rented as of midnight. He and other members of the group would be reading. George Jaszi came to pick me up a few minutes early.

"You must come."

"Pourquoi pas?" I said.

We gathered our group waiting outside and went the few blocks to the Deux-Magots where a banquet table was set up for us. George was the metteur en scène. He stood flamboyantly before the joyous group, making pronouncements, his straight hair flapping down over his forehead until he threw his poet feathers back into place like Franz Liszt sweeping into a piano crescendo. The reading began. It was sentimental, old-fashioned, enthusiastic. Jaszi was clearly the most talented of the group, despite his Parnassian delicacy. While the drinks and words were flowing, there was suddenly an obstreperous intrusion. The rest of the café was empty. The roar came from the street. I went out to investigate and saw two *fumistes*, practical jokers, revving a powerful motorcycle. As soon as they saw me they gunned the machine and took off. But no sooner was I back inside when the duo had circled the block and were again gunning the machine outside the door.

"*Deux fumistes avec leur moto*" (Two wise guys with their cycle), I reported.

George went outside and shouted at them and they were gone.

"Let's go on. Pay no attention to these villains," George said. The reading continued. The outside precincts had returned to silence. But suddenly two pairs of hands appeared on the top of the smoky glass wall separating our quarters from the main restaurant, two punk heads appeared, and finally the punk heads let loose with a torrent of insults.

"*Idiots, imbeciles, petites merdes, poétes!*" (Idiots, imbeciles, little shits, poets!)

"*Salopards!*" (Filthy bastards!)

"*A la guerre!*" the baron screamed, and rushed out, his cape guiding him in his pursuit of the villains. They were gone. Maybe for good.

It was about two, I was pretty drunk (and I wasn't used to that), so I decided to leave. As I was going out, George was on his way back in, flushed with victory.

"Where you off to, Willis?"

"To bed."

"Wait for me. Can you put me up?"

"No problem, pal."

We strolled back to my room on Cherche-Midi. The night concierge was a stout man with dark horn-rimmed glasses who sat impassively with a black cat on his right shoulder. He looked up from his book and greeted us. Once in the room, I went to the sink and threw up. George Jaszi took the cue and threw up. I took an extra pillow and a blanket, and said, "Franz Liszt, try these over there on the floor by the window." In a few minutes we were dead, sleeping it off.

As the year went on Helle and I were spending most of our nights at each other's place. Our favorite street name was rue du Cherche-Midi (Street of Seeking the Midi). In the mid-fifties I was to spend a year as a soldier in the Dordogne, which local residents like to call "Midi moins le quart" (quarter to noon), punning on "midi" meaning "noon" as well as "the Midi" or what is also called by its old Roman name "Provence." So even in that exquisite region of truffles, rust-colored villages, Montaigne, Roman bridges, and blue meadows, I was still seeking the Midi. There were street dances next to our hotel where the butcher played the accordion and the cobbler the violin. We joined in old polkas, waltzes, fox-trots; most of the people were from the local stores, and they danced with extended arms and grasping fists while rocking up and down like innocent Apachés.

At the Sorbonne, in my course on the French positivists, I got close to Francisco, a Spaniard from

Madrid whose passion, like mine, was modern Spanish poetry. He was a friend of Vicente Aleixandre, the single major poet left in Spain from those extraordinary generations of poets. Federico García Lorca was executed in his city of Granada in 1936, shortly after the uprising; Miguel de Unamuno died in his sleep on New Year's Eve, 1936, while under house arrest; Antonio Machado died in Collioure, France, in 1939, driven out of Spain, as Juan Ramón Jiménez wrote, through the back gate; in 1942 Miguel Hernández, the youngest of the great poets of Spain, was dead at thirty-one in a Spanish prison in Alicante. The other leading poets—Rafael Alberti, Luis Cernuda, Jorge Guillén, Pedro Salinas—were in exile in the Americas and Italy.

Francisco gave me two precious first editions from the early thirties of Aleixandre's poems, which I still have: *Espadas como labios* (Swords like Lips) and *La destrucción o el amor* (Destruction or Love). The Spanish poet was a revelation. A world of surrealism much more compelling to me than the automatic writing experiments of André Breton or the love and political poems of Paul Eluard, then the most revered poet in France. (Robert Desnos, who died three days after being liberated from the Therensienstadt concentration camp, became the poet I cared for most among the French surrealists.) Aleixandre shared that moment of Spanish surrealism with Lorca in *Poet in New York,* with Pablo Neruda in his *Residencias,* and Miguel Hernández in the surreal sonnets of *The Unending Lightning Ray.* After Aleixandre won the Nobel Prize in 1977, I did a volume of his poems with David Garrison, *A Bird of Paper,* 1982. We included one longish poem "Aliki," which Vicente had written for my daughter whom he already adored when he knew her in 1962. She was then only five and a pupil at the Colegio de Estilo in Madrid. I like to recall that Aleixandre, the poet I was closest to in Spain for more than thirty years, I first met through Francisco in philosophy, the kindest and most sensitive of students in France.

The Sorbonne was a rallying place for many causes. One evening there was a "Réunion des Intellectuels" to protest recent activities and statements by Charles de Gaulle. At the jammed classroom auditorium, the poet Louis Aragon was haranguing an enthusiastic audience. On stage were several speakers including a priest in his robes, sitting grimly holding a rifle in his lap. When he stood up to speak, he continued holding onto the rifle. At one climactic moment, he shouted *"Et s'il faut lutter, nous lutterons!"* (And if we must fight, we will fight!) and he jerked the rifle up over his head as everyone cheered. When it was Paul Eluard's turn to speak, we antici-

pated a few poems. He read no poems nor made a speech. He said soberly: "These are the names of the strikers who have been wounded and died in the national coal-miner strike in western France." And for the next ten minutes or so, he slowly read the names of each miner and what had happened to him. Then he sat down.

These were strange political days. Albert Camus, a resistance hero, had come out against the Stalinists and their tactics of taking over Eastern Europe. Jean Paul Sartre was an enigma. His reputation during the occupation was as a resistance leader, but even it was strangely blurry. He was increasingly Marxist in his political ideology, later paraded in the street with a poster of Mao to show his enthusiasm for the Cultural Revolution, yet in 1948 all Paris was talking about *Les Mains Salles* (The Dirty Hands), his latest play, which seemed to condemn Communist dirty tactics for political purpose.

Paul Eluard had no ambiguity in his politics. During the occupation his poems were published clandestinely by the "Midnight Press." His most famous poem is "Liberté." He writes her name on his schoolboy's notebooks, on the wings of birds, on the walls of his weariness, on the steps of death: Liberty. Milan Kundera gives us a bleak portrait of Eluard in *The Book of Laughter and Forgetting* in which he describes the French poet's visit to Prague in 1950. One of Eluard's old surrealist friends from Paris days, the Czech surrealist poet and intellectual Zavis Kalandra, was about to be hanged as a dissident member of the parliament controlled by the hardline Stalinist regime. Eluard was being feted in Prague as a special guest of the government. He marched in the street with his admirers, read his poems to large audiences, and gave prestige and legitimacy to the new leaders. André Breton wrote an open letter to Eluard, imploring him to intervene to save Kalandra, but "he was too busy dancing," Kundera wrote. Eluard refused to do so, recounting that it was sometimes necessary to take one step backward in order to take two steps forward. "In the crematorium they were just finishing off one Socialist representative and one surrealist, and the smoke climbed to the heavens like a good omen, and I heard Eluard's metallic voice intoning, "Love is at work, is tireless."

One of my close friends in Paris was Robert Payne, who had just come back from China. It was Robert who took me to Tzara, and foolishly I missed an opportunity to go with him to Brancusi's studio. Payne was already a prolific writer when I first met him. Thirty-nine years old, he was an old China hand. He had taught in Chinese universities, was a British naval officer during the war in the Far East, and had been married for five years to a sister from the extended Sung family. In those days his companion was Jamie, perhaps a decade younger, and they were a romantic pair. Jamie had a daring freshness in her stand, a dancing smartness in her eyes, and I did lust after her, all quite secretly, almost to myself. In later years Robert's fame and wealth cast him in a more conservative light. But these were days of freedom and writing and verve. The adventure of the preceding years was still invigorating his ways. Paris was his café and hotel room. We had some of the most poignant and intimate conversations of my life, dramatized by his ability to come up with dogmatic but reasonable statements on the essence of each problem and how to take decisive action. I mentioned three words about Helle, and he said, "Marry the Greek." Robert was expert in giving himself fully to the moment, to enjoying himself with no apparent stops, while at the same time retaining an English resolution of discipline. His paradoxes even pertained to his eyes which twinkled with diversity, strength, but also a glint of doubt, even sadness, which his display of character usually masked.

Robert insisted that I translate Lorca, but I felt happier with the landscapes of Antonio Machado, and began to do English versions of his poems. I owe my first experience in translation to Robert Payne. In 1973 when Harper and Row published my volume of the poems of Mao, the dedication read: "for Robert Payne who years ago when I was a student in Paris spoke with enthusiasm about a Chinese poet, Mao Tse-tung, when no one else seemed to know or care." Two years earlier Payne had been with Mao in the caves in Yenan and translated the first batch of his poems, including "Snow," into English. Now in Paris he was very excited about his poet holed up in northern China. Payne didn't speak of the Long March, the terrible civil war, politics—though later he was to write a biography of Mao—but about this talented Chinese poet, with superior calligraphy and fearful politics, whom he had discovered living in a cave in Yenan.

The first American author I knew in Paris who earned his living from his writings was Bernard Freckman. A tall, tormented, generous man, given to mild snobbery and dramatic candor, he lived upstairs in a room scattered with manuscripts, books, and coffee cups, just above my own place in a hotel opposite the Jardins du Luxembourg. I don't know why he was tormented, but he carried it with dignity. Freckman was a pro. His work had been published in leading periodicals. He translated books by Jean Paul Sartre, but his center was his translations of the novels and plays of Jean Genet. Jean Genet in 1949 was

serving a life sentence in a Paris prison. Bernard read my poems and suggested publishers. He introduced me to literary friends. Although I took my work seriously, I was not prepared to find an older writer to show belief in it. When I left America six months earlier, I knew no writer my age or even close. Now in France, and soon in Greece, Spain, and England, most of my friends for the next five years would be poets. We were the gypsy Jews of the world, under every carpet, in a nearby room across the street, as a guest at a quirky supper.

One evening Freckman came downstairs with some black-and-white art photographs of Genet. Innocently, I remarked that the author of *The Thief's Journal* had a handsome, striking face, as indeed he did. The following day Bernard was there, all smiles.

"Hi, what's up?" I said.

"I've just come from the jail. Jean wanted to tell me that he was very happy that you, a young American writer, thought that he, a common thief, was good-looking."

Sartre along with André Gide and Jean Cocteau were working to get Genet pardoned, which eventually they were able to do. For the moment Genet wanted to get his hands on some good books. Freckman explained a little conspiracy. Sartre chose the volumes and gave them to the warden. The warden cooked up an enticing delivery plan—perhaps only a literary French warden could be so mad. Rather than present the books to Genet as a mere present from Sartre, since the inmate was a thief by profession, he, the warden, would put the books in the prison library, make Genet a library worker, and so place him in a situation where he could steal the books, thereby giving him much more pleasure and also allowing him to practice his life's trade.

Freckman and I had become pals. His friendship, encouragement, just his presence was important. When I left France, we exchanged letters for some years, and then it stopped. A decade later a French writer told me a long story of a break-up Freckman had had with a girlfriend, a depression, and then an ugly end. I asked what it was, thinking it must have been some terrible disease.

"No, he took a gross rope and hanged himself over the staircase."

One evening Helle told me she was pregnant. We were too young to have a child, we agreed, but abortion in France was illegal. In Denmark abortion was legal. The Greek Consulate in Paris was completely unwilling to make her passport valid for Denmark on the grounds that the civil war was still raging in Greece. Incomprehensible as the Greek position was, it was real, and we had no options inside or outside France. Some weeks later I said to Helle, "Let's get married."

"Good. How about in the *mairie* of the *sixiéme?*"

That was it. We did what had to be done in those days, which was to obtain thirty-three signatures and documents. The assistant at the American Embassy who gave us the checklist marked the places where a bribe was proper; the suggested currency was American cigarettes. We called our friends—my two best men were Norman Rudich and Robert Payne; Artemis, Helle's Greek aunt in Paris, was her bridesmaid—and on June 1, 1949, we were married by the mayor of the sixth *arrondissement* in his office across the street from Saint Sulpice Cathedral. The mayor was full of verve in his rough Marseillais speech and pronounced his wish to see us in a year, pushing a perambulator in the Luxembourg Gardens. (Our daughter, Aliki, did not come until seven years later, in New Haven, but at least she was conceived in Periguex, France.) Our friends gave us flowers. Like the fool I often was, that same day I lost the key to my

hotel room, so after celebrating at the Cité, around midnight we took a cab to Helle's room that now was in a proper bourgeois apartment. In the morning I brought the locksmith, got a new key for my own room, and left for class at the Sorbonne.

When we met at my hotel in the afternoon, Helle had a story for me. Her dignified landlady had confronted her formally with, *"Qui était ce garçon avec qui vous avez passé la nuit?"* (Who was that boy with whom you spent the night?)

"C'était mon mari." (It was my husband.)

She was asked to leave that very day, which was not at all inconvenient. We laughed a lot.

Initially I was not happy about marriage, although I didn't convey this. Helle was wonderful, her Greekness a fable; she was a person who knew no subterfuge. Fully frank, intelligent, and irrepressibly cheerful. Her beauty only increased over the years. She cared for me as I did for her. But at twenty-one I had romantically thought of wandering for years in Europe and Asia, getting lost someplace in India, knowing many places, women, adventures. It was the

"Our wedding picture in front of the Mayor's Office, Sixth District, Paris: (front row from left)
Robert Payne, Katherine Harper, Norman Rudich, Helle Tzalopoulou Barnstone (bride),
Willis Barnstone, Jack Sanders, James Emmons," 1949

duty of a writer to know the world, to be alone. I never got over some of those feelings. From now on we would do those things together. Precisely because of the early marriage, perhaps we wandered more, adventured more, experienced more deeply. Soon we were to experience the worst.

Jack Sanders lived in a hotel across the street. Jack was a novelist, in Paris on the GI Bill as a student, but really writing his first novel, which he was to publish a few years later. Jack was my buddy. He told me one day that he had talked about the abortion matter with Jeannie, the maid in his hotel, who was his girlfriend. Jeannie knew a Lebanese doctor who could do the operation. We'd been married a week, had no plans to do anything but go soon on a honeymoon to London, and then go off to Greece. We decided on the abortion. The place was way out on the outskirts of Paris. The doctor was cold and nasty. He asked for the cash ahead of time, which we gave to him. Then with minimum anesthetic he performed the operation, which was painful. His only words afterward were, *"Voici votre chef-d'oeuvre."* (Here is your masterpiece.) We went back to our hotel. Helle was in bed a few days and recovered quickly. We went to the park often those days. Soon we would be in London, cheerfully lost in the Scottish lowlands, and hitching back to London again on an English lorry carrying blankets, taking us Pullman to our destination at the home of Peter Russell, the English poet with whom we were staying in the city.

Years later when I wrote about the operation in the sonnets, for rare reasons of discretion I changed the nationality of the person from Greek to Polish. In fact I had a very close Polish friend in my class, on a scholarship from Warsaw, and we did go to secret meetings in hotel rooms where there were reunions of Poles in Paris with Free Poland war veterans, and she did love the delicate nineteenth-century Spanish poet Gustavo Adolfo Bécquer—but I never had romantic ties with her. By changing the name and nationality, the poem took on an artistic independence from the actual event, combined outside material, although in a deeper sense it did not stray at all from its meaning and spirit:

In a Paris Faubourg

My Polish classmate at the gray Sorbonne
loves the romantic poet Becquer. She
wears heavy wool, is Chopin thin and fun
in Paris rain. One night she secrets me
off to a grim free Polish Army party
up in an orange room. We're comrades and
march behind banners down Boule Miche. Hearty
and generous in bed, she takes my hand
a Sunday morning, we go to a faubourg,

a sleezy house. I don't guess why. "It's clear,"
she says. "I'm pregnant and abortion's not
a legal act in France." Up in the morgue
the foreign doctor cuts her up. "So, here
is your chef-d'oeuvre," he tells me. We are rot.

Greek Civil War and Island Fig Trees

A year in Paris is good to have when one is twenty. Ernest Hemingway went there when he was twenty-one and stayed five years. He was married, poor, earning a living as a writer. He had some good things and some bad things to say about Gertrude Stein who accused him of being a member of a lost generation. I also stayed five years, but shared it with other countries. I could have happily stayed another year or two in Paris, my French was good, I was writing. But I was just married and wasn't a newspaperman to support my wife on newspaper articles. And so I went to Greece where I could get a job. I suppose I could have hung on in Paris, as I did in Mexico, and each day in Paris the city and the friends meant more to me. But Greece was not only a job. It was a light. I didn't know what kind of light, but it was a light I knew. And it was good to live in and with that light. As for Paris, it was not only education, writers, a marriage. It was an atmosphere, a smell, a rain, and a delicate spring both in the Jardins du Luxembourg and in villages we explored at random, only to return to the deep air of the Paris atmosphere. Hemingway said it definitively in his letter to a friend in 1950: "If you are lucky enough to have lived in Paris as a young man, then wherever you go for the rest of your life it stays with you, for Paris is a moveable feast."

In Paris I had made such a pest of myself at the Greek Consulate that the director outright refused to issue me a visa to enter Greece.

"What can we do?" I asked Dr. Vassilios Tzalopoulos, my father-in-law. There had to be some way around the bureaucracy.

The phone connection from Athens was good. Vassili said, "Go to Genoa." Then we were cut off.

So we took a train to Genoa where with no difficulty I did get the proper entry visa. All to the good, for it gave us a chance to walk around the stone streets of that beautiful city, to eat in its *tratorias,* to sit back in the kitchen and talk and listen for a few hours to the cook and maids of the *pensione* where we were staying. In the morning we boarded our Italian ship that stopped for a day in Napoli. From the city of Napoli, with huge gloomy city buildings and unknown sunny sidestreets, we took a bus to nearby

Pompeii, a mirror of the Bronze Age city in Thera /Santorini, which had not yet been discovered and uncovered from its lava blanket. In the Pompeii Museum a guard took us aside, as apparently he did everyone, and revealed the erotic decadence of those early Roman inhabitants by showing us a statuette of six naked men facing each other in a circle, whose erect penises upheld a bronze plate.

We boarded the ship again and sailed for Athens.

At first daybreak I woke as we were rounding a turbulent Peloponnesos. That turbulence I could see through our water level porthole. I climbed in the half-light to a place on the portside deck, and looked with amazement at the water a few feet below. The color and texture were like no water or liquid I had seen. Its uniqueness made me struggle to find a comparison as a way of identifying it. Only through metaphor, by likeness, by indexing, does the mind leap to the next meaningful perception. Finally, the image made sense. The water was like the inside of a purple grape. It had the pulpy thickness, the soft glow, the sweetness. Its brine must have been only an illusory surface attribute, for under it all the water was grape. Then I realized that others were forced into the same simile. There was the first writer we record in the West, Homer, and he anciently called it the "wineblue sea."

By mid-morning we edged into the port of Piraeus. The brightness of the morning even softened fumes from the "satanic mills" contaminating the atmosphere with poisons. To either side of the city were the bay islands and the dry green coasts of the mainland, always with their underlay of marble dug out by the sun. As we got to a sign-reading distance of this industrial base, it was thrilling to see the frenetic waterfront speckled with little vans, some pulled by smoky motorcycles, others by respectable small truck motors, but each bearing a similar logo boldly scrawled on the side panels: *METAFORA*. The sign in modern and ancient Greek means TRANSPORTA-TION, or literally "to carry across," as well as "translation" and "metaphor." So metaphor and translation are really moving vans. How good to arrive at an ancient port where even motorcycle trucks carry signs promoting the jargon of literature.

In September 1949 Athens was still a beautiful city. Antiquities were everywhere and everywhere seen. The splendid medieval section called Plaka lay alongside the Agora, and under Plaka another ancient city (which still can be unearthed only by destroying the oldest living section of Athens). Downtown was eighteenth- and nineteenth-century small mansions and townhouses. As in most cities of the ruined world, the earlier centuries have given way to tasteless apartment houses that age disastrously. But Athens in the fall of 1949 was still beautiful.

While the buses poured their black smoke out then as now, one could still see the mountains of marble Penteli and honeycombed Hymettos every day of the week. A few minutes outside of Athens was all olive trees amid wheatfields. Every day I drove a half hour through those fields framed by the changing mountains and Greek skies. Every day it was another gaze at beauty. The olive trees have been axed and all those wheatfields have turned into cement, giving way to small industry and urban housing as Athens exploded and darkened in order to take in fifty percent of the nation's people.

In 1949 Greece was coming out of ten years of world war, German and Italian occupation, and civil war. Italy attacked from the west in 1940. It was a farcical invasion. The Italians had the dignity of being disinterested in warfare. The Greek army drove them back deep into Albania. Then Germans invaded continental Greece and Crete. When I arrived in Greece the postage stamps still showed Cretan peasant women catching descending German paratroopers on their pitchforks, and in the countryside many houses still had numbers scrawled on the walls in witness of the hostages executed at that spot. 1942 was a famine year when the food stocks of Greece were sent north to the German armies. Athens starved. Helle's family hid a young Greek Jewish girl for a while. A week later her father came to take her away to another safe house. After the war her father came to thank the family. She survived as did most of the Jews of Athens. However, some 70,000 of the 75,000 Jews of Greece, mainly Spanish-speaking Sephardic Jews living in Salonika, were murdered. With the end of the war came the December Athens rebellion of the EAM-ELAS Communist guerrilla forces, which Churchill crushed with British tanks. By 1946 guerrilla warfare had become civil war. Some 35,000 Greek children were taken to the Socialist countries with the aim of re-education and return to Greece as future rulers. When Tito broke with Stalin, at least the kidnapped children in Yugoslavia were sent back to Greece. The other "socialist" countries kept their future janizaries. By late summer of 1949 the war was essentially over when Markos's army made a stand in the Atlas Mountains and, with no sanctuary to disappear into, were defeated.

When I reached Greece, there were just a few sporadic mopping-up operations. The closest I came to a war zone was on a trip to the Byzantine monasteries at Mount Athos in the north, when I went on muleback through the forests and up the mountains, escorted by a military patrol guiding us through the December snow. The front walls of Helle's Athens house on Tzortz Street were riddled with bullet holes from the 1944 December rebellion. Vassili told me that guerrillas were popping in and out of their house, firing from the front living-room windows or shooting down from the roof.

So Greece in that autumn was a country recovering from its wounds, and it showed in the most obvious way: the unusual number of amputees one saw in the streets. Greece was exhausted, poor, ruled by the right-wing Tsaldaris gang. Yet there was plenty of food and Greece was at peace. The common people dressed poorly in patched gray clothes. Having described the hardships of the people, I confess that it was a wonderful time to have been in Greece. No tourists at all. I was part of a Greek family. There is a saying in modern Greek that a husband comes from the village of his wife. So my village was Athens. I felt similar excitement when I spent much of a year in Buenos Aires with writer friends and Borges during their "dirty war" and more dramatically when I was in China during the Cultural Revolution.

White Island

Though Greece is blue I think of gray
and one-armed men after the War,
the Civil War, smoking and poor,
crossing Omonia on their way
to some raw cold cafe. No more
spears of the Persians; no more Franks
or Turks burning up towns. The pranks
of history mute, some pigeons soar
barbarous and WHITE! Now only gods
lurk on the islands. Artemis
and her gray lions fire the night
of terrorists and gleaming cheese,
her moon. Meanwhile, blue Theseus plods,
threading our village maze with light.

But Greece was something else. The arts were flourishing as never before. The poets Nikos Gatsos, Yannis Ritsos, George Seferis, and Odysseus Elytis were in their prime. The latter two would win the Nobel Prize. There was wonderful theater, Greek and international theater—more lively and varied than New York. In one week you could see John Steinbeck's *Of Mice and Men*, Lorca's *Blood Wedding*, and *Oedipus at Colonus*. Very soon I knew the painters, poets, and composers. I have never felt so completely integrated in the artistic community of any city or country as during those first few years in Greece.

The language I used with Helle's family was French, even after I learned modern Greek. Helle's mother, Maria, went to a French lycée in Constanti-nople and though she studied piano for two years in Vienna, French, not German or English, was her second language. Vassili had studied medicine in Paris. It took a few days to settle. One morning in the sumptuous living room of the Athens house with its eighteenth-century French furniture and oriental rugs (a room Maria normally kept locked and allowed access to only on worthy occasions), Vassili asked me, "What do you want to do in Greece?"

"I want to write poetry."

"I mean, what do you really want to do?"

"I want to learn the landscapes of Greece and a language of symbolic images for poetry."

"How do you want to earn a living?" he said impatiently. Vassili had published a small volume of stories and poems about his region in Epirus (and a medical book on nutrition), so he wasn't unsympathetic to the arts.

"Maybe I could teach. I did that in Mexico."

We went to the American College at Arsakian, which is really a good high school. They had filled their positions, but they suggested I speak to the director at Anavrita, a new school near Kifissia. This would be perfect, since in a few days we would be moving to the country house on Mount Penteli, outside Maroussi, which was a five-minute bus ride from Anavrita. That same morning I saw the director of Anavrita Academy, a school of thirty-two students, including Crown Prince Constantine then nine years old (for whom the school was established), and I had the job. I was to teach French and English.

It was a good job. The director was an Englishman, the teachers Greek except for myself. They were obsequious, almost reverent, to the prince and even to the secretly adopted German prince Karl, who also attended the school; by contrast, you usually heard the pupils screaming, "Get over here, your highness, or I'll bust you in the mouth!" *Ypsilótàte* (your highness) was for them just another name like Dimitri or Fálena, meaning "whale," which is what they called the school's fatso. I didn't teach Constantine because he already knew French and English, but I did eat lunch with him each day.

The Queen would drop in my class and we chatted about poetry. She lent me the *Faber Book of English Poetry,* which I was very glad to study. Frederika was the granddaughter of the kaiser and a cousin to Queen Elizabeth. Her accent in Greek was German. Her English was much better than her Greek. She was married to King Paul, Pavlos Glückberg, a member of the Danish royal family. It was commonly said that dynamic Frederika was the power behind the throne, and sometimes he was called "O Frederikos," which is not only Frederick but Frederika in the masculine gender, implying that not Pavlos but a masculine Frederika was boss. Publicly she was on many charity committees and initiated a campaign to raise dowry money for poor women without dowries, so helping to perpetuate the repugnant tradition of women as negotiable marriage property.

For a while I started to grow a beard—not an unusual practice in Europe, though still rare in modern America. When I had lunch one day with the Queen, she told me that she had been instructed by her son not to look me directly in the face because I was trying to grow a beard and it might embarrass me to be stared at.

The Greek government was as bad as the guerrillas in the treatment of prisoners. "Why do you execute prisoners of war?" I asked Frederika.

"They are not prisoners of war. They're thieves."

"But they're human beings, and Greece has had enough death."

"They're just common thieves."

"Do you execute common thieves?"

"There are thieves and there are thieves. These are common thieves who are killers."

"If I answer you we will have gone full circle again. So let's talk about Louis MacNeice."

When we finished lunch, I began to think of the islands, and how good it would be to live on one of them. In my room in Paris, I had put up large photographs of the islands, of Mykonos, which came from a set of twelve black-and-white photos in a boxed edition, taken by some German photographer before the war. I knew the houses in those photos so well I felt I had lived there. And I began to count months until we could go and live in one of the white buildings.

When Frederika spoke about the rebels as thieves, she was translating from *klefti* (thieves), the common Greek word for guerrillas, a title the Greek Communists proudly assumed, since the word goes back to eighteenth-century rebellions against the Turks in which the Turks called the heroes of the Greek uprising *klefti*. On a personal level I liked talking to Frederika. And to dispute politics with her was after all a privilege. She in turn, I think, liked the fact that I did not feel the inhibitions of her Greek subjects, though I wasn't sure I knew when to stop. (I don't think I've ever learned that.) Politically she represented the source of many of Greece's problems, which is to say, its history of disasters.

My father-in-law, Vassili, was a strong antimonarchist and fed me his ideas about the unpopular Greek monarchy. At the end of World War I, Constantinople was liberated by the Allies (it had fallen to Ottoman Sultan Muhammad II in 1453) and Allied forces occupied the city from 1918 to 1923. Crown Prince Constantine's grandfather, Constantine II, pro-German during World War I, managed to muddle Greece into what Greeks call the *catastrophe* in which Constantinople and Anatolia were again and now definitively Turkish territory, confirmed by a huge exodus of Greeks from Asia Minor, including that of my family-in-law. The last move of the Greek monarchy was in 1936 when George II, King Paul's older brother, dissolved parliament and appointed pro-German General Yannis Metaxa dictator of Greece for life. After the war the English engineered the return of George II and his blemished monarchy, in part as an instrument against the Communist rebellion.

After the transition period from civil war to peace in 1949, there would be a series of increasingly liberal governments, which engendered an extreme reaction by the right, culminating in the successful coup by four colonels who ruled Greece from 1967 to 1974. By then this crown prince was king. He sided with the colonels. The day after the putsch, there appeared in all the papers a picture in which the king is standing with his arms on the shoulders of the colonels. Once in power, however, Colonel Papadopoulos had no further need of the young king. Constantine tried a coup of his own. It failed and he fled into exile, leaving his monarchist aides behind to linger in Greek prisons. When the colonels fell and democracy returned with Karamanlis in 1974, there was a referendum and Constantine and the institution of monarchy were banned from Greece. Unlike his cousin Juan Carlos in Spain when the generals threatened, Constantine did not prove to be a good king. During the period of the junta, I was involved in the resistance to the dictatorship to the extent of editing an antijunta book, *Eighteen Texts*, published by Harvard University Press in 1972.

Louis MacNeice arrived in Greece in October of '49 to be the new director of the British Institute. In those days in England there were four poets from Oxford who called themselves the "new poets" and who said they were writing the "new poetry." They were Stephen Spender, Louis MacNeice, C. Day Lewis, and W. H. Auden. When a few years later Dylan Thomas came on the scene, very young and marvelous, with his *Eighteen Poems* in 1934—he was only twenty—it took the new poets by surprise. In his review of the book, MacNeice said *Eighteen Poems* was the confused work of an author out of control, who reeled out images like a drunk. For the rest of his life he praised Thomas and publicly lamented his mistaken review.

MacNeice was a classical scholar from Ireland, a member of the "new poetry" four from Oxford, less politically committed yet more of a social observer than the others. He published books of poems, translated *Agamemnon* and *Faust,* was a producer for the BBC. His wry understatement and ironic humor gave his poetry popularity. He lacked Auden's killer punch and doggerel brilliance or the fullness of Spender's Spanish Civil War poems, but many in England preferred MacNeice's newspaper eye. Greece was to give him a new imagery for his late book, *Ten Burnt Offerings.*

Louis MacNeice called me one day for tea, and I went to his apartment. Constantine Politis, a young political scientist, was there. I said, "What do you think of the political situation in Greece?" I might just as well have said, "What do you think of the planet earth?" His answer was stupendous. A gesture of futility accompanied by a weary, contemptuous sound I wish I could reproduce: a nasalized "eeenhhh," followed by *"Plus ça change, plus c'est la même chose"* (The more it changes, the more it's the same).

It was not the French cynicism but the Greek "eeenhhh" that cracked us up.

"Why don't we go to the Acropolis," Louis proposed. "I haven't been there yet."

"That's a scandal," Kostas scolded.

So we took a cab to the hill dominating Athens called the Acropolis, "high point of the city." Since it was a weekday, the site was deserted except for a few guards. There were no fences, no admission booths, no tourist buses. The Pelasgian walls were gone. We started up the western slope to the Propylaea. The breeze from Hymmetus carried with it wild herbs and honey and the sun was sweet. The climb was not made easy by regular steps. Louis, tall, handsome, one of the black Irish, seemed to be drinking the air. Suddenly he stumbled, fell face forward, and hit the ground. He cracked his forehead on a piece of marble lying about. As he pulled himself up, he wiped the blood off his face. With a tremendous smile, he said, "What luck for a Greek teacher! On the first day to mix my blood with marble and sun!"

We reached the Parthenon. It stood there in marble patience. Pericles's buildings have been much abused by Persians, Turks, Venetians, Brits. The last massive indignity was in the eighteenth century when a Venetian general lobbed cannon balls at the Parthe-

Visiting the Acropolis in the company of classical scholar and poet Louis MacNeice, newly arrived in Greece to direct the British Institute, 1949

non where the Turks had stored munitions and gunpowder. In the nineteenth century the British Museum safeguarded Caryatids and other Acropolis sculptures by placing their loot in the polluted London air of their grand building, only to sandblast them back to cleanliness in the twenties, thereby altering the marble patina of sensitive Greek skins to coarse Roman brutality. Unlike the Brits, the Turks didn't steal the women. In fact they added some of their own, turning the Erechtheum into a harem.

The Acropolis is monumental art on high. In the Near East, "high places" among the Babylonians and Canaanites are associated with adoration. The traditional site for Baal worship was on a hill or upon a monumental structure. The Sumerians, who are said to have come from the hills, worshiped hill gods on high places or on ziggurats which they built, and in I Kings 3.3 we read that "Solomon sacrificed and burned incense in the high places." That the Greeks also chose all over Greece to place their sanctuaries magnificently on high places should not surprise us. Often we find a temple between bullhorn mountains.

As for the great monumental aspect of the Acropolis, I felt uncertain, since I have usually preferred less to more. Of course the collective, major statement is impressive, in art as in government, but I usually favored a piano over a symphony, a trek through intimate rhododendron forests in the Himalayas rather than the Grand Canyon, a brook in a Wang Wei poem more than the splash and thunder of Niagara Falls. But the Parthenon is a victory for calm grandeur. Above the city and gazing out on the far Aegean, the Parthenon is the surviving god of Greece on that Athens hill; and even in its mutilated state it has, in keeping with its name "purity," immense harmony of proportions and imposing peace. It is a symphony, but each instrument is heard with clarity. Moreover, the irregularly tall columns deprived of their roof—in contrast to the almost intact and therefore gloomy Temple of Apollo at Didyma—harbor the sun and clouds and even all the translucent winds. The air over the Acropolis—at least until the diesel buses poisoned the atmosphere—as over the sea around the islands, has an intoxicating logic. It is ecstatic. There is no indoors on the Acropolis, except for the small museum with its select pieces.

A few days later, at lunch, Louis was raging against Stephen Spender—his person, not the poems. When I began to read recent poetry, I read everything Spender wrote. I liked his first book best, *Twenty Poems,* and then the volumes grew increasingly rhetorical and sentimental, and always with a struggling, uncertain ear, until he gave up altogether as a poet. Yet some extraordinary poems about Spain, some lines here and there were enough to make up for the weaknesses. Louis blamed Spender for bisexuality, for pettiness, for arguing about every single piece of furniture when he divorced his wife. Having thought of Spender, Auden, MacNeice and Day Lewis as a quadrumvirate of harmony, of social conscience and personal ethics, I was forced to understand that all people have their frailties. The Spender tirade was in part in anticipation of a visit by the poet, who had once published a book of stories many of them set in Greece. A few evenings later Louis asked me over for an evening with Spender. They were old pals again, genuinely so, and surely what was constant and significant in their old friendship took over. Spender's wife Natasha played the piano. They told intriguing stories about Eliot, Barker, and Dylan Thomas. It was a good evening.

As soon as I went into the barber shop, I realized I didn't know how to say how I wanted my hair cut. Sure enough, the barber smiled and said, "How do you want your hair?" I knew he must be saying that, and accepted that even if I were deaf and dumb, but at least a Greek, I could have explained myself perfectly well with at least half a dozen different gestures. The few words I'd picked up in these first days I learned at cafés. I had it. I'd make the barber tell *me* the word. When he asked me again how I wanted my hair, I resorted to a newly acquired language of how to order coffee, *"Ohi pikró, ohi vari glikö."* (Not bitter, not heavy sweet.)

The barber said, *"Metrio!"* (Medium!)

"Málista!" (Yes!), I shouted.

In Europe the café is where you carry on much of your social life, and in Greece the cafés are everywhere. If there is one house on a remote hill or farmland or beach, there are bound to be a few round marble tabletops (or humble aluminum ones) perched on metal legs, waiting for a customer. I saw the pianist Yannis Papadopoulos in his apartment. Then we would go to a café and chat with the composer Manos Hadjidakis. We did this regularly for two years. Manos tended to stay up all night composing and so we could never count on him showing up before late afternoon or early evening.

In those first years in Greece, Yannis Papadopoulos was our closest friend. He knew languages, speaking Greek, French, and English natively. His father had been the Greek ambassador in Washington and Yanni lived seven years in Johannesburg when married to an English-speaking South African. I had turned twenty-two when we met and so his forty years seemed to me the age of a prophet.

Yanni was a Byzantine mosaic, and perhaps a prophet. He had the large dark eyes of the Ravenna saints, his hair was very black and conservatively parted, his nose thin and slightly bridged. When he laughed he showed his front teeth, which were not bucked but seemed big and made the smiler bigger, and then, in slight embarrassment about the fun of a good story, he shut his mouth, but the smile still showed through. Sitting or standing, Yanni had the calm and erect posture of the Buddha. He was a Buddha, an idiosyncratically spiritual one, which combined nicely with his endless doctrine of anecdotes in Greek, French, and English. When he started on a story, he savored every dramatic twist and each event was worthy of the *Arabian Nights,* but he gave a wise, ironic curve to every turn of phrase so that the tale became a parable. All this wealth of aphoristic experience came out whether he was recounting what happened to nation, world, or friends—who were usually in the arts or in diplomacy, or sometimes in both. The best example of the Greek poet-diplomat was George Seferis, but that combination was not uncommon in Greece and Europe, and even Latin America where critical examples were Carlos Fuentes and Pablo Neruda, ambassadors to France, and Octavio Paz, ambassador to India. As the son of a diplomat, Yanni carried the burden of worldly behavior, which he had put aside in order to carry out his personal existence as a pianist and original thinker.

"Have some yoghurt," Yanni offered. The rituals of food and drink offerings were very important to him. "I mean the good kind that we make in a *sack.* By the way *sakkos* is an ancient Greek word given to us by the old Phoenician merchants who carried their things around in a Hebrew *sak.*"

"So a *sack* is a *sakkos* is a *sak.* Sounds older than Gertrude Stein's triple rose."

"Things haven't changed much, you see. Even when you think so. Words are disguised but they go on forever. What changes is the recognition of the masks we put on words or that we wear ourselves."

"How do you know so much about words?" I said.

"I like to browse in dictionaries. They are my newspapers. Dante is also a good newspaper. He gives you all the gossip and national doings of popes, scholars, and villains, who are often one and the same. At least in Dante's editorial."

"If you come from the East in America they say 'bag' where the rest of the country says 'sack.' We'd say 'a bag is a bag is a bag.'"

"But you know, Willis, 'sack' is more appropriate, at least for yoghurt, since we in the Balkans, including Turkey, make the best yoghurt. And it's best when you let it hang up and drain thick in a heavy sack. Then it's like cheese, but better, and better for you. Yoghurt is one of the few things we peoples can claim after Plato and Greek Fire. And at least 'sack' also comes from our part of the world, from the Near East, while 'bag' is an Icelandic word. You need real sunlight and a marble table to enjoy sack yoghurt with honey on top of it. Iceland won't do."

"Let's find Manos," I suggested.

Manos Hadjidakis was already a great composer, and then as now, Yanni kept his music in his head and wrote it down for him. It wasn't that Manos couldn't score his works. He did when he had time. But he didn't like to find the time, since he preferred to talk to friends till one or two in the morning, go home, and compose. So when was there time, with rehearsals and concerts, for writing things down? When his first ballet *The Enchanted Serpent* was to be performed in

Athens, the piece was choreographed *en scène* while the composer played the piano. The afternoon preceding the evening performance the orchestra was there waiting, but all the instrumental parts for the orchestra were not yet completed. Manos arrived right after lunch, early for him, went to work scrawling the remaining parts while the orchestra tuned up, smoked, and enjoyed itself; by five he had completed the missing instrumental scores, in time for an hour-and-a-half complete rehearsal, an early supper, and a splendid, flawless premiere at eight.

Yanni the mental note bank, Manos the mad inventor. Variations of the ballet scene occurred regularly. Once Manos was in Paris and wired for a piano suite only Yanni had in his head (Yanni learned the pieces as they practiced together on two pianos). Yanni sent it and the concert took place on schedule. Manos the outrageous—who always came through. When he wrote music for the film *Never on Sunday,* it was more of the same.

Manos was overweight, smoked between words, wore heavy dark lines under his eyes from his casual sleep habits, and was a man of endless energy, wit, and poetry. The words he wrote for his songs were as significant as the music. Like Federico García Lorca who went to Andalusian popular song (folklore) to find lost words and melodies, Hadjidakis, like Mikis Theodorakis, went to Greek popular song. He was singular in reviving the taverna songs from Smyrna and Constantinople, the *rembetika* (solo man's dance) and *hassapiko* (the butcher's dance from the medieval butcher's guild). These city songs and dances *(zembekika),* like the blues, are distinct from the regional folk songs, usually line dances by both women and men, for *paniyiri* (festivities) of baptism, saint's day, marriage, or whatever pretext there was for a party. The city songs are love songs, some macho-proud—the Greek macho is a *palikari* (a young hero) which rhymes conveniently with *fengari* (moon) and so many heroic acts take place at night with the connivance of the moon; others sing about thieves, drugs, prostitutes, death. One of the most beautiful songs that Manos rescued is "Sinefiazmeni Kiriaki," whose refrain begins: "Cloudy Sunday, you are like my heart, which always has clouds in it. Christ and my Vir . . . , Christ and my Vir . . . , Christ and my Virgin."

Before Hadjidakis and Theodorakis, the rembetika songs were very much alive and after World War I, as a result of the massive influx of refugees from Asia Minor, it had spread everywhere in Greece, including to the islands. Masters of rembetika, like Nikos Tsistanis in Piraeus continued to write new songs, which gained national popularity, but the music was still associated mainly with the city down-and-outs and could be heard live mainly in the taverns in the poor neighborhoods or among the fishermen in the islands. It was purer then. Yet when the artists discovered their popular song heritage, they did so with taste. You heard and hear "Europeanized" commercial songs. But the music that brings stadiums of people together now, from all classes, is the popular music. Greece is unique in authentically joining the popular and the sophisticated. Spain's Falla went to the same popular sources, but the beautiful suites and operas are classical, not popular and so are the audiences. On the amphitheater on top of Athens's second hill, Likavitós, the poems of Elytis, Gatsos, and Seferis are sung in compositions by Greece's composers. There is no compromise. It is a Greek art.

"Mano, I hear Greek music, and immediately recognize when European elements enter it. Sometimes in your music I hear Peru or Paris. But mostly I hear Turkey, North Africa, India, all those places Greek music came from. . . ."

"We did come from the synagogues and mosques and temples of the East. Although now we *are* our own music. And not European. Not yet. There is a difference. Even flamenco music, which at times seems to be Moorish or gypsy, meaning northern India, is European—with the exception of the Holy Week *saeta*, an almost pure Arabic chant. Almost. But Greek music is different."

"What's the magic difference?"

"It's not magic. Magic is quick and sudden. And we're patient. You see even the flamenco comes to a climax, it peaks sexually, and then the song dies. Our music doesn't die. It persists. It endures. Our orchestra (we give our three or four musicians that lofty ancient Greek title) may play a song for five minutes or an hour, and people may dance for an hour. Time in Europe is now horizontal. We have a timeless memory. It endures. But it is not historical like the Chinese. It is only eternal like India, where centuries of imitation are indistinguishable."

"You mean a Greek musician is really an Indian holy man?"

"Yes, a holy Indian with a lewd secular look and a sense of humor. Our dirges from Crete or Epirus are pure ancient drama, choral song, and timeless."

With poets W. S. Merwin (seated) and David Wade (in beret), 1964

"What's your dream project?" I asked.

"To go to the Andes, lie on a hammock, and listen to the birds playing the flute."

"And after the Andes?"

"I want to write a musical drama called 'The Street of Dreams.'"

"I'll bet on the latter."

"Yanni will collect your money, if I don't come up with it," Manos offered.

"Don't be stupid. Yanni will have it in his head before you even dream about it."

There were certain cafés, bookstores, and yoghurt shops where writers hung out—in the back of Ikaros Bookstore and Publisher, the Brazilian (a coffeehouse), and one big yoghurt establishment that reminded me of the classic New York Horn and Hardart automat on West Fifty-seventh, which had a balcony where I'd go for hours to read novels. Upstairs on the balcony in the Greek establishment, I used to sit with Nikos Gatsos and Odysseus Elytis, and sometimes Katsimbalis, Henry Miller's hero in *The Colossus of Maroussi,* would also be there. Katsimbalis was indeed a wild-speaking colossus. I had a run-in with him once, and he said some nasty things I remember with pain, but later, on the islands, we spent an afternoon talking, and there was no sign of anything but adventure. In fact he lay flat on his lounge chair and spent some hours telling me about a trip he took on his back, floating in a boat down the Blue Nile.

Nikos Gatsos was very tall, his face sculptured and severely handsome, big features, including a nose excessively noble. He sat draping back in his chair. It was difficult to know whether he was deeply bored or meditative. I'm sure both guesses are right. I was told that Gatsos came from a titled, rich Greek family and that as a young man, after receiving his inheritance, he went to Monte Carlo and gambled it away in a few days. What I know for certain is that he wrote a major poem in modern Greek, "Amorgos," a 3,000-line surreal poem about the far Cycladic island of Amorgos (which I later included in *Modern European Poetry).* In late '49 and the early fifties when I met Gatsos, his friends lamented that this most promising and perhaps most accomplished of the new Greek poets had abandoned poetry. It disturbed me. When we spoke, he was courtly, kind, and weary, though he could not have been more than forty. He did give up poetry. There have been no later books, at least none that have been reviewed. But to my great surprise, this most wonderful and difficult poet, whose images were clean shots of island Greece, beautiful as they were, in their totality, elliptically obscure, began a

new career writing transparent lyrics for popular songs. Gatsos collaborated with Manos Hadjidakis in his musical *O Dromos tou Onírou* (The Street of Dreams) and the lyrics are amazing. My judgment is so passionate when it comes to the good lyrics in Greek popular song that I fall back on John Steinbeck's lame excuse in *Travels with Charley* when he comes upon the beauty of northern Maine. He has no words for it.

Greek gods and goddesses are fashioned after men and women. So the gods are imitations of humans who are their makers. Angelos Sikelianos was a model for that imitation.

The revolution in our century in modern Greek letters occurred when the poet Kostis Palamás championed the demotic language, *dimotiki,* as opposed to *katharevousa,* the purist language—a melange of ancient and modern Greek and the nation's official language. In 1927 Angelos Sikelianos and his American wife, Helen, revived the Delphic games and drama festival at the ancient site of Delphi. Sikelianos was the first great modern poet of continental Greece. (I say continental so as not to forget Constantine Cavafy, 1863–1933, who lived in Alexandria.)

Helle and I had been translating poems by Sikelianos into English. Mainly as a result of my teaching job, where I used Greek most of the day and had to know the Greek grammar for each lesson before I could teach the equivalent English or French forms, my Greek was getting reasonably good. We translated about seven or eight longish poems. (Eventually we gave them in Spain to the English poet Laurie Lee who had them broadcast on John Lehmann's BBC program "New Soundings.")

Aphrodite Is Born

In the happy fire of daybreak, look, I'm rising
    with outstretched hands.
The holy ocean calm summons me to step out
    into blue regions.

But sudden earth-winds ram against my breasts
    and shake my body.
O Zeus, the sea is heavy, my loose hair like stones
    weighs me to the bottom.

Breezes, hurry! O Kymothoe, O Glauke, come, lift me
    by the hollow of my armpits.
I have not foreseen such quick surrender
    to the sun's embrace.

One day Helle said, "Why don't we see Sikelianos?" So we called and went to his house.

Sikelianos had just come back from the hospital. He had had a stroke and his right side was partially paralyzed, enough to force him to use his left hand for writing new poems. He lay in his bed like a god. Not only the face and its expression but even the expression and posture of the reclining figure. He couldn't help it. He had walked too long on the soil of Greece with his head in antiquity to be free of divinity. Cavafy also recreated the past and, like Sikelianos, saw Homeric, Periclean, Alexandrian, Byzantine, Modern Greece as part of one continuum. Cavafy would speak about Greeks in a Roman satrapy in Syria or Anna Komnina, author of the *Alexiad* and daughter of Emperor Alexios I Komninos, and, like Sikelianos, Cavafy made the past indistinguishable from the present. Sikelianos a classical figure, and Cavafy an Alexandrian, and Seferis in his Homeric world, couldn't do otherwise. They were Greek and their memory and identity of a few millenia were no different from what they knew or learned about their great-grandfathers. The fall of Constantinople in 1453 or 1921 is a learned fact to most Greeks, and both losses occurred indistinguishably yesterday.

When Eliot, Pound, or Joyce recreated or alluded to a past, it was to show us that there was a past, to contrast the ages, but not make the past present—and this despite Eliot's frequent meditations on time past and present or Pound's lively depiction of Chinese, Ancient Greek, and Anglo-Saxon figures. The time gap is not obliterated but emphasized through exoticism. This is not a defect in Eliot and Pound, simply another approach by authors who were not, and could not be, of the times they described.

Sikelianos gave us a colossal smile. He knew that we had translated his poems. He beckoned us over to his bed and somehow managed to reach out with his one functioning arm and pull us both on top of the bed in order to embrace us. What do you say next?

"What are you writing these days?" Helle asked.

"The last book of a poetic drama trilogy. Do you have the earlier ones?"

"No. I'm afraid we don't."

"Take these," and he took two books from the side table and handed Helle two magnificent editions of the plays.

"Do you have copies for yourself?" I said. "These aren't your last ones?"

"Don't worry. I have many friends with copies." And the other people in the room smiled assuringly that he was safe.

"You're being very stingy," I said to him. "I mean to yourself, Angelos Sikelianos. You're taking his last books away from him."

"That's all right. He too is an old friend of mine, and will understand." And the god winked.

Two years later, Sikelianos was back in the hospital for a routine treatment. The attendant gave him the wrong medicine, actually a cleaning solution, and though as soon as the mistake was discovered they pumped out his stomach, it was too late and he died.

A month before Christmas the director of Anavrita Academy called me to his office. The Englishman was not going to renew my contract for the spring semester.

"What's wrong?"

"Nothing's wrong."

"Let me ask you again. Why aren't you renewing my contract? Why are you firing me?"

"If you insist . . ."

"I do."

"You are an antimonarchist. It is not appropriate. There's nothing more to be said."

"There is nothing more to be said."

I wasn't happy. Here was my first job, and I was out. I was always a spontaneous person, which is a way of saying I couldn't keep my mouth shut. But in Greece and at that age I couldn't have done otherwise. I also got into hot water when the sculptor Dimitri Hadzis, then a Fulbright student at the Polytechnion, took me along to a party at American Ambassador Purifoy's house. In the receiving line I asked the ambassador why the American government didn't support the democratic forces in Greece. The gentleman was furious. Hadzis later told me that he got rebuked for bringing me and Helle along. Within a year a moderate government actually prevailed in a national election and the old gang was out; and since then, except for the seven years of night under the colonels, Greece has not had extremist governments. Purifoy became notorious a few years later as ambassador to Guatemala when he openly directed a coup against the reformist government of Jacobo Arbenz Guzmán, leading to the rule of Colonel Carlos Castillo Armas, whose last names, meaning "castle arms," was a wise, well-chosen title for the military leader or for the series of governments which for the next three decades would decimate its people.

I had saved some money from my job and was still dreaming of those black-and-white photographs of the islands. We left for Mykonos a month after the new year.

Mykonos was not visited by Greeks or foreigners in 1950. The islanders called both Athenians and foreigners *xeni*, so we were the only *xeni* on the *Eleni* that crawled and rocked through the winter seas to reach the island. The ship interior was stuffy and fascinating like a small village square: plump peasant women with bandanas in their hair, many in mourn-

"In Asia Minor, at the ruins of Troy, continuing my life as a vagabond, despite and because of the academic life," 1970

ing black; old men in wool waistcoats and leggings, and carrying solid crooked canes which they used to walk around with and to keep their goats and chickens quietly in place. There was no "nylon" prosperity in their dress—"nylon" being the word for the most costly polyester clothing of the coming generation. When the sea was rough, with each long rocking there was a communal moan, retching, and a lot of vomit on the deck. But no one complained. We spent most of the day up on deck, enjoying the passing islands, the cold whale clouds overhead, and the intimate fury of the untamed February sea.

It was dark when the ship dropped anchor a hundred fifty meters from the dock. The harbor was too shallow for us to come in closer to the amphitheater of white houses lighted bright for the three-time event of the week: *Eleni*'s arrival. Big rowboats with glaring headlamps began to pitch toward us through the windy sea. Sailors were shouting orders to the boats, and boat captains were shouting back their version of the argument. We descended into one of the rolling craft, under screaming orders to hurry and be careful, and before the cheerful noisy

chaos diminished the *kapetanios* was rowing us to shore.

Theodoros, age twelve, was waiting for us. His mother, Kiria Maria Hartopoulou, had a place for us. And who were we to argue? Theodoros grabbed our suitcases and while the wharf pelican monitored us we hiked by the dog chapel into the twine of alleys on the eastern side of the island toward the great eyeball dome of Paraportiani. We passed through the darkened igloo streets, under a loggia crossway, and in a few minutes the cobbled paving led us to Kiria Hartopoulou (Mrs. Daughter-of-Paper), who was waiting for us on her second-floor door stoop.

"Eláte mesa." (Come inside.)

We obeyed. We went inside, passing through a maze of geraniums potted in white-painted cans.

Without any negotiation or questions, Maria took our luggage to our room, showed us the washbowl and the pail of water to refill the water cabinet over the bowl, the closet for our clothing, and the toilet which was a miniature chapel facing the sea. Into that chapel came a cutting smell of brine and urine rising from the hole at the bottom of the red toilet bowl and another current of briney sea air came blowing in through the paneless chapel window. All the stucco floors were covered with blue Mykonos-woven rag rugs.

Our supper was soon served. We would eat with the family—Katrina, Theodoros, Maria, and captain Andonis when he came back from the sea.

"*Ávrio* (tomorrow) we'll talk about finances, but they'll be no problem," Maria shouted in the particular singsong of the Mykonian speech. And there was none. Maria tended to shout even when she was whispering, although she was a mild, even-tempered lady. At our late supper that night we consumed stewed lamb, boiled carrots and tomatoes, country green salad, and plenty of good bread and yoghurt. The retzina was harsh and tasty and it washed the food down with perfect authority. I ate about twice what I normally eat. Seeking our sea legs, we gobbled everything, including the crème caramel in honor of our arrival. In a few days Captain Andonis would be home from the Dodekanese Islands where he ventured during much of the winter as long as the local *melteme* winds were dangerous. Spring was only a few flowering almond trees away.

"When Andonis returns, we'll hear good stories," Maria promised. "Now, go to bed," Maria ordered.

Very quickly we passed into deep island sleep.

Dawn was tentative. It broke the darkness with a few rays. Then it dropped into clouds and night returned. Some gulls began to alarm the sky. Their screeching called the sun and Apollo slowly came up from the Aegean, icy and dripping dew across the stone back of Mykonos.

I slipped out of bed. Went quickly into the freezing toilet chapel, then walked down into the street to see this whitewashed village whose only reality had been pinned on my Paris hotel wall.

Minoan Crete was far to the south. Here in the Cyclades the statues were far more primitive, geometrically plain, and modern than anything found in that ornate Minoan civilization. But Mykonos shared one phenomenon with Crete: a labyrinth. The Mykonian labyrinth was not underground with fearful mysteries of a Minotaur who fed on virgins, but outdoors, under the sun glazing every irregular boulder shape into whiteness. It was only 5:00 A.M. yet the whiteness quivered. Some black cypresses stabilized the streets. Intermittent small churches poked the sky with half circles and triangles of ice. Astonishing peace. I stopped and the island halted. As I walked about, the perfectly measured shapes of the labyrinth contracted into hard fire. Wandering lost in circles, I got used to

the fire and it calmed into a constancy of ordinary light as full morning diffused the maze of iceberg sculptures. Light shifted to fishermen carting nets, black widows carrying water in clay jars, donkeys loaded with trash, a cheese peddler, my own steps. As the orchestra of noises grew, the building settled back into magnificent passivity.

Nearing Maria's again, I paused near the cupola of the white glob of Paraportiani, with its five churches connected under that stucco eyeball dome sending its rays to the entire firmament. Amid the acacia I heard the morning priest singing a cappella from the chapel.

The Small White Byzantine Chapel

On this island, nude, and nearly treeless
(But for the few acacia trees in bloom
In the small white plazas of stone and sun
With their zones of salt and seaweed aroma),

On the far side, across the island rock
(And the dry wind and fresh donkey dung),
The cupola of the white chapel stares:
A stucco eyeball brightening the sky.

Inside are sparks and fumes of incense,
And candle flames before the iconostas
Where a slant-eyed virgin leans in grief:
O points of mystery in the finite space!

Through the black air (within the whitewashed dome),
The priest leads the orphans in prayer and song.
O lifelong darkness of the finite vault,
And the white dome vainly searching the sky.

"You can make money teaching the grocer's daughter, and the postman, and the teacher can find you other students," Maria was telling me. "Yes, talk to the grocer, but be careful. He'll want something you won't be able to give to him. The grocer Assimomitis (Silvernose) is cunning, but you can teach his daughter. Have absolutely nothing to do with Zoakos, the *horofilakas*. The town policeman. His name 'small animal' means he is small, though he's fat as a pig, and a vicious animal. I've told you so. When you come back I'll have carnations for Hellitza." Maria was already fond of my Helle. Not only didn't she mind that my wife was Athenian but she was clearly pleased.

After breakfast I set out to find a job on the island.

By nightfall it was done. The mailman, the teacher, and the grocer's daughter. I would give all of them English lessons. And there would be enough money for us to live on. Just about. We won't starve in Mykonos. When I announced the good news to Maria, she told me Andonis was back.

"Then let's celebrate."

"Of course, we'll celebrate. Right here. I'll go for Cyclops and for Frangisko who plays bouzouki."

"Who's Cyclops?"

"Ah, *Kýklopas*, my one-eyed friend. You'll get to know him. And his old mother he lives with."

"I guess Cyclops and I are old buddies."

"It's okay, Wilaki, you can meet his mother some other time."

Andonis was a serious man. Built like an unbreakable spike. He wore his black captain's hat most of the time. When he spoke it was worth listening to, though he didn't speak much, unless he had a few drinks and you might cajole him into telling a story. Then he was an artist. Andonis was also an artist as a dancer. He had a reputation in Mykonos. He didn't dance often, but all his seriousness came out stoically in the *rembetika*. That was another story.

We drank and ate a lot of bread and goat cheese. Andonis made me dance first. He corrected me when I slipped into something *xeniko* (foreign). I sat down and Andonis began.

The captain stood very straight and paused a very long time. Then he began moving toward a fire, which wasn't there, in the center of the small living room. He looked at that fire, he studied it intensely. He circled that fire, slapping his thighs lightly. Stooping like a drunk, a controlled drunk, he hit the side of his shoe, leapt to the ceiling, and began to dance. Andonis was captain of all his gestures. He circled, drawn into himself, a hundred miles from the island, slapped the floor. His steps were delicate and rhythmically powerful. He spun, studied, shuffled, dropped to his knees. It went on for about fifteen minutes, ending with a leap to the ceiling in which somehow his whole body turned like a high tower diver. The bouzouki stopped. Andonis sat down. Gave the slightest smile, took a drink, and then gently began to make conversation.

"How long are you here for, Kirie Willis?"

"Not for long. Ten years, I suppose."

"Not long enough. You need a few more to get used to the water. The well water's very harsh. It takes getting used to. I think you need at least fifteen years. Then you can be a Mykoniatis."

"I don't think I can stay more than ten. But I'll return."

"*Kalá*. But you mustn't fool us. It's your word that you'll come back. After tonight, Kiria Helle, you must never let him go. Who will I dance with?"

White Island

My first day at the school for Constantine
I meet a peasant father with two hooks
(wounds from Albania) and the German Queen
of Greece who loans me her blue *Faber Book
of Verse*. But soon I'm fired and so begin
to loaf and write on islands. Mykonos,
the iceberg. I'm the only *xenos* in
the village, living with a Greek, and close
to getting jailed for working without papers.
The ship comes twice a week. Down at the pier
we all watch who comes in, but lemon vapors
of broiling fish seduce me. One white night
Captain Andonis slaps his heels. Austere,
he teaches me to dance, to live on light.

Once we were settled, Helle put a cloth on the small table in our room, made it into a desk, moved the glass with gardenias to one side, and wrote short stories about Epirus. She used her father's half brother, Apostolis, as her narrator. He was a village storyteller. At Wellesley she had written a book-length memoir of her Greek childhood, including the occupation when a German motorcyclist roared toward her, running her off the road and causing her to crash her bicycle; when her father was picked up as a hostage by a military truck in Athens, held incommunicado, and released by the Italians on Christmas Day; when her mother grabbed their clandestine radio, went upstairs and crawled with it onto a neighbor's roof while the Germans downstairs searched their house; how she dreamt that when it was all over she would have a cord around her neck with cheese and bread hanging from it and any time she was hungry she would eat the cheese and eat the bread, and as often as she wished. Despite hunger and executions, the occupation was a period of hope and people lived on that hope. Issues were clear. The confusion, the new groups killing each other, came after the war. Cavafy said in 1904 in "Waiting for the Barbarians":

What's going to happen to us without the barbarians?
Those people were some kind of solution.

I envied her fluency. Although I wanted to do a book about our life on the island, none of my attempts worked. I had neither the discipline, language, nor mastery, and most lacking was the confidence or courage to do it even with fear. If I had persisted in my failures I would have found the form. Even if it took years of rewriting and reworking, which it would have. But poetry was the only center then, and enough. I worked through many stages in poetry. Although I published a book in Greece, and it was essential to do so, it was only later in Spain, and in

New York and New Haven, that I found (or thought I found) a way to speak through the landscapes of Greece. Seferis and Cavafy helped of course. Greek cypresses in cemeteries, whitewashed villages, city streets with smells and newspapers were clear when the experience was selected and intensified in memory. So in New Haven I finished the first book of poems in America, *From This White Island.*

Much later, after a lot of drafts, I learned something and a time filter wasn't necessary. I could write on the spot about the immediate.

The day began before breakfast with a walk to the Three Wells, under the windmills. I drew water from the good well for the whole family. On the way back, just before Paraportiani, I went across a small bridge where the island jutted out and Kiria Galina, the Russian yoghurt lady, lived. I was often waylaid by Kiria Karpouzi (Mrs. Watermelon), an old lady, crazy as a bat, who always told me some wild story. Staring at me through her silver wire rims, she enjoyed her extravagance and knew I was a willing victim for her harassment. At the yoghurt shop, Kiria Galina, married to a Greek fisherman, taught me a few words in Russian. She was plump as a bowl of honey, with small Slavic eyes that stood out among the Greeks, and a smile that didn't let up. I liked our exchange, especially the big *"spasiba"* (thank you), as I balanced the clay water jug and red bowls of yoghurt while crossing the bridge to go home.

We were the only foreigners on the island except for an elderly English gentleman I rarely met. There was a snarling formality to our brief exchange of words. Unhappy, in gruff, upper-class speech, he warned me about someone or other. His name was Mill, and he was said to be a grand-nephew of John Stuart Mill. A starkly lonely man, widower of a Mykonos woman, the Englishman was a smuggler by profession. I never learned what he smuggled or whether his title was just flattering gossip, but he was Mill the smuggler like Stelios the barber.

As a reward for our writing labors, if we hadn't trekked across the island to one of the deserted beaches where it was still too cold to swim but a perfect place for reading or scratching down passages, we would have a meal in one of the harbor restaurants. With spring only just coming on, there were not yet the pyramids of watermelons built outside the eating places. One afternoon we had been glancing through a big, new book, a Greek thesaurus, and came across a word Helle didn't know: *ksekolomenos.* It was under insult words, and literally meant: "the man without an ass" or, more freely, "the man who had lost his ass." In the evening we wandered

down to the port and went into a restaurant where the fish was grilled over charcoal and doused with lemon and then touched up with local herbs. Fresh fish from the wharf, beans baked in their own sauce, island bread, and a glass of beer was the meal of your life.

Stephanos the waiter was a boy of thirteen or fourteen, school-shaven hair, and staring black eyes. Very smart and funny. I said to him *"Ksekolomenos!"* Because I didn't use the vocative but the nominative case, with the final "s," the boy knew I was not addressing him personally and identifying him as assless. He squinted, looked all around the room with great intensity, checking it out carefully to see who was the guy who had been screwed so much he had lost his ass. Then he turned back to us, seriously, and said *"Piós?"* (Who is it?). We burst out laughing, we couldn't help it. We also knew the thesaurus had given us a living word.

The place was crowded, dense with spirit, noisy. Greeks like to emphasize their words with mock-angry outbursts even when they're being most friendly to each other. Most of the island restaurants don't serve coffee. That's the work of a kafenéion or a sweetshop with long names like KAFEZACHARO-PLASTEION (Pastry-Coffeehouse-Establishment), where men, mainly men, sat playing vigorous games of *tavles*, backgammon, or just sipped coffee while fingering a *komboloï*, a string of worry beads. So after the grilled fish, we went to the kafenéion right in front of the pier where the evening ship from Athens came in. It was fun to be with everyone else inspecting who emerged from the sea on those little row-boats to join the island.

When our evening was over, everyone went home. At such moments I liked to walk the wharf alone. The island was asleep except for the lighthouse and a few bits of fire on the hills that looked like low stars. I could think, feel the drama of the island's distinction from the ordinary world. And by that difference I could define myself as a transient renegade, as clearly separated from what I had earlier known as pieces of pie in a dish suddenly cut off from each other by a knife. The difference in me was a whole zone I had swallowed, as discernible as the taste of the briny air over the wharf. I didn't have the words to define it, but it didn't matter, nor the experience to make it into poems I would keep, nor into prose I could link together. These abilities I wished, but I had to wait.

Wait, yes, but actively follow the life and verbal attempts of the writer. Otherwise the wait would be futile. Time must be actively filled in order to lead to a later time of difference. Without the constant preparation, time will lead only to increased age. So the Mykonos night was a laboratory. When I feel anxiety today, unable to escape the moment, incapable after all these years of moving into a philosophy or spirit to gain me peace or perspective, I look back to Mykonos night and my ignorances, filled with fire, if not words, with immediacy that also relished its futurity of inner and outer ventures. On the quay I got into the habit of spending an hour or two just walking and thinking. Although Wittgenstein might have protested, I seemed content at times to think perfectly well without words.

An Island

By white walls and scent of orange leaves,
    Come, I'll tell you, I know nothing.
        By this sea of salt and dolphins
I see but fish in a dome of sun.

In stars that nail me to a door,
    There are women with burning hair,
        And on the quay at night I feel
But hurricanes and rigid dawn.

On cobblestones at day I watch
    Some crazy seabirds fall and drown,
        And as the bodies sink to sand
I know I pay my birth with death.

I only see some plains of grass
    And sky-sleep in the crossing storks.
        I know nothing and see but fire
In the crater of a cat's eye.

Sometimes intruders with miracles in their pockets walk right in the door. The trick is to recognize the thief, before he gets back out with the rubies and sapphires. When I woke in the freezing bedroom of my dorm in Hawthorne Hall to write a poem, I saw the thief with his pockets bulging with loot. I went back to sleep but only to dream up enough mental steam to come out with a second poem within a half hour. Then I had some help. My friends convinced me that I had rubies and sapphires, or at least fragments of those stones, and I could have a lot more. So I was lucky. If I were a believer, I'd say I was blessed.

But the opposite can happen too. Just when you have the fire in your hands (using another metaphor

"With novelist Ye Chunchan when I was a Fulbright professor at Beijing University of Foreign Studies," China, 1972

borrowed from Federico García Lorca's words about knowing what poetry was as he knew what clouds were or the feeling of fire in his fists), some blasted thief walks in and blows it out. For now, let me recall the man who delivered the treasure. It was a Swiss.

Albert Schüpbach was a painter from Geneva, who, despite his typically Swiss-German name, proudly knew no German at all and, despite the Swiss school system, claimed he could not even pronounce his name correctly. (Many years later, in his own studio-house in southern France, he settled his Swiss nationality problem by Gallicizing his name into Chubac.) The painter came in that night on one of those pitching boats. We all spotted each other.

"*Bon soir, mes amis,*" Albert greeted us.

"*Bon soir.*"

"*Je cherche une chambre. Peut-être . . .*"

"*Entendu.*"

I grabbed his dufflebag, Helle took his portfolio, and we disappeared into the back streets of the village. Cyclops had an extra room, a spacious bachelor's lodging, and Albert was delighted with both the room and the notion that he had found Cyclops on a Greek island. Then we returned to the harbor and spent hours talking about art and hearing how Swiss order and correctness had turned him into a wanderer, which was good and impossible for a painter who above all needs a studio.

"*Si le soir j'invite des amis chez moi le lendemain je reçois une amende de la police.*" (If I invite a few friends over for the evening, the next day the police slap me with a fine.) "*Tapage nocturne.*" (Nocturnal racket.) "Only my countrymen can dream up such silent evenings."

Albert knew no Greek but refused to see this as an obstacle. He spoke to everyone in French, and in most instances he managed very well. By speaking slowly, he drew people in. They listened carefully and guessed what he was saying or needed. In a few days, on his own, he set up a studio. And almost invisibly he acquired two disciples—Helle and me. When he ran out of supplies, we did help him order things through Zacharias, the local general store merchant. But he went to the butcher to buy his own paper supplies. He discovered that the butchers of Greece wrapped meat in excellent paper for his gouache paintings. Paper that withstood blood was perfect for absorbing his colors.

Helle gave up writing stories. She didn't think about it. She simply began to draw and paint. Before long she too had a studio, with easel, acrylics, gouache, inks, and a big supply of butcher paper. (I think it was her early work from Greece and Spain, the colors, that got her into Yale as a graduate

student when she studied with Joseph Albers.) I also began to paint, but it was back in Maroussi that I set up a studio. Albert was behind it all, though I don't remember him telling us to begin. It was his example. And a few words of encouragement.

Albert was then twenty-seven years old, which seemed a very advanced age. He had been working in his profession for years and in Geneva earned his living as a painter. He had hilarious habits. While we were all eating and he was sitting to Helle's right, he had the malicious skill of placing one finger on her wrist just as she was about to direct a forkful of food into her mouth. He'd say, "*Tu disais, ma petite fée.*" And the fork halted in midair, an inch from her mouth. In Athens when a beggar came up to us, he tapped the gentleman on the belly with the flat of his hand, intoning "*Bon jour, mon vieux. Vous êtes un grand comédien,*" and guffawed. The beggar's face flashed from misery to laughter, unwillingly. But the smile remained. "*Je vous dis, mon vieux, vous êtes vraiment un grand comédien,*" Albert insisted.

One morning Theodoros ran upstairs to tell me that the *horofilakas* Zoakos wanted to see me down at his office at the harbor. Maria had warned me that he was a rotten bully. I had an early lesson and then walked upstairs at about noon to the policeman's hideout. Zoakos, a chunky, ugly man in his forties, was broadly smiling.

"*Ti kánete?*" (How are you?)

"Just fine," I said. "Kiria Maria treats me like an older son."

"You're doing a fine job I hear teaching English to our people."

"Thank you. Before coming here I was at Anavrita."

"Yes, I know."

"A small village, isn't it?"

"How would you like to teach English to my daughter?"

"How old is she?"

"She's eleven."

"A good age to begin. What's her name?"

"Aglaia."

"Let's work something out." I didn't really need any more hours. A small inheritance had just come through, taking the mystery and adventure out of the next meal. But I thought it would be a good gesture.

"Of course I would expect you to do this as a courtesy to me."

"You mean teach your daughter for nothing?"

"If you wish to put it so crudely."

"I'm very sorry."

"You cannot be sorry. You will have to give her lessons if you wish to continue the other lessons. You have no working papers."

"I have temporary working papers, and they were enough for me to work at the king's school." I was angry and not at all diplomatic.

"They won't work here."

"They'll work just fine." I turned to leave.

"You're breaking the law."

"You're crazy!" I had had enough.

Zoakos seized my arms and tried to shove me into the barred room next door. I wrestled his arms off me. I wanted to say something insulting, but I didn't. I turned very slowly, walked even more slowly to the door, and descended the stairway. At the public telephone, I called Vassili in Athens and said I might have trouble.

That afternoon I gave my lesson to the grocer's daughter.

There were difficulties. It wasn't pleasant to be at war with the local policeman. Zoakos sent me a threatening letter, which I sent on to Athens. Vassili made a legal complaint against Zoakos for trying to force me into giving his daughter free English lessons, and filed the document with the Ministry of the Interior. A higher officer from the island of Syros would come to investigate the dispute.

Spring was everywhere and the sea calm. After two months, it seemed good to take a few weeks off to wander the islands. Of course we had been to Delos, a kilometer away by *kaiki,* where Apollo and Artemis were born. After Leto became pregnant by Zeus with Apollo and Artemis, Hera, Zeus's formal consort (and sister), was furiously jealous and Leto fled across the Mediterranean, seeking a place to receive her. Only Delos at the center of the Cyclades—those islands floating on giant tortoise backs—had the courage to offer Leto a sanctuary. Zeus stepped in to steady Delos for the birth of the sun and moon gods by attaching the island to the sea bottom with adamantine chains. Sun and Moon were born and thereafter Delos was a holy island, and also a treasury. One night Xerxes, a Greek general (not the Persian emperor), came to Delos on the ship *Parabola* with an offering. He brought with him a huge statue of Apollo and in the night he extended a gold bridge out from the *Parabola* on which to carry the statue to the shore. But in the morning as he set it up, lightning struck and a tall palm tree fell, bashing and cracking its chest, and today the Apollo still lies on the sand, with his chest fractured, not far from the row of archaic marble lions.

Each island has its gossip about ancient gods. We decided to go west to Ikaria and Samos and then way out to Patmos in the Dodekanes.

I gave my students some extra lessons to do on their own. On the evening of our departure, our friends were at the wharf, at the sweetshop, including the faithful students who saw my struggle with Zoakos as their contest between civilian and military authorities. We heard the dramatic foghorn announcing the ship, and scrambled to carry our few things out to the end of the pier where the passengers from the *Eleni* were arriving, under spotlights, in the rowboats.

"Eláte mesa." (Get in.) Albert, Helle, and I stepped into one of the boats that spun around and began to row us out to the steamer. There was a five-minute stretch between the harbor spots and the ship searchlights in which we were in an open sea of darkness, as in a cave with fires at both ends. It was suddenly peaceful. Spring had quieted the surf and only the gentle lift and dip of the oars was heard. The stars descended to be closer to the unlighted precinct. Another space, a transition, time for another perspective. It was good to be alone in the darkness, to have this minute of freedom before setting out on the most exciting activity in Greece: wandering the islands.

As we reached the midnight *Eleni,* the sailors shouted at us and vigorously pulled us up on board. *Eleni* would take us to Ikaria where Ikaros had his agon with the sun. And then *Eleni* would go on as far as Amorgos, Gatsos's island, with its great Byzantine monastery like a white pancake wrinkled against the cliff over the sea. Amorgos lay at the outer circle of the Cyclades where, tugging against the adamantine chain, the last tortoise lay below the surf with the white island on its back.

Ikaria was not in the Mediterranean. It was Gauguin's Tahiti. At dawn the port of Ayos Kirakos was green. Then more pastel colors on the walls appeared until the full range of the French painter's palette was shining under fresh greenery that was everywhere. Water had visited this island. The women carrying water on their heads from the wells were clearly from the Asian Pacific. As we moved closer to shore, however, we heard the surprising sound of Greek. It was Hellas after all, another of the many Greeces I found from Alexandria and Crete to Aphrodisias in western Anatolia and Cappadocia deep in Asia Minor.

Albert had a hard time accepting this different beauty. *"Oú sommes nous?* Where are we? Till now I thought we were in Hellas." We settled into a café and no sooner were we eating our bread, butter, and lemon marmalade when he had his gouache pad out and was wetting the paper with colors. Helle took out her sketch pad and I mine. Helle liked to do both landscapes and portraits. We had a camera with us, but the pad took its place.

In voyages, figuring the next step is critical. Often it's the immediate conversation. In the woods there are two roads to take, or three or four. After Ikaria we were going to Samos, just off the Turkish coast, and the ship would leave from the city of Ikaria, on the northern coast. We decided to walk slowly across the big island, stay overnight in some village, and reach southern port city the next day. After stocking up on figs, tomatoes, cheese, sardines, and bread from the *fournos,* we walked up into the high center of the island.

Unlike Mykonos or Serifos, whose beauty is its stone aridity, its starkness in houses and fields, where the few trees and cultivated meadows stand out like flowers, Ikaria is lush with water and fertile fields. And mountains are not burnt ochre and rust but Vermont green. As all over the Mediterranean, olive and fig trees grow amidst the wheat. We walked a few hours on high slopes between barley and wheatfields. The wind cooled us.

"Watch where you're going, idiot!" Albert warned me, as I stumbled.

"You need a woman to put you in a better mood."

"I can afford so many tubes of paint, so many canvases and brushes, and right now, my quota of pretty women is very low. I'll have to sell a few more pictures before I can afford films and kisses."

"You Swiss miser."

"That's my Switzerland. You see why I'm in Greece."

"I bet you count the hairs on your face so you can somehow make a razor blade last a day longer," I insisted.

"Not bad. Not good either. But I'm a meticulous counter. A champion."

"Do you think we can afford to eat some figs?"

"So it will be Willis, the jailbird poet. Zoakos will cut your feathers," Albert warned me. "And you'll plunge into the sea like Ikaros." He liked to be cruel.

"Shut up."

"Don't be nervous. Helle and I will bring books and paper to your cell. A real poet needs a few months in jail."

"So does a real painter," Helle said.

"If it's that good, I'll volunteer. But will they take me? Why waste food on a Swiss?"

"Greeks are generous. You never know when a stranger is a disguised god," Helle said.

We walked much of the day, stopping for food breaks. In the evening the stars came out very big. There was no moon. According to our map we had still a few hours to go to the next village. We were in a very isolated center of the island. Helle couldn't find her glasses, which were lost someplace in one of the packs. Albert was very solicitous. "Don't fall, *petite feé.*"

"She's a Byzantine and nimble," I said. "She won't fall."

As a matter of fact, despite her myopia she was very nimble and danced along while Albert and I were clumsy, sometimes tripping as we crossed through fields in the dark night.

"I see the village!"

"Where?"

"To the right, over there."

"Over where?"

"Just over there," she said, pointing. "On top of the mountain."

"Those are stars."

At midnight we did find the village. In those days there were few hotels and in villages there was always one way to find a bed. Knock at a door. Greeks are hospitable beyond reason. And they enjoy the ritual of the stranger. It was impossible to walk down a village street without people pulling you into their houses to offer you coffee and fruit preserves with a glass of cold water. Especially in those days when with little money, years of disaster immediately behind them, people acted humanely and with curiosity. We knocked and asked where we could find a place. The sleepy woman, said *"Kaló írthete.* You arrived well. Forgive me while I kick the children out of the room."

Before sailing to Samos, we went by *kaiki* to a very small island named *Fourni* (Ovens). It was just a happy afternoon trip to a place no one goes except the people who live there. We were walking by a blacksmith's shop and walked inside. A giant of a man was pounding a square of white-hot iron. His undershirt was sweat. Out of the blue, I said to him, *"Den fováse to sídero?"* (Aren't you afraid of the iron?)

"The iron's afraid of me!" the giant said, and he smashed his hammer down on the burning block.

Next morning we were on the coast of southern Samos. We decided to spend the day walking to Kato Vathi, the capital. One beach where we swam was marble-smooth pebbles and stones and there was a small river feeding the shoreline. The wind used the sun to sweep and purify.

We were all in the water. Albert said, "This is like fresh water. No salt," Albert said.

"The sea's a lake," Helle shouted.

By nightfall we had hiked and swum our way across the island to Kato Vathi. As we explored the neighborhoods, we came upon a French monastery with a sign stating: WINERY FOR BENEDICTINE MISSIONS IN CENTRAL AFRICA. I rapped on the door and a sallow Dutchman appeared.

"Un moment, s'il vous plaît," and he disappeared. A few seconds later the father superior came to the entrance and, addressing Helle and me, asked, *"Vous deux, vous êtes vraiment mariés?"* (You two, are you really married?)

"Oui," I said.

"Pas de blague." (No kidding.)

"Pas de blague."

"Then you stay here with us."

Turning to the sallow monk, Father Alphonse ordered sternly, "Martin, prepare the rooms for our guests and then fix the supper." Addressing us again, he said, "Please, join me in a drink." And he brought out a bottle of muscatel wine.

Samos is the island of wines. "Drink deep the Samian wines," wrote Byron. The English poet, a hero in Greece, died at Missolonghi in the cause of independence and even today Byron remains a common given name. His poem on rich Samian wines, however, assumes one period of classical glory, and blackens out the rest. As for the sweet, rich Samian wine from the muscat or any alcohol, for me a little goes very far. I anticipated a long trip in the French mission.

The mission had two monks, Father Alphonse, a jovial Breton, and his gloomy slave, Martin, the Dutchman. After twenty-five years in the monastery, Brother Martin lost his fluency in Dutch—he told us pathetically that the people laughed at him when he went home a few years before when they heard him struggle through his native language; he never learned much Greek, since he left the mission only for shopping; and he spoke imperfect French. He was the jovial Breton's cook and housekeeper. I liked Martin for all his sad fate.

Alphonse was a *bon vivant.* He drank, had many Greek friends, and his main purpose during our visit was to keep us drunk. "You must drink. Water rusts the soul but wine renews it," he told us rhetorically. "Drink."

Being three weak-willed visitors, we obeyed. The muscatel was heavy, delicious, and lethal. Even the muscat grapes seemed to add to our stupor. I never before had wine at breakfast, a full breakfast which Martin laid out on a fresh, white cloth and decorated with flowers in Greek pitchers. He did his work well. As we sipped some sobering coffee, Alphonse sent

Martin into town on an errand. With us there alone, he settled down to serious talk.

"I confess I cannot stand Brother Martin. It's a sin, I know, but I don't feel it as a sin. I'm a happy man, and he makes me disgusted. I despise him. I should be a man of charity and he makes me stingy and cruel. But I think I will outlive him."

"You always struck me as stingy and cruel," I commented. "Look how wretched you have been with us."

"You're right. I'm a profoundly abusive person, and have no desire to change. God is writing it all down in his notebook."

"I'm beginning to feel sorry for you too."

"No, no. I'm not worth the pity," he struck back. "By the way my superiors in Paris sent me a big parcel of French classics. It's very depressing. I won't live to read them all, and don't want to read any of them anyway."

"Why not, *bon pére,"* Albert asked.

"They bore me. I like solitaire and bossing Martin around. I'm so good at it, recently I've got the Dutchman to pick up a stutter. But these books you have to take some away."

And the master of the monastery pressed Corneille, Balzac, and Proust on us. "They even sent me a book by Jean Paul Sartre. Those Fernandels in black dresses must think I'm a Communist."

Hapless sea captains were routinely halted in mythical days by sirens of the sea. The ships drifted while their captains were quizzed about Alexander the Great. Where was Alexander the Great? Have you forgotten him? Any wrong answer, any forgetting, would earn the crew the immediate sinking of their vessel. Maria's son Theodoros had his own versions of antiquity which he retold in a family way.

"So what happened to your papoús when his fishing boat was sinking?"

"Well, Kirie Willis, you know my grandfather used to go back and forth between Mykonos and Delos, and one afternoon there was a terrible storm and it flooded his boat with water and he was swept away from it."

"What happened?"

"He was a great swimmer but he was in the middle of nowhere."

"So he drowned?"

"If he drowned, how would I know what happened?"

"So he was saved?"

"Shut up, Kirie Willis. I'm trying to make sense and you're killing me."

"No, just torturing you."

"Anyway, Papoús saw a dolphin swimming near and he asked him to let him hang on to his back till they got to shore. The dolphin said sure, but when you reach the shore, you must remember to give me a push so I won't choke on the beach. Well, he swam with my grandfather to Delos and when Papoús reached the beach he was so happy he started to shout and ran into the middle of the island hoping to find someone to tell his story to. By the time he came back to the beach the dolphin who saved him was dead. Since then dolphins are very friendly, talkative, you can swim with them, but if you are drowning they will no longer take you on their backs and carry you to shore."

"Theodore, when you grow up, what are you going to do?"

"I'm going to be the cook for the president of Greece."

"You'll always eat well, huh?"

"The president will eat well."

Needless to say, in 1974 when Constantine Karamanlis came back to be prime minister after the fall of the colonels, Theodoros was his cook. It was quite a few years, however, before Karamanlis became president.

The investigation of my working papers was at a standstill. But slowly the bureaucracy kicked in. The officer from Syros came to investigate. The charge now was not the working papers. That one couldn't stick. It was more extreme. Lieutenant Karkavitsas was serious, but he skillfully avoided a confrontation by interviewing us separately. Zoakos had filed a charge that I had insulted his office by calling him *agrámatos,* a word I hadn't heard before but which I immediately understood to mean "without grammar or education." Worse, I had attempted to steal his handcuffs and lock him up in the cell next to his upstairs office. I talked to Karkavitsas about other things, our recent trip to Ikaria and Samos, and he wished me and Helle a good time in Greece. He was proper and clearly embarrassed. It made me feel very good. Either by design or accident on both our parts, we did not allude to my crimes. We parted.

I had some lingering doubts. Should I have defended myself against the outrages I committed in

"With Jorge Luis Borges in Bueno Aires, when I was Fulbright professor at the Profesorado,"
Argentina, 1975

Zoakos's eyes? It was a long beautiful summer. I carried the water jugs for Kiria Maria each morning, read, wrote, and with summer came some visitors to the islands, Greek writers who are close friends today as is Yannis Papadopoulos, now eighty, and as wise, young, and anecdotally amazing as when he was forty-two. But nothing came of the conflict with the police chief. Through enlightened neglect, there was no official report. I escaped the Greek jail. The teacher told me that Zoakos was still threatening and cursing me. The teacher was cursing Zoakos. And one evening all my students celebrated at the grocer's house, since the bully was being transferred—routinely perhaps, we had no information—to some place in northern Greece.

"May he eat shit and mayonnaise for breakfast," said Mr. Silvernose with the big belly.

"You're a grocer and want to make sure he has a nice healthy diet."

"Yes. My recipe should fit his constitution. He could live to a hundred on it."

So we drank to shit and mayonnaise and his being gone. I had lost a few nights sleep over the mess, but in those days, while emotions were deep—and that was good for the well of poetry—experience was neither cumulative nor wearying. Today, a bit of bureaucracy (an IRS audit or even waiting to hear from a publisher) leaves me less philosophical and prepared than I was in those days under the eye of the police chief who wished to get me.

Greece was Helle. She gave it to me. Not only by leading me to her country, but by being herself ancient, Byzantine, modern Athenian. And I loved her for being herself and a civilization. Greeks took me as American or Greek-American (most often) or, since I am from my wife's village, Greek. The latter Greek connection made me happiest. I adapt quickly to new cultures, learn the languages almost as quickly as a child (I should get some benefits from incorrigible childishness), and feel at home, not estranged. The immediate merging is especially right in France, Latin America, and Spain, where I "look" French, Latin American, or Spanish, but it has also held up in China. In China I knew many poets—Beijing's poets lived in our rooms during waking hours. That we were all of one clan gave us a commonality superceding origins and nationality.

Helle also gave me a blood identity with a culture, later fixed by having children who are my Greek blood relatives. The initial identity was not for having picked up ethnic prejudices—I had no desire to hate Turks or wartime Bulgarians as Serbs traditionally despise Croats and Croats Serbs. My obsession was with Greek history, ritual, Greek Orthodoxy,

popular music, popular dance, the poetry. I felt like a European poet, and specifically a Greek poet who wrote in English. My ideal reader was a Greek thoroughly fluent in American speech, who would also be a reader of the Greek poets. By extension, even now, as I think of having lived eleven years in Europe, the secret reader I would be grateful to meet on the page would know the work of the poets of Europe. Such feelings probably led me to do the Bantam volume *Modern European Poetry* that appeared in 1966.

Helle also gave me the open identity with a people which, as a Jew, was not so simple to have with Jews. I wish, in a nonrestrictive sense, it were possible to be a Jew as I am a Greek. (Given this good age, in my own mind I am improving at naturalness.) I know that when I translated for New Directions the volume of the mystical poet, Saint John of the Cross, son of a *converso*, or translated the *Song of Songs* (*Shir Hashirim*) with an Israeli linguist (in a book published by Kedros in Athens) or did the Harper and Row *The Other Bible: Jewish Pseudepigrapha, Christian Noncanonical Apocrypha, and Gnostic Scriptures*, I was discovering, as I do with Philo of Alexandria, Yehudah Halevi of Toledo and Córdoba, Franz Kafka, or Paul Celan, an identification with a literary word used by Jews. And that word has given me the clearest sense of kinship with a possible Jewish ethos—more than any vague memories and inventions of blood kin from Eastern Europe. I am an outsider. In a rare moment when I hear Kaddish or look at texts that I barely decipher despite seven years of inefficient childhood Hebrew or hear snatches of wild Yiddish klezma music, do I discover any deeper cello chords that I hear constantly because of my Greek connection. A fortune in my life has been to turn into a Greek.

Helle and I, a wandering Greek and a wandering Jew from the Western rim of Asia, we joke about our imagined earlier wanderers. For good or bad, they left in Europe and the world much of their civilization.

Athens in the autumn was literary, but by now I was very committed to painting. I had a fine studio in our Maroussi house and worked there every day, doing large paintings worthy of a child's vision. (Even in recent years when I have returned to dry-brush ink drawings and have illustrated some books—for example, *Laughing Lost in the Mountains: The Poems of Wang Wei* that my son Tony and I did for University Press of New England—my work is meticulous and primitive. Color planes in painting and poetry lure me, and I feel them in my veins.) To wake each day and go to a studio was a good life. It could be done and had all the attractive impossibility of a poet who could sit down each morning, turn on the spigot of inspiration, and write.

In that same autumn of 1950 I also began to translate fiction. Helle introduced me to Rita Liberaki, an excellent novelist whose books won literary awards in their French translations. She was Albert Camus's love in Greece. Camus also wrote a fully deserved, extraordinary blurb for her second novel, *Three Summers*. Helle and I began a translation of her novel *The Other Alexander*. We worked on it in the winter spring of 1952–1953 in Andalusia, the next year in London with Rita, and then again with Rita in Paris after she had moved to France. Nine years after we began the novel, Noonday Press brought it out.

One bright fall morning I was rushing around the Monasteraki area in downtown Athens—named for a small Byzantine chapel, but not nearly so small as one in Mykonos. When a captain, sailor, or fisherman came through a perilous sea storm, the Mykonian family erected a white chapel in the village or in the countryside. One poor family could afford only a small one, a few feet high, and they built it down at the harbor by the pier, adorning it with good icons and hangings. The islanders called it the dog chapel. Just as I got to Monasteraki itself, I saw Kimon Friar walking toward me, arm in arm with an older, stout gentleman. Kimon stopped and said he wanted me to meet George Seferis.

In Paris I had read the poet's *The King of Asine* in translation, strikingly rendered by Bernard Spencer, Nanos Valoritis, and Lawrence Durrell. I told Seferis how much I liked his poems in translation. And they do lend themselves as few poets do to the hand of master translators. Philip Sherrard and Edmund Keeley have done the complete Seferis and one can read the entire corpus in English with confidence in their English incarnation. One summer I read the collected poems in Greek three times through just because I cared so much for Seferis's poetry. That day, that first day, we spoke just a few minutes. I remember his smile.

The first day you meet a poet you love—George Seferis, Vicente Aleixandre, Luis Cernuda, Octavio Paz, Theodore Roethke, Jorge Luis Borges—stays with you forever. In the case of Aleixandre, who also had a romance with the child poet Aliki, we were in Madrid in 1952, in gloomy early-Franco years when the gray *policia armada* (the armed police), with their heavy tommy guns, were on every corner. The book Vicente Aleixandre gave me had a vanquishing title of his own darknesses and light, *Sombra del paraiso* (Shadow of Paradise), and on the fly page he wrote:

"A Willis Barnstone, en el primer dia de amistad." (To WB on the first day of friendship.)

I'm not sure the kindnesses of older poets persist into our time. I hope they do.

Later Kimon told me that Seferis was very cheerful that a young American poet already knew his work. That was touching but silly. How could I be in Greece and not read him? I was not that crazy.

In *Mythistorema* he wrote:

I woke with this marble head in my hands,
exhausting my elbows and I don't know where to
    put it down.
It was falling into dream while I was coming
    out of the dream
so our life became one and it will be very difficult
    to separate again.

I look at the eyes: neither open nor closed
I speak to the mouth which keeps trying to speak
I hold the cheeks which have broken through the
    skin.
I have no more strength left.

My hands disappear lost and come near me
mutilated.

Seferis had served as a diplomat in cities of the Near East, in Europe, and in Washington. His last post was as the Greek ambassador in London. In 1963 he was awarded the Nobel Prize in Literature. I think of Seferis in the period following the coup by the colonels in the late sixties. The poet was in New York and had just given an extraordinary reading at the Poetry Center. After the reading some members of the audience volunteered questions about the colonels and the Greek dictatorship. Seferis refused to respond, stating it was not the place to make his opinions known. He would do so in the proper place. There were some boos and much discontent. Seferis returned to Greece, and in 1969 called a news conference for foreign journalists, denouncing the junta, and asking for an end to oppression. From the outset he had joined the artists of Greece in their moratorium on publication, exhibition, and performance. As a result of his declarations to the foreign press, he was put under house arrest. When Italy accorded him its highest literary prize, he could not go to pick it up.

The last period I saw George Seferis began in December 1969, on the first evening he left his house publicly. It was at a private party in Athens and he had an introverted gaze that night—not the great smile. Though he was with friends, much of the evening he leaned over a big dining-room table, saying nothing. People were shy about interrupting his solitude and he exchanged only a few words with them. But he was a mysteriously important poetic presence and his silence spoke.

A few months later Seferis called me at noon and was a joking mortal again. He wanted to talk to my daughter Aliki, to talk over her poems with her, and say goodbye to us, since we were leaving Greece. When Aliki was ten she had her first poem accepted by *Poetry,* and two years later *The Real Tin Flower* was put out by Macmillan. In the preface to it Anne Sexton wrote, "Everything is within her range from Greece to El Greco to bubblegum." And she cited lines from a poem about her Greece which was blue and white:

> Blue is Greece
> where fishermen tame their boats
> and islands stand
> like white monastery birds
> on the Greek flag
> of spinning blue.

(I suppose my happiest moment as a writer with writer friends was when my daughter began as a child to publish her poems. Then I had a writer friend in my family, soon to be followed by Aliki's younger brother, Tony Barnstone, who did a volume with Wesleyan. I've always felt a mixture of gloom and calm in regard to the fate of my own work—but as for my children's things, I've been an insufferably proud collaborator.)

Seferis's call came less than a year before his own death, resulting from a botched ulcer operation he had been putting off. But at that moment in Athens, the poet had only one thing in mind. He was taken by my daughter and her *Tin Flower.* In his deep voice he said to me, "I don't want you to leave Greece before I say hello to Aliki, to the girl who wrote 'purple makes me want to blow my nose.'"

Distant Color

Purple is a funny color. It's maddening
and I hate it. It's icky. No one ever
cares for it

but El Greco. Sun is yellow and in Greece
I saw boats and the sea and white temples
and sweet air

but purple makes me want to blow my nose.
I only like it growing in the grass
as violets

yet feel sorry for purple, a very good friend
who paints lilacs and horizons and beards
like far mountains.

I published Seferis's poems in Friar's translations in *Modern European Poetry* and "The Cats of Saint

Nicholas" in Keeley's translation in *Eighteen Texts.* "The Cats of Saint Nicholas" was Seferis's last major poem and was an allegory for Greece in its period of darkness. The story of the cats is based on a book published in Paris in 1580, which tells of a monastery that the Duke of Cyprus built on a promontory in Cyprus in honor of Saint Nicholas. The duke imposed one condition: that the monks of the order of Saint Basil feed at least one hundred cats a day. In a period of drought the cats fought snakes and reptiles that were devastating the island; though the cats saved the island, they were themselves overcome from having taken in so much poison.

Kimon Friar had become my friend a few months earlier when I spent a week on the near island of Poros where he was living in a small house on the estate of Mina Diamantopoulou. He was engaged in his seven-year translation of Nikos Kazantzakis's epic poem *The Odyssey: A Sequel,* which was to make Kazantzakis a world figure. Kimon was born on the island of Pringipos in the Bosphorus as Kimon Kaloyeropoulos ("good old man" or "friar") and came to America when he was two. He taught at Amherst, fostered the poetry there of James Merrill, whose first book was published by Ikaros in Athens, *The Black Swan.* Kimon was always pleased to tell me that *he* was the black swan. In New York he founded the Poetry Center at the Ninety-second Street Y, did a seminal anthology of modern poetry with John Malcolm Brinnen, and then moved to Greece where he has remained for more than forty years, making known the poets of Greece in English translation. I remember one evening in Kimon's small studio house on Poros—the island off the coast of the Peloponnesos whose orange trees fill the sky like the Sirens' song. Mina had it built for him for his work. Kimon showed me correspondence with Ezra Pound who had refused to correct the mistakes in Ancient Greek words in the *Cantos;* so Kimon printed them with the errors, but noted the correct spelling in his annotations. He was clearly pleased by his own censorial scholarship, and it would have delighted Jorge Luis Borges who was less generous than Kimon in regard to Pound. Despite his nippity corrections of Pound's grammar, Kimon was a prince of generosity. His place in Athens was a home to me. As I write this he is sick and I fear for his recovery.

One word was said to me in the next days that altered what I have done with my years. The predominance of pure accident in shaping lives is a fact. Initially, we determine very few circumstances in our lives—not our birth, nor our parents, nor most early decisions. And then there is chance. Our lives are a roll of the dice of luck and failure. Having said this, I still think it essential to assume responsibility—even for chance. Philosophy speaks of kinds of will or the lack thereof. Although I was given a birth name which is a homophone of will-less, I rebuke myself or sometimes praise my actions for their failures. That helps me not to give up.

In Mykonos, arriving in the afternoon from Athens, as some of the summer ships did, was Jeffrey Graham-Bell, a South African with the famous acoustic name. We were friendly. Albert had very funny things to say about Jeffrey because of his parodic snobbery. One long evening at a party in Maroussi, Albert dozed off in his chair. He was in the corner of the living room and he woke just long enough to shout to Jeffrey, *"Chante, barbu."* (Sing, bearded one.) On the fatal day of chance, Graham-Bell walked upstairs into my studio while I was painting. It was about noon. I remember it very well. The evening before I had been reading the surreal love sonnets of Miguel Hernândez. I wrote a ballad in Spanish that same night that later appeared in *From This White Island*. Jeffrey really didn't enter the studio. He stuck his nose in, looked at the painting I was doing, and said "Ugh." Nothing else. Not even a complete word. "Ugh" did the trick.

I don't remembering thinking about the comment. It was enough to reach me, however. I ceased painting. Of course there were regrets. And I cannot blame Graham-Bell for what should have concerned *my* will. I could also have regretted that after translating a novel I did not immediately write my own rather than wait thirty years to do so. And another hundred second roads not taken. Regret is worth nothing. I return to my original fortune in finding, at the age of twenty, the center of a life, poetry, and sticking to it. Every good or terrible journey has fed it. Joy and pain instigate it. I have no complaints. Whatever questions there are of publication, recognition, and all the literary hocus-pocus in a writer's years, I have had the luck of a raja. I wrote and did so with faith, and do so now. Beyond that are perhaps nice public rewards, but not paradise. If there is one, it resides only in the creation. And invisible friendship with a secret reader.

So my sometime pal from South Africa helped to center me, to give me one. I thank him.

Winter was here. Despite the weather, we decided to go into the heart of the Peloponnesos and work our way up north. Winter adds another layer of reality to Greece, a working harshness fed by bright light while Persephone's cries are still heard from the underworld. We took a ship to the port town of Monomvasia and a dawn bus toward Olympia. After we got on the road, the ticket collector sat in the back and he and the driver sang antiphonally. The bus was a chapel. Those old postwar songs had an Asian Minor pathos that later better times could not engender.

"Where are you going?"
"To Olympia."
"You have relatives there."
"No."
"Business?"
"No."
"Why are you going to Olympia?"
"To see it."
"Strange things."

Our alibi was no good. No one on the bus believed we were going to a village, in winter, at dawn, just to look at ruins.

There was no hotel anywhere near Olympia. We walked an hour to the site and had the columns and the River Alphaeus to ourselves. Pindar's odes sang resonantly about every event of boxers, charioteers, discus throwers, and sprinters before the gaze of the supreme referee, marble Apollo, but his athletes were now bones scattered under the black earth. Some have been there since 776 B.C. when the first Olympic games were held. Not far from the temple of Zeus, I found an enormous lion head with its face pressed into the ground. It was ignominious. I spent the whole morning shoving and rolling the lion head about sixty feet to a marble base next to erect columns of varying heights. Using the genius of Archimedes's levers, we succeeded in sitting the lion head up on the base so it could observe the frozen solitude of Olympia.

(Twenty years later in summer Olympia, jammed with guests staying in new nearby hotels, it was good to find postcards in the shops, displaying our lion on its base. Next to the temple columns the real beast remained constant, peaceful, and sanctified in place through untold centuries of residence.)

That evening we found a peasant house not very far from the site.

"Like to play cards?" our host Stratos asked the three of us.

"Sure," I said, speaking for the team.

"It's been so cold lately, even my goats are bellyaching."

"Roll a few cigarettes and let them light up. They'll get warm."

"I'm a rare Greek who doesn't smoke."

"Yes, but you can be sure the goats do."

Stratos didn't burn tobacco but he filled the fireplace with a formidable fire. Then he gave us animal hides as blankets and we slept a long deep night on the floor next to the flames.

There was no paved road to Hosios Loukás. In this Byzantine monastery on the way to Delphi, the two-hour walk from the highway to the monastery was divided into two paths two hundred meters apart: one for going, on the left; and one for leaving, on the right. The way traversed meadow after meadow, and the walkers and those on donkeys or mules called greetings to each other as they came near and passed by. We were greeted with *"Na pate me ton theo,"* (May you go with God), a hymn which hung in the air as it drifted from path to path. We picked mint and sage on the way. Nothing is as invigorating as walking in sunny winter in the Greek mountains.

Hosios Loukás has a great Pantokrator Christ in its main entrance, a very Greek God who would do well as sea captain of a vessel in the War of Independence. His spirit is worldly and severe, a mosaic man accustomed to giving orders and having them obeyed as he glares down on his mortal flock. And yet there is some Apollonian beauty in his face. The marble of antiquity always penetrates the Byzantine paint and mosaic chips. Only the Pantokrator's human attendants and disciples, Saint Peter, Saint Mark, the Archangel Gabriel, and the Virgin Mary, are all mind and only modestly corporeal. As we moved around the eleventh-century church, the monks eagerly waited for conversation with us. There were very few guests in those days, and in the winter none.

"You will stay with us?"

"Of course."

"You will stay with *me,* in my cell," said Brother Petros, "and I will cook you a good meal and you will teach me how to tango. I have records and a player." And indeed he did.

We were sitting outside in the patio. The most energetic of our hosts was Mitsos, the cook. He engaged us in conversation, although the other monks tried, goodnaturedly, to shoo him away.

"Trelós einai, ma kalós" (He's crazy but good), Petros said to me in a low voice, which Mitsos could probably hear. "We felt sorry for the poor devil, so we took him in to cook for us."

I agreed that Mitsos looked a bit mad, but then Petros was no boring saint.

"We have been through war after war," the friar cook began, "and all the generals are still alive. So we will go through another war after war, everywhere in the world. But I have a plan and you must take it to the United Nations and threaten to kill everyone

there or at least have them eat wood if they don't put my plan into operation."

Albert nudged Helle to ask him for the secret plan.

"It can't fail."

"But what is it?" Helle queried.

"It can't fail."

"Okay, it can't fail. Now what is it?"

"You want to know?"

"Mitso!" I shouted. "Stop and talk!" But I wasn't at all impatient. We had to play the game or the story would be no good. Mitsos drew us into his conspiracy masterfully. Finally, he saw he had worked us up enough to be worthy of the revelation.

"Here's my plan. Catch every word of it, since you must report it accurately. You begin by getting all the bombs in the world, every single one, and every bullet in the world from every country and hamlet, even from the Eskimos, electricians, and orange pickers, and then ship in every sword and rocket and warplane and tank and battleship, old and new, from Russia and America and Bolivia, and put them all in one huge pile, with dynamite and TNT and gunpowder and gasoline, in a pile so big it reaches above the holy clouds."

"Yes?"

"You look at it," Mitsos said. He was so excited by his own story he could hardly control himself. He started to walk in swift circles, yanking at his belt, and pulling his hat down over his braided hair. Mitsos's eyes now were as ferocious as the Pantokrator's.

"What do you mean, you look at it?" I said.

"You look at it and think what it all means."

"But you must do more," I said.

"Of course you do more, you idiot, pardon me, my dear guest. Of course you do more. Do you think I would bring you this far just to look at a pile of gigantic destruction? You call on me and I take out a match, light a rag torch, hurl it as far as I can into the pile, run like a demon, and BOOM, an explosion big enough to blow a hole through heaven, and we have peace!"

After Mitsos, no one could compete. But Petros was very eager. He was kind and absolutely obsessed with learning the tango from these foreign experts. Helle was from Athens, which also made her a *xeni* today. So at nightfall we went to his rooms, his cell, and after dolmades, retsina, and powdery kourabiedes, we briefly looked at his precious personal library, photographs of his brothers and sisters, and danced. Following his instructions, Albert and I danced with Helle first, and he observed, diagraming the steps so they would be permanently in his notebook. Then he would dance with our authentic Argentine female.

"Now it's my turn," Petros said. He was very short, and as he seized Helle's waist he bent his head very low, looking down intensely at their feet so as not to miss one magic movement of the tango.

Brother Petros was happy and excited. Well, we were tango masters for several hours. The mountain evening was cold, and his coal brazier didn't do much. But we were dancing, dancing Argentine. He had the volume as loud as the poor machine could shoot out the 1930s voice of Carlos Gardel.

After Hosios Loukás, Delphi, which we reached by way of a perilous road through blue mountains, was peaceful antiquity. At the site there was a guard in the museum and Patrick Lee Fermor, the English novelist hero who during the occupation had captured the German general in command of Crete. Fermor who had been living in Crete took the general to a secret rendezvous where a British submarine spirited the German off to England and safety. Fermor, an English aristocrat, spoke and sang Cretan dialect songs like a native, and was able to capture the general by passing for a Cretan peasant. He has lived his life in Greece, now in the Mani, the austerely beautiful southeast of the Peloponnesos.

Whenever I go to Delphi—and these days of crowds have deprived Delphi of its peace—I think of its Bronze Charioteer, now in the Athens Museum, who is preserved in his entirety because of having had the luck of being toppled by an ancient earthquake. Since the Charioteer was a victory statue for a Syracusan prince and the sacred property of the god Apollo, he merited a worthy burial and thereby escaped the iconoclastic wrath of the Christian emperor Theodosius II, who in A.D. 426 ordered all pagan temples destroyed. The Charioteer was not a god, but a professional athlete. Yet no athlete could win a race with his poise. His dark eyes of bone and semiprecious stone are not glancing at the competitors. And no statue of Aphrodite or Apollo has deeper grace. What is a Greek god after all? They are modeled entirely on human beings—idealized, yes, but their model could be the Charioteer. If he were not holding the reins but a sceptre, wore less clothing and had a less beautiful headdress, this handsomest man of antiquity could have been standing on Mount Parnassus, adding tales to Homer's books. As it is, he is a challenge to the gods, not because he is like them, but because they are like *him*. The gods, however, are stained by immortality and myth, reducing that total humanity which is his.

In Thessaloníki (Salonika) we rested from our hiking and wandering. We had climbed the steep

steps at Meteora to reach the monasteries on their stalactite summits. Albert was outrageously irreverent to an El Greco Saint Jeromelike father superior with whom we shared our provisions one stormy night in high Meteora. As we entered the fabulous building, perched in isolation on nature's tower mountains, we were greeted by the tall white-haired saint. Albert smiled and said, *"Bon jour, mon père,"* tapping the stern patriarch on the belly. After a flash of hesitation, the patriarch burst into laughter and we were set for an evening of history and reminiscence. I recall the monastery toilet, a tiny room which extended precariously over the mountain. The whole room trembled as you entered it. As I flipped open the cover to the wooden box toilet, the howling night rushed up at me. Sitting on its wooden box was like riding a gale of noise and skies of darkness.

Here now in Salonika, we were in the city with the old Spanish ghetto. Before the war most of the Jews in Greece lived in Salonika. As in Warsaw the Nazis built a wall around the Jewish quarter, and killed all but a few. The Jews were all Spaniards. Borges has a sonnet on old Spanish Jews who remember Toledo and the Romans.

A Key in Salonika

Arbarbanel, Farías or Pinedo,
Hurled out of Spain in an unholy sweep-
ing persecution, even now they keep
The doorkey of an old house in Toledo.
At last, from hope and terror they are free
And watch the key as afternoon disbands.
Cast in its bronze are other days, far lands,
A weary brilliance, a calm agony,
Now that its door is dust, the instrument
Is cipher of diaspora and wind
Like the other temple key someone flung high
Into the blue (when Roman soldiers bent
And charged with dreadful flames and discipline)
And which a hand received into the sky.

In Salonika the Jews spoke Greek and their maternal tongue, Ladino (Latin), which is a Spanish cut off from Spain after 1492, the year of the expulsion. Before the war, only in Epirus were there about one thousand Jews from antiquity who had not been Hispanized. These were the descendants from the earliest diaspora which began after the dispersal of the Jews into the Near East following the end of the Babylonian Captivity in the sixth century B.C. It was they who invited Paul into their synagogues of Antioch and Thessaloníki to preach to them and make them into the new sect of Christian Jews who were to multiply and take over Europe. Four survived of these original diaspora Semites. A few years ago, when I saw the Auschwitz tattoo on the arm of the guardian of the Yannina synagogue in Epirus, I said to him, "How did you survive?"

He looked at me severely and declared, *"Dioiti O Theos ton ithele."* (Because God wanted it so.)

Our next destination was Mount Athos.

Helle went to Kastoriá, Albert and I to Mount Athos, the holy mountain at the southern tip of the Halkidiki peninsula in Macedonian northwestern Greece. We had to split since no females, not even female domestic animals, are permitted in Athos.

The way to Athos was an odyssey. A small *kaiki* took us there. Each morning the gales threw our black sails against the sun and we slid ahead, almost invisibly. With bad weather we made only short distances, and from Salonika to the peninsula required four days on the sea. At night we anchored in tiny harbors or camped on abandoned beaches. One night we slept in a lodge. At dawn the sky took on the colors of a bloody Barbary fig.

On the *kaiki* there was a village storyteller and all through the trip he told his tales to the passengers. On deck, under a black-and-red wool blanket, I listened to the war adventures, the village dramas, the comic and dirty stories. He was a one-man playhouse. Even today when I find a blanket at all resembling my Greek wool one (which I lost in France when it fell from the back of my motorcycle), I'm back on the boat, wet, cold, happy, with my ears filled with oral drama.

The boat left us a few hours from the mountain area of Athos. Although the civil war had been formally over for more than a year, here and in parts of Crete there was some guerrilla activity. We were on mules and horses in a convoy through the snow into the forested area above us. The lead horse and rear horse each carried a soldier with his weapon held in readiness. I didn't think there was any danger of an ambush, yet I saw faces who appeared from nowhere and disappeared. We reached Daphni, a small port on the coast, and climbed very high into Athos.

Albert could stay only a few days, but I remained there a month. We stocked up on provisions at the general store. The monks refused to accept money. There were no visitors in those days. And then we went to a nearby Romanian monastery. Athos or Hagion Oros (Holy Mountain) is the center of medieval Orthodoxy and has sketes and monasteries representing Bulgaria, Romania, Serbia, and Russia. Some are poor, others rich. The monks have their plots of land to grow vegetables, fruit, and olives, and they are largely self-sufficient. The first night we opened sardines of our own to go with cold beans, bread, and vinegared wine.

On the first day of wandering Athos, I met a Russian hermit prince as I walked around a tall hedge. We exchanged greetings. The prince looked like Tolstoy (on Mykonos I had been close to Tolstoy's grandson Alexander, the French linguist) and he spoke impeccable British English. We went to his little hermitage and shared some bread and liqueur. It was all strangely matter-of-fact. He was perfectly at ease in his hermitage, and had no regret for lost estates or homeland or sophisticated company. I wondered what lay behind his imperiously good manners, his cheerful resignation, and wisdom. As in a story by Borges, when the seeker finds the jaguar with the invisible script on it or the Indian god in the desert or the poet with the word in the Chinese court, the author, Borges, stops, since no one can sanely blurt out words of truth. The unknown, if it is worthwhile, must remain unknown and not cheapened by explanation and summary. So I assumed there to be that huge spirit, with its keys and enigmas, into which the Russian hermit might retreat or experience at will. Perhaps it was my desire that the

Barnstone giving a poetry reading in the 1970s

spirit be there. In any case, here was a man serenely himself. He was a prince in his own room.

In the evening there was a ceremony at Lavra. The monks were in magnificent vestments. The chapel was incense, ikons, silver goblets. It was very dark and yet brilliant, the singing faces lighted as in a Mannerist tableau. My eyes fixed on one blond monk who was beardless. In his robes and the long uncut hair characteristic of all Greek clergy, he was clearly a strange angel. His eyes were fixed on the ceiling as he and the others sang the Christmas hymns.

Entranced as I have rarely been by ceremony, by the sonorous illumination of the singing monks, I thought of a much more extreme form of utopian community: the Essenes holding out on their mountain retreat at Masada by the Dead Sea. These Greek Orthodox monks, mainly of the order of Saint Basil, had gone as far as they could: to a mountain at the bottom of a peninsula in order to shun the world. The Essenes chose a mountain in the desert. The renunciation of monks at Athos, however, was tempered by centuries of their acceptance and the accumulation of art and instruments of comfort, while the Essenes and their Dead Sea scrolls and their Teacher of Righteousness fell before the long Roman assault, though not before their literate guardians deposited scriptural scrolls for storage in tall clay jars at Khirbat Qumran near the Dead Sea. Many writers must wait a long time before they are read. The Gnostics and Essenes, at Nag Hammadi in Egypt and Qumran by the Dead Sea, waited two millenia, for light to pick up their words and deposit them in books and museums.

Going Muleback in the Snow on the Holy Mountain of Athos after the Civil War and Thinking Back to Masada

Going muleback in the snow to the monasteries on the holy peak, I see
some rebel *kleftes* hiding from the drawn
weapons of the soldiers. When they spot me,
they fade. The forest groans. Once with the monks
they give me vinegared wine, bread, a bed
of straw on wood, and guide me to the crypt
where oil lamps by the icons show the blood
of converts sworn to parables and script
about some Essenes from the wilderness
who scorned the Roman weapons and were drunk
with faith and towering awe. Light gilds the hair
of one young beardless monk whose gaze and dress
mark ancient Zealots in their rebel prayer.

Albert left and I went to the great Russian skete.

The skete was a major monastery in Russian Orthodoxy, but since the monks were largely pre-1917, there were only sixty there, most of them old,

except for some Greek monks who began to fill the uninhabited cells. There was a large stone wall surrounding the skete, and just as I was about to go inside I saw a strange Greek monk, pissing against the wall. It was cold in the snow and he was wearing torn galoshes, with no stockings, which I took to be neglect rather than poverty. When he eyed me, he turned around, shoved his penis back in its proper shelter, and said, "Come to my hermitage. We'll eat fish."

He saw me hesitate. To assure me, he said, "Don't be scared. It's close by and the fish came right out of the sea this morning."

I went with him. This hermitage was a mosaic gem. The walls were rich with Christian mythology. When we entered, Brother Spiros yanked open the door, looked to his right, and shouted, "*Siko epano!*" (Up on your feet!) to a sleeping monk, his roommate. The man popped up like a mechanical toy, his feet remaining straight on the stone slab where he had been sleeping, while his torso and head moved mechanically and quickly into a vertical posture. "*Vrey Yanni, aftos einai o filosmos.*" (Pal Yanni, this is my friend.)

We shook hands.

Yannis seemed to match Spiros in wit. After the Russian cosmos, we were back on earth. Spiros went to work preparing the meal, and Yannis rushed outside into the snow, forgetting to put on his galoshes which he had kicked off into the corner, but he came back almost immediately with a pail of water, and in the cold water were his fish.

Yannis stuck his hand into the water, pulled out a thrashing fish, and said, in English, "Good fishes. My friend catch them. What's your name? My name is Johnny. I washed dishes in Detroit."

"Why did you come back to Greece?"

"The crash. Many come back 'cause of the crash."

"Why Athos?"

"I got a brother here. And I like good life. He got me in. He got me this house and this servant monk who's my friend and he listen to me. I like good life."

I couldn't shut Yannis up after the explosion in English. But I did show rare discipline and soon went back to the Russian skete to insure my lodging. They gave me a very fine room in their own quarters, where I set up the books I had lugged with me but had not been able to read, and took a nap. I was glad to know I had a place to stay for a few weeks. In the past weeks I saw so much, I needed to stop. I wanted to walk, but walk nowhere except for the walk, wanted to read, and perhaps to write. I guess those have been my real activities. Walking, reading, writing. Borges told me once that being blind gave him the opportunity to think. He could now sit on a bench or a chair and wait and think, and not feel the need to fill his time with doing and planning other things. I had or haven't reached such a plane of undirected meditation. Sometimes in the shower I think I am just thinking, with no necessary purpose. And I stay there until the hot water threatens to turn me into a peaceful rag.

At three in the afternoon there was a knock at the door, and a tall courtly monk in red-black robes, with a Tatar face, set a glass tray with food down on the table in front of my bed. I was honored. I didn't dare say I had just eaten lunch. In fact I couldn't say much, because he spoke no Greek, French, or English, and in Russian I could only utter *da* and *nyet,* "yes" and "no." Clearly we were destined to be famous friends. When he smiled, all of Central Asia spilled from his mouth.

When the Tatar left, I ate the second meal with no trouble, relishing the black Russian bread, and began to read the collected poems of Emily Dickinson. By eight o'clock I was a little hungry but my friend had not returned. There was no one in the halls. I heard snoring from many rooms. Could they have all gone to bed so early? Indeed they had. There was some misunderstanding perhaps. I could find no dining room and no one awake. Then at eleven-thirty, there came the tattoo calling the faithful to prayer. The player had a wooden stick which he beat against a block of wood in musical rhythm, a beat that came near and retreated as he moved near my room on our floor, and then, far but piercingly, on the floors below and above. The beat was once explained to me by George Gabor, the percussionist with Pro Musica Antiqua, who assured me that its complication was real, intricately good, and important in the history of sound. I found it haunting compensation for my hunger.

In the morning I needed the sun again. I roamed about, found one of the Greek monks who lived in the Russian skete, and he explained that my supper would come at two-thirty or three because by four everyone went to sleep so they could wake and be ready to descend into the crypt by midnight where they would pray until eight in the morning. As at most of the twenty cenobitic monasteries at Athos, the monks ate separately, not communally where the gospel is read aloud from a central table to silent-eating monks.

For the next few days I tried and failed to convey to my Tatar friend that we should find some other system for supper. I tried to say with gestures that I could perhaps go elsewhere for supper, but there

were no restaurants on Athos, or way of paying someone to leave me something. Nyet. Yet there was understanding. On the third day Brother Mihaili came not at three but at one. He had a big smile and I expected the worst. He led me to a grand banquet hall. Then he gave me the key and explained that he would leave the food at the central seat of the U-shaped banquet tables, and there, under large pictures of the tzar and the tzarina, he would leave the food for my supper which I could eat at any time I wished. I was thrilled. Suppers at three in the afternoon, unless we were in Lapland, were problematic. They were treating me like a Russian prince, though I had had no conversation with any member of the monastery other than Mihaili the Tatar and that was restricted to yes, no, and gestures.

I read Dickinson. I read John Hersey's *Wall,* and then, for liberation from walls and rooms, I read the Greek poets. For reading all night I had been prepared during those months in the orphanage in Mexico, behind the gate or in the street restaurants, and now, unwise of course and impatient, I was adding to the book of memory at least one winter peacefully amid monks and snow.

One morning before my regular supper there was a knock at the door. A Greek-speaking monk was there. After a week of speaking to no one, being forced to spend much time thinking, not just filling time with worthy activities, here was someone speaking Greek, my language. Curiously, despite years of study and fourteen months of China, my spoken Chinese was never marvelous. Yet in Turkestan and Tibet, where I cared for the people immensely, when someone could speak Chinese again it was almost as if there were the communication ease of English.

The Greek monk told me that a Russian novelist wanted to speak to me. He had heard I spent my days reading and writing and was curious.

"I must warn you about Brother Sasha, however."

"What is it?"

"Kirie Willis, he's a clubfoot."

"What do I care? I don't care if he's a clubfoot or a hunchback together. So much the better. Now, he's not the local hangman?"

"You are joking and I am serious."

"I'm sorry."

"But he has something else wrong with him."

"Spill it."

"He will ask you to send him things when you get back to America."

"What does he want?"

"He'll ask you for a Baby Ruth. He misses them, he says. Before he became a monk he visited your country and ate Baby Ruths."

"I'm glad you warned me."

The next afternoon I was escorted to Brother Alexander's cell. I went inside. The door closed behind me. I was sitting before a very sour-faced Russian monk who spoke excellent English. He had traveled everywhere, had several lives, and these last years of exile were on Mount Athos.

"I'm Sasha."

"I'm Willis."

"I do not like my fellow monks. They are for the most part ignoramuses. But that's my fate." As he spoke his face fell into an ugly form which spoke the truth of his unhappiness.

"I wish you could be happy."

"But I am happy. I am a novelist." And he showed me a shelf of some eight or nine thick, bound, book-length manuscripts. "This is my life's work."

"Have you published the novels?"

"I am a Russian exile and now a monk in Greece."

"So what will you do?"

"God is my publisher."

"You mean he's your reader?"

"My publisher too. He will not let these Russian works turn into worm food."

"What will happen to this monastery?"

"There will be more Russians, but we must wait another thirty years. After another thirty years there will be nobody in Russia to pull a trigger. Not even the police will do so. And the Kremlin and the Secret Police and the army will flatten into nothingness. Listen to me. It will take thirty years, but then it will be gone as if it had never been there. The statues will disappear. The city names will change. I will be dead. But new monks will come. Though I will not be sad, especially in my grave, even if new Russian monks do not come. It's lonely here."

"Do you know the Russian hermit prince?"

"He is my one reader, apart from that one," and he pointed to the ceiling. "And to tell you the truth, I prefer the prince, since the one up there makes me nervous. I've never known for sure what he thinks about artists."

At this point, I felt I owed Sasha something and didn't care about the warning. "Is there anything I can do for you?"

"You can't publish my Russian novels, I know."

"Anything else?" I was asking for it.

"They have told you I'm sure about my fetish. Some people like shoes, some adore women's breasts. Mine you already know."

"Baby Ruth."

"Yes."

At the end of January we were all back in Athens. By February bureaucracy had caught up with us again. Helle and I were married civilly in Paris. The American government recognized this marriage and gave Helle a visa in her passport to enter the United States. The Greek government also recognized that I was married to her, but since we did not have a religious marriage in the Greek Orthodox church, and Orthodoxy is the state religion, it did not recognize that she was married to me. Therefore, they would not issue an exit visa for foreign travel. In those days only Greek students and businessmen were granted exit visas. This onerous restriction was an attempt to prevent hard currency from leaving the country. It succeeded in reducing foreign travel by its citizens.

In our case the most obvious way to circumvent the visa problem was to marry in the Greek Orthodox church. I had reservations, but if this was forced upon us, what else could we do? Vassili called the Athens bishop, who had once been his patient.

"My son-in-law, an American, wants to marry my daughter in the Church," I heard him saying on the phone.

"How can he be your son-in-law and marry her again? Isn't that bigamy?"

Vassili laughed. "No, my bishop, they were married in a civil ceremony in Paris. Now we want a church marriage."

"Very good. I will do it myself for my doctor friend."

"Thank you. Oh, by the way he's a Jew."

"No thank you. It's impossible." And he hung up.

"That was short and sweet," Vassili told me. "So much for the bishop." Vassili had no more love for the clergy than he did for the monarchy.

"What next?" I asked.

"Go to some other city, as you did for your visa to get into Greece. But not as far as Genoa."

Helle and I talked over every angle. I was glad to have to stay in Greece longer. A second year was already getting language, friends, and places deeper in place. But we had to have the option of leaving. Crete was the most tempting destination. I longed to go to Amorgos and the Dodekanese, not to mention Mani and Epirus. But Crete had many cities, and one straight road connecting everything horizontally. Besides, there was the labyrinth at Knossos and the

Minoans. So we took an overnight boat and rocked our way like Allan Bates on his way to meet Zorba.

Hanniá is one of the most attractive smaller cities in Greece. Nafpleon and Nafpontos are others. Relentlessly Venetian, it is port, snakey streets, Greek-Italian mansions. Red is the color of many buildings, an Italian memory. Lingering in Hanniá— its harbor cafés and walking the cobblestone amphitheatre curve of the port itself—is a distinguished occupation. But we left the lovely city quickly, for we had a mission, and took a bus going west. After a few hours we were both dozing—even the beauty of Crete will not keep you awake all the time, though shutting your eyes when traveling through that land is folly. Suddenly we heard gunshots and pellets came flying into the open windows.

"What is it?"

"Walnuts," Helle said.

"Walnuts?"

"Everyone out of the bus," a man was ordering the driver. He was carrying a rifle.

"What's going on?" I asked the driver.

"A baptism."

"Do they make war when they baptize?"

"No, they eat and they dance."

So all of the passengers on the bus got out, joined the circular Cretan dances, made lots of noise, sat down and feasted, and an hour later we were on our way again. No one complained.

Crete was so lovely in this moment when spring comes. It comes not quite as early as in Andalusia, that is, in December when the Málaga almond trees blossom, coinciding with the coldest moment of the year as well as the winter solstice. We were in Greek February and all the fruit trees were frolicking serenely. We asked the driver to let us out at some small village. It looked nice. We didn't know the name.

The road lay above the village which extended down a long fertile valley and eventually to more meadows and the sea. We started along the sloping main village road. Before we knew it there were cries from women: *Xeni!* "Foreigners! Who's going to put them up?" We didn't get very far, since people insisted on drawing us into their open doorways and feeding us mezedes, coffee, and water. As in China, water is a fundamental drink, though in China it comes in thermoses and is hot. Greece is the country of cold fresh water.

Three sisters in black finally cornered us. We had to stay with them. We couldn't argue. We went inside. The bareness of the living room, the large white wall spaces with a few choice pieces of furniture make Greek houses beautiful. The nakedness of the

outer white geometries is repeated in the interior. There is a natural taste. The interior of Greek peasant houses and sophisticated new ones is designed to make a plain internal sculpture of light and wall space match the exterior play of lines. In this house, however, there was a dramatic digression. The living room mirror was covered, a black cloth draped over it. A death in the family.

The sisters' brother had been through ten years of war, from 1940 through 1949, and was never wounded. At last he came home for good. One day while picking olives from their olive trees, he slipped off the ladder, fell to the ground, hitting his head against a rock, and was killed instantly. So there were three sisters and the mother, already a widow, all in black. But we had a good time. They prepared a special chicken dish for us. After supper we played *tavli* at which I was no good but Helle an avid player. We didn't tell them our mission of marriage and how we were already married. Yet I think if we had explained that the government was obliging us to do something ridiculous, they would have been in sympathy and fully believing.

In the morning the sister who was silent was up earliest. She brought the ironing board into our room and began to iron the family's clothes. Her name was Elektra. She had an amazing beauty. Her eyes were large and peaceful. Her classical nose fashioned by Phidias, strong but more gentle than the Parthenon sculptor's faces. The black dress set off her marble features. And when she smiled there was a quiet eroticism of the sea.

But Elektra said nothing. We didn't speak to her but we did exchange glances. One of her younger sisters told me casually when I stepped outside to eat an orange for breakfast, Elektra didn't speak. They didn't know if she was smart or dumb, but she had never spoken. She was not deaf and had no apparent speech defects. At the market she pointed at what she wanted and pronounced numbers, very clearly and naturally. Those were her only spoken words. The family was so adjusted, as was Elektra herself, to the beautiful woman who was unspeaking that they scarcely noticed, or didn't appear to notice, anything out of the ordinary.

We left this family reluctantly. Elektra kissed us both. And we took a bus to one of the towns, and stopped at the first church. Everywhere it was the same. You must spend six months studying how to be a Christian and then come back, or nothing doing, or we don't know what to tell you, or wait till the bishop comes and we will ask him. In Greece there is negligible anti-Semitism compared to most of Europe. A boy may hit a donkey with a stick and shout *evréo,*

Jew, to make the animal move, but have no idea what the word in that linguistic tradition means. Such a boy on the island of Spetsais had rented me a donkey for the afternoon and was helping me to get it started on its walk by cursing it with *evréo*, which I'm certain he felt was a courteous way of helping a stranger. But the church had no experience, or didn't in my uncomplicated case, in marrying a Jew to a Greek Orthodox.

So after reaching Irakleion and the museum housing Sir Arthur Evans's restorations of the Minoan wall paintings and in Knossos the labyrinth itself, the work of Daedalus who had also fabricated the fatal wax wings for his son Ikaros, we gave up, and went back to Athens. As before our journey I remained, in Greek eyes, legally married to Helle, and she remained a sinner living unmarried to me. As Cavafy might have said, as he did say about Odysseus and Ithaki, Crete gave us the trip and we were not cheated, and now we knew what journeys to Crete were all about. Moreover, we had seen the labyrinth, chatted with the bull and with its horns in the maze's very center, and learned that labyrinths are constructed, even by masters like Daedalus, primarily for purposes of escape.

George Orwell was really down and out in *Down and Out in Paris and London*. He was attracted to that life and wrote about those more down and out

"Our children Robert, Aliki, and Tony in Turkey"

than he. Even then his earlier experience told him that his plight was momentary. In his terms I've never been really down and out. I went to Mexico and sold blood, and to Mykonos with the need to pick up room-and-board money someway on the island. But I never worried about it, about food, or where I'd sleep, even though I slept on many floors in many countries. And I'm glad I didn't fret, since when you're young you should be broke, and nothing in my past, even my father's bankruptcies, had given me any fears. I shared Orwell's attraction to real down-and-outs. I also felt sympathy and compassion for them, notions I scarcely saw in Orwell's work. Their absence doesn't mark meanness in the Englishman but Orwell the writer's hardnosed style. He wouldn't be caught in any old-fashioned sloppy emotions.

Maroussi was the town down the road from Mount Penteli where our house, with its vineyard and sixty cypress trees, was. At the bottom of the road was a small restaurant, with a roast on turning spit, and the men sitting on a few wooden tables in front. There, sitting on the ground, was Babi, a blind beggar musician from a town in Anatolia up near Trapezon, by the Black Sea. I began to speak to him. He stopped after a while and sang. People greeted him. He was as well known as the mayor of Maroussi, then not much more than a town.

During the two years we had been living in Vassili's country place, I often walked the few miles down Penteli into Maroussi. Penteli (pronounced Pendeli) still had the mines from which marble was quarried in antiquity. The island of Paros (where was born Archilochus, Europe's earliest lyric poet, surpassed only perhaps by Sappho) and the mountain of Penteli gave their marble to ancient columns and statues. The classical period dynamite for breaking the marble was water placed in strategically drilled holes, which in the cold of winter would expand and crack the marble into useful blocks. Although we still heard an occasional blast as the old mines were ravaged for their remaining good stone, in the last years Penteli was a center for sanitariums. In those days there were no antibiotics to cure tuberculosis, and men living in these hospitals near the top would stroll down the mountain, usually in their pajamas, sometimes in slacks and undershirts. Opposite our house was the Sikiaridion Preventorium, a school and clinic for children in the first stages of the disease.

Babi normally sat outside the small souvlaki restaurant, his guitar lying on the ground beside him, absorbed in reading a braille volume with his fingers. He didn't spend much time in begging. He was about forty, short, and he stared intensely, if one with no eyeballs can be said to stare.

"What are you reading?"

Answering in good English, he said, "The book."

"What book?"

"The book, the only book."

"That makes it hard on any other writer where there is only one book."

"There is only one book and one author, but God permits others to write as well."

"Yes, sometimes he's been a good sport. When did you learn English?"

"I learned English after the Red Cross in Anatolia plucked out my diseased eyeballs. I had to learn English since they had no Greek bibles in braille. The set of bibles they gave me is in English."

"And whom do you speak English with?"

"With God."

"Anyone else?"

"With the people in His book."

"And with me?"

"Yes, sir, with you."

I was soon able to break down Babi's defenses and stern biblical speech as we got to know each other. Once we met, it was easy to find him in his regular spot on the sidewalk outside the souvlaki joint, where at night he slept in the kitchen, under the sink. He also washed dishes there on weekends when there was more business. The owner was a good man, he told me.

We talked often, but the visionary speech never left him for long. Sometimes every sentence was Isaiah. The Bible *was* his English.

"What happened to you during the occupation?"

"The Lamb in his Paradise looked my way and made me happy."

"Come out with it. What did you do?"

"I chopped wood for the Italians. They gave me a regular job every day. I could work, and I slept in a bed. The Italians gave me the only full-time job I ever had. People don't want to let blind men work."

"And now?"

"I am not unlucky. Several times a week a young woman leads me around town and we even take the bus to Athens, just so we can walk. I like to walk."

"Is she a religious freak like you?"

"I think she is not a religious freak like me."

Babi was so bright, no word, however slangy, went not understood, and he would normally throw it right back at me, testing it out.

"What would make you happy these days?"

"I am happy."

"And happier still?"

"To have a safe place to store these big volumes. Braille books are bigger than ordinary books, and I don't like storing them in the kitchen with all the dampness and water spilled everywhere. Even Noah wouldn't feel comfortable when we have a flood of customers and the kitchen turns into a zoo on a lake."

"I wish I could help you."

"You cannot."

"I cannot," I agreed.

"Kirie Willis, I like talking to you, although I know you don't believe a word of my visions." Babi wrinkled his brow.

"On the contrary, I believe they are your visions. Others claim to be visionary, but yours I know are real pictures in your head. They are really yours."

"They are not mine. I take my sight from this book," and his fingers struck the Bible.

Babi was the first blind Borges I knew. Like Borges, he also had endless humor, and twisted words to his individual vision. Borges as a Socratic was looking and found no answers, but let his characters come upon truths—at death, in a dream, in some way they would not reveal to the reader. But Babi was convinced that all the answers were there. The Devil threw up smoke screens but Christ danced across Lake Tiberius with all the parables and their meaning dropped into language and the soul. Borges the blind man would permit no such clarity. There were no keys. Only enigmas. Of course Babi's miseries helped him to find and hold onto his truths determinedly. Both men were saved by their intelligence, which even in the instance of Babi's faith (in contrast to Borges's skepticism) led him always into speech, which is never absolute.

Blind men sometimes beg and are sometimes wise. I don't think aristocratic Borges, who had a romance with his knife-dueling *compadritos*, would have been angry with me had I compared him to Babi the beggar. In fact, I know what he would have said. He would, in total false modesty, have tried to prove how Babi was the wise man, and he Borges, well, another imposter and failure. I saw the pattern constantly.

I spoke to Vassili about letting Babi live in a largely empty storage room in the basement of our Penteli house. Vassili, a kind man, who went each year to attend the sick, free of charge, in his native Epirote village and to supply them with medicines, would hear nothing of my suggestion. There was no point in argument.

"I will chop wood in the forests on the clouds," Babi said to me. He was often talking about his death, though I think he could throw off any ailment. "God

Aliki, Robert, and Tony in Kashgar, Chinese Turkestan, near the Afghanistan border, 1985

will replace my empty sockets with soft glass and I will see for horizons around."

Some months later I did begin to worry about Babi. I saw him with the young woman walking around the square in Maroussi, and he looked awful, coughing, feverish.

"Kirie Babi, how are you?"

"Happy, Willis. I am going to die. I have been waiting a long time to live well again. Up there the bed is real and very comfortable. The lambs lend their wool for covers, the mulberries lend their silk for sheets."

"Babi's just a little out of his mind," the young woman said. "He's got an awful cold and a fever, and is spitting like a Turk."

"I'm glad you have someone with you who won't listen to your apocalyptic complaints," I told the musician.

"She knows me pretty well," Babi smiled.

Then for some months Babi disappeared. The restaurant owner told me he was in the hospital. He did come out again, thinner, and was back on his spot on the pavement, playing the guitar. He sang the

songs of Asia Minor. He sang very well. His rough high voice was a perfect lament. It was dark, shrill, ecstatic, very low. A *rebetis*.

"We are leaving, Kirie Babi, in just a few weeks. Our papers are ready."

"You are leaving my books? Do you realize that I just touch the pages and I hear God talking? You must come back to hear the pages again."

"I'm a bad coin. A wooden nickel, we say. I always come back."

Babi stood up. "Good-bye." He stretched out his hand. Blind men are used to touching, so he held mine quite a while.

A Blind Beggar-Musician of Anatolia

Mr. Babi's indrawn eyelids cannot move.
The watery craters scar his baby face.
They are sewn-up holes of Bible light.
Glory burns inside; yet the Devil's close.
The Devil's friends who make him trip and fall
will grovel in the burning grease of Hell.

Dogs and cats are daughters, sons of Christ.
All love him. He loves every simple being.
He would fondle lambs, bears, tigers, lions,

any furry, felted hide or flying thing.
Mr. Babi's fingers (firebirds in black space)
dance on the necks of donkeys eating grass.

Mr. Babi boasts of death. He's sick of pus
and tonsilitis. Now he cannot swallow.
Wiping his wasted cheeks with a hot hand,
he walks alone and stumbles into furrows.
Saint Francis singing for his brother sun,
he founders in a ditch of carbon flowers.

Mr. Babi's eyelids feel a blow of light
as yellow angels plummet through his sleep.
The fig trees freeze in silver candelabra,
the black moon boils up into coughing seas,
heavens open to the bright wool of summer,
and death is home, health. Dying's cheap peace.

In 1959 when *From This White Island* came out,
Cleanth Brooks wrote a long, extremely praising
blurb for the volume—"these poems are drenched in
the light of the mind"—and ended his piece with
"and 'A Blind Beggar-Musician of Anatolia' is a small
masterpiece." "Masterpiece" is kindly absurd, but
thanks. As for small, in my vanity I wished "small"
were an easier epithet to receive, though I am sure
that Brooks's qualification was quantitative and good-
willed. I've felt sustained by his words on a book I
care about.

A writer's life and writing are always entangled
in clear metafiction. In a conversation with the other
blind man, Borges, he said a character is a string of
words, yet a real character. "Alas, poor Yorick, I
knew him well, Horatio," and with those words
Shakespeare, through Hamlet, brought Yorick into
being forever. Brooks's reference to "A Blind Beggar-Musician of Anatolia" has helped keep Babi alive
for me. And now Babi is more alive, since the needs
of a memoir have forced me to remember his words
"God will replace my empty sockets with soft glass
and I will see for horizons around." A memoir is all
about memory and its trickery. Once I accused
Borges of having a monstrous memory when he had
repeated the first stanza of Hopkins's "The Wreck of
the Deutchland," after having heard it only once, the
week before, and he replied, "There are lines harder
to forget than to remember."

By a series of good events in Athens, the L'Institut
Francais d'Athènes offered to publish a book of
my poems. It was paid for by the office of the
American Cultural Attaché. As I look back at this
enthusiastic and eclectic book, *Poems for Exchange,* I
am glad I had the chance to write all these things
away. From the book a few poems were preserved
that appeared in my first American volume, *From
This White Island,* put out some years later by

Twayne. (Before Twayne got into the authors series
books, they did regular trade books and John Ciardi
was their poetry editor.) *Poems for Exchange* also
contained six poems by Antonio Machado, including
his elegy on the death of Lorca. I feel very good
about all the Machado poems and am proud to have
been identified with Don Antonio from such an early
age. In 1951 when the book appeared, I was twenty-
three.

I followed the book through each stage of its
typesetting, design, and printing. It was an elegant
volume, hand set, with all the care of a limited edition
of five hundred copies. It helped me. Not particularly
publicly. But now, had I any doubts, I knew this was
my work. Borges would have said his destiny—
though Borges is usually not caught uttering such
pompous words. But he did say many times that his
destiny was to be a writer. As I write this memoir and
have added other kinds of writing to my obsession—
scholarship on noncanonical apocryphal scriptures
and Spanish and other poets, fiction writing, libret-
ti—at last I too feel like a writer as well as a poet. It's
a good feeling and in no way threatens the lyric. It
helps.

When the book was out, it was as if my destiny in
Greece for that first étape was completed. We still
couldn't leave because of the visa, but then, like the
abortion in France, someone said a few words and
there was a solution. Instead of going through the
church, through the ministries, all futilely, we discovered that a travel agency off Syndagama Square could
obtain an exit visa in twenty-four hours, if you bought
your ticket through them. They knew how and had
the connections. Years later, though I got into China
for special reasons during the Cultural Revolution,
others met only silence when their applications were
sent in. But then a few people discovered the secrets
of entry. Some Hong Kong travel agents could obtain
a visa within twenty-four hours or less into mainland
China, if you purchased your train or plane ticket
through them.

So we bought a ferry ticket from Corinth to
Brindisi, and left for Rome, our papers in good order.

Greece was not behind us, however. For me it
had begun.

For the purposes of this memoir, the narration
about the formation and adventures of a young
poet is already too long for this format. And so a
summary is in place. We left Greece for Italy. I
bought a Lambretta motorbike in Florence and we
went to Geneva where I worked for Les Editions
Skira for a summer translating French texts into
English for their art books. Then we spent a year in

The author in Kashgar, 1985

"Lapland"), the Amazon jungle in Brazil, and spent time in countries of Southeast Asia—Nepal, Burma (my preferred), Thailand, Java and Bali in Indonesia, the Philippines, Japan. *Holiday* and *Saturday Evening Post* sent me to Peru, Easter Island, China, Egypt, and Portugal for pieces for which I did the photography and story. I won some prizes for my work in poetry. I am publishing in a few months a book on the history, theory, and practice of literary translation with Yale University Press and a memoir biography of Jorge Luis Borges. My son Tony and I translated Wang Wei's poems from the Chinese, and my daughter Aliki and I edited *A Book of Women Poets from Antiquity to Now*. The poems have been and remain the center, though in the last years I have been doing fiction with great joy. I see poetry, fiction, and scholarship as Borges did. They are the work of a writer and move into each other, separated superficially by typography. Along with other books of poetry and scholarship, on November 13, 1977, I began a book of sonnets which has turned into a three-volume trilogy: *The Secret Reader*, consisting of *Gas Lamp, 1893, The Solitude of Planets*, and *To Find You at the End of This Strange Walk*. From that collection I inserted the sonnets in this memoir, which serve as a parallel memoir. Although I now wish to desonnetize myself, I hope I have the luck of finding you at the end of this strange walk.

Spain, mainly south of Granada on the coast, where I wrote and published a book of poems in Málaga, and Helle painted. We spent the summer in Tangiers, then a free city port in Morocco. In 1952 I was a full-time student in London, in Bengali, at the School of Oriental and African Studies of the University of London. I took an M.A. in English at Columbia from 1953–1954, was drafted into the U.S. Army which sent me back to France for most of two years. In 1956 I entered the Comparative Literature program at Yale, receiving the Ph.D. in 1960. But in 1958 I took a full-time job in the Romance Language department at Wesleyan University in Connecticut. In 1961 I was back in Madrid on a Guggenheim. Indiana University wrote me in Madrid and I took a position in Comparative Literature and Spanish at Indiana University in 1962. In subsequent years I was a visiting professor at the University of Massachusetts, the O'Conner Professor of Classics at Colgate, a visiting professor at University of California at Riverside and the University of Texas at Austin, a Fulbright professor at the Profesorado in Buenos Aires, and a Fulbright professor at Beijing University of Foreign Studies in China. During this period I wrote, edited, and translated some forty books. I continued my life as a vagabond, despite and because of the academic life. I spent more than a decade in Europe, went to Poland, Finland, Lapland (the *New Yorker* published a poem called

BIBLIOGRAPHY

Poetry:

Poems for Exchange, Institut Francais d'Athenes, 1951.

Notes for a Bible, Hermanos Hernandez, 1952,

From This White Island, Twayne, 1959.

A Sky of Days, Indiana University Fine Arts, 1967.

Anti-Journal, Sono Nis Press, 1971.

A Day in the Country, Harper & Row, 1971.

New Faces of China (poems and photographs), Indiana University Press, 1973.

China Poems, University of Missouri Press, 1976.

Stickball on 88th Street, Colorado Quarterly, 1978.

Overheard, Raintree Press, 1979.

A Snow Salmon Reached the Andes Lake, Curbstone Press, 1980.

Ten Gospels and a Nightingale, Triangular Press, 1981.

The Alphabet of Night, Frederick Brewer Press, 1984.

Five A.M. in Beijing, Sheep Meadow Press, 1987.

Critical writings:

The Poetics of Ecstasy, Holmes & Meier, 1983.

The Other Bible: Jewish Pseudepigrapha, Christian Noncanonical Apocrypha, and Gnostic Scriptures, Harper & Row, 1984.

The Poetics of Translation: History, Theory & Practice, Yale University Press, 1992.

With Borges on an Ordinary Evening in Buenos Aires: A Memoir, University of Illinois Press, 1992.

Six Masters of the Spanish Sonnet: Quevedo, Sor Juana Ines de la Cruz, Antonio Machado, Federico Garcia Lorca, Miguel Hernández, University of Southern Illinois Press, 1992.

Translator:

Eighty Poems of Antonio Machado, Las Americas, 1959.

(With Helle Barnstone) Margarita Liberaki, *The Other Alexander* (novel), Noonday, 1959.

(And editor) *Greek Lyric Poetry,* Bantam, 1962, revised and expanded edition, 1967.

(And author of introduction) Ignacio Bernal, *Mexico Before Cortez: Art, History and Legend,* Dolphin Books, 1963.

Physiologus Theobaldi Episcopi de Naturis Duodecim Animalium, Indiana University Press, 1964.

Sappho: Lyrics in the Original Greek with Translations, Doubleday-Anchor and New York University Press, 1965.

(And editor and author of introduction) *The Poems of St. John of the Cross,* Indiana University Press, 1968, revised edition, New Directions, 1974.

The Song of Songs, Kedros (Athens), 1970.

(With Ko Ching-po) *The Poems of Mao Tse-tung,* Harper, 1972.

(And author of introduction) Pedro Salinas, *My Voice Because of You,* State University of New York Press, 1975.

(And author of introduction) *The Unknown Light: The Poems of Fray Luis de León,* State University of New York Press, 1979.

(With David Garrison) *A Bird of Paper: Poems of Vincente Aleixandre,* Ohio University Press, 1981.

The Dream Below the Sun: Selected Poems of Antonio Machado, Crossing Press, 1981.

Sappho and the Greek Lyric Poets, Schocken, 1988.

(With Tony Barnstone) *Laughing Lost in the Mountains: Poems of Wang Wei,* University Press of New England, 1992.

Editor:

(With Hugh A. Harter) Miguel de Cervantes, *Rinconete y Cortadillo* (college text), Las Americas, 1960.

Luis de Gongora, *Soledades,* translated by Edward Wilson, Las Americas, 1965.

Modern European Poetry (anthology), Bantam, 1966, revised edition, 1978.

(And author of introduction) Edgar Lee Masters, *New Spoon River,* Macmillan, 1968.

(With Mary Ellen Solt) *Concrete Poetry: A World View,* Indiana University Press, 1969.

Spanish Poetry: From Its Beginnings through the Nineteenth Century (anthology), Oxford University Press, 1970.

Eighteen Texts: Writings by Contemporary Greek Authors, Harvard University Press, 1972.

(With Aliki Barnstone) *A Book of Women Poets from Antiquity to Now,* Schocken, 1980, revised edition, Random House/Pantheon, 1992.

(And photographer) *Borges at Eighty: Conversations,* Indiana University Press, 1982.

Contributor of some 150 translations to anthologies and books. Also contributor of poems, translations, and articles to numerous periodicals, including *Antioch Review, Arizona Quarterly, Kenyon Review, Nation, New Republic, New York Book Review, New York Times Sunday Book Review, New Yorker, Nine (London), Points (Paris), Prairie Schooner, Sewanee Review, Tulane Drama Review,* and *Yale Review.*

Raymond Barrio

1921-

REACHING BACK

Raymond Barrio, 1990

We are born. We wither. We die. And in between? We do the best we can. Darwin's answer is pretty good: we like to monkey around.

Most of the time it's very quiet here in Guerneville. We're on the Russian River, under the redwoods, eighty miles north of San Francisco. My dear wife Yolanda and I have been hibernating here the past fourteen years; we've been married thirty-four. Except for a few trips here and there, I've lived most of my life here in California, my education, my teaching, retired now, my art and writing, my wife and our lives, our worn-out cars, and our five fine children, grown now and out of the home, plus four nifty little grandkids. There, that's the nut in the shell . . .

Fourteen miles west is the tiny coastal village of Jenner, where the Russian River spills into the vast, restless Pacific. Nearby, in Monte Rio, roosts the Bohemian Grove, the Bohemian Club's lush redwood campground. Every July a number of the nation's top leaders gather, the wealthy and the powerful, good ole boys, no ladies, the rich and famous, the most conservative and the most Republican. They come cruising in on their private jets, scooters, and limousines, to romp and ape their ways under these unsuspecting forested giants. The original origin of species. Darwin would have been so proud. They come to forget all their cares. That's right. That's all right.

The high point of their carousing is a fiery frenzied ritual they call "The Cremation of Care," featuring a wise old owl who goes hoo? hoo? hoot! all through the night. I haven't yet heard if they've invited this century's most creative financial wizards, Milken, Boesky, and Keating, but they'll probably slip in. They usually do.

"Father, Saturnino, holding baby brother, Bill. I'm in foreground looking for gold," New Jersey, about 1924.

Like any normal American community, we also harbor our share of dedicated protestors here, waving placards announcing "The Resurrection of Care." The stretch limos zip by floop floop, not caring. How dare these lefties challenge the God-given right of our CEOs and VPs to rip off all the millions they can before being indicted? It's a free country, isn't it? These lefties even distribute leaflets quoting the following redlined message from TJ, Thomas Jefferson:

> I hope we shall crush in its birth the aristocracy of our moneyed corporations which dare already to challenge our government to a trial of strength and bid defiance to the laws of our country.

Way back in 1921, my birth year, my mother, Angelita, was sixteen, my father, Saturnino, twenty-seven. Both were recent immigrants from Spain, joining a little colony of expatriates in New Jersey. My mother's favorite baby story—she's eighty-seven now, living alone in San Francisco, sharper than a tack—is that when I was born, at home, the old-fashioned way, I slithered out of the midwife's hands and skidded under the bed and out of sight. I yelled. That probably accounts for the rage I was born with. My father worked as a common laborer at the U.S. Radium Corp. plant in West Orange, northwest of Newark. That's it. No more. That's about all I know about New Jersey, my birthplace, and my father.

My brother, Bill, was born a year after. Three more years and my mother called her marriage quits. She never told me her reason. I only have some intimations that my father was too severe with her, and that she was too young. She packed our baby things, said adios to poor old dad, and off we sailed back to Spain.

It was a very exciting trip, even for a five-year-old. I think the steamship was named the *Leviathan*, the name of an aquatic monster in the Bible. What luck. One night we ran into a powerful storm way out at sea. Cliff-high waves and sheets of rain thundered down on us. Someone picked up a flying fish that landed on deck. I also remember being lifted by the captain to the top of the huge steering wheel up on the bridge, thereby enabling me to steer that monstrous ship to safety. It wasn't easy. Not many five-year-olds can lay claim to that kind of experience. For a while there I felt at one with Henley that I was "master of my fate and captain of my soul." From there on, according to the second law of thermodynamics, things could only go downhill.

One more thing: with a little prescience, the oracles might have let me know that I was going to recross that same Atlantic Ocean a mere eighteen years later, in 1944, on a troopship. But that's getting a little ahead of my story.

How can I possibly deal with my seven rich decades?

There's a heady bouillabaisse here, an incredible century of extraordinary events, inventions, personalities, movements, upheavals, revolutions, wars, and what have you.

Hesiod, a contemporary of Homer in the eighth century B.C., was one of ancient Greece's great original thinkers. In his *Theogeny* he wrote an account of the origin of the world and of the gods. This was four hundred years before Socrates, Aristotle, and Plato, and eight hundred years before Christ. Hesiod knew very little; we know a lot. Are we that much better off? He didn't know about the Alexandrian Library. The Persian Empire. The Greek Empire. The Aztec and Inca Empires. And on and on, through the medieval ages, down to the modern industrial age. And yet Hesiod dared to think in cosmic terms. He was not as "educated" as we pride ourselves on today. And yet he introduced new ideals of moderation and of justice. What more could any brain want? To enlarge our visions? There is excitement to be found in the discovery of origins. Like gardeners (not commercial farmers, who are grubby ants) we keep planting and caring for new seeds, each new generation born anew, experiencing constantly the thrilling magic of continuing rebirth of seedlings.

The fruit we reap, our reward, is the insight that comes from true learning, not pedantic pits, but the succulence of joyous living ideas. Although our twentieth century is one vast garden complex of rich histories, the basic principles of justice and fairness still reign supreme in our psyche. They go back, back into dim pre-history, pre-Cro-Magnon. We know when we're being done dirt to.

Ever since childhood I've been an omnivorous reader. I even feel guilty reading a book, reading gives me such pleasure, for there are so many action things begging for attention. Chasing bugs. Feeding the finches. Watching the bull's-eye ripples on the river surface at dusk when the fingerlings feed. I get frustrated at the thought of all the thousands of good books I know about and won't get to read. What a vice.

One book that inspires and refreshes me constantly is Thoreau's *Walden; or Life in the Woods.* In 1970 I self-published a pamphlet of my favorite *Walden* excerpts, illustrated, out of love. This from my Introduction:

> *Walden* is simple. It is clean. It is forthright. It is elegant. It is above all inspiring, a key to individualized human glory . . . Thoreau raises some provocative questions. Are you content to use your life merely to make money? To "make a living"? Or would you prefer to live as richly spiritually as you deserve? If so, then a simple life is the richest life . . . Thoreau worked for one month as a surveyor in order to support himself with the proceeds for the other eleven months. *An eleven-month vacation!* We should reverse the order of the work week: we should work one day a week at whatever drudge work necessary to earn money, then use the other six days for our *real* work: to work at what our heart and imagination desire, feeding the spirit and soul, whether it's watching a sunset, studying archeology, or building your own hut. Whatever you choose to do, as a free spirit.

The vast bulk of the human race historywise and worldwide is/has been trapped either on a starvation poverty level, or in spiritually barren toil. "The mass of men lead lives of quiet desperation." What a delight it is to see a poet or a potter or a putterer

working at his/her heart's delight. The test if you do it for love is whether you get paid for it or not. I've loved teaching and have worked as a teacher over the years in order to subsidize my writing time.

The Twenties . . .

Nineteen twenty-one, Hitler's SS storm troopers terrorize political opponents, start of slide to WWII. Wolfe writes Look Homeward Angel; *Faulkner,* The Sound and the Fury. *Lindbergh flies nonstop to Paris 1927. Sacco/Vanzetti indicted for murder, executed 1927, because they are anarchists. Nineteen twenty-nine, the Teapot Dome scandal. Also 1929, the stock market crash, causing worldwide economic collapse. HCH: Harding, Coolidge, Hoover, that insufferable triumvirate of inept presidents.*

Mother spent her two years in Madrid training to be a Spanish dancer, leaving us in the loving care of our Tiabuela Margarita; our uncle owned a neighborhood corner bar. Then we got bad news: my father Saturnino, a healthy young man who worked for the U.S. Radium Corp., died of radium poisoning, as happened to a number of others. There was a public outcry. We returned to New York. An insurance settlement was made. Mother would get monthly payments for Bill and me until we reached eighteen.

The Thirties . . .

The Depression years. Twenty-five percent unemployment. Everyone sad, serious, or frightened. Bread lines. Seventeen thousand World War I veterans bonus march on Washington, D.C. Hoover orders General MacArthur to drive them out. FDR elected 1932.

My early years during the Depression were divided between two families. We stayed three years with the LaNoce family in Jamaica, Long Island, where Bill and I attended a Catholic school with lovely, caring nuns. Mother started getting bit parts in Hollywood films, a liberated woman. She shipped us to Los Angeles, where she put us in the care of a Cuban couple, Maria and Jaime, on Ninety-seventh Street, near the Watts district, and into Bret Harte Junior High.

In 1937, another jump back to New York City via Greyhound. We entered Commerce High in mid-Manhattan, a big drop after sunny California. I won several awards and made the honor society. Commerce was an all-boys school. After the sunny greenery of Los Angeles, this was like going to prison, eight stories of metal and brick, ringed by bars and steel fences. I could leap down an empty stairwell in just two or three leaps like a crazed gazelle. I never broke a leg. The goofy gods were watching over me.

I was also waking up to how crazy girls were. My first wild careen was a precocious little chick in our apartment building who agreed to meet me on the roof on a sunny afternoon. We sat on the hot asphalt in the shadow of a dirty chimney. I dared to snake my arm around her shoulder. She smiled saucily. We kissed. Holy smoke. I've never gotten over it. (My wife will crown me when she reads this.) What the hell was going on? So that's what girls were for. I ran back to the safety of my apartment to cool off. Wow. I hhhhhhad no idea—!

In my senior year my English teacher tipped me into writing. She praised my writing, not me. In later years I've been handed a number of negative compliments. Extremist. Radical. Bitter. Skeptic. Sour. Saturnine. And other nice things that remind me of Frost's "a lover's quarrel."

Early on, I came to the conclusion that I was being driven by a pair of twin engines: by rage, and by wonder.

Rage: at the cruelty of man's stupid inhumanity to man.

Wonder: at the amazing magnificence of life in all its myriad and ineffable manifestations.

While fiction and the novel have occupied my central vision and energies, I've also written hundreds of political columns, to help me get the rage out. Getting messages across successfully in fiction requires special care and subtlety, to avoid being didactic. My literary heroes are way too many to list, both fiction and nonfiction. My favorite magazine is *The Nation*, "125 years of provocative thought," and I hope this plug doubles its circulation overnight.

Curran said it right: "Eternal vigilance is the price of liberty," as it is of democracy. And it is democratic socialism that most appeals to me. Raw unregulated capitalism, America's favorite playtime, is far too destructive to people, to society, to nature, to nations, and to the planet. Cooperatives work on a human, a social level. Corporations work too, but only too well, on a ruthless level. We must find a way to close the gruesome gap between rich and poor. In fact, the wage system should be slammed into reverse. Those at the bottom should receive comfortable—not minimum—wages, while those at the top should be satisfied with the psychic rewards of fame and respect, and forego huge salaries, as dollar-a-year

industrial leaders did during WWII for FDR and, incidentally, for America.

Worst of all is the indecent and wasteful armaments industry. This past generation has thrown one half of our gross national product away on goofy armaments—$350 billion for 50,000 atomic missiles and bombs! come on!—when schools are groaning for help, when health, highway, child care, drugs, and a host of other social problems abound. Even the Bible, as usual, is full of admonitions: "What does it profit a man if he gains the whole world and loses his soul?" Goethe dramatizes this idea in his powerful Dr. Faustus. And Agur's wish: "Give me neither poverty nor riches." And Tom Paine: "Civilization makes some individuals more affluent, others more wretched than would occur in nature." And still, and yet, the modern descendents of Kings Midas and Croesus keep on getting greedier and bolder. Oh no . . . not *another* bank!

NRB. The three most reactionary American presidents of this century are being honored by the U.S. Navy. The navy is commissioning three brand new pocket destroyers (whose mission it is to destroy pockets of resistance)—the USS *Nixon*, USS *Reagan*, and USS *Bush*. It is widely rumored however that Bush can still sneak in another pocket veto. Here, now, is some more fiction from my political series which appeared in our local paper a few years back:

"I, Fred Sherwood, American . . ."
(inspired by a CBS documentary
1 September 1982)

My heart overflows with pride and gratitude at this grand honor you are all bestowing on me.

I, Fred Sherwood, am an amiable man. I am also a humble man. No one has ever accused me of being an honorable man, at least not to my humble face. As I gaze upon your bright beaming faces, you hope-filled young people about to graduate from this splendid University of the Universe, I want only to express my deepest gratitude.

Despite my colossal immodesty, I haven't the faintest idea why I was chosen for this invocation. Perhaps it's because I may serve in a seditionary way as a role model, as a symbol of America's exploitative capability at its best.

If so, I couldn't be more highly honored.

When I first went to Guatemala, now my secondary country, about thirty years ago, I set straight to work. By diligence and perniciousness I worked my way up to where I'm now pretty well off, well, obscenely rich, if I may say so. And all by horsing around with some good investments, and by paying strict attention to the almighty, the almighty buck that is. And that is how I now hope to inspire all you young Americans about to graduate. Work hard, and you too will benefit and gain the riches that the almighty meant you to have.

Way back in 1954, President Eisenhower bravely took up the cudgel against the dirty Communist rats infesting my golden Guatemala egg.

Guatemala's President Arbenz kept lying through his teeth, the few he had left. Yes, he was a leftie too. The usual Commie crap. You know, crying that he'd been elected honestly, that he was a legitimate president—he even dared compare himself to our beloved Ike, the nerve!—and that he was no Communist. But we know better. He had at least two known pals who were seen reading *The Star*. Anybody need any better proof than that?

Then our beloved Vice President Nixon said to the world, "World, you just watch what we do, not what we say." And by gum we sure set up Guatemala nice and fluffy for us Americanos. Think of it! We are now 10,000 Americans living happily in Guatemala, running everything, with some $300 million invested.

Some snoopy CBS reporteros came up to me and asked, what about the killings? What killings? I shot right back. Well, they said, thousands of poor Guatemalans have been killed at an average of 500 a month. Well, I said, you got proof? Anyway, they're just Commies. Sure, maybe five or six peasants might have been killed at my company, PROKESA. You know, these people just aren't ready for our kind of democracy. Death squads? I'm all for it, live ammo and all.

Let me tell you bright young Amerigringos just how good Guatemala is. I mean, like my comfy life style, my ranch, my mansion, my li'l ole jet. And my workers NEVER complain. Nossir, they're too tired or too happy. Hundreds of 'em, saying si snore and no snore. I'm a robber, I mean I'm in rubber and cement. I pay them good, more than they're worth, the worthless peasants, a standard $4 a day in good days, that is, whenever they's work. I mean, I'm not running no charity rancho. They don't have to meet the bills I have. What have they got to crab about in them thar hills, eh? Those illiterate, unambitious, uneducated Indians, they don't want no TV. No education. They don't want no cars, that's for sure. See? See how sweet and simple a life they lead?

And I intend to fight for the country of my choice, Guatemala. That's why, as president of the Guatemala Chamber of Commerce, I like to support their patriotic police patrols. They keep law and order. Those dumb CBS reporteros, what do they know, why do they keep calling them death squads? Why, they ain't killed 120 peasants in a year. Oh, a couple of loudmouthed peasant politicos were killed accidentally last year. Sure. But they are OUR ENEMAS. They want to destroy OUR WAY OF LIFE, as we know it. They want to wreck OUR government and OUR freedoms and, my goodness, my grand mansion and OUR great liberties. That's why we need more helicopters, machines, machine guns, and machine-gun parts, to keep our law in order.

In closing, I implore you young people. Guard your liberties and guard your God-given freedoms well. Guard your right to do as you please anywhere anytime to anyone.

WE ARE ALL AMERICANS!

Meanwhile my other engine—wonder—has been going full blast. I wonder about dawn and midnight and and crickets and the roiling surf and the moon's pull on our tides. I wonder at the human brain's being barely half a million years old while Lucy, our humanoid ancestor, may be four million. And that dinosaurs go back from 60 to 160 million years ago, in the reptilian age when there were no mammals. I am lit up by Eiseley's *Star Thrower*. I wonder about our educational system and the First Amendment and sorcerers and sand dunes in the Sahara. Everything is mist and shrift and grist for my small windmill. From the sternest science to the most poignant paeans. The classics are telescopes to our minds. They help us see far beyond the foraging, calculating, copulating animals that we are, that we need to practice to survive.

All these forces come together, our DNA, our total education, both formal and informal, to form some sort of eyepiece squinting at the universe. For me, my magic magnet was writing as honestly as I knew how to. And to ponder on the immortality of the ant.

The Forties . . .

Europe explodes into war.

In 1940, when I graduated from high school, I'd just barely finished reading about WWI, when I had to face II. The headlines were black with Hitler's deceitful, shocking aggression.

Now what? I take a boring office job for a year. I want to go to college, a natural student. But how? I make a plan. I'll return to Los Angeles. On my own. My mother is hurt. Disappointed. Still is. Even at this late date. Her gist: why go to college when you can keep working and make all that money out there? She had been doing her thing all her life, going for dancing and acting and show business, and good for her. But now I wanted to do mine.

Summer 1941. My friend Charlie is going to Mexico City with his uncle. I can go along and pay my share of gas. From there I could go on to L.A. This is the first time I am entirely on my own, an uncaged bird. An exciting feeling. We travel without incident.

*"At Yale University, just before joining
the 78th Division," 1943*

I rent a room in a cheap hotel in Mexico City and stay a few days. At a neighborhood dance I meet a lovely young señorita. I fall in love with Mexico. She agrees to let me visit her. Her mamacita sat at the opposite end of la sala, the salon, concentrating on her sewing.

Well, I had to get on. I took the train from Mexico City to Guadalajara, north to Mexicali, and a bus to L.A. where I took a room at the downtown YMCA. I hadn't the vaguest idea how to get started in college. I remembered that the University of Southern California was on Vermont Avenue, not far from where I'd gone to junior high. I found the registrar's office and enrolled in two morning classes. I found a rooming house with other students just off campus. Then I found a part-time afternoon job. I was all set. I did it, and I did it by myself. Except for one thing. I was letting myself float in a dream world.

On a grim Sunday afternoon, I was in the stadium watching a football game, December 7, when war struck. As students, all registered for the draft of course, we were allowed to continue our studies. In the spring, in midterm, we were all gobbled up,

cannon fodder, in one fell swoop (great string of cliches there, eh?).

Then I crossed the country again, to basic training in Virginia. I qualified for an intriguing special program called ASTP for Army Specialized Training Program. Several hundred of us were selected to be trained in one of four oriental languages and Russian. I became a Russki at Yale. I was back again, unexpectedly, in my kingdom of heaven, a student, and immersed in the most concentrated course I'd ever known: concentrated conversation in the Russian language, Russian literature, history, art, music, the works. An excellent top quality program, for almost a year. We were all convinced we were all going to be commissioned captain or better and go directly to Moscow as official liaisons. Another dream exploded.

Instead, typical army, we were rounded up to flesh out the 78th Lightning Division in North Carolina. What? You never heard of the Lightning 78th? We were shipped over—I left a sweetheart at Yale, one in New York, and another in New Jersey—and, remember my earlier childhood crossing? This time, five thousand of us cannonballs were sardined into a troopship on convoy and I tell you I sure am glad I knew nothing about the success ratio of German U-boats. Not only did we all get seasick but we all came down with diarrhea at the same time. Don't even try to imagine the horror of that cruise, waiting in long lines for the heads and crowded against the bent rails. Not even Dante could have handled it.

We were dropped off at friendly, war-weary Southampton, England. Our Normandy boys had gotten across the channel ahead of us. In October we landed at the wretched wrecked harbor of Le Havre, which I'd crossed at five and seven. We were trucked to Belgium and the German border, facing the sick Siegfried Line. I was a telephone wireman with the 903d FA Field Artillery battery of 105 howitzers. Among other close calls I had one wartime coincidence that reminded me of my literary leanings. In that winter 1944 we were dug in under a blanket of snow in the Hürtgen forest, gateway to Nazi Germany. It was my turn to go for my meal. The cooks had set up our kitchen under a canopy of pines. As I cut across the white field, toward the woods, I heard the buzz of a small plane. I looked up and spotted, I thought, one of our observation planes. Then I heard a short burst, the unmistakable burst of a machine gun, just as I reached the first tree. A sudden *thwack!* smacked the tree next to my innocent head. The plane vanished. It was a g.d. Nazi flier *strafing* me! What marksmanship. I remembered Remarque's *All*

Quiet on the Western Front. In the movie Lew Ayres sticks his head up for one moment in the lull of fighting to catch a butterfly, when *wham!* a German sniper zaps him in the forehead. The end. Lady Luck let me keep going.

In January we started piercing Germany again and raced across the Cologne plain. Our division participated in the dramatic capture of the unexploded Remagen Bridge am Rhein, which George Segal in the movie seized nearly singlehanded. From there it was home all the way. I eventually got to Berlin, a mass of rubble, to Paris, and even got to attend some classes at Swansea University in Wales, on leave. Finally it was my turn to return. I got to Berkeley and received my B.A. at the University of California in 1947. That same year, I even had a fling at a brief marriage which lasted only six months.

Now, finally, I had to start thinking seriously of how to "make a living." 'Tain't easy being a thoroughgoing Thoreauvian, feathers and all. Graduate work didn't appeal to me, but art did. I enrolled in Art Center College for another three years. Again . . . now what was I going to do?

The Fifties . . .

McCarthyism. Korean War. Hersey's Wall. *Color TV. Governor Faubus closes schools in Arkansas. Castro in Cuba.*

"Inside Germany, a soldier at war's end," 1945

It was on to San Miguel de Allende, for the second time, in the middle of Mexico, where I experienced one of the most beautiful bursts of pure freedom in my life. The small, loosely jointed art school there, run by a very friendly Sterling Dickinson, catered to veterans on the GI Bill. It had a distinctly wild, undisciplined, hippy flavor. As long as you signed in and made some reasonable effort at painting or drawing, why, you were in. Nobody made you do anything. You disciplined yourself, which is the best kind of freedom there is. My greatest delight was coming true: I didn't have to answer to anyone either out of fear or concern. I was neither boss nor bossed. I could laze the days away or become a star. I could walk, waltz, or wobble. The dim, yellow nightlights over the dark street corners intrigued me. I had access to all kinds of sociable contacts, students, residents, tourists, Euripides, Socrates, epiphanies. I had, and have, no interest in any myth or religion, mystic or occult, but I felt the full power of a spiritual awakening in me. It was incredible. I could see how religions and mysticisms came to be invented. I was highly charged, enlightened, glowing. Religious fanatics insist that you join them. I joined nothing. I had my health, my intellect, my brain, my neurons, my social being, and I was rich beyond Croesus.

Everything turned on the sun: light, energy, warmth, photosynthesis, life. San Miguel was a small village, maybe two thousand souls, easy to walk to anywhere, el Parque Frances cool with lush overgrowth. El mercado merited a visit every day, with its great moments of brightly colored fruits, vegetables, parrots. And oranges and lemons and avocados and apples from Yakima and peanuts and frijoles and okra and tomatl and chokolatl and and and. In the plaza, a cool, verdant paradise, the grim Presidencia faced the soaring parroquia. On either side were shops, a friendly barbershop, an appliance store, zapateria, abarrotes, a bank, and so on.

The art school occupied what had been an ancient convent, two stories around a huge, open, central patio filled with flowering bushes, palms, and fruit trees. A small Eden. The classrooms and art studios had been the nuns' private cells. The curriculum was mostly inferential infernal ah informal. The walls gave off a humid, musty odor that I found richly intriguing, in contrast to the hot, dry, outside air. Here, I don't have a country to run or a shoeshine stand. I'm not making gigantic savings and loans ripoffs. Even the military establishment ignores me and hoo hoo Hoover too, I hope. (Either one.) I sleep at any time, dropping off like a baby when I feel like it, totally unworried about the upkeep of my land yacht.

Yolanda Ocio and Raymond Barrio at their wedding reception, Mazatlan, 1957

Then again, how free am I? Really? Is a bat free in its belfry? Wasps, trout, hummingbirds have wide ranges of flight and movement. Some whales, I hear, travel from the north to the south poles, round-trip. Nature pushes the excitement of trees to the maximum, and all wild creatures. Yet that freedom is concentrated only in one single overriding purpose: survival.

I still seek something more, deeper, wider, far out.

What I seek is a sense of self-conscious awareness, which is denied our wilder cousins.

I wish I could capture whole that extraordinary rapture of nature in all its exciting ripples, passages, and shadings. I may be a mayfly, maybe a barfly, a predator, a mitotic cell, a total failure, or a complete success. The magnificent end product of my race, the humanoid supremus. It was my responsibility not just to stay alive, but to sense and contemplate self-consciously. Perversely we moderns torch the house of intellect, of sensorial experience, of repose. We box ourselves in soft cushiony boxes, and ignore the stern snap of thunder and lightning.

One lazy morning I cross the sun-dusted plaza, in my native huaraches, heading for my abode, drawing pad under my arm. A small urchin comes up to me. *"Señor Barrio,"* he says. I'm surprised. He knows me. *"Si! Pues, señor, el señor cura allí,"* and he pointed at the Parroquia, "would like the honor of a brief word with you, if you are not indisposed." What polite correctness. *Por supuesto,* of course. I go up to the dignified priest, who invites me to his office. At his invitation I sit in a deep leather chair. He compliments me for being the only norteamericano who speaks Cristiano, meaning Spanish. Behind him the wall from floor to ceiling is loaded with the thick tomes of his personal library. Here, he says simply, is the total refutation of Freud. I am startled and impressed.

He offers me a cigar which I stupidly accept, as I've never smoked cigars. He also offers me a small shot of brandy, which I have no trouble with at all, at all. He draws me into friendly conversation. As a Latino, yes, of course, I am Catholic. I refrain, however, from telling him that I am a cultural Catholic, not a religious believer. At the door, as I'm leaving, he says, "By the way, señor Barrio, could I ah beg a very small favor of you?" *"Por supuesto,"* I reply. He hesitated, then murmured, "I'd very much appreciate your covering your drawings when you walk across town. You see . . ." I saw instantly. I'd just finished a drawing of a nude, and—I was in old Mexico. I thanked him and left.

Back in Los Angeles once again, I hired myself out to a kind, gentle artist named Guy MacCoy. Guy taught me—and many others—the art of serigraphy, or silk-screen printmaking. I entered my paintings, drawings, and prints in numerous art competitions, and built up a list of acceptances and sales.

Then, restless, I was off to Mexico again. I was becoming a Mexican in my soul. This time I drove my light Studebaker down the west coast. I stopped over in Mazatlan, vaguely intending to go on to Guadalajara or Ajijic or Lake Chapala or Morelia. I never made it. A nice, friendly gringo named Jim Reagan, lean as a beanpole and an endless chainsmoker from Santa Cruz, was living his own life of Reilly there as free as any bird on a pension.

We ate pyramids of iced raw oysters from a pushcart street stand, cracked open by the happy vendor with his large, wicked knife, and squirted hot chili salsa on them. I thought, wow, what I've been missing. Jim also got around to introducing me to my dark-eyed beauty Yolanda, who was killing time clerking in her cousin's curio store designed to ensnare happy turistas.

Yolanda was not all that impresionada with my impressive presence, I gathered. I made believe I couldn't speak Spanish and communicated in fractured gringo phrases. Soon after, at a New Year's dance, which she attended with family and friends, she spotted me coming in with a couple of pals. See that gringo? she said jokingly. That's the one I'm going to marry. She was just ajoshing for, as I soon found out, she was very very haughty. *Altiva* in Spanish. We met. We danced. I asked if I could. Could what? she said. Visit you, I said. One thing led to another. Soon we were betrothed. All correct. All proper, both civil and church wedding. Her mother, who had separated from her father, had died of an accident. Yoli and her sister were then raised by her uncle, Dr. Rodolfo Ocio (QEPD, Spanish for RIP) who was then one of Mazatlan's most respected physicians.

Soon we had to leave for points north. Ay, the sighs! I took my bride to my modest rented house in Chatsworth, in the northwest corner of Los Angeles's San Fernando Valley, on the edge of a vast wilderness. I continued working for Guy, selling my prints and paintings.

Yoli became pregnant right away with our first born, Angelita. What a thrill, a beautiful, brand-new baby girl. (Lita is now thirty-three, and herself the mother of three of our four delightful grandchildren.) As might be suspected, I wasn't exactly getting rich off my paintings. Now I *really* had to get out and earn some hard tack for a change. I was still trying to start my heavy writing. But first I had to bring in baby fruit jars. Filled. Right away. I took a job as a social worker for a year. If I had to work earning money in the marketplace, I much preferred doing it teaching. Eventually, into the future now, through my teaching I was going to be able to raise our brood of five magnificent children, all now grown and out of the home.

The Sixties . . .

Nineteen sixty: American U-2 spy plane shot down over Russia. JFK elected; assassinated 1963. Martin Luther King Jr. assassinated 1968; also Robert Kennedy. First weather satellite. Summer of love, 1967.

We moved north to teach at Ventura College. Next I was hired in 1964 to teach art at University of California Santa Barbara. While there I was awarded a special faculty Creative Arts grant for a year's self-study. What a tremendous break! Yoli and I immediately worked out an overall plan. We

bought a used pickup camper and spent the entire summer on a vagabond trip up the West Coast to Canada and back. We'd never had a vacation. Our three babies, Lita six, Gabriel four, and Raymond two, were happy as larks. Kids go goofy camping. Well, and so did we. Our best camping spot was on the flank of Washington's resplendent Mount Rainier with its radiant ice cap. We spent a couple of delicious weeks there, just floundering, cooking, eating, walking, waking, oohing, and grunting. We even joined corny campground sings by campfire light led by rangers, "OH Hanapecosh is the CAMP for us, is the CAMP for us," and so on.

The summer flashed by in one second. From Canada, Vancouver, we drove down to San Diego, more crowded there, and then back to Santa Barbara, to settle down for a year. In nearby Carpinteria we rented a nice, light, airy house surrounded by a huge yard, and there we experienced a new kind of freedom. Yoli and the babies, and I to write as I pleased. I dashed off several articles for art magazines and got them published. I wrote up our travels, with many photos, *These Woods Are Mine*. A Santa Barbara

"A serious moment at requisite 'author' typewriter," 1960

publisher saw it, liked it, took it, and then reneged, souring me some more.

Next I concentrated on writing serious short fiction for little liberated—I mean literary—magazines, "little" because of their small circulation, but very big in ideals, honesty, aspiration, and independence. My very thing. I learned that they are just as tough to break into, just as competitive as the big-paying general/commercial magazines. And they don't pay. There are hundreds of them, so you never run out. It's a hassle keeping track, but you have to. Soon I started getting in.

Meanwhile my first novel, "Wolf Boyd, Artist," came ripping off my midnight flier like a smoking marlin. On the very first submission an editor said he liked it, right away. A month later it was rejected. His boss didn't like it. I sent it out faithfully every three months for five years, meanwhile starting other novels. Then I figured out the mathematics. You could consume your entire lifetime sending manuscripts out cold. There had to be a better, a different way.

The *Atlantic Monthly* loves getting 2,000 submissions every month. They pick two, for odds of 1 out of 1,000. The rest of their stories are by known writers, with an in. They have to. That's how they keep the magazine going. Readers respond to known writers. *Mademoiselle* pays $1,000 a story, same odds. Talk about cream. One editor of *Sun & Moon* wrote: "Our most exciting young writers, left high and dry by conglomerate publishers, are unable to get their work published." It figures. You could spend fifty years just sending manuscripts out every three months, supporting the post office, and NEVER get accepted.

One other way is through literary agents, but they can't handle you unless you sell, and you can't sell unless you get published. And you can't get published unless . . . catch-22.

I finally woke up in the real world and realized that UC Santa Barbara wasn't going to rehire me. We moved north and rented an apartment in Santa Clara. I quickly lined up some part-time adult education classes and, later, at community colleges. I taught all phases of art, painting, drawing, and then history, humanities, and Chicano studies. Also creative writing, writing the novel, and self-publishing. I covered the world. My teaching reflected my broadening interests. I was, and am, a generalist, not a specialist.

Self-publishing. I put a little booklet together, "The Big Picture," based on painting lessons I'd developed. By this time I was a far-out advocate of modern expressionistic art, pushing Franz Kline,

Hans Hofmann, Jasper Johns, and others I admired. My book encouraged starting artists to first see what was going on in the world of modern art, and how it happened, and then to plunge in and try it for themselves. I always had plenty of students, which speaks well of the subject matter.

Despairing of finding a publisher, I went to a print shop and ran off a thousand copies. One frenzied morning I was at the print shop, unshaven, supervising my layout, when I received a hurried call from my wife: a classroomful of students was waiting for me to show up! I broke every speed record getting there. The devil always insists on his dues.

I didn't have a thousand students, but by word of mouth my one-dollar booklets were soon all gone. Hey, a best-seller! Then I lurched into an important lesson: I started sending out twenty copies each week to different publishers, in effect bypassing the single submission rule which all publishers sternly insist upon, and making multiple submissions of the same story at the sizzling rate of eighty a month. Much better odds. And I said as much in my cover letter. And doggone it if in the third week I didn't snag a publisher, Sterling Publishing Company, who not only accepted my booklet enthusiastically, but turned it into a large, handsome hardcover and, to top that, with color plates of my paintings. I was fromboobliated (don't look it up, it's a neologism). Unfortunately, it didn't become an international best-seller. It was now called *Experiments in Modern Art;* I achieved what I was sure was impossible: handsomely born and distributed.

I kept finding out more about self-publishing. It was, and is, spreading all over the country, challenging the big conglomerate publishers. I even bought a small offset press, and actually taught myself to run it. I produced several small booklets and even learned how to make perfect bound paperback covers. I could easily have made my living at this, but that wasn't exactly my point. Writing/editing/publishing are where the creative juices flow. Distribution is mechanical, physical, raw animal jungle.

On Fiction. Every writer gravitates naturally to the method, menu, medium, and style that s/he is most comfortable with—the sum total of one's personality, beliefs, ambition. No apologies. No excuses. I find the writing of fiction wild. Pure gold. A newscaster once compared a jury to a bear—"It can do anything it wants to." So with fiction. You make it do anything. But getting readers and critics to agree is another matter. Fiction is a strange, exciting, magnificent literary animal. It slinks. It whispers. It roars. It prances. It penetrates. It excites. It goes up.

Down. Backward. Any which way. You follow. Entranced. What happens next? Characters come alive in their settings, natural or unnatural, real or wholly fantasized. Never equate fiction, no matter how wild, no matter how imaginative, with the false or the unreal or untruth. Fiction, like poetry, can and often does achieve far higher levels of truth than nonfiction. Good war novels often have far more truth than any journalistic account.

Unfortunately, the intense commercialization saturating all aspects of modern living—variously called materialism, specialization, greed, technology, etc.—does great damage to the tentative aspiration of young idealistic writers. Fame and Fortune, Incorporated: Wreckers.

No writer can possibly be all things to all people. *Alice* comes pretty close. Is there anyone who doesn't like Lewis Carroll's *Wonderland?* A serious writer concentrates on his/her own private inner voice, and then is satisfied if s/he finds even the smallest sliver of the reading pie out there. The Best-Seller syndrome does great damage to aspirants young and old. Once a writer's imagination is seized

"Our first born, Angelita, with husband, Ron Swietek," 1990

by a vivid theme, a dream, a vision, and finds the way to plan it into writing, then—the story born should first of all be its own reward. If it's done skillfully enough, emotionally, powerfully enough, then the story will find its own readers.

The Seventies . . .

In 1969, a lot of dramatic events. Nixon in. Armstrong lands on moon. Ike dies. The Chicago Eight indicted. DDT barred. 1970, Vietnam protest at Kent State, four students killed by National Guard. Watergate break-in. 1974, Nixon out.

I really got ambitious in 1969. Earlier in Santa Barbara, I had come across Ernesto Galarza's extraordinary documentation of the exploitation of Mexican farm workers (which is still going on) in California, facts, figures, statistics. Another vivid, appalling example of man's inhumanity to man.

I started writing *The Plum Plum Pickers,* my sixth or seventh novel, all still in manuscript. The cold statistics were Plum's invisible skeleton. I invented a Mexican couple and their children, and described their simple everyday life, getting up, cooking, loving, fighting, housed in a splintered shack in sunny, prosperous, affluent Santa Clara, picking apricots endlessly. I also experimented with language.

Here's young Ramiro:

> From predawn blackness Ramiro picked ripe his fruit. He picked to dusk. He picked from prehistory into glass bright civilization. From pre-Columbian artifacts to freeways to the future. From Aztec elegance to the latest word in slums. Man dumb. Inverted man. Man invented Ramiro to exploit him in order to fleece him and float his own cheap alter image and gild the cage and call it survival and social justice to fit the punishment of birth and control of crime that doesn't pay. Ramiro was also part—pure devil . . .

My dear, hardworking, superbusy wife Yoli was floating up to her molars caring for our four energetic children, soon to be five, lunches, clothing, band-aids, caring love, and feeding. She was also keeping a keen eye on my efforts to break into publishing. I proposed and she accepted: we would finance and publish *The Plum Plum Pickers* ourselves. (The title is poetical alliteration.)

She understood the deadly rejection rate as well as I. I rented an electric typewriter, set the type, went to a local printer in San Jose, and ordered one thousand copies. They were delivered at the end of July 1969, just as Armstrong was stepping out on the moon. Some omen. We packed the kids in the family wagon and spent a whole day going up the San Francisco peninsula. I stopped at every bookstore I could find, about twenty of them, mostly small independents. Half of them, to my surprise, took five copies each on trial, and let me bill them.

The chains (including Waldenbooks, ironically) wouldn't take any. We crossed the Bay Bridge to Berkeley, my old academic stomping ground, where several bookstores took copies. I also took five copies over to the campus bookstore at San Jose State University, where the manager was a writing colleague of mine. Sure, he said. He put five copies on the shelf for browsers to pick up and look at. That was all I did.

In less than a week I received an order from Professor Mario Garcia at San Jose State for—100 copies! I was amazed and elated. The following week, two more 100-block orders. Before the month was out, I was getting orders from UCLA, Stanford, UC Berkeley, UC Santa Barbara. Then from Texas, New Mexico, Minneapolis, all across the country. I was soon out of books. My printer advanced me credit based on invoices which aren't paid for two or three months. I boldly ordered a run of 2,000 copies, and another, and another, until I'd gone through 10,000 copies that first year. Since short runs are costly, I was losing money with every short run. What was happening?

Plum was getting picked up by the newborn Chicano movement. It was/is my pride and honor to be associated with the Chicano movement. Chicanos are Mexican-Americans who accept their Americanness but who also want to express pride in their Mexican origins. The term Hispanic encompasses the entire Spanish-speaking or Latino world. A growing number of Chicano and other Hispanic writers are finding their way into America's literary stream. Antonio Villareal's *Pocho* (also of Santa Clara) was the first precursor of the Chicano novel. And now we have a growing list: Rudolfo Anaya's excellent *Bless Me, Ultima;* Tomas Rivera, Arturo Islas, Sandra Cisneros, Nash Candelaria's *Memories of the Alhambra* addressing his New Mexican origins, and many others. These, in addition to exciting Latin American writers: Octavio Paz, Carlos Fuentes, Gabriel Garcia Marquez.

Now here's another interesting story within a story. In the meantime I was also sending out multiple queries to publishers begging them to please take this book off my hands. I queried every fiction publisher in New York I could find in the *LMP (Literary Market Place)*. They ALL turned me down. This was just like getting rejected by the whole world. So I've learned

"Son Gabriel with wife, Alka Atal, at their Hindu wedding," 1987

to compensate for that insensate iniquity by bragging modestly that my *Plum* has received more rejections than any other book in history. I don't fool around. I aim for the top.

Now I was tinkering with the machinery and with the odds. Four single submissions a year to two hundred publishers would take fifty years and I wasn't about to take that route any more. So I compressed the fifty years to two months. Faster, no? Finally, on the second turn around (all publishers have several editors, so I'd really never run out) a second Harper and Row editor said he'd look at it. He took it, gave me a lunch cum margarita, a contract, a hand-shake, and a thousand-dollar advance. They ran off handsome paperback and hardcover editions for the next two years; relieving me of the box-boy syndrome (wrapping, shipping, billing) so I could get back to writing.

Then another happy thing happened. Requests from compilers and publishers of high school and college literary anthologies started coming in, with print runs of tens of thousands across the country. Excerpts from *Plum* began appearing alongside my literary heroes since my high school days. I'd gotten my message out, straight and honest, with my integrity intact. Eventually Harper and Row gave it up, and now Bilingual Review Press of Arizona is still keeping *Plum* in print, after twenty years.

I still had to keep right on teaching for I was not swamped by floods of dollars. I was gratified at being invited to teach Chicano studies courses, and also had the joy of doing research in Mexico's extraordinary history. The Aztec and Maya are but two of many fascinating pre-Columbian civilizations. These civilizations, like the Incas of Peru, were founded independently, and deserve every bit as much original credit as the ancient civilizations of Mesopotamia and Sumer. No, the Mexican pyramids were not engineered by visiting Egyptians, Vikings, or aliens. Out of my research I produced a third self-published book, *Mexico's Art and Chicano Artists*.

Some of the terms of that history still need to be straightened out. The word "Conquistador" has a romantic ring to it which Europeans and Americans love to hear, but which is demeaning to the victims. At the time of the brutal destruction of the Aztec Empire in the early 1500s, one unique Spanish explorer named Alvar Nuñez Cabeza de Vaca was shipwrecked off the coast of a wild, unknown Texas. Barely surviving, he was taken in by a tribe of friendly Indians. It took him eight years to get back to Mexico and *in that time he became an Indian himself*. In his later years, as a retired official, he wrote his memoirs, and almost alone of all those destructive thugs euphoniously called "Conquistadores," he expressed his great sorrow for the Indian people he came to know and love so intimately. Claiming they were more Christian than self-proclaimed Christians, he wrote:

> Spaniards are as spiritually barren as the barren fields of Castile . . . A day came when our friendly Indians said they watched from behind some trees as our countrymen took many of their people away in chains . . .

The Black Legend of Spanish/Mexican history exposes the stark cruelty of the Spanish conquest. In my *Mexico's Art* I wrote: "[The Spaniards invaded Mexico and] they wrecked their temples, their art, their religion, their deities, their sculpture, their calendar, their crafts, their skills, their architecture. They melted down every precious artifact they could find, all the gold and silver, regardless of how exquisitely fashioned it was." The great German Renaissance artist Albrecht Dürer (1471–1528) expressed amazement at the artistic splendor of the numerous Mexican art works he saw, better, he said,

"Son Raymond, Jr., with his guitar," 1990

than anything he'd seen in all of Europe. One six-foot disc of gold represented the sun, another of silver, the moon. They were both melted down, to pay for still more Spanish cannons.

All of this also holds true for the indignant resentment of the Red Man, Native Americans, who understandably are not all that thrilled about the coming 500th anniversary celebration of Columbus's "discovery" of America. Where the Spaniard intermixed with the native Mexicans and produced the current mix, or Raza, the English brought their own women and children and gradually pushed surviving Indians into reservations.

On Retirement. In 1977 I became eligible for an early pension, and my dear Yoli, despite her misgivings, agreed to let me retire. At the same time, my mother offered us her spare Russian River house, where we've been living for the past fifteen years.

Another thing I can't figure out is how we managed to raise our fine brood of five, two boys and three girls, all through the '60s and '70s without medical insurance coverage. I don't know how we managed. It was crazy. Luck, mostly. I paid cash for births, broken bones, baby shots, colds, chicken "pops," "wumps," one pneumonia. My hernia operation finally knocked me out. I'm glad to see that now for millions of undercovered Americans there is serious talk about national coverage, yes, socialized medicine. Even those conservative pharmaceutical corporations are expressing enthusiasm. Well, why not, just look at all those nice new millions they stand to gain.

All our five children are now grown and out of the home, and dipping into their own American experience. Firstborn Angelita, 1957, became a computer and microchip specialist at National Semiconductor in Silicon Valley, where she met and married Ron Swietek, who is CEO of his own small computer firm. They live in faraway San Diego with their three lovely tots. Next, Gabriel (b. 1959) got through high school with high honors, got his B.A. at Cal Poly, Pomona, and attended Stanford Medical School, now an M.D. He is married to our lovely daughter-in-law Alka Atal who, to our delight, also graduated M.D. from Stanford in the same class—two Barrios for one! They are in their last year of residence at Stanford.

Next, Raymond Jr. (b. 1961), has stayed on here in the Russian River. He likes to be called a River Rat. His passion is music, lead guitar, and he earns his living as a skilled carpenter. Married and split, his baby daughter, Delia, is our delight. Our second daughter, Andrea, (b. 1967) has lived these past seven years at Santa Cruz. She delighted us last summer by finally graduating from UC Santa Cruz. She's still hanging on there. Maybe she'll become a teacher. And finally, our baby, Margarita, now twenty (b. 1971) is approaching her third year at UC San Diego, and living with her older sister Lita. She majors in political science and has law as her career goal.

Nasario Garcia interviewed me in the spring 1985 issue of *Revista Chicano-Requena*. Following are excerpts:

NG: What kind of person are you and do these traits surface in your writings? How?

RB: I am an open, enthusiastic, and voluble advocate of liberal causes and concepts. I like the legal admonition: "Do you promise to tell the truth, the whole truth, and nothing but the truth?" All writings have moral, judgmental overtones, even if by default. It's up to the artist in every creative writer to choose the essential direction: to be a hack writing commercial potboilers, if he so chooses—or to try to reach the greatest idealistic heights

possible . . .

The art of writing is something quite different from whatever information is being imparted. I am full of gripes. I can't stand gothic romances. I am a real crank when I want to be. My writing shows it . . .

I want my life and career to serve as an example and as a catalyst for young idealists everywhere. For Chicanos and Hispanics, yes, and for every ethnic minority, but especially for all idealists, young and old . . . I do my best, my passionate best, to try to persuade young people to reject the materialism of technocrats now flooding our society, and to pursue the idealism of humanism.

The following comments were made by Eli A. Rubinstein, a retired professor of mass communication, in his article "The Not So Golden Years" (*Newsweek* 7 Oct/91):

> My retirement community . . . in North Carolina, is a case study of the trials and tribulations that come with growing old. The 380 residents are an elite group, retired professors, deans, etc. Despite all the social and sports activities here, an air of quiet resignation lurks under this blanket of convivial interaction . . . We're shifting the deck chairs around waiting for our ship of life to hit an iceberg and sink.

How incredibly depressing. What a gloomy gus. What a miserable group of dried-up clods. Shame on these aged yuppies.

Consider now the exciting creativity of a local artist named Raymond Barnhart who is eighty-eight. He lives in his own hand-made home in nearby Sebastopol, California. Barnhart "makes things." His recycled junk is described as "relief construction" and "conceptual art." He has been an artist all his life, an art instructor for thirty-two years. He and his work are widely loved and respected. He juxtaposes wind-blasted, sun-bleached, and burnt materials against rusted and tarnished discards, which become "the poetry of deserted places." One three-dimensional work entitled "Op-Art" evolved from a wood-munching gopher's stealing fruit from a prune tray. Barnhart maintains that nothing can mimic the natural aging process of nature, which gives his works a characteristic patina.

In sharp contrast to those decaying decrepitudes in North Carolina (and elsewhere) lolling in their fur-lined hot tubs, Barnhart serves as an eternal and refreshing inspiration for all young spirits everywhere no matter of what age. The gray panther barks. Good for him!

Now I have another confession to make. I never really retired. When I reached retirement age I simply activated my pension, but that was so I could concentrate more innocently on my real work, which is writhing, I mean writing. A form of self-torture. My pension is liberation liquified. Another creative arts grant. Another shaft of light in the great cavern we call learning. Another level of freedom.

I see people, young and old, rolling their eyeballs down the boob tube, minute after minute, year after year, lost. I see senior city citz glide into empty meaningless retirement, afloat on generous savings, equity, and pensions (OK, not all senior citizens), only to find themselves not really free, but trapped within themselves, barren spiritually, drained psychologically, hollow barbizons. Gaunt. Empty eyes. Maybe puttering with a little golf here or a little lotto there. Sure, I admit that's their thing too, but—come on—that's because they haven't sculpted or gardened or written poetry or sung to the spheres or created new pottery, skills they could carry on to greater heights

in their new age of wisdom, and share with others. Senior citz periodicals bark shrilly for still more material rights and flavors, usually for those who already are surfeited. So everybody's ding dong doing it. Grab bag. More comforters, more garbage, more loafers, while inner-city denizens remain trapped in poverty struggling just to stay alive. The sickness called materialism, like the poisons drummed into our rivers, oozes everywhere, into our pores, into our fat heads, into our innermost psyches.

The cure? Simple. More social justice, more eternal vigilance, more planetary care.

I'm still deep in the gestation of my latest octo opus, a novel I call *Carib Blue.* My central character Maxwell Kennfield is dropped off innocently enough at a business conference on a small Caribbean island, only to learn he has been rudely severed from his plush WashDC job. Flustered at first, he gradually realizes he is liberated, out of the cage, amused at being able to examine the foibles of modern man in a

"Our three daughters—Andrea (top), Lita (with her daughter Jennifer), Margarita—and Grandma Yoli holding Lita's son, Ronnie. Not shown are Raymond Jr.'s daughter, Delia, born later that year, and Lita's other daughter, Katrina, born the following year,"
Guerneville, 1986

very leisurely manner. Maybe I'll just print it up and get copies onto supermarket shelves. Look for it.

The Eighties . . .

Nineteen seventy-nine. "The Gypper" elected President.

In the summer of 1979, our second year of hibernating in the Russian River area, a couple of friends started up a spry little weekly which they called *The Paper*. It was newsy, colorful, and locally entertaining. In April 1980 I approached editor Nick Valentine with an idea for an irreverent political column. "Sure," he said. "Let's see if it floats." He looked like a young Santa Claus, full, rich, brown beard. And float it did. For the next six years, I punched out a free-swinging raucous weekly political. Free. No pay. I was given complete freedom. Wham the hell, let it all hang out.

This was an extraordinary growth experience for me.

I'd always liked reading anthologies and opinion and op/ed columns, and I always wanted to stick my pin into political foibles, events, and well-known personalities. The truth above all! As I saw it. I eventually got more than three hundred columns out. I gathered seventy-two of them into another self-published paperback titled *Political Portfolio*. I tried my best to be as logical as possible, as factual, and as inspiring and accusative and indignant as I could.

Whenever I sounded a little bitter or sour, as some readers noticed, it was because I was, yes, indeed sour and bitter and enraged at the incredibly selfish ripoffs of so many of the country's leading financiers and industrialists in our elite socialite structure. Why should top crooks escape, or get only a wrist slap? And there's our boyfaced vice president in the White House, secretly helping the business congloms wreck the country's pollution laws. Bitter? Is that what capitalism is all about? To keep quiet? Keeping quiet just compounds the crime. Is that what our beautiful democracy is all about? So, yes, I rant.

In one column, I raved over the excellence of W. A. Swanberg's incredible biography of Henry Luce, cofounder of *Time* magazine, and one of America's greatest intellectual thugs, along with the old Hearst.

I wrote: "Luce, America's most vicious manipulator of news in our time, had a brilliant mind. A supreme elitist, fascinated with fascism and nazism, he scorned democracy. This antihumanist aristocratic snob loved power and loathed humanity."

Luce believed in Great Men. By Great Men he did not mean the likes of Washington, Jefferson, or Lincoln. He meant Businessmen, Industrialists. The ones he praised in *Fortune*.

Luce wrote: "Business is what we in America believe in more than any other agency of society. Business will never be run on a democratic basis. Business must be aristocratic. There must be a top, and the best men must get there." And, he might have added, they must be Wasps, White Anglo-Saxon Protestants. Business was his religion, and only a false modesty prevented him from admitting who God was. Cal Coolidge also had his two cents' worth: "The business of America is business." Followed by Hoover and the Great Depression.

Luce's greatest crime was the slanting of news. One of his persistent public phrases was, "The Russians stink." It was Luce, short for Lucifer, who stank. He never allowed any favorable comments to be made about the Russians (or liberals, or humanists), only unfavorable. Well, a steady diet of that and what do you get? You get a warped readership, as Hitler also well knew. Incidentally, the *Reader's Digest* also practices this kind of hidden bias: to this day, they won't print any positive articles about unions, only negative, even though the Wallaces have been long dead gone.

Well, I've also had my share of admirers. Example:

> Editor: There are some who will be happy to know that Raymond Barrio's dream is becoming a reality in America, a cancer spreading across the face of the land. Humanists can take credit for eliminating religion from classrooms. Humanism denies God and defies man. It embraces evolution, occultism, witchcraft, mysticism, and satan worship. Yes, Mr. Barrio, your dream is becoming reality.—C.C., Monte Rio, CA.

To quote The Bard, Oh were that it were true! This rogue C.C. sure knows how to dish it out, even as he steals from my own style. Au contraire, I would say: "Humanism decries superstition, bypasses deism, and defines man."

Another letter writer to the editor, Ross Grossman of Sebastopol (Sonoma County, please, not Russia), wrote: "In defense of Barrio's columns, it seems to me they are in the best tradition of American radical journalism—they go to the root. Barrio's world-view is a healthy balance to the pseudo-objective, thoroughly biased conservative view of the world's owners."

And who, the Bible asks, shall inherit the earth? Thanks, R.G. I proudly admit to being highly biased,

The author and his wife at home, 1990

in favor of The Good, social justice, honesty, fairness, democracy, evolution, abortion, and to being equally prejudiced against the warped twisted richies who can only think of sopping up more riches, the ugly greedies who say to hell with humanity.

As a sideline, for years I kept sending out copies of my irascible columns to major newspapers across the country. I got some interesting feedback, but no proposals. I got the feeling that my potatoes were too hot. Even Ben Bradlee (name pushing) of the *Washington Post* turned me down. Well, I tried.

Finally, here's my farewell column for *WOW, Writers on Writing,* out of Florida:

One Writer's Dilemma

Usually you won't catch me dead reading the obituary columns, but then I came across this intriguing bit about a famous New York publisher whom I shall refer to as X, giving up his ghost at 97. One devil of a long rich life, I'd say.

X founded his own publishing firm in 1921 at age 29.

A 1913 graduate of Columbia University, X made several generous gifts over the years to his alma mater. He began his foul career by publishing pulp magazines, "Cupid's Diary," and comic magazines, and other such trash. He sold more than 30 million copies a month, and became rich. After WWII, X became a major publisher of paperback books. Soon he was a multi-millionaire. In 1963 he formed his own press, publishing such well-known authors as Kurt Vonnegut, Danielle Steele, Irwin Shaw, James Clavell, and others.

For $350,000 X built a 400-foot geyser on Roosevelt Island in New York. It spewed polluted water into the air. He was forced to chlorinate it. Then the chlorine killed the nearby trees. Local residents became even more enraged. X liked to say he liked to see something for his money.

And now for this jewel in the crown of his tremendous accomplishments: asked once about helping the poor, X said, "People are poor because they're dumb or because they're lazy. If you feed them you just keep them in the same strata."

Somehow I expected higher ideals from a mogul publisher. Where did I go wrong?

Retiring in 1976 at the age of 82, he sold his firm to Doubleday, another conglom, and was named to the publishers Hall of Fame.

This, then, is your publishing world's superleech. He became a multimillionaire by slurping around in the lowest depths of illiteracy, and then he had the gall to set himself up as social arbiter as well as literary genius. Bad role model. Destroyer of high standards.

In all fairness, this dorp was really no different from vast numbers of honored American businessmen, Henry Luce's heroes, robber barons, fanatic industrialists, financial manipulators. Some day, I keep promising myself, I shall compile a Devil's Encyclopedia of Dirty Capitalists, and leave Ambrose Bierce behind in his dust. Trouble is, I'm overwhelmed by the sheer quantity of the material.

Now, for contrast, to show that famous writers are equally capable of equal ignominy, consider the following excerpt from Patricia Holt's review in the *San Francisco Chronicle* of 4 August 1991:

> [Harold Robbins' new novel *The Pirhana* is] so awful it's not worth reviewing . . . Robbins' 20 novels have sold something like 685 million copies. Why is it necessary then to show a voluptuous nude woman [on the cover?]

While I'm at it, I'd also like to raise the question: Just where does the wholly fabricated and enormously profitable sequel to GWTW, *Scarlett*, fit into the literary scheme of things? Or is it just . . . plain lucre?

We're talking fame here and big megabucks and a superfluous flood of orgiastic writing. Yes, that's obviously what the people want, and what the people should be free to choose, yes, yes. But then the annoying question keeps arising, like Lazarus: *isn't literature important?*

What is a serious, dedicated writer to do, one who has not only paid his dues, but who has sacrificed even the comfort and security and well-being of his family for years for the unproven aspirations of his serious writing efforts?

To keep his own integrity, a serious writer must subsidize himself. Which means years, perhaps a lifetime, of eking out the money and the time to pay for his vainglorious writing time and the printer through some external means, and with the loving support of his family.

So what's left, O writer of epics and paeans and ethos and great American novels? What's left is you. You have to do it yourself. Like an artist. A singer. A poet. A sculptor.

You devote yourself to producing your cherished dreams for your own pleasure, holding the line against tackiness, no pandering to what's selling, to what's hot, but to your own private inner beam of inspiration. You stand your ground against the philistines and the Xs. You stay in the barrio.

The writer who decides to take the higher road should consider (unless he can snag a good agent) going into self-publishing. This way you can experience the thrill of self-expression. In fact, the majority of those we honor as great classical authors—Melville, Thoreau, Carroll, Dreiser, a long, long list—started by self-publishing themselves. True, the creeping conglomerates hadn't taken over then.

The printed book is itself your greatest reward, your triumph.

Anything else that follows is just dessert.

BIBLIOGRAPHY

Experiments in Modern Art: Lessons in the Art of Painting, Sterling, 1968.

The Plum Plum Pickers (novel), Bilingual Review Press, 1969.

Mexico's Art and Chicano Artists, Ventura Press, 1975.

Devil's Apple Corps (drama), Ventura Press, 1976.

Also contributor to anthologies, including *American Literature, Arrangement in Literature, Gallery, Insights: Themes in Literature,* and *Values and Voices: A College Reader.*

Germaine Brée

1907-

Germaine Brée, 1991

First and always, at the beginning, is the tortoise. Head thrust out, it was making its way across the garden under the fascinated eyes of two or three small children. The event took place in the village of Lasalle, where I was born, in the Cévennes mountains, north of the better-known Côte d'Azur, the Riviera. I can't have been more than three. There were other wondrous creatures in Lasalle: the silkworms spread out on trays in the "magnaneries" (the silkworm breeding barns) relentlessly chewing on mulberry leaves as they turned into cocoons, a feat punctuated every year by a jovial village celebration; and the sheep, hundreds of them it seemed to us, preceded by a cloud of dust and the tinkling of their bells, filling the narrow street from edge to edge as they made their way up to their summer pastures. We knew they would come down again at the end of summer, complete with shepherds, dogs, and the awesome rams, on their trek home to the coastal plain. But the unexpected passage of that tortoise in our garden, accompanied by the semianguished cry of one of my playmates, "Oh the silly thing, it *walks!*" was different. It was not frightening, just strange. It was the first time, I think, that I glimpsed the fact that other beings, unconnected with people and their activities, could live quietly in the space which we thought of as ours. That sense I have never lost; a familiar garden may harbor who-knows-what mystery.

As I look back some eighty years to Lasalle, it still seems a rather enchanted place: there were wild meadow flowers, mauve and white violets and gold "coucous" (cowslips); olive trees, the ubiquitous chestnut trees whose nuts turned up in all manner of dishes—soups, stews, and the great Cévenol specialty, "la confiture de marron" (chestnut jam). We were to leave Lasalle just before I turned five. Today, at first sight, it doesn't seem greatly changed, with its single narrow street, walled in on both sides by the austere façades of houses that afford not a glimpse of the sunny gardens in the back, a typical centuries-old Cévenol village. But the silkworms have gone; the chestnut trees are dying out, prey to some deadly disease; and cars block the road in place of the sheep that, no doubt to their satisfaction, go by truck to their summer pastures. "Summer people" or retirees inhabit the dour old châteaux and many of the farmhouses that dot the slopes around the village. But the tortoise, I feel sure, lives on, undisturbed, in the garden which once we had thought of as ours.

I cannot claim the Cévennes as an ancestral home, much as I might like to. The past of this region is very much alive for me, with its legend of an age-old resistance to intrusions from outside, reactivated again at the time of World War II when it sheltered many refugees. It is because of another episode in its history that I happened to have been born there. It was in this natural fortress, in the seventeenth century, that the Protestant "Huguenot" mountain folk stubbornly fought off the dragoons of Louis XIV sent out to eradicate the Protestant "heresy." My father was the minister to a small Methodist group with ties to the English Wesleyan church. But he was not a Cévenol. He was a Channel Islander, from the island of Jersey lying off the Norman coast. Though French in origin, no doubt, he was of British nationality. The small cluster of prosperous Channel Islands enjoyed a certain degree of autonomy. They were the last vestiges of the French possessions of the dukes of Normandy still attached to the British crown. As such, besides a measure of self-government, they had retained their Norman dialect, laws, many of their customs, and their pride in a somewhat mythical independence in regard to British rule. The rapid modernization of world trade and a five-year occupation by German troops (1940–1945) shook their sense of self-sufficiency rooted in a history they could trace back to Neanderthal man. On occasion though, it could still assert itself: "When did the British conquer the island?" inquired the German officer sent in 1940 to take over a territory whose only importance was symbolic. "We conquered England in 1066" was the answer, an exchange duly recorded in the Jersey archives.

At the turn of the century, the relations between Jersey and France were active. My grandfather owned the "Brée Royal Hôtel" in St. Heliers, the capital of Jersey, and through his wife's family had interests in a small company of freighters which under the Jersey flag sailed beyond the British Channel as far as the Gaspé peninsula in Canada. He was in close touch with the Mont-Saint-Michel community on the Norman coast just fifteen miles offshore, and he enjoyed participating in the regattas in Dinard. This information was relayed to me by my father, for both my grandfather and grandmother died before I was born. The nine-year-old I was when we moved to Jersey was rather nonplussed at the sight of the family name inscribed on the hotel façade. It has long since disappeared. But, much later, when driving through the Gaspé to visit one of my father's cousins there, I ran across a number of settlers from Jersey who immediately recognized my name and knew just who I was; that was more perhaps than I knew myself. "Cousin Amy," I inquired, "have you been to the United States?" "Yes," she answered firmly, "I once went to Virginia to see a Jersey man." She, at least, had no trouble with identity. My grandfather had sent his sons to France, to the lycée of Coutances in Normandy, for their secondary education, after which, presumably well-grounded in French culture, they would go on to some English university. My father chose to pursue his theological studies in Paris. His three brothers went their differ-

"Walter Brée, my father"

ent ways. One, a medical doctor, settled in England; another, an architect, moved to Argentina; the third went to Aldershot and to a career in India, rising to the rank of general and, for a brief time, governor of a province. Troubled by the French resonance of his name, he adopted an older spelling "Bray"; my father in contrast took out French naturalization papers. Caught up, as it were, in this duality, which he coped with differently, was a cousin whom I greatly admired. As a young Oxford student during World War I, he volunteered in an ambulance unit attached to the French army, losing a leg in the fray. I was in awe of him, of his courage, of his Oxford cap and gown, of his status as professor of French at the University of Belfast, Ireland; and I treasured an early article of his on Marcel Proust written years before Proust had come my way.

My mother's family was one of a small group of Protestants in Lorraine, a province which, though predominantly Catholic, harbored no prejudices against other affiliations. According to my mother, the family had achieved some notoriety at the time of the Napoleonic wars when a cousin, Augereau, rose from the rank of soldier of fortune to become general and marshal of France. But they were not drawn to the military. As part of a minority, they tended to look beyond their narrow circle for cultural sustenance: to the vigorous Jewish community in Nancy, to Switzerland (my grandmother was Swiss), to Germany, but preferably to England. As an adolescent, my mother had been to England to learn the language, one of her sisters married an Englishman who had a job as professor in Adelaide, South Australia. My mother, in her early twenties, had undertaken the long sea voyage to visit her sister "down under." She enthralled us by her stories of the Suez Canal, the Red Sea, the stopover in Ceylon, now Sri Lanka; with stories of moonlight picnics, of black swans on the Darling River, of koala bears. When I, too, visited Australia, though, alas, by plane, they were still all there. Another sister married into a Huguenot family in southern France, establishing thereby our link with that part of the world and its history. If I recall in some detail my heterogenous background, it is because I see how well it prepared me for the cosmopolitan and mobile world which was to be ours. Both my

"Lois Marguerité Andrault, my mother"

parents and their siblings on both sides had moved away from their family homes. My world could hardly be parochial. But it was real, inscribed on maps and peopled, it seemed, by our relatives. As for us, my father's church shuffled its ministers around on principle every four years or so. Consequently, the houses we lived in were not ours, nor was much of the furniture. We were, in fact, nomads. When I say "we," I speak of six small girls; later seven; then came my brother, the youngest and last child. In spite of dire predictions as to his future which, inevitably, destined him to become a spoiled brat, he turned out very well indeed. Like his father, he became a minister. He was later to help many a refugee find shelter from Nazi persecution; he is known as a man of integrity and courage.

In 1912, we began our first migration. We left the Cévennes for what was to be a ten-year sojourn in the Channel Islands, four spent in Guernsey, six in Jersey. We were nine travelers: five small girls; their serene, completely deaf grandmother; our perennially absent-minded father; and our mother, the infallible source of our security. We didn't mind the uprooting—rather to the contrary. For we took along our own rituals: family prayers at night; grace sung in French before each meal, a habit which was mightily to intrigue our new neighbors for we sang grace in French to the tune of "God Save the King"; observance of the year's festivities; birthdays, of which there were many; shoes laid out in front of the fireplace, French-style, at Christmas; the Christmas tree which appeared miraculously on Christmas morning, fully decorated. We played, quarrelled, communicated with each other endlessly, far more aware of each other than of our parents. A subtle web of complicity linked child to child. Beyond, was the reassuring emporium of our parents. Large families perhaps escape Freudian fixations and anxieties? So we moved without anxiety into a new way of life and a new language, English.

My memories of the journey to the islands are vague; except for the uneasy pleasure of sleeping in the luggage net. Above all, I remember the curious sensation of moving on the sea in a boat, my first boat trip, then the excitement of docking in Guernsey's St. Peter's Port and going by carriage to our new home. The Channel Islands, in those years, even more perhaps than the Cévennes, were a child's paradise. There were few cars as yet, so we could freely roam the lanes, watch the farmers' horse-drawn vans carrying the potatoes to the port, the cows being milked, and the apples or cherries being picked. Best of all were the bays and beaches swept by the tides, happy hunting grounds where the low tides left behind puddles in the rocks inhabited by small shellfish, limpets and sea anemones. We all learned how to swim. Fascinating and dangerous, the sea was a vast, independent force, stretching all around. We wanted to know, what lay behind the horizon? We made up stories of lost sailors returning after years of travel and, in fact, sometimes identified them on the beach. The First World War passed by almost unnoticed. But something else was happening, *school!* I became a precocious and passionate reader, determined to keep up with my two older sisters, half sisters actually, who were three and four years older than I was. Both my parents, on occasion and differently, were storytellers, and there were many books in my father's library. My parents never supervised our reading or our games as long as we did not become obstreperous. As large families are wont to do, we attracted many other children, boys and girls, who came to play. We were never bored. Nonetheless, my older sisters were fast growing up and distancing themselves from the "little ones!" "It's not for children," they would announce of a book. "You wouldn't understand." A case in point was *The Scarlet Letter* through which I stubbornly ploughed and which I did *not* understand: what was wrong with the scarlet letter? and why did the minister stand on the scaffold? *Little Women* was more fun. So much so that my younger sisters took to impersonating the characters, acting out their stories, adding unexpected episodes.

The real crunch came for me when, at nine, I was enrolled with my two older sisters as a weekly boarder in a "public" (English sense) school, rather pompously called, at the time, the Jersey Ladies' College. Taught at home by a governess, my younger sisters continued to live their own way. Somewhere between reality and fantasy, the cohesiveness of our world began to erode, although, as I discovered, the bonding between us never failed. When, six years later, I left the college with the requisite "matriculation" for admission to a British university, presumably Oxford, I had been metamorphosized into that peculiar product: an English schoolgirl! At the outset, the frocks, white underwear, long hair and white hair ribbons had given way to the school uniform: blue gym tunic, "bloomers" of the same material, long black stockings and gym shoes, pleated hair and barrettes, completed by a "basher," a stiff straw hat adorned with the school colors: red-and-white ribbon and school crest. When we came home on weekends, we now tended to be seen as "outsiders," or as someone once put it, "outsiders-insiders," by our home-centered siblings. At school, there were gym classes, team games, netball, rounders, volleyball, the

ancestors of our powerful athletic games today, hockey, tennis. In spring, we walked two-by-two in a "crocodile" to swim in the pool flushed out twice a day by the tide. Or, as "girl guides," we followed the scout programs, which I never quite took to. There were piano lessons and, of course, classes that I enjoyed, more especially English and history classes, Latin, and French, which I was rapidly forgetting. Most enthralling was the poetry, reams of which we were required to learn by heart and recite on special occasions, such as Parents' Day. I still dispose of a vast and uneven repertoire touching on poets from Chaucer to Kipling and the poet laureate of the hour, Sir Henry Newbold, whose martial verses ring in my ears: "Admirals all, for England's sake. . . ." Though I am careful to spare my friends, I can still declaim those poems today when I hit a depressing hour: "How weary, stale, flat and unprofitable / Seem to me all the uses of this world. . . ." "Great stuff," a friend of mine used to say; more especially for a world-weary adolescent. My successes were clearly academic and easily come by.

Something else was taking place. Many of the boarders were the daughters of colonial administrators, from India mostly, sent to Jersey because of its mild climate. To be "French" was not exactly a quality in their eyes. The French were clearly an inferior breed. My name "Germaine," besides, could easily be transformed into "German." I had to fight for it, and did. Thereby I earned another name, "Jimmie," which my English sisters, their children and grandchildren use to this day. The teasing was too puerile and sporadic to constitute a threat. My schooldays, broken by weekends and holidays at home, were happy. But they raised the disturbing question of the connection between language and the historical conflicts of nations discussed in history classes. English and French had never been compartmentalized in my mind. *Alice in Wonderland* and the *Contes* of Perrault occupied the same space in my imagination. The adventures of "Little Red Riding Hood" were no different in French or English. My return to France, at fifteen, would raise the question again dramatically. Since I was too young for admission to Oxford, it was decided that I should spend a couple of years in French schools before taking off for England. But postwar economic conditions intervened. Oxford, economically, was out of the question. I spent the next ten years getting thoroughly integrated into the French educational system, a difficult process which absorbed most of my energy. And it was there that my life took a decisive turn. The English schoolgirl, at first rebelliously, became French.

"The family in Guernsey. I am the one kneeling on the left," 1912

I was not quite fifteen, in June 1922, when I took the Jersey boat to St. Malo, en route for the Cévennes, for the small town of Le Vigan to which my father had been posted the year before. His church was one of the seven Protestant churches that shared a dwindling and aging constituency. The younger generations of Cévenols were leaving for more promising areas. It was then, I think, that I moved toward an unaggressive, unvoiced agnosticism which I have not relinquished. It entailed no rebellion. There had been a time when we judged my father's humor and freedom from clerical solemnity rather sternly. We wanted him to look important and be beyond human frailty. As we grew up, we learned to prize his imperviousness to all forms of cant and dogmatism. He was an island unto himself, a natural nonconformist who respected other people's beliefs. My patient and perspicacious mother, though not always without trouble, furnished the ballast that kept his enterprises going in parish and family. Life at Le Vigan soon established its own rhythms. We took long hikes up the mountain sheep trails—"the drailles"—sometimes walking all night to reach the high summits from which one might catch a glimpse of the rising sun reflected on the glinting Mediterranean sea. Or we explored old villages, some of them former Roman camps on the arid plateaus of Les Causses. To the south, the larger towns were rich in Roman monuments that I never thought of as "ruins," so well integrated were they with the cities—Nîmes and Arles for instance—temples, portals, arenas, baths, and, not least among them, the Pont du Gard aqueduct. The Jersey dolmens could hardly compare with such landmarks. I had been living in a timeless world. I took things as they were, for granted. The school curriculum in those years was not focussed on the arts; nor were the arts visible in the Cévennes villages or the Channel Islands. I had not thought of the books I read or the poems I learned as "literature." No one spoke at the time of the "creative arts" nor of "creative writing." Human activities were puzzling, of course, but now the arts, and especially the literary arts, began to seem particularly enigmatic. I smile when I think of the fifteen-year-old fresh out of school who knew nothing of radio, television, computers, word processors, or airplanes. As an "unknown" author put it, for us "pot" was "something you cooked in," and "grass" was "what you mowed." Our classes and books were our main sources of knowledge, besides conversations with adults. When one started to ask oneself what in fact a book was, one's intellectual horizons were changing.

Besides, I had run into an impasse. Since I was supposed at first to be only temporarily staying in France to brush up my French, I attended the local primary school. For the only time in my long academic career, I fell upon an inflexible xenophobic teacher. England and all things English were her pet bugaboos. She seemed to think I was responsible for all England's misdeeds, chief of them the burning of Joan of Arc. The confused adolescent I was took her disparaging attacks to heart. I was becoming disputatious and angry. My pleasure in learning and my sense of security foundered. I dropped out. Luckily my parents came to my rescue. A friendly tutor came to teach me at home. Learning was no longer reduced to an invidious confrontation between English and French. Both were OK. Today we might say that I had had a glimpse of the snares of "cultural diversity," or maybe "pluralism." The concept would have meant nothing to me at the time.

So I embarked on what was to be a remarkably rich program of study involving four years in Nîmes and one in Bordeaux, until in the fall of 1928 I landed on the threshold of the Sorbonne in Paris. I realized I had been on the wrong track all that time, enrolled in a program for primary school teachers. However, my teachers, almost all of them women, had been great. They placed meticulous emphasis on precision and accuracy of language, and consistency of thought. The general goal of their teaching was to foster a sense of value and continuity in the long history of French civilization. In literature this meant the reading, analysis, and discussion of chosen texts or excerpts from the "great authors," a classical nineteenth-century model. It was all very reassuring. As a child, I had read for the fun of moving in imaginary lives and worlds. Now I was asked to analyze how literary works were put together and how they fitted into an evolving historical continuity, a cultural statement, of "universal" significance. It would take some fifty years to sort out the implications and the limits of this assumption, which, in fact, transcended national and linguistic frontiers, and literary "genres," and attributed value of high order to certain forms of writing. In my last year of study in Bordeaux, jumping beyond the chronological boundaries of the formal canon, a small group of students had plunged into the reading of contemporary writ-

ers: Gide, Proust, Valéry. . . . The "mandatory" reading lists, we knew, did not exhaust the never-completed enterprise of literary expression, of modes of thought and perception. My five years' detour was now to prove most profitable. I had acquired a solid background in French culture which was invaluable when I became a teacher of French literature in higher education in the United States.

At the Sorbonne, I opted for a major in English literature. Well ahead of some programs in the USA, the syllabus comprised a section on American literature. Attendance at the lectures was optional. Students were given reading lists upon which the examination questions would rest. The examinations were fiercely competitive. In order to get to Paris, I had done what students have always done the world over. I had taken a job as governess in a family of the "grande bourgeoisie" that had three sons. The time I could devote to study was limited. I was treated with consideration, even affection. I reacted to the constraints on my time and my freedom with increasing restiveness. Three years went by as, year by year, I passed the required exams, preliminary to the "agrégation." But I had discovered a haven in the overcrowded student world of Paris, the American library. When I had to present what was the equivalent of an M.A. thesis, I chose a topic on Henry James; the American library, with its kindly librarians and its comfortable reading room, became my refuge.

Of Paris, seething with activity in those years, only echoes reached me: of ballet, opera, concerts, painting exhibitions, debates, and manifestoes, I managed to catch only a glimpse. Like Simone de Beauvoir who, unbeknown to me, was one of the fast-growing minority of women students of my generation, I worked with a small group of students, friends who helped me by sharing the notes of those courses I could not attend and keeping me informed of university events. But all in all, I was almost desperately tired of what seemed to me by then the grinding drabness of my daily life. Then, suddenly, a door opened and determined the course of my life.

One day, a fellow student wandering in the maze of Sorbonne corridors asked me for directions. She had just come back, she explained, from a year of study in the USA. As I showed her the way, I asked her how she had got there, and I headed forthwith to the office in charge of the exchange programs for foreign students interested in studying in the USA. In France, in those years, students were deeply interested in the USA, its first films, jazz, and history; more especially in the vision of the Far West shaped by Jack London and many a novelist. One French novelist in particular had fired my imagination by stories of Salt

Lake City and the Mormon community. I settled for Bryn Mawr College. I had never heard of it before. Among the American professors interviewing the French applicants was the dean of the small graduate school of Bryn Mawr. Dean Eunice Morgan Schenck, a Flaubert scholar, was one of a great generation of American university women I would come greatly to respect. She was impressive, decisive, and kindly impersonal in action, wise to the ways of the "foreign" students she interviewed. Overlooking, no doubt with amusement, my abysmal ignorance in regard to Bryn Mawr, she offered me a one-year graduate fellowship. It was perhaps, I later thought, because of Henry James.

I finished my thesis, said good-bye to my job and, with a small group of French students, embarked in midsummer, on the SS *de Grasse* of the French Line, for the fabulous city of New York. As we sailed out of Le Havre, nothing was further from my mind than the long vista of exams I was leaving behind me. It was 1931; life was great. And I had not given a thought to the Great Depression or America's struggle with the Prohibition laws, to say nothing of the racial problem. My USA was a semi-imaginary land. Surprisingly, the segment of America I now came to know in many ways surpassed the dream.

There were to be many transatlantic crossings for me in the next few years which witnessed the rise and fall of the great transatlantic liners. Travel by air which replaced them would never give the same feeling of being suspended in time, between sea and sky. My first crossing in the late summer of 1931, however, stands out in sharp contrast to the last on the SS *France*, seven years later. The French line cast a tolerant eye on students. We roamed the decks at will, played deck tennis and shuffleboard and enjoyed whatever entertainment was forthcoming. We greeted the Statue of Liberty and the "Manhattan skyline" with exuberance. In 1938, in contrast, the mood was grim. We approached New York to the rhythmic beat of male voices coming over the radio, chanting "Sieg, heil! Sieg, heil!" interminably, no doubt the broadcast of one of the Nazi Nuremberg rallies, a prelude to the annexation of the Sudetenlands. A group of silent German passengers gathered around the radio. One of them, standing near me, murmured: "I am ashamed. I am so ashamed." This was my introduction to the distinguished theologian Paul Tillich who shortly after would be in exile in the United States.

In 1931, nothing was further from our minds than war. Taken in charge by the competent and dedicated Institute of International Education, we toured New York, went to the top of the Empire State Building, attended an impressive event—*Tris-*

tan und Isolde at the Met. We were then taken to Storm King College by bus for briefing before betaking ourselves to our respective universities. There were other "foreign" student groups at Storm King, notably a large German contingent which we held in awe because of the vigorous choral sessions with which they entertained us in the evening. We were no match for them in that area and had to make up for it in the discussion groups! The atmosphere was friendly. The beauty of the setting, the sense of discovery we shared, were exhilarating. We were very optimistic. True, the twenties had not been easy; but the future seemed to us promising, at least as perceived from the banks of the Hudson. The League of Nations had opened its doors to Germany. The cordial talks between the French and German statesmen—Aristide Briand and Gustav Stresemann—were showing the way to the making of a "United States of Europe." In 1926 the two men had even shared a Nobel Peace Prize. Gandhi was a hero for our time. The precarious economic situation in Germany and the Wall Street crash seemed past; Russia was far away. By 1938, the "postwar years" had become "the interwar years." But in 1931, our minds set on the present, we were not, any of us, as I remember, in a doomsday mood. Seen retrospectively, the years between '31 and '38 marked an ominous transition in world affairs, to say nothing of personal destinies. We were hardly aware of it. Because the Bryn Mawr fall semester began a little later than most, there was a gap in my schedule. I was befriended by one of the generous volunteer workers on the Institute staff. She introduced me to her cottage in the Catskills, then to New York. By the time I reached Bryn Mawr, I felt I was a seasoned American, enchanted with the USA I had glimpsed. It was, to be sure, a selected fragment of the whole nation, one that would later be branded "élitiste," but it was *real*. The spaciousness of the land seemed to be matched by the openhanded American generosity; I had begun to grasp something of its diversity. Though this was an all-white America, it was cosmopolitan in outlook and tolerant. Bryn Mawr College with its carefully groomed campus and staid buildings did not in any way reflect the image of university life projected in films. After four years in Paris, it seemed, at times, all too quiet. In contrast, it offered a life of luxury, where devotion to academic work, the respect for scholarly achievement and intellectual integrity were prime values. The experience of working in small seminars, with distinguished professors, was exciting. The camaraderie between students, some of them like me, "foreign," who were engaged in similar studies and lived in the same dormitory, inspired lively discussions. I also became acquainted with the often admirable and prosperous community of "Main Line" Pennsylvania Quakers; with the quasi-fabulous Philadelphia orchestra and its director Leopold Stokowski; and with the Bach-Bethlehem chorale, to whose annual performance I was invited, and shall never forget. All in all it was a rich experience. Later, I would realize that there were powerful disruptive forces at work in a society of which I had seen only the most privileged strata. Still, it communicated to me a sense that the words "the American way of life" designated something more than a myth. The "groves of Academe" might not always prove idyllic. Yet, despite the ritual "bashing" of academic institutions that American intellectuals seem to relish, my respect for the academic community has not flagged. Its dedication to learning, to integrity, and to freedom of thought are, I believe, active forces in shaping the American mind. Later I would discover the diversity that makes any discussion of "the American university" as such, a rather gratuitous rhetorical exercise.

When the academic year drew to its end, heralded by the then traditional and beautiful College May Day Celebration, I left Bryn Mawr with no great qualms concerning the final exam awaiting me in Paris. My friends, with the generous solidarity of student life, had registered me as required for all candidates; and they had secured a small room for me on the sixth floor of a house overlooking the Luxembourg gardens. It was a "maid's room," which enjoyed the privilege of a single cold water faucet shared by all on that floor. Furthermore, it had no access to the elevator: so much for social equality! But it was all I needed. I occupied it for the duration of the exam: the written session was followed, after a pause, by the oral exam, and by the final public posting of the names of the successful candidates on a bulletin board. It was like a rather tense ritual of passage. The candidates, often with family or friends, assembled in the courtyard waiting for the calling of the names. Jubilation and resigned despair intermingled as the successful candidates made off for the summer vacation assured of a teaching position for the fall, while their unlucky fellow students went back empty-handed with no prospect but to try again a year later. Within the French system, the "agrégation" entitles the holder to a permanent position in the lycée structure. As one of the lucky ones that year, I left for a glorious vacation "en famille" on the coast near St. Malo, where my parents were now living, and waited for the notification of my next destination. The Ministry of Education had sent a

questionnaire concerning our desiderata in the matter. I had opted for the lycée of Hanoi in what was then known as French Indochina, now Vietnam. The novelist André Malraux, among others, had awakened our imaginations to the majesty of the great Khmer temples—more especially Angkor Wat, lost in the jungles of Cambodia. I wanted to find out more about the East. I would be less than candid if I failed to mention the incentives of a higher "colonial" salary, and of travel at the expense of the French government. Like many young intellectuals, I was not in favor of colonial exploitation; but I detached my own profession, teaching, from the general reprobation: it was a nonexploitive activity, as we saw it. We would soon be enlightened as to the ambiguity of our outlook. In any case, there being no opening in Hanoi at the time, and luckily for me, I was appointed to the girls' lycée of Oran, Algeria, rather closer to home. There I taught English for four years, broken by summers in France and England and, during the other vacations, forays into Tunisia, Morocco, and the oases in the South.

Commencement Day, Bryn Mawr College,
late 1930s

There were very few, if any, Muslim girls in the lycée; in contrast to their brothers, they were kept at home. But, apart from this, an Algerian classroom offered a wide diversity of origins: Spanish, Italian, Maltese, Polish, Jewish, all of whom had come in successive waves as political or economic circumstances determined, some recent, others century-old. The French were of different kinds; some known as the "Français de France," the "French from France," belonged to the administrative French cadres, whether military, legal, or educational. Then there were the "Français d'Algérie," born in Algeria. Among those were the "grands colons," or powerful landowners, and the "petits colons," who ran small businesses or were employed in a variety of jobs. One thing was clear: the young girls in Algeria were far more mature, "worldly-wise," than their counterparts in France. Whether teaching the rudiments of English to the twelve-year-olds or *Hamlet* to the older students preparing for the "baccalauréat," I found they were a lively bunch, some of whom I have kept in touch with to this day. Their English, such as it was, served them well when, only a few years ahead, Oran unexpectedly became a bustling American military base. But no one foresaw, at the time, the drama of their future existence: the Algerian war was to play havoc with their fate. One of my Algerian colleagues at the lycée had a younger sister who was to play a role of some consequence in my life. She married a promising young man by the name of Albert Camus.

Life in Oran, with its Mediterranean beaches and sunshine, was pleasant. More fascinating were the vast stretches of land to the south: the beauty of the landscape, whether mountain or desert; the "golden towns," remains of the Roman outposts, the oases. To the west were the famed cities of Morocco, Fez and, way south, Marrakesh; to the east, the Tunisian holy city of Kairouan. At the lycées—the boys' as well as the girls'—there were many young professors in their mid-twenties. In small groups, according to affinities or convenience, we took off as soon as the classes were over for the Christmas and spring vacations. It would take me far beyond the limits of this narrative to describe our travels to the south, through the Sahara to oases, no one of which resembled the others. We took local, rickety busses; on one occasion a twenty-four-kilometer camel ride. . . . At no time, as I remember it, did we meet with any hostility. Only once did I feel jittery. Somewhere in the desert, our bus suddenly stopped amid great shouts from the Arab travelers who leapt out and began to run around. Why, we did not know. They came back, triumphantly holding a large desert lizard, a welcome addition to their evening meal. The captor of the lizard rode in the seat behind me, clutching the lizard right behind my back. I was happy when we arrived and we went our separate ways. The vitality of the Arabic and Berber villages, their cohesion within a broad diversity, the dignity so often lost in the Europeanized coastal towns were compelling. Theirs was a completely distinct "way of life," a culture not easy to penetrate but which commanded respect.

But, under no circumstances, being a woman, could I endorse that culture's conception of the place and role of women in or outside the family. I knew I would always be an alien in that society; an alien, too, I also discovered, in the colonial society.

I shall recall only briefly the events bearing down on the world at large in those years. From 1933, when Hitler became Chancellor of the Reich, to 1936, when the Spanish Civil War broke out, violence was erupting everywhere. Stalinism triumphed in Russia. Mussolini's army conquered Haile Selassie's Ethiopia; Hitler was preparing to occupy the Rhineland and to annex Austria. Fascism was contagious. In France, to counter the belligerence of the rightist factions, the left-wing groups formed an alliance, the Popular Front, which won the 1936 elections amid strikes, brawls, and manifestoes. The agitation spilled over into Algeria. There, in a region where Muslims and Jews had established a kind of modus vivendi, it took on a nasty anti-Semitic coloring. Young French professors in general were convinced anti-Fascists, supporters of the Popular Front in France and the democratic Spanish Republic. Spain was a close neighbor. We often took the Spanish route on our way to and from France and liked its way of life, its museums, and its great past. It was a shock to watch a dissident general, aided by Moroccan mercenary troops, destroy an elected régime, while the democracies, including France, looked on. The bombing of Guérnica (1937) later commemorated by Picasso signaled, we felt, the appearance of a new form of human ferocity. So, more or less consciously, we entered an era of political confusion and technical brutality. One book, Céline's *Journey to the End of the Night,* caught the mood of derisive hopelessness that would become pervasive. In the mid-thirties, we signed manifestoes, engaged in lively discussions and demonstrations, and learned that we were helpless, at least in regard to short-term political issues; women more so, who, incredible though it seems today, enjoyed no voting rights. I remember the discomfort we felt at living simultaneously on two levels, interlocking but contradictory. We enjoyed the freedom and joys of our life as full-fledged adults; yet we were haunted by a sense of impending disaster that we wanted to deny. Euphoric when the Popular Front carried the day, we despaired as we witnessed the vociferous and hostile fascisms develop on three of our frontiers. I felt the need to fashion for myself a vague philosophy, a theory of what I called "alternative lives." A life took certain paths, by the chance of circumstances, but might have taken others equally available, and turned out quite differently. Might I not be living in Hanoi? or England? So every now and then one might chance upon perspectives leaving room for the play of freedom; while remaining fully engaged in present tasks one should not be committed. I was in a pre-existentialist mood. Chance now intervened.

In 1936, Bryn Mawr College offered me a one-year lectureship. I welcomed the offer. Instead of working as an English teacher in a French lycée, I was now to work as an instructor of French language and literature in a prestigious liberal arts college in the United States. It was the first step in what turned out to be a fifty-year career.

I now saw Bryn Mawr from a different angle, both as an autonomous, private, self-governing enterprise and as part of a vast and diverse network of American institutions of higher learning. The ritual debates which periodically blow over the United States concerning the perilous state of "*The* University" always puzzle me, so diverse are the institutions, so tailored to so many needs. Bryn Mawr, faithful to its Quaker origins, was a liberal arts college whose curriculum was centered on the humanities. Its president, at the time, was Marion Edwards Park, a Boston intellectual and aristocrat in the best sense of the word, fully attuned to the academic ideal of democratic governance. The dean, Helen Taft Manning, had spent part of her childhood in the White House, a fact that impressed me. She was an outspoken and broad-minded woman impervious to petty intrigue. Faculty meetings I rarely understood at first, so obscure did the procedures and debates seem to me. I could nonetheless, had I the time and place, align a roster of faculty personalities, women and men, nationally reputed in their fields. Formed in the less research-oriented French Sorbonne, I was somewhat vague as to the function of the "fields" in our profession and how a professor came to own one. On my arrival, the head of the French department and dean of the graduate school, Professor Eunice Morgan Schenck, enlightened me. I was assigned two "fields," the seventeenth century and twentieth century contemporary literature, the latter including a graduate seminar I would conduct on Marcel Proust. I blanched. My acquaintance with Proust was limited to "Combray," the very first section of the monumen-

tal *A la Recherche du Temps Perdu.* It was also suggested that I should attend the meetings of the Modern Language Association and consider "publishing." The only texts I had ever written, outside those assigned, were poems, either lyrical or parodic, all definitely expendable. I had never kept a diary either or even class notes. So I discovered an activity that I found I enjoyed. The first paper I wrote was an essay on "Racine and Violence." Violence and its effects on human lives was one of my preoccupations. The voices of Racine's tragic heroes, raised in protest against injustice, had inspired my rereading of the structure of Racine's tragedies. But it was Proust who captivated me, subsequently eliciting from me two books and some articles. Teaching too was proving quite exhilarating.

The Bryn Mawr students were excellent, many of them were intellectually sophisticated, more so, it sometimes seemed, than their teacher. They came with the three or four years of language study then required by Bryn Mawr, with, often, a background in Latin. I am still in touch with some of them: Margaret Otis Guiton, with whom I later co-authored a book on the French contemporary novel *An Age of Fiction;* C. J. Richards who, in cooperation with a friend, translated my first book on Proust; Elaine Marks, who is an outstanding figure in the academic world today. Though I missed the freedom of my life in Algiers, intensive intellectual work now made up for it. At the end of the year, my appointment was renewed. I was put in charge, for a couple of years, of the newly founded French House. In 1937 came a first visit to the Middlebury College summer language schools. As Dr. Stephen Freeman, their humane and wise administrator, lately reminded me, I taught there for six summers between 1937 and 1947 and was appointed director of their first graduate school in Paris during its second semester: Middlebury honored me later by awarding me an honorary degree of Doctor of Law. Besides eking out my modest salary, Middlebury brought me much: first, familiarity with the beauty of Vermont, experience, and wider horizons. There, faculty and students mingled easily with some of the most distinguished French professors teaching in America: for instance, Professor André Morize of Harvard, the genial director of the French School; Professor Maurice-Edgar Coindreau of Princeton, who almost single-handedly, through translations and essays, was introducing the rising generation of American writers to the French, thus inspiring what French critics have named "the age of the American novel." At Middlebury, French writers and critics dropped in, more particularly after 1939 when many of them had taken refuge in the United States, mostly

"With my students at Middlebury College," 1941

in New York: Jules Romains and Julien Green were among them. In New York, in 1941, Pierre Brodin, head of the French lycée there, organized L'École Libre where many scholars—such as the anthropologist Levi-Strauss—could be heard. Some of the settled academics, myself among them, were called upon to lecture there, contributing our small share to the maintenance of the school.

There were other passing figures: André Malraux, in 1937, more famous then for his involvement in the Spanish War than as a novelist, electrifying a vast mainly working-class audience in Philadelphia on behalf of the combatants against Franco; in New York, Antoine de Saint-Exupéry, pilot and writer, whose *Flight to Arras* described the plight of his small squadron of flyers sent out to stem the massive 1940 German offensive. While waiting for a chance to take up the fight again, he was writing, among other things, one small book which was to become a classic, *Le Petit Prince.* He disappeared, in 1943, presumably shot down over the Mediterranean. Presiding over all these activities, mentor often and always kindly helper, Professor Henri Peyre of Yale kept his

freedom and independence of judgment, refusing to take part in the deadly factionalism that, in the United States, was pitting Gaullists against the partisans of Vichy. Those qualities were in rather short supply among the émigré groups at the time. He was and remained, in many eyes, a kind of ex-officio representative of France.

I had other concerns, unrelated to my professional life. Between '36 and '38, I spent the summers, as in the past, in France and England. My sisters had all married: three in England, three in France, one of whom subsequently moved to North Africa. All but one had children. Shortly after he was demobilized, my brother followed suit. Nieces and nephews grew up and in turn established families, somewhat eclectically. My own bent did not incline me toward marriage. But, over the years, I would acquire, all through marriages, a much-loved Sri-Lankan—at the time, Singhalese—family; a beautiful, semi-African niece; a West German nephew. Recently, at our improvised family reunions, I can observe four generations interacting with uninhibited relish and eloquence. Family ties are still solid.

In the late thirties, in contrast, prospects were grim. An accidental fall left my father semiparalysed and dependent on a wheelchair. Then came a severe blow, most of all for my mother. My twenty-five-year-old sister died in childbirth, just as her husband was drafted into the army. My parents had sought a quiet place for retirement and opted for Vichy, a provincial town, offering the amenities of a spa, where they had friends. Consulted, we all thought the choice made perfect sense; Vichy seemed happily situated outside the danger zones. But Vichy, it turned out, was not to be the haven they had hoped for. Just before the move, in the late summer of 1938, as the time had come for me to return to Bryn Mawr, I lingered on the doorstep, reluctant to take leave of my mother: "Go now," she said to me gently, "You must go." I never saw her again.

Born in Lorraine in 1870, under German occupation, she died a refugee in central France. One of my sisters who, with her husband, had been in charge of a camp for Spanish refugee children near Paris managed to catch the last train out of Paris with their two children and join our parents. They had no love for the so-called "national revolution" proclaimed by the Vichy government and moved to a small village where my brother-in-law grew vegetables to supplement their scanty rations. My brother joined them there for a short time after his demobilization. Of course, I knew nothing of this. My English sisters, living either in London or on the east coast, were in some danger from the Luftwaffe raids. For me, life was going along comfortably while collective events and private anxieties coalesced. The kindness of my colleagues made life tolerable, in a kind of stop-time vacuum. Yet it was in those years that one of my friends, a mathematician, Professor Marguerite Lehr, invited me to her summer cottage in Mount Desert Island, introducing me to a place of unspoiled beauty I loved, also to Mount Katahdine, to the top of which I hiked regularly and which I held almost as a sacred place. I found that anxiety and wonder do not cancel each other out, they can coexist.

But time began to move again. The United States entered the war after Pearl Harbor. In 1942 Anglo-American forces landed in North Africa, which had been held in uneasy neutrality by the French. Amid much conflict, the French army began to regroup, eager to participate in the liberation of France. A group of French and American women sent out a call for volunteers to form an ambulance unit to join the French forces. I was one of the twelve volunteers selected. Bryn Mawr gave me its blessing and informed me my job would remain open for me on my return. The unit was officered by Florence Conrad, a dauntless francophile who had driven an ambulance in World War I. She was seconded by Elizabeth de Breteuil, who married Prince Chachavadze, and by Suzanne Torrès, wife of a famous left-wing lawyer and leader of the militant "France-for-ever" group in the United States. Among the "privates," Elizabeth's daughter, Laure, and her friend Nane de Bourbon, of the house of Bourbon-Parme, could lay claim to some status in the socio-political circles of Washington and New York, as also, in a different mode, Lulu Arpels, of Van Cleef and Arpels. The rest of us were not so burdened. Despite an occasional political or class stand-off, ours proved to be an easy group to live with, uncomplaining, witty, and even-tempered. In the late summer, we were finally summoned to New York for departure. It would be almost two years before I set foot in New York again.

Our first staging area was Camp Patrick Henry near Norfolk, Virginia. There we waited, along with some 40,000 GI's who considered the small group of women, Red Cross volunteers and ambulance drivers, with friendly enthusiasm. Only once did the enthusiasm overflow certain limits. While taking a shower one day, two women in our unit, hearing some unexpected sounds on the roof, looked up to see four eyes looking down from above. The army command went into action; guards were placed in front and back of our quarters and a brilliant red light was installed in front for our protection. No harm ensued. The day came when, carrying our backpacks and accompanied by the cheers of the GI's, we set out to our ship. I had no idea that, seen from ground level, a ship could tower so majestically above a traveler. It was a French ship, the *Pasteur,* which had been made over as a troop transport, keeping its personnel. We clambered up the ladders and stepped on deck. Recognizing Elizabeth de Breteuil, the steward stepped forward with a courteous, "This way, your Highness," and ushered us to our quarters on the first-class deck, equipped with some twenty bunks. The ship was filled to capacity with troops; the weather was splendid. We zigzagged across the Atlantic not knowing where we were heading. We eventually learned that we, our ambulances, complete with the pharmaceutical products generously donated, were due to disembark in Casablanca, thence to proceed to Rabat to join the Second Armored Division of General Leclerc. The Leclerc Division, a Gaullist division, was quasi-legendary. It had fought its way north from Chad and was preparing to participate in the liberation of France. The men in the division, led by their general, had taken an oath not to lay down their arms until the French flag flew again over the cities of Alsace.

We moved into our quarters, a barge anchored on the small inlet of the Bour-greg, headquarters of the Rabat yacht club. It was a beautiful spot and we were quite comfortable, once a few stray rats had been eliminated. We served as nurses in the improvised infirmary of the division. Inexperienced though I was, I was put in charge of the "dermato-venereal" ward along with a wonderful younger woman. Our ward was always full and sadly lacking in appropriate medicine. But, under the overall supervision of a highly competent member of the team, Marianne Glazer, the aspect of the ward picked up, and with it, the spirit of our patients, Arabs, Europeans, Senegalese. One day, as my coworker was bringing in some boiled water—a scarce commodity—she unexpectedly turned Baudelairian: "I feel," she announced, "as if I were watering my flowers of evil!" The delight of the ward was uninhibited. I remember, in contrast, a brief moment of panic. One of the men, a large Senegalese, was suffering from some kind of skin infection. I had been instructed to "paint" the area daily with methylene blue, one of the rare disinfectants available, and had done so meticulously. A few days later, as I followed the medical officer on his round, he stopped by the man's bedside and muttered to himself, "What does this look like?" "Chicken pox?" I queried rashly. "Well," he answered, "to me it looks like leprosy!" Aware perhaps that I was startled, he added: "Leprosy is not contagious in all its phases." Time proved that he was right.

Besides our duties as nurses, we occasionally took part in maneuvers, collected French recruits who had crossed into Spain to escape deportation to Germany as workers and whose release from Spain, it was rumored, had been negotiated by the Americans: so much wheat in exchange for so many men. Things were quiet. Once, when two of us had been sent on duty to collect the rations allotted to our unit from within the walls of the Arab "medina" (a small walled-in Arab city), we noticed a noisy crowd of men pouring out of another door. As we were driving back toward our quarters, we caught sight of them again and saw a flame shoot up from inside the crowd. We took a detour. We reached our destination to find two armored cars on guard. There had been a minor disturbance; the crowd had attacked a French military motorcyclist and set fire to him and his motorcycle. I had never liked crowds. I remember a more festive incident, bringing in, at Christmastime, a truckload of bleating and restive sheep destined for the Christmas dinner of the division.

In Casablanca, only some fifty miles away, I was lucky to find one of my sisters, with her husband who was chaplain of the navy, and their two sons. They were not in the least inclined to romanticize the situation. They welcomed the renewed activity in North Africa with slightly rueful wonder and filled in for me, in part, the facts pertaining to the tangled skein of the French Pétainiste, non-Pétainiste, and Gaullist maneuvering and the sometimes conflicting decisions of Churchill and Roosevelt. My five-year-old nephew looked upon the "Amerlos," as he called us, with affectionate suspicion ready to defend me if he thought I was not being fairly treated; his younger brother attracted much attention by briskly saluting French officers with military vigor: clearly, I was on my way home. After a short while, I was promoted to the rank of second lieutenant and transferred to the Intelligence section of the General Headquarters of the French army—in Algiers. Thence, following the rapid advance of the Allied armies up the Rhône Valley, I was assigned to the staff of the French general commanding the Dijon area where many American troops were stationed. Later, in the wake of the Allied drive into Germany, I was assigned to the Intelligence section of the supply base for the American Seventh and French First armies: Continental Advance Section, known as Conad. It set up its headquarters in Mannheim-Seckenheim in Germany. I worked there until shortly after VE-Day, during which time I was given the rank of lieutenant. In that period, the tasks were essentially those of a minor bureaucrat. The military would obviously not trust an untrained amateur with sensitive secrets. But those tasks were varied. Each stage in these last months of the war—Algiers, Dijon, Mannheim-Seckenheim—had its own atmosphere.

Algiers, in contrast with Rabat, was crowded with people: military personnel, civilians of all kinds, diplomats, agents, and black-market operators. They filled the streets and the cafés. In Rabat, within a single-mindedly Gaullist division, I had had little sense of the military and political situation whether in France or Africa, nor of the violent polarization of the Vichy-Gaullist issue. Nor did I know much of the many Resistance organizations in France, anti-Nazi to be sure, but not necessarily friendly to one another. This I was to learn. By the time I arrived in Algiers, the Gaullist provisional government had won the political battle, to the displeasure of the military who had "held the fort," as it were, under the command of General Weygand, loyal to Vichy. They later opted for the Roosevelt-backed General Giraud. My unit was no exception. They were not fond of the Gaullists. But I was made welcome by former Oran

"In the army with CONAD, front row far left," 1945

acquaintances, now fervent Gaullists working in Algiers, among them a small contingent that had been the mainstay of Albert Camus's early experimental theater, his wife Francine among them. I was introduced to *The Stranger* and *The Myth of Sisyphus* and learned that Camus was in France, active in the underground network Combat and the clandestine printing of the news sheet with the same name.

It had begun to dawn on me that something important was in the books. People came and went in Algiers. One such was a young American with whom I had struck up a friendship. One day, I was handed a file for analysis. I learned that, parachuted into France in the region around Marseille, he had been denounced, arrested by the Gestapo, tortured, and killed. It was then I began to understand the violence of the hatreds tearing France apart. Things were moving again, but at first not in my sector. On June 6, D-Day, the long awaited landing in Normandy began. We felt left out, as it were, useless though jubilant; until August 15, when a Franco-American expeditionary force landed with little trouble near Toulon, reaching Dijon some three weeks later. In the inter-

val, the much more highly publicized battle of Paris was being fought and won: for many, it was the symbol of victory. In truth, VE-Day was still a year away.

Dijon was now my temporary home, as it was, too, to large contingents of American troops. My duties then were mainly those of interpreter between the French local command and Conad under the command of General Arthur Wilson, a vigorous and generous man, with a deep concern for equity and justice in his dealing with both his own men and the French. The mayor of Dijon, Mayor Connes, was a friend of the Allies and had been a staunch anti-Nazi: disagreements were not hard to settle. The magnitude of the operations dealing with supply problems stretched far beyond my purview. Closer to me were such efforts as the screening of individuals needed as workers, problems of the ubiquitous Black Market, and so on. Among the persons we screened, I remember one, a Frenchman who had escaped from a camp in Germany. Our task was to document his story. He had been pitilessly tortured. His obsession was to find the man who had denounced him in order to kill him: he was posted to a job at the other end of France. Shortly after I arrived in Dijon, a man accused of having turned in a number of students to the Gestapo was hauled out of prison, where he had been consigned pending his trial, paraded by a crowd through the streets of Dijon, and lynched. Such an incident was, so far as I know, unique of its kind. Far more pleasant was the visit of the prestigious American troupe bringing to the GI's and the Dijon community Brian Aherne, Margelo Gilmore, and more especially, Katherine Cornell in *The Barretts of Wimpole Street.* The performance was immensely successful. The cast were delighted when some GI's waited for Brian Aherne at the stage door to take him to task for the way he had treated his ailing daughter. I accompanied the troupe as interpreter. Two short leaves punctuated my stay: the first to the center of France to visit my father and sister whom I had not seen for six years; the second to Paris.

In casual encounters with people, as I moved through France, I had sensed a numbness, a slowness in response that contrasted with memories of French vivacity. My visit to my family, after a six-year separation, made clear to me the price human beings pay when they are deprived, over a period of years, of the basic freedom and joys of human life: the depletion of energy, the anxiety brought on by isolation within a kind of vacuum. My visit was unannounced. A staff car dropped me off and would pick me up in a couple of days. The door opened into a small and dark kitchen-living room. My father, greatly aged, was hunched over a book by the table. At his side stood a little girl, five years old or so, absolutely motionless and tense, watching. Only when my father spoke my name did she move, running to get her mother, my sister. I was in uniform; uniforms, in her eyes, I found out later, meant trouble. Thence the watchfulness and the reluctance to leave her grandfather unattended. The family counted themselves, and indeed were, among the more fortunate refugees. They had taken in a couple of Polish Jews to help in the house and garden, a situation not without peril. The burden of anxiety had now lifted, leaving deep bonds of warmth and trust among them. But anxiety had left its scars, more particularly on the children conditioned to expect danger, rather than pleasure and joy, from unexpected circumstances. The modest contents of my duffle bag, furnished by the American PX in Dijon, nonetheless were a source of wonder: there they found things they had *heard* of but never seen, like oranges and "real" soap; they had been using a substitute extracted by my sister from the saporaria plant. It was as if my visit had opened the door to a world beyond, pointing to a future at last free from confinement.

Paris was more open, of course, though the weariness of the civilian population was often manifest. There was, at the end of November 1944, a bitterly cold period. Apartments were sparsely heated, if at all, and food still scarce. But the city was unbelievably beautiful. Except for a few military vehicles, its vast avenues were empty, spacious, and tranquil. I met with friends from my Oran days, and came to know the flats they were living in. One of these Camus made famous in his short story "Jonah, or the Artist at Work." People dropped in and out. It was a good place to pick up on literary gossip and political debates. This was the dawn of "existentialism," signalling the advent of an upbeat new "generation" of writers—Simone de Beauvoir, Sartre, and Camus among them—determined to restore France's confidence in its spiritual values. They were not a large group, but they were rich in talent. Yet, uncertainties with regard to the future and the deep cleavages within their ranks colored their not too sanguine expectations. One cold afternoon, I took off on a private venture. Among my Philadelphia friends were the Paul Crets. He was a distinguished architect, a friend of Eisenhower with whom he had worked on the American Battle Monuments Commission, more particularly on the Valley Forge monument. "If you are anywhere near General Eisenhower," he said to me as I left for Africa, "call him and say that Paul Cret had sent you." Eisenhower's headquarters were in Versailles. I headed for Versailles and I informed the sentry at the gate that I had come to pay a call on General Eisenhower; I said that Paul Cret had sent me. The message worked like magic. Within minutes, Colonel Lodge, Eisenhower's aide-de-camp I believe, appeared with a program for me: I was to see Eisenhower the next morning. In the meantime, I might perhaps enjoy a hot bath followed by dinner in the officer's mess? I would be driven back to Paris, and a car would pick me up in the morning. This was utopia. I did, indeed, enjoy the hot bath that came accompanied by a whisky and soda; the dinner in one of Versailles's luxury hotels seemed sumptuous. The few minutes I spent with General Eisenhower the next day were memorable. I still marvel at the courteous generosity of a man so burdened with responsibilities, a great man in my eyes, if ever there was one. I returned to Dijon in high spirits to find that, north of us, in the Ardennes, the "Battle of the Bulge" had just begun. It was a fierce and costly battle. It was followed by the spring Allied offensive that drove across the Rhine into Germany. For a short interval, the outcome of the war had seemed in question. Understandably, the civilian population was nervous. Guns, that supposedly had been turned in, suddenly reappeared. By the end of the year, it was apparent that the German offensive had bogged down. The guns disappeared.

Come spring, I was on my way again. With a small group of officers from the French First Army integrated with Conad, I drove north via the valley of the Moselle River, Nancy, and Trier, and across the Rhine to Mannheim. It was early in April, I believe, and the drive offered a strange amalgam of wrecked tanks framed by the white blossoms of fruit trees. A curious smell hung over the scene. Once, a sudden volley of shots brought our cars to a brusque halt. The men jumped out, scattered briefly and returned with a prisoner, a German soldier who was carrying on his lonely war. He was turned over to the German authorities in Trier. I had been intrigued by the sound of sporadic shooting along the way. I was reassured. It was only the Moroccan troops, I was informed. After a battle, they enjoyed a twenty-four hour reprieve from military discipline. They were probably rounding up a few women for collective enjoyment. I was appalled. Perhaps my informant was pulling my leg? I was later to see quite extensive looting, and *not* by the Moroccan troops only. But very little rape.

There was no question as to what war meant when we approached Mannheim. I had seen ruins, of course, but no destruction of that magnitude. The German V-1's and V-2's were even then landing on English territory. Hiroshima, about which we knew almost nothing, was in the works. The sight of bombed-out cities would become familiar. That day, only some three months before Hiroshima, the sight literally tore at my eyes. As we drove past, shaking his fist violently at our small convoy, a demobilized German soldier shouted a stream of insults at us: I realized I was now part of that universally hated entity, an "occupying force." I was billeted with two or three women of the French First Army in a house requisitioned for the purpose. We saw almost no Germans, carefully guarded within the area designated as "Conad City."

The tasks of Conad were immense. Among them was the problem of caring for the Displaced Persons and liberated prisoners of war now pouring through in the tens of thousands. They often came on foot, pushing small carts on which they had piled their few belongings. Sometimes, a more or less crudely painted flag proclaimed their nationality. They had to be fed, screened, lodged in camps, and when possible, repatriated. Language was a major stumbling block. Let me quote here from a Conad report: "Poles,

Italians, Dutch, Greeks, Russians, Ukrainians, Czechoslovakians, Estonian, Lithuanians, French, Yugoslavs, Germans, Danish, Americans, Turks, Belgians, Nicaraguans, Finnish, Hungarians, Armenians, Swiss, Canadians, and Latvians"; a dismal spectacle and a compendium of many distressing stories. This is a face of war we too often pass over as marginal. I have come to think it is perhaps the most truly revealing.

In the G-2, our task was to assure the exchange of information between the French First Army of General DeLattre de Tassigny, and the Americans. It culminated in two memorable trips to Lake Constance, headquarters of the French forces. The first trip was an escapade. General Wilson, perhaps to give us a break, sent a small group through the Black Forest to find him a cuckoo clock. The mission was not as simple as it sounds, since GI's in mass had nursed the same ambition. There were four of us in the general's car, two of whom had been members of a Resistance group. It was clear that they had their own mission in mind: to reach Lake Constance and the husband of one of the two, stationed there. At one point, our car suddenly emerged near an inn at the top of a hill. A dramatic moment ensued: a hundred or so German soldiers were enjoying beer at the inn. At the edge of the road was a solitary French tank; it had broken down and the driver was clearly nervous. So was the innkeeper. The sudden arrival of an American car showing four stars was a shock. The two women from the Resistance took over. It was made clear to all that we were going to Lake Constance to report on the whereabouts of the tank, which had better be there when the men of the French First Army came to the rescue. Therewith, we also got the cuckoo clock and made off for Lake Constance, found our companion's husband there, and delivered our message.

The second trip was official. With the G-2 officers, I attended a fête given by General DeLattre de Tassigny as a token of gratitude to a large number of American generals. It was a quasi-imperial show which took place on the banks of the lake. It culminated in a play of red, white, and blue projectors which created a kind of ballet of light around us. The war seemed to be coming to an end. I have memories of other trips, one to the Italian frontier; one to Paris and the Ritz, as General Wilson prepared to take on to a new post; one brief foray into central France to see the family. But my memory here fails me. On May 8, VE-Day, I know I was in Seckenheim. There was no dearth of libations, but there was not much change either in the rhythm of the work, as those of Buchenwald and Dachau who could travel came through our headquarters with many others. I do not remember exactly when I left for Paris on my way to demobilization and Bryn Mawr. There, still in uniform, complete with a Bronze Star Medal and an Army commendation-ribbon generously bestowed, Lieutenant Germaine Brée waited in Paris for the liberty ship which was to turn her back, to her delight, into Assistant Professor Brée at Bryn Mawr College.

After two routine years in various war zones, what struck me on landing in New York was the vibrancy of colors: the rich colors of the big food stores, the variegated color of the taxis, of the women's clothes. After Europe, it seemed unbelievably rich. I arrived in Bryn Mawr exactly on time for the opening of the fall term, and was at work immediately. In the back of my mind, I had often pictured the moment when I would move back into my room, shut the door, turn on the light, and read in bed. That is just what I did. I was taking possession of my life again.

I had gained much confidence in American efficacy and good faith. The Americans I saw in the army were, on the whole, admirable. It was not surprising, therefore, that a short time after the war was over, I decided to become an American citizen. The decision implied no rejection of France, a country to which I remained deeply attached and which never seemed to me, in any deep way, antagonistic to the United States.

In 1945, on my return to America, I was thirty-eight years old and aware that academic life was the life best suited to my temperament and capacities. I still thought so in 1985, when I retired. To begin with, a professor of contemporary literature is engaged in a fascinating adventure. Contemporary French literature, my "field," was, along with the other arts in France, in a transitional period and in one of its creative phases. I sometimes think of the pattern of French literature when I began to teach: of that "literary space," as it is sometimes called—without Sartre, Camus, Saint-Exupéry, and Marguerite Yourcenar among others. Who had heard of Henri Michaux, Francis Ponge, Léopold Senghor, Aimé Césaire, or René Char among the poets? The work of Proust was just becoming visible as it were. I find it exciting to discern new literary constellations joining the familiar established ones; as if to test them. This, no one does alone. In France, the task of discerning the significant work from within the proliferating mass is often left to sophisticated forms of literary journalism. In America, we turn to academics. In the thirties, there were only a handful of

twentieth-century specialists in the field. Since then, as the century came of age, they have greatly multiplied. To discover, *not to compile,* was our main concern: to discover and communicate. The first writers I dealt with, Proust and Gide, were now known as the last classics. Next appeared the writers of my generation, not the "Surrealists" that I enjoyed, who were older, but the "Existentialists," so-called at the time. Camus was a case in point. I have spoken of him often and written about him, and can only refer readers to my bibliography. Today, I scrutinize the work of the new and younger women and men. Besides, it is an extraordinary experience, though sometimes an aggravating one, to see books acquire ever new dimensions as new readers and critics scrutinize them. Critical theories come and go, but they cannot alter the text. They provide new, more or less convincing readings and renewed interest. Ours is a collective enterprise rewarding in its rich vitality. It was that preoccupation which culminated in my attempt at drawing together in a volume, however incomplete, the course of fifty years of French literature, from 1920–1970, transmitting a sense not of literature in isolation, but of the literary enterprise as it developed within a socio-historical complex in relation to a nexus of cultural activities. Planning anthologies, editions of texts for teaching purposes, or textbooks with eminent colleagues—

"With Professor Tom Bishop at my farewell party,"
New York University, 1960

Carlos Lynes of the University of Pennsylvania, Charles Carlut of Ohio State University, Alex Kroff of Wisconsin—or with bright research assistants was rewarding in friendship, fun, and the development of professional standards. It was a period when French writing of the present and present French thought appealed to the young Americans preoccupied by the war, and, later, by its extension in Vietnam. Of those writers, Albert Camus was one of the most appealing. And Camus was a friend. When it was suggested I write an introductory essay on a figure so widely known in the United States, I was able to do so with his help. He kindly gave me access to his papers, manuscripts, correspondence. I saw him regularly every summer until his death. I treasured his friendship and trust. Quiet, soft-spoken, sometimes devastatingly funny, always attentive to others, Camus was deeply reserved, entrenched one might say, within his own demanding conscience and inflexible integrity. It was a privilege to know him; though the fact has sometimes been insinuated in our sex-obsessed society, there was no erotic connection between us.

In the meantime, I moved from Bryn Mawr to New York University. Thence, after seven years, to the newly founded Institute of Research in the Humanities at the University of Wisconsin, two quite different assignments. Under vigorous new leadership, NYU was upgrading its curriculum, its buildings, and equipment. My task as chair of the Romance Languages and Russian Department in that context was facilitated by the surging interest in education, and more particularly languages, that followed the war. I think there was, at the time, only one other female chairperson in the Liberal Arts School. The deans of the graduate and undergraduate schools gave me their full support. That is how I was able, with the help of William Willis, then a young assistant dean, to set up, in a charming house in Washington mews, a French cultural center. The French community in New York responded generously to our modest campaign for funds, fully backed as we were by the French cultural services. Lucien David, a French architect, remodelled the house gratuitously, as I remember. It was really rather fun to wander through the more affluent sections of New York with Bill Willis, armed with introductions furnished by the quiet and powerfully efficient French cultural counsellor Edouard Morot-Sir, a friend, if ever there was one. So, in 1957, the French house of NYU was inaugurated. It has grown and prospered beyond all expectations under the direction of two men directly connected to the department of French, David Noakes and Tom Bishop. The French government awarded me the Legion of Honor for founding the French House; and, a couple of years ago, the award of Commander of the Order of the Academic Palms in recognition of my academic work. At the same time I should mention that my work has been acknowledged in America with some twenty-five honorary doctorates, which it would be a bore to enumerate. I am grateful to both countries.

The NYU students were quite different from those at Bryn Mawr. Many worked long hours for a living; their intellectual and social backgrounds were different. Yet among them were two future poets. I remember John Ashbery, one of my teaching assistants for a short time, presenting me with a copy of his first volume of verse, *Some Trees,* and Marilyn Hacker, who was to have a brilliant career as a poet. My teaching assistants were young and devoted: among them, Elaine Marks and George Borchardt, who was to become one of the leading literary agents in New York. It was he who, as editor of a volume of essays entitled *New French Writing,* was among the first to draw attention to a new constellation of poets and fiction writers presented in translation. It was he who spoke to me of the rich harvest of postwar French poetry, suggesting that I contribute to the volume an essay entitled "New French Poetry." NYU was a demanding job but a rewarding one for, in those years, the university, as a whole, grew rapidly in strength and quality, and salaries were moving up fairly rapidly. All this favored easier relations for a newly appointed head. New York itself was rich in cultural activities, French events not least among them. Seven years as "head" of a department that spanned three schools and five languages at different stages of development and which involved some fifty colleagues could eventually prove exhausting. So, in 1960, after some hesitation, I accepted Professor Marshall Claggett's invitation to join the Institute for Research in the Humanities, in Madison, of which he was the director.

The Old Observatory, where the Institute was housed, stood on the highest ground in the university campus, with a splendid view over the largest of the three lakes that frame Madison, Lake Mendota. There, the members of the Institute worked, had lunch together, and discussed ideas and concerns with each other and with visitors from abroad and from the departments, invited for short-term residence. Professor Marshall Claggett, an outstanding medieval historian, the head of the Institute, was a genial, unpretentious friend. As a permanent member, it was my privilege to frequent, on a daily basis, besides Marshall Claggett, Emmett Bennett, a linguist, one of the decipherers of "linear B," the scrupulous and gentle philosopher Julius Weinberg, and Fritz Solm-

Ayres Rock, Australia, 1962

sen, the eminent Greek scholar from the University of Berlin who, accompanied by his wife Lise Lotte, had left Germany in 1932, in protest against the Nazis; later came Kenneth Setton, the historian of the Popes. Both Claggett and he eventually moved to the Princeton Institute. It was a stimulating group. And the students too were stimulating: when, shortly after my arrival, a student group asked me to lecture on André Gide, I was surprised to find an audience of some thousand interested students. Campus life in the sixties was lively. The fifties had marked the end of colonialism, exemplified by the confusions of the Algerian War and the French defeat, in what was to become Vietnam. In the United States, heralded by the assassination of President Kennedy, the sixties were disturbing, as the USA got bogged down in the Vietnam War. Campus unrest was flagrant on the Madison campus, and faculty opinion divided. I felt in sympathy with the students. The university in those years was fortunate in having as president a great liberal, in the best sense of the word, President Harrington, ably seconded by the dean of the Liberal Arts School, Dean Young. Faculty members, Profes-

sor George Mosse among them, organized "teach-ins"; I was asked to discuss the existentialist key word, commitment. Eventually, the student movement died down. The violence in Madison was minimal.

Simultaneously, almost as a counter-theme, other initiatives of positive value to the academic world were taking place: the establishment of the National Endowment for the Humanities, for instance, under the leadership of two vigorous personalities, the president of Brown University and Henry Allen Moe. The architect I. M. Pei was on the planning committee, to which I, too, was appointed. It was an education in itself to see such a committee at work. I have sat on many committees; few could compare with that one. It was particularly gratifying, some years later, to organize two summer seminars under the auspices of the Endowment, on the question of "l'écriture féminine" for a vocal, brilliant, and articulate group of teachers, mostly women.

There were other opportunities in those years, thanks to the generous Fulbright program and others. I taught one semester (winter for them, summer for us) in Australia, visiting the "town called Alice," and the famous meteor Ayres Rock in the central desert. "We pay for the most direct route in economy class," the Australian Fulbright representative informed me, "but plan to go around the earth; Madison is almost exactly halfway!" So I did; from Madison, to Hawaii, to the Fiji Islands, to Sydney and Adelaide—my destination; returning via Perth, Malaysia, Sri-Lanka, which I visited at some length, Madras, Delhi, Istanbul, Paris. This was the most extensive of my university-connected travels of which I shall give no further account, in case I should sound like a restless globe-trotter. They are examples of the heightened internationalization of university life in the postwar era of expanding communications. Thus, I taught for one semester at the American University of Cairo, and at King's College, London University. My "field" was in great demand; and I lectured extensively. Thanks in part to two small grants from the American Philosophical Society, I was able, on occasion, to rent a small villa for the summer in an especially attractive place, like Caldurà di Cefalu in Sicily, Cascaïs in Portugal, Cabris, north of Grasse, in France. There, I could spend many hours working in

peace. A last such period, I owe to the generosity of the Camargo Foundation, beautifully located on the Provence coast. I remember, too, the excitement of driving from coast to coast twice on my way from New York to teach in summer school at Berkeley and Los Angeles University. So condensed, this account of my wanderings might transmit an impression of frenetic instability. In fact, they were spread over many years; my life was peaceful, and my main concern throughout my Madison years concentrated on my graduate students, the seminars, and the theses on which their future careers would in part depend. When, in 1975, I became president of the Modern Language Association, a group of these former students presented me with a handsome volume of their essays, *Twentieth Century French Fiction*, prefaced by Henri Peyre, who underscores their diversity and excellence, and the quality of their professional achievement. What more could a professor wish?

In 1973, I moved one last time: Wake Forest University, a small liberal arts school in Winston-Salem, North Carolina, had invited me down to lecture, and to participate in its Honors seminar. I

"The 'Family' in the Cévennes, including sisters, brother, brother-in-law, nieces, nephews, grandnieces and grandnephews," France, 1981

"With the National Endowment for the Humanities summer seminar. I am the one with the glasses, second row left," 1981

had been impressed by the quality of the students in those seminars, the ambiance of faculty-student relations, to say nothing of the beauty of the place, and the mildness of the climate. I was reaching retirement age; deeply attached though I was to the Institute, when the provost of Wake Forest, a man of unusual sensitivity and courtesy, came all the way from the warm South to speak to me about moving to Wake Forest, for a Kenan Professorship, I accepted. The much vaunted hospitality of the South is not a myth. I was offered the opportunity of building a house for myself in a quiet, wooded section of the college grounds. For the first time in my life, I considered owning a house of my own. While in Wisconsin, by chance, I had been able to acquire a cottage on a lake in Interlochen, Michigan, a cottage that I could reach from Madison by taking a night ferry. It is strictly a summer place which I cherish. The Winston-Salem house, beautifully designed by an architect-poet, John Ramsay, well known in North Carolina is, in a way, the happy realization of a latent dream. Here I have found a community of friends, as in all the places I

have taught, but more accessible—living at a quieter rhythm, more human lives.

As I was looking through my papers in anticipation of this essay, I came across a lecture I gave in Oxford, the Zaharoff lecture a dozen years ago, entitled "Narcissus Absconditus: The Problematic Art of Autobiography in Contemporary France," then a popular theme in avant-garde speculation. One of the many seekers of a satisfactory definition of the genre, Philippe Lejeune, whom I had quoted, spoke of an "autobiographical pact" between autobiographer and reader: "as he undertakes the sincere project to seize and understand his own life, the autobiographer . . . guarantees that the writer, the narrator, and the protagonist in his story are one and the same, that the events recounted have in fact been lived and that he/she has dutifully recorded them." How, I wonder, have I performed? To begin with, lucky is the person who "seizes and understands" her own life . . . or, in truth, anybody else's. . . . I have found the life that opened before me wondrous, not because it was "mine," but because it was there, a "many-faceted thing," without regard for the just or unjust effects of its cruelty and indifferent beauty. It is to human friendships, love and solidarity, that I owe the sense of the values of those "human ways of life," imprinted in what we call human "cultures," made up of millennial human efforts to "figure out" our human relation to the world, which so many living creatures, like and unlike, inherit.

BIBLIOGRAPHY

Nonfiction:

(Translator) Jules Romains, *Seven Mysteries of Europe*, Knopf, 1940.

Du temps perdu au temps retrouvé: Introduction à l'oeuvre de Marcel Proust, Belles Lettres (Paris), 1950, translation by C. J. Richards and A. D. Truitt published as *Marcel Proust and Deliverance from Time*, Rutgers University Press, 1955.

André Gide, L'insaisissable Protée: Etude critique de l'oeuvre d'André Gide, Belles Lettres (Paris), 1953, translation by author and published as *Gide*, Rutgers University Press, 1963.

(With Margaret Guiton) *An Age of Fiction: The French Novel from Gide to Camus*, Rutgers University Press, 1957, also published as *The French Novel from Gide to Camus*, Harcourt, 1962.

Camus, Rutgers University Press, 1959.

(With Georges Markow-Totevy) *Contes et nouvelles: 1950–1960*, Holt, 1961, revised edition published as *Contes et nouvelles: 1950–1970*, Holt, 1970.

Albert Camus (critical essay), Columbia University Press, 1964.

(With others) *Literature and Society*, edited by Bernice Slote, University of Nebraska Press, 1964.

(With Micheline Dufau) *Voix d'aujourd'hui* (instructional language aid), Harcourt, 1964.

The World of Marcel Proust, Houghton, 1966.

(With others) *The Modern French Novel*, Purdue University Department of English, 1970.

(With René Jules Dubos and Louis B. Wright) *Essays in Honor of David Lyall Patrick*, University of Arizona, 1971.

Camus and Sartre: Crisis and Commitment, Delacorte, 1972.

Women Writers in France: Variations on a Theme, Rutgers University Press, 1973.

Le Vingtième siècle, sole author of vol. II (1920–1970), Arthaud (Paris), 1978, published as *Twentieth-Century French Literature*, University of Chicago Press, 1983, revised edition published as *Du surréalisme a l'empire de la critique . . .*, Arthaud (Paris), 1984.

Le Monde Fabuleux de J. M. G. Le Clézio (critical study), Rodopic, 1990.

Editor:

(With Carlos Lynes) Marcel Proust, *Combray*, Appleton, 1952.

Culture, Literature, and Articulation, Northeast Conference on the Teaching of Foreign Languages, 1955.

(With Lynes) Albert Camus, *L'Etranger*, Appleton, 1955.

(With Charles Carlut) *France de nos jours* (textbook), Macmillan, 1957.

(With Sidney D. Braun) Anatole France, *Le Crime de Sylvestre Bonnard*, Holt, 1958.

(With Anne Prioleau Jones) *Hier et aujourd'hui: Premières lectures littéraires*, Ronald, 1958.

Great French Short Stories, Dell, 1960.

Camus: A Collection of Critical Essays, Prentice-Hall, 1962.

Twentieth-Century French Literature: An Anthology of Prose and Poetry, Macmillan, 1962.

(With Eric Schoenfeld) Samuel Beckett, *En attendant Godot*, Macmillan, 1963.

(With Schoenfeld) Alain Robbe-Grillet, *La Jalousie*, Macmillan, 1963.

(With Philip Solomon) *Choix d'essais du vingtième siècle*, Blaisdell, 1969.

Gustave Flaubert, *Madame Bovary*, translation from the French by Lawrence Merloyd, Houghton, 1969.

(With Alexander Y. Kroff) *Twentieth-Century French Drama*, Macmillan, 1969.

(With George Bernauer) *Defeat and Beyond: An Anthology of French Wartime Writing, 1940–1945*, Pantheon, 1970.

Albert Camus, *La Chute*, Schoenhof, 1986.

Philippe Jaccottet: Poems, Wake Forest University Press, 1988.

Pierre Reverdy: Poems, Wake Forest University Press, 1991.

Also editor of Albert Camus, *De l'envers et l'endroit à l'exil et le royaume*, and editor of "French Language Library," Dell. General editor of the newly inaugurated series of contemporary French poets in translation (facing French/English versions), including *Philippe Jaccottet* and *Pierre Reverdy* above.

Elizabeth Brewster

1922-

I have often used material from my own life in poems, short stories, and a semiautobiographical novel, *The Sisters*. Also I have had to provide, from time to time, the stark, impersonal summary of information required in biographical dictionaries: birth date, parents' names, education, positions held, awards, publications. I take it that what is required here is something fuller than the summary, something more strictly factual, less intimate than the semifiction piece or the confessional poem. How shall I proceed? Perhaps in as dry and factual a manner as that employed by one of my favourite fictional characters, Robinson Crusoe, an "I was born . . ."

Well, then, I was born August 26, 1922, in Chipman, New Brunswick, Canada, in a room in my grandmother's house. The village doctor arrived after I was born; I had already been delivered by my grandmother and my mother's cousin Maggie. I was the youngest of five children born to Frederick John and Ethel May (Day) Brewster. My mother was over forty when I was born, my father not quite forty-five. My father, at the time I was born, was in Saint John, watching by what was to be the deathbed of my other grandmother, the one for whom I was named. Maybe some awareness of the shadow of death came into my mind even in infancy. I was told that I was a very frail and tiny child, that my mother doubted if she would manage to keep me alive. My sister Eleanor (four years old when I was born) tells me that I cried constantly. She herself, I think, was grieved that she was no longer the baby of the family.

My father had at one point been a fairly prosperous merchant, but had gone bankrupt, suffered a breakdown in health, and at the time I was born was unemployed. Later, he worked as a store clerk for a time, and during the Depression of the thirties tried unsuccessfully to farm. We nearly starved, but at least I spent some of my childhood in a beautiful physical setting on the shores of the Washademoak Lake. I have written about that period in my novel *The Sisters*, where the Washademoak is called Moss Lake.

Both my parents were kind and gentle people, and I was devoted—almost too devoted—to both of them. My mother was the stricter of the two, with a

Elizabeth Brewster, 1989

strong religious sense. My father could be lively and amusing, but was given to depression and melancholy. His mind was more restless and unorthodox than my mother's. He was fond of books, especially the novels of Dickens, and used to recite the poems on which he grew up, Gray's "Elegy in a Country Churchyard," Tennyson's "May Queen" or "Lady Clara Vere de Vere," fragments from Walter Scott or Byron or Longfellow or Whittier. (Whittier, he said, was a distant relative, by way of the Greenleaf family.)

My brothers, Percy and Cyril, were teenagers when I was born, and were too far removed from me to be much of an influence. The elder of the two, Percy, went suddenly deaf when he was around sixteen. One of my more frequently anthologized poems, "Jamie," is about him. He was my favourite of the two, probably because he played with me more often, getting down on the floor with me when I was three or four to make castles out of blocks, or carrying me around on his shoulders when he went for a walk. Cyril, my other brother, sometimes took me for rides on the handlebars of his bicycle. Marion, the elder of my two sisters—"the pretty one," as they said—was eleven years older than I, a lively girl, though given, like my father, to fits of depression and with an unpredictable temper. Most of the time she made rather a pet of me; but she could become impatient, especially with what she called my cowardice, for I was rather a timid child. I remember her disgust with me (I was around four years old at the time) when she swung me—I thought—too high on a swing, and I howled to be let down. The swing could never have gone too high for her. I was fond of her, though somewhat wary of her, and followed her around admiringly. Although she was not academically inclined, she was, like my father, fond of poetry, and used to write little verses. Perhaps I caught the notion of writing poetry from her.

With my sister Eleanor, the sister nearest me in age, I had a more troubled relationship. As she told me later, she resented me when I was a baby; very naturally, for the fact that I was such a frail child meant that she was somewhat neglected by my mother. However, we played fairly happily together for a few years, until I was eight and she was twelve. Then she began to withdraw from me, thinking that she was grown-up and I was still a baby. I felt this withdrawal as a rejection, and was very unhappy about it. However, I was discovering books and writing, and consoled myself with paper and pencil.

I can't remember a time when I couldn't read. I do remember getting blocks with letters and numbers on them the Christmas I was three years old; and I seem to remember my brother Percy helping me to make simple words with them—CAT, MAT. Around this time I was also given a book of Bible stories, with an alphabet and some simple readings in front and a group of illustrated Bible stories in the back. It may have been my first real reader. Eleanor's old primer from the first grade was still around the house, and I read it and some other school textbooks. We had Grimm's fairy tales, with black-and-white illustrations, and I coloured them with beet juice.

Because I was a delicate child—and perhaps because she herself was somewhat overprotective—my mother had not wanted to send me to school when I was six. Although I had learned to read without much help, she wasn't sure that I had learned

to spell; and I recall standing by her rug frames while she was hooking a rug with one eye and "hearing my spelling" with the other. She also tried to teach me the addition and multiplication tables, for which I did not have an affinity.

It was not until I was eight and we had moved to the Washademoak that I began to attend the one-room school there. Although I could read fluently by this time, and had read some grown-up novels (including Hawthorne's *Scarlet Letter*, for the sake of little Pearl), I had not learned to write, could print only awkwardly, and had no notion of arithmetic. The little Hammtown School had, at that time, only nine students, running from the first to the eighth grade, taught by a young woman who was in charge of her first school. During the four years I attended it there were five successive teachers, only one of whom had any previous experience. They were mostly kind people, and, if they did not teach much, did no harm. During January and February, the little school was too cold for classes, and I buried myself in books at home. They were usually books from an earlier time, novels by Scott, Dickens, Charles Kingsley, Mrs.

"Great-aunt Rebecca, about whom several of my poems were written"

Ewing. My father gave me Burns's poems for my tenth birthday, and I still have the copy, marked by my struggles with the dialect. I read my way doggedly through my mother's Bible, partly as a religious exercise, partly (I think) to prove my stamina; but much of it I enjoyed for its poetry, going back often to Job, and Ruth, and Ecclesiastes, and the Psalms, as well as favourite passages from the New Testament Epistles. I also read most of Shakespeare, and especially read and reread *A Midsummer Night's Dream, The Tempest, As You Like It,* and *King Lear,* all of which seemed related to fairy tales. I think that early reading of Shakespeare was the deepest source of my addiction to poetry.

Pastoral tradition

Reading *As You Like It* reminds me
how I read it as a child, and thought
it could take place in the bush somewhere
beyond the cow pasture
where there were deer and chipmunks
and the fern-tasting blueberries grew.

But Orlando never came wandering
past with poems to stick on trees,
and I never saw Rosalind sitting
on the log fence of the pasture
making witty conversation
with melancholy Jaques.
There were no dukes eating picnic lunches,
or courtiers to sing to them,
and not even Touchstone
on a day's jaunt from the city
gingerly avoiding the
dried pats of cowdung.

But "What is poetical?" Audrey asked.
"Is it honest?"
Touchstone said no.

(From *In Search of Eros*)

I began writing diaries, fiction, and poetry at more or less the same time, when I was a child of nine or ten. I had read a novel in diary form, a "dear diary" novel, and thought I should keep a diary too. But nothing happened. What was I to do? I filled out the entries with poems. I wrote a long, rambling fiction, a fantasy about two children, a boy and a girl, who wandered away from home into an enchanted forest, where they encountered a princess who lived in a castle and sang to the accompaniment of a harp. I could not imagine what song the princess sang. I asked my sister Marion to write one for me, but she wrote instead a song for fairies dancing in a round. I had to write the princess's song myself, and invent another episode in which the children saw the fairies

dancing. Much later I wrote a small poem about this story.

Fairy Tale

I had a story that I told
Myself when I was nine years old.
Two children, walking in a wood,
Lost themselves one day for good
From home, and bed, and food.

They wandered here, they wandered there,
Through the sweet midsummer air;
And dragons made of fire
Passed them by with flaming wings
And stupid, sidelong stare.

And fairy princesses sang songs
To moonbeam harps, and merry gongs
Rang for a dinner, where bright throngs
Sat eating air and drinking dew
From thimble cups and plates of new
Green leaves. It was no dream, but true.

And they were there forevermore:
The homeward path, the schoolhouse door
Vanished from thought forevermore.

Only the lake's dark motion came
Dimly to them in a dream
Sometimes, they went again.

(From *Five New Brunswick Poets*)

I wrote other things: attempts at plays, fragmentary sermons, even a newspaper (though nothing happened). Two poems from *Passage of Summer* recall this Washademoak period:

Make-Believe

The child, playing all day in the summer fields,
Was an Indian lying in a teepee with roof of timothy
And floor of vetch and clover; the smell of grass
Was sweet and hot and tickly in her nose.
Or, dressed in a straw hat and a blue sash,
She was the young Victoria in a portrait
Painted in childhood, princess blonde and good.
The Lake was the Sweet Thames, or it might be
Deerslayer's Lake, where Hutter had his home.
The growth of bush where blueberries darkly grew,
Spicy with ferns, was a woodchopper's forest
Where Hop-My-Thumb might wander;
And a deserted house in lonely fields
With broken windows and its walls unpainted
Was the bewitched tower where the lady slumbered
Through mouldering years, waiting a brown-eyed
    prince.
In dewy pastures steeds—not horses—whinnied;
Cows were bucolic in their patient ease;
And in the dim barn, smelling of hay and manure,
The barnyard cat with wizard yellow eyes,
Peering for mice, was lithe and gluttonous,
Cunning as any cat in ancient story.

(From *Passage of Summer*)

Poem to my Sister

Do you remember the houseboat that came and
    anchored
Out in the midst of the lake, one day in summer?
One of the boys rowed us out. We climbed on board,
And the skipper, old John Brown, showed us around.
"Just like a house," we said, and saw his kitchen,
With mugs and pancake flour stored on the shelf,
And his tidy bedroom with his bunk and books.

And always after that we envied him—
I did at least—able to drop his anchor
Out there on the Lake and look across the water
At ordinary householders on shore.
It must have been like living on an island
In a world separate as a rounded shell.
Water lapped him to sleep and dawn awoke him.
The fibrous yellow lilies floated near,
And trees along the shore cast green reflections.
The daytime sun was lazy on the ripples,
And in the evening all the farmhouse lights
Glinted like warmer stars fallen from the skies.
Perhaps those houses seemed enchanted too
To one who watched their lights shine on the water
And wondered who had lit the yellow lamps
Or stood beside the windows looking out.

(From *Passage of Summer*)

"My sister Marion standing under an apple tree,"
about 1940

In 1934, when I was twelve, we left the Washademoak, and spent the next four years at or near Chipman. Chipman I've also written about in *The Sisters*, my long narrative poem *Lillooet*, my short story "Visiting Aunt Alix," and some of my poems, such as those about my great-aunt Rebecca.

This was the most painful period of my growing up, and probably the most painful period for my parents, too. It was harsh enough as I narrated it in *The Sisters*, but harsher still as we lived through it.

We lived for the first year or so in an old dilapidated house outside of town, called the Pest House because a group of people had been quartered there in the distant past with some disease. It was a long distance to school; I had not good shoes or overshoes; somehow I dropped out of school for three years. If I had been ambitious, no doubt I would have found a way to go, but I didn't. Of course I went on reading. I remember sitting with my feet in the oven of the old wood stove to keep them warm, while I read *A Tale of Two Cities* and *Great Expectations* and *Oliver Twist*. My father tried to make a little money selling magazine subscriptions. My mother helped a number of housewives with their spring cleaning, or her nieces with the birth of their babies. I went along on these excursions, helped out with a little dishwashing, read any books on the premises. Sometimes the pickings were slim: Cousin Myrtle had

only the Bible, the collected poems of Tennyson, and *Eatons' Catalogue*. Cousin Remona had the *Books of Knowledge*, which I brought out one by one from the frigid, unheated parlor where they were kept. But Isaac Baird's family had a whole array of books: that's where I first read *Pride and Prejudice* and *Jane Eyre* and Boswell's *Life of Johnson* and *Journey to the Hebrides*. Frank Baird (was he Isaac's brother or uncle?) had been Moderator of the Presbyterian Church in Canada and the author of historical novels. One of Isaac's sisters had married the president of the University of New Brunswick. The idea of university first entered my mind then, especially when a Baird grandson with a scholarship visited. I told my mother that I would like to go back to school, though by this time I was fifteen. So we moved into town—on the wrong side of the tracks, of course, but town all the same—in what was nicknamed Rabbit Town. "Bridge" recreates something of the uncertainty of my early teens:

Bridge

I remember walking the bridge across the river
one evening in spring with my mother
when I was thirteen.
We took turns carrying a suitcase
which had in it just about all we owned,
and we were not sure with which relatives
we might spend the night.
It was a high, clear evening,
with the new moon out and all the stars,
and we stopped halfway over the bridge
to look down into the quiet water
so still and so deep.

I thought my mother,
who liked beautiful things,
was only admiring the stars
reflected;
but now I know
she must have been thinking
how peaceful it would be
down there
far below the bridge.

(From *Sunrise North*)

The onset of adolescence, during the period when I was twelve to fifteen, had brought on a great flood of verse. I had my first publication when I was twelve, a poem in the Saint John *Telegraph*. My father had sent the poem off without my permission. I was angry with him, but pleased to see myself in print. School temporarily halted the flow of verse, while I caught up with arithmetic and history and geography.

In 1938 we moved to Sussex, King's County. Sussex also serves as a background in *The Sisters*, as the town of Milton, and is the background of the title story of my collection *A House Full of Women*. A pleasant, idyllic rural small town, it was somewhat changed in 1939, when war revitalized the army camp which had been there in the first Great War. The beginning of the Second War coincided with my entry into high school. In the Sussex High School I was lucky enough to have several good teachers, especially Nane MacNeill and Ethel Singer. Miss MacNeill lent me books of poetry and books about poetry and, eventually, was the person most responsible for persuading me to apply for a scholarship to university. Miss Singer nagged me into writing an essay for a Provincial contest run by the Press Club, which I won. I was helped also by my friend and rival, Phyllis King, who was in my class in school. Phyllis and I were both omnivorous readers, reading books aloud to each other. We borrowed books from the small village library (upstairs over the fire station) and my father also brought me home books from the army camp, where he worked in the army canteen. One of the enthusiasms I've kept from that time is for

Katherine Mansfield, especially for her poetic stories of childhood, and I like to think that I learned something from her technique.

One person I met during this high school period was P. K. Page. I sent some poems to a contest of the New Brunswick Authors Association in Saint John. Pat, a young poet herself, was one of the judges. She wrote to me, and a visit to Saint John was arranged. I used this visit, very much changed, as the basis of my short story "Essence of Marigold." Pat was my "first acquaintance with poets," and her work has always been important to me.

I graduated from high school in 1942, and that autumn entered the University of New Brunswick in Fredericton. I had a small entrance scholarship, but could probably not have managed to go to university if my parents had not moved to Fredericton, where my father worked in the army canteen and my mother cooked doughnuts for the soldiers.

The account of Jane Marchant's arrival in Fredericton, as told in *The Sisters*, is similar to my own:

My parents and I moved to Fredericton in August. My father went first, to rent a house. My mother and I stopped for a few days in Lillooet, visiting Cousin May. I was rather disappointed that, as we weren't there on a Sunday, we didn't see Mr. Cranshaw.

My father met us at the station with a taxi driven by a fat, dour taxi-driver named Guy. Guy and my father later became close friends, so that for years afterward I came to associate arrivals and departures with him.

The train arrived in Devon, across the river from Fredericton. Guy drove us across the Devon bridge into the small, quiet city, with its church spires and clustered wooden houses and squat, ornate legislative building. It was a bright, hot August afternoon, but the summer had been moist and lawns and trees were still green, even though drooping a little. The house my father had rented was a small grey frame house on Charlotte Street with a picket fence and an old-fashioned flower garden that had run wild. We had the downstairs. The upstairs was rented to a young couple, a truck-driver and his wife.

My father had bought a wood stove and a kitchen table and chairs, but otherwise we had no furniture. There had been none to move; in Milton we had lived at old Mrs. Patterson's and used her furniture. For a night or so we slept on mattresses on the floor. Then my mother and father went off to a shop that sold second-hand furniture, my mother carrying her worn old navy-blue purse with the money, as she and my father agreed that she was the better bargainer.

They came back pleased and beaming, with the purse somewhat thinner, and the next day their purchases were delivered: two bedsteads, a kitchen cot, a bureau and a chest of drawers (made by hand), a dining table and chairs and a buffet. The dining-room furniture was heavy and Victorian, and somehow had a happy look of having belonged to us for years. Something was wrong with the catch on one of the doors of the buffet, so it always had to be closed with a bit of paper; but my mother was delighted with it, and polished it vigorously. Later a rocking chair and an arm chair were added, battered but comfortable, and a new sofa with a cretonne flounce. We used the same room as living-room and dining-room. In the evening I did my studying there, at the dining-room table or on the sofa, while my mother read or sewed in the armchair. But that is to look ahead, to the time when I had started classes.

My father, as he had hoped, got a job working nights in a canteen at the military camp. We were settled in.

All three of us took walks around the campus and looked at the buildings. If I had had any experience of other campuses I might have been disappointed; but to me, and to my parents, it looked imposing. It was certainly bigger than Milton High School. Besides, the view over the town and the river was beautiful, and all the more beautiful when September came and the leaves began to change colour.

I wandered all over the town, reading the epitaphs in the little graveyard on Carleton Street, near which we lived, peering into the cathedral, crossing the Devon bridge, visiting the parks and the Green, prowling around the Market outside the Town Hall on a Saturday morning. I had a sense of freedom and anonymity. Nobody in town knew me yet, except maybe the young couple upstairs, who weren't paying much attention to anybody but themselves.

I loved Fredericton and the university. Fredericton of that time was a gentle, elm-shaded small city of only about eight thousand people. The university itself was small and intimate, probably smaller even than a few years earlier, because of the War. Although there was no formal course in creative writing, several members of the faculty were writers: Edward McCourt, who later published a number of admirable novels; Desmond Pacey, chiefly a literary historian, but also a writer of short stories; and A. G. Bailey, a talented poet who was the chief faculty adviser of our small poetry society and the person most responsible for the founding of the little magazine—*The Fiddlehead*—which we started and which still survives. One of my classmates, Donald Gammon, was the first editor; a few years later Fred Cogswell took it over. Fred arrived on the campus in 1945 as a returning veteran, after the conclusion of the War. He is now well known in Canada as a poet, translator, and editor.

Fredericton served as part of the setting for *The Sisters* and (under the name of Georgetown) as the principal background of *Junction,* my time-travel novel. It also is present in some of my poems and short stories. The title story of *Visitations* is set at the university.

In 1946 I graduated from the University of New Brunswick. I received a travelling scholarship from the Canadian Federation of University Women, and in September of that year entered Radcliffe College (Harvard), from which I received a master's degree in June 1947. This was the first time I had ever been away from Canada (or, for that matter, from New Brunswick) and some of the time I was violently homesick, though I also enjoyed the stimulation of a large university community. I was impressed by some of my professors (F. O. Matthiessen, Walter Bate) but was more impressed by visits of T. S. Eliot and Robert Frost. I was too busy to do much writing of poetry myself, though I had some poems accepted by *Poetry* (Chicago).

I returned to Canada that summer, and in the autumn of 1947 took a teaching position in Hatfield Hall, a small private school in Cobourg, Ontario. Hatfield Hall was the model for the school in my short story "A Perfect Setting." However, I did not stay there long. Three weeks after I arrived I fell off a horse (I can't really say I was thrown) and was shipped back to my parents' home in Fredericton with a broken back. I was in a cast for eight months, but in January 1948 started to work in the library at the University of New Brunswick, and worked there until August.

In September 1948 I went to Bloomington, Indiana, where I was enrolled in the graduate school at Indiana University, taking courses towards a Ph.D. in English and doing some teaching of freshmen. I enjoyed Bloomington and intended to stay there until I received the degree but was tempted by the opportunity to apply for a Beaverbrook Overseas Scholarship to the University of London. Bloomington is the setting for one of my stories, "Her First Apartment."

I spent the academic year 1949–50 at King's College, London. Several of my poems and three short stories ("Strangers," "Voyage Home," and "A Question of Style") make use of this setting and time frame. It was a mixed experience. In some ways I fell in love with the England of the time (still a period of postwar shortages and a certain gallantry of spirit in enduring them). English theatre was good and cheap. I loved the little bookshops, the early English spring, the *Times* crosswords. However, I was disappointed that the experience was not very useful to me academically. I could not work towards a degree except to obtain a second master's degree; and this did not seem to be worthwhile. I did attend some classes, especially one on critical theory run by Geoffrey Bullough, which was also attended by my compatriot and contemporary, Norman Levine (later known for his short stories and novels). I also spent time in the British Museum Reading Room, reading around in the background of one of my favourite poets, George Crabbe, and his contemporaries of the late eighteenth and early nineteenth centuries. One of these contemporaries and friends was an Anglo-Irish Quaker writer, Mary Shackleton Leadbeater, whose personality interested me, and I spent a week or two in Dublin reading her unpublished diary. I met some of Mary Leadbeater's distant Shackleton relatives, descendants of her brother, and thought of using them as models for fictional characters, but never did. Perhaps I shall yet.

I returned to Fredericton in the summer of 1950, shortly after the beginning of the Korean War. The next year was unsettled and unhappy. Unable to get a suitable academic position, I filled time by taking a business school course in typing and shorthand. For a short time I worked at a stopgap job typing in a lawyer's office. In the autumn of 1951 I moved to Kingston, Ontario, where I worked at Queen's University, part-time in the *Queen's Quarterly* office, part-time for the Government Documents section of the university library. It was very shortly after my move to Kingston that my first tiny chapbook of poetry, *East Coast,* was published by Ryerson Press. Although it did not attract much attention at first, the fact that it was eventually reviewed very favourably by Northrop Frye was cheering to me. I needed cheering, as I was still suffering from the previous year's depression and felt that I was in a dead-end situation. My story "Comfort Me with Apples" reflects in part my feelings of the time. My depression gradually diminished, however. Both the people I worked for were interesting to me. George Herbert Clarke, the editor of *Queen's Quarterly,* was a minor poet and something of a character. Douglas Fisher, in charge of Government Documents at the university library, later became active in national politics and as a journalist. The Fishers were my closest friends in Kingston. I later regretted not having become better acquainted with George Whalley, poet and Coleridgean critic.

I decided that, since I was working in a library, I should have a library degree, and spent the academic year 1952–53 in the University of Toronto Library School, where I obtained my B.L.S. in 1953. I also received the E. J. Pratt Award for poetry from the University of Toronto for selections from my poem *Lillooet,* which I had written in Kingston but which was not published by the Ryerson Press until 1954. Pratt was a poet whose work I liked, and I was pleased to receive an award with his name attached to it.

From 1953 to 1957 I worked in the library of Carleton University, Ottawa. Although Ottawa is the national capital, it did not at that time have much of a writing community. However, I did make several acquaintanceships with poets in Ottawa. The first was with George Johnston, a witty poet who later acquired a reputation as a translator of several of the sagas *(The Saga of Gisli, The Faroe Islanders' Saga).* George and his wife Jeanne became my closest friends in Ottawa. The second friendship was with the poet Jay Macpherson. Jay did not actually live in Ottawa at that time, but had formerly lived there and returned in vacations to visit her mother. Jay introduced me to Daryl Hine, then a very young poet, on a visit to Ottawa. Another acquaintanceship was with Peter Dale Scott, then living in Ottawa with his wife Maylie, with whom I worked in the Carleton University library.

Elizabeth Brewster, about 1944

A large conference of Canadian writers in Kingston in the summer of 1955, organized by Frank Scott, was the scene of my first meeting with a number of Canadian poets: Earle Birney, Irving Layton, Dorothy Livesay, Louis Dudek, Raymond Souster, James Reaney, Frank Scott himself, Phyllis Webb. Livesay, Scott, and Souster have all appeared in my poetry or had poems addressed to them.

Of importance to my writing was a psychoanalysis that I went through during this period. The psychoanalyst was Marta Wassermann, widow of the Austrian novelist Jakob Wassermann. She had formerly written novels under her maiden name of Marta Karlweis. She had been analyzed by Carl Jung, and I suppose could be called a Jungian analyst, though I don't think she belonged exclusively to any school. Something of my relationship with her, though fictionalized, appears in my short story "Understanding Eva." She helped me to get rid of a writer's block that had been preventing me from writing poems, largely by getting me in touch with my dreams. She encouraged me to draw the details of dreams, but I wrote them as poems instead. An interest in dream, myth, and archetype has continued with me ever since. Two dream poems written during this period:

Dream Landscape

What is this dark landscape of my dreams,
These mazy paths where it is always hard walking,
In country lanes or on some city side street,
A dark alley lined by crowded tenements?
What are the scuffles in the dark, the muted
    violence?
What are the bridges that are so hard to cross?
What are the rooms I walk through, the empty
    corridors
Hollowly echoing to uncertain feet,
The unfurnished apartments always to be let,
The dining rooms where meals are never served?

What are these crowds gathered to see a play—
Comedy or tragedy, nobody knows which—
Where the blonde and beautiful heroine weeps and
    smiles?
Or are they waiting for a symphony to begin
While the instruments tune up but never play?

And what is the name of this grey, restless sea
By which I walk, escaped from crowds and houses?
How beautiful and perilous the path
Along the rocky coast, watching the gulls dip
From a patch of lonely sky, watching the spray
Tossed high by the wind against the waiting rocks.
What are these rocks? What is this tossing spray?

(From *Passage of Summer*)

Dream

I dreamed that I was buried live.
My spirit took a spade
And dug the earth where deep
My body had been laid.

If I arrived in time
I knew I had a spark
Would light my fainting life,
Even in that dark.

But when my spade had struck
The coffin, I was dead,
Body and silent heart.
Only my severed head

Cut from my naked neck,
Still lived, and faintly spoke
With senseless, twittering tongue.
Its eyes, with clouded look,
Stared at me and implored
My help by deed or word.

(From *Passage of Summer*)

In 1957 I returned to Bloomington, Indiana, where I worked for a year in the university library, and then went back to the graduate school to pick up my work for a Ph.D. My dissertation was on George Crabbe. My third small book of poems, *Roads,* was published in 1957, and I continued to write poetry. A young poet from India, A. K. Ramanujan, was in the graduate school at the same time, and we had lively discussions and comparisons of each other's poetry. A group of poems, "Nine Poems for Raman," written at this time, was not published until my 1982 volume *Digging In.* The title poem of my 1974 volume *In Search of Eros* was also written at this time. It is a long poem on the "Cupid and Psyche" story. Unfortunately, I discarded parts of it, so that it remains only in fragments.

I came back to Canada in 1960, accepting a teaching position in the Department of English, Victoria University, Victoria. My father had died in 1959; my mother came out to Victoria from New Brunswick to live with me. We stayed there for only a year. In 1961 I took a position in the Mount Allison University Library, in Sackville, New Brunswick, and we moved to Sackville. I had by this time completed the work for my Ph.D., though I did not receive the degree until 1962. My mother died in May 1962; I received my degree in June. My story-essay "Collage," in *Visitations,* is about my father. "Victorian Interlude," published in the little magazine *Event* (Spring 1990) is about my mother. ("Victorian Interlude" will appear in my next prose collection, *The Invention of Truth,* due to be published in autumn 1991.)

Sackville is a beautiful little town with a view of the Tantramar Marshes. Mount Allison is a small liberal arts college. It has (or had) a lively arts community. The artist Alex Colville was one of my neighbours. Michael Collie of the English department wrote poetry, and so did William Aide, although Bill Aide is better known as a musician. It was a town of characters, such as Miss Ella Smith of the local bookstore, who had been in Spain at the time of the Spanish Civil War and managed to get into trouble with both sides. "August Afternoon" gives some of the atmosphere of Sackville:

August Afternoon

Summer is almost over now. The fountain
Still sprays its untired coolness on the grass,
And grass is lush, and clover what it was,
And ducks still move like squadrons in formation,
Stepping downward to the water's brink. They
    paddle
As young as ever on the waves. And yet
One's lame now. Something's happened to his foot.
Ducks and ourselves are not as fit as fiddles.

Fall's not in air; frost has not hit the leaves;
But the marsh smells of blackberries and hay.
The goldenrod waves thick; the jewel weed
Winds its small orange horn powdered with red.
Cling to this sunshine, pile the summer day
Close pressed for winter under mind's dark eaves.

(From *Passage of Summer*)

Parents, Frederick John and Ethel Brewster, sometime in the 1950s

I stayed in Sackville for four years, from 1961 to 1965. During this period I was vainly attempting to get a larger collection of poems published. Except for a few poems in magazines, my only publication during this time was a group of poems in the anthology *Five New Brunswick Poets*, published by Fiddlehead. Alden Nowlan, one of the five poets, had recently married and moved to Saint John. He wrote me a warm and enthusiastic letter about my work. Later I visited the Nowlans in Saint John, and formed an enduring friendship with Alden and Claudine. My poem "For Alden," in my *Selected Poems* (1985), is a tribute to that friendship.

In 1965 I moved to Fredericton, where I worked for three years as associate librarian in the Legislative Library. I used the background of the Legislative Library in the title story of *It's Easy to Fall on the Ice*. I wrote both poems and stories at this time; but it was not until I had left Fredericton in 1968 that a substantial collection of poems was accepted for publication. This was *Passage of Summer,* published in 1969 by Ryerson Press. I might not have persevered in trying to get the book published if it had not been for the nagging of Dorothy Livesay, then writer-in-

residence at the University of New Brunswick, and my old professor, Desmond Pacey, who wrapped the parcel up to send to publishers.

I moved to Edmonton, Alberta, in the autumn of 1968, to work in the university library. Edmonton had quite a lively literary community at that time. Margaret Atwood, near the beginning of her literary career, arrived around the same time as I did. I was already acquainted with her poetry, and knew that she was a former student of Jay Macpherson. Dorothy Livesay had moved from Fredericton to Edmonton. Henry Kreisel, whose novels *The Rich Man* and *The Betrayal* I had read before with admiration, was vice-president academic at the university. Wilfred and Sheila Watson were a lively writing couple. Rudy Wiebe had already begun his writing career, though his most impressive novels were yet to come. Later, the poets Stephen Scobie and Douglas Barbour arrived on the scene.

I worked in the library for two years, but decided in 1970 that I wanted more time for writing. I was then working on the novel that eventually became *The Sisters* as well as on a new collection of poetry. I had thought of taking a year off entirely, but Marga-

The author with Dorothy Livesay and Desmond Pacey, Fredericton, New Brunswick, about 1966

ret Atwood, who was leaving at that time, suggested that I might teach the section of creative writing in poetry that she had been teaching the previous academic year. I had not been happy teaching in Victoria ten years earlier, but I enjoyed this experience. Margaret also influenced the choice and arrangement of poems in my next book, *Sunrise North* (though this did not appear until 1972), and suggested the title. She enjoyed fortune-telling at this time (palm reading, Tarot pack, horoscope). I still have a horoscope she drew for me at that time, though I don't know how to read it. Perhaps the fact that she foretold that my later life would be happier and more prosperous than the early part, and that I would have more fame, fortune, love, and friendship in the later part of my life, helped me to face the future cheerfully. One rather comic poem I wrote at this time was "Tea Leaf Reading" (in *Sunrise North)* about a visit we paid to a woman who told fortunes in the tea leaves. I have always admired Margaret's work, wrote reviews of several of her books of poetry. Even though she was a much younger writer than I, I felt that I learned something from her about arrangements of poems and arrangements of lines.

Poem for a young sorceress

The witch is young.
Her uncoiled hair
slides down her back.
Her gaze is clear,

her forehead smooth,
her smile discreet,
her manner guarded,
distant-sweet.

The spirit who
obeys her spell
I think is tricky
Ariel.

She reads my palm
my horoscope.
I listen with
half-mocking hope,

but wonder
what her fate will be
who smiles and tells
my fate to me.

(From *In Search of Eros)*

I had joined the League of Canadian Poets in 1968, when it was a very new organization. Among other things, the League encouraged poetry reading tours by its members. The first I took part in was a series of joint readings in autumn 1971 with Frank Scott and Douglas Barbour. Scott's witty and humane poems had always attracted me. Later I wrote an essay on his work, "The 'I' of the Observer."

Earlier that year, in the spring of 1971, I received a Senior Arts Award from the Canada Council which freed me during the academic year 1971–72 to work on my writing. I spent the rest of 1971 in Edmonton, but went to Ottawa for the first four months of 1972. One writer whom I saw a good deal of at that time was Joy Kogawa. Joy had not yet written her novel *Obasan,* but was working towards it. Both of us were very much interested in dreams at that time and kept dream journals. We were also interested in the *I Ching,* and I wrote a poetic sequence, "Consulting the *I Ching,*" which was published in my collection *In Search of Eros.*

I renewed my acquaintance with my old friends the Johnstons at this time, and also with Frank Scott, now retired from McGill but sometimes coming to Ottawa to lecture on constitutional law.

Before I left Ottawa, my poetry collection *Sunrise North* was published by Clarke, Irwin. Most of these poems were written in Edmonton. However, one, "Block of Silence," dated back to 1950, and had been intended to be the title poem of my first little book, *East Coast.* "I Thought of You" is also an earlier poem. A number of poems, though written during the Edmonton period, deal with past experiences, sometimes of childhood or adolescence ("Family Quarrel," "Blueflag," "Inheritance," "Bridge," "Cold Tea"), sometimes of other periods ("Voyage Home," "Poems for Psychoanalysis"). I thought of these memory poems as mostly antinostalgic, an attempt to explore some of the pain of the past.

I returned to Edmonton from Ottawa in late April 1972, immediately after the publication of *Sunrise North.* In Toronto, on my way back to Edmonton, I received a telephone call from the head of the English department at the University of Saskatchewan about a position in the department. I came to Saskatoon in May to be interviewed for the position, and moved to Saskatoon the end of August. I have lived in Saskatoon, except for brief absences, ever since. When I came, I thought that I might stay for a year or so, and then (in my usual restless way) move elsewhere. However, I continued to teach in the university until 1990, and have stayed on in Saskatoon after my retirement, though I have spent some of the winter in Victoria.

When one lives in the same place, years and experiences tend to run together. I have lived a quiet, rather dull life, teaching, writing, having books published, sometimes taking a year off.

Has teaching helped or hindered my writing? I'm not entirely sure myself of the answer. Contact with young minds ought, perhaps, to have helped. I taught chiefly courses in Canadian poetry and fiction which kept me in touch with the writing being done by other Canadians. A university environment does provide communication with civilized minds. There were also disadvantages. I found teaching a demanding profession which doesn't provide much free time during the academic year, whether for writing or for the sort of vagrant, quirky reading that aids poetry. I tended to do my writing either in summer vacations or in the years I took off. I had grants from the Canada Council in 1976, 1978–79, and 1985–86, which enabled me to take time off. I also had sabbaticals in 1980–81 and 1988–89.

I had two books published in 1974, my novel *The Sisters* and a book of poems, *In Search of Eros.* I had worked on *The Sisters* for a number of years and it had gone through several revisions. Many of the poems in *In Search of Eros* had been written during my 1972 period in Ottawa; others had been written in Saskatoon; the title poem dated back to Indiana days.

My first real Saskatoon book is *Sometimes I Think of Moving,* a collection of poems published in 1977. Most of these poems were recent poems, although there were a handful of earlier date, such as "Lady with a Creative Imagination," "Where I Come From," "Woman on a Bus," "Elegy for Jean," "The Green Grass Grows All Around." One sequence, "Scenes from Abandoned Novel," was based on notebook scribblings from my time in Sackville, back in the sixties. Other poems connect with childhood or youth. But the present is also there in the book, a coming to terms with the new place in the Saskatoon poems. My first book of short stories, *It's Easy to Fall on the Ice,* was also published in 1977. Some of these stories were written in Saskatoon, some at an earlier period. None was set in Saskatoon. In prose, at any rate, I have always found it easier to deal with the past than the present. And I still felt unsure, I think, about the voices of prairie people in dialogue.

I had no books published between 1977 and 1982. However, I had quite a bit of periodical publication; and in 1980 I won the President's Medal and Award from the University of Western Ontario for the best Canadian magazine poem of 1979, a poem called "The Hoop," published in *Fiddlehead* (later reprinted in *The Way Home*). My novel *Junction,* though not published until 1982, was begun in the summer of 1978, during a lengthy visit to Frederic- ton. It began as a short story suggested by a dream, was expanded to a novella, and eventually was completed as a novel. A time-travel novel, set in 1948 and 1910 (the year of Halley's Comet), it was concerned (among other themes) with the theme of war and its effects and with the yearning of people to change their pasts, to have a second chance.

Some travel experiences entered into poems of this period and later, especially from several visits to Australia and New Zealand. I was interested in the parallels and contrasts between the writings of (espe- cially) New Zealanders and Canadians. Mansfield, of course, was an early favourite; but I was also interest- ed in the work of Janet Frame, of C. K. Stead (whom I met), of James K. Baxter, Maurice Gee, and Fiona Kidman, among others. Poems on Mansfield appear in *The Way Home,* in the group of "new poems" in my *Selected Poems* (1985), and in *Spring Again* (1990). Stead and Baxter were influences on the group of unrhymed sonnets among the "new poems" of the *Selected Poems.*

Travel is both a subject and a major metaphor in my work, which is often concerned with quest. This can be seen in a number of my titles: *Roads, In Search of Eros, Sometimes I Think of Moving, The Way Home, Junction, Digging In.* Another major metaphor is the seasonal cycle: *Passage of Summer, Sunrise North, Spring Again.* Gardens and houses recur. Ancestral

voices are important—parents, grandparents, literary ancestors. Poetry itself is a subject, and also the nature of fiction.

The title of *A House Full of Women* suggests the strong interest in women's lives present especially in my fiction, but also in my poetry. *Visitations* (1987) is also mainly fiction, but includes one frankly autobio- graphical piece, "Collage," about my father's life.

Most of my books of poems from the seventies and eighties include poetic sequences; but the two most recent, *Entertaining Angels* (1988) and *Spring Again* (1990), are especially dominated by sequences. The title sequence of *Entertaining Angels* is mainly addressed to my sister Eleanor in her serious illness, though it is also a poem about words, working its way through the alphabet. "H. D. Analyzes Sigmund Freud" is a tribute to one of the women poets who impresses me. (I often like to write letter poems, especially to the dead.) In *Spring Again,* "Garden Cantos," "Nausicaa Cantos," and "Ordering Verses" form a major part of the book. "Ordering Verses" is in part a response to the Salman Rushdie affair.

My most recent poetic sequence, "Wheel of Change," won an award in January 1991 in a Canadian Broadcasting Corporation literary competi- tion. It is a group of thirteen poems, largely con- cerned with the problems of Canadian unity (or disunity).

"With three younger colleagues from the University of Saskatchewan," 1990

Decline and Fall

Empires rise and fall. I suppose Aurelius's
was already on its long long decline
as he battled barbarians and whatever disease
killed him in army camp.

When I was a child in the thirties,
the British Empire also
must have begun its descent,
though the trappings were still there,
even in the one-room schoolhouse
in New Brunswick back woods
where Blanche Corcoran and I
stood in front of the wall maps
pointing out to each other
the pink British countries

and we studied British history
with all its kings and battles
and Canadian history with a picture of General Wolfe
dying a hero's death

and drew the Union Jack in colour
carefully in our scribblers.

The holidays were half British:
Victoria Day, King George's birthday,
the embattled Orange Twelfth of July
with a local farmer
as King William on a white horse.

I had never been outside of New Brunswick.
Quebec was far and picturesque,
and people there spoke another language.
Louis Hemon wrote about it,
and Gilbert Parker.
Ontario was where Uncle Cecil went
when he was angry with his brothers.

Saskatchewan was far and flat.
Someone sent me a post card of wheat fields
under a harvest moon.
I kept it for months, maybe years,
on a shelf in my room.

Alberta was home on the range

and then there were mountains.

That was Canada.

Newfoundland was not Canada.
It was out there in the Atlantic
        (but part of the Empire, of course).

And India was Empire too, with maharajahs,
and Australia and New Zealand,
and South Africa, where my father remembered
older men going to fight,
and there were strange words
like kopje and veldt.

Somewhere on the other side of the water
was London, which was the heart,
a great dark blob on the map,
and Paris, another heart

where the blood came from
that had poured into those
blank spaces on our map
and made them
still pink.

"Civis Romanus sum."

Europe packed up and carried
in trunks and boxes
aboard vessels tossed on the Atlantic:

Shakespeare's plays, a Wedgwood tea set,
the *Meditations* of Marcus Aurelius,
Moliere, Racine, a Latin Grammar,
ABC, Mother Goose.

Shadow of the Roman Empire
behind those later Empires, French or British.

"Thine, O Roman, remember . . ."

Grandmother said we had Dutch blood,
Cousin Pierce said French Huguenot.
And of course all those Scots and English,
including Puritan William Brewster.

Roman? It's always possible.

Quest

Do you find a country
by negotiations?
By constitutional amendments?
By expert legal opinions
on the meaning of certain words and phrases?
Will a Canada clause give us
our missing identity?

I think of Psyche searching
for her lost love,
the love she lost
because she insisted on seeing
what he looked like;

because her sisters
made her doubt his nature,
suspect him of being a monster
instead of the beautiful
god of love.

The Land

The land is not ours.
It will never belong to us—
English or French or Chinese or Ukrainian
or even Cree or Algonquin.

It owns itself.
Our cities cannot subdue it,
though they may spoil it.

It is a green idea of itself.
It is a white snow
in which our footsteps
vanish without trace.

Our arguments, the words
we use to bruise each other,
diminish into snowy silence,
inaudible, invisible.

Wolfe and Montcalm,
Montcalm and Wolfe
are buried long ago
under the land's
indifference.

Elizabeth Brewster, "on retirement from university, with Dean Art Knight," May 1990

Surely also
our ten premiers and Mulroney,
News commentators on television, waving
the flags of the provinces,
our white banner
with its dying maple leaf
blood red

they too . . .

I retired from teaching in June 1990. Retirement may have given me more leisure for writing; yet it also warns me that time may be short, that it might be foolish to aim at *Paradise Lost* or a four-volume novel. In the last dozen years or so, many of my relatives, close friends, colleagues, or casual acquaintances have died. That fact is reflected in poems or stories over the years. The time has come to sum up; if I have something I want especially to say, I must say it now. Or perhaps I should just have fun with writing.

What I have written here is the skeleton of a life. Anyone who wants to put flesh on the skeleton should take a look at some of my other poems and stories, at my novel *The Sisters,* and at the volume of prose

pieces, *The Invention of Truth,* that Oberon plans to publish in autumn 1991.

BIBLIOGRAPHY

Poetry:

East Coast, Ryerson (Toronto), 1951.

Lillooet, Ryerson, 1954.

Roads, and Other Poems, Ryerson, 1957.

Passage of Summer, Ryerson, 1969.

Sunrise North, Clarke, Irwin (Toronto), 1972.

In Search of Eros, Clarke, Irwin, 1974.

Sometimes I Think of Moving, Oberon (Ottawa), 1977.

The Way Home, Oberon, 1982.

Digging In, Oberon, 1982.

Selected Poems of Elizabeth Brewster, 1944–1984, two volumes, Oberon, 1985.

Entertaining Angels, Oberon, 1988.

Spring Again, Oberon, 1990.

Fiction:

The Sisters (novel), Oberon, 1974.

It's Easy to Fall on the Ice: Ten Stories, Oberon, 1977.

Junction (novel), Black Moss (Windsor), 1982.

A House Full of Women (stories), Oberon, 1983.

Visitations (stories), Oberon, 1987.

Other:

(With others) Fred Cogswell, editor, *Five New Brunswick Poets,* Fiddlehead (Fredericton, New Brunswick), 1962.

The Invention of Truth (stories and essays), Oberon, 1991.

Abelardo B. Delgado

1931-

Abelardo "Lalo" Delgado, 1975

Growing Up in Mexico

The priest tries to explain the Blessed Trinity in his sermon. I listen. He is saying it is the same God performing three different functions: one creates, one redeems, and one maintains. It is the same God seen doing different things. Humans, too, do various things at various times. They are seen by others in different roles. When I read poems I actually believe myself to be a different person. I can easily be seven different persons and keep each one separate from the others.

I am a few months from reaching my sixtieth birthday. I feel it is a good time to take inventory of the many persons housed in me. This brief autobio-graphical attempt can be part of the inheritance I will be leaving my eight children and fourteen grandchildren.

Many people know me and see me as Lalo the poet, Lalo the writer. They see me respond to that inner desire to share the written word.

That Lalo happens to be a hard one to describe. The other Lalos must be equally hard to understand, even by myself. My own children and grandchildren do not know me. To them I am simply Dad or Grandpa. Surrounded by them in one of those many cookouts we make I feel a stranger. My wife of thirty-plus years knows me the least even after having shared so many intimacies. This autobiography is for her as well.

I was born in a little town in Mexico. It is in the state of Chihuahua and called La Boquilla de Conchos. Conchos is a river which feeds into a dam famous for its bass.

I owe my having become a writer to having grown up without a television set. The biggest factor was my great-grandmother Andrea. She was near a hundred years old and was bedridden. She was blind but she could spin a yarn, or cuento, as we call them in Spanish. Her stories kept me close to her bed. I would even get her water and light her cigarettes. I got to the point where she would start a cuento and my imagination would take off and finish it. When it was time for me to go to sleep I would actually recall her many cuentos and make some of my own.

I am an only son on my mother's side. My mother was just a teenager when I was born. We grew up together. I remember her as a very beautiful woman. She still is. On my father's side I ended up with seven half brothers and sisters. They are all living in Mexico. Most of my half brothers and sisters are teachers or professionals in other fields. They seem to be doing all right despite the bad economy in Mexico.

My grandmother Luz did most of the task of raising me in those early years. She was my mother's mom. I guess she loved me a lot but she was overly protective. She did not even let me go to school, afraid someone would beat me up. I had to learn to read and write right at home. Mexican comic books were one of the reasons I strived to learn to read in a hurry.

Most of what I recall from those twelve years in Mexico is often reinforced by what my mother tells me. Other memories are a bit obscure. I may change them at times to suit me. My mom wanted to have a little girl but had to settle for me. She actually would dress me up as a little girl. This made me very angry. It must have been then when I developed my mean look.

My grandmother used to tell me of a time she took me to the molino to grind some corn. Some of the women there began to comment about what a nice-looking little girl I was. She tells me that in anger I raised my skirt and showed all of them my tiny manhood proof. I was a boy regardless of how my mother decided to dress me.

Lalo, seated to the left of Father Gilly, El Paso, 1949

One thing I remember of Mexico is that I did not stay long in rural settings. We moved to Parral, which was a city. Because we were poor we often walked from one city to the other. We spent many a night sleeping on dirt floors. We seldom had the luxury of running water or toilets. Later on we landed in Ciudad Juárez, which is a rather large border city.

We had many rough times economically but we also had some good ones. My mom even tried her hand at being an entrepreneur. She opened up a grocery store, and later in a small mining town she opened up a restaurant and a bar. I used to tend the cantina at night. I was barely six or seven but was selling beer. I did my part to help the business along by filling beer bottles with leftover beer and recapping them. The unsuspecting patrons did not know the difference. This is but one of the many survival skills many Mexicans have to learn to stay alive.

I ended up having about two years of formal education. I started going to school after my grandmother Luz passed away. She died in a Juárez hospital from cancer. She always smoked too much.

I loved my grandmother very much. I guess that is why I remember her humble funeral so well. She was the one who fussed at me those first years of my life and took the best of care.

We had no money for the funeral. She ended up inside a cheap wooden box, unpainted yet. She had to be buried at the pauper cemetery without a cross or a priest there to say a few kind words. She had to be carried there in a city garbage truck. My mother and I followed in a taxi. A twenty-six-year-old woman and an eleven-year-old boy had lost all the family they had. We were very sad and very scared but ready to face the world nonetheless.

The times after her death were rather prosperous in comparison to our past. This was the beginning of World War II. My mother used her English to land a job as a curiosities vendor in one of the many shops in Juárez. She sold souvenirs to the many soldiers who were stationed in Fort Bliss in the neighboring border city of El Paso.

My mother ended up marrying one of them. He was a Chicano from Arizona. He took a liking to me. He did not know if he was going to return from war or not. He wanted to do a good deed. Her marriage to this soldier was more of an arrangement than love. He knew that and accepted it as such. He made it easy for us to come and live in the United States.

While in Juárez I began my puppy-love years. I had a crush on a couple of young girls I had met in the movies. These two girls caught my eye. I say that literally. I was born with only one good eye. The other is scarred and allows only minimal light. To this day I have lived with this handicap, doing my best to ignore it. This makes my bad eye cross as it tries to help my good one.

I had to get used to the fact my grandmother Luz was no longer around to protect and spoil me. I began the task of learning to love my mother, a task which still continues.

In Mexico it is almost a given that most children are raised as Roman Catholics. I was no exception. I went to catechism and made my First Communion before coming to the U.S. Just to make sure, I made it again in El Paso. At that age I became fanatic about my religion. I used to pray with extraordinary fervor and constantly. I would pray for eternal life not even knowing what the word *eternal* meant.

The Mother of All Barrios

To borrow a current phrase, I landed in the mother of all barrios in the U.S. To this day this barrio is known as El Segundo Barrio.

Crossing the Santa Fe Bridge to the United States is a ritual done by millions of Mexicans who have to escape the misery their own country offers them. My mother and I did it in a rented pickup. That was more than enough to hold our belongings. My mother had rented a two-room flat.

The pickup was unloaded in front of our two-room apartment on Oregon Street. We had rented this flat from a Black family. This was in the barrio, which was all Chicano with the exception of a couple of blocks on Oregon Street where some Black families lived. Rent was fifteen dollars per month then.

I was in awe of my new country though I did not notice much difference from the barrio of the arroyo Colorado I had just left. Both barrios basically encased poverty.

El Segundo Barrio, mother of all barrios, is considered the stepping-stone for the many Mexicanos who naturally aspire to the greater things this country can offer.

At age twelve with no knowledge of the English language I started school. I wanted to attend a Protestant school because some of my friends from Juárez were attending there. The tuition was more than my mother could afford. I ended up in Aoy Elementary. I was lost in my new world of written and spoken English. Fortunately all students were Chicanos. We spoke Spanish to one another. Speaking Spanish in the school grounds was against Texas law in those days. We spoke Spanish anyway. We were punished for doing it. We took many paddlings from the principal and from some well-meaning teachers with heavy hands. We kept on speaking Spanish because Spanish was all we knew.

At the same time I entered school, began my experiences in the world of work. Because I began to work at such an early age I have thought of asking the social security people for an early retirement. I am sure they would tell me that it doesn't work that way.

My first job in the United States was at a bowling alley. I did not even know how the game was played but I knew it paid three dollars per night. I started as soon as I got out of school and worked until past midnight. My job was as a pinsetter. In those days pins were placed into a machine and lowered manually. By looking at the kids next to me I soon learned at least the basics. I knew I had to pick up the pins the bowler had knocked and place them in the machine. I did not know that if he didn't knock them all with the first ball I was to leave the remaining pins standing. The first few times doing this job I would reset even the spares. This angered the players to no end. It also drove me crazy trying to set the right pins which had remained up. They would yell at me and cuss me out. I think they were saying, "You dumb sonofabitch." It did not bother me since I didn't know what they were saying. I always thought they were praising my speed and dexterity.

I learned quickly the way it should be done. Soon the same players who used to cuss at me were giving me tips.

I did not like the job too much. I soon switched to restaurant work. There I could at least eat. I could also make a little more money. I worked as a dishwasher, a busboy, a porter, and as a cook's helper. From grade three in elementary school I began to work steady. I worked almost every day and often worked full time.

I remember a teacher sending me to the principal because she noticed I had a lot of money. She thought I had stolen it.

Teachers encouraged us to buy war bonds, a quarter a week. I used to buy twenty dollars worth of bonds at a time.

I learned at a very early age to have my own money. With it I would buy things I needed and things I wanted. This earning power I had as a youngster also did much to alleviate my mother's needs, as she was having a hard time making ends meet.

I went back to looking at girls with a gleam in my eye. I found out that here in the U.S. I could actually embrace and kiss them on the first date. In Mexico you would not have dared do that. I began to write love poems to many of the pretty girls in my school. My English was not up to par then for love poems, it

still isn't. Many of those early poems had the word "gay" in them for happy, just so they would rhyme.

I had a crush on a freckled-face Chicanita with long black hair. Her name was Lucy. To this day her initials L.G. are still tattooed on my right arm. Once I showed my teacher a few of my poems. I did this with much pride expecting a compliment from her. She must have been having a bad day because without looking at them she tore them up and threw them in the trash can. She sent me to my seat saying, "Learn to spell before you try writing poems."

Many years have gone by since that clunk. I still misspell a few words and don't often catch my typos but I believe that now, like long ago, I have many good ideas and thoughts to share with people.

Instead of feeling down I got angry at her reaction and took that as a challenge to keep on writing.

Those early years in elementary and middle school I also began to display some leadership qualities. In Mexico I had been a Boy Scout and active in church organizations. In the U.S. I was not only a member of groups but the leader of those groups. I was never a patrol boy but the captain of patrols. Even in those early years I began to challenge and question authority.

One example of these challenges was the time I refused to stand up for the national anthem in music class. Not only did I refuse but got the rest of the class to do likewise. This was done during wartime, too. To my surprise the teacher was understanding when I told her that most of us had our roots in Mexico and we would like to hear the Mexican anthem as well. She told me that if I got her the music for the Mexican anthem she would gladly play it for us. I did. We stood up from then on for both anthems.

In the fifth grade I remember starting a newsletter. I even did some war cartoons which made fun of Hitler, Mussolini, and Hirohito.

Teachers tolerated much from me because they saw I could do my work and influence other students to do theirs too. I got three double promotions in my school years. This allowed me to catch up with those my age, and even pass a few who had been born here. That couple of years of school in Mexico helped a lot because I knew my math very well. It was all a matter of picking up the English language.

My early education was highly complemented by the work I did after school. In the barrio I was receiving yet another kind of education. I was picking up on a third language, called caló. This was the lingo of the Pachucos. It is made up of combinations of English and Spanish and some other very innovative coinage of words. The word "Chicano" may well be one of them.

"El Chuco" is the way to say El Paso. This is probably where the word "Pachuco" came from.

La Bowie

By the time I got to Bowie Junior High the war had ended. Many Chicanos who had interrupted their education to join the service returned to school. This created a good blend of students. We younger students were very proud to have them around in our classes.

"La Bowie" is how we referred to our school. We ex-students always speak with much pride of la Bowie. It was the barrio high school. It had 100 percent Chicano students. Only the teachers and principal were Anglo. Competition in all sports with schools which had all Anglo students was always fierce. So were some of the fights that took place after the games.

I kept on working after school during my junior and senior high school years. My schoolwork never suffered because of that.

I also kept on writing during those years. In my senior year I was the editor of the school paper. I won some awards for my writing and represented the school in writing competitions with other city schools. I was awarded the medal for journalism on graduation night.

My essay, "What Democracy Means to Me," won third prize in a citywide competition. I also indulged in writing lyrics for songs. I was suckered into sending money to Hollywood so they would add music to one of my lyrics. They sent me hundreds of music sheets of my lyric, "Magic Lips." I asked the hotel piano player where I worked to play it for me. I didn't like the way it sounded.

With the money I earned I was one of the only teens in the barrio with a brand-new typewriter. It was an Underwood. I paid one hundred dollars cash for it. It typed in two colors with its black-and-red ribbon.

Other writing activities included entering contests which romance magazines often sponsored. They did not know I was a mere teenager providing adults with advice.

During those years I enjoyed, or thought I did, my first sexual experience. My mother had a lot of young beautiful friends who often visited her. One morning as I was typing poems one of them showed up. She must have been partying all night because she still smelled of liquor. She asked me if it would be all

right to lie down for a while in my mother's bed. I told her she could. She beckoned me to help her undress. Curious and excited I rushed to her to comply with her request. No instructions were necessary. As I urgently fumbled with her dress I became aroused, to no end. I don't know if my fear was greater than my arousal. She was a beautiful woman, short but with ample chichis, just like the ones I had seen in the *Sunshine and Health* magazines, only her bust was real and bouncingly alive.

I cannot truthfully say it was a good experience. In my excitement I finished in seconds with what I had dreamed for years. Obviously my quickness did not satisfy her. Sex is not the one-hundred-yard dash, or so I later learned. She wanted more. I did not know I had more to give. I had to let my fingers do the walking. She guided me to this activity. It seemed quite pleasing to her. The only part of this episode that is vivid is that we ended up losing her panties.

I ran a couple of blocks down the street to tell my close friend that I was no longer a virgin. He came home with me to examine the scene of the crime. By then she was quite asleep and it was getting time for

High school graduation, 1950

my mother to come home for lunch. This thought kept me from waking her as by then I was the one wanting more.

I went back to the poem I was typing. I did that with a quicker pace that kept in tune with the excitement in my heart. That day I had woken up a teenager and by noon I was a man, or so I thought.

Sex, said Freud, makes the world go around. That morning it even made my barrio go around.

In the summer of 1950 I graduated from high school. Teachers had talked to me about the possibility of some scholarships so I could go to college. I knew college was not for barrio people. I thanked them but did not take them up on their offer. I was just eager to continue with my work, maybe find some better, steady job.

My dream was to be a postman. I liked to walk and the job was with the government. I signed up to take the test. I was so happy because I scored at the top. Soon I was disappointed because to work in the post office you needed to be a U.S. citizen, which I wasn't.

I did what most high school graduates from the barrio did. I went to the employment service to be tested for aptitudes. I was told what all of them were told. I was supposed to be good with my hands. I should have known they were lying because I could not even masturbate properly.

I played the game and got a job in a steel plant. I was to be a helper for the welders. The company had just gotten a contract with the government to build thirty storage tanks of one-half-inch steel the size of a home. That job almost got me killed. A steel structure fell on my head and split it open.

I don't have much to recall when it comes to having novias. I did not have a steady girlfriend. My love life was going nowhere. One day in a barrio dance I met the girl who was to become my wife and share my life.

Courting my wife, Lola, in the barrio was hard. We had to spend our most precious moments in alleys by trash cans just to be alone with each other. Most other teens had to do the same. Lola came from a big family. They, like the rest of the barrio dwellers, only had two nine-by-twelve rooms to call home. In the barrio privacy is at a premium. Besides it wasn't culturally cool to go to your girlfriend's house unless you were a novio oficial, a steady boyfriend. This meant having passed the scrutiny of her parents. In Lola's case I only had her father to worry about.

Lola had lost her mother when she was fifteen. At that age she was forced to quit school and care for her younger brothers and sisters. Lola had also suffered a fall from her second-story apartment. It

was a serious fall. Her father obtained a lawyer to sue the landlord. She was hanging up clothes to dry when the old wood gave in. The lawyer managed to get a five-hundred-dollar settlement for her. It was exchanged for government bonds. With this kind of money you can be considered rich in the barrio. Lola and I still joke about the fact I may have married her for her money.

Lola is her nickname. Her real name is Dolores. With the similar nicknames of Lalo and Lola we knew we belonged together. Lola's father was one of the first in the barrio to buy a television set. In the barrio most good things are bought in abonos. Installments on whatever one buys in the barrio seem to go on forever. After I became her steady boyfriend I did visit her a lot. Some nights I don't know if I went to see Lola or the next episode of "Dragnet."

Meeting My Father

I took a few days off and a bus to Camargo. I went back to Mexico to meet my father. I was curious to know him. When I arrived in Camargo it was late in the evening. I did not get to see him until the following morning.

I inquired and found out his brother-in-law ran a restaurant. His brother-in-law allowed me to sleep right there in the restaurant that evening. I also learned I had some half brothers. I was also anxious to meet them. It never dawned on me they could be quite angry to learn I was the firstborn. I learned their address and walked over to take a peek at them.

My father and I finally had a good while to talk. He was somewhat apologetic about not marrying my mother. He blamed my mother for not wanting to settle down and my grandmother for meddling in their lives. I understood. Knowing my mother I knew that perhaps not even now was she ready to settle down. I had not gone there to fight with him or to ask him for anything. I had gone there to compare notes. It turned out that besides the great physical resemblance we had a lot in common in the way we thought. Our personalities were quite similar.

The following day I guess he broke the news to his family because my brothers and sisters started to come to the restaurant to meet me. They were as curious about me as I was about them.

Some years later after my father suffered a major economical setback with his cattle, I helped him get a visa to come and work here in the U.S. I also helped one of my sisters come and study in El Paso. My father was a cattleman who was ruined, along with many others, when the United States stopped buying their cattle because of the hoof-and-mouth epidemic.

After many years of struggle and work my father has gone back to ranching in Mexico. He worked here for the gas company and retired. I still visit him once in a while whenever I happen to go back to El Paso.

Back from Camargo, Lola and I began to plan for our wedding. We tried to save some money towards our proposed marriage but we knew that at the rate we were going we would never get married. The minute we saved a few dollars a good movie came along and we spent them going to see it. We loved movies.

I had worked for a coffee shop away from the barrio. There I was a busboy. Busboys earned very little then, I suppose they still do. The wages were small but were complemented with a couple of dollars the waitresses gave us from the money they made on tips. I had read in a Los Angeles newspaper what busboys earned in California. Armed with that bit of information I got the other busboys to confront the boss and ask him for more money or we would walk

off our jobs in their busiest hour. He did not care much for our demands. He knew he could easily replace us. We walked, or rather took off to L.A. in a bus. The very day we arrived we got placed in a coffee shop or hotel.

I got lucky and ended up at the Huntington Hotel in Pasadena. That job provided me with room and board. I got very good wages and I found out the tips were enough to equal what I was making in El Paso from both wages and tips.

I told Lola that I was going back to Pasadena to save money for our marriage. She did not like the idea of my leaving her even if it was just for a few months. I promised to write her daily and call her. That, plus the promise of an October wedding, eased the pain of being apart from one another.

This time I was even luckier and got promoted to room-service waiter. The tips were even better as a waiter. In a few months I had saved enough for the wedding.

I used to write Lola daily and send a dollar in each letter. With those dollars she bought her wedding dress. I also started to save some bottles of

Wedding day, El Paso, 1953

champagne left over from some of the expensive weddings we catered in the hotel.

It was in Pasadena that I came to the realization as to the power the written word can have. One day I was showing my roommate an old poem I had written in Spanish. He read that poem over and over. He suddenly got up and packed his clothes in a suitcase and took off. He was going to his wife and family he had left behind in Mexico. I am sure my poem alone did not provoke such a response. He may have been thinking of going back to his family and the poem was merely the last straw in his determination to go back. The poem, by the way, spoke of the futility of looking for love elsewhere when often we have it right in our own home.

On another occasion I wrote a poem for the family of a German waiter who had died suddenly. The family was very moved by the words I had chosen to talk about him in the poem. They were very thankful.

Very early I learned the good habit of writing daily. I used to include a poem in each of the letters I sent my wife. Most of them were love poems and very personal. A few of them were on other themes. Some were in English and some were in Spanish. It was after we got married that I learned my wife does not know how to read in Spanish. She had one of her sisters read them for her.

I asked for time off from my job to return to El Paso and get married. I promised to come right back after the ceremony. There was to be no honeymoon. I barely had time to go back and make the marriage arrangements.

The wedding was at the barrio church. It was the same church where I had been a member of the San Luis Sodality. Ours was not a fancy wedding but it was one that met most of the traditional demands. It included a big number of padrinos and madrinas. These many best men and maids of honor were to have helped a little with the expenses. They didn't, most of them were broke. I even had to help some rent their tuxedos.

We had a nice reception in one of Lola's aunts' house. We had plenty of food and drink for the invitados. Later on we had a big dance with a band.

Lola and I escaped before the dance was over. We were more than ready, biologically speaking. I don't think we could have waited one more hour for the wedding night. We had not enjoyed any of those sexual sneak previews most people enjoy nowadays.

My mother, poor soul, slept out in the car just so we could enjoy her bed and the privacy we needed on our wedding night.

With firstborn, Ana, El Paso, 1955

The very next day we took a bus to Los Angeles. Lola had decided to bring along her little brother. I had no objection, especially since I remembered her saying the doctor told her she may never have children because of the fall she had taken. Besides, the little boy saw his big sister as his mom and he could keep her company since my job was going to keep me away for long hours.

We had gotten married October 11, 1953. That very winter we returned to El Paso. Lola missed her family and was quite lonely and somewhat upset because she had not gotten pregnant immediately.

Back in El Paso my mother helped us rent another of the two-room apartments. I soon found a job as a shipping clerk for a record distributor. In January Lola got pregnant.

I believe I stuck it out with that job for almost a year. My firstborn, Ana, was born in October of 1954. My wife, who according to her doctor wasn't supposed to have any children, went on to give me eight healthy children in the years that followed.

My life was to change drastically for the first time. I went back to being active with the church organization, which by then had a young Jesuit at the spiritual helm. He came to El Paso from San Antonio and had a clear vision of what he wanted to do with his mission as a priest. We had had a lot of problems with youth gangs in South El Paso. The young Jesuit named Harold J. Rahm thought he could end that. He set out to open up a youth center. He obtained the use of an old building belonging to the Knights of Columbus. This building was at Fourth and Kansas Street.

I was earning forty dollars a week at my job as a shipping clerk. Lola, our new baby, and I had enough to get by with the little I was earning. Father Rahm was rounding up some staff for his youth center and he put the tap on me. I was afraid to leave my nice, but low-paying, steady job. I stalled with my answer. I was really afraid to leave a sure thing for an untested one, even if he had promised to top my salary by ten dollars a week.

I was already volunteering at the youth center a few nights a week and enjoyed working with the youth, even if most of them were little rascals. I finally agreed to join him and I gave my boss the customary two-week notice. He had grown to like me and did not like to see me go but he never did offer any more salary in order to keep me.

I soon learned that those few extra dollars per week the priest had promised me were not enough to make up for the long hours I had to work, weekends included. I did not know it then but a pattern, which has endured, was beginning. I have not had many nights to spend at home with my family since then.

The first few nights at my new job I almost quit. The young thugs had decided to give me a baptism of fire. They emptied the trash cans in the middle of the basketball court and turned off all the lights inside the building. They wanted to test me, maybe have some fun, as surely I would start chasing them.

I survived those few nights and went on to give that priest ten years of my life. I was a youth worker, a special activities director by night, and during the day I ran an employment office for domestic workers and laborers. I also helped to run the thrift store the Jesuit priest had opened.

It would take a novel-size book just to write about all the experiences those ten years contain.

I received enough inspiration during all those years that made me keep on writing. I actually wrote three one-act plays which I went on to direct and win first prize for in a citywide competition. Under that priest we preceded the war on poverty by a good ten years. We had volunteers, we grew into a large staff, and we were successful in getting enough financial support. Father Rahm was a literal genius when it came to getting people to help.

That Jesuit priest of German origin, besides being my boss, was my mentor and spiritual guide. I learned many things from him but the most important was to love and care for people who need help.

He was the living gospel, love personified. He was a very spiritual and saintly person but he was also very practical. He told me once that if ever the Roman Catholic church stopped making sense that it would be a cue to leave it.

All good things come to an end. The Jesuit priest got assigned to Brazil. He learned Portuguese with the same ease he had learned Spanish. He had a tremendous love and devotion for Our Lady of Guadalupe, the patroness of Chicano people.

A strong embrace, a handshake, and many tears, and I lost the man who had inspired me so much, my spiritual foundation. Since then I have fallen many a time and gotten up because of him.

Life after Father Rahm

While at the youth center I was encouraged to go to college. I took the advice of a Mormon sociologist, who died a couple of years ago, and entered through the back door one summer session.

Graduation from Texas Western College (later the University of Texas at El Paso), 1962

My first college classes were with him and an English professor who has also died.

I received a degree in secondary education with a major in Spanish and a minor in speech and drama. I received this degree from Texas Western College in El Paso, which is now the University of Texas, El Paso. During college I received some encouragement from some of the professors to keep on writing. I also managed to get quite a few of my poems in the college magazine. It was named after the college mascot, *El Burro*. I began to write "Abelard" at the end of the poems. This was meant to ask for no quarter for being a minority. I wanted to compete with Anglo writers without their knowing that I was a Chicano. All this was silly and during the Chicano movement I went back to putting the "o" at the end of my name. I was Abelardo again.

Instead of merely having a high school diploma, after Father Rahm left, I had a college degree with which to face the future.

Soon after Father Rahm left I quit my job at the neighborhood center. Another priest was running the show and I did not care much for his ideas. I had been teaching during the daytime. I taught one year in high school and one year in grade school. I wasn't much of a disciplinarian, but I was one hell of a teacher. The El Paso school system did not care much for my innovative ideas.

I entered a very depressive period of my life. I had to prove to myself that I could still earn my living with my hands without the aid of that college degree I had acquired.

I left my wife and kids and headed back to the Western Mecca of Los Angeles. I had ten dollars left after I bought my bus ticket. While I was there I bummed around in skid row. I got up at 5:00 A.M. with the winos to get to the employment agency. There we would be sent on odd jobs which paid us at the end of the day. I tried doing this for a couple of months but got real homesick for my wife and kids. I went back empty-handed but not discouraged. I must have written some good stuff those days. I manage to lose most of my original work.

Back in El Paso I got a job with a moving company. Later on I got a good job with the Texas Employment Agency, my old enemy. It was then that Lola lost her father.

I had not even warmed up my seat as a job interviewer when Sal Ramirez aka "el Huevo" asked me to work with him. He had gotten a grant from HEW to try a method of preventing gangs from forming in the barrio. He, like Father Rahm, offered me more money. I ignored him but did take a job with the government to help people resettle after

Mexico and the U.S. had finally agreed to a settlement to resolve the Chamizal border dispute. This issue was finally resolved under the Kennedy administration.

Huevo was not a man to take no for an answer so he kept on persisting, in a very convincing way, that I should go back to what I could do best, organizing in the barrio.

I did take his offer. Again I found out that while it was more money there were quite a few extra demands on my time. Once more I was working nights and weekends.

Our work plan under the project was to divide the barrio into four key target areas. The project became known as the El Paso Juvenile Delinquency Study Project. For short we called it the J.D. Project. The money had come in through the El Paso Boys Club where Huevo was the director.

What was to be only a one-year pilot project, turned into three and one half years of organizing, as we got refunded and were given more funds than initially. This was a good time to be doing what we were doing. Soon after our project the war on poverty followed.

In this project I learned much more about organizing. The philosophy was quite different than that of Father Rahm. We no longer provided services but we educated, informed, and organized so that people had a better understanding as to why they were in the situation they were. Huevo turned out to be a master at the task of organizing. Where Father had been wise, Huevo was smart. In the J.D. Project I met Andy Mares, a fellow staff person who had left the school system to work with us. From him, I learned much about poverty, its causes and social issues.

In this job I grew wings for higher and longer flights in the area of organizing and confronting the institutions. In a racist manner institutions excluded minorities and did not service our communities well.

Towards the end of the project, in 1968, I did a twenty-one-day fast. This meant no food of any kind, just water. I had fasted before on liquids. To get ready for this fast I had stopped taking solids nineteen days prior. This fast was to bring attention to the inhuman dwellings called presidios in which most people lived in the barrio. The fast was aimed at the Catholic church, to force them to take a stand and speak out against these living conditions.

This fast provided me with an opportunity to assemble a booklet of the poems I was writing while I fasted. At the end of the fast I had one hundred xerox copies of the book for sale.

I was very successful in attracting national media attention to the problem of the presidios. I also got the bishop from El Paso to come down to the barrio and say Mass. He ended up saying those living conditions should come to an end.

There has been a lot of housing reform in El Paso since my fast. I would like to think my small contribution helped towards those positive changes.

After the J.D. Project ended Sal left El Paso and started to work with students at the University of Colorado in Boulder. Prior to his leaving, he tricked me into making a presentation before a congressional hearing. He said he had lost his voice and would appreciate it if I would speak from a paper he had prepared by way of testimony. I agreed to speak before the congressional committee but told him I would prepare my own testimony. The gist of it all was to use the opportunity to poke at the neglect from our state senators. I guess I overdid it. Suddenly Huevo regained his voice and wanted to cool things down.

You do not insult a Texas senator and get away with it. I was blackballed from working on any other

Receiving an award from Güero, one of the J.D. Project youths

project in El Paso after J.D. ended. People knew I was a good organizer and wanted to hire me but the word had gotten out that I was not to be hired. I couldn't believe it was because of that one incident but I finally confronted the political boss who told me right out that it was because of that. I would not work in El Paso.

I finally landed a job in New Mexico. This meant I had to drive forty miles to and from work daily. It was a job with Project HELP, a migrant organization. I was to be an education director.

The job provided an opportunity for me to keep on writing. I was able to think a lot on those drives. At times I even stopped the car to catch those dusk landscapes for which New Mexico is famous. In those days my first book was being developed and I did not even know it.

A man I had met when I had accompanied Huevo to a meeting in Colorado called me long distance. His name is Jim Allen. He is another person in my life who helped me along with one of those destiny turns which are good. He wanted me to work with the Colorado Migrant Council. He wanted me to run his program.

Colorado and Beyond

It was a challenging proposition. In September 1969, I took the job. I went to Colorado by myself and when I had secured a place for my family I went back to El Paso and got them all moved. I had seven children by then. One, the last one, was to be born in Colorado the following year.

My job consisted of supervising a team of individuals who worked along with migrant workers. They were undercover migrants who would look out for abuses of the workers, organize and assist the workers. After a few months there I fell in love with their cause.

After a couple of months with the Colorado Migrant Council my organizing skills were put to a test, not to mention my leadership. The council was in serious trouble. It seems it had overspent $100,000. It had another problem. These programs were meant to have boards of directors which were to reflect the clientele they served. Our board was basically white and included all professionals. The challenge that the Office of Economic Opportunity gave us was to reorganize the board. If we did that by the end of the year we might be allowed to continue our operations.

The executive director resigned. I took the helm and tried to comply with the OEO's request. With a skeleton crew I succeeded in organizing a new board. One of the new board's first actions was to elect me as the new executive director.

Once I had a moment to reflect on all that had happened to me since I had gotten to Colorado, I was quite surprised. Here was the boy born in Mexico, the dishwasher from El Paso, running a poverty program worth $2.5 million and with a staff of over two hundred throughout the state and outside the state. It was scary.

My first love has never been far behind anything I do. The winter of 1969 I came out with a chapbook called *Chicano, Twenty-five Pieces of a Chicano Mind.* That was the book which was forming even before I came to Colorado. It was well received because the time was right. This was the heart of the Chicano movement time and sitewise. That book went on to be reprinted and over ten thousand copies were sold. It sold so well that I don't even have a copy myself.

I did much those days to gain the respect of my peers in Colorado and outside the state. I had gone once to visit the prisoners in Cañon City Prison. I dared share some of my poems with them. Here was

Delgado, J.D. Project youth Jesus "el Kan" Jacobo, and Sal "el Huevo" Ramirez, El Paso, 1965

an audience of supposedly hard men in tears. I promised them to keep on reading works wherever I would go. I returned a year later to read some more poems and to renew my promise. I was much in demand to do readings all over the nation. I had also acquired a reputation for being a man of integrity. A man others could trust and ask for advice. People knew of my dedication to improve the working conditions and earning power of migrant workers, to prepare them for other jobs and to prevent their children from becoming tangled in the same vicious cycle of poverty.

I did not know the importance of what I and a handful of Chicano writers were doing. We were instituting a new literary art form now widely known as Chicano literature. In many colleges and universities, particularly in the western states, Chicano literature is included as one of their regular courses, one which can be taken for credit in English literature.

The task of doing this was complementing American literature in general by truly making it representative of the population make-up, of the diversity of American people.

Others, like Alurista, Ricardo Sánchez, and Corky Gonzalez, as well as novelist Rudolfo Anaya, were also pioneers in this important and historical literary venture.

I had hardly flown in an airplane prior to coming to Colorado but in the decade of the seventies I quickly accumulated one hundred thousand miles of flying time on just one airline. I stopped counting on my way to a million miles. Many of these trips were to attend national literary festivals sponsored by Chicanos. These festivals also included other artistic disciplines, and the week-long events were meant to inspire the local artists and writers to keep creating. They were held annually and were known as Flor y Canto and Canto al Pueblo. The first name was borrowed from the one used by Aztecs to refer to their poetry festivals. Literally it means "Flower and Song." The latter title of the festivals was a bit more revolutionary in nature and means "Song to the People."

These festivals served the added purpose of meeting other writers and artists. The number of talented Chicanos in all disciplines has by now multiplied. The festivals, held in various cities, were our Chicano Woodstocks.

After being the executive director of the Colorado Migrant Council for over a year I decided to take a position back in my hometown. By then Western College had become the University of Texas, El Paso. The students had invited me to work for them in a project designed to help minority students make it through college. I was contracted to be the director of the program. It included being a member of the faculty.

In retrospect maybe I should not have left my job with the migrants. When I left I had rebuilt the program. We were running over $4 million worth of services.

I wish that when I speak of the many persons which I have been I could speak with equal pride of all. There are some sides of me which in fact are quite shameful. As an executive director for a poverty program I did a lot of traveling. I spent so much time away from home and began to meet some women who awoke the sleeping worm of desire living in me. Some relationships outside my marriage were light but some shook the foundations of my marriage. The many promises of faithfulness I had made to my wife were thrown out from many hotel windows.

Back in El Paso my writing fever continued. This time I had the advantage of linking myself with the university, where most of my writing had started. I returned a writer, with broader perspective.

While at UTEP, one of my short stories won first prize in a competition in New York. The Council on Interracial Books for Children had sponsored the contest. I wrote it based on a true incident. A Chicano had hijacked an airplane. He was interested in getting publicity to speak of the hardships of Chicano people. I wrote the story based on that and titled it, "My Father Hijacked a Plane."

Once back in El Paso I had saved enough for a down payment on a nice home by the airport. It was far away from the barrio where Lola and I had met and married, from the barrio where our first children were born.

In those days I felt like a Chicano Don Quixote riding his Rocinante, only I was riding jet planes. I went wherever I was invited and took whatever jobs were offered me. I also did much consulting with various firms.

After working at the university for a while I quit to go work in the Northwest. My territory was the three-state region of Idaho, Oregon, and Washington.

There my mission, as I saw it, was to set up health services for migrant workers under the banner of the Northwest Chicano Health Task Force, Inc.

This time it was a long haul, thirteen thousand miles to travel with our U-Haul. To reward my family for such a long jump I got lucky and had secured a beautiful home in Kirkland, right by the lake and across from Seattle. It even had a sauna.

I was invited to make a reading and a presentation at the University of Utah in Salt Lake. The

Lalo and Lola, El Paso, 1972

students challenged me to stay and work with them. That was more of a challenge than a job offer. It was to be with the Chicano Studies department. Much to the displeasure of my family I accepted to go work in Utah. Seattle is a nice place to live and for my children it was a nice place to go to school. My firstborn, Ana, graduated there from Juanita High School.

I was not as lucky to secure a home for my family to follow me and move into. I had to stay with a teacher and his family. Eventually I did find a home and once more it was a nice one by the skirt of a mountain. You could see deer come close to it at times.

I was very happy in Utah and the other-Lalo, the teacher, emerged with much zeal. I would even design courses which I was allowed to teach. I also got a bit serious about myself pursuing a Ph.D. I began to attend some courses to take a doctorate in the cultural foundations. I guess I was not serious enough because one more time my roaming ways returned. I was offered the position of a directorship to do nationwide research on farmworkers. I accepted.

Before I moved back to Denver I had published three books of my poetry and prose. I had also won first prize for a short novel I had written as a series of letters I sent a woman. The title truthfully describes what is in it, *Letters to Louise*. These were actual letters that went through the mail. She typed them for me.

I joke about spending three years in Utah. I say I went there to do penance for all my sinful ways. Speaking of sinful ways this would not be a complete autobiography if I did not at least mention another side of Lalo. This side is Lalo the gambling man. I have wasted more time and money in horse races, dog races, and bingo halls. For that, gambling is bound to be sinful. My fascination for numbers and their combinations has me trying to outguess the lotto machines. So far they manage to elude me.

Since my return to Denver I think of myself as completing a cycle of life activity. I am much more mellow and my various affairs outside of marriage have turned into one big love affair with my fourteen grandchildren. You could say I've anchored here for good.

After three and one half years of doing the research on migrant workers I stayed for a while longer with the Colorado Migrant Council. I even got back to being the executive director. This time I was not as successful at keeping it alive after some fiscal problems. The mood in the whole country had changed and after many years of service the council folded while I held the helm one last time.

Since then I have been a part-time college instructor. For the last two years I have been the client services specialist for the Justice Information Center.

I have a couple more books under my belt. Many of my poems have found their way into anthologies and other publications.

In 1988 I received the Mayor's Award, presented on behalf of the city of Denver to deserving artists, for promoting literature. More than a writer, I have been promoting and teaching Chicano literature for a lifetime. That may very well be the side of Lalo which has been more productive.

Entering into my sixties I am a much more reflective person. I have boxes and boxes of my writing which beckon me to rework them, make an effort to get them published. I am a romantic at heart and am looking for a fairy godmother or a king to subsidize the effort. Economically speaking I do not believe I am in any better shape than when I started all these efforts.

Physically speaking, other than diabetes, hypertension, and thyroid problems, I am all right. I have a tremendous fear of going blind just before I die, if not sooner. This was the fate of my great-grandmoth-

The Delgado clan, Denver, 1989

er on my mother's side and that of my grandfather on my father's side.

My spirit is much healthier, my mind as sharp as when I was young. I believe sincerely that we have not seen all of Lalo's many persons yet. Recently I have been convening poetry and acting. Presently I am in a play in which I recite and narrate.

Any of the avenues that I have touched briefly in this sketch of the many persons that live in me beg for more detail. Maybe in the same autobiographical format, I could do it in book size.

Loving the written word is perhaps where I have been unfaithful the most. To my wife and children. I apologize.

BIBLIOGRAPHY

Chicano: Twenty-five Pieces of a Chicano Mind (poetry), Barrio, 1969.

The Chicano Movement: Some Not Too Subjective Observations (essays), Colorado Migrant Council, 1971.

(Editor with Ricardo Sánchez and contributor) *Los quatro: Abelardo Delgado, Reymundo "Tigre" Pérez, Ricardo Sánchez, Juan Valdez (Magdaleno Avila)—Poemas y reflecciones de cuatro chicanos* (poetry), Barrio, 1971.

Mortal Sin Kit (chapbook), Idaho Migrant Council, 1973.

Bajo el sol de Aztlán: Veinticinco soles de Abelardo (title means "Under the Sun of Aztlán: Twenty-five Suns of Abelardo"; poetry), Barrio, 1973.

It's Cold: Fifty-two Cold-Thought Poems of Abelardo, Barrio, 1974.

A Quilt of Words: Twenty-five Quilts of Abelardo (prose and poetry), Barrio, 1974.

A Thermos Bottle Full of Self-Pity: Twenty-five Bottles of Abelardo (poetry), Barrio, 1975.

Reflexiones: Sixteen Reflections of Abelardo (poetry and short stories), Barrio, 1976.

Here Lies Lalo: Twenty-five Deaths of Abelardo (poetry), Barrio, 1977, revised edition, Barrio, 1979.

Under the Skirt of Lady Justice: Forty-three Skirts of Abelardo (poetry), Barrio, 1978.

Siete de Abelardo, Barrio, 1979.

Totoncaxihuitl, a Laxative: Twenty-five Laxatives of Abelardo (prose and poetry), Barrio, 1981.

Letters to Louise (novel), Tonatiuh-Quinto Sol International, 1982.

Unos perros con metralla (Some Dogs with a Machine-gun): Twenty-five Dogs of Abelardo (poetry), Barrio, 1982.

La llorona: Twenty-five Lloronas of Abelardo, Barrio, 1991.

Contributor to numerous anthologies, including *Canto al Pueblo: Antología* (Arizona Canto al Pueblo IV, Comité Editorial, 1980) and *Chicanos: Antología histórica y literaria* (Fondo de Cultura Económica, 1980). Contributor to periodicals. Founder and editor of *La Onda Campesina* (newsletter) and *Farmworker Journal*, both Denver; editor-at-large, *La Luz* (magazine), Denver.

Michael Gilbert

1912-

Michael Gilbert with his sister Felicity, 1913

The roots of a tree go down into the earth; and the deeper they go and the more widely they spread the greater are the chances of the tree surviving. I was not very old when I discovered that with a human being the picture is reversed. The roots of the family tree run upwards. It is upon his forebears that his chance of a tolerable life may depend.

This is the dark side of the picture and I have no wish to over-paint it. Millions of children then, and now, live with famine round the corner and starvation an ever-present threat. It wasn't like that with us. This was England in 1918. It was not yet a welfare state, but death by starvation was rare. What was at stake was something different. It was a question of status.

Let me map it out for you.

My mother (who is one of the two heroines of this story) was the fourth child of a typical Victorian upper middle-class family. They lived in an old-fashioned house in Harewood Square where the Marylebone main line station now stands; a happy and comfortable life, from which anything sordid or dramatic was as rigorously excluded as the draughts from their day nursery.

My grandfather, Goymour Cuthbert, was the youngest of five sons of a Suffolk squire. He had wanted, from earliest boyhood, to enter the regular army, but accepted the need to earn his own living and became an architect; fulfilling his military ambition by joining the London Rifle Brigade, one of the

Father, Bernard Gilbert, 1910

great City volunteer regiments of "spare-time soldiers" and rising to command it. My mother writes in her memoir:

> To us, my father's appearance in full uniform always seemed quite splendid, for he was over six foot tall and when to this height was added the Rifle Brigade shako and plume of cock's feathers he certainly was a notable figure.

This was the plateau. The level ground along which one might, with average luck, make one's way; or from which, with energy and enterprise, one might ascend; or from which a turn of the wheel might precipitate an unexpected and uncomfortable descent.

The first such downturn occurred when my mother, aged fourteen, was at boarding school in Eastbourne. Her father, needing to convalesce after an accident, came to stay at the Hydro.

> And that was the last time I saw my father, for the very next day he suddenly fell down dead from heart failure.

This was a serious but not a fatal blow; a premonition, perhaps, that life was not going to continue in the same easy way. My grandmother, a woman of spirit, was able to cope. She had enough money to send her son, Roy, and her oldest daughter, Enid, to Oxford and her second girl, Hazel, who had medical ambitions, to the London School of Medicine. My mother, for her part, was packed off to become a student nurse at the Evelina Hospital for Sick Children. All of this was in accordance with my grandmother Cuthbert's philosophy. Children—girls in particular—had to be given some sort of training after they left school and before they married.

At the Evelina Hospital life was far from easy. My mother writes:

> I was always tired and always hungry. The food was poor and there was never enough of it. Lectures were a dead loss, because I took good care to sit at the back and fell asleep as soon as they started. I was so tired that I couldn't help myself and in spite of all my efforts to stay awake when Matron was explaining the circulation of the blood, I never heard more than the opening and closing sentences. To this day I have only the vaguest idea of how this fluid starts on its journey and where it ends.

She stuck it out for the stipulated year, and it was at the end of it that the wheel took a further turn. The whole family had gone for the Christmas holidays to Smedleys Hydro at Matlock. Among the guests was a young seed merchant from Billinghay in Lincolnshire. In a television programme his first appearance on the screen would have been heralded with a disturbing chord of music. For if my mother is the first heroine of the story, the seed merchant, Bernard Gilbert, must, reluctantly, be cast as the villain.

He was a remarkable man. From farming stock and almost entirely self-educated, he was one of the few notable writers that Lincolnshire has produced. His output was impressive. He constructed a whole district, running inland from the Wash and equipped it with villages, farms and churches (particularly churches; in Lincolnshire few villages boasted less than five different denominations). He drew up lists of the inhabitants, describing with precision what they did and what they said to each other and about each other. If this sounds dull, I can only record that having reread them recently they seem as fresh as when they were first minted. His scope was large.

At first it was mostly poetry. There are people in Billinghay alive today who will quote to you "Cunning Jim," which describes how a farmer, irritated by the fact that the sparrows always seemed to be on the other side of the haystack, bent the barrel of his shotgun into a right angle so that he could shoot at them round the corner; with results which pleased only the sparrows.

There were short stories, novels and one-act plays. A handful of the plays were included in Nelson's well-known collection and are acted by amateurs to this day.

My mother records the sequel to that holiday.

> With a singleness of purpose which he later transmitted to his son, Bernard proceeded to propose marriage to me practically every day and was not at all put off by my saying that I had no particular desire to marry and certainly not to marry him. I pointed out that I was going on a long trip abroad and had no wish to tie myself up with any commitments before I started. I did, however, mention the places at which we should be calling—and I never failed to find, at each, a postcard addressed to me and consisting simply of a large question mark.

Such a man usually gets his own way in the end. By 1909 they were engaged. Four months later they were married. Five years of married life produced four children; myself and three sisters. It also produced the First World War, which started in August 1914 and affected, for better or worse, the life of almost every family in England.

It certainly affected the Gilbert family. By the end of the first year the situation, if not desperate, had become serious. My father's literary work was at a standstill and the money he had made by the sale of his business was nearly gone. He was medically unfit for any form of military service. There was only one solution. He had to take some form of government work, and where they sent him there he had to go. It turned out to be the Ministry of Munitions and a job at Bristol.

My mother had just received a small legacy and she decided that she, too, would come south. A house within her means was found, in the London suburb of Upminster, and thither we trekked—she and her children—Felicity aged four; myself three; my two younger sisters, Monica and Noel, two and under one.

Although she may not have admitted it, even to herself, I think that her real reason for moving was not to be near her husband—after all, Bristol was almost as far from London as Billinghay—but to reestablish contact with her own family. She must by then have realised the truth about her husband. He was clever, single-minded and charming. He was also completely, almost pathologically, selfish.

His point of view was simple. He liked writing. His wife liked children. Very well. He had done his bit by presenting her with four of them. The sort of money he could earn, now and in the foreseeable future, was likely to be enough to keep him in modest comfort. His wife would no doubt be able to find some job which would support her and the children.

Years later, when I was old enough to understand these things, my mother told me that the truth had not dawned on her slowly. It had presented itself to her suddenly, as a fait accompli. One fine summer day in 1918, when she was getting off a bus in the Charing Cross Road, the truth had risen up and hit her. She could expect no further support from her husband. She was on her own.

I asked her what she did. She said, "I went into the nearest tea shop and ordered a cup of tea. Whilst I drank it, I thought out my plans. Clearly they all turned on my own family."

The first step was to get out of Upminster. She had never liked it, or what she called "the horrid little house" she had bought there. No difficulty there. With the war just over, houses were doubling and

Mother, Berwyn Cuthbert Gilbert, 1910

redoubling in price. With the sale money she could buy a flat in London and have a bit to spare. Her mother would keep house with her and share the running expense. There were other sources from which help could be evoked.

Both of her older sisters had married remarkable men.

Hazel, now a qualified doctor, had married a Russian, Alexis Gregory. I was never clear exactly how or when he entered medical practice in this country, but he must have been fully qualified by 1914 since, on the outbreak of war, he enlisted as medical officer to the London Scottish Regiment and went with them to France. After the armistice he married Hazel and set up a highly successful practice, conducted from a house which he had purchased in Russell Square. Nor am I technically equipped to explain how he established a practical monopoly in the treatment (then in its infancy) of rheumatoid arthritis, but of its success I had ample evidence. It provided him with a manor house in Huntingdonshire and a collection of pictures which included original works by Constable and Utrillo. He was particularly attracted by the latter and I can remember him showing me one of Utrillo's studies of the suburbs of Paris: "Just look at that wall, Michael. Isn't it wonderful? So accurate in every detail. Why, you can see where the dogs have pissed against it."

I have jumped ahead and must return to 1920 when, at the age of eight, I had begun to emerge as a person. I find that I am only mentioned twice in the first fifty pages of my mother's memoir. The first is when I climbed a tree, having been forbidden to do so—and possibly for that reason alone. The second is my appointment by the vicar of Upminster as thurifer or "boat-boy" to carry the incense. "This," she says, "was a very successful move and Michael loved it. His angelic expression when pacing down the aisle was gratifying to all; though completely misleading."

I was, I think, a difficult child. But I return to my uncles.

The second, and equally outstanding personality, was Enid's husband, Arthur Wynne. In 1914 he had been a classics master at Dover College. When war broke out, the boys and a handful of the staff had been evacuated to Devonshire, where they joined the well-known West Country public school Blundells. Here the reign of a famous headmaster was drawing to a close and it was necessary to choose a successor.

This produced endless debate among the senior housemasters, all of whom were, or supported, candidates for the job. In the end, when the votes for each one had cancelled each other out, a compromise solution was arrived at. The post would be offered, for the duration of the war, to a "caretaker" headmaster; and my uncle was selected for the job. He had formidable qualifications. A double first at Oxford, a mathematical bent which enabled him to deal with the complications of timetable construction and, above all, that imponderable quality of "gravitas." This was in 1915. Far from being a "stopgap," he remained headmaster until 1930. When he finally retired he decided to take orders, with a view to acquiring what he described as "a comfortable curacy, preferably close to a golf course."

He lived to be a hundred.

The third of my supports was Uncle Roy, now vicar of St. Margaret's, near Twickenham. He became my godfather, and used to take me to the "varsity match," groaning for the frequent successes of Cambridge and reacting so enthusiastically to the occasional triumphs of his own university that he once rubbed off most of the buttons from his ecclesiastical raincoat against the barrier behind which we were standing.

So, with potential support from medicine, academia and the church, I set forth into the world of school. For my mother was implacable. Her son was to be properly educated, and the first step was to enter him at a good preparatory boarding school. It was not a step which many people, situated as she was, would have contemplated. Although the fees at such places had not reached today's astronomical figures, they were none of them cheap. However, with the residue of the money made from the sale of the Upminster house in her pocket, which would, she reckoned, pay the fees for a term or two, and fortified by a belief in providence and the support of her family, she set out for the South Coast to find a school for me.

In 1920 there were plenty to choose from. She could not have chosen better when she picked St. Peter's, Seaford, which was resettling itself after the war. The headmaster, Rolf Henderson, liked her and with rare perspicacity seemed to detect in me, at the age of eight, a scholar who might be a credit to his establishment.

Before pursuing my school career I must turn aside to make one point plain. Although my father might be a hissing and an abomination to the rest of my mother's family, she refused to hear a word against him. She appreciated his point of view. She would go her way; he would go his. To us children, he was not a demon, but an amiable, if distant, figure who very occasionally emerged from obscurity to give us a treat. A visit to the cinema, a high tea at Lyons Corner House; on one notable occasion lunch at the Authors' Club. Children think in visual terms and to me he was epitomised in the glitter of his gold-rimmed spectacles, and a kindly smile, viewed through the smoke of his cigar.

We enjoyed, too, his recitation of Lincolnshire nonsense rhymes:

> As I went down my umelly-jumelly
> My umelly-jumelly jeeny
> I met Sir Rat-me-fat
> Eating my allego feeny

"What's an umelly-jummelly, Daddy? What's allego feeny?"

"A vegetable garden, of course. And asparagus."

> Oh, if I had my whip-me-jig
> My whip-me-jig me jeeny
> *How* I would whip Sir Rat-me-fat
> For eating my allego feeny

I spent six years at St. Peter's. My mother's plans for meeting the fees were successful. When, at the end of the first year, she told the headmaster that she might have to remove me, he promptly offered to reduce the fees—and since even reduced fees were beyond her, Uncle Alexis paid them. He evidently approved of the school and sent his own son there later.

What sort of school was it? At a later stage after decades of success it became—I almost displayed my prejudices by saying it degenerated into—a rich school for rich boys. In the early 1920s we were a mixed bag. There was a Siamese prince called Rang, who came the same term that I did, and a Central European boy called Schidrowitz, who lost all tolerance and esteem by farting during the Two Minutes Silence on Armistice Day. There was a rich parent called Mr. Cann, who, at half-term, took out not only his own son, but any boys whose parents had failed to arrive. I was frequently in this position and after young Cann had left was taken out by a parent who had just concluded a term as Lord Mayor of London. When we asked him whether he had enjoyed it he looked thoughtful. He said that there were so many grand lunches and dinners that he often found himself dreaming about scrambled eggs on toast. A sensible sort of dream, we considered.

Then there was Mrs. Previté, who was even richer than Mr. Cann. Her money was said to come from Trinidad. On one occasion she provided a picnic for the whole school with two footmen to serve it. This must have been towards the end of my St. Peter's days because I was by then head of the school and had to call for three cheers for our hostess; cheers

"Me at five years old with my sister Felicity at six"

most liberally accorded by sixty boys full of cold game-pie and strawberries and cream.

On the other hand, there were the sons of clergymen, and of officers in the army and navy, demobilised after the end of the war. None of them could have had a lot of money. But of all of them I was unquestionably the poorest. Her family having behaved so handsomely over the fees, my mother did not feel able to approach them for help with the inevitable extras; and I can remember her pointing out to me the pawnbroker's establishment near Victoria Station where, she said, she had regularly pawned her wedding ring to raise the money needed to pay my fare back to school and to provide a modicum of pocket money for me.

At the time the fact that I was so much poorer than the other boys made little impression on them or on me. Young boys do not normally measure their friends in terms of money. It was only in retrospect that I became ashamed of the shifts my mother had been put to.

She constructed a number of my garments herself. She was a keen, but inexperienced, knitter and one scarf which she made me had a curious ability to prolong itself. Even when it was wound twice round my neck the ends trailed on the ground. At the time this did not worry me. But years later, when I was commanding one of the HAC batteries in Italy, a perky regular captain who was seconded to us remembered that scarf and reminded me of it. That was when I felt the sting.

For the most part my six years at St. Peter's passed swiftly away in the routine of work and games. Only a few scattered incidents remain in my memory. My first dormitory was under a benevolent head. My second was run by a genial bully, a tyrant whom we admired, but feared. Late one night he woke me and told me to get into his bed. I was slightly surprised when he then suggested that we both take off our pyjamas. However, the night was cold and we should be able to keep each other warm. When I woke in the morning I surveyed the rest of the dormitory with considerable pride from my position as the captain's chosen friend. Unfortunately the news got out and reached the headmaster who put a rapid, and painful, end to that liaison.

I made at that time a more profitable and permanent friend in Christopher Pirie-Gordon, son of the foreign editor of the London *Times;* a friendship which lasted until his death more than sixty years later. We fell into the habit of telling each other stories which we made up as we went along. The characters were the boys and staff of the school and the crowned heads of Europe, of whom there were more available then than now. This was my first effort at improvisation and the construction of romances. It proved a wonderful way of mitigating the boredom of the long school walks over Seaford Head or down to Exeat Bridge.

In the end I was able to justify the hopes of my mother and the headmaster; and this is where Uncle Arthur steps into the picture. He suggested that I should be able to tackle an open scholarship at Blundells. I was to stay at his house for the few days involved. Every evening after supper, he introduced me to the comforts of alcohol in the shape of a large glass of port. Instead of worrying about the exam, I enjoyed a dreamless night's sleep and came fresh to the starting post each morning.

I am sure that my uncle had nothing to do with the marking of the papers, so there can be no suggestion of nepotism in the result, which was that I got one of the two top scholarships. They were known as the Temple scholarships, after the archbishop. The next two were named after an equally distinguished Blundellian who had started life as a highwayman—thus demonstrating the well-deserved reputation of Blundells for brains and brawn.

Payment of fees presented no problem. A family connection with the Haberdashers' Company in the City of London entitled me to sit for one of their scholarships. These were particularly useful, since they could be added to scholarships at other schools. I had taken this exam a year before I left St. Peter's and had gained, against little opposition, one of the top awards of £40. This could now be added to the Temple scholarship of £100. A year's fees, in those far-off days (a gasp of incredulity from parents now paying school fees), was £135. So I was actually in credit by £5 a year which may have accounted for my mother keeping me at school for an extra year.

When I left, the new headmaster, A. R. Wallace (subsequently dean of Exeter), wrote at the foot of my report—"A very creditable finish to a creditable school career." This was kindly meant, but was quite untrue. I had accomplished nothing. I was to discover a little later how badly I had bungled the scholastic side. I had played for no team—not even for a house team, let alone a school side. I had passed the qualifying test for swimming colours, but had not been awarded them since my diving was an ungainly flop with my rebellious legs spread widely behind me. My time for a hundred yards' sprint was nearer twenty than ten seconds. I had strong wrists and shoulders and gained a few qualifying points by heaving the weight, unscientifically, for the appropriate distance. At the end of five years I was, so far as accomplishment and promise went, behind the point at which I had started.

I had been placed in School House, which was a stroke of luck, since the housemaster Charles Edward Fisher had come from Dover with my uncle and was always friendly and helpful. He was a gruff, but agreeable, old man, popularly known as "Cabby" after a supposed resemblance to the cabmen which the artist Belcher drew for *Punch.* He was a bachelor, which meant that we fed well, since he had less incentives than married housemasters and their wives to make a profit out of the catering.

During my second term my father died, of pneumonia, which modern medicine would easily have controlled. I was in Latin class, conducted by "Jimmy" Hall, the classics and choirmaster, when a message arrived that my housemaster wanted me. "Cabby" gave me the news in his simple and unaffected way, saying, "I know that you and your father were never very close." When I got back to my seat "Jimmy" Hall, who was famous for his jokes and comments, said, "Well, Gilbert, I see you are still in one piece. So nothing too serious, I gather." I said, "Not really, sir. I was just told that my father had died."

For once in his life J.H. was bereft of speech.

The happiest part of my life at Blundells came in the closing months of my last summer term. I was sharing a study with a boy called Eric Gibbon. (He was as tall as I was and sixty years later, when we went back to look at it, we wondered how on earth we both got into it.) Eric came of an army family and was to have a distinguished career in the Armoured Corps, winning the Distinguised Service Order in the desert and a second one for escaping from the Strafe Camp in the north of Italy, making his way south through Jugoslavia, engaging in some fighting for Tito and being finally put across the Adriatic into the British Zone.

We decided that cricket was not for us and set out to explore the country north of Tiverton. We found that by walking hard for forty-five minutes, mostly along a disused railway track, we could reach a village on the upper reaches of the river Loman, perfect for bathing. Our towels and a rug could be left in charge of the village shopkeeper whom we rewarded with purchases of chocolate and biscuits. The only snag was that the hour-and-a-half spent in walking there and back left too little time for lazing and bathing; and bathing naked in a peaty stream is not a pleasure to be skimped. However, if we could get leave off the four o'clock roll call, that would give us four perfect hours. The temptation was too great to resist. Leave comprised a chit from one's house-master, and "Cabby" Fisher's initials—a simple, rounded C.E.F.—were ridiculously easy to copy.

So I finished my inglorious career at Blundells. A layabout *and* a forger.

It is now 1932. In England and America, the Depression is in full swing. By rights I should be depressed, since I had left school without any reasonable prospect of making a living. But I refused to be depressed. I was young. I was fit and the weather was gorgeous.

At that time we were living in a bungalow on the Thames, above Staines. We kept our own boat at the landing stage and I was now in it paddling slowly upstream towards Runnymede, followed by a swan, hopeful of food.

It was at this moment and none other that I made up my mind. I would be a lawyer. Not a lordly, bewigged barrister, but a humble and businesslike solicitor.

The obstacles were formidable.

The first step was to become an articled clerk—that is to say an unpaid slave to a firm of solicitors. And not only unpaid. To enter serfdom you had to pay a premium to your masters. The amount varied, but with a good firm could be £300 to £500. Nor was this all.

The period of articles was normally five years. In other words, before I could earn anything I should have to scrounge on my mother for five years. And there was a final obstacle. It had been erected about a century before and was so typical of its time and its outlook that it deserves a moment of consideration.

The powers-that-be had decided that although solicitors ranked lower than barristers this did not mean that any riff-raff could be admitted. They therefore laid it down that articles of clerkship should bear a stamp duty of £80. In terms of modern money say, if you like, £800 or £1,000. A golden filter to keep the intake pure.

I had not the most distant prospect of obtaining any such sums of money, except by applying to my uncle Alexis. This, though acceptable when I was a child, was now, somehow, unthinkable. But there was another, barely feasible, solution.

If—and it was a big if—I obtained a law degree, the period in articles would be reduced from five years to three. And once I was able to write the letters LL.B. after my name, a firm might be induced to accept me without payment of a premium. This degree could be obtained "externally"—that is to say without actual attendance at a university. It would, I realised, take some time, maybe four or five years rather than the three-year course for internal students, but that, too, could be useful. It should be possible in five years to save enough money to keep me for the next three.

The figure which floated before my eyes was £380—say £100 a year for my out-of-pocket expenses, living at home, and £80 for that bloody stamp duty. It might be done and the job which automatically suggested itself was an assistant mastership at a preparatory school. My report from Blundells would be useful there.

This first step proved simple enough. A letter to a firm of scholastic agents, an interview, and, behold, I was a wage earner. The salary was £90 a year. The school was the Cathedral School at Salisbury.

"The teaching," said the prospectus, "is based on the general idea that apart from mere preparation for examinations, a boy, in addition to a memory to be stored, has an imagination to be fired, a moral sense to be trained and developed and individual possibilities to be guided and encouraged." Splendid. I could manage all that.

During the Christmas holidays I hastened up to London to enrol myself at the university. Here I discovered the final futility of my school career. Although I had passed School Certificate once and Higher Certificate twice, it seemed that I had not done so in the subjects which would exempt me from matriculation. And until I had passed this comparatively elementary examination I could not start the degree course.

Accordingly that summer I descended on Southampton University and duly gobbled up the matriculation papers. But an additional year had been added to my programme.

At the time I had few regrets about this.

Salisbury was a most agreeable interlude; particularly after the first year when a consortium of parents succeeded in removing the headmaster—who was a bit of a bully—and the second master, Laurence Griffiths, reigned in his stead. I am eternally grateful to "Griff" for his tolerance and help as I ploughed slowly through the outlying fields of Contract, Tort and Constitutional Law.

In many ways, what I was enjoying was a substitute university life. As well as my pursuit of a degree I was playing rugby football for Salisbury in term time and for the Saracens in the winter holidays. I had discovered the pleasures of squash and I had learned to drink beer.

By 1938 I had my degree and only the final obstacle remained. Helped by a kindly gift of £50 from the Dean and Chapter, I had managed to accumulate, to the last penny, the £380 at which I was aiming. But there was still the question of a premium.

Enter the third of my uncles, Uncle Roy. One of his church wardens, Roland Hazel, was a solicitor, Pickwickian in figure, but robust enough to have started in 1914 as a motorcyclist orderly and ended the war as a major with a Military Cross. In his youth Roland had himself been presented with his articles and had always resolved to pass a like benefit on to some other impoverished young man. I was the lucky recipient. So, on 3 September 1938, I signed my articles, paid the £80 stamp duty with a snarl of rage, and started to work for the firm of Ellis, Bickersteth, Aglionby and Hazel of Portland House, Basinghall Street in the City of London.

The next twelve months proved, in two respects, to be of decisive influence.

That autumn I presented myself as a recruit to the Honourable Artillery Company, otherwise universally known as the HAC. It is the oldest regiment in the British army having, at that date, been in continuous existence for more than four hundred years. It has an associated body in America, the Ancient and Honourable Artillery Company of Boston, Massachusetts, which is the oldest military body in the New World.

At the time when I joined it the HAC comprised an infantry battalion and a gunner regiment of two batteries. In earlier times it may have been regarded as a lot of City gentlemen playing at soldiers, but its

accomplishments in the South African War and in the First World War had silenced such criticism. By 1939 it was a serious military school.

My fear was that my short sight—I had worn glasses since the age of ten—might cause me to fail my medical, but I pointed out to the examining doctor that since it did not prevent me from playing rugby football it should not prevent me from fighting. In normal times this disingenuous argument might not have succeeded; but the times were not normal. The shadow of Hitler was over Europe and few people doubted that we were heading for war. So all went smoothly and I became Gunner Gilbert, the latest of a flood of recruits to "B" Battery HAC.

The second important development arose out of the first. When I looked at my fellow gunners, with their well-cut suits, their expensive cars and expensive girlfriends, I started to hunt round for some method of increasing my spending money of £2 a week.

Of that great crime writer, Margery Allingham, it was said that she took to writing naturally. "Indeed, in her family no other occupation was considered natural or even sane." The same might have been said of the Cuthbert clan. My grandfather had written a number of plays for his friends and family to act; thus following the example of Charles Dickens twenty years before. One of his outstanding successes was a dramatisation of Jane Austen's *Pride and Prejudice*. His wife said that he had made Mrs. Bennet so like her that she could hardly bring herself to act in it. Whilst my mother was employed by Glaxo Laboratories—her salary from whom had supported her and us for twenty-five years—she had written all their mothercraft books. When she finally left she had added to the generous pension they gave her by producing a monthly article for Hulton's publication "Housewife," about the upbringing of children; an article in which she regularly libelled her son. At the Cathedral School I had myself written a series of one-act plays for performance by the boys at Christmas.

Turning my mind now to more serious endeavours, I decided to try my hand at a detective story. This was a normal development since a young man's first book will almost always be a reflection of his favourite reading; and the masters—or, rather, the mistresses—of the craft in whose steps I sought to follow were Dorothy Sayers, Margery Allingham and Ngaio Marsh.

The form of the whodunnit was well established. The essential characters were a murderer, a murderee, a detective and a number of suspects. The setting would usually be one well known to the writer.

Murder, being an amateur crime, could take place anywhere you chose.

I decided, inevitably, that the location of my first book should be a Cathedral Close. The detective should be a professional from Scotland Yard. (The silk-dressing-gowned amateur was becoming a little dated.) And what an admirable collection of suspects paraded before me: one Dean, one Archdeacon, three Canons residentiary, numerous minor Canons, three Vergers, two Organists and the Close Constable. All that remained to be decided was who should murder whom.

At this point I have to be careful.

I am well aware that there are two schools of thought about writing. One is to regard it as a matter of inspiration, of waiting until the destined moment arrives and then pouring out one's thoughts onto paper in a fury of creation. Many masterpieces have been written in this way. The other school looks on writing more coldly, as the manufacture of an article; something which the factory of the writer's mind constructs, working factory hours, and hoping that the conveyer belt will ultimately bear off a product which the market will accept and pay for.

"The young officer," 1939

I stress this difference—no doubt exaggerating it—in case I am accused of being a dilettante, of not taking writing seriously. Nothing could be further from the truth. The "perspiration" school, to which I belong, is every bit as serious as the "inspiration" school. It is only more realistic in its outlook and more regular in its hours. A leader of this school, and a shining light to me, was Anthony Trollope. Having to hold down a job in the Post Office, he disciplined his writing habits with military firmness. So many words, filling so many sheets of paper, at such and such a time each day. When, in his autobiography, he not only explained this, but even went so far as to tabulate how much money each book had earned him, he became an object of much critical hostility. He suffered by being too honest. If only he had left his readers imagining that his novels somehow wrote themselves, no one would have thought of questioning his preeminent position.

This was a matter which did not affect me at that time, but which was to become important later.

Meanwhile I settled down, every evening, to write the book to which I gave the punning title *Close Quarters*. I began it around Christmas 1938 and by the third week in August 1939 fourteen of the projected sixteen chapters had gone to the typing agency. The story had reached the point at which the detective announces that he has arrived at the solution. He knows who the murderer is, and how the crime was committed. The last two chapters would, of course, have passed this information on to the readers. But it was not to be.

By registered post that morning arrived Army Form E 623 B, headed "IMMEDIATE AND IMPORTANT," notifying me that I was called up for service and was required to report immediately at the headquarters of the HAC. To the back of this blue leaflet I subsequently pinned a second one, dated 28 December 1945, starting, "Now that the time has come for your release from active military duty, I am commanded by the Army Council to express their thanks for the valuable services which you have rendered to your country at a time of grave national emergency."

These two documents, comprising what an actor would call his entrance and his exit lines, frame six years of military service.

One of the privileges of the HAC—a privilege which vanished on the outbreak of war—was to commission its own officers. And on 2 September, for reasons which were inexplicable at the time and will remain unexplained until the Day of Judgment when all books are opened and the Adjutant is called upon to justify his choice, I was forthwith commissioned as a second lieutenant into "D" Battery, 12th (HAC) Regiment RHA.

There followed three years of training, by regular RHA officers with strict standards and whiplash tongues. This could be unpleasant, but when we thought about the civilian soldiers in the previous war who were hurried into the trenches, sometimes with less than three months training, we started to appreciate our good fortune.

By the time we sailed for North Africa in November 1942 we were as efficient as peacetime training could make us. All that we needed was sharpening on the whetstone of active service. This the regiment received, in full measure, in the ensuing six months. But I saw very little of it. An unhappy sequence of events started with my driving over an unmarked minefield at a point some miles in front of our own lines. The signaller and I escaped comparatively undamaged. My assistant, the driver and his vehicle were all *hors-de-combat.* There was a farmhouse nearby which proved to be deserted. We deposited the two casualties in it and I promised to come back, as soon as possible, and pick them up. This proved to be a crowning disaster. Going back that night I lost my way, stopped at another farmhouse to make enquiries, and stepped straight into the hands of a detachment of German parachutists.

Six hours later I was in a German cage in Tunis and six days later in an Italian prison camp at Capua, north of Naples. There I was joined by one of my oldest friends, Tony Davies, picked up in the messy fighting round Medjez-el-Bab.

From that moment we had only one thought. To remove ourselves as expeditiously as possible and rejoin our regiment. This might seem to be a tall order. There were only two ways out of Italy. North to Switzerland or east to Jugoslavia. And as a preliminary, we had to shake off the attentions of our hosts, who seemed to be unwilling to part from us.

The first opportunity occurred when we were being transported by train from Capua to a more permanent camp on the Adriatic side. This involved a train journey across the Apennines, with numerous stops and starts. After one such we departed through an open carriage window and took to the mountains. This expedition did not last long. We lost each other in the dark, were totally ill-equipped and both recaptured after a day or two of precarious liberty.

July saw us in a camp even further to the north; at Fontenellato, in the valley of the Po, between Parma and Piacenza. It was a comfortable and well-run camp, with an efficient senior British officer, Colonel de Burgh, R.A., hand in glove with a

sympathetic Italian commandant. These facts were to prove important in the days that followed.

I see that in a letter to my mother of 13 August 1943—which was, curiously, allowed through uncensored—I said, "The news continues to be good and it is not outside the bounds of possibility that we might be seeing something of each other soon." What I meant, of course, was that we had heard of Mussolini's downfall and were certain that the Italians would slide out of the war. What would happen then was anyone's guess.

What did happen was that as soon as the Italian armistice was declared, a section of the barbed wire was removed and we marched out and dispersed around the countryside. Other camps were not so lucky. In them, for reasons which have never been fully explained, the prisoners stayed put, were picked up by the Germans and removed to Germany.

We had heard on the wireless that the Eighth Army had landed on the toe of Italy and that there had been some fighting south of Naples. It was a confusing situation, which offered at least three choices. We could stay put, undercover, and wait for the British to arrive. We could go north to Switzerland—a matter of about one hundred miles. Or we could go south to meet up with our troops, advancing steadily, we hoped, but at that moment many miles away.

People talked to their friends and made their individual choices. Tony and I, with a third gunner, Toby Graham, decided that we would go south, sticking to the mountains and trusting that the Germans would be too busy getting on with the war to bother too much about us.

I described the events which followed in the last two chapters in the English edition of a book which I wrote some years later, which I called *Death in Captivity,* a whodunnit set in a prison camp. The earlier details are fiction, but the last bit is as truthful as I could make it. For forty days we walked, hobbled and crawled along the backbone of the Apennines. We covered around fifteen miles each day, which might only have measured ten miles on the map; but if you advanced ten miles a day for forty days you got somewhere in the end.

What we got into was a loop in the line which the Germans had established above the river Sangro. They clearly intended to stay there for the winter. We pushed on cautiously, but soon ran into trouble and Tony was recaptured. Toby and I were luckier. Five days later we encountered an uninterested squadron of Canadian armoured cars occupying a village in what was temporarily our own front line. We were glad to get back onto army rations.

"On the run in Italy; Tony is standing third from the left, Toby, fifth, and I'm on the right"

That was the end of October 1943. By the end of November I was back in England. In the latter part of my journey, through North Africa towards Algiers, I had managed to slip out of the convoy and make contact with my regiment, who were enjoying a well-earned rest from their labours, in the sand hills, behind Bone. They extended me a warm welcome, but I was aware that authority was on my track. It was a rigid rule that escaping prisoners of war went back to the United Kingdom. Knowing this I took the precaution of getting letters from my own commanding officer, John Barstow, and from the Divisional Commander (who invited me to tea), both stating that a vacancy awaited me.

It was well that I did so. England at the end of 1943 proved almost more difficult to get out of than an Italian prison camp. However, armed with my letters and clearly determined to go on making a nuisance of myself indefinitely, in the end I succeeded. Grudgingly I was put in charge of a batch of anti-tank gunners who thought they were going to Iceland. "When you're out at sea," said the smooth young officer from AG6 Postings, "you can break it

to them that they're going to North Africa. I hope they don't throw you overboard."

Once in Algiers I was safe. The HAC network which covered North Africa from Algiers to Cairo soon had me back with the regiment. I believe that a certain amount of paperwork followed me, but since by the time it arrived we were in action in Italy, John Barstow, by now commanding, was well placed to lose or destroy it.

The rest of my war, though it involved some exciting episodes of action at the third and final battle of Cassino and the breaking of the Gothic Line, seemed something of an anticlimax. The episodes which I remember best all belong to the lighter side of soldiering. A tumultuous reunion party when we found ourselves alongside our sister regiment, the 11th RHA; a battery concert south of Florence; a Christmas party for Italian children when we were spending a few quiet weeks in reserve, in the course of which the Regimental Sergeant Major, dressed as Father Christmas, was lowered from the balcony into a screaming horde of Italian boys and girls. This was the only occasion on which this imperturbable man was seen to look apprehensive.

"The much older officer," 1949

After the armistice, by which time I was a major and in command of "C" Battery, we moved up to Carinthia in South Austria and spent a pleasant six months shooting, fishing and riding. I was also taking a correspondence course in the law, which proved useful, since, when I got back to London in October, I discovered that the Law Society, either kindly disposed towards returning soldiers or anxious to recruit solicitors as quickly as possible, did not insist on my completing the statutory term of articles. I could take the final exam as soon as I felt equipped to do so. I think that the standard of admission at that period was designedly low.

John Barstow, who had already done me a number of good turns in the HAC, now did me another by introducing me into his firm, a first-class solicitors' partnership which prided itself on being a "Lincoln's Inn" firm, not (with a slight curl of the lips) a City outfit. King George III had been one of their clients and their basement was stacked high with black boxes painted with distinguished names. I described such a firm, with a measure of exaggeration, in my fourth novel, *Smallbone Deceased.* More of that later.

Meanwhile John had done me a final good turn which eclipsed all the others. He introduced me to his secretary, whom I lost no time in marrying.

(Introduction—January 1947; marriage—July 1947). She is the second heroine of this account. My mother, abandoning the normal captious attitude of mothers-in-law, wrote in her memoir, "Michael was fortunate enough to marry Colonel Barstow's secretary, Roberta, for which I have never ceased to be thankful. She has made him a wonderful wife." She was more enthusiastic about Roberta than Roberta's parents were about me. Her father was a brigadier in the regular army and I fancy that he had visualised her marrying a well-breeched cavalry officer, not an impecunious solicitor. This didn't bother us and Roberta demonstrated her enthusiasm for the married state by presenting me, in rapid succession, with four plump daughters. Becoming worried about this preponderance of females, she consulted an old Indian army friend of her father, a general in charge of army remounts, who told her, "It's perfectly simple. I've proved it with thousands of horses. If the child is conceived whilst the moon is waxing it will be male; if waning, it will be female."

Following this little-known obstetric principle, and keeping a careful eye on the moon, we produced two sons and a fifth daughter. On that last occasion it must have been a full moon, presenting us with an even chance.

I must now retrace my steps a little to let my literary career catch up with my domestic life.

One of the first things I did on returning to my mother's flat after the war was to take out the fourteen chapters of *Close Quarters.* Attached to them was a note from Uncle Alexis's son Basil, a medical student, who had occupied the flat from time to time during the war. It said, "I much enjoyed your book. Its abrupt ending, cutting out a lot of tiresome explanations, was particularly effective."

This was encouraging, but if it was to be published I saw that the explanations would have to be added. Here an unexpected difficulty arose. *Close Quarters* was a complicated whodunnit with a large number of suspects. It was full of hidden clues and suggestive hints and these I had now to disentangle. I think, and hope, that I got the right man arrested; after which it went off to the well-known literary agents, Curtis Brown. The head of the firm, Spencer Curtis Brown, invited me to his office. He displayed a moderate enthusiasm for the book, but said that it had one fatal drawback. It was too long. Could I cut it by, say, 20 percent?

This was on a Friday. I set to work with a blue pencil over the weekend and deleted some fifteen thousand words—including the whole of the first chapter. A treatment, incidentally, which would improve most books. Spencer seemed pleased by my

"The Gilbert family complete, 1960: my wife, Roberta Mary, holding Gerard, Richard, myself holding Laura; (from left) Olivia, Kate, Victoria, Harriett"

drastic surgery and promised to do his best for me. One of his lady readers, a formidable team of bluestockings, had apparently described it as "Dorothy Sayers, milk and water"—but, as Spencer informed me, that particular lady recognised no authors but Proust and Henry James.

A few weeks later the letter arrived that no author, however sophisticated, ever forgets. Messrs. Hodder and Stoughton had accepted the book. The sun shone, the birds sang and the whole world was suffused with a golden glow.

Encouraged and sharpened by my army experience, I rapidly peeled off two books of a type which John Buchan described as "shockers." These were not received with any great enthusiasm, but Hodders published them, hoping for better things. I then returned to the detective story proper and produced one of my most successful novels. It was called *Smallbone Deceased* and was set, inevitably, in the premises of an old-fashioned Lincoln's Inn firm. They had mislaid one of their trustee clients and were distressed to find him in a deed box.

Almost everyone in the firm, from the office boy to the senior partner, quickly identified themselves as characters in the book. They were wide of the mark. Insofar as any of the characters were based on real people, they were based on members of the City firm, in which I had been articled eight years before. This seems to be a common process with writers. An interval of years blurs the outlines of a real person, leaving behind a type, perhaps even a caricature; very suitable for a crime novel in which, as many practitioners have pointed out, it is a mistake and a waste of time to delve too deeply into characterisation.

I spoke of a "crime novel" as though this was a single type of book. I soon discovered, to my pleasure, that the field was spacious. There are at least four types of crime book, each with numerous subdivisions. There is the detective story, or whodunnit, mentioned above, which is totally different from the adventure story, or thriller, in which the emphasis is on action, not on ratiocination. Both types have offspring.

The whodunnit can develop into a whydunnit, a study of motive rather than motion. The thriller can diverge into two fields, the spy story and the police procedural. In the past forty years, I have dipped into all these promising pools.

The best received of my detective stories, apart from *Smallbone Deceased,* was *Death in Captivity* based on my prison camp experiences. The whodunnit element centred on the identity of the traitor in the camp. An added thriller element described the eventual escape of three of the characters and their trek to safety.

At this period I was being regularly published in America by Harper and was in the hands of the only real editor that I ever encountered. This was the redoubtable Joan Kahn, a woman who took endless trouble with her authors. She was not bothered about minor mistakes. These could be picked up by line editors. She concentrated on two things. Causation and shape.

Were the actions properly integrated, or did they depend on mere happenstance or (worst crime of all) on coincidence? In other words, did the plot hang together. If it passed this test, did it present an agreeable and comprehensible shape, starting at the

right point and ending at the right point? If it did not, she could be ruthless in her corrections. She decided that the final escape in my prison camp book should be omitted altogether. The puzzle should be worked out in the camp and stay there. An American reader who wants to follow the adventures of Tony Davies, Toby Graham and myself (for that is what the last two chapters really are) will have to buy the English edition. He can do so. It is still in print.

I came to the spy story late; no doubt as a result of enjoying Le Carré and Deighton. This addiction produced two collections of short stories, *Game without Rules* and *Mr. Calder and Mr. Behrens,* and one full-length novel, *Be Shot for Sixpence.* Philip, the hero of this, was markedly antifeminist, a point which so enraged one reader that she sent me a three-page letter explaining how disgusting and intolerable she found him. She mitigated her wrath by telling me that she had enjoyed my other books and by sending me two excellent bottles of claret.

On the whole I found it much easier to write detective stories than thrillers. In any thriller the difficulty is the relationship between the hero and the

Daughter Victoria, father-in-law Judge Edward Clarke, son-in-law Peter Clarke, 1981

villain. In a police procedural or a spy story it was easy. Policemen and criminals do exist and do come into conflict; spies are pursued by counterintelligence agencies. A straight thriller is much more difficult.

One has not only to invent a plausible villain, but to give the hero an understandable reason for getting after him. In the early days, when the dew was on the grass, readers seemed to accept that a man like Bulldog Drummond would be unhappy if he were not tangling with Carl Peterson. This would not have done for Joan Kahn. The first question she would have asked is why doesn't Drummond leave Peterson to the police and enjoy Phyllis and his comfortable house on Half Moon Street? A difficult question to answer.

The bibliography at the end will demonstrate that the twenty-six novels and seven collections of short stories are fairly evenly divided between the types mentioned above. Lately I have found myself diverging from all of them into what might be described as a straight adventure story with criminal or legal trimmings. Perhaps, in the end, the criminal will disappear altogether. I hope not. He is such an old friend that I should hate to part company with him entirely.

One agreeable result of ploughing in this field was the receipt, shortly after the end of the war, of an invitation from its secretary, Dorothy L. Sayers, to join the Detection Club. My fellow invitee was Michael Innes, already well known as an author of crime books, which I certainly was not. It may have been the appearance of *Smallbone Deceased* which prompted the offer, which was a flattering one.

The Detection Club had been formed twenty years before, at the instigation of John Dickson Carr. Its first president had been G. K. Chesterton of "Father Brown" fame. It was at that time a genuine club, with a club room behind Regent Street and a list of around twenty-five members which included all the well-known names in that golden era of the detective story. Dorothy Sayers's sisters in crime, Agatha Christie, Margery Allingham and Ngaio Marsh. H. C. Bailey, Freeman Wills Crofts, R. Austin Freeman, John Rhode, Arthur Morrison, the Baroness Orczy of "Scarlet Pimpernel" fame, and A. A. Milne, who had written one detective story which was subsequently severely panned by Raymond Chandler.

By its constitution it excluded writers who produced only thrillers, spy stories and other unacceptable variations; which may have accounted for the formation, some years later, of a more broadly based body, the Crime Writers Association (CWA). This corresponded to the Mystery Writers of America (MWA). To neither of these bodies did you have to

be elected. If you had written a qualifying number of novels or short stories you were entitled to membership. There was also the Screen Writers Guild, which, in its inception, was devoted to the interests of film and television writers. I joined them all.

Undoubtedly the Detection Club was the most prestigious. The procedure was that, once a month, if there was business to discuss, the members met briefly in the club room and then proceeded to one of the modest Soho restaurants where a private room was reserved for them. The few guests who attended on these occasions would have been told to proceed directly to the restaurant. On one occasion this produced an embarrassing situation for my wife. Either she arrived early, or club business had been unexpectedly lengthy, because finding the dining room empty she decided to fill in time by taking a walk round the block. In Soho, at night, this was not perhaps a wise decision. Before she had gone far she saw that she was being followed by what she described as a sinister woman in black. She quickened her pace. So did the woman. Both were nearly running when she got back to the restaurant. Her pursuer turned out to be Ngaio Marsh who had also arrived early.

In an interview with the press, John Dickson Carr once reported me as having adopted "a novel Malthusian principle." One child to every two books. I cannot remember making such a dangerous prediction, but by 1951 it was roughly correct. I had two children with a third on the way and my fifth book, *Death Has Deep Roots*, had just been published. It was then that we decided to leave the small North London terrace house that we had been married into and get out into the country.

Roberta's godfather, a well-known Rochester surveyor and estate agent, suggested the Old Rectory at Luddesdown, a fairly isolated Kentish village. Most old rectors being philoprogenitive, it had eleven bedrooms. We had plans to fill most of them. It was a dilapidated building, set in an uncared-for garden. This offered full scope to Roberta's talents as a wallpaperer, painter, bricklayer, general decorator and gardener. We have lived there in continuing contentment for forty years.

There was one drawback. The station was two miles away. The journey to London took just under an hour. Once in London I had a full day's work as a solicitor ahead of me and by the evening would certainly be too tired to do much writing. The weekends would be free, but I felt, somehow, that this was not the answer to the problem of regular production. My writing plans were Trollopian. A measured quantity of words every day. An hour would be just enough. But where was an hour to be found, preferably at the beginning of the day, when the mind was fresh and alert?

Trollope's solution was to get up very early and write before breakfast. Early rising has never appealed to me, but there was a possible variation of this.

On the journey to London I had become accustomed to sharing a first-class carriage with a group of friends: a barrister, a journalist, a civil servant and a businessman or two. We were not talkative. The barrister studied his briefs; the journalist read his rivals' newspapers, with occasional snorts of disgust; the civil servant started on the *Times* crossword puzzle. In this studious and helpful atmosphere I started to write.

My daily rate of production was two pages in a counsel's notebook. Each page was two hundred words. Five days a week was two thousand words. Thirty-five weeks was seventy thousand words. Seventy thousand words was a novel. Which left several weeks over for short stories and radio or television scripts as demanded.

If anyone, fixed with a day-time job and a regular journey to work, should feel inclined to adopt this system, I would give them this warning. You can only make it work if you know, at all times, exactly where you are in the book and exactly where you are going, so that your pen starts writing when the train starts and continues quite steadily until you arrive. This involves a good deal of careful plotting and synopsising, which can be done on weekends, especially on long and solitary walks. It is also useful to bear Ernest Hemingway's advice in mind: "Treat your writing like an old car. Always leave it pointing downhill."

I have gone into this matter at some length because when, years later, in a newspaper interview I confessed that my last fifteen novels had all been written in the train on the way to work, a lady, who was evidently a disciple of the inspiration school, accused me of vilifying crime writers and, incidentally, of telling lies. I had no defence. Except that what I had said was the truth.

Was being a solicitor helpful to me as a crime writer? In detail, certainly not. Your clients' affairs are totally confidential and to write about them even under the guise of fiction would have been a breach of that confidence. In any event, mine was not a criminal practice. Two of my most notable clients were the Conservative party and the ruler of Bahrain. A third—the Society of Authors—was indirectly productive, since through it I became the adviser of a number of authors who were having trouble over contracts, copyright, libel and other pitfalls of the writer's trade. In this way I encountered Gavin Lyall and his wife, Katharine Whitehorn; Cyril Hare, who was really Judge Gordon Clark and P. D. James. Of all of them the one I remember best was Raymond Chandler.

I had an introduction to him from a mutual friend, Dorothy Gardiner, then secretary of the MWA. I telephoned his hotel on the evening that he was due to arrive and went to meet him. I had read all that he had written and expected a formidable, wisecracking gangster. In fact I found a charming middle-aged gentleman who reminded me in many ways of my own father. Two days later I had a letter from him which started, "Are you a real lawyer?" and went on to suggest that if I was, I could help him in the running fights he was engaged in with the Inland Revenue and the Immigration officials.

This was the first of a series of letters which brightened my working day. In dark blue type on light blue paper (the colours, as I told him, of the Old Etonian tie) he discussed his legal problems, breaking off occasionally to insert a paragraph describing the technique for impressing a girl you were taking out to dinner in New York. One of my jobs was to make wills for him. I made several, but not as many as he did, since it seemed that in America, as in Scotland, a so-called holograph will—which is a will without witnesses or any other formalities—could be admitted to probate provided it was totally in the handwriting of the testator. After his death several of these were produced, some of them scribbled on the back of menus or other even odder sheets of paper. I am

Sons Richard and Gerard

"My wife, Roberta Mary (née Marsden)"

glad to say that when the matter finally came before the court in California, the version drafted by me in full Lincoln's Inn style was the one which gained the day.

I mentioned that some weeks each year were available for productions other than novels. Of these the one I found most compatible was the crime short story. At that time there was a market for them in England. It was not as lavish as in the old days when the *Strand,* the *Grand,* the *Windsor* and other respectable monthly magazines adorned every station bookstall. But it had survived, in *John Bull* and *Argosy,* which would accept stories of around four thousand words, and in the *Evening News and Standard,* which took stories of twelve to fifteen hundred words.

All these markets have now disappeared, which is sad, since short stories by such masters as Conan Doyle, G. K. Chesterton, H. C. Bailey and Lord Dunsany were among the glories of the genre. Thanks largely to the efforts of the late Eleanor Sullivan (to whom a statue should be erected by grateful crime writers) a flourishing market still exists in America in the form of *Ellery Queen's Mystery Magazine.*

The writing of plays, whether for stage or film, television or radio, did not prove to be my forte. I tried them all. Least successful were my stage plays, although four of them were produced in the West End. The only one which showed any evidence of stamina was the first, *A Clean Kill.* This started life at the Criterion, was transferred after a couple of months to the Duchess, and, following a month there, to the Westminster. A kindly critic then described it as "the most moving play in London."

Television, when it was flexing its infant muscles in the days just after the war, was a more exciting medium than it has now become. Plays were not prerecorded. They were acted out, on the floor, in front of the cameras and sound booms, and if something went wrong there was really nothing anyone could do about it. One of my first producers, Gerald Glaister, had been in the RAF and he admitted that he was more frightened as he sat sweating in the producer's box than he had been in a Spitfire during the Battle of Britain.

To give some idea of the conditions under which we laboured, I recall one play in which I had written a scene depicting the heroine, a secretary, in the office taking dictation. At the end of the scene her boss, who was clearly becoming enamoured of her, invited her to dinner at a restaurant that evening. Cut to restaurant set, ten yards away, boss and secretary approaching the dinner table.

When, in rehearsal, we reached this point, the young lady raised an objection. Was it to be supposed that, having been invited out to dinner by her boss, she would appear in the clothes which she wore in the office? Perish the thought. Her objection was sustained. I offered to insert a short discussion scene at Scotland Yard. How long would it take her to change? She thought that ninety seconds would be sufficient. I have sometimes reminded my wife of this.

I wrote plays for broadcasting and still try my hand at them from time to time. They seem to me to be the ideal medium for transposing a short story. I once expressed this opinion to Agatha Christie, who agreed with it. She said that the idea of *The Mousetrap* had first occurred to her as a short story and had then been rewritten as a radio play. I gathered that rehashing it as a stage play was something of an afterthought. Which proves what a lot of life there is in a sound plot.

So what of the future? Another novel, possibly. A short story or two if asked for. Then I shall turn my mind to drafting my own epitaph.

Suggestions are welcome.

BIBLIOGRAPHY

Fiction:

Close Quarters, Hodder & Stoughton, 1947, Walker, 1963.

They Never Looked Inside, Hodder & Stoughton, 1948, published in America as *He Didn't Mind Danger,* Harper, 1948.

The Doors Open, Hodder & Stoughton, 1949, Walker, 1962.

Smallbone Deceased, Hodder & Stoughton, 1950, Harper, 1950.

Death Has Deep Roots, Hodder & Stoughton, 1951, Harper, 1951.

Death in Captivity, Hodder & Stoughton, 1952, published in America as *The Danger Within,* Harper, 1952.

Fear to Tread, Hodder & Stoughton, 1953, Harper, 1953.

Sky High, Hodder & Stoughton, 1955, published in America as *The Country-House Burglar,* Harper, 1955.

Be Shot for Sixpence, Hodder & Stoughton, 1956, Harper, 1956.

Blood and Judgement, Hodder & Stoughton, 1958, Harper, 1959.

After the Fine Weather, Hodder & Stoughton, 1963, Harper, 1963.

The Crack in the Teacup, Hodder & Stoughton, 1966, Harper, 1966.

The Dust and the Heat, Hodder & Stoughton, 1967, published in America as *Overdrive,* Harper, 1967.

The Etruscan Net, Hodder & Stoughton, 1969, published in America as *The Family Tomb,* Harper, 1969.

The Body of a Girl, Hodder & Stoughton, 1972, Harper, 1972.

The Ninety-second Tiger, Hodder & Stoughton, 1973, Harper, 1973.

Flash Point, Hodder & Stoughton, 1974, Harper, 1974.

The Night of the Twelfth, Hodder & Stoughton, 1976, Harper, 1976.

The Empty House, Hodder & Stoughton, 1978, Harper, 1978.

Death of a Favourite Girl, Hodder & Stoughton, 1980, published in America as *The Killing of Katie Steelstock,* Harper, 1980.

The Final Throw, Hodder & Stoughton, 1982, published in America as *End-Game,* Harper, 1982.

The Black Seraphim, Hodder & Stoughton, 1983, Harper, 1984.

The Long Journey Home, Hodder & Stoughton, 1985, Harper, 1985.

Trouble, Hodder & Stoughton, 1987, Harper, 1987.

Paint, Gold, and Blood, Hodder & Stoughton, 1989, Harper, 1989.

The Queen against Karl Mullen, Hodder & Stoughton, 1991, Carroll & Graf, 1991.

Short-story collections:

Game without Rules (includes "The Road to Damascus," "On Slay Down," "The Spoilers," "The Cat Cracker," "Tremblings Tours," "The Headmaster," "Heilige Nacht," "Upon the King . . . ," "Crossover," "Prometheus Unbound," and "A Prince of Abyssinia"), Hodder & Stoughton, 1962, Harper, 1967.

Stay of Execution, and Other Stories of Legal Practice (includes "Back of the Shelf," "The Blackmailing of Mr. Justice Ball," "Murder by Jury," "Xinia Florata," "Weekend at Wapentake," "The System," "Cousin Once Removed," "Modus Operandi," "The King in Pawn," "The Rich Man in His Castle," "Where There's a Will," "Mr. Portway's Practice," and "Stay of Execution"), Hodder & Stoughton, 1971.

Amateur in Violence, edited and with introduction by Ellery Queen, Davis Publications, 1973.

Petrella at Q (includes "The Elusive Baby," "The Banting Street Fire," "The Death of Mrs. Key," "Why Tarry the Wheels of His Chariot?," "Rough Justice," "Counterplot," "To the Editor, Dear Sir," "A Thoroughly Nice Boy," "The Cleaners: Inquest on the Death of Bernie Nicholls: A Lively Night at Basildon Mansions: The Peripatetic Birds: St. Valentine's Day," "Captain Crabtree," "The Last Tenant," and "Mutiny at Patton Street"), Hodder & Stoughton, 1977, Harper, 1977.

Mr. Calder and Mr. Behrens (includes "The Twilight of the Gods," "Emergency Exit," "One-to-Ten," "The Peaceful People," "The Lion and the Virgin," "The African Tree Beavers," "Signal Tresham," "The Mercenaries," "Early Warning," "The Killing of Michael Finnegan," "The Decline and Fall of Mr. Behrens," and "The Last Reunion"), Hodder & Stoughton, 1982, Harper, 1982.

Young Petrella (includes "The Conspirators," "Who Has Seen the Wind?," "The Prophet and the Bird," "Nothing Ever Happens on Highside," "Cash in Hand," "Source Seven," "The Night the Cat Stayed Out," "Breach of the Peace," "Voyage into Illusion," "The Oyster Catcher," "Dangerous Structure," "Death Watch," "Lost Leader," "The Coulmon Handicap," "The Sark Land Mission," and "Paris in Summer"), Hodder & Stoughton, 1988, Harper, 1988.

Anything for a Quiet Life (includes "Anything for a Quiet Life," "Black Bob," "Vivat Regina," "The Reign of Terror," "The Admiral," "We've Come to Report a Murder, Sir," "Holy Writ," "The Bird of Dawning," and "The Freedom Folk"), Hodder & Stoughton, 1990, Carroll & Graf, 1990.

Plays:

A Clean Kill (three acts; produced on the West End, London, 1959), Constable, 1960.

The Bargain (three acts; produced on the West End, London, 1961), Constable, 1961.

The Shot in Question (three acts; produced on the West End, London, 1963), Constable, 1963.

Windfall (three acts; produced on the West End, London, 1963), Constable, 1963.

Editor:

Best Detective Stories of Cyril Hare, Faber, 1959, Walker, 1961, published as *Death among Friends,* Perennial Library, 1984.

(Collected with others on behalf of the Crime Writers Association) *Crime in Good Company: Essays on Criminals and Crime-Writing,* Constable, 1959.

The Oxford Book of Legal Anecdotes, Oxford University Press, 1986.

Prep School, John Murray, 1991.

Contributor:

Herbert Brean, editor, *The Mystery Writers' Handbook,* Harper, 1956.

George Hardinge, editor, *Winter's Crimes 1,* St. Martin's, 1969.

John Ball, editor, *The Mystery Story,* University Extension, University of California, 1976.

H. R. F. Keating, editor, *Agatha Christie: First Lady of Crime,* Weidenfeld & Nicolson, 1977.

Dilys Winn, editor, *Murder Ink: The Mystery Reader's Companion,* Workman Publishing, 1977.

Miriam Gross, editor, *The World of Raymond Chandler,* Weidenfeld & Nicolson, 1977.

Otto Penzler, editor, *The Great Detectives,* Little, Brown, 1978.

Julian Symons, editor, *Verdict of Thirteen,* Harper, 1978.

James Hale, editor, *The After Midnight Ghost Book,* Hutchinson, 1980, F. Watts, 1981.

Mark Dixon, editor, *Crime Wave,* Collins, 1980.

Alice Laurance and Isaac Asimov, editors, *Who Done It?,* Houghton, 1980.

Hilary Watson, editor, *Winter's Crimes 12,* St. Martin's, 1980.

Other:

Dr. Crippen, Odhams Press, 1953.

The Claimant, Constable, 1957.

The Law, David & Charles, 1977.

Author of radio scripts: "Death in Captivity," 1953, "The Man Who Could Not Sleep," 1955, "Crime Report," 1956, "Doctor at Law," 1956, "The Waterloo Table," 1957, "You Must Take Things Easy," 1958, "Stay of Execution" (based on his story of the same title), 1965, "Game without Rules" (based on his story of the same title), 1968, "The Last Chapter," 1970, "Black Light," 1972, "Flash Point" (based on his novel of the same title), 1974, "Petrella," 1976, "In the Nick of Time," 1979, "The Last Tenant" (based on his story of the same title), 1979, and "The Oyster Catcher," 1983.

Author of television scripts: "The Crime of the Century," 1956, "Wideawake," 1957, "The Body of a Girl," 1958, "Fair Game," 1958, "Crime Report" (based on his radio script of the same title), 1958, "Blackmail Is So Difficult," 1959, "Dangerous Ice," 1959, "A Clean Kill" (based on his play of the same title), 1961, "The Men from Room 13" (adapted from a story by Stanley Firmin), 1961, "Scene of the Accident," 1961, "The Betrayers" (adapted from a story by Stanley Ellin), 1962, "Trial Run," 1963, "The Blackmailing of Mr. S.," 1964, "The Mind of the Enemy," 1965, "The Man in Room 17," 1966, "Misleading Cases" (adapted from stories by A. P. Herbert), 1971, "Hadleigh," 1971, "Money to Burn" (adapted from the novel by Margery Allingham), 1974, and "Where There's a Will" (based on his story of the same title), 1975.

Also editor of "Classics of Detection and Adventure" series, Hodder & Stoughton. Contributor of short stories to *Ellery Queen's Mystery Magazine.*

Sam Hamill

HOMECOMING

The day my new mother drove me from the orphanage in Ogden, Utah, down to the farm in Holladay, I ran away. It wasn't really an orphanage, I guess, since no one has ever found any official records. Call it a short-term foster home. I'd been abandoned at the beginning of World War II—according to a juvenile-court psychiatrist—by a transient carnival fry-cook. A frightened three-year-old child, I had been abandoned, then physically and sexually abused, and was bloated from malnutrition. I must have had some vague memory of a father and a dog, because I was told they would meet me at the end of the journey with my new mother. When we arrived at the farm and I was greeted by Big Sam, a tall, handsome rangy man with a pipe and a cocker spaniel, I cried, "You're not my father and that's not my dog, and you can't keep me here!"

I was given a new name, assigned a birth date, and hauled off again to doctor and dentist to be examined. "Gotta watch this one," the Doc told my mother, "He'll grow up to be a fatty if you don't watch his diet." Soon I was given my own tiny table beside the one where the adults—mother, father, aunt, and grandmother—ate their meals. Big Sam ate enormous meals that always included desserts eaten along with the main course, usually something made with chocolate. Everyone agreed it was best I didn't see. Thus, my own low table. Within the family, I was to be an only child, separate from the family.

I was returned to the doctor immediately for circumcision. "It's dirty," I was told. I thought they cut it off. And there were chronic sinus problems: weekly treatments including strapping me into a chair and forcing a saltwater solution through the sinuses, treatment that caused vomiting, incredible pain, and intensified my claustrophobia. My mother and old Doc Maw were apparently amused by my screams. For some reason I've never understood, they laughed as they strapped me down. They made jokes about it. They simply didn't understand my terror.

The dentist reported that a number of secondary teeth had failed to form, probably the result of malnutrition, and he prescribed a sugar-free diet with lots of milk, running counter to the doctor's instructions to limit milk and bread.

Sam Hamill, about four years old

Within the first year or so, I was bitten in the face by my father's dog. Not long thereafter I was kicked in the face by the girl who lived next door. She was wearing ice skates at the time, and her kick left a ragged crescent scar on my forehead just below the hairline. I worried that these people planned to kill me. I suffered intense somnophobia, fear of sleeping, because of chronic nightmaring, probably the result of early sexual abuse. My terror at the thought of lying alone and vulnerable in a dark room led my mother to begin reading to me at bedtime, and I began to find solace in the stories and poems I heard every night. Even now, nearly half a century later, I can hear the opening of Steinbeck's *The Red Pony*, a story I would read to my daughter over and over twenty-five years later: "At daybreak Billy Buck emerged from the bunkhouse and stood for a moment on the porch looking up at the sky." I still have my mother's slipcased, 1945 edition with illustrations by Wesley Dennis. There were a series of farmhands who served as big brother or Billy Buck in my imagination, mostly with disastrous results. A couple died in Korea, one in a jail fire in Nevada. Events seemed to conspire to underscore my sense of isolation, a separateness overcome only when I assumed a persona.

Along with Steinbeck's stories, I loved the Brothers Grimm, and a large illustrated volume of Greek myths, Twain, Dickens, and Robert Louis Stevenson. But most of all, I became enchanted by Big Sam's recitation of poetry, mostly the Romantics: Byron, Keats, and Shelley. He could recite for hours. There were poems of Wordsworth and Longfellow; there was "Bobbie" Burns—Big Sam's middle name was Burns—sung in a funny pseudo-Scottish brogue; there were poems by Robert Service—probably the first poems I memorized. Before long, I had established certain favorites and would ask for them over and over again in the evening after Big Sam's final round of the night, putting to bed some five thousand chickens. "Tell me 'Ode to the West Wind,' tell me 'The Village Blacksmith,' tell me 'The Ballad of Sam McGee!'" I would cry, and then I would try to say the

words along with his rich, resonant baritone, trying desperately to lower my voice to sound like his. I "made up" poems while working with my father, pitchforking chicken manure or loading hay for twenty cents an hour, and we would revise them together, and later, after dinner, write them down.

It wasn't long before "Sam Patrick Hamill" rejected even his name, Patrick. Everyone insisted on calling me "Pat," a name I disliked—I thought it a girl's name. So I simply refused to answer unless addressed as "Sam." My adopted father became "Big Sam." A change of name is a change of life—or, at least, a change of primary metaphor. I lived in a state of perpetual fear and rage my new family often thought was "awfully cute." I despised being cute more than anything else in the world. Being cute means being witless; being cute means one's suffering or anger is trivialized; being cute means not being heard. I was also told time and again that I was "chosen," that I was "lucky to have a family that cares," and other similarly well-intentioned but nonetheless devastating comments. When told I was "lucky to be adopted," I wondered how lucky it is to be abandoned; when bawled out for being insufficiently grateful, I offered silent resentment. I was told "You'll never amount to a damned thing" until I began to believe it.

Thirty years later I would realize that I had been surprisingly aware of the politics of living in Utah in the late forties and early fifties. In Utah, the senator from Wisconsin, Joe McCarthy, was treated as a media hero, but my father spoke of him with considerable contempt and brought me to our new television set to see Edward R. Murrow go on the offensive. I remember wondering whether Big Sam may have had "communist friends" like the men McCarthy persecuted. In school, there were "atomic bomb drills" that sent us under our desks. Russophobia colored everything we learned. Liberal to the core and agnostic in Mormon Utah, my parents cheered when Adlai Stevenson said, "Losing causes are the only ones worth fighting for." Poor Adlai with a hole in his shoe. He was "too smart to be electable." There were a lot of political discussions in the family. The Mormon church taught that "Negroes carry the mark of Cain." Everyone was frightened of "the bomb," afraid the Russians were knocking at our borders and in a "world-wide communist conspiracy," the billion Chinese would join the Russians in an attack that would obliterate us all.

When we children played games of cowboys and Indians, I always loved playing Indian, learning stories—relatively *truthful* stories—about Geronimo, the great Sioux leaders, the Five Nations, and others.

"Big Sam and Little Sam," Christmas, late 1940s

When we played war, I was John Wayne "slaughtering the Japs," until I got a summer job weeding strawberries for old Mr. Mitsunaga, who had lost grandsons on both sides in the war. A gentle, hardworking man, he carried an enormous grief in his face. He had come back to the Salt Lake Valley after spending the war years in a camp somewhere; I don't remember which one. His land had been taken from him, and he had begun again as a tenant farmer. I stopped playing war.

I was sent off to "experience" a little Mormon religion—which I despised—and joined the Boy Scouts. While on a camping trip, I was molested by a scout leader. And within weeks or months, my grandmother died in her bed. I had just come home from a scout meeting, frightened to death of the man who had molested me and keeping his dirty secret out of sheer dread. I was too terrorized to quit the troop. And I came home one evening to a solemn house.

"Poose," as she was called, had been bedridden for months, sick for as long as I could remember. A handsome old woman possessed of great inner strength, she had been the family matriarch. Her estranged husband, Otto Empey, lived in a "retirement hotel" in downtown Salt Lake City—in those days, a long way away. He had been a coal miner, half his fingers lost to blasting caps, and was tough as an old goat. But Ott was there in a little bowler hat and dark suit. There was a modest funeral and burial in the Holladay cemetery. I felt guilty as hell, thinking about my parents moving into her newly vacated upstairs bedroom and me moving into their large room in the basement. In some way, Poose's death eased my guilt and grief over what had happened on that camping trip and several times after. Poose's death was the end of the Boy Scouts for me. I had almost, but not quite, been an eagle.

There were also a few childhood friendships, and games, sports, camping; and I loved animals, especially dogs and horses. There were creeks for swimming or fishing, a lot of open country to be explored, and I enjoyed a wealth of imagination, turning a barn into a pirate ship, a shadow into a demon.

At my mother's family's cattle ranch in Moab, the Bar-A, Lester Taylor, the family patriarch, a large, rawboned man with the family's strong features, made an enormous impression on me. His temperament ran somewhere between stubborn and tenacious, and riding with him through hills and canyons, watching him work cattle with his border collie or mend fences or break horses, I began to understand the twenty-four-hour workday, an attitude that would eventually inform my discipline as a

"My grandmother, 'Poose' Empey, beside ocotillo cactus,"
about 1948

writer. Running a ranch meant no vacations, no escape from daily responsibilities. Although Lester lived but a mere half-hour drive from Arches National Monument, had grown up in "red rock country," he had never been out to view the famous red rocks. "Nothin' out there but a bunch of damned rocks!" Even as a boy, I intuitively understood something about that stubborn desert frontier spirit that would feed my soul in my own struggles many years later. In my mother, it expressed itself simply in a refusal to give up. If I learned something about inner strength, tenacity, from Lester Taylor, I also picked up a lot of what his wife called "his plain damned cussedness."

There were all kinds of well-intentioned, unspeakably dull organizations I was pushed into trying for a summer or for a meeting or two. I built a ham radio. I rode with a western-riding drill group and rode in some rodeos, despising and resenting being a child at all. Every group increased my own sense of powerlessness, alienation, and rebellion. In retrospect, I think I expected to die at any moment, either from invading Russians' atomic bombs, or at the hands of those who prey on children. Violence was power. Danger was romantic. Death was fascinating.

I watched over and over again as my father hung chickens upside down from an old plum branch and slipped the narrow blade of a boning knife down their throats. They thrashed a moment and then hung there as blood poured out. Later, cats would come and lick the ground for their blood. A favorite evening game was made of killing nests of mice in the chicken coops, my father peeling back hay bales to reveal them so I could smash them one by one with a four-foot length of heavy rubber garden hose.

I rode horses with another kid, Rex Hintze, roaming the foothills shooting rabbits and rattle-snakes for fun. We used to "go frogging," catching little swamp frogs and using slingshots to send them flying into the grills of passing trucks. His father once beat me unmercifully with his fists for "talking back," and I wasn't terribly surprised when, a few years later, my childhood chum beat two girls to death with a claw hammer in the desert when they didn't know how to change his flat tire. He was a nut because his father was a nut, I thought. I was not unacquainted

with madness. The mother of another close friend was finally hospitalized after dozens of episodes in which she ran screaming from ensuing, imaginary Nazis, arms flailing, down the street in her nightgown in the middle of the night. She was both frightening and heartrending, a gentle woman with prematurely white hair and pale gray eyes.

I ran with a very dangerous bunch of loonies from time to time, and not a few certifiable psycho-paths, the majority of whom ended up in jails or prisons. We were a generation of adolescent nihilists. The death of James Dean on September 30, 1955, came to symbolize the Romantic ideal of a rebellious generation. Faron Young sang, "I wanna live fast, love hard, die young, and leave a beautiful memory." And it was out of that cry of desperation that rock'n'roll was born. There was Marlon Brando of *The Wild One* and *On the Waterfront.* Violence was practical: it brought dinner; violence was power: John Wayne or Marlon Brando, it was publicly glorified; the threat of violence could be worn like a suit of armor. I practiced being inarticulate and wore a motorcycle jacket and boots. I rode a motorcycle.

"On the Bar-A cattle ranch, a pensive child on buckskin, far right," about 1948

And there was Johnny Cash, who had recorded an album for Sun Records, and who was seeing the mother of a girl I knew, and he brought us a record by Elvis Presley. Funny name. I had studied piano, mostly under duress. Once I heard rock'n'roll, my classical training was dead. But, rather than guitar, I took up the trumpet, wanting to sound "like Miles Davis or Rafael Mendez," rock'n'roll or not. Trumpet music was decidedly "cool." Even musically, I was a little out of sync, something of a misfit. If I loved to dance and sing to rock music, I loved jazz and blues as much or more. In the middle of lily white Utah in the muddle of the paranoid 1950s, I listened to Little Richard, Miles, Coltrane, Cannonball, Ray Charles—I listened to music that was Black; and, often, white guys *sounding* Black: Elvis and Jerry Lee to Dave Brubeck and Gerry Mulligan. There was an emotional intensity in Black soul, blues, rock, and jazz that almost never informed mainstream popular radio music like "Your Hit Parade." Who could ever forget Snooky Lanson trying to sing, "You ain' nothin' but a houn' dawg," an "Elvis tune" first popularized by Big Mama Thornton. It was *our* music, and white, middle-class adults couldn't stand it. Ed Sullivan wouldn't show Elvis below the hips. Being "dangerous" meant being both powerful and attractive. Elvis had four gold records in 1956.

On October 13, 1955, Kenneth Rexroth introduced several poets at a reading in San Francisco's Six Gallery, including Gary Snyder, Allen Ginsberg, Phil Whalen, Michael McClure, and Philip Lamantia, and began a literary revolution that made nationwide news during most of 1956. Jack Kerouac would deliver an indelible impression of the evening in his 1958 novel, *The Dharma Bums*. I skipped a lot of school in favor of Kerouac novels, "Beat" poetry, shooting pool, and drinking beer. At fourteen, I began hot-wiring cars for "joy rides" beatniks glamourized. I was busted, jailed as a runaway in Casper, Denver, Las Vegas, in several Rocky Mountain towns I've long since forgotten, and spent a wild couple of weeks in an adobe cell with a half dozen other delinquents in Fredonia, Arizona. Nobody would come to get us. I'd already stolen and wrecked my parents' car. So we sat in there, passing Bull Durham cigarettes back and forth, until they simply gave up and turned us loose.

I spent a frightening, frozen Thanksgiving weekend camped in a stolen car, out of gas in a canyon outside Price, Utah, so cold my fingertips got frostbitten. I finally tore the stuffing out of the back seats and got a fire started that probably saved my life. Life on the streets, even in the mid-fifties, was tough. In a Colorado jail, I was gang-raped, a sock stuffed in my mouth to stifle screams, tattooed on my cheek, icepicked in the face, and left for dead after a quarrel with a Pachuco gang. There were gang fights and street fights. In a parking lot war at Olympus High School in Holladay, I was kicked in the groin so hard my scrotum split open. Of only average height and weight, I managed to intimidate through pure tenacity. I was "crazy" in a fight, they said. I "wouldn't quit," an image I worked hard to encourage even at the expense of a few broken teeth, a gash or two.

A fourteen- or fifteen-year-old kid doesn't take to the streets merely out of naive romantic dream. The romance of "freedom" lasts about twenty-four hours. Homelessness and hunger provide hard lessons. Violence wears a hundred disguises. One takes to the streets only when life at home becomes intolerable. While still in elementary school I had begun to defend myself when "disciplined," whether in the case of spanking or in the case of more severe physical threats such as the paddle a teacher wielded enthusiastically on boys like me. My mother could no longer "swat" me without retaliation. When discipline was turned over to Big Sam, my defiance was intensified. In our last angry encounter, I stood him off with a pitchfork.

Like most adolescents, I was self-conscious and insecure, feelings that were complicated by my embarrassment over the stench of chickenshit at home. The family farm, once a source of inspiration, suddenly made me feel ashamed. What girl wanted to date a guy who shoveled manure after school? The romance of "seeing the world" soon yielded to the need to escape from my own life. On the road, I could be anyone, anyone at all.

The Beat writers gave me a sense of purpose, a more comfortable identity. They made being smart respectable in a perverse kind of way. Intellectual rebellion was more exciting than adolescent rebellion. They wrote poems that produced an immediate emotional response I had never found in Wordsworth or Burns, poems that were aware of the conditions of *my* life. Streetwise and tough, on the run, I read, memorized, recited, and wrote poetry in exactly the same way a decent young jazz musician practices scales. I wrote hundreds of sonnets; I wrote imitations of "Howl" and horny adolescent ballads, memorizing Ferlinghetti's wonderful "Underwear" and Rexroth's magnificent "Letter to William Carlos Williams."

There were also periods when I made serious attempts to adjust. I fulfilled a probation period, including making restitution for a wrecked car. Street life went nowhere fast—that was self-evident. So I went back to school, determined to be a decent student. But it didn't last. It couldn't. Blue jailhouse tattoos on face and hands and arms set me irrevocably apart from the pastel faces and decent lives of Holladay, Utah, high school students. I had been around, had seen some death, had been beaten and raped. And I had survived. I was suspended for reading *On the Road* in school.

I went to San Francisco to be a beatnik. I had been reading Kenneth Rexroth's poetry, and had memorized most of Ferlinghetti's *Coney Island of the Mind* poems, and the stink that was raised over publication of *Howl* also carried news of beatniks and something called "free love" when marijuana smoke and wine and poetry lasted all night. Drunk on Kerouac, I stole a car in Holladay, another in Wendover, another in Sacramento, and took to the streets of The City. I sacked out in cars, played pool for money, got an odd job swamping now and then, and got thrown out of jazz clubs every night until every bouncer knew who I was.

And I put a lot of heroin up my nose. I never had the nerve to stick needles in my arm and that's probably the only reason I was able to beat the addiction. Everyone in the world of jazz was on smack, and Chet Baker, who was called "James Dean with a horn," became another self-destructive hero to a lot of young men like me. He was supremely *hip*. He did drugs, we did drugs. We ate uppers—"little white crosses"—like Kerouac, and stayed up all night drinking bad wine and talking East Coast jazz and West Coast jazz, Beat poetry, the hot and the cool, until we collapsed where we sat. And I learned something about free love: drunks and junkies don't get laid. And they don't even care.

I met Kenneth Rexroth on Columbus Avenue outside City Lights Bookstore and asked him to autograph his *Thirty Spanish Poems of Love and Exile*, and during our conversation he learned of my predicament. He took me to his home near the old Jewish center and fed me and invited me to stay for one of his evening gatherings. He gave me a thorough tongue-lashing about heroin without inspiring my ire and without making me feel ashamed. I felt that I somehow mattered a little *to him*. I saw him regularly over the next few weeks, and looking forward to seeing him was all the impetus I needed to stay clean. I devoured his books, and it was through Rexroth that I first began to see poetry not only as a discipline, but as a way of life. Poetry became a *connection*—between the living and the dead, between the heart and the soul, between a poet and the world. Poetry clarifies one's response to the world, it becomes a form of emotional discipline as well as an intellectual "artistic" act. Through poetry, I began to

"*Fresh from the streets and cleaned up for a last crack at high school,*" about 1959

feel, I could resolve the hurt and the anger that left me so conflicted.

But I was still on the street. I got a little work as an artist's model, but all the "artists" turned out to be pedophiles—or at least those who prey on adolescent boys. It was clear that I would either have to start turning tricks or get the hell out of North Beach and the Tenderloin. Other street kids told me about "pulling a daisy chain" and other forms of child prostitution. A lot of the beatnik fringe was psychotic and self-destructive, including Saint Jack. I got the hell out. The world was full of predatory pederasts, Salt Lake to San Francisco, Tucson to Missoula.

Going back to Utah for a final crack at high school was a last desperate suck. I cut off my greased-back hair, got some decent clothes, and tried like hell to pass for white. The only problem was, all those pale Mormon boys and girls had never seen the inside of a jail. They had never read Allen Ginsberg or Robert Creeley or Catullus. They didn't dig poetry or jazz. Introduced into a new middle-class crowd, I learned quickly that "frats," unlike "greasers," had a lot of cash and a lot of expensive booze. If they frowned on smoking weed, and if they didn't dig soul music, they could always be counted on for a bottle of Cuervo Gold or Jack Black. And for several months, I played my newfound friends like an old violin, telling them poems, introducing them to jazz. I dragged them off to the only coffeehouse in Salt Lake City, The Abyss, a tiny club in a downtown basement, to listen to locals read from Baudelaire, Beckett, Artaud, and Ferlinghetti. We wrecked some pretty new houses on the East Bench of the Salt Lake Valley that winter, and even a couple of ski lodges. Most of those guys went on to law school or whatever, and all the pretty blonde girls married them and made lots of pretty babies, and now they all live together in pretty new houses on the East Bench of the Salt Lake Valley and ski in paradise.

The sixties began with my classmates utterly unaware of Rosa Parks and Martin Luther King, Jr. Their consciousness would be raised by young folk singers like Bob Dylan and Joan Baez a couple of years later, while I was in Japan. At the end of the Eisenhower era, they listened to Pat Boone and Bobby Darin and began to get interested in folk music, especially the Kingston Trio. I was immersed in Robert Johnson, Leadbelly, and Cannonball Adderly's hip blues. Blue Note records and City Lights Pocket Poets and New Directions books were primary accoutrements among the "hipeoisie." Being hip also meant being too cool for violence. Duels were duels of wit only. I loved telling poems to these "children of god," these jack-Mormons, these innocents, especially *Coney Island of the Mind,* with all its good humor and jive.

I got busted by a cop who'd busted me several times before. We had a little meeting with a judge, and it was determined that I would enlist in the Marine Corps for a minimum of four years, upon which time my rather considerable juvenile judicial history would be expunged. So I enlisted, with the added bonus that I would be sent directly to Japan once I completed basic training. Rexroth and Gary Snyder had made Zen very attractive to me, so the USMC would be my ticket to the world of Zen. For the first time in my life, the folks around Holladay seemed to approve of something I was doing. But then, they didn't know about the bust. And besides, I figured, it was as much a case of "good riddance" as "good-bye." In any case, I couldn't imagine anyplace farther from Utah than Japan. And that was good. That was fine with me. There was a world I wanted to see.

To this day, I can still close my eyes and see Gunnery Sergeant Smith, his flat-brimmed drill instructor's "smokey bear" hat level with his eyebrows,

white spittle from the stomach medicine he drank flaking at the corners of his mouth as he screamed, nose-to-nose in my face, "You are living proof your mother fucks billy-goats, private!" Little sprays of spittle made me blink, but I never wiped. I really don't know why I thought push-ups and sit-ups and being screamed at and insulted was so much fun. But I did it and enjoyed doing it until I got to Okinawa. I wasn't much of a patriot, but I was, for a time, a marine's marine. The regimen appealed to all my baser instincts. Intimidation as the foundation of respect. The United States Marine Corps is *not* hip.

In 1961 and '62, there were a lot of rumors floating around the marine bases on occupied Okinawa, many having to do with "advisors" in Southeast Asia. Okinawa was a devasted country. The villages were full of bars and whorehouses, drugs were rampant, and the general poverty was unspeakable. I was reading Camus's *The Rebel* and a lot of existential writers and began studying Zen, especially R. H. Blyth and Suzuki. A suite of essays Camus wrote for *Combat* in 1946 brought me to make the decision of a lifetime: I read "Neither Victims nor Executioners" over and over again. Do we want to live in a society in which murder is considered trifling? Camus asks. He asks us to consider whether means justify ends, and calls for an international code of justice that would begin with the abolition of the death penalty—including the mass death penalty called war. "Hope remains only in the most difficult task of all: to reconsider even from the ground up, so as to shape a living society inside a dying society." A young marine doesn't romanticize the idea of nonviolence. Marines who don't follow orders go to prison or get shot. I read Gandhi. Violence is a consequence of fear, just as fear is a consequence of ignorance.

My Zen teacher told me about Japanese Zen master Dogen, who learned to read Chinese poetry at the age of four at his grandmother's knee, and who wrote a collection of Chinese poems at the age of seven. "Study the self," Dogen taught, "to forget the self." The fundamental teaching of Buddhism is codependent origination, the idea that nothing—people, nations, objects, ideas, *nothing*—is entirely self-generating. Sitting *zazen,* I began to be free of the persistent ache of having been abandoned. I began to feel like I meant something, to feel at peace. Years later, I would read a late poem by Rexroth in which he says, "The question is not / Does being have meaning, / But does meaning have being." Sitting *zazen,* I began to understand that I am a part, not apart. "Meaning" is a koan; it is a knot the mind unkinks. Camus says life is absurd, that only our commitment gives meaning. He was for me, perhaps, a kind of bridge between Asian and European philosophical traditions.

I went to company headquarters and turned in my rifle. In the Marine Corps, *every* marine is a marksman; every marine is expected to qualify every year with his weapon. I declared myself a Buddhist and a Conscientious Objector, fully expecting to be sent to prison or simply be shot. In a Marine Corps brig, there are six yellow lines outside the door to the guardshack. The prisoner is required to stop, stand at attention, and repeat, "Sir! Prisoner 1944738 requests permission to speak, sir!" (That was my number.) Some Pfc or lance corporal says, "Speak, maggot," and the prisoner says, "Sir! Prisoner 1944738 requests permission to cross the yellow line, sir!" And the guard says, "Go, shit-head," and the prisoner steps to the next line and repeats the indignation. Marine Corps discipline.

Since I expected to be shot as a traitor and a coward anyway, I just stopped at the first yellow line and said, "You better kill me. Because you can take my life, but you can't take my dignity." Solitary confinement. Permitted three books, I had Pound's

Confucius, Camus's *The Rebel,* and Blyth on Zen. I sat *zazen.* I managed to overcome self-pity after the first few days, and if I did not come to any profound realization, that in itself was profound in a modest way, and I found something deeply satisfying about having made the initial decision. It was a decision that would focus the remainder of my life, a decision that would affect my every waking hour. I had staked some sort of claim to "dignity," some sort of defined commitment, for the first time in my life. Writing and music were as much a part of my life as drawing a breath, whereas conscientious objection places demands on everything one does, requiring a deep personal *conviction.* Locked up, convicted, I felt good about myself.

I sat in solitary until a Catholic chaplain was touched by my case and began making appeals on my behalf. In the end, I was issued new dog tags that read "Buddhist" under the category *religion* that previously read "none," and I became an office worker, saved from prison only because I could type seventy words per minute and think in complete sentences, *rara avis* in the U.S. Marine Corps of 1962. Because some brass desperately needed an articulate typist, another "criminal conviction" was expunged.

I spent a couple of years in the Orient, learned some Japanese, and began the discipline of *zazen.* During my last two years in the armed forces, I got the best treatment possible. The corps simply recognized that I posed no threat and used me to its best advantage. I wrote reports and handled all sorts of paperwork and came and went largely as I pleased, an outsider, a civilian dressed in fatigues. But I was deeply troubled. Didn't I, by continuing to serve the corps, simply free some other clerk-typist who could then be sent into the fields to be cannon fodder? Deep inside, I felt that I had no honorable alternative but to refuse to cooperate with the business of death. I completed my enlistment obligations torn by conflicting emotions.

Stateside once again in my last assignment before discharge, I took my final leave to visit my family in Utah. While there, a high school friend called on the phone. She had married young and was in a terrible situation. Her husband beat her, kept the checkbook in his name, and she didn't drive. She had nowhere to turn. A high school dropout, she couldn't even hope to find a job. So I took her to Las Vegas on my way back to California, and we got her a quick divorce and married, intending to get her some government-sponsored training so she could begin a life of her own.

The trouble was, "we" got pregnant. Eron was born a month after my "honorable" discharge.

"My boot camp photo—before long, 'C.O.' would take on a whole new meaning," 1961

Troops were being sent to Viet Nam. Stone broke, a high school dropout myself, I returned yet again to Utah, begging bowl in hand. If my parents would help me, I could work and go to school. Eron Hamill was born in Cottonwood Hospital in Murray, Utah, in the midsummer of 1965. I wept with joy, then drank a bottle of whiskey, frightened out of my wits. I wouldn't have wished me as a father on anyone. My life was nearly overwhelmed by unnamed desire and what everyone around me agreed was "an utter lack of direction." I read poetry, obsessed with Robert Duncan's idea that a poet's real work is to "study thru, to deepen the experience." How could I explain the urgency I felt when I opened a book of poetry? My new wife didn't understand. I didn't understand myself.

I suppose Eron's mother and I *wanted* to be in love. But I doubt we ever were. No two people could harbor more diverse notions of what is meant by success. I wanted to write a poem. She wanted a house in suburbia with several bathrooms and closets you could walk in. I got a job collecting bad debts for a loan company and lasted a couple of months. We moved back to southern California and bought a car on credit, moved into the usual southern California apartment with a palm at the gate, and I went to work for loan companies again, despising every minute of my life until I started attending classes at Los Angeles Valley College on the GI Bill in 1966.

Everything on campus pulled me away from the bourgeois life Eron's mother was determined to enjoy. The civil rights movement was in high gear, and I became an activist, Norman Thomas, Martin Luther King, Jr., and Michael Harrington providing primary inspiration. I studied history and philosophy, taking Camus as a kind of model upon which I could build. There were voter registration drives in California and Mississippi, food drives after Delta floods, marches in the streets, confrontations with police and police dogs. And there was the burning of Watts, the burning of Detroit. We told people time and again, "If you're not part of the solution, you're part of the problem," a slogan that means as much to me today as it did then. I became active in antiwar activities. In short, I became socialized—in every sense of the word.

In 1968, I ran for the California State Assembly on an antiwar, socialist platform, campaigned for Gene McCarthy, and began to become feminized, thanks largely to *Second Sex,* a book given to me by a teacher I greatly admired at LAVC, Cecile Forbes. She was the only member of the English department who understood why I studied journalism, and she shared my enthusiasm for Camus. We had long conversations about Sartre and de Beauvoir, Camus, and Ignazio Silone. *Second Sex* shook my life; it clarified my conscientious objections. Social equality *ought* to mean equality. Joan Baez was telling women, "Don't make love to men who make war." I had grown up sexist in a sexist environment and I saw in myself attitudes I despised.

My two closest friends during those years were Chuck Jorgensen, a radical history professor and social activist, and Willie Davis, a leader in the Black Student Union. I learned more during long nights at their house in the San Fernando Valley—gallon jugs of cheap wine and stacks of Taj Mahal and Coltrane records—than in any classroom. I read Malcolm X and Eugene Debs and the poetry of Thomas McGrath and D. H. Lawrence.

Our little "family" toughed it out for a couple of years, but it was clear that my wife wanted a different life than the one beginning to open to me. I had a lot of time with Eron while she was small. But her mother and I were headed in opposite directions. I edited the college newspaper and the literary magazine and published bad poetry in other college journals. But—as my wife and family reminded me constantly—what kind of *career* was I headed for? Would I go into journalism? Teach English? I didn't know. I wanted to write some poetry. I wasn't looking for a career, I was looking for a life. The serious and strenuous study of poetry, along with Willie Davis, Chuck Jorgensen, and Cecile Forbes, did a great deal to help me begin to define what I wanted to do with my life. I immersed myself in Ezra Pound studies, and in the Black Mountain poets, especially Robert Creeley, Robert Duncan, and Denise Levertov. I wrote a small history of Black Mountain, fascinated with Charles Olson's notion of *polis* and myth—the politics of poetry reflected already in Amiri Baraka and other Beat and post-Beat poets—and I began to see feminism as an important political tool, a *primary* development in a move toward worldwide nonviolence. Poetry is a form of bearing witness, and Simone de Beauvoir and the U.S. Marine Corps and the Viet Nam War and the civil rights movement intersected in the poetry I wanted to write. A poem could be a "field of action," and Olson talked about the poet's "stance toward reality" both inside and outside the poem—so that the two would be fused. A love poem becomes the quintessential antiwar poem in such a context.

My reading brought me into a long conversation on the nature of violence, a conversation that spanned political and literary boundaries. I broke with the Peace and Freedom Party over the issue of

Eron Hamill, age five, "my only blood relative in the world," 1970

violence. Violence remains the primary political problem that supercedes all others. Those who finance violence at home or at the ballot box or in the church pews cannot escape its unspeakable consequence. If I am not part of the solution, I am the problem.

My real "homework" was with the poetry of Pound, Williams, D. H. Lawrence; and Rexroth and Creeley and Levertov, with Everson and Duncan and H.D. The writer Deena Metzger introduced me to a number of southern California writers, including the local glitterati at a surreal bash for Anaïs Nin. And I particularly remember a wonderful drive to Santa Barbara to hear Galway Kinnell read a new poem from *Poetry* magazine, "The Bear," an indelible event for a young poet. There were regular readings at the Metzgers' large house on a canyon hillside, until Deena lost her job at LAVC over a controversial poem. There were a couple of memorable encounters with the elderly Dalton Trumbo who talked about the blacklist and about writers like Tom McGrath and Meridel Le Sueur. I soaked up influence like a sponge.

We moved to Marin County, north of San Francisco. I was happy to be in the country again, out of the miserable excessive mania of L.A., but my job with the San Raphael *Independent Journal* ended abruptly over a strike. I got a job installing telephone systems for Western Electric in San Francisco and bought my daughter a pony. I read her *The Red Pony* and the poetry of Dylan Thomas. I tried to be a father and I tried to write a poem. But I was dying inside. I was creeping up on thirty and, with no degree, had no future in journalism. Zen practice had been all but abandoned. I longed for literary conversation. My wife had never talked about her terrible childhood and abusive marriage; I didn't talk about mine; we never talked politics; she didn't read poetry; she wanted to buy a house. Nothing could have been more frightening to me than the idea of a thirty-year mortgage on a life.

One morning at 4 A.M., driving to work across the Golden Gate Bridge, I suddenly realized I was smoking a joint to brace myself for the day ahead; I realized I had a six-pack of beer, three for lunch and three for the drive home, stashed in back. I walked in to work, told my boss my mother had just died, and asked for an emergency paycheck. No questions asked. I had a check within an hour, drove to the airport, mailed my wife the car keys, and left with one paycheck and the clothes on my back. I figured, what the hell, my parents would never speak to me again, I was abandoning my daughter knowing full well what abandonment means, abandoning her just as my father had abandoned me, and it made me so crazy I was suicidal for several years. But I simply could not survive life as a telephone systems installer and buyer of cars and houses on credit.

I returned for a semester at LAVC simply to get GI Bill money and take classes, and lived for months sleeping on the couches of various friends. When a friend from my journalism class was murdered, I completely fell apart. We hadn't been terribly close, but he had taken a number of photographs of my daughter, and they were all I had of her at the time. I couldn't shake the guilt and grief. But I couldn't face any other life.

Eventually, I got a 1954 Ford panel truck, filled it with books and camp gear, and lived in it off and on over the next two years. I saw Eron in the summer, between summer school sessions, while I was at the University of California, Santa Barbara, where I'd gone to undertake Pound studies with Hugh Kenner, and to be near Rexroth. Eron was a kid who could talk and could listen. When she was only six or seven, I could explain to her how I felt about my life, and she seemed to understand. Her mother was making good money and generously freed me of financial responsibility at the time.

I explored the northwest coast up to and including Horseshoe Bay, north of Vancouver, British Columbia, and spent a lot of time camping along the Novarro River on the Mendocino coast, immersed in the literature and history of the American west, including most of Frances Densmore's multi-volume study of Sioux culture, books by Frank Waters, Vine Deloria, and Dee Brown, and the folklore and truth—as much as can be determined—about the mountain men, especially Hugh Glass. The "long crawl" of Hugh Glass—more than a hundred miles—following a devastating encounter with a large bear became a personal myth, a figure of survival and rebirth, and figures prominently in the mythmaking of *Triada*—somewhere along one of those journeys in that old truck, probably while traveling with my daughter, I began to conceive a long, lyrically intense poem that would interleave personal myth with historical episodes—like the *Pisan Cantos,* but in a "purely American idiom" as Williams called for. I felt like I was beginning to get somewhere as a poet.

But I was also involved in a devastating, mutually abusive relationship with a woman. I believed, naively, that I could save her from herself; and I hoped she could save me from myself—each seeking salvation in an *other.* Our mutual attraction was centered in the physical, except that the emerging feminism of 1970 was a major force in both our lives. We antagonized each other, started terrible fights, then "made up" with a passion that could almost, but not quite, obliterate all the pain we inflicted upon each other. I drank too much, trying to "drown the grief." We split up. I had begun to understand the problem of domestic violence, to recognize the cycle, and had named it for the first time. I felt like a complete fake. I had betrayed myself and her and all that I thought I believed. How could I talk about nonviolence or feminism and still give in to male jealousy, to the need to control?

There were no books to read about battering relationships in 1970. There were no shelters for battered women, no community domestic-violence programs, nothing. I knew that if I was to *really* practice nonviolence, I would have to undertake a personal moral overhaul, a major self-transformation. And the university curriculum offered very little that would be of much use. What we now recognize as the "cycle of abuse" was then still largely unnamed. A friend suggested that I try to become the kind of man I would want my daughter to marry. I called all my friends and organized a big party where I burned a dozen large notebooks filled with pieces of poetry and fiction and personal journalism, but mostly with hundreds of sonnets I had written since returning from the Orient. The burning of my journals represented a death and rebirth, a rejection of the old male dominance over women, a rejection of the old

personal politics of fear and jealousy and rage. Finally, it represented an almost religious commitment to poetry as a tool for personal transformation.

Unfortunately, everything at UCSB was geared to another universe. Since the university had no journalism department, my journalism credits had been disallowed. I had been admitted only by obtaining a permanent intercampus transfer from UC Irvine, where I was admitted as a writing student. At UCSB, I was deemed "too old and unsufficiently malleable" for Professor Marvin Mudrick's College of Creative Studies. In the two years I attended classes, the English department managed to drive away Scott Momaday, Hugh Kenner, and Kenneth Rexroth.

When I became editor of the university literary magazine, *Spectrum,* there was serious talk about discontinuing it. No one cared for the journal that had printed W. C. Williams's most famous essay, "The Variable Foot," for a journal that had published Samuel Beckett. But when I received the Coordinating Council of Literary Magazines' College Editor's Award for producing "the best journal in the country," the dons of the English department actually tried to keep me from getting the award money by telling the council that I had left and asking it to make the check payable to the magazine. I learned of the CCLM award only through a reporter covering the story for the student newspaper. Rexroth called the English department "the fog factory," a rare example of Rexroth understatement.

At Santa Barbara, I made two great, lasting friendships: one with Tree Swenson, who became my partner in life and cofounder of Copper Canyon Press; one with Bill O'Daly, who would eventually devote seventeen years to translating six books by Pablo Neruda, books Tree and I would publish at the Press. In the Unitarian Church in Isla Vista, just off the campus, there were wonderful, powerful poetry readings against the war, and I first heard Galway Kinnell, Philip Levine, Denise Levertov, Robert Bly, William Everson, the young Diane Wakoski, and many, many others in that church. Bill and I were ever-present enthusiasts, both of us immersed in poetics ranging from Garcia Lorca's *duende* to the "projective stance" of Charles Olson.

On one of many regular walks through the art department, I met Tree as she worked on a large painting. It was "like at first sight" for me, despite being lost in a fog of grief over failed relationships. She was my first love based upon respect. Despite being ten years younger, Tree mothered me through my pain; she was sympathetic toward my struggle to overcome decades of machismo, and sexist, racist culture; she understood my guilt and remorse over my daughter, and my desperate need to write, an almost uncontrollable sense of urgency intensified by the war, by student protests, and the gassing of students during riots when the Bank of America was burned. In the midst of all this turmoil, Tree became my friend and lover, my confidante, deep waters discovered in the midst of a swirling Sahara.

And there was Rexroth—by now a grand, old, white-haired man, a rogue patriarch who, despite his own personally troubled history, espoused feminism and anarchism, Buddhism and Gnosticism, who spun out stories and poems and wisdom, delighted to be despised by his English department colleagues. Sometimes he was almost infantile in his paranoid, reactionary behavior: one night during a reception at the home of Melissa Mytinger, publisher of Christopher's Books in Santa Barbara, Rexroth punched the English-American poetry theorist Frederick Turner in the nose for espousing his neo-formalist aesthetic. Rexroth read positively everything, knew everyone, and had almost total recall. He remained a sixty-five-year-old *enfant terrible,* the only breath of life among a gang of aesthetes and pedants and Yvor Winters's sycophants. When Rexroth told me that the greatest tragedy is that it's no longer possible to know the poetry of the whole world, I set out to prove him wrong.

UCSB taught me all I ever have to learn about snivelling and malicious backbiting, ignorance, la-

ziness, and cowardice in the university community. A professor who taught poetry writing had never heard of "projective verse" and had not read Olson, Creeley, Duncan, Levertov, or Pound; he knew William Carlos Williams only through Imagist anthology pieces, the literary bric-a-brac of the Poetry Morgue. I was to put my "career in verse" to nest under this benevolent wing? Frederick Turner insisted that there is no such thing as organic verse while simultaneously insisting that the iamb is born of the heartbeat. This was the English department that pink-slipped Rexroth on his birthday, and had never permitted him to teach more than two classes. This was the English department that would try to steal my little $500 CCLM award for the months of work O'Daly and I invested in *Spectrum.*

If LAVC had expanded my horizons, UCSB was discouraging at every turn; if my professors at LAVC were accessible, helpful, and personable, those who ran the English department at UCSB were inaccessible, unfriendly, even contemptuous. More than one expressed resentment over my interest in Rexroth and/or Kenner. If my years at LAVC were wonderfully invigorating, my experience at UCSB was enervating and depressing. I was simply in the wrong place at the wrong time. Having grown up reading the very poets the department dons all taught, I was enthralled by *contemporary* poets I was discovering almost every day, poets no one at Santa Barbara read.

With Tree Swenson in Colorado high country, 1973

I was interested in Jerome Rothenberg's notion of the "deep image" from a short essay in *Trobar* in 1961. "The power of the image is its ability to convey a sense of two-worlds-in-one: directly: with no concept to come between the inner experience and its meaning." No one at UCSB (other than Rexroth, of course) had ever heard of Rothenberg or *Trobar* or deep image poetry. No one read *any* contemporary poetry as far as I could tell. There was no creative writing program and no interdisciplinary studies program flexible enough to prepare a serious writer for a life of writing. The students—mostly ten years younger than myself—knew more contemporary verse than the department dons. Together, we soaked up Merwin, Creeley, Levertov, Kinnell, and Levine; we read *everything* we could, much of it read aloud in our small group of afficionados. There was Pound's "A Few Don'ts" and other important critical essays, especially *The ABC of Reading* and *Confucius.* We students gathered regularly to drink wine and read poetry aloud. The university, clearly, was fucking up my education. After the episode over *Spectrum,* I left in disgust, everything I owned still in that shaky old panel truck. With the departure of Kenner and Rexroth, several of the best students also left the campus.

I migrated to Denver, in part to get the Rocky Mountains back inside my skin and "write the long poem," in part to escape the last vestiges of imagery from "Surf Bored Tech." From several notebooks, I began working seriously, three hours each day, at writing *Triada,* a poem of three long parts that would take nearly ten years to complete and run a hundred pages. I lived in a tenement with several other happy misfits, and bought a printing press—an antique proofing press—with the CCLM prize money and began to learn. The press was installed in our cockroach-infested kitchen in November 1972. I called Tree in Santa Barbara and begged her to come, and she walked out of her last year of college. O'Daly came for a while. That little award from CCLM fed my spiritual fires for a long time; it gave me faith that I could someday write or edit or publish something of value, even if that value could not be measured in dollars or fame. It was a vote of confidence that came at a perfect time.

It was hardly surprising I had failed to make the grade at UCSB. The poets I most admired, had chosen as models all my life, were all academic rebels, from the Romantics to Pound, Williams, and Rexroth; from Sappho to Catullus; from Whitman to Levertov; from Socrates to Camus. I was also plagued by minor and not-so-minor physical problems. Tree had driven me down from our little house at the

"Father and daughter, Eron, and the house we built together," about 1977

summit of San Marcos Pass one night as I thrashed around her car in the pain of kidney stones, neither of us knowing what it was that brought on my groans and cries. I suffered chronic pinched nerves in my lower back, and had trouble with my teeth, and no money for doctor or dentist. A decade had passed since I had become a conscientious objector; at college, despite my total opposition to the war and to university business connections with the machinery of war, I had tried once again to pass for white. A relatively unpublished poet with an "incomplete" education after nearly six years of full-time college including summer school, I was thirty years old and through—forever through—with trying to pass.

In Denver, I worked as "the straight man" for a dirty-book distributor. Every "adult" bookstore had a large section of "straight books" for, presumably, "socially redeeming value," and I bought, warehoused, and supplied all the dirty bookstores in Denver and most of the West with all their "straight" stuff. It was incredible. Surreal. A sales representative gave me the advance copy of *Our Bodies, Our Selves* there in the midst of pornographic magazines and 8-mm movies, and within weeks, I would be selling copies of it through bookstores owned and operated by the same porno distributor—known to employees only as "the Cleveland mafia." I was reading Adrienne Rich and Susan Brownmiller while these submafioso-types were showing "Deep Throat" on the warehouse wall. The money was so good, I couldn't leave. It paid our early printing bills. O'Daly worked briefly for the same people. Tree worked at a big art supply store.

We were all crazy as hell. When Tree and I married, we all went off to a strip joint and got bombed. We read Samuel Beckett aloud, and thrived on a shared passion for poetry. But I continued to have nightmares over my daughter who remained in California. And I had yet to resolve my own inner rage and sense of alienation. Classical Chinese poetry and philosophy emphasized clarity in language and taught reverence for tenacious artists who persist against odds. I was gaining discipline, but occasionally lost control and exploded.

One night, drunk, I got into a shouting match with Tree and hit her and cracked a rib. She swore that if I ever raised a hand again she would leave. Whatever self-respect I had found in the CCLM award went down the drain that night, and I would spend several more years rethinking my convictions, years of grief and guilt over harming everyone I had ever loved, from foster parents to my own daughter, and now my partner who had given up so much for me. Zen practice and feminist studies continued to clarify things, but I knew that I would overcome only through long and patient practice. It was time to rededicate myself to "studying thru," to "deepening the experience." In the midst of what was a kind of de facto small commune of literati, I extended that "almost religious commitment" to include a life of study, a commitment shared by my partner.

If self-respect allows me to feed my ego on a CCLM award while lacking the self-control to avoid terrorism in my own home, what the hell use is poetry, and what is the meaning of nonviolence? I turned to Confucius. "All wisdom is rooted in learning to call things by the right name." I never called Tree my wife; she was my partner. Together, we began working on establishing a true partnership. Only a coward resorts to violence in the home. The root cause is fear, and fear can be faced; it can be overcome when it is properly named. To be named, it must be faced unblinkingly. Humility before the task of running the press could save us when we were too egocentric to resolve personal conflicts. As Hakuin Zenji says, the work is part of the koan.

Women in America every day try to forgive the men who batter them, and they remain when they should rightly flee, often paying with their lives. All the odds against her, Tree stayed. Some part of me—that old redneck strain—wanted desperately to give

in to the bottle and to rage, jealousy, and self-hate, but Tree's friendship and the work of the press wouldn't permit that kind of self-indulgence. Tree made a dangerous decision, but one for which I am grateful every day. She wasn't the first woman to point out to me a tendency to present myself in the worst possible light so as to make it easy for people to reject me, thereby saving myself from the pain of being rejected by people I had learned to love. Of course it was true. But changing the behavioral patterns of thirty years is a tough act.

Duncan and Rothenberg called for an "ethno-poetics" of deep imagery in which—in Duncan's phrase—"all the old excluded orders must be included." I who had felt excluded every day of my life began to see in poetry a great communal sense of purpose, of vital purpose, in which I could participate fully, but only at the risk of utter self-exposure. Camus stressed the importance of "recapturing the two or three primary metaphors of a life." To stand utterly naked before the task of poetry became the work, the glue that held my life together.

For a while, we were a kind of anarchistic commune; there was talk of being several different presses so each could publish what he or she wanted. We finally settled on Copper Canyon Press, a name drawn not from Mexico, but as a moral, social, historical, and ecological reference to the Bingham Copper Mine near Salt Lake City, once a holy place to Northern Utes, now a huge, open-pit mine. We bought a house and moved the press into the basement and published our first book, a few poems by Gerald Costanzo, *Badlands,* in 1973. We all worked day jobs, then came home and worked all night. Through sheer manic tenacity, we published an astonishingly sane, quiet little book of poems, *The Berrypicker,* by Marianne Wolfe, also in 1973. And by the end of the year, W. M. Ransom's *Finding True North,* and the first section of my long poem *Heroes of the Teton Mythos.*

By the early spring of 1974, my life had become intolerable once again. I was not, at heart, communal. O'Daly had married and moved to San Francisco. Denver seemed cold, indifferent, and dead. I didn't know anyone. To call my boss at Sundial Distributors "a sexist, racist pig" would be a generous understatement. Devoted as I am to the first amendment of the Constitution, I could no longer face dirty movies day after day, could no longer bear to walk through huge stacks of pornographic magazines to get to my own work area. Tree and I talked about moving to the Northwest, perhaps to the Oregon or northern California coast. I finally quit my job.

Sam Hamill and Tree Swenson—"preparing to leave for Japan," 1988

Just as things looked desperate, we got an offer from Bill Ransom in Port Townsend. He was setting up a large summer poetry symposium for Centrum, a nonprofit arts organization just starting out. It would be useful, he thought, to have a resident press and editor. Centrum would provide housing for the press, but no money. Tree and I had talked about living in the country, about rejection of capital-intensive economics in favor of labor-intensive publishing, and about building a small house in the woods somewhere within reach of the Pacific. It was a risky proposition. Several small presses in the Northwest had already declined the offer as too risky. But in the spring of 1974, we set up shop in an old barnlike building at Fort Worden State Park in Port Townsend.

Here we would build that little house in the woods, and build a publishing program. My daughter would come to live with us. Tree would become my teacher and collaborator in the art of the book and publisher of Copper Canyon Press. I would build the house myself, and my life as a writer and as a man, remembering examples set by Sam and Freeda Hamill, by Lester Taylor, by all those who made art out

of "silence, exile, and cunning." Coming home, the real work is the koan.

BIBLIOGRAPHY

Poetry:

Heroes of the Teton Mythos, Copper Canyon, 1973.

Petroglyphs, Three Rivers, Carnegie-Mellon University, 1975.

The Calling Across Forever, Copper Canyon, 1976.

The Book of Elegiac Geography, Bookstore, 1978.

Triada, Copper Canyon, 1978.

animae, Copper Canyon, 1980.

Fatal Pleasure, Breitenbush, 1984.

The Nootka Rose, Breitenbush, 1987.

Passport, Broken Moon, 1988.

A Dragon in the Clouds, Broken Moon, 1989.

Mandala, Milkweed Editions, 1991.

Essays:

At Home in the World, Jawbone Press, 1980.

Basho's Ghost, Broken Moon, 1989.

A Poet's Work: The Other Side of Poetry, Broken Moon, 1990.

Translator:

The Lotus Lovers (from the Chinese), Coffee House, 1985.

Night Traveling (from the Chinese), Turkey Press, 1985.

The Same Sea in Us All (from the Estonian of Jaan Kaplinski), Breitenbush, 1985, reprinted in English, Collins Harvill, 1990.

The Art of Writing (Lu Chi's *Wen Fu*), Barbarian Press, Canada, 1986, revised edition, Milkweed Editions, 1991.

Catullus Redivivus (poems of Catullus), Blue Begonia, 1986.

Banished Immortal (poems of Li T'ai-po), White Pine, 1987.

The Wandering Border (from the Estonian of Jaan Kaplinski), Copper Canyon, 1987.

Facing the Snow (poems of Tu Fu), White Pine, 1988.

Narrow Road to the Interior (Basho's *Oku no hosomichi*), Shambhala, 1991.

Only Companion (poems from the Japanese), Shambhala, 1991.

The Infinite Moment (poems from ancient Greek), New Directions, 1992.

Editor:

Selected Poems of Thomas McGrath, Copper Canyon, 1988.

Collected Poems of Kay Boyle, Copper Canyon, 1991.

Death Song (posthumous poems of Thomas McGrath), Copper Canyon, 1991.

Contributor:

Geoffrey Gardner, editor, *For Rexroth,* Ark, 1980.

James Hepworth and Gregory McNamee, editors, *Resist Much, Obey Little: Some Notes on Edward Abbey,* Harbinger, 1985.

Ray Gonzales, editor, *Crossing the River,* Permanent Press, 1987.

Lex Runciman and Steven Sher, editors, *Northwest Variety,* Arrowhead, 1987.

Wood, McDonnell, editors, *Classics in World Literature,* Scott, Foresman, 1989.

Stephen Mitchell, editor, *The Enlightened Heart,* Harper & Row, 1989.

James McCorkle, editor, *Conversant Essays,* Wayne State University Press, 1990.

David Weiss, editor, *In the Act: Essays on the Poetry of Hayden Carruth,* Hobart and William Smith Colleges Press, 1990.

Helen Frost, editor, *Season of Dead Water,* Breitenbush, 1990.

Kent Johnson and Craig Paulenich, editors, *Beneath a Single Moon,* Shambhala, 1991.

Howard Junker, editor, *Roots and Branches,* Mercury House, 1991.

Audiotapes featuring Hamill's poetry include *Blue Moves* (Paul Herder, piano, and Michael Phillips, acoustic bass), Rainshadow, 1986; *Historical Romance* (music by Jon Brower, synthesizer), Rainshadow, 1987; *Watching the Waves* (featuring Christopher Yohmei Blasdel, shakuhachi), Rainshadow, 1989.

Videotapes featuring Hamill's work include *Passport* (music by Jon Brower, paintings by Galen Garwood), 1987, and *Poetvision Presents Sam Hamill,* Rohm & Haas, Philadelphia, 1988.

Contributor of poetry, translations, and essays to numerous periodicals, including *American Book Review, American Poetry Review, Chariton Review, Literary Review, Mid-West Quarterly, New Directions Annual, Northwest Review, The Paris Review, Parnassus, Ploughshares, Poetry East,* and *Tri-Quarterly.* Poems and essays have appeared in English and Japanese translation in the Japanese journals *Blue Jacket, Kyoto Journal, Fune,* and *Blue Canyon Press.*

Daryl Hine

1936-

Above the fireplace hangs a large oil painting of the seventeenth or eighteenth century, too uneven in execution to be a copy or a fake. It obscurely illustrates an episode from the eighth book of Ovid's *Metamorphoses:* the showing-up of Callisto, who is trying to hide her obvious and illicit pregnancy from her virginal mistress, Diana or Artemis. According to Sir James George Frazer, Callisto ("loveliest") is a pseudonym of Artemis, Apollo's sister, who had many guises. Like dreams, mythology shows the same entity in different rôles, victim and avenger, seducer and seduced. When Diana set her hounds on Callisto to punish her unchastity, Jove or Zeus, whose child the nymph bore, raised her to the heavens as the Great Bear, the first constellation I learned to recognize among those phosphorescent luminaries pasted on my nursery ceiling by my adoptive father, Fraser. In the celestial Rorschach test, the son of Jove and Callisto became the star Arcturus, guardian of the she-bear. My Mother's name was not Ursa Major, but Elsie May; my other mother's name I do not know. I shall distinguish them here by upper and lowercase initials, the capital distinguishing the elective Mother, while the natural one lurks in minuscule.

Briefly fostered eighteen years later by Mother Church, which my forebears would have called the Scarlet Woman, one text that entranced me was the prayer of the Latin Mass, so soon to be obsolete, that begins: *"Deus, qui human naturam mirabiliter formasti et mirabilius reformasti* (God, who wonderfully formed and more wonderfully reformed humankind)." Happy those for whom Callisto and Artemis, nature and grace, are the same! A more familiar, domestic myth pictures me at six months, naked, starveling, and alone, but seraphically smiling, in the midst of a great brass bed, not unlike the one I sleep in today (or tonight). Finding me there at the baby farm to which my mother had reluctantly relegated me, my Mother, childless at thirty-six, is said to have picked me up and refused to put me down during the subsequent formalities of adoption, which in Canada in 1936 may have been formidable. Certainly a few months later I was a plump and healthy child, secure enough perhaps even to cry. The adoption authorities then strove to match children ethnically to their adoptive

Daryl Hine at two years, Christina Lake, British Columbia

parents. So my Mother's descent was mere English, like my mother's, and both my fathers' Scots, Fraser being related, through his clairvoyant mother, to the eponymous explorer, if not, as I used to fancy, to the Fraser River itself. By Canadian standards at the time I was thus, like Arctophylax, the product of a mixed marriage.

Many children, even happy ones, invent an exotic parentage for themselves, as imagination stirs and the familiar palls; few are confronted with the appalling realization of their fantasies. Directly questioned, neither of my hitherto supposed parents—who remained after all my "real" parents in all but the biological sense—could have lied. This shocking

At about four years, Grand Forks, British Columbia

verification left me with a superstitious fear that anything I dreaded might be true—and worse, that anything I wished might, on coming true, prove to be what I dreaded.

It must seem strange that my younger brother, my memory of whose adoption when I was two prompted intimations of my own, plays no part in this memoir; all the more so in that it was a brother I sought from adolescence on, and finally found, not a parent. We could not have had less in common had we been genetically related.

Of my birth parents I was to learn no more for thirty years, and then only the most generic facts. They proved not, as I had always assumed, carefree teenagers but careless adults. My mother in her thirties had operated a "boarding-house" in Saskatchewan; my father, fifty-three at the time of my birth and a native of Glasgow, taught technical subjects at the local high school. So I come by my interest in poetic technique legitimately (or rather illegitimately) enough; and there have been moments of harried hospitality when I felt as if my home were a boarding-house. No one who has ever scanned the Canadian

prairies would question my nameless mother's next step, a migration to the maritime anonymity of British Columbia, where I was born, adopted, and brought up.

I can almost reconstruct the house I lived in till the age of five, in Grand Forks, a tiny town at the confluence of the Kettle and Granby Rivers in the arid interior of British Columbia. Built of wood (a material one could count on always in B.C.), this bungalow belonged to one of the pillars of Grand Forks, where the only other uprights, and the only shade, were provided by the great deciduous trees that lined the riverbanks. As principal of the sole school, Fraser joined the small Anglo, mostly Anglican, elite, the bank manager, dentist, doctor, veterinarian, and owner of the feed store, whose insipid children I was encouraged to play with. The "natives," even less indigenous than we, called themselves Doukhobors, or "sons of the spirit," an enthusiastic Russian sect settled upon us by that charismatic crackpot, Count Tolstoy. Excellent neighbours in their way (which, it was early emphasized to me, was not ours), they practiced three sectarian precepts, with two of which I was in wholehearted accord. They refused to send their children to secular state schools; from time to time they burnt down their own houses; and on occasion they paraded all together down the main (and only) street of town in what was tactfully called in my hearing "the altogether." I am not sure if this was the only parade in Grand Forks, but it was certainly the most popular, though clandestinely observed. Never permitted to watch it myself, but bundled off to the back of the house to get on with *The Water Babies* or *The Jungle Book*, I am told my Mother did not deign to spy, but sat out on the front porch and waved in a neighbourly way to such of the naked marchers as she knew by sight. If this seems hard to reconcile with her protective prudery towards me, it certainly illustrates her forthright contempt for hypocrisy and social subterfuge.

Since all children are criminals, if minor ones, well-brought-up children must be kept under more or less strict supervision. Custody backfired one afternoon when my baby-sitter, the twelve-year-old son of our Russian maid, Olga, unable to shake me off, took me to a nearby field and told me not to look while he approximated the beast with two backs atop a girl of his acquaintance. Naturally I peeked, puzzled but fascinated by this demonstration unaccompanied by any lecture. I had a long-standing, infantile crush on the boy, as on Prince Valiant and Mowgli, which makes it all the odder that I cannot remember his name, as I can his mother's. Later, at a birthday party of the bourgeoisie, I tried to expound something of the great if mysterious revelation to my overdressed coevals, rocking and weeping on a rocking horse because they would not listen.

Summers we removed to the shady shores of Christina Lake, not far from the dusty glare of Grand Forks, but another, better world. There my Father had built a log cabin, as he used to build me igloos during our bitter winters. This consisted of a solid, central, inner room, kitchen and parlour combined, surrounded by a screened sleeping porch perched over the dulcet waters of the lake as they lapped the pebbly shore, and open to the cool and fragrant breezes of the dense forest. There must have been many other summer houses on this not inconsiderable body of fresh water, but I don't remember any, only the impression that the precondition of paradise was that it be depopulated. Each June when we arrived in our clumsy black Chrysler, top-heavy with the essentials of summer, Elsie took us two boys down the unpaved, overgrown road a while whence we could hear (but were adjured to ignore) the rifle shots betokening Fraser's massacre of the pack rats that wintered in our summer retreat. Deploring, like any small child, the slaughter of small, furry animals I never saw, I was thrilled one year by the recovery from one of their nests of my Mother's wedding ring, missing all winter.

The days of childhood seem endless, but it is not easy to say now how one spent them. From my fourth year I read whatever came to hand, books, papers, and magazines, quick to recognize what was not yet for me and might never be, but I never saw a comic book, apart from the Sunday funnies that had started me on the precocious path to literacy, nor ever a children's book as such, unless the puerilities of Kingsley, Kipling, Defoe, Twain, and Thackeray could be so described. Permitted, even encouraged to browse *ad lib.* in the serendipitous home library, with no condition but the iron rule that still compels me today, that I must finish anything I began, I read with rapidly increasing speed and pleasure. By recognizing words rather than spelling out letters, I developed an analphabetic almost ideogrammatic knack for which I credit my poetic sense of the solid worth of words.

The last time I saw him shortly before his death in 1984, my Father told me a story I do not quite know how to take. Sagas of rescue from the lake I was familiar with, such as the time our red setter, Red, had saved Fraser's life when that normally strong swimmer suffered a cramp. Father, who had an experimental turn of mind, and was understandably jealous of all the attention I got from Elsie, tested some current theory by dropping me, at a tender age, into the water to see if I could swim naturally and

untaught. I sank as I should sink for years; this would not be the last time he had to rescue me—Red not being on the spot. This time he found me lying on the bottom, six feet or so deep, still and smiling, with my eyes wide open. He was well enough read, perhaps, to have plagiarized a similar story about Shelley, not that he would ever consciously lie.

Fraser's acceptance of a post as principal of a school on Lulu Island in the delta of his namesake river populated densely by "new Canadians" of every stripe from Sikh to Swede, involved our removal not only from the dry interior with its climatic extremes to the wet, temperate coast but from a straggling village to a small city laid out on the standard North American grid, with numbered streets and avenues: from paradise to suburbia. Less an adjunct of Vancouver than today, "New Westminister," as it was vulgarly miscalled, tumbled down the steep north bank of the wide and muddy Fraser. Our house on Eighth Avenue perched just above the declivity. Seeming larger than it was because of its generous proportions and deep verandas, my true childhood home squatted between a glorious but unkempt rose garden in front and a small but prolific orchard of apple, plum, and pear trees built for climbing in back. The large, rather dark rooms seemed to be furnished mostly by books and worn Turkey carpets, with an occasional solid, scuffed sofa or table. Heating through grates in the floor, though almost optional in the mild climate, emanated from a furnace burning that most British Columbian of fuels, sawdust, which, unlike oil and gas, smelled nice. This fragrant but never excessive central heating was augmented year round—for the summers were as damp and cool as the winters then—by a massive, black, wood-burning stove in the kitchen. In addition to the usual kitchen fixtures, this largest and most frequented room was furnished with a blackboard for me to draw and write on, and a card table holding poster paints, plasticine, the old Underwood on which I learned my letters, and the higgledy-piggledy products of my unchecked play—plays too, typescripts a few pages and a few minutes long of *Cinderella, Ali Baba, Hansel and Gretel,* and *Aladdin,* for puppets to perform at the public library. In a pantry off the kitchen Mother spent much of her time, when not reading the Book of the Month, confecting cakes and pies and other *friandises,* and listening to me; this was my true classroom, though I never did learn how to bake. By report an inspiring schoolmarm before her marriage, she found in me her favourite, and only, pupil.

Another comedown soon followed our descent to the coast. I entered Lord Kelvin Elementary

School, two blocks from home, not only already knowing how to read but doing so well enough that I was sometimes left to read to the restive class while teacher slipped away for a cigarette. Having taught myself to write on a typewriter, I saw no point either in the alphabet (QWE rather than ABC seemed the normal order of letters), until I came to consult a dictionary, or in the endless lessons in penmanship that, with cutting out and pasting, made every period latency period. With nothing as I thought to learn in elementary school, I learned nothing there; a muff at the MacLean's Method and busy work, I had nothing, the vestal faculty assured me, to look forward to but failure in adult life, which was all copperplate and collage. Yet more than one of these spinsters suggested that I be advanced—or "skipped"—a grade or two, doubtless in hopes of getting me out of their forties hairdos. Though Fraser and I were spared the mutual embarrassment of his presiding as principal over the trireme in which I toiled as galley slave, his position as an educationist both prejudiced him against academic acceleration and empowered him to enforce his views. It would prove traumatic for me,

he said, to be separated from my coevals; worse, unspecified evils would ensue from enforced contact with boys and girls one or two years my senior. In this, despite his experience and best intentions, I thought and still think he was mistaken. Although I played with other children, suggesting and scripting our games which surged from playground to back alley to garage, I preferred being with adults. I disliked being a child and wanted to be a grown-up, though mercifully ignorant of what growing up would entail. Thus I formed a strong one-sided attachment to a young soldier who manoeuvred with his mates in Moody Park near our house. Their presence was, with the redundant and halfhearted blackout and rationing, one of the few signs of World War II, which would date this infatuation to my tenth year or before. My unwitting inamorato may have been a decade older, and gave his name as Tommy, possibly a generic pseudonym. When I invited him to our house for dinner—was it not our duty to entertain the troops?—he first asked if my Mother was good-looking. I allowed that I thought so, but he saw through this paltering with truth and loyalty, and

On Mother's lap (left), with Father and younger brother, about 1941

declined, alleging "night work," an excuse that I in turn penetrated: not even his leer could spoil his cocky beauty.

In *Academic Festival Overtures* I rehearse a puberty muted by the fatal illness and death of my Mother, guilt, repression, and the first notes of my poetic vocation. At the same time glasses were prescribed for a myopia that had rather magnified than dimmed the boredom of school. What they did enlarge was the self-consciousness of an age of acute if abashed physicality. Specs still make one invisible to certain people in certain situations. The family catastrophe was signaled as in melodrama by a change of scene, a shift literally downhill from the shabby, cosy house of childhood to the cramped apartment of pubescence, which had however advantages in location, being two blocks in different directions from the public library where I spent so much of my adolescence, the home of my platonic friend, and the hospital where my Mother, a lifelong antipapist, languished in the care of nuns. Presently, as the course of her incurable cancer forbade further visits, after a long interval of suspended grief and apprehension, I learned of her death, as I would of my Father's nearly forty years later, on the telephone, henceforth always a two-edged instrument. Apartments were my lodgings for many years, but for me only a house is a home: a throwback perhaps to my genetic mother, the "boarding-house" keeper. It would be twenty years before I found another one, this one.

The new proximity of the library, where I had discovered with equal enlightenment the poetry and psychology shelves, more than compensated for my increased distance from junior high school. Bringing together from scattered elementary schools students of an age not merely awkward but unbalanced, Central, as it was evocatively called, while providing a broader selection of potential friends and enemies, necessitated busing, though not for racial ends. Alternatives to the bus, in the back of which romantically bad boys of thirteen and fourteen practised such manly vices as smoking and swearing, were walking and the bike. A romantic but far from bad boy I have called Don Wisdom saved me from the former, by offering me a lift on the latter at thirteen, thus lifting me from pedestrian sorrow onto another cycle.

One legacy of my Calvinist background, besides a work ethic which scorned mere ostentatious employment (inducing me for instance to read an improving book under the desk rather than listen to the twaddle up front), was a painful preponderance of guilt over shame—painful because, as Kingsley Amis might have put it before a prudish revision ruined his best poem, Shame stops when you pull up your pants,

Mother, Elsie, 1942

Guilt never lets you go. On her deathbed, my Mother filled me with enough sexual guilt to last a lifetime, leaving no room for mere social shame at the direction of my sexuality. Chaste, I saw nothing shocking or funny in the merely optative, which Don's disability rendered doubly doubtful. Though I continued to search, and encountered mutual love, briefly, in college, I did not form a lasting attachment till my thirtieth year.

I escaped from being teased as a cissy not so much as a "brain" but as a wit; bullies dreaded sarcasm like nothing else. Anyway I had nothing save my ineptitude at games to be reproached for. Not my proclivities but my loquacity risked ostracism and, worse, the loss of tacit opportunities. My perhaps pedantic penchant for putting things into words made it seem natural that my closest companion during these theoretical years was one with whom that was all one could put things into.

*At age thirteen, New Westminster,
British Columbia*

Words were more and more where things belonged. I always wondered how anyone could just live, without a poetic commentary. That I must have done so once makes those years memorable mostly for external circumstances. To the triple epiphany of puberty, death, and love supervened a superior revelation, poetry as the universal medium. The possibilities and peculiarities of language went far beyond any crude translation of my feelings and predicament. Plastic as the paints and clay I played with till I recognized my true talent, language early became for me an end not a means. A spontaneous impulse soon had for its expression recourse to imitation, the way we learn to speak or walk or do virtually anything. To find my models I paged through as much modern poetry as the New Westminster Public Library afforded, picking not the best (mine would be a most uncritical anthology), but what was best suited to my obscure purposes: Prufrock rubbed shoulders with Aurora Leigh, Pocahontas with Miniver Cheevy, and "The Making of Americans" went down with "The Wreck of the Deutschland." The obscurity resulting from such rapid, serial

mimicry, my inchoate feelings, and infatuation for language for its own sake shadowed my poetry until I learned enough cunning to feign clarity, or some interest in the illusion of content. *Le mot juste* was not *obscure* but *opaque.* I prefer a poem that is not a pushover, though the apparent simplicity of Wordsworth or Baudelaire hides much complexity. As my poems have grown clearer, they have grown rarer. Instead of pages of free verse such as I scrawled at thirteen and fourteen in which I strove to catch every fleeting phenomenon as on a sketch pad, I now write a metred poem every few weeks, an ephemeral prose diary, a few lines of whatever I am translating at the moment, and the occasional prose command performance like this. In high school I formed the indispensable habit of writing every day. Then I did so in the afternoon; today I do so in the morning.

My first publication, at fifteen, in *Contemporary Verse,* led to my being invited to join a small Vancouver writers' group that met fortnightly at its members' homes, to read and discuss each other's work. Hitherto, since my Mother's death, I had had no readers, except the odd curious librarian, and fewer critics, and while I needed the latter more than I wanted the former, I found out soon that for most modern poets these are the same. It took me longer to psych out that my first reader remained my ideal reader, and that my life's work is only a way of talking to her. Every poet is the Muse's son, Callisto's as well as Calliope's, Ursa Major's as much as Melpomene's. The Writers' Club was social as well as literary, so for the first time I had not just an audience and a sounding board, but the society of my peers. All older than I, some with children my age, the members treated me, most of the time, like another adult, overlooking my youth as they would a physical infirmity, like Don's. The heady sensation of having been suddenly advanced by several grades after all acted on me like an intoxicant.

Language engenders language. Careful never to acquire inerrant fluency in any but my own, intuiting that a poet is hobbled to his mother tongue, I found that other idioms, like other countries or a little infidelity, cast light upon the beauties of one's own. I met French early enough (one of the real superiorities of Canadian education) and pushed the acquaintance so rapidly that I was enfranchised of French poetry just when I needed it most. My next infatuation, and one I recommend to all young poets, was Latin, which comes as near to the fabulous universal grammar as any. As soon as I saw at once that one cannot begin to read Latin without a grasp of syntax, I was taken out of the introductory class and sent to the office of the principal, who taught me four years of Latin in one—another gratifying instance of acceleration. However, I could find no one to tutor me in Greek. I do not claim that the only good language is a dead language, but it is certainly the best kind to learn on one's own. Always a better reader than a speaker, quick to read sheet music which I could not play and pictures I could never paint, I absorbed the elements of Greek as greedily as once I had mastered the mysteries of English and with even less assistance. This time, dependent on the lexicon, I learned the alphabet in sequence.

One day when I was fifteen my Father caught me smoking, a habit acquired from Don Wisdom or Huckleberry Finn, and reading *Ulysses,* a notorious work I had picked up on my own, with the collusion of a sympathetic librarian. Considerably less indulgent, Fraser cut off my small allowance then and there. Uncertain which activity he disapproved of more, I saw no recourse but to get a part-time job. Though it would cut into my writing time, this may have been his purpose all along, as he mistrusted my scribbling more than tobacco or Molly Bloom. He later destroyed my forty-page pastiche of Joyce's last masterpiece, along with all my other juvenilia: three novellas, a number of plays, and innumerable, perfectly terrible poems finished and unfinished, in spotty typescript and illegible manuscript. Through the intercession of a member of the writer's group, I got a job as a page at the Vancouver Public Library, picturesquely and educationally situated between Chinatown and skid row. Getting there after school and on Saturdays required little less than an hour's ride on the interurban, a quaint and rickety form of rail transport I preferred to the bus, as for all the sway and rattle it was easier to read on it. It was also, I found, easy to read if not to write on the job, whether I was supposed to be fetching volumes from the reference stacks for impatient readers or snipping up newspapers for the clipping file. Regarding anything save my vocation as avocational or worse, I made a reprehensible employee. Most workers, unless their jobs and vocations coincide, goldbrick without the excuse of another talent. What strikes me is that I knew so early and with such absolute conviction what I could and would and must do. If nothing else (and I stole a liberal education from the bound volumes of literary reviews when I should have been clipping the *Christian Science Monitor),* the library where I worked for approximately three years afforded me the means of escape, in the form of savings that would pay my bus ticket across the continent. My native parsimony has stood me in good stead when it came, as it always comes, to buying my freedom. On graduation from high school with an effortless (and meaningless) gold

medal for academic excellence, I tacitly overrode my Father's wish that I take up a bursary at the University of British Columbia in favour of a full scholarship at McGill—not because it was a better university (it wasn't), just because it was farther away.

What wonder if I found "back East," as we beyond the Rockies called it, cosy? Montreal, though it might have been—and may still be—in a foreign country, reminded me of Grand Forks in everything but size and style of architecture. Both topographically named, instead of with the nostalgic nomenclature of the colonies, both sprawled upon the banks of great rivers and dominated by a modest royal mountain, enduring a manic-depressive climate of severe winters and sultry summers, each had its large, disaffected, foreign-speaking population, Doukhobor or French-Canadian, for Montreal before it became Montréal under the regulations of the language police was a linguistically divided city. Built of stone and brick, unlike the fly-by-night encampments of the far West, it gazed wistfully across the Atlantic rather than across the undefended border to our South for cultural inspiration. Many of my classmates returned from an almost mandatory year in England with absurdly posh accents and attitudes, yet not only the Francophone expected enlightenment from Paris. Even at exclusively English-speaking McGill, I picked up French from the night school of the city.

Much of what one remembers and experiences at the deepest level escapes the mesh of language; the more skilled the trawler, the better he knows the capacity of the net. Heat and cold, relative humidity, barometric pressure, atmosphere, light and dark and all the colours of the spectrum, sound, silence, with the subtle associations of scent, regulate our feelings and lives subliminally everyday. If everyone talks about the weather, it is not just because it is banal but because it is basic. However, only the syntactical life, including those actions which are mimetic of language, involving a subject, an object, and a verb, can be framed in words. The rest, irrelevant sense impressions we hardly notice at the time which may haunt us everlastingly, frustrate the most veracious and articulate annalist. I can barely describe let alone convey the exhilaration of those first crisp, vivid fall days in Montreal, with their flamboyant foliage and brilliant chill, both unknown back West. The tang of a Northern Spy will always represent the first taste of independence, as a bite of apple is said to have done for our genetic forebears. Yet while the eighteen-year-old's vistas seemed to expand, I rather enjoyed than otherwise the contraction of the days and the year towards my first Christmas without a Xmas tree.

Like a white dwarf McGill had long outlived a reputation still brilliant elsewhere, its afterlife more socially than academically stimulating. Wisely I forswore further formal study of my own language, but with misguided Anglophilia modelled my program on that called "Greats" at Oxford, honouring in classics and philosophy. Most of the classicists, recruited from the British Isles, combined a solid foundation in Latin and Greek with a stolid refusal to treat the immortal works of Aeschylus, Homer, and Thucydides as anything but repositories of grammatical anomalies like "the dative of hairpulling." Yielding to no one in my respect for grammar, I saw it always as a means rather than an end. Pedantry could not quite ruin these ancient monuments for me, fortunate in predating the ennoblement of such critical methods into theory.

The philosophy faculty, on the other hand, approached their subject with appropriate respect. There were no original thinkers in the philosophy department, no philosopher in residence, but ideas were taken as seriously as texts, whatever their provenance; and ideas held for me what may perhaps seem strange in a poet, an irresistible allure. As I worked through the texts of Western philosophy (and in those days we did not consider any other), I reeled like a hypochondriac through the symptoms of the *Physician's Desk Reference,* from system to system, in turn a realist, a nominalist, an idealist, a sceptic, and I don't know what, till I came up against the granite of Kant, whose first *Critique,* lovingly and rigorously expounded by the best and least pretentious of professors, stumped me as the summit of mental exertion. Newly inducted, following his death in 1951, into the pantheon, Wittgenstein provided both a spectacle of departmental disagreement instructive to the nascent playwright, and several one-liners worth pilfering. Moreover among philosophical graduate students, I made several friends at what was, as it is for most people, the age of friendship.

Of my most intense undergraduate friendship I have already written, and of its aftermath. *In and Out* relates in unrhymed anapaests the impetuous leap I made in my freshman year from the griddle of passion into a dubious *auto da fé.* My experience hitherto had split between hopeless romantic attachments and amicable hanky-panky. True promiscuity—intimacy with strangers—frightened and repelled me as much as the public places in which I heard it was usually initiated and often consummated; my choice of partners, restricted by the hang-ups of our culture, has always been confined to a small

circle. Chaste in thought, word, and deed during my months in the preconciliar church, as I had been for a rather longer period about the time of my Mother's death in 1949, I found myself liberated from longing at the primitive monastery where I spent most of my Catholic summer of '55, and where I wanted to stay. Ordered back to McGill to complete my degree, at which time there might be an opening in the choir, I felt my faith crumble before my vocation. Today my life remains monastic, regular, reclusive, and reasonably industrious, modelled rather on the Carthusians, whom I was prevented from joining only by their not yet having established a Charterhouse in North America, than on the rather too cenobitic Benedictines. Expelled from the cloister, I would soon be stranded by Vatican II, whose improvements seemed to me dubiously cosmetic and whose depredations devastating. Meanwhile love and reason had inveigled me away. Hyacinth Star, as I shall continue to call him, was also a Catholic, albeit a Jew. I don't think I had ever known one before Montreal, where I became a lifelong philosemite. One's preferred physical type, the icon of desire, appears not so much in conscious predilection as in the photographic record: a matter of height and build, colouring and cast of feature, as well as character and intelligence. Hyacinth's portrait and his tragic fate are sketched in *In and Out.*

There were other friendships, none so close. A poem in an undergraduate magazine led to my being asked to join the McGill Literary and Philosophical Society. Less serious and purposive than the Vancouver writers' circle, this was at last the society of my coevals. Amid the novelties of adult life, I noted the publication of my first pamphlet, *Five Poems,* in 1954, and the encouraging reviews it received. My second book, *The Carnal and the Crane,* coincided with the end of my affair with Hyacinth, and thus attracted less notice from its unhappy author than from the critics. I had in the next two years, in a close-knit if far-flung country on the verge of national puberty, an inoculation of fame, for which I have never ceased to be grateful. Hardly worth pursuing, and perhaps to be avoided almost at any cost, this echoic phenomenon makes fools of all but the best and simplest, as the grandmotherly adage about names and faces in public places warns us.

Besides an undemanding academic schedule and the demands of social and sentimental propaedeutics (a word gleefully lifted from Kant), not to mention all the poetry I was writing at a time when my style was forged (though my voice is idiosyncratic in the earliest scraps), I had a living to eke out.

With Antony Stern ("Hyacinth," left), Montreal, 1956

Scholarships covered room and board and tuition. For the luxuries indispensable to the most monastic *modus vivendi*, I had to work. My experience and bespectacled bookishness secured me a sinecure presiding over the periodical room of the university library. Libraries, which harboured the first universities, have played a role in my history unlike any other institution, but even that most perdurable of institutions, the Church of Rome, with its uneven record of librarianship, offered me labour as well as prayer. In my brief sojourn within its gates I performed, for purely spiritual recompense, domestic drudgery at a settlement house in the slums, stoop labour in the vegetable garden of a monastery, and a hurried translation of *L'expérience Bénédictine* for the same institution, which published it as "by a friend of Sweet Savior Priory." Translation also played a rôle in the jobs that, safe back in the world, I undertook next summer. The Hungarian refugees to whom I tried to teach English in 1956 proved puzzled pupils, perhaps because, like the other refugees at my Father's school on Lulu Island, whom I used to play at teaching, they were older than I. Hardly more successful was the translation of snippets of Aldrovandus, though I did get to work with a magnificently illustrated folio. As the zoologist who commisioned this knew no Latin and I knew next to no natural history, our joint addition to the store of human knowledge cannot have been impressive. Nor was my contribution to journalism, during my mercifully brief but instructive apprenticeship one summer at United Press International. In a noisy, unventilated sweatshop, from 4.00 p.m. till midnight, I, who had not read a newspaper since I grew big enough to hold a book, toiled at putting the raw news plucked from the teletype wires into journalese—a form of translation at which I signally failed, as one can only translate into one's native tongue. Too flowery, prolix, and grammatical, I was, after a short misadventure as a reporter, demoted to monitoring the wires themselves, harried between the conflicting claims of Ike's heart attack and the baseball scores. If I remember no other news that summer, I must have been still callow enough to believe nothing newsworthy unless it happened to me. This experiment disabused me of any illusions concerning the compatibility of journalism and literature, a confusion that bedevils more journalists than writers. Much pleasanter, if less remunerative, was a tour of Quebec at Hyacinth's side in pursuance of his summer job in market research. Conscientiously we took turns questioning provincial shopkeepers in our stilted French, and filling out the forms afterwards. Filling in the map from Lac Saint Jean to Trois Rivières, we slept together in country hotels crowded with rowdy commercial travelers and in rustic cabins beside rushing streams.

In my senior year the irreconcilable lures of life, art, and study became too much for me. Imagining two allegorical figures, one winsome and holding out a wreath of bays, the other grimly proffering a mortarboard, I put off my inevitable decision, even as I did everything to incline it to one side. Every lifeline diverges in directions no less crucial for being as a rule not quite deliberate. The first such option in my case, between life or death, was exercised in the cradle. I have never felt that I chose either my poetic or my affective vocation, indubitable as both appear to me; but having been chosen is equally decisive, as the Old Testament testifies. My choice of universities at eighteen in opposition to parental pressure indicated some exertion of will, and altered the course of my life again. The direction in which I drifted at twenty-one, deplored by all who claimed to know better, may have made less difference than the fuss at the time and my defiant stance suggested. Promised a job in the classics department if I returned from Oxbridge with another B.A., and promised another scholarship to get it, I spent the year writing plays, on classical themes, but in colloquial language. To complete my ruin, I saw and, on the Canadian Broadcasting Corporation, heard my efforts performed, an episode likely to turn the head of any closet dramatist. Not only modesty deterred me from taking the title role in my *Minotauromachy,* where as in a proleptic psychodrama, the part of Theseus was played by Hyacinth and that of Ariadne by his future widow. Attacked for blasphemy (a charge I thought obsolete), the play owed more to Cocteau than Genet. Backstage life brought me the flirtatious, gossipy camaraderie of the large, contentious, gifted family which I had always hankered after. Moreover, the seductive facility of dramatic writing, harkening back to the puppet plays of childhood, with its metrical mimesis of speech, tapped the lyrical vein that was my first fixation.

The gloomy yet brilliant winter of 1957–58, holed up in my first cramped apartment, on Prince Arthur, I produced a record number of brilliant but gloomy poems, which make up the best part of *The Devil's Picture Book.* Looking at these and all my early lyrics, I am most struck by their impersonality, in a genre and at an age that is ordinarily so confessional and egoistic. The first person singular hardly appears at all, so that in the poem or two where it does, it comes as a shock, functioning primarily as an indispensable introduction to the second: *I* as a precondition of *you,* the true subject and object of the composition. At the same time that my touted obscurity cleared up like an adolescent blemish, a formalism outmoded already in the late fifties established itself. I have never entertained the least illusion of conscious control over my manner of work—the matter being only slightly more optional. No more could I write free verse, not even the semimetrical rhapsodic lines of yesteryear. Little as I once admired certain poets, unrecognizable today, who changed their style with the decade and the mode, now I despise them. Whitman after all wrote as he did when such rambling verse was not only unchic but unpopular, unlike his faddish imitators. The bad and mediocre verse of any period reads all alike, as a glance at any anthology reveals; the exceptional strikes one as just that. Standoffish as well as off-putting in its obvious difficulty (for an effortless ease was rapidly becoming prevalent), my poetry passed out of fashion just as it came into its own. Though I should never lack for a publisher and a few appreciative critics, a wide readership would not be mine.

In addition to homegrown laurels, fate or fortune (so often difficult to tell apart) held out a grant from the Canada Foundation, precursor of the Canada Council, one of four awarded each year, with no strings attached. Still hesitant, while it was not quite too late to redeem my academic honour, I asked Northrop Frye, who had praised my early work and whose own works had meant much to me long before I met him, whether a career in classics scripted to the last iota subscript would be soul-destroying. His Delphic advice, that "only the soul can destroy the soul," encouraged me to take the step or leap which he, along with everybody else, must strongly disapprove. Contrary to all well-meaning common sense, I kept my own counsel. No degree I decreed better than a bad one, nor could I really see what use a B.A., or even two (the second English), was likely to prove; and against all odds I was right. Skipping my finals, I steamed abroad on a tiny Cunarder whose name, like the date of my departure in late May '58, I forget.

Before "Eurocentric" became a term of abuse, I looked toward the cradle not of my race but of my culture. However beguiling the native or exotic product, such achievements of Western civilization as perspective and the alphabet, printing and polyphony, still seem to me worthy of the respect of its heirs. In those days (and this is one of the real changes in my lifetime, like Vatican II and the begrudged emergence of black and gay pride), nearly no one crossed the Atlantic by air. Hyacinth and I once met the only person I ever did who had, Graham Greene, at the Montreal airport, on behalf of Hyacinth's father, psychoanalyst to the Catholic intelligentsia. Staggering off the plane, the author of *It's a Battlefield* and *England Made Me* assured us that he had drunk up the difference between first- and second-class fare in free spirits. Comparable economy as well as boredom on shipboard prompted widespread gluttony, for the price of drink was not included in tourist fare. One endured or enjoyed a week of tedium and indigestion in place of the hours of discomfort and anorexia separating affluent modern travelers from their goal.

I had, like most Canadian emigrés, three patrimonies to choose among, as in the memorable joke: American culture, British know-how, or French politics. Neighbourly and pervasive, the United States, which I had visited and had not been enthralled by, loomed too near for immediate interest, a glitzier, more anarchic Canada. Never one to befriend the people next door, I could not know that I would spend the better part of my life here in quasi-exile. England (not Britain, despite the prevalence of Scots in Canada), reverently referred to as the Motherland, exerted an ambiguous appeal which the drab, stale reality soon dispelled. Food, weather, morality, and manners better suited my notion of that other worker's paradise, the Soviet Union. Unprepared for

English rudeness and unschooled in the nuances of class accent of the most stratified society since the Forbidden City, I recoiled from a vaunted eccentricity masking hypocritical conformism. My few introductions notwithstanding, I was made to feel, as I was, a shabby stranger on brief sufferance in an exclusive club. As for that other exclusive enclave, the microcosm of English letters, though still twitching in pub and publishing house, it seemed at its last gasp; certainly insular poetry since the death of Dylan Thomas had become literally unspeakable. One explanation of the prevalent clannishness posited that most of the people I met not only knew one another from school, but were related by blood. Thus a son of Angela Thirkell sent me to see the grandson of Ada Leverson, somehow connected through Sir Edward Burne-Jones. It would take an anthropologist to straighten out the kinship patterns, but the effects of chronic inbreeding were everywhere patent.

Of France, my unsuspected future home, I had the briefest, beguiling glimpse one summer evening from the Pont d'Austerlitz on my way to Majorca. I rued the folly that had made me rent, sight unseen, a hovel on a Mediterranean island from that most plausible of confidence men, the friend of a friend of a friend. A pig in a poke (and what else is the world to ingenuous youth?) almost always turns out a bad bet, no matter how persuasive the pig. If earnestness entrapped me—the lure of a hideaway in which to write the *magnum opus* for which I felt I had the talent if not yet the title—duty (undiminished by the shenanigans of the last semester) kept me to my commitment. This crash course in the school of hard knocks, however padded, earned me the diploma of disillusionment. In my bijou residence on the barren hillside, I who had sometimes scribbled all night through the busy winter and spring dried up. Nothing inhibits inspiration more than subvention, though in an underwritten, overwritten life I have learned how to get around the gag order. That the muse hates most a well-made bed no one had told me, but then I knew no one familiar with her likes and dislikes. Our local Polyphemus, Robert Graves, wasn't talking, jealous and fickle in his suspicions of younger poets. Anyway, I suspect our muses had different temperaments if similar habits. Perhaps I alienated him by writing the masque for his sixty-fifth birthday, *The Tunnel of Love,* later broadcast on the BBC, and the only work completed that summer; its staggering silliness might have emphasized the generation gap, had silliness not been one of the hallmarks of his own work. Fragments of a novel and scraps of verse turn up in other notebooks. I have always, after such barren stretches when I remember writing

In Paris, 1959

nothing discovered that someone has been forging my script, sometimes with astonishing prolixity. This period of unproductive fieldwork produced, the following winter in a cold and rainy climate more conducive to literary composition, *The Prince of Darkness and Co.,* a novel very different from the one abandoned on the spot. The characters' actions are as obviously fictitious as their names, and the book, deemed too libelous to be published in England, where it was written and might have found a readier readership, is out of print.

My youthful infatuation with Paris, to which I returned as soon as I could, partook of that strange snobbery of place, whereby a mere address enhances so many people's self-importance. Other cities, like London and New York, boasted the same prestige, but though I had to live there, I would just as soon be buried in the country or even more ingloriously in the suburbs, had not my exile in Xanadu convinced me that cities are the proper habitat of the young.

Sexist propaganda notwithstanding, *le Paris* is masculine, albeit a transvestite. Unlike his Trojan namesake (no etymological connection), my Paris could not decide among beauty, wit, and wealth, but while bringing me little of the last, at least proved affordable. If during our three years' liaison I did not prove strictly faithful, indulging in brief flings with Venice, Vienna, Amsterdam, Warsaw, London, and Edinburgh commemorated in poetic *billets doux,* I always came back to the Seine reenamoured. To Paris I owe many of the lyrics in *The Wooden Horse,* as well (or ill) as a second unpublishable novel in which I discovered the fictional pitfalls of psychic cross-dressing as well as of the simpleminded substitution of the third person for the first. Proust's advice to Gide, "Never say I!" belies his compulsive practice. Pursuing *la recherche du temps perdu,* I often got stuck in *la porte étroite.*

Hastily written in Paris, *Polish Subtitles* details a month in Warsaw, where I rewrote the subtitles for a Jagielonic horse opera and was offered the English editorship of *Polonia,* a propaganda magazine, which I had just enough political savvy to decline. Also scripted in Paris, a series of radio plays—*The Power Failure, Defunctive Music, A Mutual Flame,* broadcast on the BBC Third Program and the CBC—eked out my second, modest Canada Council grant; here the challenge was to represent a whole action through one sense. Endlessly revised decades later, *Arrondissements* attempts to conjure up a pre-facelifted grey Paris not yet impassable to pedestrians, rationally and seductively organized in concentric circles round the Ile de la Cité.

These seem disproportionately eventful and memorable years in a life where memory has loomed larger than event. Many of my Parisian friends were artists, what the French call *artistes-peintres,* at a time when the fine arts contributed more to my ongoing education than what passed for French letters, a modish method of mirth control. The painstaking attachment of the artists I knew to representation suited my own old-fashioned practice and theory. My ally in both and guide to social circles neither infernal nor celestial *(ni tasses ni Vicomtesses)* was an American, Virgil Burnett (what else with such a name?), who remains my ideal illustrator. I had met him and his classicist wife Anne in the summer of 1958 at a party aboard a houseboat moored in the Seine opposite the Musée de l'Art Moderne, to which I was taken by the Canadian Bonnard, Joe Plaskett, a long-standing expatriate from my hometown. On frequent visits to Joe's studio, first on the Boulevard Saint Germain and later on the rue Pecquay in the Marais, I envied his ability to work for hour after hour, daubing away at his eternal still lifes while gabbing with guests, cooking, and listening to the radio. My own creative

concentration, demanding silence and solitude, hardly lasted till lunch. Visual artists appeared to me, as Rodin did to Rilke, like those fabulous persons who can indefinitely prolong the pleasure of coitus.

Friendships, uniquely human phenomena, involve concatenation; one leads to another, and I can more readily trace my acquaintance to a common source than my ancestry. Plaskett presented me to the affably acerbic master of *trompe l'oeil,* David Hill. Both painted my portrait, but Hill undertook my education in the arts, decorative and otherwise: the difference between porcelain and faience, silver and pewter, glass and crystal, woven' and embroidered fabrics. I cannot pretend I absorbed all this (I was not after all preparing for a career at Sotheby's), but I picked up enough not only to stiffen my sales resistance at the *marché aux puces* round which David led me after a long Sunday metro ride to the Porte de Clignancourt, and at more upscale and less rewarding antique emporia today, but to glimpse other material realms of marvellous workmanship equalling the most ingenious verbal intricacy. A diverting *cicerone* to out-of-the-way museums like the Palais de Soubise and the Hôtel du Chatelet, in which Paris, itself a vast and various museum, abounds, he illuminated architectural styles from flamboyant Gothic to the crushed tulip period, explaining how glass was painted and marble falsified, tricks of the trade at which he was adept. Much as music meant to me—and David was an unabashed amateur who, scorning the "canned music" of the gramophone, rattled off eighteenth- and nineteenth-century tunes on the old Pleyel in one of the warren of rooms he inhabited on the ground floor of a pavilion overlooked by the Paris Observatory—the plastic arts (strange label for one who did not have to be taught to abominate plastic) taught me more. Language for me has substance, weight, colour, and dimension, and not mere significance—though its significance is something I learned to slight at my peril. Words have a taste on the tongue and a smell in the nostrils, but above all they resound in the ear—a dimension that many modern poets ignore at their peril. Even the almost inaudibly accented words of French have their rhythm as well as their perfume, as in that supreme line of Baudelaire's which so often came to mind on Paris evenings: *Tu reclamais le soir: il descend, le voici.*

Though he liked to keep his friends in distinct compartments, like the separate waiting rooms of a pricey psychiatrist, David's kindness often belied his asperity, and had farther-reaching effects than even he could guess. So he summoned me in summer 1960 to meet the American poet James Merrill, whose *First Poems* I had been toting about in my compendious travelling library. The best poet I had met so far, and the best I was ever to know so well, he consolidated an influence, astral in effect, which began before we met. The industrious example of one who did not need to work impressed me as much as his Promethean generosity. In a life sustained largely by handouts, I did not always find it easy to follow the gospel injunction to take no thought for the morrow, what I should eat or what I should drink, topics of passing interest. It was David Hill who taught me that as long as one did "God's work"—strange phrase from a doctrinaire atheist, which needed no elucidation—the rest would follow, not fame and riches but one's daily bread. Once I was complaining that I had only enough funds to see me through the week. "That's that, then," said David, pouring cold tea from a lovely but cracked China pot into exquisite china cups without handles (a European refinement), "you'll just have to commit suicide!" Though, like Mallarmé, I have found the notion of suicide a comfort on sleepless nights—which were not so frequent then, at twenty-four—I never considered it seriously, and my *fou rire* restored my sanguine *nonchaloir* almost as well as the check that arrived next morning from some anthology.

Monastic, if not always so by intent, my years in Paris followed no regular rule. The two rôle models of whom I saw most were not just *célibataires* but celibate. David used to declare that he had given up sex at thirty, some years before, hinting that he had had much to give up; Joe was vaguer as to the nature and extent, if any, of his erotic experience. The human figure appeared seldom in Plaskett's work, the nude never, possibly because he did not really draw well enough, whereas Hill's superb technique delighted in depicting the male and female forms in all their anatomical splendour. It was while sitting for my portrait that I was introduced by accident to a further argument for celibacy in the form of a dark-browed Scot my age studying at the Sorbonne. His name, Sandy, was evidently not an adjectival sobriquet but an abbreviation of Alexander, the pseudonym of Paris. Far from "the best of men" (as that translates) however, he proved dry, abrasive, and insinuating. Nevertheless he shared, or divided, my life and sometimes my tiny seventh-floor flat on the Ile Saint Louis till we both left for different parts of North America. From the back of his Lambretta I saw rural France, hobbling round churches and chateaux and eating in delicious unstarred restaurants. In our economical hotel bed at night I never knew whether to expect the frozen North or a Caledonian volcano. Then after freezing me out all night, Sandy would abruptly pull over en route next day into a copse or

field to make love in the hay or bracken. Once he summoned me to London, where he was teaching at a summer language school, met my train, took me to the flat where I was staying in exchange for use of my *pied à terre* in Paris, only to announce that he was leaving for the weekend with a wet English friend whom I never met and of whose existence I only wished I had doubts. Perhaps it was this episode that cured me once and for all of jealousy.

Less of a letdown proved a visit to his family home in the Highlands, an ancient stone croft in a remote glen above a bleak loch among the treeless braes where the prickly heather furnished our bracken on those few occasions when Sandy could overcome his guilty ambivalence long enough. Here I saw for myself the extraordinary social mobility of my ancestors, the almost mediaeval meritocracy that took clever boys from the byre to the Bibliothèque Nationale, without apparent envy on the part of siblings, parental pride notwithstanding, or snobbish repudiation on the part of the paragon. It comes in part from the excellent, universal education: I met a shepherdess once who quoted Virgil. At the same time, brought up as I was in a blether of Burns and Scott and haggis and Hogmanay, of tartan plaid, Loch Lomond, and Harry Lauder, I marveled at the independent and austere yet free-spoken originals of our prim and straitlaced race. The Scots, like the Irish in America and perhaps all immigrants, undergo a sea change. No doubt my month in the real Scotland influenced my choice of dissertation topic a few years later: George Buchanan, the sixteenth-century Latin humanist whose career bore points of resemblance to Sandy's, though I doubt Buchanan ever wore a kilt in Paris, as Sandy occasionally did. His resorting to my country, like so many Scots, after showing me his, seemed the sole reciprocal arrangement in an unbalanced relationship.

"G od's work" did not require a *permis de travail* even in godless Paris. My only job there Virgil procured me. Maurice Darantière had been a famous printer, originally in Dijon, who had produced among other rare and beautiful books the first edition of *Ulysses*. About eighty, he now lay, whenever I saw him, on an iron cot behind a tapestry screen under a frescoed ceiling by Mignard or Lebrun on the *piano nobile* of the Hôtel Mansart-Sagonné, Paris house of the great architect of Versailles, amidst the bric-a-brac of a lifetime. On the floor below a carpenter's shop opened on the cobbled court; the worn, stone stairs were broad and shallow. To complete the Balzacian *mise en scène*, the aged but cheerful housekeeper, who let me in some minutes after I tapped at the double doors, the time it took to cross the vast salons, was called Madame de Sèze. Darantière took a fatherly interest in Virgil and had organized a show of his drawings. His project of an album of *fleurs vénéneuses,* to be researched at the Jardin des Plantes, versified by me, and illustrated by Virgil, never got beyond the *solanacea.* However, the old man advised us on the production of a limited edition of Virgil's etchings and my poems, *Heroics* (1960); the poems would reach a wider, North American readership in *The Wooden Horse* (1965). Informed of my difficult if not desperate straits, Darantière hired me to catalogue his library, a task he must have known exceeded my patience and competence as much as its completion exceeded his life expectancy. Privileged to browse through the priceless florilegia of corrected proofs and autographed letters from the likes of Claudel, Cocteau, and Valéry, written on thin blue paper in blue ink still exquisitely legible, it never occurred to me to pluck a few, as perhaps I was meant to, to preserve them from the Balzacian heirs. Dandified in silk ascot and dressing gown, as if expecting a more distinguished visitor than I, as indeed he was,

In Chicago, 1969

while awaiting death Darantière delivered himself of the gossip and wisdom of a long life. "Les grands ennuis," he used to pronounce, "ce sont le lire et le voyage." Not having as yet sampled all the other miseries of life, I could not argue. I have since come to see his point about travel, but reading, however tedious, remains my favourite pastime.

About, myself, to suffer a sea change, I did not see it coming till the last moment. There is an art in knowing when to leave, and one good time to leave is when your friends do. As it was, I tarried after Sandy took his kilt and guilt to Moosejaw or Medicine Hat. The Burnetts too were preparing to go to Chicago, where Anne had a job at the university of the same name. Next in the curriculum of the open university in which I had automatically enrolled upon dropping out of McGill, she recommended as finishing school New York. "The great Rome / Of those who lost or hated home," as one newcomer's *New Year Letter* termed it, proved nothing if not hospitable, if less indulgent to youthful poverty than Paris. But the city of light had begun to lose its lustre; return visits in 1965 and 1971 revealed it as noisier, more mephitic, and way beyond my means. Only Joe and David did not change, still patiently painting their modest masterpieces and living from hand to mouth.

If Paris had been a sidewalk café, with its casual contacts, leisure, and easygoing evasions, New York was like a noisy party. I rarely frequented cafés, and never felt at home at parties, especially those which one would be ashamed to leave alone. Many pages have been drafted in cafés; parties do not encourage composition. Crowded with names and faces, these months offer less story than inventory; but lists, the primary use of literacy, have little literary appeal. Nonetheless a catalogue, however partial, is indispensable at an exhibition. The most private parties became public showcases for the show-offs of conspicuous presumption. Seldom does one have the sense of a definable era as it unfolds. Perhaps what I experienced was less New York than the early sixties.

No place for reading and writing, a party presents an occasion for drinking and meeting people. I did more of both in my short stay in New York than at any other time. The scene recalled reduces to a few essential, crowded hours. Through the smoke which he puffs like a dragon, the corrugated mask of W. H. Auden glowers amiably. Asked to call him Wystan, I remark how we authors have degenerated from the standoffishness of initials to the cutoffs of nicknames. Equally Anglo-Saxon, ours do not suffer abbreviation. "You don't," he grumbles, as I light my second Gauloise of the evening, "smoke enough to make it worthwhile. Do you want to live forever? For your age you think too much about the past," he gainsays, "otherwise you might just be my successor." In view of the competition, literally, for some of it is present—James Merrill, my host and the only person I know to have been born in New York, listening with every symptom of interest to Robert Lowell or is it Kenneth Koch? John Ashbery swaying glassy-eyed beside Anthony Hecht, and John Hollander encyclopedically lecturing a bilingual (or forked-tongued) translator—I demur. Dreading a proposition, which I could never learn to handle, I breathe more easily and stop blushing as the great man, most of whose *obiter dicta* find their way into print if they are not there already, turns to a husky young hustler whose tattoos Marianne Moore, tiny in black tricorne and cloak, is also admiring, in that scientific spirit which informs her curious verse. Wystan, whose gruff courtliness twenty years in the rude new world have not effaced, introduces me to Miss Moore, but not to the stud. Instead he presents me to his publisher, with the suggestion that he become mine. An inveterate, well-meaning, and sometimes inspired matchmaker, he proves less successful than usual this time. "I only did it out of respect!" a soon-to-be superstar of stage and screen defends his homage to age and genius. I look round in vain for his dead-pan puppet master, the soup-can king, wondering how much respect my privately proclaimed status as heir presumptive will win me? Perhaps Wystan has conferred the same accolade on this young pretender, who is seven years my junior, for favours rendered? It would appear not, nor was I ever called to account. But there are many superior pretenders to respect here, some so famous that I thought they were dead. Anita Loos and Lotte Lenya, Peggy Guggenheim and Peggy Atwood, Jerome Robbins in animated dispute with Lincoln Kirstein look, though legendary, surprisingly alive. Rather less so, a clutch of art historians, honorary art historians, critics and dealers, some with bifurcated names (a blessedly rare distinction in this democratic land where immigrants are more likely to shorten their names than to augment them, but hyphenate their nationality), are debating the price of Bacon and Egg in illustration of Gresham's Law. A quieter if marginally sober group surrounds a portly, florid man whom I recognize from his oratorical style as Marius Bewley, whose complex and eccentric essays I had read when I was supposed to be shelving periodicals. A Leavisite from Saint Louis, he becomes more high table with each bourbon and branch. "The trouble with you, deah boy," he greets me in his Lady Bracknell voice, on next to no provocation or indeed acquaintance; but I am not to learn my shortcomings tonight from him. Semiaudible as the murmur of self-

criticism, Elizabeth Bishop, a fantastic poet disguised as an ordinary woman, peers up at me from the vicinity of my elbow, to emend, "Your problem is, you're too regular." While I am wondering if one can be too regular, or if I ought to worry about it at my age, a practicing polyglot known to the language police of the P.E.N. as Rosetta Stone emends, "En matière de métrique, meint sie." The party has shown no signs of breaking up since Wystan, who does everything like clockwork, left hours ago, at 9.30, and alone. Forever audible outside, the city does not sound like shutting down either.

I couldn't work there, hard as I did. What else was I to do with those mornings-after? My sole semblance of a job, reading and rejecting manuscripts for my sometime publisher, did not count as real work: nothing for which I was paid ever did. A handful of poems, some quite pretty, like pebbles picked up on some polluted beach, glint in my collection. Digging desperately but no deeper day by day into the sand of my unfinished fiction, "A Still, Salt Pool." I could not write convincing dialogue, create the supreme illusion of coherent character, or plot beyond short scenes and situations. Moreover not all the advice of Percy Lubbock and Marius Bewley, not all the novels I pondered, could help me do so. Prose clearly was not my forte, yet my handwriting, in the notebooks in which I drafted this drivel, reached the roundest, most ornamental legibility it would ever attain. Not since Majorca had I experienced such writer's block; rather, the writing flowed all too freely, but tasted brackish. Manhattan was an island, too, and the milieu in which I moved had all the disadvantages of a retirement village, though no one retires to New York, the Mecca of almost as many hopeless dreams as Hollywood. Perhaps I should have gone to Cambridge after all? Marius, who had, was not discouraging; nevertheless would I be given that rarest of surprises, a second chance? Anne Burnett urged me to apply to the graduate school of the University of Chicago, saying that it seemed a pity to have learned Latin and Greek as I had and not use them. As for my not being a graduate, Chicago had a tradition of bending the rules for exceptional cases. My growing bibliography helped, but nothing so much as the advocacy of the distinguished professor of classics. Alone among the chorus of dismay at my selling out to the academy, Auden observed that as the nature of our craft prevented a poet from writing poetry all the time, he needed a secondary occupation that would afford him a living. Since I had failed at prose fiction and showed no aptitude for the precarious practice of literary journalism by which Wystan himself made ends meet, he considered textual criticism more respectable than teaching creative writing (as he had done and I was doomed to do) or writing advertising copy. In any case, accepted on probation, I packed my steamer trunk with the meagre accumulation of a gypsy life, mostly books, for my third crucial displacement in five years.

"Don't you see anyone but other homosexuals?" a censorious Canadian visitor asked. Now some of my best friends, like her then, have always been heterosexual; but the point about New York was that one could, if one wished, associate exclusively with one's own kind. The babble of languages would have baffled even Rosetta Stone, and the ethnic and cultural variety and vitality showed me what this great country of theirs was all about. I received a further demonstration the week before my departure. Followed home by three hulking young male members of the proletariat and satirically propositioned, I was called upon to defend my honour in my front hall, possessed by a fury I hadn't known I possessed till physically attacked. Pummeling, slapping, scratching, kicking and—most effectively—kneeing them in their precious manhood, I broke all the Queensbery rules as if in revenge for what that brute had done to Oscar Wilde. More suddenly than they had struck, my assailants limped away. Not for a moment did I consider calling the police, who I felt sure would have sided with my assailants; but I did the next day see a doctor, not so much for my bruises and cracked ribs as for the anxiety, more severe and persistent than any physical assault, consequent upon such an uninhibited access of rage.

From a similar predicament a couple of years later on the waterfront that is one of Chicago's surprising amenities I extricated myself with more finesse. On a warm spring afternoon I had taken an apple and Aeschylus's *Choephoroi* down to the megaliths scattered along the lakeside to study for my upcoming Ph.D. preliminary examinations. A play a day stretched my Greek to the limit, while affording the innocent and ingenious amusement of a detective novel: Aristotle's prescriptions in *The Poetics,* the basis then of all work in the humanities at the University of Chicago, applied equally to the whodunit. Having discovered who did it (Orestes) and thrown my apple core in Lake Michigan, I mounted my one-speed bike and started back. Cycling had proved as hard to forget as Greek. Athwart my path I spotted a swarthy band, individually less bulky than the boys from the Bund, but more numerous. Their postures were obstructive but, despite the decade, they did not look as if they were holding a civil rights demonstration.

As I braked by pedalling backwards, they seized the handlebars and pushed the bike over onto the turf— their turf, I daresay. Remembering the advice of Mungo Park or somebody, to identify and address the leader, I had no trouble in picking him out: a slender, black youth, perhaps sixteen, of great beauty and aristocratic bearing, whose eyes blazed with generic hatred. Fingering the bicycle chain he had taken from the basket of my Raleigh, he taunted, "Ever been beat with a chain, honky?" I assured him, with respect, that that was not at all my thing, and asked what it was he really wanted? During this dialogue I kept trying to stare him in the eye as recommended in such half-remembered manuals as *Man-Eaters I Have Met* by Claude Baddeley; for he looked well on his way to becoming a Black Panther. "You got any money?" one of his more simpleminded sidekicks piped up, giving me my cue. Without missing a beat I said, "Sure, I had lots in my pocket but it fell out when you pushed me off the bike." I too had read Uncle Remus and knew about Br'er Rabbit. In seconds all seven were scrambling through the weeds and cinders while more quickly than thought I bestrode my battered vehicle and pedalled furiously away. "Come back!" they cried when they noticed my absence from their midst and the dearth of any plunder in the grass. At a safe distance, without ceasing to pedal, I called back, "Why?"

Such isolated incidents notwithstanding, I found Chicago an unexpectedly agreeable place to live, making up for what it lacked in cachet by a shabby kind of cosiness. Glimpsed first from the bus taking me to Montreal in '54 (there was no direct trans-Canada route at that time), it evoked the literary enormities of Studs Lonigan, Nelson Algren, and Saul Bellow, a fictional side that I never saw when I moved there ten years later, even in conversation with its creators. That there is this myth of what politicians like to call the "City of Chicago" has put it on the map of popular imagination; but one can live there or nearby as I have done for half my life now without encountering any corresponding reality. The charming park, dotted with neoclassical whited sepulchres that, to my perfervid eighteen-year-old imagination, masked imaginary horrors, turned into the harmless pleasure ground discernible through the curved window of my little corner flat. Yet I never walked there after dark, though I cut across it daily on my way to class.

Graduate school proved, in a phrase of my wartime childhood, a piece of cake: rich, striated, fattening, frosted with scholarships, and less crumby than advertised. I strongly recommend an intermission between the acts of higher education. I do not however suggest trying to sneak back into the auditorium after the intermission, as I did, without a ticket. If I found every step in the curriculum easier and pleasanter from elementary to postgraduate school, this owed as much to the sympathetic excellence of my preceptors as to the free choice of courses and ultimately of thesis topic I was allowed. I confined myself academically to verse, Greek, Latin, and French, which I continued to write in English. I even dallied with my undergraduate undoing, the theatre, when my translation of Euripides's *Alcestis,* disembodied on the CBC and BBC, took costumed flesh in an amateur production, and my radical revision of Tristan l'Hermite, *The Death of Seneca,* featured in a university arts festival. All the while I practised my vocation I was glad to add another string to my academic *violon d'Ingres.*

Everyone, however amative and domestic, should take a course in solitary survival, as an emotional Crusoe, till Friday comes along; previous experiments in cohabitation had given me a tolerance for my own company. At first I returned quarterly on the bus for a week's dip in the social whirlpool of New

Samuel Todes, Evanston, Illinois, 1980

York. My daily relations with the Burnetts soon became almost familial, while I made many acquaintances if few friends at the university. There were of course visitors, even intruders, but they seldom stayed long. After 1964, when I tried to catch up by reading the *Argonautica* at a giddy rate in Greek (the pace that pastiche deserves), and pondering the mysteries of *Un Coup de Dec N'abolira Jamais le Hasard* while weathering a sultry middle-American summer without an air conditioner, I estivated elsewhere. In '65 in Paris it rained everyday; but in '66 in Stonington, Connecticut, the weather stayed equable, though the folkways of that upscale seaside enclave might have been of more interest to a novelist like Mary McCarthy, whom I met there, than to a poet.

The hot, dry August of '67 at last I spent under a centenarian cedar on the lawn of my Father's bungalow in Langley, B.C., writing my dissertation on a rickety card table with the minuscule help of a duodecimo edition of George Buchanan's *Poemata.* Thirteen years absence on my part ensured not just a truce but a reconciliation. Retired now from teaching, my Father and stepmother devoted their Scottish skills to the garden that rampaged over an acre or more adjacent to their Dunroamin, not that they had ever roamed very far. Gardening, a hobby or art I never cottoned to, lacking the patience indispensable, bears a resemblance to education, but whether Fraser and Mary ever dreamed amid the alien cornflowers of the noxious weeds they had extirpated, the errant vines they had trained to grow upright, the growths they had dwarfed and the precocious blooms they had nipped in the bud, they didn't say. Fraser did grant a grudging approval to my thesis topic, because it was Scotch, albeit Latin, and because a doctorate (originally a teaching certificate) was one achievement he recognized. However when I asked about the trunk of juvenilia I had left behind in '54, he shrugged: lost, like the scribblings he now denied having burnt earlier.

When he in turn inquired if I intended to get married, I retorted that I was already engaged, to Sam. Having told him at fourteen of my proclivities, when they were nothing more, I had not credited his glib but kindly comment then, that it was just a phase. So, I pointed out, was the Ice Age. Sam he knew by name from my habit of smuggling him into the conversation à propos of anything: "Sam says that friendship is the only uniquely human form of association," "Sam believes not in God but in the divine," "Sam thinks that the soul is subject to the body, I think." Unable to speak to the absent beloved, one adopts the consolation of talking about him, as better than discretion. I had met Samuel

Judah Todes the previous August in New York, through mutual friends, of which we turned out to have a number, none of whom had thought to introduce us sooner. True, he was teaching philosophy at MIT, having completed a few years earlier his doctorate at Harvard with a thesis that even I could see was brilliant, original, and profound (if at times impenetrable) on *The Human Body as Subject of the World,* while I was tied to Chicago and my more particular and pedestrian dissertation. In fall '67 I should begin teaching there too, and for the better or worse part of two years we had to carry on our instantaneous commitment by long distance. Love at first sight the second sight of a quarter century has not dimmed. His name, the German genitive of "death," signifies "gratitude" in Hebrew.

Taking my degree in '67, I had just begun teaching at the University of Chicago when offered the editorship of *Poetry,* about the time Sam came to teach at Northwestern. This post, which has seemed to many the peak of my career, resembled rather an arid, treeless plateau. The drudgery of journalism is never done. No sooner had I chosen the poems for each monthly issue—say, thirty from the ten thousand unsolicited manuscripts received every month—and cajoled reviews from coy reviewers whose copy often had to be rewritten for grammar and coherence, read two sets of proofs and put, in professional jargon, the periodical to bed, than the whole gestation began all over again. A monthly magazine perpetually skirts trouble, and as with all pregnancies there were complications. The heights of Parnassus, snow-capped and serene, overlook treacherous lower slopes strewn with pitfalls, sheep, and goats. Our few first-rate contributors (barely a quorum in any generation, even if the numbers of the living now equalled what used to be called the majority) gave no trouble, submitted work flawless in every respect, and demanded nothing but their due; lesser lights were wont to blink and splutter.

If tractability diminished in proportion to talent, it reached vanishing point in some of the incumbents on the board with which Pegasus was lumbered. Founded in 1917, and thus venerable by Chicago standards, *Poetry* could not compete for conspicuous patronage with the symphony, the opera, the art institute and the zoo. Unlikely to attract civic-minded big spenders, the little magazine that never missed a deadline must settle for their poorer or stingier relations. Why *Poetry,* supported by subscriptions which hovered about nine thousand and the generosity of two or three Maecenases only nominally on board or not at all, needed a tutelary body, I failed to see. Founded long before my time by a more upward-

ly mobile editor, the board perpetuated itself, as useless as the House of Lords but less picturesque. Few of its splinters contributed more than a pittance, hardly enough to pay for their bubbly at the annual "Benefit"—whoever benefited, it was not the magazine. This excruciating shindig exhausted the fitful interest of most of the trustees, but a few, contrary to the unwritten rules of their trust, showered me with unsolicited poetic munificence. There were modest, helpful, generous, even literate and likable members of the overseers, of course, but the virtuous are everywhere outnumbered.

Perforce I met many poets by virtue of my awkward position. My predecessor had warned me that this job would not further my career; "You don't make friends in the White House," he wisely if rather grandiosely admonished me. *Poetry* was not the White House, but might be likened to some foreign consulate where visas were in great demand and short supply. Inept at logrolling, I never saw so much as a twig of that power with which detractors credited me—a myth, glamour, prestige, and flimflam. I did make some friends, mostly fair-weather, and many acquaintances among *die Meistersinger.* One paradox, subject like all rules to validating exceptions, soon became apparent: the better the poet, too often the less likable the person. This I had already noted in Majorca and New York, not to mention London. What I had not foreseen was the frequent amiability of poetasters whose works left me tepid. Not all of them, naturally, beguiled, any more than all of the greats or near greats chilled one's admiration with their egotistic self-adulation. On a tour of the States, John Betjeman remarked, shrewdly and, for an Englishman, humbly, how poetry flourished in the most unlikely climes.

In the fall of 1971 Sam and I, who had been living in a picturesque but cramped turn-of-the-century architect's studio near my office, moved to Evanston to be near his. The swing and sway of the (mostly) elevated train on which I commuted suffered me to read, and since that constituted much of my work I got a great deal done before I got to work. There I wrote rejection and (much more rarely) acceptance letters, put together the next issue (much my favourite task), and fudged up News Notes, the silly page to which I fear most of our readers turned first. The telephone, which the trustees favoured, and the mail, the contributors' chosen vehicle, did not alone prevent me from doing my own work, that is God's work, there. Where having always been as important to me as when to write, I worked for an hour or so every morning at home, primarily on translation, which can be put down and picked up like embroidery. A text does not go away as an idea may; besides how else could I use the dead languages so patiently and pleasantly acquired, which I should never get to teach? *The Homeric Hymns, Theocritus: Idylls and Epigrams,* and *Ovid's Heroines* represent the residue of those classical tastes and skills; I never had a practical use for my Ph.D., just as I never missed a B.A., but I thoroughly enjoyed earning it. My part-time teaching during and after my tenure at *Poetry* drew more upon my poetic reputation than my academic qualifications; though these may not have done me any harm, I doubt they did me any good.

A few months short of a decade on duty, I quit as editor in 1977. Long meditated yet impulsive, this gesture could not be termed wholly rational; but like all such leaps into the void, including my acceptance of the job in '68 when a well-meaning mentor at the University of Chicago warned me that I was "stepping off the academic escalator," it was to prove as right as it seemed irresistible. Free at last to do the work I in fact had never ceased to do, I completed two long poems (*Academic Festival Overtures, In and Out*) and any number of short ones (*Daylight Saving, Selected Poems, Postscripts*), two translations respectively from Greek and Latin (*Theocritus, Ovid's Heroines*), and an unpublished novel about my misadventures in PoBiz, "The Wastebasket." In this busy leisure I was, and am, sustained by my own meagre savings and earnings, teaching part-time at University of Chicago, University of Illinois (Chicago Circle), and Northwestern, Montreal, and various local libraries, where if I tired of the workshop format I delighted in the maturity of my students. I also read verse translations for Princeton University Press, and picked a number of prizewinners. Agreeable as all this was, with the odd royalty cheque, I should have starved but for Sam's generosity and financial acumen and subventions from the Ingram-Merrill Foundation, the Guggenheim Foundation, the Canada Council, and Canada's enlightened Public Lending Right whereby authors are paid for the circulation of their books in libraries. Finally the MacArthur Foundation in 1986 gave me enough money that I could stop worrying about it for five years. There may have been more deserving Fellows, but there can never have been a needier.

While I have lived here for twenty years, during the preceding thirty-five I must have had easily as many addresses. This ramshackle house in its overgrown plantation, built in 1908 (mediaeval by Evanston standards) round a massive brick fireplace as the clubhouse of a vanished golf course and added onto whimsically since, by us as well, is my habitat rather

"*With Samuel Todes (right),*" *Evanston, 1981*

than town or country. The paucity of local society has made me a semirecluse with a huge telephone bill; I remain a Canadian as much for the sake of critical detachment—residential alienation—as out of attachment to my native land, which anyone seeking a "kinder and gentler America" would do well to visit. Though the hearth has been superseded as traditional centre of every home by the kitchen, the focus of mine, for me, is my study, a smallish room whose sliding glass doors open on the tangled thicket that serves us for lawn and garden and grove. Itself a kitchen of sorts, walls lined floor to ceiling with staples and condiments, from Attic salt to modern MSG, this is where I stew and brew my wordy concoctions and distill my poetic spirits.

BIBLIOGRAPHY

Poetry:

Five Poems, Emblem Books, 1954.

The Carnal and the Crane, Contact Press, 1957.

The Devil's Picture Book, Abelard-Schuman, 1960.

Heroics: Five Poems, Grosswiller (France), 1961.

The Wooden Horse, Atheneum, 1965.

Minutes, Atheneum, 1968.

In and Out, privately printed, 1975, Knopf, 1989.

Resident Alien, Atheneum, 1975.

Daylight Saving, Atheneum, 1978.

Selected Poems, Oxford University Press (Toronto), 1980, Atheneum, 1981.

Academic Festival Overtures, Atheneum, 1985.

Postscripts, Knopf, 1991.

Translator:

The Homeric Hymns and the Battle of the Frogs and the Mice, Atheneum, 1972.

(And author of commentary) *Theocritus: Idylls and Epigrams,* Atheneum, 1982.

Ovid's Heroines, Yale University Press, 1991.

Other:

The Prince of Darkness & Co. (novel), Abelard-Schuman, 1961.

Polish Subtitles: Impressions from a Journey (nonfiction), Abelard-Schuman, 1962.

(Editor with Joseph Parisi) *The "Poetry" Anthology, 1912-1977,* Houghton, 1978.

Author of a play, "The Death of Seneca," produced in Chicago, 1968. Also author of two radio plays, "A Mutual Flame," 1961, and "Alcestis," 1972, both broadcast in the United Kingdom. Contributor of poems to the *New Yorker* and other magazines. Editor, *Poetry,* 1968-78.

Harold Horwood
1923-

The big, white bungalow overlooking the distant harbour of St. John's, Newfoundland, was designed for Barbados, with shady verandas and spreading eaves, but my grandfather, Captain John Horwood, liked the look of it, so he reproduced it on a windy hill where you could look out and see icebergs drifting by, instead of palm trees.

Here I had the great good luck to spend the first eight years of my life in an extended family that included, besides my brother and parents, grandparents, aunts, great-aunts, and visiting uncles and cousins literally by the dozen.

Captain John, who had sailed to fifteen foreign countries, was the unquestioned head of this clan, but there were strong-willed women, his wife Leah, his sister, Great-aunt Anne, and my own mother, Vina (who was always unhappy that she wasn't a man), to keep him within bounds. Captain John spent his retirement writing about the sea, progressing about the city's sidewalks meeting other VIPs for talk about politics, often with me trotting beside him, for though he was abrupt and impatient with adults, he was unfailingly gentle and patient with children, and I was undoubtedly his favourite grandchild—the eldest son of an eldest son of an eldest son, on whom the future of the world sat lightly.

When Captain John finally left that house in a teak box with silver handles, he still hadn't finished it. The sons and grandsons for whom he had planned its seven bedrooms had departed; the job was finally completed by my brother, Charles, after his marriage. My father, Andrew, at the age of ninety moved back there to spend the last months of his life and to die in the same room where his parents had died a generation before. Today my brother's grandchildren scamper through its corridors, and wonder at the name "Kalmia" in gold leaf above its door.

I have flashes of memory going back to infancy—my brother brought from the hospital in a blanket when I was a year-and-a-half old; my mother training me to use a pot, teaching me to hate the very sound of her voice; whipping my legs with a switch as I stood in a corner in disgrace for some misdeed; wheeling me around in a wicker stroller that I always believed was going to tip over and kill me; scolding

Harold Horwood, St. John's, Newfoundland, 1925

me for dressing in front of my grandmother beside the kitchen stove in winter. If there was any way to warp a child's attitudes toward the human body, Vina was well equipped to do it.

Vina was tone-deaf, but all the Horwoods believed they were musical—they played instruments in bands, sang in choirs, and sang around the piano at home. Even Captain John could sing. He also knew some old rhymes, including what may have been the original of the famous King William nursery rhyme:

> King William was King George's son,
> And many a gallant race he run.
> He loved the rich, he loved the poor,
> Had many a maid on a bar-room floor.

The sons he got in St. John's town
Are mariners bold of great renown.
They wear the cap, they wear the star,
So here's a toast to Billy the Tar.

Grandmother Leah and Great-aunt Anne would have been scandalized by such rhymes—"on a barroom floor indeed!"—and though Captain John generally cared little whom he scandalized, he saved his rhymes for such times as when the women had gone to church. He never did explain what the rhyme was about. It must have come down from his own grandfather's time when Prince William, afterwards King William IV, was in Newfoundland fathering illegitimate children who later became naval officers.

Horwoods lived in Carbonear from the middle of the eighteenth century, the first of them probably moving there from the Virginia colony, where a Horwood had been governor back in the time of Sir Walter Raleigh. They were all fishermen and shipbuilders from Devonshire, but were an established Carbonear clan by 1740. From Carbonear my great-grandfather Captain Hugh Horwood sailed to the icefields, seal hunting. When his ship was sunk by

Captain John Horwood, "head of the household" into which his grandson Harold was born, 1923

colliding ice floes, he and his crew walked ashore, and then around the coast for a hundred miles to Carbonear.

Here my great-grandmother Levinia Burke died in childbirth when her daughter Leah was ten years old. Here another great-grandmother, Mary Powell, owned what was perhaps the first sewing machine in Carbonear, and sewed suits for all-comers at one cent for each yard of seam.

Here my grandfather built his own schooner, the *Lord Kitchener,* in his backyard, with Leah as his only helper. He then sailed it to the Labrador fishery, but soon sold it and began sailing in the foreign trade. His wife's father, John Burke, taught him navigation, solid geometry, and spherical trigonometry. He was a captain in the international trade before the age of thirty.

Leah, who had lost two brothers at sea, insisted that her sons would not become sailors. When Andrew was old enough to work, she got him a job in a merchant's house at Carbonear. A year or two later he moved to St. John's to work for another merchant, and the rest of the family soon followed him. There Captain John got a job as a customs officer, and built his house on the edge of the little city, where the wild country, filled with lakes and woods, stretched off to the north and west. Among those lakes and woods my brother and I wandered with our aunt Lillian throughout all the years before we went to school.

We went boating among the islands of Mundy Pond, a mere quarter of a mile away, and saw much older boys swimming there as nude as young Greeks (nothing of the kind would be permitted to us—those were Irish kids, from a different social order). We brought home armloads of white water lilies that filled the house with perfume.

In those days the family ran a small dairy farm (five cows) as a sort of hobby or "sideline." Lillian ran the operation, while the rest of us helped with milking, taking the cows back and forth to pasture, and so on. Captain John also raised geese, including half-wild Canada geese that successfully drove all children from the field where they grazed.

Captain John was, of course, the great archetype of my childhood, and the principal model for Joshua Markady in my first novel, written twenty years after his death. His sister, my great-aunt Anne, served as model for another character in that novel; her death also became fiction, for she died very slowly and very peacefully while I sat on the edge of her bed and held her hand and her breathing slowed to a final halt.

Because Captain John loved children, he could teach them all sorts of things. My brother and I could read the clock and the compass, recite the names of the capes on a map of Newfoundland, and the number of sea miles in a degree of latitude long before we went to school. As a young man, Captain John had made two trips on sealing ships, then flatly refused ever to go again. Killing baby seals while they looked up at you with tears flowing from their eyes, crying for mercy was, he said, "beneath the level of human decency." He was saying this in the 1920s, forty years before humanitarians around the world took up the same cry.

Twenty years after his death I began a campaign to end the atrocity of the seal hunt. My first anti-sealing article, "Tragedy on the Whelping Ice," appeared in *Canadian Audubon* in the spring of 1960. I later wrote articles that were reprinted and translated around the world, calling for an end to the seal hunt. By 1965 there was an international clamour to stop the massacre. People with great gifts for visibility and publicity had joined what was at first a one-man campaign. It took more than a quarter of a century from the date of my first article until the sealing industry in Canada folded up. I am truly proud that this campaign was initiated in Newfoundland by a native Newfoundlander, not, as most people suppose, by Canadian mainlanders such as Brian Davies with their gifts for media manipulation. The fate of the seal hunt is a striking example of one man's moral influence reaching down through two generations and across the world to change the world's conscience.

As children, my brother and I spent time in Carbonear, where many of our extended family still lived, and on the St. John's waterfront, where our father was a department manager for a merchant, with free access to the small coastal ships that tied up at the docks, restlessly moving like horses at a hitching post, smelling of the sea and of far places, coming to us from Moreton's Harbour and Sagona and Isle aux Morts, filling us with the desire to wander, to stand on the bows of a ship as it rose and fell in the sea, hissing with foam. From as far back as I can remember I knew that some day I would sail, perhaps own my own ship. Later, when we began handling first boats and then ships, we seemed to know how to do it without being taught. Just visiting them in childhood, wandering through cabin and fo'c'sle and galley, somehow taught us all we needed to know. The sea was in our blood like the soil in the blood of a peasant.

I was eight years old when we went on our first real voyage—all the way to Canada on the SS *Nova Scotia,* and back on the SS *Fort St. George,* which operated between Liverpool, St. John's, Halifax, and Boston. It was not only our first time travelling on a

Father, Andrew Horwood, with sons Harold and Charles "at the house on Campbell Avenue which was being rebuilt after destruction in the fire of 1924"

real ship, but also our first time living on a real farm—one owned by our maternal grandparents at Gagetown, New Brunswick. There we milked cows, picked apples, tried to learn to swim in the "crick" which was part of the great St. John River, and helped to harvest hay on the "interval"—a long island in midstream.

I was spared school until the age of seven, when I started in grade one the same day my brother started in kindergarten. I could already read a bit, and Great-aunt Anne had taught me to write script by the same methods that had been passed down through generations of outport Newfoundlanders who never saw the inside of a school.

School was not just a rite of passage like circumcision among the Arabs or dream-fasting among Amerindians; it was a shock, not because of the teachers, some of whom were decent enough, but because of the children, who were barbarians, and had been raised that way. Those kids had been taught from birth that life was a jungle, and there was no supervision in playroom or playground. Outside the classroom the savages were left entirely to their own devices. I was plunged into this mob world at the age of eight in grade two, the year I also encountered a teacher who beat the children with strap and ruler every day.

Actually the threat was worse than the reality—the strapping was rarely severe—but there was always the threat of being sent to the principal, the dreadful Miss Fanny Badcock, for a *real* whipping, from which you'd come back with your eyes red and your hands swollen. For such ultimate crimes as playing hookey, even Fanny Badcock was insufficient. The burly male principal from the senior school would then be called in, bringing his strap with him, and the culprit would be hauled off to the office to be reduced to a blob of whimpering contrition.

Humane teachers somehow survived in the midst of this terrorism. In grade four we had a woman with a science degree who invited us back on Saturday mornings to do experiments with sprouting seeds and developing tadpoles. She never whipped anyone or sent anyone to Miss Badcock. But what she taught on Saturdays was not regarded as education—rather as extracurricular fun, like Boy Scouts.

Our lives hadn't changed much from the nineteenth century. We owned a car, a radio, a primitive washing machine, but looking back to the 1920s and '30s the thing that strikes me most forcefully is how little change there had been. My great-uncle caught and cured fish for a living, using gear that had been improved only a little since the Devon men had come to Newfoundland in the eighteenth century. Kids walked back and forth to school, often half an hour each way; most men walked to work; almost everyone walked to church, summoned by a chorus of bells that rang out over the city on Sunday mornings.

The odd miracle came fluttering by. We saw Charles Lindbergh fly over the city on his way to Paris, and I dreamed that I might one day fly a Gypsy Moth like the first small mail planes that flew off a lake in the city. The thought that I would one day fly nonstop to Vancouver, Moscow, Trinidad, and Baffin Land never once crossed my mind.

By grade six I was placing first in class, taking music lessons, winning the occasional sprint at track, but refusing to work at anything. I learned to read music, but rejected the swatting at the keyboard that might have made me a performer. I did badly in team sports, but made friends readily. A little later, some of those friendships would ripen into emotional affairs of great power and glory.

When I was "going on nine" the extended family split up. Mother, Father, and two kids moved off to the shell of a new bungalow on Oxen Pond Road—"in the woods" as Great-aunt Anne scornfully called it. It was a move to a wholly new world of myth, a plunge into raw nature, almost wilderness, woods and streams and lakes and ponds, a hill that looked a little like a mountain, a river that rose in the back country and ran off through distant lakes and steadies and over roaring waterfalls to the faraway sea. Here my brother and I became cowboys and pirates and naked Indians, learned to run barefoot, to build bowhouses, to climb trees, eventually to swim across full-sized lakes.

Here we returned to primitivism, to a shallow well with a hand pump, a privy instead of a toilet, a galvanized washing tub instead of a bath. I don't know when Andrew and Vina took baths—I suppose after we kids were asleep. Neither parent ever undressed in our presence, or touched us when we were naked.

A couple of years later, Andrew had installed an electric pumping system and a septic tank, and our sister, Ruth, was born. An accident? perhaps. They were practising "rhythm." Seven years after Ruth's birth, they slipped up again, Vina became pregnant and miscarried.

Hot water, a bathroom with a stove that would heat the air to 90° F, and a six-foot tub provided sybaritic luxury. For some reason, Vina never realized the sinfulness of such bathing, or the fact that it usually included masturbation, which I had discovered about then. In other respects she was still Spartan, sometimes whipped us with a piece of cord, and even persuaded Andrew to keep a two-foot leather strap for discipline. I can't remember that he ever used it, and in any case it soon disappeared because I cut it into small pieces and threw it in the garbage. Perhaps because his own father had never whipped him, Andrew was quite unsuccessful at child abuse, but he was equally unable to love a child, or win a child's love. Love—giving and receiving—first came to me from outside the family.

My brother and I were still milking a cow each, morning and evening, and now began to share in the "milk money" as profits from the dairy were called. Out of those profits my brother and I bought a light horse, and since Andrew was now manager of a fuel company, it was easy to get work for the horse, making small deliveries of coal to customers who bought by the quarter ton or less. Out of the proceeds came the horse's feed and the driver's wage, and the surplus made the two of us inordinately rich in the midst of the Great Depression.

I bought my first bicycle, cowboy hat, accordion, fancy clothes, and my first pair of skis out of the horse's earnings. I never learned to ride or drive a horse properly, but on the bicycle I became a rider of the purple sage, almost a creature with wings. Except for the short time I was in politics and journalism and fancied myself a man of affairs, I have ridden a bicycle ever since. My son Andrew and I go for ten-mile rides on our mountain bikes even now. I was one of the first St. John's boys on skis, followed by a chorus of barking dogs who had never seen such a novelty.

On a corner a quarter of a mile from our house was Linegar's Store, a dingy little place with a wooden counter where a wonderful old Irish woman sold peppermint knobs, Hershey bells, and drugs. Here, when we were old enough to be tempted, we bought our first Irish Porter, sold in eight-ounce bottles, just right for apprentice drinkers. Here too we bought our first cigarettes one at a time from an open pack of Flags. Cash was so scarce that even grown men often bought cigarettes singly.

Smoking was not only sinful, but also bad for your health, and this was well known even in the thirties. Cigarettes were "coffin nails." People didn't get lung cancer, but they got "smoker's cough" and died of it anyway. Andrew told me, as soon as I was old enough to know where babies come from, that the babies of smokers were born underweight and sickly. Despite such knowledge, everyone got hooked, me included. We didn't really believe that smoking was all that deadly until the hard statistical evidence confirmed all the horror stories during the 1950s. Old Mrs. Linegar was a darling, the most innocent of drug peddlers. The age of innocence was still with us.

What sex education we got was sketchy, fallacious, and harmful. Vina warned us against the wickedness of girls and the dangers of syphilis, but didn't even know the meaning of the word "fuck" when her younger son brought it home from school. She asked Andrew, who was flabbergasted.

"You actually don't know? It's . . . well . . . it's like fornicate."

"Oh . . ." Long pause. "I won't let him say it again."

"Of course not."

Andrew wasn't as bad as Vina. He saw nothing wrong when we swam or played in the nude, and said so, though Vina thought it shocking and indecent. But if it actually came to talking about sex, he was as tongue-tied as she. When I complained that the rooster was attacking the hens he tried to explain: "That's how the chickens get into the eggs. If he

didn't do that there wouldn't be any germ of life in the egg."

All very well, but what I saw the rooster do was jump on the hen and grab her comb in his beak, often drawing blood. So this was the sex act. I knew what bulls did to cows because I saw it happening, but I was well along in adulthood before I realized that birds copulated like mammals with organs near their tails. I had always assumed that sex in birds was a matter of beaks and combs.

Despite Captain John's writing, and the few history books that he treasured, you could hardly call us a literary family. Our first taste of imaginative writing came from the daily press—Thornton W. Burgess's "Bedtime Stories." Later there was "Little Bennie," also in the daily press, and the smorgasbord of delights offered by the *Family Herald and Weekly Star*, to which we turned for its page of children's

"The three Horwood kids: Ruth, age three, Charlie, eleven, Harold, twelve, at Freshwater Valley, near St. John's," 1936

stories and easy-to-solve puzzles. Aunt Lillian worked its embroidery patterns. Andrew read its lines of music, whistling the tunes from its page of "Old Favourites." A weekly magazine issued on newsprint, it appealed to almost every rural and small-town family in British North America, and influenced a whole generation of Canadians and Newfoundlanders. Everyone from Harold Innes to Harold Horwood grew up on it.

There was also *The Pocket University,* a thirty-six-volume anthology of fiction, poetry, plays, essays, and biography sold to Andrew by some door-to-door salesman. Andrew scarcely touched it himself, but his two young sons read it to tatters. Here I encountered Thackeray's *Book of Snobs,* Kipling's *Man Who Would Be King,* and the full range of American popular writers from Ben Franklin to Bret Harte. Prejudiced by this early reading, I have never gotten rid of my preference for American over English writers.

Later Andrew supplied us with an eight-volume illustrated dictionary and a twelve-volume encyclopedia that we devoured from cover to cover. And with those came, free, a *Complete Works of Shakespeare,* on onionskin paper in double columns—forbiddingly hard to read, yet it was here, not in school, that I encountered Lady Macbeth, grand and villainous, the incredibly silly Othello, and the senile Lear; here, too, my first taste of pornography, *Venus and Adonis* and *The Passionate Pilgrim;* and the dark splendours of the sonnets.

No one in our family had ever read the classics. It was virtually an accident, like a stroke of providence, that I encountered at home some of the greatest things in the English language. By the age of fourteen I was lost forever to the abandoned life of the poet, and was purchasing, with money earned by milking cows, such things as the poetical works of Milton, and Gibbon's *Decline and Fall.*

A little later I had the good luck to encounter one teacher who did something useful for me. Bill Blackwood, an English scholar from Edinburgh University, loved the language. He taught me not to split infinitives, demonstrated the utter vulgarity of a dangling participle, the absurdity of a floating adverb, and the contemptible illogic of such phrases as "under the circumstances." I still squirm when TV announcers use "hopefully" in place of "we hope that," or, even worsely, tell us that some superstar once worked surprisingly in a strip joint.

In our late teens, my brother and I began reading literature that was almost contemporary— plays by Shaw and Ibsen, novels by D. H. Lawrence, Steinbeck, Joyce, the essays of Aldous Huxley, modern French writers in translation. Before long I was

discovering such rarities as Sacheverell Sitwell's wonderful, rambling meditations on European art, and the prose works of Dylan Thomas. My brother and I even read Henry Miller before anything he had written was in print in North America.

In high school we had a science lab, quite well equipped, and a real library, with travel books and books on science, including one that discussed models of the atom by Rutherford, Neils Bohr, Erwin Schrödinger, and others. I still marvel that a Newfoundland high school in the 1930s possessed a book discussing the Copenhagen interpretation of the quantum theory. But there it was. I haunted that library after class, even contrived to be left behind, sometimes, after all the teachers had left and the school was supposed to be empty at five in the afternoon.

Captain John died in the autumn of 1938. The last summer of his life he made a trip to the fishing rooms of Labrador. The women of the household all called him an old fool and suggested he was senile, but he did it anyway, then came home and died quietly in bed of kidney failure. Somehow, he had communicated his strength and self-confidence to me. Long before he died I had chosen writing as my life work and had begun to endure from my family the same disbelief, belittlement, and incomprehension that he had endured. The only member of the family who believed writing could be anything but a spare-time hobby was my younger brother. Long before I actually encountered it, I was prepared for the discouragements of publishers and editors and the ignorance and stupidity of critics. After being right when my father and mother and all my uncles and aunts and cousins were dead wrong, it wasn't difficult to believe that I was right when some publisher's hack or semiliterate reviewer failed to understand what I had written.

The year I was seventeen we moved "out of the woods" back to a new house that Andrew planned and built in St. John's. My brother and I worked full-time building it. It was spacious, with five bedrooms, two bathrooms, dining room, sitting room, and library. The library started out as a fair-sized room that would have housed a couple of thousand books, desks, typewriters, and so on, but was soon reduced to a cubbyhole because Vina decided she needed a "sewing room." So most of the library was partitioned off, leaving a small built-in desk with drawers, a couple of bookshelves above, and some other shelves on the wall. In this cubbyhole my father worked at radio broadcasts, and I wrote the first sketchy draught of the book that, forty years later, would become my third novel, *Remembering Summer*. It is a simple fact that I never at any point abandoned that book, but went back to it again and again over half a lifetime, adding, deleting, rewriting, rearranging. It became the only true Canadian "novel of the sixties" with much of what seemed to be the peculiar ethos of the sixties in it, but even when it was finally published in 1987 it contained long passages that I had written just at the close of the Second World War.

My first romantic relationships, in my middle and late teens, were with boys of my own age, or somewhat younger. I sometimes walked home with a girl, and talked with her on levels of surprising intimacy, but the deep emotional relationships were with boys. My first sexual affairs were with women somewhat older than myself—but these came later, and, later again, with women of my own age. It all seems common enough, I suppose, but it was not common at the time: it was an emotional adventure of apocalyptic intensity, a series of love affairs involving the whole spirit, bringing both great happiness and great suffering. Perhaps because of the puritan background, a sexually segregated school, a mother who preached the evils of the female sex, I did not develop mature relationships early; my whole development toward maturity had to be a revolt against everything that I had been taught.

The people most important to me in early adulthood were Janet and Irving Fogwill. Insofar as I had a master and teacher who shaped the direction of my life, it was Irving. He was twenty-two years my senior, but not a father figure—rather the senior sorcerer. He and his wife, Janet, were the only people in Newfoundland at that time in touch with fully contemporary literature. Irving introduced me to the work of Djuna Barnes (who influenced me profoundly) and the work of Henry Miller (who perhaps influenced me even more) at a time when virtually nobody in Newfoundland or Canada had heard of either of them. Barnes we secured in print; Miller's *Tropic of Cancer* we could get only in mimeograph. But soon we were buying by mail order from *The Gotham Book Mart*, and subscribing to such journals as *The Briarcliff Quarterly*, where we encountered the poetry of Saint-John Perse, and—at about the same time—the weird and wonderful anti-books of Kenneth Patchen. Fogwill was a poet and short-story writer. In his whole lifetime he produced only two small books, but he was the direct ancestor of the Newfoundland renaissance, which became, in the 1970s, such a major event in the Canadian renaissance of the same period. In addition to avant garde literature, Fogwill read such novels as *City of Night*,

The World of O, Last Exit to Brooklyn, The Man with the Golden Arm as they were published. I never read any of those books. On the other hand, I read the full, extended text of *The Golden Bough*, and all the translated works of Pierre Tielhard de Chardin. I even went to the length of reading some of his essays in French, a language I could only "spell out" with difficulty. I read some of the literature of Buddhism, Taoism and Vedanta. I was very early departing from the tastes of my teacher. Lastly, I read everything written by Faulkner, and to back it up everything written by Conrad, who became my connection to the past of the English novel. Except for Melville, and a few isolated works by Hawthorne, Henry James, and Samuel Butler, I never read the novels of the nineteenth century. In recent years I've looked at them and judged them unreadable.

The other great friend of my youth was a man named Charlie Halfyard, an intellectual who read philosophy and theology, and was so frail as to be virtually an invalid with a leaky heart valve. Through Halfyard I encountered the English philosophers, the Greek dramatists, and even undertook (briefly) to *read* Greek, but I never went far with this—the last thing I wanted to be was a scholar. Halfyard died suddenly a few days before the destruction of Hiroshima.

Meanwhile, again through Fogwill's influence, I had become a union organizer. I first organized and led a union of unskilled labourers at St. John's (the General Workers' Union) which achieved great success, later unions of truck drivers, painters, fish-plant workers, and others. Between the years 1945 and 1948 I was the *enfant terrible* of the Newfoundland labour movement, and was employed successively by the Newfoundland Federation of Labour and the Canadian Congress of Labour as an organizer. I helped to lead a number of successful strikes, and, through the labour movement, got involved in politics.

In 1945 I was campaign manager for the St. John's District Labour Party, but by the end of 1946 I was one of the founders of the Newfoundland Confederate Association—the organization led by Joey Smallwood that brought Newfoundland into federal union with Canada. Newfoundland at that time was an independent British Dominion with its constitution in a temporary state of suspension, and its government in the hands of an appointed commission. Union with Canada had been tried twice before and soundly defeated, and seemed a very unlikely future. But Smallwood was a political genius, and that made all the difference.

With members of the executive board of the General Workers' Union, which the author organized in 1945–46. Standing: Jack Fitzgerald, Clarence Harding, Angus Caines; seated: Jack White, Jack Lewis, Harold Horwood, Charles Horwood, Harry Constantine.

When he came to town looking for votes in 1946 I was at the peak of my career as a labour leader—chairman of the biggest local union in St. John's, and also of the crafts' council that controlled the whole building industry, then getting into its postwar boom. He struck me at once as a winner, and we joined forces. Four members of my executive board, and six other labour leaders came with me.

It took us two years, and many political twists and turns, to con Newfoundland into confederation with Canada. We had to fight a campaign in which the real issues were obscured by a split between people of English and Irish descent, between Catholics and Protestants, between the back country and the city, and so on. We had absolutely no money to run such a campaign, and no way of raising it in Newfoundland, where all the wealthy people were against us, but we had a couple of excellent contacts inside the Liberal Party of Canada, and they, in turn, put us in touch with their own best patrons. And that was how the Canadian liquor corporations came to finance a political campaign in Newfoundland. They

coughed up some quarter of a million dollars—a lot of money in the 1940s—and permitted us to put on a razzle-dazzle campaign that just barely turned the trick. We won by seven thousand votes, and Newfoundland became the tenth province of Canada.

I then went to Labrador and won a seat in the Newfoundland legislature, but I had neither the wish to continue with politics nor the ability to remain loyal to Smallwood. After a little more than two years I went back to private life while he went on to become the most successful political leader Newfoundland had ever produced. I got out of politics what I went looking for—experience. I never did write the political novel that I briefly considered, but forty years later I wrote a highly successful biography of Smallwood.

My travels in Labrador were of even greater value to me than my experience in politics. I travelled the subarctic coast by boat in summer, by mail plane and dog team in winter. I met Indians and Inuit as well as fishermen and trappers. The Indians taught me to use a canoe, the Inuit to hunt seals and caribou. I even learned to sail my own ship, the forty-five-foot ocean-going auxiliary sloop *Fort Amadjuak,* formerly owned by the Hudson Bay Company. Above all, though, I learned something of the lives of people who existed on what they could wring directly from a barren coastline and an unfriendly sea, with a cash income of less than five hundred dollars a year per family. Here were true third-world people in North America. My first two novels came directly out of that experience, one of them set in Newfoundland, and one in Labrador.

My principal service to the people of Labrador was the organization of a new division in the civil service—the Division of Northern Labrador Services. It became responsible for the people of the north in many fields: a supply of trade goods at reasonable prices, assistance to fisheries, public housing, education, health, and welfare. Over the course of a quarter of a century the division gradually transformed the living conditions in northern Labrador from that of the Stone Age to that of twentieth-century Canada. Having successfully launched the

"*Self-portrait—at the beginning of my career as novelist and nonfiction writer,*" *1962*

division, I walked away from politics and applied for a job as a reporter on Newfoundland's largest daily newspaper. The next step in my education as a writer was to be the experience of meeting publishing deadlines five days a week.

I began by reporting the legislature, and since I was still friendly with Premier Smallwood, he suggested I do a daily column of political chit-chat. That was how "Political Notebook" got its start, but within a year or so it had developed into the most devastating column of political criticism ever published in Newfoundland. Not just criticism, I went in for investigative reporting, too, and learned the ins and outs of every scheme by which the government kept its party coffers full and its rascals in power. Smallwood not only quit speaking to me, he threatened publicly to have me thrown into jail. He and his ministers sued the *Telegram* for libel on several occasions. At one point all thirteen members of the government sued us collectively. But we stuck to our allegations and brazened it out and fought our court battles and won—not once in six years of being the government's principal opposition did the *Telegram* have to back down. In our last and greatest battle over the liquor trade and organized prostitution we were found not guilty and awarded costs by the Supreme Court.

It was great stuff for circulation. The *Telegram* quickly eclipsed all other papers in the province, tripled its size, doubled and redoubled its sales, bought a new press, began computer typesetting. And then, suddenly, I was tired of the whole thing. I was now editor of the editorial page, and I could see the unpleasant gleam of the gold watch forty years down the road.

I had discovered by now that I couldn't combine journalism—full-time, staff journalism—with other writing. I wrote a few paragraphs from time to time, and these grew to a few pages of what would eventually be my first novel, but it was obvious that I would never finish it unless I quit everything else and worked at it full-time. Then Farley Mowat arrived on his first visit to St. John's, and told me I was wasting my time working for a provincial daily. Late in the summer of 1958 I drove to Stephenville Airport and met Mowat for a camping and drinking tour of Newfoundland. The day the tour ended I handed in my resignation. Mowat and I have been the closest of friends ever since. We write books in each other's houses, read each other's first draughts, criticise and edit each other's manuscripts. He tried to teach me to manipulate the media, and I tried to teach him to sail a boat; neither of us was too successful.

I sold my cruiser, my skiff, and my outboard motors, took my tent and canoe and headed into the backwoods. I returned with a beard, a few pages of notes, and the conviction that I had to get out of the city to as quiet and primitive a place as I could find. I began searching for what turned out to be Beachy Cove.

While working at the *Evening Telegram* I met three other people who were crucial to my life and my career: Les Tuck, Marguerite Reid, and Tom Buck. Tuck was a field biologist, working for the Canadian government, who enlisted me in a newspaper campaign to stop the deliberate dumping of waste oil at sea. It surprised us how quickly we secured Canadian laws against this practice. After I left the *Telegram* I worked briefly as Tuck's field assistant, helped to edit his monographs *The Murres* and *The Snipes,* took up bird-watching, and, under his influence, began compiling the notes that would eventually grow into *The Foxes of Beachy Cove* and *Dancing on the Shore.* Besides being a field biologist, Tuck was an enthusiastic wildlife photographer. One of my jobs was to carry a loaded .303 rifle to insure that he wouldn't be killed by a rutting stag caribou under whose nose he was working, or by a grumpy black bear with whom he was sharing a blueberry patch.

Tom Buck and his wife, Helda, gave me generous, long-term support in my career, provided me with a second home in Toronto, a house always open to me for weeks or even months at a time in the publishing capital of Canada. It is hard for me to imagine how I would have managed to get through the difficult stage of publishing my first four or five books without them.

Marguerite was my long-term mistress. When I first met her in 1956 she was a free-lance journalist and a stunningly glamorous woman. We enjoyed a relationship that lasted for about ten years, and it was she who said to me one day, "There's a little place for sale in Beachy Cove. If you like I'll take you there and we can look at it. It might suit you."

When I bought the little house at Beachy Cove I was nearly thirty-eight years old and at the decisive point where I had decided to stop drifting and begin living my own life. For after leaving the *Telegram* I continued to drift, doing a little free-lance journalism, doing some portrait photography, founding and running a weekly paper, the *Examiner.* Abandoning the city was a truly symbolic act—a leaving behind of *all that.* I didn't go to the country as an experiment. I went once and for all, in a lifelong commitment that has lasted (as I write this) for more than thirty years. Beachy Cove, in those days, was true wilderness, beyond the reach of the power lines, surrounded by woods and sea, approached by a one-lane dirt road. Marguerite and I lived there with oil lamps, well

water, and a house heated by firewood which I cut myself from the forest. Wild foxes regularly visited our yard; on occasion a lynx or a moose came wandering by; all within fifteen miles of the city.

While writing my first two books, *Tomorrow Will Be Sunday* and *The Foxes of Beachy Cove,* I managed to support myself by the thin pickings of Canadian free-lance journalism, writing the occasional article for *Maclean's* magazine or *Weekend,* doing TV scripts for the Canadian Broadcasting Corporation. Numerous Canadian writers had tried this route and failed. It was almost impossible to make a living from that kind of writing. I succeeded because, like Thoreau a hundred years before, I reduced my wants to the barest minimum. I had no rent to pay, no utility bills, and a willingness to live at a level somewhat below that of my neighbours who were on welfare. My first year at Beachy Cove my income dropped below two thousand dollars. It was one of the happiest years of my life. It was several years before I got up to four thousand dollars. During that time I managed to keep my car, my one and only luxury. By the time it had to be replaced I was able to give it away to a friend in need and buy a good used one from a dealer.

Those years were euphoric. We had a garden full of half-wild flowers and an acre of vegetables, an old bed I'd brought from the city, a few old chairs, stacks of books, and a little battery-operated record player grinding out Vivaldi and Scarlatti and Prokofiev and Dave Brubeck. Clothes mattered hardly at all: lumberjack's shirts and pants, logans for winter, bare feet most of the year. Almost at my front door there was a river with a wonderful pool for swimming. There were crops of wild berries on the hills, fish in the sea. I divided my time about equally between living like a pioneer and working at the typewriter.

Visitors from the city were sometimes a problem. They seemed to think I was on perpetual holiday. They would arrive at any hour of the day or night, bringing their bottles of booze with them. Margaret Laurence, facing a similar situation in her cabin in rural Ontario, laid down the law that there were to be no visitors except on weekends. Somehow, I managed without such a rule. Sometimes I could "get inside" my novel for almost a day at a time; at other times I could hardly touch it for days at a stretch. But by 1964 it had gone through three draughts and had grown to 100,000 words.

At the same time I made improvements to the house—added a huge stone chimney and stone fireplace, built an attached greenhouse facing south, insulated the walls and roof. On sunny days in winter the greenhouse provided more heat than the house could use, and we opened windows and doors.

Flowers bloomed there all year, and I worked there in winter wearing only a pair of shorts. By 1964, in fact, I had what must have been one of the first "passive solar houses" in Canada; the term wasn't current for at least another ten years.

Unlike the back-to-the-landers who came fifteen years later, I had no support from the government or any other agency: no incentive grants, no unemployment insurance, no university backup, no welfare cheques. Like the Irish settlers who had gone to Beachy Cove a century earlier, I was on my own, enjoying the happiest years of my life while I reached the age of forty with still no sign of success in my chosen career.

By 1967 Marguerite was suffering serious drug-related problems, on a cycle of uppers and downers, using two separate sets of prescriptions from two doctors, filled at separate drugstores. Late that summer she walked out on me. Shortly afterwards she was in a psychiatric ward getting insulin shock. When they released her she was forty pounds overweight, and sliding into the final twilight of her life. Eventually she committed suicide with an overdose of drugs.

Travels with Farley were always an adventure. I visited him at Palgrave, Ontario, before he and his first wife, Frances, had become estranged. I had trouble finding the place, getting past his "Radiation Hazard" signs and the nude department-store dummy that graced his gateway. Farley and his boys were as naked as the dummy. "You mustn't mind him," Frances told me. "It's just his way. I've given up

trying to civilize him." But they weren't really compatible. A year or two later they were living apart.

Another time he was with me he went cavorting along the cliff tops on a wild stretch of Newfoundland coastline wearing nothing but a pair of waders. A crew of Irish-Newfoundland fishermen who passed by in a trap boat later reported that they had seen a spirit.

We prowled along the south coast of Newfoundland in his tiny schooner, *The Happy Adventure,* which he later celebrated in his book *The Boat Who Wouldn't Float.* I drove him and the woman who became his second wife, Claire Wheeler, to Mexico City, where Farley got a divorce from Frances. We then spent several weeks at Manzanillo on the Pacific coast of Mexico, and on the way north Farley and Claire were married in Texas.

Farley wrote the final version of his juvenile novel *The Black Joke* in my house at Beachy Cove, and Claire did the illustrations there. That same winter I joined them at their new home in Burgeo, on the remote southwest coast of Newfoundland, and wrote the final (fifth) version of *Tomorrow Will Be Sunday* there, while Farley worked on the first draught of *Never Cry Wolf* and did the research for *Westviking.*

At Farley's suggestion I submitted my first novel to McClelland and Stewart of Toronto (who have published all his books). They accepted it and paid a small advance, but I was quite unable to agree with Jack McClelland's ideas about revisions, so I refunded the advance and took the book to Doubleday, who published it in New York and Toronto in 1966. The book received elaborately good reviews in both countries, and won the Beta Sigma Phi first-novel award, which helped to bridge the financial gap to my next book. *Tomorrow Will Be Sunday* became a best-seller in Canada, and especially in Newfoundland, where it received a fantastic amount of publicity in the daily and weekly press and on radio and TV. Its success made it possible for me to continue as a freelance writer. If it had failed I would almost certainly have been forced back to full-time journalism.

Tomorrow Will Be Sunday took me about four years and five rewrites. *The Foxes of Beachy Cove,* my second book, was completed in three months—one month to write it, one month to revise it, and one month to draw the illustrations. It was published by Doubleday in 1967, and by Peter Davies in 1968. It had universally great reviews, but disappointing sales; "nature" books just didn't have the audience, especially in Canada in the 1960s, but nine years after first publication it became a national best-seller in Canada in paperback.

With his son, Andrew, and Farley Mowat at Mowat's home on Cape Breton Island, Nova Scotia, 1983

The Committee of the Arts advisory panel to the Canada Council, at Horwood's home in Beachy Cove, Newfoundland, 1978. From left: Jean-Pierre Lefabvre, film; Horwood, writing; Micheline Chaput, arts administration; Phyllis Mailing, music; Roger Jones, dance; Sharon Pollock, theatre; Bruce Ferguson, visual art. "The task force proposed policies for the third and fourth decades of the Canada Council's existence."

While my first book was on press, CBC-TV offered me the opportunity of a lifetime, the chance to become not a mere writer, but a TV personality, with a daily interview show, and a thirteen-week half-hour series. The money was so much more than I could hope to earn as a real writer, that I couldn't even afford to give myself time to think it over. Before I could yield to temptation I said, "Sorry, I just won't have the time for it," and that was that.

I was by now thoroughly at home in front of the cameras. Living temporarily in Toronto with the Bucks allowed me to promote my books in the only way that seemed effective in the late sixties and early seventies: nonstop appearances on radio and television. In one week-long publicity binge I was on thirteen TV talk shows in Toronto, Montreal, Ottawa, and Peterborough, with radio interviews in the three major cities as well. I was then promoting my third book, *Newfoundland*, published in Toronto by Macmillan (St. Martin's Press in the USA) in 1969, and still in print, still the major travel book on Newfoundland, twenty-two years later.

At that time I was suffering the usual agony of the second novel. *Remembering Summer* was still languishing in my filing cabinet. I took it out from time to time and did a bit of reworking on it. But I didn't want to publish a wild experimental novel immediate-

ly after a straight novel and a straight success like *Tomorrow Will Be Sunday*. My second novel, I felt, needed to be in the tradition of Conrad or Lawrence, a novel that had a chance to sell to the reading public, not something that would appeal only to the readers of Patchen and the subscribers to New Directions.

Tomorrow Will Be Sunday was a story of personal salvation, cast in the mode of the autobiographical novel, though in fact it contained scarcely a trace of autobiography in the strict sense. The novel I was now trying to write, "One Door into Darkness," was to be a novel of damnation, of personal failure to be true to inner convictions, and it was to include the theme of capital punishment, at that time a very lively topic of public debate in Canada. But at no point did the book begin to move of itself. At no point did the characters begin to take charge of it, as had happened in the earlier novel. And then it appeared that the whole question of capital punishment in Canada might become passé by legislation. A novel about the death penalty and the moral dilemmas surrounding it, a novel in which a hanging would have to take place at some point, would be a curious anachronism if it appeared shortly after the death penalty had been abolished.

So I used the first draught of my second novel to light the fire in my kitchen stove. A sacrifice? I suppose. But I couldn't afford to be sentimental. My writing had to succeed. Though I made false starts on other stories, I never went far with them. "One Door into Darkness" was the only large piece of adult writing that I ever destroyed.

My third book, *Newfoundland,* was commissioned by Macmillan, and was written in thirty days, making use of materials from my files, much of it newspaper and magazine features that I had written a few years earlier for the *Evening Telegram, Maclean's, Weekend,* and other journals. I wrote a chapter a day, and revised immediately, so that the book never needed a second draught.

Someone at *Reader's Digest* read it, and asked me to do a travel piece on the province. When they discovered that I could turn out an article that required very little editing, they kept asking me to do others. I did the article on Ontario as well as Newfoundland, one on the Cape Breton Highlands, a whole series of dramatic sea rescue stories. They sent me to the Canadian arctic, and to the north coast of British Columbia twice. Besides magazine pieces, I did sections for their books: two on Newfoundland's national parks, one on the St. John River, one on the Upper Churchill. In all, I must have done between thirty and forty assignments over a period of fifteen years, and picked up from this source something like fifty thousand dollars well spread over the period. I was able to do this without any kind of compromise. I never pretended to endorse the politics or social views of the *Reader's Digest.* The work was easy, consuming only a tiny fraction of the time I spent writing my books or growing my gardens or exploring the back country. And it paid the expenses of most of my travel to places I would have wanted to go anyway. As Evelyn Waugh had said a generation earlier, the real reason for writing books is to get yourself into the lucrative magazine market. I wrote pieces on commission for various other magazines in Canada and the United States. Some of them were translated and published in Germany, Italy, Norway, Spain, Portugal, Argentina, and Japan. Yet I never spent more than a few days on any magazine piece, or took that kind of writing seriously. But it was an important factor in keeping me solvent—far easier than teaching, which seems to be the resort of so many writers who cannot pay their bills from book royalties alone.

With "One Door into Darkness" out of the way, I returned, part-time, to *Remembering Summer.* I picked it up and worked at it and put it down again throughout the first twenty years of my writing career, never being satisfied with it. It went through more draughts and rewrites than I can remember, but my faith in the book was never shaken in the least.

It remained my favourite project throughout a period when I wrote and published fifteen other books. In part, *Remembering Summer* is one more tribute to life at Beachy Cove, where I spent seventeen years—the longest I have ever lived in one place. Mainly, it deals with life there at the end of the sixties when "humanity was going off like a bomb," as I expressed it, and Beachy Cove had become one of the Meccas for disaffiliated youth from all parts of North America.

Children of all ages—including those at the edge of adulthood—always flocked around me. This, together with my ingrained radicalism and tolerance for the unconventional, made me a guru of the sixties. In a sense I was already a hippie before the first hippie was hatched, already in love with music, birds, flowers, and even butterflies, already bearded and barefooted, already loving people by the score, instead of only the woman who shared my bed.

I saw my first acid trip at Christmas near the end of the sixties, and had visits from a handful of students the rest of that winter. Then one sunny evening in June I returned from the city to find fifteen teenagers in my sitting room playing the Fugs and the Doors on my record player. Most of them I had never seen before. Soon there were tents in my backyard, and a tarpaulin that had once been a cover for a transport truck now converted into a kind of community centre. The floors, as well as the beds, davenports, and chairs, were filled with crashers. Day and night I was surrounded by people from half a dozen Canadian provinces, and occasionally by some from as far as Georgia and Alaska, all of them on pilgrimage to Beachy Cove, directed there by the underground telegraph.

The kids, of course, were followed by the police doing drug searches, looking for runaways, adding to the pandemonium. And in the midst of it all, between the smoke clouds of the hash pipes and the visions of mescaline and LSD, I started work on my next novel.

White Eskimo, the Labrador novel, and one of my most successful books, gave me no trouble at all. I started in the middle and wrote it backwards and forwards, and after I'd done the whole thing I did one complete rewrite; that was all.

While this was going on I was acting as friend and protector to bearded giants and maxi-skirted young women, some of them drug freaks, some of them poets, some of them quite capable of stealing cars or looting deserted houses. I put up bail when they needed it, and once or twice parents phoned me in states of murderous fury because I'd bailed out kids whom they wanted to see punished by imprisonment without trial. Explaining that bail was everyone's civil right drove them to states of even greater

Horwood and Canada's Governor-General Ed Schreyer, at Government House, Ottawa, 1983— "on this occasion we escaped from the security guards through a hole in the fence and went cross-country skiing like common mortals"

Perhaps surprisingly, Animal Farm received a lot of support from people in the Department of Education, from some of the professors at the university in St. John's, and from a number of teachers who were unhappily trapped in the public school system. All of our teachers were volunteers; some of them devoted a great deal of time to a project that could never bring them any personal gain, and was quite likely to win them public hatred and contempt.

At the end of 1970 the manuscript of *White Eskimo* went off to my editor, Doug Gibson, at Doubleday, and I was able to turn my attention to *Death on the Ice,* a manuscript by Cassie Brown of St. John's that Doug had put into my hands. The research on this story of Newfoundland's greatest sealing disaster was impeccable, but the writing was impossible. I not only rewrote the book, I reshaped and recast it, and Cassie and I published it as coauthors.

White Eskimo appeared in September 1972, and was a national best-seller in Canada for seventeen weeks. A month later *Death on the Ice* appeared, and also became a best-seller. Total sales of both books, in hardcover and paperback, quickly ran into the hundreds of thousands of copies. Twenty years after publication, *Death on the Ice* is still selling around three thousand copies a year.

That autumn I also published a small anthology of poetry by four young Newfoundlanders, *Voices Underground.* It was published in Toronto by New Press, and went to a second printing. One of the four—Des Walsh—has since become a full-time writer with an established reputation.

fury. The spirit—the essence of it all—is recorded in *Remembering Summer,* the one true Canadian novel of the sixties, written from the inside by an insider.

At the same time I helped to organize, and then to defend against the attacks of the public and the police, the only free high school that Newfoundland has ever known—Animal Farm, in St. John's. Other "alternative" schools tended to serve little kids. This one was for people who had been thrown out of high school, or had dropped out, or just couldn't hack it. It was a wild and wonderful school, where wonderful things happened, and immature kids turned into mature people, and some of them got a certain amount of academic education, too. At least twenty of our students finished high school and qualified for university. One of them today is an established poet and dramatist; at least one is a university professor; a few still lead the free and impoverished lives of the sixties; most have retreated to featureless places in society. I'm not aware that any have become yuppies.

I lived in Ontario for three summers and two winters—the summers at Mowat's cabin in Brighton on Lake Ontario, and the winters at Schomberg, north of Toronto. Each year I made lengthy visits to St. John's and Beachy Cove. In the autumn of 1972 I returned to Newfoundland, and the following summer began living with a neighbour of mine, Cornelia (Corky) Lindesmith, recently divorced from Bill Cohen, an American biochemist working in St. John's. I had known Corky slightly from the time of her arrival in Newfoundland in 1968. After our marriage I sold my house, moved a quarter of a mile downhill to her much larger and newer house overlooking Conception Bay, and bought her husband's equity in the property. Along with Corky came three grown daughters and a daughter and son who were still kids. I tried at first to use our bedroom as a workroom, but soon found it impossible and built a working cabin in the woods near the house. Our son, Andrew, was born May 20, 1974.

Like me, Corky had been a magnet for the "heads" of the sixties, and the older of her children were of an age to associate with them. My nephew John was living with one of her daughters (and still is, after twenty years; they have three children). Many of our tastes were identical. We both liked serious reading, classical music, camping, travel, swimming, boats, and flowers. We both liked children, cats, and dogs, and were interested in scientific discoveries. She was enthusiastic about sex, hated housework, and had none of the old-fashioned feminine fixations on dress or personal adornment.

When Andrew was five weeks old we took him on a canoe trip down the St. John River in New Brunswick. Partway through the trip I began suffering from renal colic; six weeks later, after many such attacks, I passed a kidney stone, the only serious illness of my adult life.

In my new work cabin I wrote *Beyond the Road,* a story of Newfoundland outports in transition. It was illustrated by a wonderful young American portrait photographer, Stephen Taylor, and published by Van Nostrand Reinhold. There I also did the final versions of my short story collection, *Only the Gods Speak,* published by Breakwater Books, and one more rewrite of *Remembering Summer,* this time with the cabin itself in the opening sentence.

Before he was two years old I knew that Andrew was dyslexic. I coached him in special ways, with wooden word blocks that he could arrange into simple sentences. He worked hard at learning to read, spent three years in a special class for dyslexics, and another three years in a private school for dyslexics, and by the age of sixteen he was able to read novels by Hemingway and H. G. Wells, nonfiction books by his father and Konrad Lorenz, and anything else he wanted to read *at a pace perhaps one-tenth as fast as a skillful reader.* In my view, this was an enormous accomplishment, achieved by determination against very long odds. Emotionally, Andrew remained stable, self-possessed, and self-confident. He also acquired, largely through his mother's reading to him, a level of education far beyond his years, and was treated by his schoolfellows as a sort of walking encyclopedia.

In 1975 I had two national best-sellers in mass-market paperback, *White Eskimo* and *The Foxes of Beachy Cove. Beyond the Road* was on press. *Bartlett,* my biography of the great ice captain who took Peary to within one hundred and fifty miles of the North Pole, was under contract. Next year I was invited by the University of Victoria to spend a year as a visiting teacher of creative writing, but before I could accept I was offered a residency by the University of Western Ontario for slightly more money and decidedly better working conditions. I took it, rented a house in Grand Bend, some forty miles from the campus, and there my second child, Leah, was born on December 13, 1976, at home, without medical help or any kind of professional birth attendant. Leah was never attended by a doctor for any reason whatever until the age of twelve, when she broke an arm in a sliding accident. When Corky reached her fiftieth birthday she was still breast-feeding this child. Neither of our kids ever tasted baby food or formula or sucked from a bottle (or from a thumb, either). And they knew nothing about sibling rivalry. They were each other's best friend throughout their entire period of growth to maturity.

In addition to serious books in the seventies and eighties I wrote potboilers—a history book on colonial Canada for McClelland and Stewart, a short history of Canada for an American package publisher, Bison Books, two local histories published by Breakwater Books, and two books on pirates, privateers, bandits, and outlaws, coauthored by Ed Butts of Mississauga, Ontario, and published by Doubleday. In addition I wrote a little volume of folklore, *Tales of the Labrador Indians,* published by Harry Cuff of St. John's, and edited the writings of Gregory J. Power, a sensitive poet and skilled satirist who had begun his career as a colleague of mine in the Newfoundland Confederate Association. This book, *The Power of the Pen,* was also published by Cuff.

I had gotten involved in cultural politics in the early seventies, and was very active in the organization of the Writers' Union of Canada. I was vice-chairman of the union three times, and chairman in 1980–81. That year I was also invited to be writer-in-residence at the University of Waterloo, and while there founded the literary journal the *New Quarterly* (now in its eleventh year). I spent two years at Waterloo as writer-in-residence, and a third as a resource person in one of the university departments. In 1980 I received the Order of Canada for contributions to Canadian literature.

Meanwhile Corky and I sold our house at Beachy Cove to members of our own family, and moved with our two children to a new house which we built on the shore of Annapolis Basin in Nova Scotia—a place where we could practise our common passion for gardening with much greater success. The new house, a passive solar design which we created ourselves, sits on thirteen acres of parkland that we developed from a former hayfield. It includes a seafront beach, two ponds, and eight acres of forest planted from nursery stock. Part of the money used to build this place came from the sale of my research papers and manuscripts to the library of the University of Calgary.

In 1985 I was invited by the Union of Writers of the USSR to attend an international convention of writers in Leningrad, celebrating the fortieth anniversary of the end of the Second World War. There I met writers from every continent except North America. Writers from Canada and the United States were conspicuously absent, perhaps because the Cold War was not quite over, though pretty well on its last legs. I went to the convention without any great hopes, but the Russians proved to be the finest hosts I have ever encountered—utterly generous and anxious to please. I had the services of a full-time interpreter, time to visit Moscow, and several other cities and towns, as well as Leningrad, tickets to opera, ballet, puppet theatres, and musical performances. I encountered a complete willingness and freedom to discuss any issue whatsoever, and a surprising amount of good will toward the West, including the United States. At the conference itself the government provided simultaneous translation in eight languages. I was interviewed for radio and television in Czechoslovakia and Bulgaria, as well as in the Soviet Union. I wandered around Moscow on my own, and a number of people, recognizing me by my dress as a North American, came up to me and spoke to me in English. Everyone seemed anxious to make use of this universal second language and particularly anxious to dispel the ill will of decades of cold-war propaganda.

The Bartlett biography was published by Doubleday in November 1977 with disappointing results—at least for me. Sales the first year were limited to about four thousand, and this great explorer, who had done so much to open the Canadian arctic, remained virtually unknown in Canada. To the credit of the publishers, they refused to allow the book to die. The following year they brought out a new edition in quality paperback, with revisions, and finally in 1989 a third edition, also in quality paperback and larger format, with a more attractive cover.

During the 1980s at Annapolis Basin I wrote two books in addition to the popular histories published by Doubleday and Breakwater. Those were *Dancing on the Shore* and *Joey*. *Dancing on the Shore* might,

Harold Horwood with son, Andrew, sixteen, and daughter, Leah, thirteen, in the conservatory of their house at Upper Clements, Nova Scotia, 1990

perhaps, be called nature writing, like *The Foxes of Beachy Cove.* But it was about much more than nature unless you include the nature of man and the nature of the universe. More than anything, it was a book of evolutionary philosophy, a book of visions, a book of wisdom. It was beautifully published by Doug Gibson and McClelland and Stewart, and by Dutton in New York. The summer following its first appearance, I was invited to talk about it at Chautauqua, in New York, where I had an absolutely euphoric experience with the most receptive audience I have ever encountered, anywhere. Sales were modest—a total of seven or eight thousand in both countries—but the mail I received, and the personal visits from people who had read the book, were far more rewarding than any returns in royalties could possibly be. No book that I have written, with the possible exception of *Remembering Summer,* published by Pottersfield Press that same year, has given me such satisfaction. Once these books were both in print I could have retired, contented.

But, of course, one doesn't retire. My next book, a biography of Newfoundland's political genius, Joey Smallwood, appeared in 1989, based on my experiences with him of thirty and forty years before. After that? Well, I have two other books in process, right now, but they are the kind of books, like *Dancing on the Shore,* that accumulate, rather than rushing onto the page, so they may take several years to complete.

It has been a rewarding life, so far, one I wouldn't exchange for any other that I can imagine. I have met and become personal friends with all the most interesting people in Canada—all of them writers, none of them in any sense competitors, but all engaged in their unique ways in the common task of creating a national literature for one of the world's young nations.

BIBLIOGRAPHY

Fiction:

Tomorrow Will Be Sunday, Doubleday, 1966.

White Eskimo: A Novel of Labrador, Doubleday, 1972.

Only the Gods Speak (short stories), Breakwater, 1979.

Remembering Summer, Pottersfield, 1987.

Nonfiction:

The Foxes of Beachy Cove, Doubleday, 1967.

Newfoundland (travel), St. Martin's, 1969.

(With Cassie Brown) *Death on the Ice* (history), Doubleday, 1972.

Beyond the Road: Portraits and Visions of Newfoundlanders (travel; photographs by Stephen Taylor), Van Nostrand, 1976.

Bartlett: The Great Canadian Explorer (biography), Doubleday, 1977, revised edition, 1980, 1989.

The Colonial Dream, 1497–1760, McClelland & Stewart, 1978.

Tales of the Labrador Indians (folklore), Harry Cuff Publications, 1981.

A History of Canada, Bison Books, 1983.

(With Edward Butts) *Pirates and Outlaws of Canada, 1610–1932,* Doubleday, 1984.

Corner Brook: The Social History of a Paper Town, Breakwater, 1986.

(With John de Visser) *Historic Newfoundland,* Oxford University Press, 1986.

A History of the Newfoundland Ranger Force, Breakwater, 1986.

(With Butts) *Bandits and Privateers: Canada in the Age of Gunpowder,* Doubleday, 1987.

Dancing on the Shore: A Celebration of Life at Annapolis Basin, McClelland & Stewart, 1987.

Joey: The Life and Political Times of Joey Smallwood, Stoddard, 1989.

Editor:

Voices Underground: Poems from Newfoundland, New Press, 1972.

The Power of the Pen (writings of Gregory J. Power), Harry Cuff Publications, 1989.

Also contributor to *New Canadian Stories,* David Helwig and Joan Harcourt, editors, Oberon Press, 1973, 1974; *Voices Down East;* and other anthologies. Founding editor, *New Quarterly* (Waterloo, Ontario). A collection of his research papers and manuscripts are housed at the University of Calgary.

Jack Matthews

1925-

THE EYE OF THE HORSESHOE

"My great-grandparents: John A. and Lydia (Macomber) Matthews. John served four years in Company I of the 36th Ohio Volunteer Infantry Regiment in the Civil War. My grandfather Sam is far right, back row."

To Begin with, Before Beginning

Portions of what follows may seem too amiably comfortable for credibility. I am aware that there is no practical, common sense, "real" perspective from which my childhood, for example, could be viewed as quite so lyrically untroubled. But if the imagination cannot illuminate the past, where is its power? So if I have idealized my childhood, there is a deeper truth in the account; because idealization is natural to me, and what I am is memory.

My title may also need explaining. A horseshoe doesn't have an eye any more than a rope or a pond. But it doesn't have any *less* than a rope (posing as a lariat, for example) or a pond (a circle with a theoretical center). Here, we find ourselves in the intensely human world of metaphor. My focus is upon the image of a horseshoe, whose center of gravity is empty space—an invisible, unreal eye gazing at us.

This speaks of what I am and where I live, and the twofold focus is central to my title. Both imaginary and real, the horseshoe's eye is a perfect symbol,

"My father, John Matthews, a star third baseman and aspiring attorney"

therefore perfectly human, for as symbol users, we are never quite real to ourselves and are forced to live flanked by otherness in all directions, including the temporal.

The eye of the horseshoe, then, is the image, the symbol, and the process itself. It is the center of the implement of memory and the ceremony of recall. It occupies time and watches us from out of its center. It is what we essentially are, embraced by past and future and bracketed in the iron arms of artifact.

Stirring Awake

I was born on July 22, 1925, in my family's house at 164 Glencoe Road, in Clintonville, a far north suburb of Columbus, Ohio. My great-uncle Elwood had built the first four houses on Glencoe, then no more than a country lane, and ours was the fourth. My parents had moved there the year before. I remember my mother reading the Bible to me in bed at night before I went to sleep. I remember winter evenings when I was asked to stand in front of the

fireplace and recite for company. What did I recite? I have forgotten.

But in 1931, visiting my grandfather Sam Matthews, in Vinton, a village in the wooded hills of Gallia County, Ohio, I do remember singing "The Big Rock Candy Mountain"; and when he asked how old I was, I answered, "Eight." This amused and scandalized my parents, because I was six, and had always been taught to tell the truth. "Jack," my mother said, "don't tell stories." Sam Matthews had a feed store in Vinton, and I can remember standing there in the warm, golden shafts of sunlight that shimmered with the fragrant dust of grain.

I also remember visiting my grandmother Grover on her farm near Bidwell, a town whose name, at least, was immortalized by Sherwood Anderson in his story "The Egg." My grandfather Augustus Grover, known countywide as "Bub," was a legendary, larger-than-life character, a big, flamboyant, 285-pound cattleman with over one thousand acres of land. He was a passionate baseball fan, and when the home team was losing, he simply could not bear it and left the stands to hide out amongst the buggies and Model T's, asking passersby who was winning.

The fact that the home team starred his son-in-law, my dad, along with his own son, my uncle Ray, was at the heart of his attitude. He was passionate and impetuous, with little use for objectivity, and once horsewhipped a democrat. When he was old and asthmatic, he trained a horse so he could shoot quail from its back. When I was born, he said, "Thank the Lord! Another baseball player!" He died when I was two years old. He had a gift for sentimentality, which I inherited, along with a certain impetuosity.

Half a century after Momma Grover died, I was driving by her house and saw a garage-sale sign. I stopped and asked if they had any old books for sale; they did not. I told them my grandmother had lived there fifty years before. But I didn't tell them about one dark Halloween night when my sister and girl cousins undertook to frighten me. My cousin Elizabeth put on a sheet and came moaning out of the dark mist of the orchard. Long afterwards, I remembered this in my story "The Terrible Mrs. Bird" (in *Crazy Women*).

All my girl cousins were affectionate and great fun, and almost as close as sisters. My sister, Dorothy, and all but one of those girl cousins are now dead. Momma Grover was a wonderful, spirited, loving old lady, although I was too young to ever tell her something like that. I couldn't have said it anyway, except in some such distant translation as this. But she would have understood.

I remember going to Clinton School, where pretty Miss Wing was my first-grade teacher. When I was eight or nine years old, my mother taught me auction bridge, which I enjoyed playing with adults. People said I played well; but I've never been any good at card or board games since then, because my mind wanders. I remember the families on Glencoe Road gathering to play bridge every New Year's Eve, with servings of pie and cake and soft drinks and coffee. Never booze; not even beer or wine. At midnight, Jake Meckstroth, editor of the *Ohio State Journal,* would fetch his carbide cannon, set it in the middle of the street, and fire it. All of us boys liked the beautiful, loud *bam* it made.

Liking noise, I took trumpet lessons, and in 1935 my father bought a seven-foot Steinway grand piano for my mother, who liked to play and sing such popular sentimental favorites as "In a Little Spanish Town" and "On the Isle of Capri." Dad bought the piano from Otto Heaton, a hunchbacked music-store owner who was legendary in Columbus and had signs placed all over central Ohio, saying, TEACH YOUR SON TO PLAY A HORN AND HE WON'T GO TO PRISON. The piano he sold us had been used by Rachmaninoff for practice in his suite at the Deshler-Wallick Hotel, while he was on tour as a "Steinway artist." Rachmaninoff signed the metal plate, to signify his approval of the piano's tone.

Gripping the handle of my trumpet case on the right handlebar, I rode my balloon-tired bicycle south into the university district, where I took lessons from Mr. Saumenig, enjoying the odors of dinner cooking as I blundered through the week's lesson. I never practiced, although I knew what valves to press to play the notes. Occasionally my mother would convince me that we should play "The Gayety Polka," as a duet. That, and Dad's favorite, "The Bells of Saint Mary's," may have been the only two pieces I ever got all the way through without a mistake, although that probably didn't happen very often.

My parents, older sister, Dorothy, and I enjoyed travel, and in summers we took fishing trips to Michigan, Canada, Minnesota, and Wisconsin. In 1937 we visited Fort Ticonderoga and later ferried across the St. Lawrence on a rainy night into Quebec, where I was interested to learn people really spoke French. On the Martin River, north of North Bay, Ontario, Dad and I trolled for great northern pike with daredevil spoons. We saw wild bears feeding in a garbage dump, and Dad took their picture with our new 16-millimeter movie camera, which attracted a lot of attention among the people, although the bears weren't impressed.

Back home, I remember hiking in the woods and fields north of Acton Road. I also went to Boy Scout camp on the Olentangy River in Delaware County, the same county where our family would one day own a farm. I was interested in Indians and pioneers, and my favorite century was the eighteenth. I remember drawing pictures with soldiers wearing knee breeches and tricornered hats. I liked books, and read *Cardigan,* by Robert W. Chambers, *Northwest Passage* and *Arundel,* by Kenneth Roberts, and, of course, *The Deerslayer.*

I went to movies at the Clinton Theater, where children were admitted for a dime. Already I showed a gift for absent-mindedness. For a while, streetcar tickets were a problem. Going to the movies one evening, I presented a streetcar ticket at the booth, and the woman and I both gazed at it a moment before she told me I wasn't on a streetcar. At another time, arriving home after dark, I tried to put a streetcar ticket into our front door lock to let myself into the house.

Henry James's belief that a writer is one upon whom nothing is lost, should be amended to "nothing *germane* is lost"; although who can say what is germane? Or what *might* be? I was constantly missing obvious things. Once, having visited Doc Stevens's office several times, I went to get a poison ivy shot, but took a wrong turn and walked all the way to

Parents, Lou Grover and John Matthews, about 1913

"With my mother and sister, Dorothy," 1926

Olentangy Park, looking for it. What was I doing? Thinking of other things.

On hikes I pretended I was either an Indian or a pioneer; it seemed to make little difference, as if I could already sense the mysterious and secret collaboration of opposites. All that land north of Acton Road is now covered with urban sprawl, as if it, too, had once yearned to change into some theoretical, though hardly conceivable, opposite. Still, part of its image remains in my memory, as if beyond the reach of change.

I feel privileged to have survived so many years and to have experienced so many transformations; and I am thankful. I have mentioned elsewhere (see "The Bracketing of Time," in *Memoirs of a Bookman*) that I can remember standing at the window of my father's suite of law offices, on the eighth floor of the Outlook Building, at 44 East Broad Street, directly across from the old State Capitol, looking down upon Armistice Day parades. I remember the old Grand Army of the Republic veterans marching in front, and how their ranks thinned yearly. My father seemed to know everyone in downtown Columbus,

and when he took me to lunch, he would stop often to chat with friends, always introducing me to them and telling me stories about them afterwards.

As a child, I was blessed in many ways: growing up in a stable and loving family (although we didn't use the word "love"), in a stable neighborhood that was safe for roaming and irresponsibility; cold winters when we would eat clean snow ice cream, and autumns that were fragrant with sunlight and rotting leaves; and listening to the weekly installment of "Og, Son of Fire" on our big Zenith radio. I was spoiled and had an enduring egocentric feeling that I was not only liked by people, but *paid attention to*. I remember the adults I knew as a small boy as generous and courtly and decent. Men joked with me and asked me questions. And sometimes, when I was very small, women would grab my head and hug it to their warm bodies, embarrassing me as it gave me secret pleasure.

Growing up in such a world, how could a boy not be happy?

Crestview Junior High School at Calumet and Weber

At Crestview I won a medal from the Daughters of the American Revolution for my essay on the Constitution. This caught everyone off guard. Even teachers told me they were surprised, and I believed them. Exasperated, Miss Ashmead stopped me in the hall one day and said, "Jack, if *I'd* had anything to do with it, you wouldn't have even been recommended to *take* the test!" I could see her point. I could never sit still and had a short attention span, so I was pretty surprised myself.

In junior high, I was very short in stature, but also very strong for my size. When I was twelve or thirteen, Miss Ashmead had us produce a play in English class, and she assigned me the role of an evil dwarf, which filled me with embarrassment, humiliation, and helpless wrath. (Evil dwarfs will know how I felt.) The hero was a tall, inoffensive, milky-limbed boy who towered over me, but wasn't nearly as strong; and to me it was a terrible injustice that we were so woefully miscast.

It seemed unfair; but it would prove useful, for it taught me the valuable lesson that the world would not always want to hug my head to its warm body. Our lives are filled with such trivial wrongs, but they have a special significance for two sorts of people: the dismal tribe of injustice collectors who pant after their share of the inevitable human nastiness . . . and future writers, who remember in unique ways and for unique reasons, as they instinctively gather material.

So Miss Ashmead may have had a part in my becoming a writer, although I'm sure she didn't intend it. But I've never resented her; I believe she was just nervous. In fact, many of my teachers seemed nervous, now that I think about it. I remember most of them fondly, although I was never a teacher's pet. My homeroom teacher was gentle and seldom smiled; she talked in a rapid whisper and wore heavy makeup to conceal burn scars on her face. She was a sensitive, warmhearted woman, with the wonderful name of Hedwig Bretz.

After Crestview, I went to North High School, where I remained indifferent to grades and often, alas, subject matter. And yet, there were moments. Miss Corbin was my English teacher; she was short, round, erect, and had snow-white hair. I remember her aristocratic nostrils and her wonderful eloquence in expressing genteel scorn. She assigned Conrad's novel *The Rover,* but I read it anyway. Later, I decided that this book first inspired me to become a writer. While reading it, I paused and thought: "How wonderful it would be to create something like this!"

North High was a very large school, and a great power in the city football league. I tried out for the team as a senior, and although I was the smallest boy on the squad (I would keep growing for several years), I was second-string strong-side guard behind Harry Ackley, who had been in the Civilian Conservation Corps and was a nineteen-year-old man. A few days before the first game, however, our family bought 121 acres of farmland in Delaware County, upon which there was an orchard thick with gnarled, old apple trees, badly in need of pruning.

The boy who'd once read *Cardigan* and *Northwest Passage* was excited by the thought of owning so much woodland and pasture. And since all those apples needed picking, I dropped off the team shortly before our first game. My career as a football player ended then, one of the many roads not taken, one of the lives not lived. I speak of those little theoretical lives, ignored and going to seed, thick as unpruned orchards. I speak of those mysterious little lives, each centered upon the image of an eye, a center of gravity in empty space.

Buying our farm was a symbolic return for my parents, who were born and reared in rural Gallia County in southern Ohio. For my father, leaving the farm and going to the city symbolized growing up. This was a familiar myth: the farm was childhood's Eden; the city, adult reality. Because of the modern demographic identification of reality with population, in leaving the farm, a boy left his youth; in the city he

grew up and proved himself. Eventually successful, he would buy land and become a "gentleman farmer," closing the circle and returning to the felicity of first awakening.

The house on our farm was built in 1821, and its stairways and the mantels of its three fireplaces were beautifully carved out of solid cherry. When the farm was sold after my father's death, Alum Creek was dammed to create the Alum Creek Reservoir. Now, all of that familiar woods and wild pasture land is underwater, transformed into the Past, another world, another realm. Water is the medium of time, and the remembered Past a sunken empire. I have often used this image in poems and stories, thinking it was mine alone until I read and rejoiced in Conrad Richter's magical novel *The Waters of Kronos.*

At a country auction, many years after I had last walked upon those wooded hills and pastures, I bought the *History of Delaware County,* Chicago, 1880, in which I read about our farm (originally "the Eaton Place") where, in one of the back buildings, an old black woman named Sarah Brandy lived. She had been a servant in George Washington's household, and died at the age of 125 years, somewhere on the land where I would one day pitch hay, grow corn and potatoes, and prune apple trees. We keep learning what we have been; and bracketing events enables us to structure time out of simple duration, and connect the generations in the long, slow dance of sequences.

The Past is never really completed; it keeps happening over and over, even though it's never quite the same. So is it any wonder I would become a fiction writer and try to retrieve something of all those quondam and unlived realities that are now submerged in the water of time, and understand them as they once were? Or might have been? Or might be?

Semper Paratus

For a while after graduation from North High, I drove our family's second car, a black 1936 Olds coupe, sixteen miles to work on our farm. Then in December 1943, I went into the Coast Guard. Like many eighteen-year-old boys, I had never lived away from home. Boot camp was at Curtis Bay, Maryland, outside Baltimore. I was assigned to Company I; my great-grandfather, John A. Matthews, also served in a Company I; only he was a teamster in the 36th Ohio Volunteer Infantry Regiment in the Civil War.

My Company I included many boys from Tennessee, some of them probably descendants of rebels, who at night before lights out, filled the barracks with happy, loud, whang-dang guitar music. By day, we learned to march in close-order drill, handle oars in a Monomoy surf boat, disassemble a .45 automatic, and step into a gas-filled shed, remove our gas masks, then give our names and serial numbers before being dismissed.

After boot camp, I was assigned to the bull gang at the shipyards in Curtis Bay; after that I was a firefighter. There were no fires, but I enjoyed climbing up the gigantic shipyard cranes to inspect their fire extinguishers. Those cranes were so lofty, I thought you might be able to see Finland and Madagascar from their gear shacks; but if you could, they looked exactly like Chesapeake Bay.

I was then assigned to Radio School in Atlantic City, where I learned the Morse Code, radio theory, and Q signals, and got a temporary, after-hours job carrying furs out of the basement of Gettleman's Furriers, on the boardwalk. Those furs had been soaked by the tidal wave of the 1944 hurricane. Standing in briny water, Steve Schwantkowski, a fellow coast guardsman, and I were moving a heavy, metal fur-drying machine when there was a short circuit, tickling us mercilessly for a few seconds. Steve was wearing metal plates on his heels and passed out. He was brought around with *crème de menthe*.

From Radio School I went to Alaska. I was stationed at Point Higgins, outside Ketchikan, after which I was assigned briefly to the U.S. Coast Guard Cutter *Maclaine*, a 125-foot patrol boat on antisubmarine patrol. She was a tough little ship, but a rolling and pitching hard rider that always moved in more directions than forward. She alternated week-long patrols with the *Aurora*, out of Sitka and Juneau, and before I joined her had been credited with destroying a Japanese sub in an Alaskan bay. The sub had fired a torpedo right on target, but the *Maclaine* didn't draw enough water to catch it, so it went under her forward hull, giving her time to throw depth charges until engine oil surfaced.

In Sitka I heard about openings for part-time orderlies in the Old Pioneers' Home, and I could have arranged to work on alternate weeks, when we weren't on patrol. I was tempted, but eventually decided that giving baths to old men wasn't my idea of man's work, let alone fun, so I decided not to apply. Later, I regretted my decision, thinking of the stories I might have heard from men old enough to remember the Alaskan gold rush. The sins of omission are hard for all of us to bear, but they are a special burden for one who wants to become a writer.

I remember wonderful days of cool, invigorating wind and hard, bright sunlight, while the Mighty Mac, with sonar pinging, wallowed heavily in the

"With my parents on the porch of the Grand Hotel," Mackinac Island, Michigan, early 1930s

ground swell off Mendenhall Glacier. I remember the blue dark fissures in the glacial ice, piling away upwards toward the sky—a virtual mountain range itself; and then, above that, a line of the jagged peaks of real mountains, topped by a cloud bank . . . above which Mount Fairweather towered, solitary and majestic. I remember how we would stand on the fantail, eating apples and throwing the cores at the seagulls that squawked and fluttered like frowzy pennants above our foaming wake.

I remember reading the Armed Service paperback editions we had in our ship's library. I read Mencken's *Happy Days* and *Newspaper Days,* and Jack London's *Sea Wolf.* I sat in the radio shack as we rolled creaking and groaning in the North Pacific, reading London's classic variation upon *Moby Dick,* in which the fictional schooner *Ghost* sailed, with Wolf Larsen its mad captain, upon the very waters I could see through our portholes, actuality and latitude only slightly edited.

I remember all those lyric moments as true. But of course, they're not the whole truth. Their usefulness extends to more than the simple retention necessary for our human identity; as symbolically charged images they define the past, a little like those dots in children's games that become pictures when they are connected with straight lines. Or a little like the still frames that constitute a moving picture in the gestalt formation of a rapid series.

But more than these, each image is the eye of a horseshoe, which is to say, a point bracketed by the iron of inexpressible fact. As symbols, each is ultimately definable in terms of all that surrounds it. In this way they evoke rich complexes of potential memory, so that to explicate them perfectly would be to evoke all about them. Bachofen said that myth is the exegesis of the symbol—a potent idea of artistic synthesis and integrity that rests at the heart of much I have tried to express as a writer, long before I came upon Bachofen's formula.

So the images I have given of those Alaskan coast guard days are partial and limited, omitting much; for like every young person I can imagine, I crawled with turmoil, guilt, confusion, and *Angst*. Those images of lyric perfection do not convey everything; and the extent of their omission can be measured by the following anecdote. I remember being awakened in the blackness of night to go on watch, with the ship rolling and pitching and the dim glow of the night lights in the fo'c'sle, an indifferent infinity of black, frigid water beyond its hull. I remember thinking at the very instant upon awakening that dying would be a return to that warm oblivion I'd just been pried out of. I remember thinking, "This is the time to contemplate death, because now, for an instant, the thought of it is comforting."

The two qualifications in that formula are essential to its validity, but the idea has stayed with me. Thinking of death at such times brings the idea into a context in which it appears familiar and attractive rather than the alien and threatening transformation that appalls the imagination. At that brief moment, the thought of death is internalized, domesticated and possessed, nullifying its distant and mythic power.

That dark formula notwithstanding, it is obvious that my tour in the Coast Guard had nothing approaching the grandiose horrors of war. And yet, we instinctively seek out our own tragic limits within, regardless of what fate provides without, so that some version of our capacity for experience can be realized.

Life in the Mine Fields

When I think of the difficulties boys face in becoming men, I am appalled. I think specifically of that wild chasm they are thrown into at puberty, made to sink or swim—metaphors flying—with few folkways or institutions to support, edify, or comfort them. Sometimes I think the best method of discipline would have them deprived of all leisure, kept in solitary confinement, providing no more than minimal comfort, a good reading light, and edifying books to read, along with forced physical labor every day to the pitch of exhaustion. But of course that wouldn't work any better than any other conceivable program. Obviously, the situation is hopeless.

What I am talking about is the wild turbulence of youth, the hormone wars, the blinding explosion of energies that can no more be capped than a geyser can be stuffed into a beer bottle. This problem is especially acute for boys raised in an idealistic but repressive, Protestant, middle-class environment. It's no wonder many of them riot when the constraints are lifted; it's no wonder that they get drunk so they can explore the wild reaches of possibility—trying out such sins as drinking, blasphemy, and fornication to see how they fit, becoming other people in bars and telling outrageous lies . . . even "admitting" to sullen crimes and nasty adventures they have not committed, nor could *ever* commit, drunk or sober. Like nascent fiction writers, they yearn to satisfy the terrible hunger for possibilities that transcend every individual's life.

An old Irish triad states that for twenty years a man is an ignorant child; for twenty years mad with lust; for twenty years a rational creature; then he's ready to die. Triads have to be symmetrical, which distorts those times allotted; but there's truth in the saying. The frenzied lust of youth is the subject of my poem "Eros Oikoumenikos" (in *An Almanac for Twilight*) which begins, "No drunkenness like the drunkenness of this." And what was my cure for "lustguilt"? It was twofold, both desperate and inadequate: "For this fever, I'd prescribed bleeding into the centuries of men long turned to words; or even an actual liquor to bring sobriety, compared to this."

Adolescence does not end at age twenty-one; its vestiges are with us to the end. Unlike the vermiform appendix, it cannot be removed; although part is rubbed away with experience, another part sublimated. All, however, is encoded in the Myth of Self, to be replayed again and again, trying always to be gotten right. Herakleitos said that our character is our fate; which is true, but it explains only so much, for the one turns out to be just as mysterious as the other.

Adolescence is an *Angst* beyond the dreams of nightmare. Years later, I thought of a cartoon image that perfectly expresses what it is like—walking through a mine field, and with every step you step on a mine and are blown up. That's a hard way to walk, a hard way to get anywhere. But somehow, we do it, sort of . . . and eventually, if we're lucky, grow up; and that is a great mystery, too.

Signing Up for Philosopher

In 1945, as one of that great horde of veterans returning to college, I consulted the Veterans Administration advisor at Ohio State University about what I should study. His name was Mr. Buechler, and he had a small, thin mustache. He asked what I was interested in, and I told him philosophy. He picked up a list of vocations and studied it. After a moment, he put it down, saying "philosopher" wasn't listed.

Both of us contemplated this fact. In a better world the occupation of philosopher might be listed. But this was not the case in the world that existed then any more than today. Mr. Buechler asked what I would like to do in life. I said, "I would like to write philosophical novels somewhat like those of Joseph Conrad."

Once again he studied the list of vocational majors. After a moment, he looked up and said, "How about Creative Writing?"

"Creative Writing"? It had an odd sound to it. Creative Writing courses were scarcely better known in those days than courses in fainting or mugging. Obviously honorific, the term "creative" had not yet become the shibboleth of today, so I thought Mr. Buechler's question might be a put-on. But a glance at his earnest face told me otherwise. "Well," I said, "sure. Why not?"

In so casual a manner was one of the critical decisions of my life made. But I didn't realize it at the time. Like so many important events, it happened while I was psychologically absent, thinking about girls or beer at Larry's Bar at High Street and Woodruff or *Philosophy in a New Key*, by Susanne K. Langer. It's too bad we're so often absent at the great turns in our lives.

My first three freshman courses at Ohio State were physics ("Introduction to Classical Mechanics"; my advisor had commented upon my Ohio State Psychological Exam score in physics, surmising my abilities might lie there, that nonsense about Joseph Conrad notwithstanding), philosophy (it was a beginning course in ethics), and classical Greek. What an odd trio, people said. And I thought it was pretty odd myself, but tried not to be too proud of the fact.

I was still trying to warp the world to fit my whims. Like literary texts of great density, which they insistently reflect in an inverted representationalism, human lives can be viewed as intricately plotted, possessing latent as well as overt meanings. Part of the latent meaning of my life was that I was one who would insist upon marching to a drummer who was, if not necessarily different, inaudible to common sense.

So I attended most of my classes in philosophy, physics, and Greek, and finished my first quarter with a *D* in philosophy, and *C*s in physics and Greek. A sturdy 1.66 grade point average. "Why were your grades so low?" you ask. "Why were they so high?" I answer. For the fact was, whenever I happened to pay attention, I argued with my professors. Especially in ethics—a fact which might conceivably help explain that *D* grade. But then how could anybody *not* argue in an ethics class? I certainly didn't know how to manage it.

Being contentious and scarcely opening a book, I was not a model student. Just like high school. We keep repeating ourselves over and over, which is character, or the Myth of Self still trying to be gotten right. Einstein once defined insanity as doing the same thing over and over, expecting a different result. Well, most of us do this, running in the squirrel cage of habit. After all, it's what we are. Certainly, *I've* always done it, and have continued to this very moment, without even having to step outside the squirrel cage to say so.

Physics and philosophy soon gasped, sagged, abandoned all metaphorical integrity, and collapsed by the wayside. But I continued to take courses in classical Greek, as well as some in English literature— a new instrument added to the score. Every quarter, I signed up for the next course in Greek. My grades soared to the *B* range, and then, for some utterly mysterious reason, occasionally even higher. Generally, however, I might just as well have been playing the trumpet.

But I trudged on, so that by the third quarter of my sophomore year, I had exhausted the undergraduate curriculum in Greek, and started graduate courses. I was now the only member of the class, sitting at a table with Professor Robert Jones, a mild, gentle, scholarly man, obviously puzzled by my persistence. But how could he not have been? If I'd ever stopped to think about it, I would have been pretty puzzled myself.

There were two jokes about my taking classical Greek: "Was I going to open a restaurant?" and "It's all Greek to me." In their way, these jokes were harder to bear than the study of a language which everyone concedes to be very difficult, with something like 1500 irregular verb forms or disguises. (As I remember it, there were practically no regular verbs—which I guess means *they* were the irregular ones.) Its complexity brings to mind what Heine said about Latin—that if the Romans had had to learn it first, they could never have found time to conquer the world.

When I graduated, I was surprised to discover I was unemployable. But what had I expected? Had I assumed that I'd be hired simply to Think Great Thoughts? Or perhaps, for somewhat less pay, Pretty Good Thoughts? Gazing back over the decades, it's hard to imagine I could have been capable of such folly. And yet, I obviously *was* capable of it; and not simply *capable* of it, but capable of it with a certain *panache*—which is the only way to do it, if you have to do it at all.

Not all my actions were foolish, though. In 1947, I married Barbara Reese, and we are still married. This is sufficiently unusual for the general populace; but for a writer, it's almost as grotesque an embarrassment as having a happy childhood. Barbara was working for the Ohio State University Research Foundation, and continued until I graduated. Our first daughter, Cynthia, was born in 1948, followed by Barbara Ellen in 1950, and our son John in 1959.

Jack and Barbara Matthews on their wedding day, 1947

In 1948 we bought a new Anglia, an English Ford, which in those days was a startling sight. We drove it everywhere, visiting our farm in Delaware County, and travelling all over the beautiful, back-country roads of central Ohio, eating apples, with me smoking cigarettes or a pipe as we drove, reciting Wordsworth sonnets that had been memorized, and talking idealistically and dreaming extravagantly about how wonderful it would be if someday I could teach in a university and we could live the academic life—a life rich in culture, stability, and peace. Sure. But also, *excitement!* For what is more exciting than ideas and the institutionalized leisure in which to study them?

One of our favorite movies was *The Third Man,* and its zither theme song plunked enchantingly through our heads for several months. I was a door-to-door Fuller brush salesman, then. That song still surfaces, occasionally—if sounds can be said to surface. (Recently, we saw the film again on TV; and what a disappointment *that* was! I guess you had to be there.) I worked at a variety of other jobs in those days, some to be itemized in the next section. We enjoyed reading mysteries and popular novels. Along with Hugh Walpole's *Rogue Herries* and the mystery novels of Theodora DuBois, I read Emerson's essays and Boethius's *Consolation of Philosophy* in translation.

They were wonderful years. Filled with anxiety and uncertainty, of course; but that's only as it should be, for young people should have to pay for being in love and charged with all the excitement and promise of youth.

On Being a Husband, Father, and Worker at Various Jobs

Most of the anxiety and uncertainty had to do with the trouble I had getting my head in focus. A later generation would have said I was trying to find myself, but we didn't have the vocabulary then, so I didn't know where to look. I tried a number of things, becoming increasingly frustrated and demoralized; even though I shared in the proletarian cult of experience, or at least some romanticized, middle-class version thereof. I liked the idea of working at a lot of various things, absorbing *real life* in all its rich and raw variety. I was doing what young writers were supposed to do back then, accumulating job experiences the way Kiowas used to gather *coup* feathers.

Off and on, I worked on the loading docks of the Big Bear Warehouse, just off Olentangy River Road, in Columbus. Whenever I needed a job there, there

"Our children Barbie, John, and Cindy," 1965

was one waiting, for one of two reasons: it was hard work and they always needed help, or because my aunt and uncle owned the trucking company that served all the Big Bear stores throughout Ohio. So much for my proletarian experience, you might say; still, the literal nepotism ended at the loading docks, for I still had to be at work at two or four in the morning, depending upon the loading schedules, and I had to work as hard as the other workers.

Maybe there were times when I worked a little harder, for I liked the idea of using my muscles. *Mens sana in corpore sano* seemed a pretty nifty motto, until I saw it quoted in an issue of Bob Hoffman's *Strength and Health,* which kind of took the fun out of it. Like just about everything else, hard physical labor was *interesting;* and I can remember sitting on the loading docks and reading a school edition of Aesop's *Fables* in the original Greek during lunch hour, which was at eight o'clock, therefore a sort of breakfast.

Years later, I would use these experiences on the Big Bear produce docks to write *The Tale of Asa Bean,* a novel about a hopelessly quixotic, sexually starved intellectual who lived with his married sister (née Earlene Bean) and brother-in-law, Roy Scobie, and worked in a produce warehouse, where he quoted Latin to the cabbage crates and proved generally whimsical and feckless as he played clever though impractical games with reality.

I took a door-to-door job selling *Brittanica Junior* encyclopaedias—making two sales the first week, which surprised me. I didn't think money should come that easily; and as it turned out, it didn't. Then I became a Fuller Brush man, carried my sample suitcase from door to door, took orders from yawning housewives, and read philosophy over lunch in a neighborhood restaurant. Our district manager was Leon Wedluga, a relentlessly sanguine man who talked a lot, and smiled and chewed gum with his mouth open, and said "Fine and dandy" so often and with such gusto that I figured it must be a Fuller Brush slogan.

I was still selling Fuller Brushes when I worked briefly as a gumshoe, which is to say, a shamus or private eye. Guy Houston owned a farm near ours in Delaware County, and he had his own detective agency. One day he asked if I'd be interested in a job that paid one dollar an hour, and since I wasn't selling many Fuller Brushes, and since after the episode in Sitka I'd learned not to despise the gifts of chance, I told him I would. Guy's wife was the daughter of the eponym of the Chase Investigating Agency, and both of them had worked in private detection for years.

So I took on a few cases, and managed to use my Fuller Brush suitcase as a cover for knocking on doors and finding out things that people usually don't want to be known. This was a perfect job for nosy people, or people who are interested in other people . . . or people who have a vague but sometimes powerful hankering to write philosophical novels somewhat like those of Joseph Conrad. A hankering to do it *some* day, maybe, though not necessarily too soon.

In Ohio at that time, private detectives were not licensed. They were essentially hired witnesses (thus, "Private Eyes"). I worked on a few insurance frauds, and one domestic relations case that required me to sit in my little 1948 Anglia and watch a house for ten hours a day. Once the man in the case took off in his car, driving fast, and I had to tail him in my Anglia, about as inconspicuous as a fire engine in need of a ring job.

I remember one difficult insurance fraud case in Springfield, Ohio, fifty miles away. A woman who'd sued for injuries she claimed to have suffered in a car wreck was said to have chased some marauding urchins out of her yard, running after them and waving her crutches. Stories like that get the attention of insurance companies; but our subject wouldn't let anyone in her house, and of course we had no legal right to enter. Guy and several other agents failed to get in. I also gave it a shot, but got nowhere.

Then Barbara, who became an agent for this single case, tried and was freely admitted. The results were not what everyone expected; not only did the old lady refrain from brandishing her crutch and chasing my wife off the premises, she gave a very convincing display of physical debility. Since that time I've never trusted the word of marauding urchins worth a damn.

My next brief and largely inconsequential adventure was working as a piano salesman at Lyon and Healy's Music Store in downtown Columbus. There I met a woman, the manager of the sheet music department, who was the most extraordinarily gifted specimen of relentless, perverse, committed nastiness I have ever known. Today, they'd say she probably didn't feel good about herself. But then, there's no reason she should have.

I sold virtually nothing at Lyon and Healy's, although I do remember reading Milton while I was seated at my desk trying to look knowledgeable about pianos. By this time I should have figured it out: if I was supposed to sell pianos, I did lessons; if I was supposed to do lessons, I drank beer at Larry's or ate cheeseburgers at Ptomaine Tommy's, on High Street across from the OSU campus, with a sign announcing a "seating capacity of 10,000, 30 at a time."

Lyon and Healy's was located on Gay Street. That name didn't mean a thing to me at the time, because the word's homosexual reference wasn't yet part of the language; but even if it had been, its significance might have eluded me, for there is a lot I don't notice. I've always believed that missing what everybody else notices is a gift. For example, it had never occurred to me when I was growing up that "Fallis Road," only two streets north of Glencoe, was oddly named.

Awareness is admirable, of course; but there's a lot to be said for obliviousness, too.

Why I Worked at the Post Office

In 1950, I finally settled down and got a job in the United States Post Office, working as a clerk in the Parcel Post Station, on Spring Street in Columbus. It was while working there that I began publishing in literary quarterlies. My first published story, "The Lieutenant," appeared in an Irish periodical, *Envoy,* in June 1951.

Literary quarterlies were the first and have remained virtually the only market for my short stories and poems. I came early to believe that in spite of paying little or nothing for contributions, they publish most of the best in literature. Perhaps my idealization of academic life has carried over to these small magazines, for they are mostly university-con-

nected. Whatever the reason, I still honor them. In spite of their occasional decadence, kookiness, and overly specialized audiences, they have been for me the real thing, and not a mere "training ground for writers," as they're labelled in market listings.

No doubt they have subtly influenced my writing, since I have always believed that *here* is where literature should happen, and not in the large commercial magazines whose real business is perfume and carpet ads, articles on diet and sexual attractiveness, and photos of the current crop of immortal celebrities. If quarterlies and little magazines are sometimes committed to exotic silliness and goofy causes, the great commercial magazines are always more or less vulnerable to the superstitions of fashion, which may or may not be compatible with literary value. Relevance is a terrible trap; and it's the sole business of the commercial media.

I'm usually content to have paid the price for writing noncommercial fiction, but there are times when I feel bitter about the neglect of my work. But then, for a writer to feel neglected is as natural as for a dog to have fleas. Not only that, generally despising the popular market on principle, I have no just complaint against its neglect of me. Furthermore, I have no particular reason to expect popular success, for most of the people I instinctively write for are either dead or don't read books.

The literary quarterlies of the fifties and sixties were wonderful. My stories began to appear in *Accent,* the *Chicago Review,* the *Southwest Review,* the *Sewanee Review,* and others. They shared issues with the work of J. F. Powers, Wallace Stevens, Babette Deutsch, Wallace Fowlie, Iris Murdoch, Nat Hentoff, T. S. Eliot, Lorine Niedecker, Albert Cook, Donald Hall, Isaac Rosenfeld, and whole hosts of other writers of promise and substance . . . hosts as richly heterogeneous as the above sampling.

Meanwhile, I continued to support my family by working as a clerk at the Parcel Post Station. I discovered that I could make that my life's work, and be reasonably happy, for it left me free time to write. Along with writing, I earned my master's degree in English from OSU. My thesis was "The Legal Comedy of the Ring and the Book," directed by Richard D. Altick, a first-rate scholar and inspiring teacher, whose book *The Scholar Adventurers* is something of a bibliophilic classic. Although my degree in English literature was almost as impractical as one in classical Greek, it was nevertheless an accomplishment, and it made me proud. I believed then, and still believe, that the world of letters is elegant and worthy of our idealism; and a scholarly commitment to that world is an enduring privilege.

"Cindy, Barbie, Barbara, and my mother with John at 164 Glencoe Road, where I was born,"
1969

It was said that whoever worked five years in the post office would never leave. The annual one hundred dollar increments to one's salary were so small that quitting was a demoralizing thought. Nevertheless, I left after nine years when I was offered a job by a neighbor, Ralph Gauvey, who had just been named president of Urbana College, a small Swedenborgian school in Urbana, Ohio. Gauvey had read some of my stories and offered me a job teaching English, even though I had never taught.

The next year, we moved to Urbana, thus beginning a new life. That's the way it always happens, isn't it? Just one new life after another.

Notebook Days

While working in the Parcel Post Station, I carried a small notebook in my hip pocket for jotting down ideas. I have kept these tattered old notebooks, and occasionally take them out to see what my head was doing all those years ago. They are filled with epigrams, perceptions, story ideas, drafts for poems, jingles for advertising contests, and notes I made for writing feature stories for the *Columbus Dispatch*. There are also a few invented names. I've always liked to think of names as onomastic codes, so that whatever happened to a character named J. Dan Swope could not happen to one named Rex McCoy (protagonists, respectively, of *Pictures of the Journey Back* and *The Charisma Campaigns*). This is nonsense, of course; but it can be an interesting and sometimes useful game. Which means it isn't nonsense, after all.

The notebook entries are short, and some are almost Delphic in their enigmatic laconism. For example, what could one make of this entry, from one of the 1958 notebooks? "Broken toe lying there like the bloated corpse of a mouse." Or this one: "Keeping alive the handsome (tender?) logic of the veins"? And what about such creepy entries as "A blind tick climbing my neck at night" and "Saurian in the green leaves"?

Most of the entries, however, are not enigmatic. In fact, many are so clear as to be banal—although I don't see any reason for apology, since we go through life more or less constantly forgetting the obvious.

Not only that, the world changes, and a few of today's platitudes may have been real wowsers four decades ago. Therefore, the law is: trust yourself enough to be honest. But then, if you're tempted to quote from your jottings when your career is ripe, be judiciously selective, without being *too* selective; if something seems worthwhile, repeat it. If our messages were confined to the genuinely creative, we'd all starve for information. Here is a sampling from those old notebooks:

Epigrams

The reason people are dirty is they're afraid of death.

There are some people to whom presents are given and there are others to whom presents are not given.

One of the purposes of acquiring knowledge is to learn how to be overwhelmed by the complexity of life.

The poor survive because they're anonymous.

The worst thing: to be locked inside oneself.

For most men, it requires courage to be happy.

Characters

Man who can't stop sneezing.

College prof, with unhappy family life, "kills" himself (identity) by disappearing and becoming a laborer with his hands.

Brilliant woman married to a sleepy-eyed man who frequently sighs and says, "You're a fool, Martha." She needs this.

Hunchbacked girl playing a violin in an amateur show.

Drunken business man always goes to driving range "to hit a bucket of balls."

Gestures, Expressions and Mannerisms

He always had a business-like look on his face . . . the look of a man wiping the windows of his car.

She walked with her head to the side, as if she had forgotten something.

Professor shoots firecrackers when he sees class drifting off . . . or some boy looking drowsy.

Young girl before summer shower. Afraid that the rain will turn her into a witch?

Little girl sobbing inside vast, grinning Halloween mask.

Names

Irish Joe Schmidt.
Paula Popinsky
Sisters of the Sick Poor
John Roger Simes

Perceptions

Light hums within the eye and sound glimmers.

The moral obligation for self-fulfillment.

Families seen as small, pathetically embattled groups against a world conceived of as hostile.

People get divorced because they have different philosophies.

The mystique of an institution (school)—perpetuity.

Synthesis is at the very core of human experience—to wit, sights, sounds, etc. No wonder, then, man craves unity.

Images

Two butterflies dancing inches apart in the air.

Bricks: cherry red, dirty pink, amber, pastel blue, dull orange, nutty brown, walnut, fuchsia, dirty ivory, cream, purple, tan, gray, lavender, dun, maroon, honey.

Piano in an old saloon—nobody knows how to play it.

Dogs and Cat

We have had four dogs in our marriage, and I have always walked them on a leash, a civilized ritual. Reggie was an Airedale, lord of all he surveyed. He was smart, loyal, and gentle with people; but to other dogs an egregious tyrant. He once attacked a German shepherd, destroying his morale for life, maybe longer. He attacked another dog of dubious parentage, frightening him so much, the dog fainted. My wife, who had the disadvantage of being a witness, claims the dog didn't faint, but was almost killed before Reggie could be talked out of canicide. Its owner, ashamed to tell the vet his pet had been so seriously incapacitated by another dog, claimed he'd been hit by a car.

I've heard of only two Airedales fighting pit bulls, and both won. One was attacked by a pit bull in his own yard, but the Airedale jumped over it, seized it by the back of its skull, and crushed it. Now, no sensible person wants a killing machine for a dog; but it's good to know that such intelligent and amiable companions as Airedales have proved capable of doing The Right Thing when called upon.

We also had a genial and gentle 165-pound Rottweiler, years before that breed became fashionable. This was Duke, aka Elm Blight, and he came to us with a thirty-pound rock he thought was his mother. After that was an Irish wolfhound, Cormac. When he stood on his hind legs, he looked like the Eiffel Tower without a haircut. And finally, another Airedale—this one a bitch named Cecily, who still abides with us and prances to inaudible bells. Our only cat was a Siamese named Hecate. She lived sixteen years and kept her figure to the last.

We've loved all our pets. One of the great advantages they have over people is that they're not people. I am especially moved by the profound sadness of dogs. They want to discuss politics, talk about the old days, and listen to Mozart; but they don't know how, and we can't teach them. Otherwise, they ask for little: to be fed, watered, spoken to, and walked. They are faithful in a perfidious world, and like having their ears rubbed.

College Life Again, Within and Without

Urbana College was operating as a junior college and had almost expired in 1959 when I began teaching there. The student body numbered sixteen, the faculty five. Within a few years, enrollment ballooned to over one hundred. The campus was beautiful, with elbow room for the tall oaks and shagbark hickory trees on its rolling lawns. There were three academic buildings and one dormitory. I was the English department.

For five years I taught all English classes, designing them as follows: the first quarter, rhetoric and composition; second quarter, general semantics or formal logic; third quarter, literature. I considered this a good system then, and I still do. The abandonment of traditional college composition courses as a freshmen requirement has proved an utter disaster. The concession to "relevance" by skewing the curriculum was a shameful abdication of intellectual responsibility. College is meant to change lives, not reinforce ignorance and prejudice in a craven spirit of social accommodation.

But I still love university life. A professor once began every lecture by bowing to his students, signifying the honor he felt in teaching them. I often contemplate that courtly and elegant gesture, and might perform it myself if my classes were big enough . . . and if the male students wore coats and ties and the females wore skirts and dresses, and they all used correct grammar and took their pleasure in silently reading books rather than in the verbigeration of rock music.

Many students at Urbana were quiet, Ohio farm boys who liked cars instead of English. I gave a lot of *C*s and *D*s to those boys, sometimes just to pass them. I doubt if they got much from my classes, but from them I got the idea for the hero of *Hanger Stout, Awake!* Hanger was humble, kind, hopelessly nonverbal, and something of a funny saint. Hiram Haydn,

Wife, Barbara, in period costume for Athens County Bicentennial of the Northwest Ordinance, 1987

my editor at Harcourt Brace, called Hanger "all of us before we've eaten the apple."

In 1964, when Scribners published *Bitter Knowledge*, my first book of short stories, I was invited to come to Ohio University to teach Creative Writing. Hollis Summers was already here; and in the ensuing years, Walter Tevis, Daniel Keyes, James Norman Schmidt, Wayne Dodd, Stanley Plumly, Paul Nelson, Eve Shelnutt, and many other writers have taught in our program. In the early days, when meetings were unavoidable, we held them at our homes, opened a bottle of bourbon, and sat and smoked and enjoyed ourselves, comrades all. Most of that amiable assembly are now dead, retired, or living elsewhere. But I still teach and grumble about the modern world in the way of all old men. This is a ridiculous role we play, to be sure—even though old men have often turned out to be right.

So Athens became our home. The Jeffersonian elegance of our college green is an enduring inspiration. Surrounded by depressing rural poverty, we are nevertheless part of a university community. And for people who are mindful, mature, and intellectually unfettered, it is a good place to live. We can enjoy peace and comfort and read any book we could read anywhere else. We also have electricity, central heating, and a good sewer system.

Our children, Cindy, Barbie, and John, are married and live elsewhere. We have seven grandchildren—several may become presidents of the United States if they can work it into their schedules. My wife and I spend many hours in the car, driving on country roads to sales and auctions in a relentless search for old and rare books, along with whatever antiques and old paintings we can gather. Riding in our car is something we've always enjoyed, and it's possible that we have eaten more meals in fast food places than the entire population of Tobruk or Sligo.

What does all this have to do with being a writer? Well, it depends upon the writer. As for me, I think of such homey details as the fabric of reality. In a media-drunk age, our life in a small southeastern Ohio town could easily be judged provincial and escapist, partial and socially erroneous. But that's all right, for *sub specie aeternitatis* all human lives are temporally as well as geographically provincial, and the partiality and error we inhabit are our realities—as good and true, in their way, as any other.

Exorcising the Great Bitch Goddess of Success

Upon rare occasions through the years, editors of large commercial magazines have written to me, asking to see something they might publish. I've always complied, but whatever I've sent has been utterly and obviously not the sort of thing they would ever conceivably use. Why didn't I send something appropriate? One reason may have been a certain ambivalence about success. Even the idea makes me jumpy.

I have sabotaged my own interests in a hundred ways. In 1974, in connection with some film interest in my novel *The Charisma Campaigns,* my agent set up a meeting with a production company in Hollywood. I visited them and was asked to do a treatment. So I mailed them one a week later. The only thing is, I didn't have a clear idea of what a treatment was, and didn't bother to find out. I didn't particularly want to know. I simply sat down and wrote several pages of text that seemed to me kind of, sort of, *maybe* what a treatment might be. If it worked, fine; if not, why, no problem.

I'm uneasy about institutionalized celebrity, afraid of being destroyed by it as so many others have been. I distrust the change of focus it brings into one's life; I distrust its phoniness, its glitz and make-believe. Celebrity distorts one's basic relationship to others, and people who want to understand something of their lives are wise to abjure it.

Part of my fear of publicity is superstitious, but superstition can be intellectually and psychologically healthy. There are ways in which it can promote a sane and wholesome wariness, reflective of how limited our grasp of reality is. Superstition can also be fun, interesting, a fascinating reality game. And yet, it is always more than that, for it keeps the doors of possibility open, allowing the spirit to breathe.

All of this having been said, it's obvious I don't find publicity entirely repugnant or you wouldn't be reading this account. And yet, my ambivalence is very real and defies a clear explanation. No doubt the world awaits some clarification, but it won't be found here.

Bibliophilia

I bought my first old book in the summer of 1942, on Oakland Park Avenue in Columbus, next door to the North Broadway Methodist Church . . . where I had once won a Bible contest in Sunday school, and where good old Boy Scout Troop 28 met once a week for several years, during which time I was a First Class scout and leader of The Flaming Arrow Patrol. (It came to me already named, just like Duke, our Rottweiler.)

However, it is not the church, but the house we are concerned with. There was an estate sale there, and on the third floor, filled with hot, stale air and smelling like an attic, there were bits and pieces of things lying about, including several books for a dime each. Two were leather-bound and I bought them. One was *A Renunciation of Universalism* and the other was the Dayton, 1845, edition of Lewis and Clark's journal, in the back of which was a short lexicon of "Indian" words. I've kept the Lewis and Clark book, for it is the first antiquarian book I ever bought.

There would be many more through the years. In the early 1960s, in Findlay, Ohio, I bought an entire semitruckload of 10,000 books. I climbed through them, selecting a box or two, after which I sold the remainder to a used-book store in Columbus. That was the greatest number I have ever bought at one time, although there have been other moments of plenitude. Once at auction, I bought fifty-two boxes of books, about 1500, and sold one of them, a first edition of Book Two of William Carlos Williams's *Patterson* in dust jacket, for more than I'd paid for the entire lot.

Such boasting is fun, but it does not reflect the great adventure and dignity of book collecting. There is an energy and style in wheeling and dealing for books, and playing the game of profits; but the real genius of collecting is aesthetic, spiritual, *bibliophilic.* To build a great collection is to enter upon a quest and accept some of the conditions of art. It is an act of quiet elegance, virtually independent of subject matter. If you choose to collect books about fire engines or cathode ray tubes or Victorian underwear, others may wonder at your choice; but if you "learn the field"—and are shrewd, knowledgeable, and patient—you will create something worthy and honorable.

And yet, collecting need not be coherent, much less elegant, to be fun. While I have been a serious collector of rare books since my days at Urbana College, I have never achieved that admirable discipline and focus that characterize great collections. Still, this is a limitation I am happy to accept. I collect by spending time instead of money, travelling and responding to whatever books surface by chance. This aleatory strategy suits me well, for it is a grand adventure; and I wouldn't trade my method for any other—even one resulting in a collection that has achieved fame and renown in the small but intense and vivid world of bibliophily.

How is my passion for collecting old and rare books connected with my writing? One connection is obvious: I *write* about collecting old and rare books; not only should I know something about that odd and intricate world of enterprise, but I should keep fanning the fires of enthusiasm. And yet, that isn't how it really happens; that's too contrived, too calculated. If I kept collecting books merely to keep my interest stimulated so I could write convincingly on the subject, it would be simply a means to an end; and that's not the way it is at all. Building a personal library (which means constantly changing it as well as adding to it) is an act of freedom, commitment, and self-definition. Just like living.

It is also a scholarly undertaking, and in a unique way, artistic. Furthermore, it can be a form of investment. All of these aspects of bibliophily are interesting; all are worthy of mindful and reflective people. Books map all that we can know, and much that we can't. They map time, space, and as much of eternity as we can imagine. In short, they reflect the world itself, so that no matter how specialized a collection is, it is a kind of microcosm.

I also collect old and rare books as a writer, gathering whole worlds of information from which I am constantly drawing material. For example, my novel *Sassafras* was originally inspired by my reading

about the burial practices of Plains Indians. This was long before I'd begun to collect western Americana, but the idea lay dormant in my mind for years until I did start to collect actively, absorbing all sorts of information that would eventually prove useful . . . such as the nineteenth-century books on phrenology that always seemed to crop up in the piles I sorted through while looking for treasures.

For me, "collecting" includes reading widely and accumulating all sorts of odd facts. Much that I gathered in those years was from western historical documents, and would prove essential to *Sassafras,* which is about a phrenologist in Kansas in 1853. His beloved Wuyoomi-Yaki, a Comanche girl, is killed while digging up the corpse of her brother which had been buried by a U.S. Cavalry unit. In creating this version of the Antigone story with the burial customs reversed, I returned to my first idea for the novel, for it was this variation upon the classical motif that I had found interesting.

The author and his wife, shortly before their forty-fourth wedding anniversary, 1991

After You Get There, It All Looks Different

I collect memories as I collect books, and much of my mental life is reminiscence. This is neither simple passivity nor easy self-indulgence, but a philosophical undertaking, for I keep trying to get the Past right. My oldest memories reach back to when I was a very small boy, drinking in the world as fast as I could gulp, innocent of any thought that I might be "gathering material" as I now think of it in writerly terms. And yet, we keep our grip on the thread of self as we grope our paths through time; and I can remember as a boy trying to communicate with the man I would someday become . . . as if, somehow, I needed to clarify and justify what I then was, in all my confusion and ignorance, to some wiser future self, who loomed in my imagination somewhat like another father.

That old man is not what I thought I'd be, for how could I have known? But then, I'm sure the boy I remember—a boy necessarily focused through the lens of all those subsequent decades—would seem strange to that real boy, at that time. You can forget, but you can't unremember. And now, I greet him as one tenuous and evanescent reality to another, and confer retroactive blessings upon him, as I feel his proactive blessings upon me. After you get there, nothing looks the same. And yet, none of it looks very different, either. This is one of the great mysteries of time and self; it's one of the things I have always written about, and always will.

BIBLIOGRAPHY

Novels:

Hanger Stout, Awake!, Harcourt, 1967.

Beyond the Bridge, Harcourt, 1970.

The Tale of Asa Bean, Harcourt, 1971.

The Charisma Campaigns, Harcourt, 1972.

Pictures of the Journey Back, Harcourt, 1973.

Sassafras, Houghton, 1983.

Short-story collections:

Bitter Knowledge, Scribners, 1964.

Tales of the Ohio Land, Ohio Historical Society, 1980.

Dubious Persuasions, Johns Hopkins University Press, 1981.

Crazy Women, Johns Hopkins University Press, 1985.

Ghostly Populations, Johns Hopkins University Press, 1986.

Dirty Tricks, Johns Hopkins University Press, 1990.

Nonfiction:

Book Collecting and the Search for Reality (essay), privately printed by Library Associates of Wichita State University, 1972.

Collecting Rare Books for Pleasure and Profit, Putnam, 1977.

Booking in the Heartland (essays), Johns Hopkins University Press, 1986.

Perhaps the Greatest Incomparable Autobiography in the World, Northern Ohio Bibliophilic Society, 1986.

Memoirs of a Bookman (essays), Ohio University Press, 1989.

Poetry:

An Almanac for Twilight, University of North Carolina Press, 1966.

In a Theater of Buildings (chapbook), Ox Head Press, 1970.

Private Landscapes (chapbook), Croissant, Pamphlet No. 1, 1975.

Plays:

An Interview with the Sphinx, Dramatic Publishing Company, 1991.

On the Shore of that Beautiful Shore, Dramatic Publishing Company, 1991.

Editor:

(With Elaine Hemley) *The Writer's Signature: Idea in Story and Essay*, Scott Foresman, 1972.

Archetypal Themes in the Modern Story, St. Martin's Press, 1973.

Belden, The White Chief (autobiography), Ohio University Press, 1974.

Rare Book Lore: Selected Letters of Ernest J. Wessen, Ohio University Press, forthcoming.

Contributor of short stories, essays, poems, and reviews to such periodicals as *Gamut, Kenyon, London Review of Books, Mademoiselle, Malahat Review, Michigan Quarterly Review, Nation, National Review, New Republic, New York Times, Poetry, Review, Sewanee Review, Southern Review,* and *Yale Review.*

Jim Wayne Miller
1936-

"My great-grandfather and great-grandmother Miller (back row, left and front row, second from right), my grandmother and grandfather Miller (front row, right), and my father's older brothers and sisters, spring 1913. My father is an infant in his mother's arms."

I don't remember it, but my mother tells me that at about the age of three I would dance when my uncle played his fiddle. That would have been when we were still living with my grandmother and grandfather Miller, on the Sandy Mush Creek Road, in Buncombe County, about fifteen miles from Asheville, in mountainous western North Carolina.

I do remember my grandmother Miller reciting—Kipling's "If," "The Little Match Girl"—and repeating what she called "declamation pieces"—set speeches on subjects like truth, courage, and virtue remembered from her school days. Her repertoire was extensive; she could recite, it seemed, for hours without repeating herself. My grandfather Miller was a quiet man who read Zane Grey novels, newspapers, and commented laconically on religion, politics, and any foolishness at the national, state, or local level that caught his attention.

I remember my parents and grandparents discussing whether or not I would be permitted to enter first grade in the fall of 1942, for the term began in late August or early September, and I would not be six years old until late October. I was allowed to enter, and I recall being full of anticipation the evening before school began. By this time I had a younger sister, Judy, and two younger brothers, Jerry and Douglas (Joe and Debbie would come later), and we had our own house on a small farm about four miles from my grandmother and grandfather Miller's farm. My maternal grandparents, Grandmother and Grandfather Smith, had come to live with us there on the Leicester Road between Hanlon Mountain and High Knob. They had built their own house, within sight of ours, and ran the farm on a share system. (This arrangement is presented, in a telescoped fashion, in my novel *Newfound.*) My father worked in Asheville during the war years, exempt from the draft either because his job was considered defense-related or because he had four, then five, and finally six children. But sometime after I started to school my mother's brother, Uncle Arnold, came by our house before daylight one morning to say good-bye. He was leaving for the army. My mother wept and I cried because she did.

My father took us to a war bond rally at the Leicester School, a redbrick 1–12 school built by the Works Progress Administration during the Depression. Mr. Bascom Lamar Lunsford, a neighbor from the South Turkey Creek community, emceed the program from the school stage. Local entertainers picked guitars, played fiddles, sang, and danced. Then everyone was asked to buy war bonds. My most vivid recollection of the war bond rally was a guest entertainer from Kentucky, a man with salt-and-pepper hair and thick black eyebrows, named Virgil Sturgill, who stood on the stage unaccompanied, his hands behind his back, and sang the ballad "Barbara Allen." I think the performance permanently altered me. My blood ran cold. I felt, in Emily Dickinson's words, "zero at the bone." The ballad sounded like many of the poems my grandmother Miller recited—in the kitchen or in the parlor at her house on Sandy Mush Road. But until I heard Virgil sing I hadn't realized how powerful the old poems and songs could be.

So much about my place and people there in Leicester, in western North Carolina, a part of the southern Appalachian region, I would realize only gradually as the years passed.

The novelist Saul Bellow says a writer is first a reader who has been moved to emulation. Or first a listener, I would add. I had heard my grandmother's poems and declamation pieces, Bascom Lamar Lunsford's and Virgil Sturgill's ballads, and I was constantly listening to my parents, grandparents, and neighbors, whose discourse consisted chiefly of anecdotes. Any explanation might involve a story: "I'm by that the way the old lady was who kissed the cow." And

"My grandfather Smith with his foxhounds, in the 1950s"

now I was reading stories and poems, in and out of school, and listening to radio dramas evenings and weekends. Reading, listening, and writing. I remember reading a poem describing dark woods—and drafting my own unabashed imitation of it, which I carried to my grandmother Miller, who read it with enthusiasm and approval. She encouraged all her grandchildren to bring her samples of their school work. She filed our papers, rolled up and tied with red ribbon, in back bedroom bureau drawers. (Years later, when the house was cleaned out, drawers full of these papers were found.)

In third grade I became a teaching assistant. Miss Duckett, our teacher, who must have been in her early twenties and just out of teachers college, held silent reading periods in her room. She designated me and two of my classmates helpers during these reading sessions. We were assigned two rows each and we stood at the front of our rows waiting until a classmate came on an unfamiliar word or phrase and raised a hand. Our job was to go to their desks, pronounce the unfamiliar word in a whisper, or explain its meaning in a hushed voice. During these sessions Miss Duckett typically worked at her desk, filling out report cards or maintaining other records. Sometimes she used a typewriter at her desk. The typewriter fascinated me. (Miss Duckett fascinated me, too. I was in love with her and intended to marry her when I grew up.) She noticed my interest in the typewriter and introduced me to it, rolling in a clean sheet of paper and helping me type my name. But repeatedly during the reading sessions I incurred the wrath of my fellow teacher aids, two girls, who complained that they often had to help students in my two rows because I was always watching Miss Duckett type, or staring out the window while students in my rows had their hands up, waiting for help. I don't recall Miss Duckett ever reprimanding me for my negligence. We must have formed a mutual admiration society of two. She taught me a short list of Spanish vocabulary and at lunchtime pulled me out of the cafeteria line and drilled me on my Spanish words before other teachers. "Amigo?"—"Friend." "Amiga?"—"Girl friend."

But I think Miss Duckett despaired when, for our third-grade play, she cast me in a role that required

Grandmother Smith, about 1900

skipping backwards. I couldn't do it, at least not dependably, and our play would be performed before the entire school. She switched me to the role of a minister who held an open Bible and married a couple onstage. On the morning we performed our play I suddenly found myself onstage in front of the waiting couple, two of my classmates—without my Bible! I froze. In that instant Miss Duckett's hand, holding the Bible, appeared miraculously through a slit in the sidestage curtain. I took the Bible, opened it, and after the entire school—grades one through twelve, plus teachers and principal—had stopped laughing, performed the marriage ceremony.

Miss Duckett forgave me everything. Despite my shortcomings, she arranged with other teachers in the school to have me come to their rooms as a storyteller. I recall how she would take me outside our classroom, give me directions to another teacher's room, then go back into her class and close the door, leaving me standing in the hall, where the wooden floors smelled of linseed oil. These visits were daunting excursions, for sometimes they entailed going up on the second floor, and facing a room full of seventh or eighth graders, who, in the hierarchy of grade school, were alien and superior creatures who could do long division and fractions. I recall knocking on classroom doors, having them opened by teachers who were still lecturing the class, textbook in hand, finishing up some comment on American history or the chief exports of a South American country. I would whisper the reason for my being there. The teacher might seem puzzled at first, then remember the arrangement with Miss Duckett, and announce to the class that I had come to tell a story. I don't remember actually telling the stories, or even what stories I told. I must have gone on automatic pilot for the telling. But when I finished I would turn to leave; at the door I can remember looking back at the faces of students who seemed to be having difficulty understanding the odd interruption of their lesson.

We also wrote stories in Miss Duckett's third grade, and I believe some of them were published in the school newspaper. I seem to recall taking a story of mine that had appeared in the school paper to my grandmother Miller, as I had done with my poem, and getting a rave review. We continued to write stories in fourth grade, with Mrs. Davis, and in fifth and sixth, under Mrs. McIntyre (who taught both fifth and sixth grades in the same room, doubling up because of a space and teacher shortage). We learned a new group of twenty to twenty-five words each week, and the assignment, routinely, was to write each word in a sentence and underline the new word. Mrs. McIntyre had no patience with students who

"My mother holding me, 1937"

fudged and wrote something like, "What does *statute* mean?" She disqualified such sentences. We had to show by the way we used the word that we understood its meaning.

Instead of writing unrelated sentences, we had the option of using all the new words in a story or an essay. I preferred this assignment, for it was fun to look over a new list of words and imagine a scene, situation, or subject that would require using the whole list. Sometimes it was possible to use two or three new words in a single sentence. "Jack wanted to learn more about his *environment*. He decided to learn the names of all the *individual* trees on his father's farm. He did not want to be *negligent* and *omit* the name of a single tree, no matter how *nondescript*."

Neither Mrs. Davis nor Mrs. McIntyre used students as teaching assistants, as Miss Duckett had done. In their classrooms I don't recall having silent reading periods in preparation for reading aloud. But such study sessions would have been useful, for

students were forever stumbling over words in the text. A veteran teaching assistant, I noticed every mispronunciation. Once, as we worked our way through a passage describing a performance by Stephen Foster, a girl read: "A wave of applesauce arose from the crowd." "Applause," I thought, anticipating the teacher's correction.

During those years Miss Vittorio came to our school once a week. A former opera singer who had retired to the Asheville, North Carolina, area, she brought musical culture to nearby schools. For a quarter per student. Students who brought their quarters were dismissed from regular classes to attend Miss Vittorio's sessions in the auditorium, where she taught us a variety of songs, including hits from current Broadway musicals. She also produced an occasional operetta at our school, and an annual musical evening to which the entire community was invited. Black-haired and bosomy, Miss Vittorio dressed vividly, was theatrical and outspoken. Our country school and community had never seen anything like her, except maybe in a movie. At her musical evenings, when she showcased our talents, she did mildly outrageous things like running down the auditorium aisle in a spontaneous gesture of gratitude to Mr. Wilde, our principal, and kissing him on his bald head. The audience of students, parents, and grandparents loved it.

I was cast in one of Miss Vittorio's operettas. (The role did not require skipping backwards.) Dressed in a vaguely Spanish costume my mother had made for the occasion, I walked arm-in-arm with a girl from another grade and together we sang—something. Right after the program we had recess. I changed out of my costume, went out on the playground—and immediately got into a fight with a bully who made fun of the costume I'd worn and called me a sissy.

What with being unable to skip backwards, the humiliation of the suddenly appearing Bible in the third-grade play, and the fight I got into as a result of my part in the operetta, I lost any enthusiasm I'd had for theatricals. (I believe a recitation of Whitman's "O Captain! My Captain!" for a Lincoln Day radio program in Asheville along about then was my last performance for a long time.) I hadn't been thrilled going door-to-door in third grade telling stories. I did it because Miss Duckett told me to. I liked reading better, and writing something once in a while.

But even writing got me in trouble at school, at least once. I grew impatient with our games of cowboys and Indians, cops and robbers, or war games. They seemed to me sloppy and lacking in direction. I proposed that we come up with what amounted to a scenario before we started playing, so we'd know who was supposed to do what, and how things would turn out. This worked fairly well, but I wasn't altogether satisfied. One afternoon after school, while waiting for the "second" bus we rode home on, I was sitting at the edge of the playground with a buddy writing out a script for next day's game—when a bully came by. His discovery that we were *writing* somehow angered him; he picked a fight. I remember rolling with him down the bank at the edge of the playground, over honeysuckle, under a barbed-wire fence, and out into Mr. Brown's pasture. I managed to get on top of him, then, thinking I'd won, made the mistake of letting him up. He jumped on me again and I had to fight him all over. I almost missed my bus.

Many of the boys I grew up with were contemptuous of literary efforts, mine or anyone else's. They scorned poetry by repeating doggerel such as "Between your thighs / Your beauty lies. Snakeshit." They sang bawdy songs like "Ring Dang Doo, what is that? / Round and fuzzy like a pussy cat. / She went to Baltimore / to be a whore / Tacked her sign out on the door." Etc. But there was poetry in their language when they least knew it, and in the stories they told that were not thought of as literature. Still is.

In summer, when I wasn't helping my grandparents in fields and gardens, I often lay on my bed at a shaded open window and read. I read Ernest Thompson Seton's *Rolf in the Woods* there, glancing anxiously at the remaining pages, not wanting the story to end. I read *Black Beauty* by flashlight under the covers at night, after my parents made us turn off lights. As often as not, I lay across my bed hot afternoons and read the dictionary. In third and fourth grade during the summer I would fetch the newspaper when it arrived and carry it, with a jar of cold water, to a field where my grandfather Smith would be working, and read him the war news while he rested and quenched his thirst. Uncle Arnold was in General Mark Clark's army in Italy, so Grandma and Grandpa Smith had a special interest in following war news from there. (My grandmother Smith read, especially her Bible, but Grandpa Smith did not read.)

During one of these summers I heard a radio drama I thought was so good I wanted to write something like it. I walked to the crossroads store, bought a new tablet of lined paper, and new pencils. Back at the house, I made a desk of my mother's Singer sewing machine and set to work. Something interrupted me, or I lost interest, for I don't recall ever finishing the story, although at the time I thought it would be a good one.

After World War II ended and my uncle Arnold returned, he went to work for a news company in Asheville. He became a source of remaindered comic books and outdoor magazines such as *Field and Stream.* Whenever he came to the country to visit us, he'd bring me stacks of comics and outdoor magazines, all with the front cover torn off. I accumulated so many magazines, I set up an office in the top of our well house, where I cobbled a couple of secret compartments in the walls (for treasured possessions) and read comic books and outdoor magazines. I supplied comics to boys all over the scattered community. I'd carry a stack to school and trade or sell them. On weekends and in summer boys would ride bicycles to my office, to trade or purchase comics. They would stand at the foot of the steps leading up to my office over the well house and I would wheel and deal from the superior position of my seat on a middle step, a stack of magazines beside me. Of course, I read other things in my office, too. When I read *Tom Sawyer*

"My father, same year"

there, I laughed so hard at the scene involving the turpentined cat, my mother heard me from the house and came to see about me, thinking I had hurt myself somehow.

Although I had my office, I spent a lot of time outdoors. After all, we lived on a small farm, and there was work to be done. I milked two cows, morning and evening, and helped wean calves. I worked with my grandmother and grandfather in the cornfields, potato patches, the garden, and in the raising of burley tobacco, our cash crop. Whenever one of our cows came in heat, and walked the fencerows restlessly, bawling, I would have to lead her along the road by a rope to a neighbor who owned a bull, and get her bred. This was embarrassing—and potentially dangerous, for cows in heat, walking behind you, were capable of attempting to mount you. So I always had to walk along constantly looking back.

I began to range farther and farther from home. I spent a lot of time at the crossroads store, where men gathered in the evening to pitch horseshoes and talk politics. I went fishing with my father and my uncles. When I was younger, I would stay the night with my grandmother Smith when Grandpa went foxhunting with his cronies. Sometimes he would be gone just one night; but in autumn he always went on a week-long hunting and camping trip farther back in the mountains to a place called the Bearwallow. Now I began to go hunting with him, while one of my younger brothers or my sister Judy stayed with Grandma Smith. I roamed the woods, day and night. I cut pulpwood and timber for wages by day, then hunted possum and coon with the same crew of men and boys at night. We grabbled suckers in the creeks. I trapped muskrat and mink in winter and sold the furs on Lexington Avenue in Asheville. Once I sent a shipment of furs to a company in Pennsylvania and a couple of weeks later received a check for over $100.00—a fortune for a boy at that time, in that place.

I had no idea that many Americans would have considered me, along with my relatives and neighbors, quaint mountaineers. I didn't know that our speech was considered colorful (although I had long recognized a difference between "school" English and the way we talked at home). My grandfather Smith would say things like, "I *holp* him put up his hay and he *holp* me house my tobacco." (It sounded as if he were saying *hope* but he meant *helped.)* My grandmother Smith would refer to a neighbor as "clever," meaning generous or hospitable. If I went to her house early in the morning, she might say, "Well, did you come to borry fire?" When I walked

across Early's Mountain to my aunt Velma and uncle Roy Robinson's, to spend Christmas vacation there, and trap and hunt, old great-aunt Vashti might spy me coming into the yard, and although I was on foot, she would invite me to "Light down!"—as if I were arriving on a horse.

I didn't think about our speech much then. I knew it wasn't school talk. I mostly *felt* it—as a warm, friendly, sometimes jocular way of talking. Later I would discover that a lot of our talk was archaic English and could be found in the works of Shakespeare and Chaucer. Scholars came to our area to find people who still used such language. I also discovered later that the English musicologist Cecil Sharp came to western North Carolina around the time of World War I to collect ballads, and that he had found them in great abundance—and in the eastern Kentucky mountains, as well, among people like Virgil Sturgill, who sang "Barbara Allen" at the war bond rally.

I didn't know, until much later, that Bascom Lamar Lunsford, our neighbor on South Turkey Creek, who not only emceed the war bond rally, but probably organized it, as well, had established the Mountain Music Festival held in Asheville every August. In the late 1940s he went to Washington, D.C., and recorded his repertoire—more than 360 traditional songs and ballads—for the Library of Congress. All I knew during those years was that Bascom drove a new green Hudson Hornet around the community.

I had heard something about Thomas Wolfe, who had caused a furor in Asheville when he published his first novel, *Look Homeward, Angel.* My source was an uncle who ran a garage in Asheville, knew the Wolfe family, and said he'd worked on Wolfe's car once when Wolfe returned to Asheville. I learned later that F. Scott Fitzgerald had spent a lot of time at Asheville's Grove Park Inn, and that his wife Zelda died in a sanitorium fire there in the late 1940s. In those years I would come across a curious one-inch advertisement in the *Asheville Citizen* (I think it ran daily for a long time):

> Goat Milk
> Fifty Cents the Quart
> Carl Sandburg
> Connemara Farms
> Flat Rock, North Carolina

But I noticed it only because it usually appeared near the comics or the baseball scores.

After seventh grade, with Mrs. Sams, who had also been my mother's seventh-grade teacher (and

"The Leicester High School baseball team, 1954. I am in the first row, second from right, beside the catcher."

who remarked that on state exams I had "shot the moon"), after that year I ceased to be a student. I answered the call of woods and water, hunted, trapped, worked in timber. I was sent home from school in eighth grade because I had trapped a skunk and got the odor on me. (I thought I'd got it all off, but I'd merely ceased to be able to smell it myself; then, too, my desk was by the radiator and as I warmed up, I became intolerable.) I drifted through eighth, ninth, tenth grades. In school I was interested in baseball; away from school my interests ran to hounds, horns, lanterns, guns, girls, cars, and girls in cars.

My best buddy in high school came to me with a proposal. His uncle had been a pretty steady moonshiner in past years, but he'd given it up now, and his old whiskey still was hidden in the barn. Yeah? So? Well, my buddy said, we could clean up that old still, make moonshine, sell it, and buy us a car. His uncle would show us how to do it. He did, and we did. (On the sly, of course. My father would have been outraged and concerned about the possibility of my going to jail; my mother horrified at the certainty of

my going to hell.) We made enough moonshine, sold to a local bootlegger, to buy a car. And as soon as we had the car, we got out of the business. But by the time I came across Horace Kephart's *Our Southern Highlanders,* with its chapter on moonshining, I was able to check the text for the accuracy of his description.

My moonshining buddy and I were not above sampling our own wares. We did some mindless, dangerous, perfectly dreadful things, for which I am still apologizing. An incident involving the car bought with the proceeds of our moonshining project appears in one of several apology poems I wrote in memory of my father, after his death in 1985:

Thanks. I'm Sorry

I'm sorry I took your buffalo head nickels
and bought candy with them when I was eight.
Didn't I know they were part of your collection?
I was only sure that I loved Milky Ways.

I'm sorry I ran over Jess Teague's turkey
when I was sixteen and in love with speed.
Feathers in the rearview mirror—that's all I saw.
I hear you paid Jess fifteen dollars. Thanks.

Thanks, too, for taking off from work
and driving out to see the baseball game
I hit the home run in. I still remember
how you cheered and cheered from the third base
    bleachers.
Thanks. I'm sorry. And sorry you had to die.
You know that boy you were a father to?
He died, too—a little while after you did.
I wonder if you've seen him where you are?

I had not thought much about what I might do after high school. My father assumed I would go to college, but no definite plans had been made. Then in the spring of my senior year two college recruiters visited the Leicester School. One representing a business college in Asheville stressed opportunities in traffic management, which turned out to be the routing of long-haul trucks, not what it sounded like. The other, a Dr. Willis Weatherford (he said we could remember his name if we thought of sunny weather and Henry Ford), was a trustee of Berea College in Kentucky, a school, he explained, that drew 80 percent of its students from the southern Appalachian region. You didn't have to have a lot of money to attend Berea; you could work your way through. In fact, all Berea students had to work at something. He described the college's several industries, including something called Fireside Industries. That interested me. Sounded cozy.

I filled out an application for admission to Berea College, took some tests (monitored by the principal, since we had no counselor), and later in the year received a letter of acceptance. Now, of course, I can appreciate how important that letter was, for it made possible a formative undergraduate experience at Berea. But at the time I didn't entertain the possibility that I wouldn't be admitted. The bliss of ignorance! The confidence of the immature!

I entered Berea College in the fall of 1954 and became a student again, something like the student I had been during the first seven years of grade school. I worked in the college bakery that year, took required courses, and wrote a lot of themes during the second semester, including a research paper on the biblical city of Nineveh. Back home for the summer, I worked in a restaurant—and wished I were still in Dr. Carol Gesner's composition class, reading and writing. For ten dollars I bought a secondhand typewriter (like the old table model Miss Duckett first let me type my name on) and tried writing a few things in the evening. But my room at home was hot, and like the time I used my mother's sewing machine for a desk, I never finished anything.

But I carried the old typewriter back to Berea with me for my sophomore year, and along with other courses, among them German, enrolled in advanced composition as an elective. Early on, I wrote a piece for the composition class about guys I'd worked with that past summer. Dr. Hughes, the instructor, read a passage from it in class and called for discussion. After one of my classmates volunteered that the details in the passage were "too vivid," Dr. Hughes wondered if my classmate didn't mean the details were unpleasant; we should not be afraid of being too vivid.

The German class proved interesting. Three days a week Professor Kogerma introduced new material; two days a week we had a student instructor who led us through our reader or drilled us on material already introduced. This student instructor, a junior named Mary Ellen Yates, was stunningly beautiful, and smart, too. I discovered that German grammar was fascinating, especially when Mary Ellen illustrated it. Teaching German was part of her labor assignment, although she was really an English major. She also wrote for the newspaper and was a member of Twenty Writers, the campus literary group. I learned all this as I walked with her from our class to the cafeteria; as we drank coffee and talked about books, writers, and writing in a student hangout; as we studied together; as we went off campus to films and dinner, when we could afford it.

The Twenty Writers group had a couple of openings, Mary Ellen told me. I should submit something. The current members, together with the faculty sponsor, Dr. Thomas Kreider, read manuscripts not knowing the authors' names, and voted blind on the writers to admit to the group. The typical amateur, I wrote a story on a subject about which I knew nothing—combat in the Korean War—and submitted it. A week or so later Mary Ellen called me at my dorm. I thought she might be calling to suggest we go out for coffee; instead, she had called on behalf of Twenty Writers to say I had been admitted to the group. (The faculty advisor, she told me, had thought my story must have been written by an older student, perhaps a Korean War veteran.)

I had gone to Berea with the vague assumption that I would become a doctor or lawyer. Rather, my parents and grandparents had assumed that. I was relieved that they did not appear disappointed when, by the end of my sophomore year, I was committed to majoring in English. Which is what I did. I worked again during the summer, but also managed to write the obligatory dreadful, unpublishable novel (I called it *Doves in the Grapevine*), returned for my junior year, enrolled in upper-division English classes, including

Wife, Mary Ellen, as an undergraduate, 1957

creative writing, and started contributing a column to the school newspaper (Mary Ellen by then was editor). I worked at the college theater getting out programs for the weekly one-act plays and the two major productions we staged each academic year. Mary Ellen and I worked together on the newspaper, and on the Twenty Writers publication. I recall hawking copies of the books to guests on the porch of Boone Tavern in Berea.

In the spring of my junior year I was awarded a summer homestay in Germany by the Experiment in International Living. I was able to go only because my parents helped out, providing pocket money and money for the following year at Berea, which I would otherwise have earned from a summer job. I spent the summer in Minden, Westphalia, living in the home of a kind and generous German family, one of ten American students in similar situations there that summer. A story about us appeared in the Minden newspaper. I identified myself as someone who "had already written a novel and had another one in progress." I had seen Mary Ellen in June, in Columbus, Ohio, where she was working. When I returned

from Germany at the end of the summer, I came home by way of Indiana, where Mary Ellen, who had graduated in June, was teaching English in a high school. We corresponded, but didn't see one another again until Christmas, when she came to Berea and from there went on to Leicester with me to meet my family and stay for a good part of the 1957 Christmas break.

In the spring of 1958, my last semester at Berea, I finished another terrible novel as part of an independent-study project. And after I was assured there was a position for Mary Ellen, too, I signed a contract to teach German and English in the Fort Knox Dependent Schools, on the military base at Fort Knox, Kentucky. Mary Ellen and I were married on August 17, 1958, at her home in Willard, Kentucky, and soon afterward moved into an apartment in Elizabethtown, Kentucky, south of Fort Knox.

The opening of school was prefaced by five days of faculty and staff orientation. On Friday afternoon, as we were concluding—finally—this elaborate introduction to the academic year, I received a call requesting that I come by the superintendent's office before leaving for the day. I went. The superintendent leaned back in his chair and with an expression blending disbelief and pained inconvenience informed me that I had no professional education courses on my transcript. That was correct, I said. I had taken all "subject matter" courses, in English and German language and literature. And I thought the superintendent had been aware of my qualifications, or lack of them, when he hired me at Berea in April. Besides, he had been in possession of my complete transcript since June and now it was late August. Well, no, he had just become aware of this situation, which presented a difficulty. The upshot was that I had to project a program of summer study over the next seven years (on a fold-out form as big as a road map), a program which, if I followed it faithfully, would allow me to teach on an emergency certificate.

I actually implemented that program the following summer. While Mary Ellen taught a summer term at Fort Knox and lived with a friend we'd made in Elizabethtown, I enrolled in education courses at a college near Asheville. But mostly I fished and scribbled, for the courses were not demanding. At the end of the summer Mary Ellen began an M.A. program in English at the University of Kentucky in Lexington, and I, legitimized by my summer of pedagogical studies, but still in a state of emergency certification, returned to Fort Knox, lived in the bachelor officers' quarters, and taught a second year. I wrote evenings and drove to Mary Ellen's tiny apartment in Lexington on weekends and holidays.

We had a plan. Mary Ellen would have her M.A. by the end of the summer. After that, it would be my turn to do graduate study. Foolishly, I had thought I could save enough money teaching to pay for graduate studies! Now I knew I would have to have a scholarship, like the one Mary Ellen had at the University of Kentucky, or a fellowship or assistantship—something. I sent out several applications.

And received two good offers: a National Defense Education Act Fellowship in English at Washington University in St. Louis, and a similar NDEA Fellowship at Vanderbilt University—to study German. But I had applied to Vanderbilt's English department. Nevertheless, I found myself standing in a telephone booth in the bachelor officers' quarters at Fort Knox returning a call to Dr. Josef Rysan, head of the Department of Germanic and Slavic Languages at Vanderbilt. He explained to me that Vanderbilt's English department offered no NDEA Fellowships. (For some reason, I'd assumed it did.) But Dr. Rysan's department offered NDEA's. He had seen my dossier in the graduate-school office, noticed that I had studied German at Berea College and had lived in Germany as part of an Experiment in International Living program, and was prepared to offer me an NDEA Fellowship in the Department of Germanic and Slavic Languages.

I preferred to study at Vanderbilt, because at Berea I had learned about the Fugitive/Agrarians, the Vanderbilt group that included John Crowe Ransom, Allen Tate, and Robert Penn Warren. In my naivete (yet again) I assumed the Fugitives were still there. (Of course, Ransom had long since moved to Kenyon College, where he founded the *Kenyon Review.* Tate had gone first to Princeton, then to the University of Minnesota. Robert Penn Warren was by that time at Yale.) I wanted to study at Vanderbilt, but in the English department. After Dr. Rysan pointed out that I could study American literature as a minor field in a program at Vanderbilt, I accepted the offer. Mary Ellen and I moved to Nashville, Tennessee, in the fall of 1960 and I began a three-year residency.

I had misgivings about studying German literature. Surely others would have a better command of the language than I. And, in fact, some of the other graduate students were native speakers, but my acquaintance with literature generally, and the experience of writing literary essays at Berea, stood me in good stead. I pursued my studies in German successfully, in combination with courses in the English department under Randall Stewart, the Hawthorne scholar, and Donald Davidson, the Fugitive poet and essayist, the only member of the Fugitive/Agrarian group still at Vanderbilt by that time. I also published stories and poems in every issue of the Vanderbilt literary magazine during the 1960–63 residency.

In the spring of 1963 I sent a sheaf of poems about my grandfather Smith (he had died the previous summer) to Maxine Kumin, who was then conducting "The Poetry Workshop," a bimonthly column in *The Writer.* In the July number of that magazine Kumin commented at length on the poems I'd sent, and printed one of them entitled:

Hanlon Mountain in Mist

Ril Sams came by, but now the house is still
and cold with dread. Unless this weather breaks,
I look for another grave on Newfound Hill.
Rain rumbles from the roof, splashes from the eaves,
and foams and bubbles into tubs below
the spouts. The barn, shingles on the crib
drip black with rain. Springhouse mosses grow
frog-green, and Hanlon's top is lost in mist.
Ril Sams climbed Hanlon with his hounds last night,
but when they winded something below the top,
and wouldn't go beyond the lantern light,
and trembled on the lead, then he came home.
I trust the hounds: they know what made them stop,
what waits there in the mist on Hanlon's top.

"The detail," Kumin wrote of the poem, "even without the cumulative bolstering of the other poems, quite easily conveys the setting. This is hill country, hunting country. . . . The proper name Ril Sams, the place names Newfound Hill and Hanlon evoke to me . . . a backwoods section, the Ozarks, possibly."

Though the setting might well have been the Ozarks, those place names came from western North Carolina. But I think no one would suspect that many of the poem's details came to me from New England, for just before I wrote the poem I had been reading Hawthorne's *Mosses from an Old Manse.* I consciously borrowed from this passage:

All day long, and for a week together, the rain was drip-drip-dripping and splash-splash-splashing, from the eaves, and bubbling and foaming into tubs beneath the spouts. The old unpainted shingles of the houses and outbuildings were black with moisture; and the mosses of ancient growth upon the walls looked fresh and green, as if they were the newest things and afterthought of time. The usually mirrored surface of the river was blurred by an infinity of raindrops; the whole landscape had a completely water-soaked appearance, conveying the impression that the earth was wet through like a sponge; while the summit of the wooded hill, about a mile distant, was enveloped in a dense mist; where the demon of the tempest seemed to have his abiding place, and to be plotting still direr inclemencies.

Hawthorne's nineteenth-century New England landscape struck me as much like my twentieth-century western North Carolina landscape, so closely identified in my thoughts and feelings with my grandfather. To make my poem, I borrowed Hawthorne's tubs and spouts, his moss, even his spook on the hilltop. But I left him his river, his Latinate diction ("direr inclemencies"), and combined what I took with my own barn, crib, springhouse, and neighbor, Ril Sams. The poem is a *combination* of things, some from direct experience, some from reading. But reading is an experience, too, and for me always had been. Hawthorne's passage was something I experienced no less than my grief over my grandfather's death. I dwell on this because the poem seems to illustrate the close connection in my poems, stories, and essays between reading and writing, as well as the important role place has always played in my work.

The poems Maxine Kumin commented on were published in my first collection, *Copperhead Cane,* the following year, by which time Mary Ellen and I, and our two boys, born in 1962 and 1963, had moved to Bowling Green, Kentucky. I had disappointed my major professor at Vanderbilt by not taking positions offered at Haverford College and at Sweet Briar. But I was reluctant to leave the region. Besides, in Bowling Green, where we began teaching, Mary Ellen in the English department and I in the Department of Modern Languages at Western Kentucky University, I could be close to Vanderbilt's library while finishing a dissertation on Annette von Droste-Huelshoff, a nineteenth-century German poet.

The period between the spring of 1954 and the spring of 1964, when my first collection of poems appeared, amounted to a dizzying decade. At the beginning of that period I was running the mountain roads of western North Carolina in an old car bought with money made in a moonshining venture. At the end of it I had completed four years of college, married, taught two years in a high school, completed a three-year graduate residency, become the father of two sons, published a little collection of poems, and was teaching in a state university and working on a dissertation that would be completed by the end of the 1964–65 academic year. I had always combined the writing of poems and stories with my work as student or teacher, but once the dissertation was completed I was able to devote more time to creative work. And I was becoming increasingly interested in the history of the upland or Appalachian South,

"Our son Jimmy, early 1970s"

which, it became clearer and clearer to me, was quite different from that of the lowland South. Even the Vanderbilt Fugitive/Agrarians, I had come to see, were more concerned with the lowland South than with the mountain South, where I came from.

I had first read about my own region in high school, when I checked Horace Kephart's *Our Southern Highlanders* out of the library. And it was impossible to attend Berea College without learning something about southern Appalachia, for the school's mission, as Dr. Weatherford had pointed out, was to serve the region. I had entered Berea in the fall of 1954, the year Harriette Arnow's *The Dollmaker,* a kind of Appalachian *Grapes of Wrath,* appeared. Those of us majoring in English at Berea, and interested in writing ourselves, were urged by our professors (especially Emily Ann Smith, head of the English department) to acquaint ourselves with writers and writing reflecting our region. At Berea I became acquainted with the work of Arnow, and of Jesse Stuart, James Still, Wilma Dykeman, and others. I began reading a regional magazine, *Mountain Life and Work,* which was published in Berea, and published a story in it during my senior year. Now, as national attention was beginning to be focused on southern Appalachia as a result of the War on Poverty, and through books like Harry Caudill's *Night Comes to the Cumberlands,* and Jack E. Weller's *Yesterday's People,* I began to look more seriously into the history of my own place, a region of America, according to John C. Campbell in *The Southern Highlander and His Homeland,* about which there was more misinformation and misunderstanding than any other part of the country; a region, according to the historian Carl Degler, which had a complicated "triple history"—a history shared with the rest of the United States, one shared with the American South, and a history all its own as a kind of separate South. In *Mountain Life and Work* and elsewhere I began to come across stories, poems, and essays reflecting the Appalachian region, its history and heritage, problems and promise. This work caused me to examine my own experience more carefully than ever before.

Again it was a matter of reading *and* writing. I began contributing to regional publications regularly, writing out of my mountain South background—in combination with whatever came my way. Reading Eckermann's *Conversations with Goethe,* I came on Goethe's pronouncement that a poet ought to take an interest in *Aberglaube,* superstitions and beliefs, for these were often the poetry of ordinary folk. I knew all sorts of beliefs and superstitions, picked up from my grandparents in western North Carolina. I remembered how I used to hoe garden plots with my grandfather Smith, standing opposite him in a row, and recalled a belief he passed along once when we got our hoes tangled as we worked. I drafted a poem called:

Meeting

My shadow was my partner in the row.
He was working the slick-handled shadow of his hoe
when out of the patch toward noon there came the
     sound
of steel on steel, two inches underground.
My shadow's hoe must be of steel, I thought.
And where my chopping hoe came down and struck,
memory rushed like water out of rock.
"When two strike hoes," I said, "it's always a sign
they'll work the patch together again sometime.
An old man told me that the last time ever
we worked this patch and our hoes rang together."
Delving there with my hoe, I half-uncovered
a plowpoint, worn and rusted over.
"The man I hoed with last lies under earth,"
I said, "his plowpoint and his saying of equal worth."
My shadow, standing by me in the row,
waited, and while I rested, raised his hoe.

Freud says somewhere that writing has its origin in the voice of an absent person. Many of my early poems, like the ones Maxine Kumin commented on, were elegies *to* an absent person, spoken in a voice that was not quite mine. After "Meeting," the absent person, my grandfather, began to speak in his own well-remembered voice—as if answering because he had been spoken to. The conversation became part of my second collection, *Dialogue with a Dead Man.*

The late sixties and early seventies were busy years for Mary Ellen and me. We were both teaching and writing (Mary Ellen had worked as a copywriter in Nashville while I studied at Vanderbilt, and now, in addition to her teaching, she wrote news releases for a dyslexia program headquartered at our school and was working on her own teaching manuals and educational film scripts). I was writing poems, stories, essays, and translating the work of Emil Lerperger, an Austrian poet, as well as the work of other German and Austrian poets. Our daughter, Ruth, was born in 1967, so now we had two active boys and a young daughter whose schedules and appointments, together with ours, along with unscheduled demands, kept us busy. I remember being called at the office and told our oldest son, Jimmy, had torn his shirt at school. I ran by the house, got another one, and delivered it to the school. Jimmy was our athlete (and later a musician). I made home movies of him at diving meets, and after repeatedly loading the eight-millimeter film for viewing, admiring his control of his body and recalling that I was the fellow who, in third grade, lost a part in the class play because I couldn't skip backwards, wrote:

Diver

When he strides to the tip of the board and turns,
poised in silence,
unruffled as the waiting water,
his dive is a film darkly
coiled, intricately threaded through his body.

When the dive unrolls over a looping
track invisible in the air
his body becomes frame after frame
of flight, pure vision
projected by the hot bulb of his concentration.

I remember when Jimmy's brother Fred went through phases so fast I couldn't keep up. In his carpenter phase, down in the basement, he sawed in two a leaf from a prized table that had belonged to my great-grandmother Miller. Occasionally, we treated the kids at a bakery/delicatessen on the way to school. One morning, as we entered, Fred fell on the floor writhing. I was stricken. I bent over him and asked him what was wrong. Gasping, he pointed to a bakery display case. "Hot cross buns!" he managed. And when I didn't get it, he repeated, "Hot *cross* buns!" I had forgotten he was in his vampire phase. Later he was a magician, Fredrico the Great. I took him with me to a summer institute I worked in at Berea College when he was a magician. He stopped people on the street and showed off his sleight of hand. Once I found him in front of Boone Tavern where he was demonstrating his legerdemain to the novelist and social historian Wilma Dykeman, my colleague in the institute.

Later Fred's sister, Ruth, sometimes accompanied me on readings, summer workshops, and institutes. Once at Berea, as I prepared to make my opening remarks at a summer workshop, I positioned Ruth, who was about nine, in the back of the room and told her to hold up one finger if she needed to leave to go to the restroom, two if she got bored and wanted to go outside. I checked my notes and began greeting the assembled workshop participants. Scanning the room as I uttered my first sentence to the group, I saw Ruth in the back—already holding up two fingers. At an evening reading a local bookseller

sold my books and I autographed them. As we walked to our little campus apartment after the reading, she announced her intention to write a book. I offered encouragement. The next morning she stayed in the apartment to work on her book, and when I returned at noon, the book was finished! By the time she was in junior high school she was distancing herself from me. She preferred that I drop her off a block from school because, she told me, we had a generic car— and she was right.

In the same way that I wrote about Jimmy on the diving board, I wrote about Fred and Ruth in a series of "about the house" poems. One of these has been included in a Scott, Foresman "America Reads" high-school text. It's called:

A House of Readers

At 9:42 on this May morning
the children's rooms are concentrating too.
Like a tendril growing toward the sun, Ruth
moves her book into a wedge of light
that settles on the floor like a butterfly.
She turns a page.
Fred is immersed in magic, cool
as a Black Angus belly-deep in a farm pond.

"Our son Fred with his wife, Lynne, mid-1980s"

The only sounds: pages turning softly.
This is the quietness
of bottomland where you can hear only the young
    corn
growing, where a little breeze stirs the blades
and then breathes in again.

I mark my place.
I listen like a farmer in the rows.

Writing this poem, and others like it, I realized how very different my own childhood was from that of my children. I grew up on a small farm, in a rural, agricultural area; they were growing up in the suburbs of a university town, the children of teacher/writers. Their lore derived mostly from popular culture; mine had come out of traditional culture. I noticed how my farm background kept coming through in the imagery of these poems, and how, in "A House of Readers," I saw myself as essentially a farmer, raising a crop of kids. (Our children have all completed college degrees. Jimmy lives in Bowling Green, Fred with his wife, Lynne, in Louisville, Kentucky, where he works in an art gallery and Lynne in children's theater. Ruth lives in San Francisco and works in an art museum.)

After first appearing in a little magazine, "A House of Readers" was included in my 1980 collection *The Mountains Have Come Closer,* in an opening section called "In the American Funhouse," along with companion poems about a typical "Saturday Morning" in the suburbs and about "Living with Children." The persona in these poems finds himself disoriented in a funhouse of distorting images. Confused in the present, he clearly recalls the girl who sat beside him at eighth-grade graduation, and remembers well enough "a horsehair hanging / on a barbed-wire fence in a mountain pasture." He dies "in a long line of traffic / on an evening in November / when mercury vapor lights are coming on," and reemerges, transformed, in the second section, "You Must Be Born Again," as the Brier, a quintessential southern Appalachian person struggling to remain free of an ascribed identity, determined to be himself. The new persona is seen first in:

The Brier Losing Touch with His Traditions

Once he was a chairmaker.
People up north discovered him.
They said he was "an authentic mountain
    craftsman."
People came and made pictures of him working,
wrote him up in the newspapers.

He got famous.
Got a lot of orders for his chairs.

"Our daughter, Ruth, with her cat Rachelle"

When he moved up to Cincinnati
so he could be closer to his market
(besides, a lot of his people lived there now)
he found out he was a Brier.

And when his customers found out
he was using an electric lathe and power drill
just to keep up with all the orders,
they said he was losing touch with his traditions.
His orders fell off something awful.
He figured it had been a bad mistake
to let the magazine people take those pictures
of him with his power tools, clean-shaven,
wearing a flowered sport shirt and drip-dry pants.

So he moved back down to east Kentucky.
Had himself a brochure printed up
with a picture of him using his hand lathe,
bearded, barefoot, in faded overalls.
Then when folks would come from the magazines,
he'd get rid of them before suppertime
so he could put on his shoes, his flowered sport shirt
and double-knit pants, and open a can of beer
and watch the six-thirty news on tv
out of New York and Washington.

He had to have some time to be himself.

I had been coming across derisive jokes about "Briers," southern Appalachians who had moved out of the region to Ohio, Illinois, and Michigan, since the late sixties. My appropriation of the figure represented a movement beyond my personal experience to a point where I could write of the collective experience of several million southern Appalachians known to other Americans chiefly through the stereotypes found in popular fiction, in movies, and on television. It seemed to me that the experience of southern Appalachian out-migrants resembled that of other immigrants in our history, a difference being that southern Appalachians had become immigrants in their own country.

While I didn't know exactly what I was doing while doing it, I could see later that my poems were indebted to old songs and ballads like those I'd heard sung by my grandmother Miller, Bascom Lamar Lunsford, and Virgil Sturgill. I came to see, too, a line of development from early poems such as "Hanlon Mountain in Mist" and "Meeting" (where my grandfather appears as a ghost-shadow) to the persona of the Brier, who accommodated my own experience, my grandfather's, and the experience of other southern Appalachians who bore ascribed identities into a period of wrenching change. A reviewer commented that I and my persona, the Brier, had been born in a folktale and grew up in a drama of the absurd, one way of accounting for the juxtaposition of the "American Funhouse" poems with the "Brier" poems.

The poems in *The Mountains Have Come Closer* seemed to clarify the experiences of readers in the southern mountains and were read throughout the Appalachian region during a time of growing regional self-awareness. The poems appeared at a time when, throughout the country, many Americans, in the wake of the *Roots* phenomenon, were in a mood to celebrate our ethnic and cultural diversity and rummage about in the flea market of our local and regional histories and traditions. *The Mountains Have Come Closer* appeared in the same year the *Harvard Encyclopedia of American Ethnic Groups* included, for the first time, as far as I know, an entry on "Appalachians." In the mid-1980s Harvard would publish the first volume of DARE (*Dictionary of American Regional English*), which includes an entry on the word *brier:* "A poor farmer or worker; a rustic." The DARE entry has a citation from around 1910 in which a woman from Steubenville, Ohio, used the term *brier* "to mean people and not plants. . . . She explained that the word was short for *brier-hopper*" and meant "a specific sort of rustic, an immigrant to southern Ohio from backwoodsy Kentucky."

By the time *The Mountains Have Come Closer* appeared in 1980 my poems, stories, and essays had already been appearing for fifteen years. They were printed and reprinted in regional magazines (*Appalachian Heritage, Appalachian Journal*). My essay "A Mirror for Appalachia," modeled after Donald Da-

vidson's "A Mirror for Artists" in the Fugitive/Agrarian manifesto *I'll Take My Stand,* appeared in the anthology *Voices from the Hills,* a widely adopted reader. I wrote essays with titles such as "A Post-Agrarian Regionalism for Appalachia," "Reading, Writing, Region." My poems appeared in Bantam's *A Geography of Poets.* I served on the staff of workshops with writers whose work I had first become acquainted with at Berea College: Jesse Stuart, Harriette Arnow; James Still, whose exquisite poems, short stories, and novels are best represented by a little American classic, his novel *River of Earth.* At these readings, conferences, and workshops I met other writers of my generation, Fred Chappell, Robert Morgan, Jeff Daniel Marion, and Gurney Norman, whose novel *Divine Right's Trip* first appeared in *The Last Whole Earth Catalog* and blends the California counterculture of the late sixties with traditions of Norman's native southern Appalachia.

For more than a decade before his death in 1985 I had the privilege of working with and learning from Cratis Williams, an east Kentuckian who in the early sixties produced a three-volume, 1600-page doctoral dissertation in the American Studies Program at New York University entitled *The Southern Mountaineer in Fact and Fiction.* Like the region it is concerned with, whose significance, it has been said, "is obscured by the fact that it is divided among eight different commonwealths," the literature of the southern Appalachian region was obscure even to those of us who were most interested in it. Williams's encyclopedic survey of fiction and nonfiction revealed this body of work to us and, by doing so, further stimulated writing in and about the region. When he completed his study in 1960, Williams said he thought he was "putting the mountaineer to bed." For it seemed to him then that Harriette Arnow's *The Dollmaker* traced the dissolution of southern Appalachians as they disappeared into the working class of the industrial Midwest—and thus completed the story of the southern mountaineer. But during the next quarter century, as national attention was focused on the southern Appalachian region during the War on Poverty, the southern mountaineer, in fact and in fiction, rose up from his bed. Writing from and about southern Appalachia (as evidenced by the success of the *Foxfire* books) reflected a renewed interest in the region's history, the values of its people, their cultural traditions, and their region's relation to the rest of the country. No one was more pleased than Williams himself when he discovered that southern Appalachia had become, by the mid-seventies, "a nest of singing birds."

One of the birds in that nest, in addition to writing my poems, stories, and essays, I've edited an anthology of Appalachian writing for the schools; assisted the Jesse Stuart Foundation in reissuing a number of Stuart's books; and served on the staff of the Hindman Settlement School Writing Workshop, a workshop with a regional focus. I have edited James Still's collected poems (and done stints with him at Yaddo, the artist colony at Saratoga Springs, New York, and traveled with him in Europe, Iceland, and the Yucatan. I wrote a friend a postcard from the Yucatan: "Still's down here studying Mayan culture. I'm studying Still").

In October 1983 I contributed an essay called "Appalachian Literature: At Home in this World" to a James Still Festival held at Emory and Henry College in Virginia. I also interviewed Still before a large audience. The essay and the interview appeared subsequently along with a James Still bibliography and other papers by Fred Chappell and Jeff Daniel Marion in Emory and Henry's *Iron Mountain Review*. Five years and three collections of poems later *(Vein of*

"Dr. Cratis Williams, friend and mentor, lecturing at the Hindman Settlement School in the late 1970s or early 1980s"

Words appeared in 1984; *Nostalgia for 70* in 1986; *Brier, His Book* in 1988), I found my work the subject of a similar festival at Emory and Henry College. I heard myself described as one of the principal spokespersons for Appalachian life and literature and for the values inherent in the culture of the region. In an allusion to one of my poems, I heard myself compared to my persona, the Brier, as someone who operated a "Mountain Vision Center." Colleagues presented papers (Grace T. Edwards, "Jim Wayne Miller: Holding the Mirror for Appalachia"; Wade Hall, "Jim Wayne Miller's Brier Poems: The Appalachian in Exile"; Don Johnson, "The Appalachian Homeplace as Oneiric House in Jim Wayne Miller's *The Mountains Have Come Closer*"—a reading of the poems based on insights from Gaston Bachelard's *The Poetics of Space*. I hadn't known the image of the house appeared so frequently in my poems until I heard this paper, and I certainly hadn't suspected my houses were "oneiric"). These papers, together with a selected bibliography, became an issue of *The Iron Mountain Review*. The number also contains the transcript of an interview I did at the festival with a friend and colleague, Loyal Jones, director of the Appalachian Center at Berea College (and biographer of Bascom Lamar Lunsford). Going back through that interview, I noticed that Jones asked me why I didn't write a novel. Remembering the inadequate novels I'd written as an undergraduate, I had answered: "I don't think I have the narrative power a novelist requires. I heard Reynolds Price make a distinction between the poet and the novelist which may be applicable. Price said the novelist is the broad-backed peasant among writers. The novelist has to bend to the task, and shovel tons of words. I would prefer to remain an aristocrat among writers!" As we say in the southern mountains, you can hear anything but the truth and meat a-frying. For less than eighteen months later I published a novel, *Newfound*, which was placed on the American Library Association's Best Books of the Year list.

Newfound, a coming-of-age novel about growing up in southern Appalachia, part might-have-been, part was, began in a query from Richard Jackson, an enterprising and intelligent editor at Orchard Books. Jackson was editing books by a colleague and staff member of the Hindman Settlement School Writing Workshop, George Ella Lyon, and he was familiar with some of my poems that had appeared in Bradbury Press and Orchard anthologies edited by Paul Janeczko (*Strings: A Gathering of Family Poems; Going Over to Your Place; The Music of What Happens: Poems That Tell Stories; Preposterous*). Jackson noticed that many of my poems were little narratives, and he

Harriette Simpson Arnow, Jim Wayne Miller, George Ella Lyon, and Fred Chappell,
staff of the Hindman Settlement School Writers Workshop, early 1980s

queried me indirectly through George Ella Lyon about possibly writing a novel. Realizing this was an unusual circumstance (ordinarily, writer queries editor), I sent Jackson a story I proposed to make the opening of a novel, and an outline. He was encouraging. I completed the manuscript and he accepted it.

Although I had declared myself unsuited for the novel in 1988, I have written *Newfound,* which has had an excellent critical reception and enjoys respectable sales, and now have another novel in progress. I'm glad I did not declare myself unfit for drama, because I recently sat through two staged readings of *His First, Best Country,* my play-in-progress based on a short story which appeared in 1987 as a chapbook.

In the future I'd like to concentrate more on writing and spend less time teaching, reviewing, editing, translating, workshopping, and preparing essays for assorted occasions and special numbers of journals and magazines. I've spent an inordinate amount of the available time on activities that are actually peripheral to writing. In a mock "Report to the Public Service Committee" in the 1980s I enumerated some of these activities:

I edited the anthology, read the page proofs.

I spoke to members of the Tuesday Book Club.

I sent the photo for the workshop brochure.

I got up at six-thirty in Virginia,
played poet-in-the-school till three p.m.,
drove to Tennessee, read poems, stayed
up all night, all the next day, too,
then drove to Kentucky in coffee-colored darkness.

* * *

In mountain backyards of five states I argued
that literature and history were good things.

* * *

I searched for my car in airport parking lots.
I passed through sleeping towns and metal detectors.

I missed appointments, interstate exits, meals.
I drank my bourbon neat in motel rooms.

I read my mail and answered some of it.

The catalog of activities runs to more than seventy-five lines. In "Quick Trip Home," also from the mid-eighties, I realized the irony of the situation I had worked myself into:

A man writes about an old-fashioned way of life he
  lived,
describes its pleasures, a certain serenity and
  knowledge
that comes from living a long time in one place—
and does this so many times, in so many places
he grows harried and distracted.

But somewhere recently—perhaps as I walked down a long hall to enter a classroom in an Appalachian school, or as I told a story as part of a reading-with-comments—it occurred to me that for years now what I've been doing is an elaborated version of those classroom visits I started making in the third grade, when Miss Duckett sent me to other rooms to tell stories. Sometimes I even include an old ballad in the readings (Bascom Lamar Lunsford's favorite, "Little Margaret," whose ghost-girl I suspect as the source of my ghost-grandfather in "Meeting"), and the presentations are often reminiscent of Virgil Sturgill when he sang "Barbara Allen" at the war bond rally at the Leicester School all those years ago, or of my grandmother Miller's recitations.

Then again I think the readings, workshops, conferences, and school visitations are appropriate activities for a teacher/writer. And the time seems well-spent when I see young people getting interested in the history and cultural heritage of their place (and becoming more knowledgeable about it at an earlier age than I did). It is gratifying to receive positive evaluations from students who think they are writing them only for their teacher—even ambiguous ones like the one-sentence critique by a high school student who wrote of my presentation: "It was hard not to listen to him."

I realize that much of the interest in my work has been of an extra-literary nature, for my poems, stories, and essays have appeared most frequently in the context of multi-discipline regional studies approaches. With regard to critical reception, I have sometimes felt myself in much the same situation as my "Brier Losing Touch with His Traditions": reviewers and readers insist on seeing me as an "Appalachian" writer and are disappointed when I am not "Appalachian" enough for them.

While it may appear to some readers that my work has been almost exclusively concerned with an old-fashioned way of life in the Appalachian South, this has never been the case. I hope readers will come to see that this writing is not only about tradition, but also about what Eric Hofer called the "ordeal" of change.

If not, I'll be content having contributed to a heightened awareness on the part of people in one of the United States' old culture regions. And I'll have the satisfaction of knowing I have never—at least, not wittingly—encouraged views about southern Appalachia that are uninformed, smug, blinkered, or parochial. I think no one will find witless yodeling about mountains in my work, or any reflection of what Roland Barthes calls a "bourgeois alpine myth" about mountains which causes otherwise intelligent people to take leave of their senses "anytime the ground is uneven."

While my work is associated with the southern Appalachian region (and, I hope, is a genuine expression of the region), I have never wanted to be associated with anything less than a cosmopolitan regionalism, an awareness of our little histories and local traditions compatible with national and international perspectives. The world is full of places like southern Appalachia, places that exist at the periphery of a larger national experience. But the periphery sometimes offers an interesting perspective on cultural and economic centers; and one can take a global view from the outer rim. The Lithuanian poet and Nobel Prize winner Czeslaw Milosz came from such a cultural periphery, a kind of northeast European Appalachia, and in recognition of this fact I dedicate a poem entitled "The Country of Conscience" (in *Brier, His Book*) to Milosz. In the poem my Appalachian persona, the Brier, surveys the multicultural situation of eastern Europe and the Soviet Union, where local cultures, folkways, and traditions have long been subjugated to ideology and imperial hegemony, and concludes:

There are two of every country.
One country is really there—
"this side of the river," "these mountains,"
a country felt and known,
a native ground and tongue, our own people.
It is a taste: burgoo, redeye gravy,
Ukrainian balik, Georgian cheese bread.
It is the smell of wood smoke, a pan of water
on the stove singing an old song.
It's knowledge we fondle like loose skin on our dog's
  neck.

The other country is a jigsaw shape
one kind of history draws on what is really there,
a shape seen on maps, or from the height of some
  idea.

Surveying Soviet socialism's attempts, for most of the twentieth century, to cultivate a uniform human type (and this was written before glasnost, perestroika, the demolition of the Berlin Wall, and subsequent changes that have taken place in eastern Europe and the Soviet Union) the Brier finds that:

> . . . everywhere the empire's overtaken
> by blooded old varieties, all kinds and colors,
> that keep coming up volunteer.

The Brier sees that

> What's really there, rooted deep,
> keeps coming back: a state of diverse nations,
> countries within a country, nations rooted
> deep in time, rooted deep in place,
> and hardier than rootless uniformity.

This view of eastern Europe and the Soviet Union is available to me and my persona, the Brier, at least in part because we come from southern Appalachia, a kind of country within a country. ("The Country of Conscience" is scheduled to be part of an international exchange between *The Sandhills/St. Andrews Review* and *Tsiskari,* a publication featuring writers of the Soviet Republic of Georgia.)

Beyond the novel and play in progress, I have no definite plans. I've never set out to write a *book* of poems. I write poems—this poem, that poem—and after they have appeared in journals and magazines, I may see certain thematic and imagistic patterns which suggest the possibility of a collection, a group of poems that belong together. Beyond that, I can't chart a course. Poems aren't the result of will and conscious intention. And as Auden has said, being a poet is a sometime thing. One is a poet only as long as one is putting the finishing touches on a poem. When the poem is finished, one stops being a poet until the next one is begun, or, perhaps, forever. But I think that if you are true to your instincts and interests, over weeks, months, and years, whatever gets written will reflect that faithfulness.

For me, writing has never been a matter of having something to say and then saying it. Rather, writing is an attempt to clarify concerns I have, questions I put to myself. Thinking of writing in this way, I've made experiments and probes, said a lot of things, and then decided which of those things I

At the James Still Festival, Emory and Henry College, October 1983: (from left) Jim Wayne Miller, Jonathan Greene, James Still, Terry Cornett, Jeff Daniel Marion, and Fred Chappell

meant! Instead of knowing in advance what I want to say, I always have to discover my meaning in and through the process of writing.

But no matter how much or how little I write in the future, I know the quality I want the work to possess. Growing up in western North Carolina, I was often amused, along with other natives, at tourists who fished the trout streams. The pools, so perfectly clear, had a deceptive depth. Fishermen unacquainted with them, wearing hip waders, were forever stepping off into pools they judged to be knee-deep—and going in up to their waists or even their armpits, sometimes being floated right off their feet. I want to make my writing like those pools, so simple and clear its depth is deceptive. I want the writing to be transparent, so readers forget they are reading and are aware only that they are having an experience. They are suddenly plunged deeper than they expected and come up shivering.

BIBLIOGRAPHY

Poetry:

Copperhead Cane, Robert Moore Allen, 1964.

The More Things Change the More They Stay the Same (ballads), Whippoorwill, 1971.

Dialogue with a Dead Man, University of Georgia Press, 1974.

(Translator) Emil Lerperger, *The Figure of Fulfillment*, Green River, 1975.

The Mountains Have Come Closer, Appalachian Consortium, 1980.

(Editor) *I Have a Place* (anthology), Appalachian Learning Laboratory, 1981.

Vein of Words, Seven Buffaloes, 1984.

Nostalgia for 70, Seven Buffaloes, 1986.

(Editor and author of introduction) Jesse Stuart, *Songs of a Mountain Plowman*, The Jesse Stuart Foundation, 1986.

(Editor and author of introduction) James Still, *The Wolfpen Poems*, Berea College Press, 1986.

Brier, His Book, Gnomon, 1988.

The Wisdom of Folk Metaphor (chapbook), Seven Buffaloes, 1988.

Nonfiction:

Reading, Writing, Region: A Checklist and Purchase Guide for School and Community Libraries, Appalachian Consortium, 1980.

Sideswipes (chapbook), Seven Buffaloes, 1986.

The Examined Life: Family, Community, and Work in American Literature, Appalachian Consortium, 1989.

Round and Round with Kahlil Gibran (chapbook), Rowan Mountain, 1990.

Fiction:

His First, Best Country (chapbook), Gnomon, 1987.

(Editor with others) Stuart, *A Penny's Worth of Character*, The Jesse Stuart Foundation, 1988.

(Editor with others) Stuart, *The Beatinest Boy*, The Jesse Stuart Foundation, 1989.

Newfound (novel), Orchard Books, 1989.

(Editor with others) Stuart, *The Rightful Owner*, The Jesse Stuart Foundation, 1989.

Other:

I Have a Place: The Poetry of Jim Wayne Miller (videotape), Western Kentucky University Media Services, 1986.

Contributor:

Robert J. Higgs and Ambrose N. Manning, editors, *Voices from the Hills: Selected Readings of Southern Appalachia*, Frederick Ungar, 1975.

Guy and Candie Carawan, collectors and recorders, *Voices from the Mountains*, Knopf, 1975.

Nancy Stone and Robert Waters Grey, editors, *White Trash: An Anthology of Contemporary Southern Poets*, The New South Company, 1976.

Higgs and Neil D. Isaacs, editors, *The Sporting Spirit: Athletes in Literature and Life*, Harcourt, Brace, Jovanovich, 1977.

Edward Field, editor, *A Geography of Poets: An Anthology of the New Poetry*, Bantam, 1979.

Guy Owen and Mary C. Williams, editors, *Contemporary Southern Poetry: An Anthology*, Louisiana State University Press, 1980.

Paul B. Janeczko, editor, *Strings: A Gathering of Family Poems*, Seven Buffaloes, 1984.

James E. Miller, Jr. and others, editors, *United States in Literature*, Scott, Foresman, 1984.

D. L. Emblen and Arnold Solkov, *Before and After: The Shape and Shaping of Prose*, Random House, 1986.

William E. Mallory and Paul Simpson-Housley, editors, *Geography and Literature: A Meeting of the Disciplines*, Syracuse University Press, 1987.

Janeczko, editor, *Going over to Your Place*, Bradbury, 1987.

Leon Stokesbury, editor, *The Made Things: An Anthology of Southern Poetry*, University of Arkansas Press, 1987.

Sally Buckner, editor, *Our Words, Our Ways: Reading and Writing in North Carolina*, Carolina Academic Press, 1991.

Janeczko, editor, *Preposterous: Poems of Youth,* Orchard, 1991.

Fred Moramarco and Al Zolynas, editors, *Men of Our Time: Male Poetry in Contemporary America,* University of Georgia Press, 1992.

Contributor to numerous other anthologies. Also contributor of short stories, poems, articles, essays, and reviews to periodicals and professional journals, including *Appalachian Heritage, Appalachian Journal, Carolina Quarterly, Chattahoochee Review, Georgia Review, International Poetry Review, Iron Mountain Review, Journal of Kentucky Studies, Kentucky Poetry Review, Kentucky Review, Mississippi Review,* and *Vanderbilt Poetry Review.*

James Crerar Reaney

1926-

James Crerar Reaney, conducting a drama workshop at the University of Windsor, Ontario, 1978

Before I go into "food and me," I should point out that I was born on a farm near Stratford, Ontario, where getting down to earth was quite easy, but rising up from it was not too difficult either, what with an Irish father who had won a prize for mime (milking a cow) when a scholar at the local one-room school ("the Irish School") and also with a Scottish-German mother who directed plays with the local young people and used children's games in what really were dramatic workshops cum wiener roasts. Her career as a teacher ended when the school trustees fired her for putting on too many plays with the local youth! so she got married.

Food

Asked to name first foods that impressed me almost to the point of saying "dietary gods," I should have to say OATMEAL, MILK, WATER, TOAST. By many a mile, oatmeal comes first although the hard, hard water from our hundred-foot well is hard to beat. Oatmeal? Let me explain why.

Being of Scottish descent on my mother's side, oats had been the Highland racial diet since Lord knows when. In our farmhouse pantry, we had on the shelves, lent by my grandfather Peter Anderson Crerar, at least a dozen volumes of one Professor Kirk's ravings on the virtues of oatmeal. They were bound in hand-sewn surgical linen, and probably obtained from the same Glasgow bookseller as *Scotland in the Days of the Druids,* a more scary book, for it showed Druids sacrificing captives encaged in a wicker giant fifty feet high to which they were applying the torch. According to Kirk, Scotland was what it was because of its national diet, even though mocked at by the heresiarch, Dr. Samuel Johnson, who implied in his dictionary that it was turning them into horses. And it certainly is an easily grown and flexible food. Do you know any other nutriment that can be eaten raw, is edible if just mixed with cold water, was sent with students to college where it

Infant James with mother, Elizabeth Crerar Reaney, and pet collie Togo, 1926

process glimpsed in these stones and very suggestive of how, if ever driven, life could be even more drastically simplified at Concession II, Lot 39, South Easthope, Perth County, Ontario.

Now, the farm actually produced oats, a beautiful crop to watch turning from blue-green mist to yellow curved spikelets to dead-white ripe spilling into the granary from the threshing machine pipe. But the pursuit of status symbols prevented us from slipping backwards into primitivism, and my parents shopped for either Quaker Oats (not instant, long cooking; instant is an abomination) or rolled oats (plain brown paper bag). Sometimes in summer (see Alice Munro) we hereticized to Puffed Oats, shot from a cannon and supported by a radio serial called "Sunny Jim." We even backslid to Kellogg's Cornflakes or even Rice Krispies—again a radio programme tugged at us, in this case Irene Wicker's "Singing Lady"; and for a box top from either of the above you could obtain a booklet called *When the Great Were Young*—stories of Michelangelo, Giotto, Bach—filled with notions of how to escape if need be from the farm one day. Grape Nuts I early drew the line at; they seemed to be tooth shattering and, even when soaked in boiling water, almost beyond chewing by jackhammers. Was it in the thirties that some food detective opened the wrong freight car at the Grape Nuts siding and discovered it to be full of peanut shells about to be ground up? I should mention Nabisco Shredded Wheat—very satisfying if eaten right beside the box, which had a dramatic picture of Niagara Falls thereupon; they were made, wheat fibre cushionettes, nearby this great natural phenomenon.

Dietary gods have melted into the idolatry of logos that is part of being young in a kitchen and particularly with a great-aunt and uncle who ran an archaic grocery store in town, the Brittania Grocery. I first learnt some French from their cans of Bon Ami household cleaning powder. There was a little chick on these who *"n'a pas encore gratigné."* My first glimpse of how to paint distance in landscape was from Cow Brand Baking Soda—the hills in the background are not green like the foreground fields, but blue!

Behind all this, logos, cereals, the first meal of the day, stood two more recognizable gods—my parents, who had given me their bodies plus the very bowl from which I ate, the chair, the table, and the idea of TOAST. The summer kitchen would be filled with smoke resulting from our toasting of thick bread slices over, top of stove lifted, lids and all, open fire. As we sat down to breakfast, the kitchen was transformed by big, blue sun ladders coming in the east windows and slanting down to the linoleum.

nourished both mind and body for term after term? Well, Pablum. When I first taught creative writing at the University of Manitoba, there was a madman there who had ten barrels of Pablum in his basement upon which he and his family flourished, but the taste of pablum is dull, dull, dull. Not so, oatmeal!

So, a bowl of porridge from a kettle of cooked oatmeal started each day on the farm and was one of the first things I learned to cook. I was frequently accused of adding either too much or too little salt. At one time in my life, I could not, myself, eat porridge unless it had just the right trace of salt in its flavour, a far more important additive than the milk and corn syrup added after the porridge hit the bowl.

After breakfast, my cousins and I were put in charge of cleaning the porridge kettle—dread task. Aged four, I remember finding some oats spilled out of the pail for the hens just south of the woodshed. I took a stone, pounded the oats on top of a flagstone, and produced, to my wonderment, oatmeal—recognizable oatmeal. Local Indians had left grinding stones for corn in the loam of our farm. My production of oatmeal was as basic and mysterious as the

Push all this ever so slightly and the kitchen becomes a temple with my parents as priest and priestess involved in beginning the day's trivial tasks. Trivial? No! Sacred. First the kindling of the fire, the pumping of the water, the boiling of the sacred meal, the domestic murmur after the blessing. It may seem commonplace, but actually it was liturgical—which means "work of the people."

If you get the first food of the day right, a society unfolds. Change at your peril. I know I'm sounding like Dr. Kirk, but in my defence I call on Goethe's "You are what you eat" and also on the contemporary *C-* student who writes like a Golden Arches hamburger. *Frumentum; ergo sum!*

A perhaps bizarre illustration of how food gets entangled with thought, and how it might form the basis for a culture, comes from my feeling, recently impelled by a remark in Northrop Frye's *Words with Power,* that I had to, at long last, read Aristotle's *Metaphysics:* "Why you can't with this philosopher even step into the same river once!" says he. As Frye had suggested, it was a spiritually refreshing experience, so delightful it reminded me of some of the desserts at the Mykonos Café in town here—say Galaktobouriko. Behind even their philosophers, there lurks a nation's cuisine?

Shelter

About half-a-dozen different houses have I lived in, besides rooms, from college residence to Toronto and Winnipeg lodgings, plus apartments, boardinghouses, summer digs (Plage Albert in Manitoba the summer of 1960). The house where I was actually born, as my father before me (midwife plus doctor), being my first shelter, deserves some coverage. But since it contained in its library the half-filled daybook that became my first diary, I thought I would use some quotations from this latter, *indirectly* to give you the feeling of that first house.

"Tuesday, January 3, 1939—Wind: east, a sleety and very cold wind. Weather: very cold, snow deep hard to get around." Two months before, we would have moved the stove and ourselves into the winter kitchen; a constant house-in-winter image, therefore, was passing through the summer kitchen, all cold and deserted, on the way to the pump or the barn. To go to school, I left the house by its formal front door, not much used, going by a hall dresser whose combination chest with seat-lid was filled with powerfully sweet-smelling grass seed. The way to public school lay first through the relic of a Victorian dooryard, uncut locust hedge reaching up farther every year,

four apple trees shaded by big maples where once, very early (1870), had been a garden. Then, the gables of the house still visible behind me, a field, the edge of a bush and swamp, Cardwell's flats—difficult to cross with high water after floods—and a ditch across which my father had sort of established a floating, single log bridge.

"Monday, June 26, 1939—painted chairs green, swam two times. Mother tried baking, washing, scrubbing at same time & it didn't work."

By this time, my mother had changed mates and had already born one child by him, my sister, Wilma. Now she was pregnant with my brother, Ronald. I was chief baby-sitter and mother-helper, getting vegetables ready to sell, washing floors, peddling peas and balls of cottage cheese on the streets of Stratford, hoeing turnips, digging potatoes, picking raspberries.

"July 23, 1939—helping at threshing, straightening up cellar, holding bags for barley, cleaning out chicken house, pulling onions."

When Mother was away in the hospital at Guelph, I got the meals for my stepfather and the hired man. Amusements were swimming in our pond,

With father, James Nesbitt Reaney, "off to get my first pair of real shoes," 1927

an abandoned claypit once part of a brickyard filled with prehistoric white cedar stumps, and collecting wild bird feathers and birdtracks (Ernest Thompson Seton, *Two Little Savages);* also, trying to ride my bicycle—this was crucial since my getting to high school next term depended on the skill. Two summers away, I would sell potatoes on the market, Saturdays, and on July 5, 1941, with my share of the proceeds, buy a copy of *Wuthering Heights* (Pocket Book Editions) for thirty-nine cents. The piano finally came home from being lent to my cousins—lessons in Miss Cora B. Ahrens's music class uptown. My only comment on all this is that every child by the age of ten should be taught how to drain boiled potatoes properly and so avoid the problem of "too wet mashed," a constant complaint when I was in charge of meals.

"Thursday, October 30, 1941—Everything is dripping wet now in this fall. The water drips in the cistern continually. Yesterday was the plowing match at Anderson's. I met several plowmen on the way, with plows on their waggons, drawn by fine high-spirited horses, sleek & freshly oiled."

High school, twelfth birthday, keeping a diary, reading *Wuthering Heights,* and having access for the first time to a good school library as well as the Carnegie Library in town, changed my style from "Swam twice to-day . . ." to whatever the above represents. I think it was a combination of the actual physical journey to school each day from an isolated farm, down a very long lane, then a busy highway (7 and 8 recently named His Majesty's Highways), then factories, workers, downtown, well-sited and arresting courthouse, St. Andrew's Church, library, and then the collegiate, for the first year of the war jam-crammed with every conceivable kind of kid and taught by a spectrum of teachers ranging from the gah-gah to people who lent you Stendhal's *The Red and the Black* and loved language. There was a massive amount of remembering and thinking to do; as my poem "The Bicycle" puts it:

> Past the house where the bees winter,
> I climb on the stairs of my pedals
> To school murmuring irregular verbs . . .

I was particularly grateful for just the chance to choose between German and Greek; someone I was great friends with took German so I took that for a year, then dreaming that I might go into theology one day, I switched. My parents always looked pale at this. I wasn't saved, although I found out years later that Knox Presbyterian church had tried twice to "get" me—once at birth, once when I was eigh-

teen—but my mother foiled them, she privately believing that the only puberty or manhood rite I should have was total immersion by a local evangelist in the Avon River!

Ah, start a new sentence. I spent the summer of 1942 catching up on Greek and finished my matriculation with it plus Latin and French, which had included some French-Canadian poetry, a rare bird then, plus the obligatory *Maria Chapdelaine*—the ultimate Quebecois pioneer novel. On the grade thirteen exam, the prose was "*Ecrivez en français* 'How to Make a Mosquito Smudge'!" I loved all the Shakespeare we took, natural in a town where all the schools are named after his plays; particularly loved ancient history, and enjoyed geometry, algebra (puzzles), modern history, *The Moonstone,* a lot of British Georgian poetry—Walter de la Mare was big; hated physical training and cadet corps. The most remarkable book in the school library was Elbert Hubbard's *Little Journeys,* the author a disciple of William Morris in upper New York State—the first handmade book with uncut pages I ever held in my hands.

Perhaps the key moment in my high school career was going with two other lads in my class all the way to Toronto one snowy day near Easter in 1943 on our bicycles to catch the roadshow version of Disney's *Fantasia,* which was the fuller version with the abstract Bach toccata left in. The epic journey (120 miles) down through snow, thaw, sunlight, then total darkness till arrival at midnight—and us with no lights—still impresses me with its mad pursuit of beauty. The Y was full, but they farmed us out with Glasgow landladies, one of whom gave me Charlotte Brontë's *The Professor and Emma* plus her poems. In roaming around Toronto before the show, another formative epiphany took place: standing on the bridge on Queen Park's Crescent, I beheld the knobby finials of Hart House, the Massey-endowed student union at University of Toronto, copied from some Oxford spire. The result was instant desire to go to college and see those knobby finials every day.

"Friday, April 16, 1943—Monster truck nearly got Garwood. Snow—took shelter in gas station at New Hamburg. When we passed McCallum's, Loie ran out and screamed at us. Little girl—schoolbag/-Ducks in ditch. Factory girls. Funny old houses with square attic windows. Lambs on white snow in orchard. A ditch prickled with new grass."

One feature of the trip down that caused division between me and my companions was that, true to the traditions of a farmhouse, my mother had packed me a series of snacks and drinks (all labelled as to time release) to have on the journey regardless of the eating places that might line the route. So, when my two friends went into a café or diner, they ordered food, while I just wanted coffee or tea or a glass of water. As I pulled out my flask of buttermilk or cut into a homemade sausage and a small loaf of bread with my jackknife, my chums would remove themselves to another table, as far away from the rural cheapskate as possible.

That fall, my mother played a splendid surprise on us all. Without warning, she suddenly moved us into town. It was my last year in high school, the crucial preparatory year for college, and the move into Stratford was supposed to rid me of the long exhausting trek into town through the blizzards and snowdrifts. It was like moving from the Seven Dwarves' cottage, all gables, carvings, thatched roof, and forest sun ladders, to Studs Lonigan's abode in some Chicago ghetto.

432 Albert Street sat squarely across from one of the largest furniture factories in the country; it was a frame two-storey box with a timid gable, a stoop, no front or backyard, no cellar. On the positive side, though, it had a flush toilet, and a bathtub where you could get a hot bath more than once a week, with privacy, as opposed to a tin tub in front of the kitchen stove. Lots of neighbours too.

To the left, in an identical house, lived ten grandchildren of a poor neighbour of ours out in the country. On our right, in a house marked Unfit for Human Habitation, lived their uncle with woman and babe in some misery; four doors down, the railway to Kincardine provided train whistles, and the two factories, very close by, started their roaring at 6:00 A.M., not ceasing until midnight.

The previous owner—some sort of sailor—had left an old New York square grand piano as well as a smooth, shiny postcard depicting the Mermaid of Aden, some really old American books for children (*First Lessons in Truth and Gentleness*, Boston, 1853), and a conch shell doorstop.

But its frame was so old, the piano had to be tuned once a month by a slender piano tuner who often paused for a cigarette in his hour-long struggle with disharmony. Since my musical commitment to the local competition festival coming up in the spring included a Bach prelude and fugue, a Beethoven sonata, and two Debussy preludes, I walked out to the farm about twice monthly, lit a fire, and did some supplemental practising on the piano there.

I notice all these difficulties now; but did I then? No. Instead, I loved the blue coke flame of the kitchen gas plate, the big horse-drawn drays that came once a week to take away everyone's cinders and ashes, and the films I could see uptown—Joan Fontaine in *The Constant Nymph,* and Salvador Dali

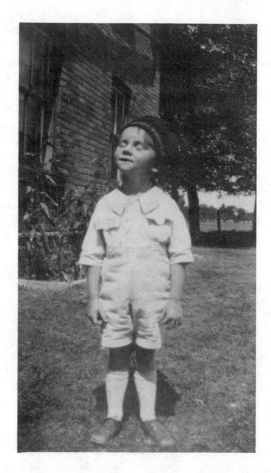

In front of Ontario farmhouse, 1930

dream sequences in Hitchcock's *Spellbound.* One day I would write an opera libretto, *Crazy to Kill,* based on the idea of a series of murders in a mental sanatorium.

There are now two turning points as big as the *Fantasia* bike trip: one, I wrote the grade thirteen departmentals—fainted during the extra cramming sessions in Latin at 8:00 A.M. souping up our handling of the subjunctive in "ut" clauses. Our classics teacher was a ferocious Roman-looking matron in rimless spectacles whose telephone number you'd expect to be Tacitus MCLX, and whose teaching of Homer's "Nausicaa" episode had unexpected sexual benefits. The editors of the British text had used illustrations from Greek vases and this time forgot to erase all of Odysseus's genitalia as, after swimming about there for months, he lurches out of the ocean towards the king of Phaeacia's daughter. At last, a straightforward glimpse of sexual excitement in an understandable context! But apparently completely unnoted by Tacitus MCLX.

Of all the courses I should have done well in, English composition somehow eluded me. I hated précis work, and my English teacher had also rebelled against the turn my style had taken after my eighteenth birthday. I now wrote sentences just jungle-like in their metaphorical growths (backwoods Dylan Thomas)—something to do with the sudden intensity of virile development about that time in young men's lives and the effect that had on wherever the soul's metaphor factory is located. So, I won my scholarships in Greek and Latin composition and literature instead and escaped 432 Albert to the aforementioned home of the knobby Gothic finials.

The other turning point was my discovery of Debussy. He made far more sense to me than the German composers—he talked directly to me—literary, sensual, poetic, collages of wit with exactly the hot bed of sudden flashes and turns that filled my own mental landscape. My playing of *Voiles* (Modéré. Dans un rythme sans rigeur et caressant) and *Minstrels* (Modéré. Nerveux et avec humour) wrung this from the usually suspicious British adjudicator: "Jolly good work though and done with a great deal of authority and insight into the subject matter. . . . It had that Debussy quality . . ."

Hearing this, playing this to a full house in Stratford's Dutch Renaissance city hall auditorium, how could it be otherwise than that I should start writing music and poems based on Debussy's style about the devil-worshippers of the town incessantly puffing black coal smoke out of their chimneys!

To sum up, one incident keeps recurring. When I was about fourteen, impelled by *Pinocchio*, I had made Cinderella puppets out of paraffin wax, stuffed rags, and old scraps from my mother's sewing basket. Used to do library story hours and Sunday school socials. One winter night, a handsome, willowy youth knocked at the front door of 432 Albert Street to tell me that, regretfully, he had to cancel the invitation for a performance at St. Swithin's (High Church, Anglican) because he had just realized the performance would be in Lent.

That was okay with me since back at the kitchen table I was gridlocking into Xenophon's *Anabasis* and memorizing the glossary to our *Macbeth* text ("Discuss twenty Elizabethan words not in use to-day in the Shakespearean play taken"), but . . . somehow or other our scene was my youth epiphanized. I think he had on a fedora too, something I couldn't bring myself to wear. And a coat with a belt.

The wind howled down the street almost drowning out the factory whine and hum with occasional thunderous modulations rattling our windows.

Love and Friendship

Skipping ahead about four years, in the fall of 1947 I wrote in my diary: "Oct 7—moved to 70 Grenville St. tonight."

I was to be very happy in that minuscule broom closet of an attic bedroom. Paul, a classmate and navy veteran, got me the room more or less to make me resident author for his little magazine, *Here and Now*, which he was printing and editing in the basement with his girlfriend Cathy. The rent was twelve dollars monthly, and my mother provided me with bedding from the farm, but there was already a batik coverlet for the mattress on the cot with matching batik curtain for the closet, all reminding one that this address was in the North Village, on the extreme edge of Toronto's Bohemia of the thirties. There was still a street of studios and craft shops (Gerrard Street) plus a restaurant serving real food as opposed to Puritan Toronto inedibles, but Mary John's, as it was called, found my hair too long and refused to let me eat there! On the ground floor of 70 Grenville was the landlord's British Israelite Press, and other lodgers with elocutionary backgrounds (Royal Conservatory of Toronto) or gay window dressers for Eaton's department stores abounded. There was a bar next door—Malloney's—which reluctantly admitted me; Fiona lodged over the way (Montreal friend Colleen recommended me when we met her in creative writing class); chestnut trees; and late at night you could hear the City Hall bell, the St. James Cathedral bells, the harbour bell, and if a stormy night, the British Israelite Press sign creaking back and forth on its horizontal rod.

By 1947, I was in the fourth year of the English language and literature honours course at University College where, in first year, I had met my wife-to-be, Colleen Thibaudeau, and took classes with her and twenty or so other friends every year until graduation. More or less, we started with Anglo-Saxon poetry and moved year by year through English until we arrived at Virginia Woolf, creative writing, *Culture and Anarchy*, Henry James, and even some Canadian poetry—I was much struck with Earle Birney's *Anglo-Saxon Street* about a real and still-existing Toronto street with "giraffe towers" in the distance (the highest building in the British empire—head office of the Bank of Commerce) and many tough navvies "jawslack for meat" lumbering home to their "bleached beldames, garnished in bargain-basements . . . spewed from wheelboat / after day-long doughtiness . . . in sewertrench or sandpit . . . Junebrown Jutekings . . . in slumbertrough adding sleepily to Anglekin." Streetcars and beds aren't so ordinary after you've made up kennings for them such as "wheelboat" and "slumbertrough." A. M. Klein, a Montreal poet, also knocked me over with "Portrait of the Poet as Landscape," which celebrated the non-status of poets in our country:

He is alone; yet not completely alone.
Pins on a map of a colour similar to his,
each city has one, sometimes more than one . . .

But, while teaching this years later, I suddenly felt, for the first time, a twinge, for in a satirical catalogue of the madness this loneliness drives poets to appears "a third, alone, and sick with sex, and rapt / doodles him symbols convex and concave." This is the result of myself publishing a poem in 1947 called "The Oracular Portcullis" which has the concave/convex bit and which fifteen years later appeared in an anthology of erotic poetry. So sick was I that, of course, I hadn't thought of it as an erotic poem, but a symbolist friend pointed out the *vagina dentata* title and thus enlightened me on the unconscious drives

that bedevil a complete innocent. But Mr. Klein—ouch!

By the time our class had reached the poetry of Ossian, Chatterton, and Blake, I had fallen in love with Colleen—stirred perhaps by E. P. Ellinger's book about Chatterton, *The Marvelous Boy,* or maybe by the fact that our lecturers kept labelling these poets "pre-romantic." I remember one fall night, she came up to my room to read me a verse play she had written about cultural goddesses of our country—Laura Secord and Mrs. Moodie—and perhaps the rebel William Lyon Mackenzie reading their lines from handfuls of dead leaves while sitting around a table. This manuscript has been lost as has the book she also wrote for a friend's children that when you had finished it, you turned it upside down and read it backwards to the title page again. We both published poetry, along with our friend Phyllis Gotlieb, in the same year in the college literary mag, the *Undergrad,* sumptuously designed by Paul Arthur with a typographical cover in red and silver, with some numbers having green-and-red or russet-and-gold covers:

With schoolmates (second from left, back row), 1938

THE
UND
ERG
RAD

We three are still published together—take a look at Peggy Atwood's recent *Oxford Book of Canuck Poetry* and you'll find us cheek by jowl.

My first poem published outside the college circle appeared in Cleveland's *Driftwind,* cover title printed on wallpaper; got accepted by *Chimaera* and *Midland Review,* turned down by *View,* the surrealist magazine from New York, available in Martin Roher's news depot on Bloor Street and, along with the British *Horizon,* my favourite source of cultural *savoir faire.* In Canada, there was *Contemporary Verse* (British Columbia, blind editor, his wife, who disliked poetry, had to read him all the poems), but despite all this, readably designed and culturally acute. Our Pacific province was goddessland for me because of Emily Carr, the great poet and writer whose last exhibit I'd been bowled over by in second year. In Toronto, there was *Canadian Forum* with Northrop Frye as literary editor; they rejected my poem on "Abortion" but took such other goodies as "Klaxon" (an anti–car driving poem that caused deep trouble with parents when it appeared in school readers) and "To the Avon River above Stratford," recently anthologized in Hong Kong. What few readers understand is that it has to be "above" because the city's sewage farm makes the rest of the river unprintable.

In Montreal, there was *First Statement,* succeeded by *Northern Review,* whose editor, John Sutherland, earned my loyalty and trust—thrilling to realize he typeset the whole shebang by hand as well as his chapbook series, in which I read my first Irving Layton poem: "church steeples, hemorrhoids on the city's anus." When Sutherland (half brother to Donald) published vanity press items for cash, he changed the name of his press from First Statement to Poison Ivy. His sister designed for him, rather more coolly than Paul's design of *Here and Now*—baroque, *Graphis* influenced. Since I hoped to be editor of the *Undergrad* next year, my fingers itched to experiment with type.

In our graduate year, Colleen decided to do her M.A. thesis on contemporary Canadian poetry with McLuhan and one weekend we entrained for Montreal to visit the coteries. Colleen stayed at Fiona's father's house, I stayed at her aunt's—Westmount, heavy with Redpath sugar and francophone servants.

Up in John and Audrey's apartment we played poetry poker with their bunch of poets and hangers-on (Guy Glover—National Film Board—"tightly rolled magazine of grief''); this was the time we noted at breakfast that a poet's wife had overnight developed a black eye—a first indication to us that marriage to the "inspired" might have its occupational hazards. Frank Scott, Arthur Smith, P. K. Page formed another coterie based on a magazine called *Preview;* there were disputes about the savage review Sutherland wrote of Robert Finch's poems (Professor Finch had taught Colleen Mallarmé), of the way Smith edited the *Chicago Anthology of Canadian Poetry* (result: Sutherland's *Other Canadians* anthology) and accusations of Westmount snobbery versus ghetto sincerity. Scott I revere for trapping monster prime ministers, such as Mackenzie King and R. B. Bennett, in his satirical portrait poems, and Page for certain poems where white-and-black Canada (snow, winter) is poised against multi-flowered Brazil and Mexico. Two other big moments were seeing my first Quebecois play—Gratien Gelinas's *Tit-Coq* at the Theâtre de Gésu, about the disadvantages of being a bastard

"Freshman Reaney," University College,
Toronto, 1944

As a graduate student, with future wife Colleen Thibaudeau, 1950

in Quebec—and the opening lines of "O Canada" engraved all around the concourse at the railway station:

> O Canada! Terre de nos aieux, Ton histoire est une épopé Des plus brillants exploits, Et ta valeur, de foi trempée, Protégera nos foyers et nos droits.

You might imagine that with all this going on, there could be some relation between ourselves as writers and the courses we were taking—especially courses in literary criticism and theory. With Colleen's teachers Finch and McLuhan, yes; but with Arthur Woodhouse, head of the English department at University College, no. The key poem for him and for me is *Paradise Lost,* which I consider a very sensuous poem ("simple, sensuous, and passionate" is what Milton says poetry should be), but Professor Woodhouse took quite a different view. The great epic poem was important because of its ideas; great poetry was written by finding great ideas, e.g., "predestination—true or false?" and metaphors

were fit only to be put in front of theology and philosophy as bait.

What stuck in my craw was that the New Testament had people in it who would have failed all exams in theology. And, as we slid through literary history, I noted that some poets I really loved—Emily Dickinson and Edgar Allan Poe—were given pretty short shrift; they were so metaphorical that of course there was no dialectic. The trouble was the power and authority of this attitude caused me to give myself short shrift. Rescuers were available—Northrop Frye, Marshall McLuhan, and Harold Innis, all thinkers who thought poetically about language, expression, communication, and culture, but not at my college. At the end of her graduate year, Arthur Woodhouse told Colleen that she would never get a job, that because of her French name and her being a woman, she would never get a job. She replied (during the war we had both worked summers in farm camps), "Not even picking grapes?"

Connected with this crux was one of the key turning points of my college career, even more crucial than the publication of my first book of poems. In my second year, to celebrate my leaving the men's residence, I wrote a nine hundred-word short story called "The Box Social." Out of the deep past it somehow came to me, I think from my mother talking about the way men treated women in our neighbourhood. They never struck back; well, in my story one of them did. This fiction caused a sensation when Paul, after some difficulty, got it published in the *Undergrad;* later it did the same across Canada when it was released nationally in a mag called *New Liberty.* The attacks took two forms—writing a dirty story, eh? and writing an untrue story—i.e., not realistic. I fought back with a letter to the *Varsity* using William Faulkner as a defence, promptly to be told (by Robert Weaver) that Faulkner was a realist! In my new diary (I'd long outgrown my grandmother's ledger) I see that I thought: "there should be something called neo-Gothic." Not for nought had I written a big essay in third year on the Gothic novel, and there seemed no reason why old farmhouses in southern Ontario could not have a Popeye sitting in the polished, engineless car out in front, or a Temple Drake lighting a cigarette up in the barn.

Fortunately, the aesthetic misunderstandings did not extend to the universities of Iowa and Manitoba, which offered me, respectively, a fellowship in creative writing and a job (took the latter), but it did turn out to be a startling confirmation of how dangerous it was to be too imaginative. I did not get to be editor of the *Undergrad;* the argument was that anyone who could write such a terrible story would not be suitable!

One night, I took my last Saturday night walk down Yonge Street. At that time, one would have heard scores of storefront evangelical preachers raving away with leather lungs, seen the scores of secondhand bookshops all dark and shut up, the butcher shops still open with sawdust on their floors and rabbits hanging down from their ceilings. Nightlife swarmed in a parade with Toronto's last barrel organ squealing out "We're Soldiers of the Queen." The princesses of the evening were stout utilitarian ladies with stockings rolled down to their knees, rollicking soldiers and sailors on their arms. At Christmas, Eaton's department store would have windows which were each decorated like a Pollock's Toy Theatre scene (tuppence plain, threepence coloured), but not after midnight when the dread Toronto Sabbath settled down. Then, the blinds would be drawn down as they were at Northway's in Stratford, for both Mr. Eaton and Mr. Northway hailed from Belfast, Ulster, whose Old Testament morals and aesthetics dominated Ontario at this time, particularly Toronto.

When we came to Queen Street, the rolled-stocking ladies thickened, and I told Colleen of my first walk there in my freshman year when an early skateboarder, an old rascal with Ronald Reagan legs cut off at the hips, tied to a self-propelled roller, slid by me "like a pair of ragged claws" and said wearily: "Oh these country boys." In one of my orange Coil-Rotary notebooks from this period I have an emblematic drawing called "Queen Street" in which a vista down to the Don Jail, symbolized by a gallows, is framed by a young rolled-stocking woman on stage right and a randy, vigorous old tramp as her opposite, sinister companion. Between them, some red lanterns guard an excavation in which the body of a suicide poet has been discovered.

With imagery like this bubbling away in my bespectacled head, there was surely no doubt I could field some sort of creative writing class at Manitoba or perhaps end up, at least, in the local madhouse, but with the skateboarder's remark still quite true of my appearance as well, would I be able to teach the other courses required, e.g., *Prologue to Canterbury Tales* in Middle English, to talkative (to each other) Home Economics young ladies ("I was talking to Audrey, sir") 120 at a time, or Remedial English to a total spectrum of dyslexics, one of whom kept sniggering every time I mentioned the copula verb, or Commerce Special English where "ejaculation" produced guffaws, or Freshman English, total atheists so far as the concept of verbal texture was concerned?

The solution was easy, although it took some years to light upon it. Copying a friend of mine (Richard), I eventually grew a moustache "to fend off evil students." That at least brought up what I looked like within striking distance of my real age.

Since I am one of those who hate change so much that I could cheerfully have missed schooling altogether and just stayed home, the Manitoba job experience was one of the toughest metamorphoses forced upon me by the inexorable god of experience, tempered at last by my marriage to Colleen (December 29, 1951) and obliterated as a problem by the happy arrival of children and an important book Colleen gave me at graduation, Northrop Frye's *Fearful Symmetry,* which helped me at last to read Blake's prophecies where my problems with Orc (energy) and Beulah (innocent joy) are handled in terms of psychologic epic.

But at first, I just wanted to go home. The big landscape alienating shock was that there were *no* Ontario foregrounds. Because of its flatness (the Red River valley is the bottom of ancient Lake Agassiz) and its savannahs, you look out a window and see a grain elevator one hundred miles away. "That's why it's such a good place to think," said Marshall McLuhan when I came back to Toronto to do doctoral work with Frye. Yes, Marshall should have known since he was brought up in Winnipeg and *there* there are no messy thickets of chokecherry bushes substituting for a clean mental slate on which to analyze our articulation problems as he was doing in *Mechanical Bride.*

Soon, of course, I would be feeling homesick for Manitoba—especially long bicycle trips up the Red through the old parishes to Netley Marsh and south as far as Aubigny, where there is a ferryman to get you across to the St. Boniface side of Winnipeg. Louis Riel's farm was just across from the Fort Garry campus and the university bus turned off at the spot where one day in 1868 a Métis farmer, André Nault, told the Ontario surveyors to stop meddling with his hay privilege. If I had stayed in Manitoba I would have done a play about the Riel Rebellion instead of handling similar figures in my own bailiwick—the Donnelly family—but. . . .

Another problem, not so easily solved, was the intrigue always potential in the academic ratpit.

Self-confidence was not encouraged by two of my colleagues whom I shall call Professor Grendel and Doctor Heremod. The latter's game was to accept my first poetry book, *The Red Heart,* for reviewing in the *Winnipeg Free Press,* but never to write the review, nor give back the book so someone else could. The rumour was that she considered the poems of too poor quality. As a result, no one in town really knew that I had published something other than "The Box Social." Incidentally, friend Robert had typed out the manuscript for *The Red Heart* (I didn't learn to type until I was forty), Colleen and Sybil edited and arranged—Sybil was literary editor at McClelland and Stewart, the publisher; later on she became my agent. Originally I had wanted to call the book *Antichrist as a Child,* but old Mr. McClelland, a Bible salesman through and through, would have none of that sort of blasphemy, so *The Red Heart,* which received nice reviews, sold out, and eventually got the Governor-General's Award, in those days a mere medal smithed at Birks, the Toronto jeweler. Trying to sell this medal when flat broke at graduate school, I was told by a monocled lady in Agatha

With sons, James Stewart and John Andrew, 1958

Conducting a seminar at the University of Western Ontario, 1963

Christie costume at the back of Birks that I would lose my amateur status!

Before I ever arrived in Fort Garry, Professor Grendel, he must have secretly approached my registration card box, lifted out the normal contents and substituted for that every problem student on campus—mostly foreign students come to see if they could squeeze into the medical school—from Nigeria, Macao, Kiev, Hong Kong, New Joisey, Tierra del Fuego. One or two were fluent in English, but the majority had terrible difficulties, each one of them different from everybody else's, some of them terminal. As a result, my freshman class had a failure rate of 90 percent; however, the sympathetic head of the department (Lloyd) realized, I hope, what was going on.

It was comforting, perhaps, to watch Doctor Heremod some years later do a superb witch in *Rapunzel*, a children's theatre production directed by a student friend of mine—the late John Hirsch. This brilliant director went on to found a professional theatre in Winnipeg and encouraged me to start thinking about writing plays. My first children's play,

Names and Nicknames, was created as an exercise for his young actors at Manitoba Theatre Centre. Also an encouragement to move from lyric to dramatic poetry was a request by a college friend, composer John Beckwith, to write him an opera libretto.

After seven years, I asked for a sabbatical so I could return to Toronto and work on a doctoral thesis with Frye. (*a*) I wanted to become a qualified teacher since I was being asked to do far more than just be a writer-in-residence or get night school students (a huge class of one hundred) to do displaced modern versions of such Grimm fairy tales as *The Robber Bridegroom*, (*b*) I wanted to become more expert in literary symbolism, structure, and genre. I can hear some readers, brought up on the Whitmanic American school that has swept Canada clean of its British-influenced poetry—"tightly rolled magazine of grief" indeed!—I can hear them gnashing at such an academic and old-fashioned approach, but it worked.

Because of my two years' work with Frye, and also, let's face it, my study of *Beowulf* with Dr. Shook at St. Michael's, it was then possible for me to organize the craft values that plays demand. For example, just to start—the garden up at the farm that I planted in 1959 after my thesis oral ("The Influence of Edmund Spenser on William Butler Yeats") was larger, easier to control, the best garden I ever have made. In the old days, I used to flake out after only digging a quarter of what I could have. As with the physical garden, so with the mental garden of one's own vocation and art. Essential to this was closeness to a large library and so the teaching made sense in the college context. Just how much sense I didn't realize until I moved to the English department at Western in London, Ontario, and discovered that their regional archives had a dazzling three hundred feet concerning the back and foreground of the Donnelly Tragedy. But now, I need a new and last section called . . .

Property and Freedom

Thirty years afterwards, in semiretirement, I sit in my office in the tower of University College at Western and look at my library (of which impressed young reporters from the *Gazette* have said, "why it's like a secondhand bookshop") as well as my theatre posters which, with the help of a research assistant (Rod—an honours history grad whom I found playing a trumpet on Dundas Street), hang from a picture railing fifteen feet up. Everything that happened to me after I left the University of Manitoba in 1960 is represented by something in this room either shelved or hanging up between the collegiate gothic dungeon windows or hidden in green filing cabinets, a jam cupboard, and the subscription desk of a now-defunct magazine known as the *Farmer's Advocate,* a once-famous local publication.

If commanded, I could produce a complete file of my little magazine *Alphabet: the iconography of the imagination,* a semiannual which lasted from 1960 to 1971 balancing documentary with myth (Narcissus/Twins as Mirror Images of Each Other, etc.) and bringing together a group of writers who came to be known as the Identifiers. In the filing cabinets and on the shelves are the paper fossils of the courses I devised to teach literacy in the culture of our country and my province. People are still alarmed that there could be such a course as Ontario and Literature Culture. Culture in Ontario?!

The play posters answer this not only with their range, from those for children to those for the geriatric, but also in their varying attempts, indirectly and directly, to "tell my region's story"; some time ago, Alice Munro made a pact with me that she was to have everything north of Exeter (farther up on Highway 4) and I everything south—which leaves me with the Pontiac Conspiracy, the Baldoon poltergeist, and the Donnellys. Continuing research on this fascinating family, whose story resembles a cross between the Hatfields and the McCoys cum *O.K. Corral* cum the *Njalsaga,* lies spread out in assembly line on two seminar tables joined together. In a cupboard are stored up not only foul papers for the twenty-odd plays I've written but also ordnance maps (mile to an inch) for large swatches of Ontario and Manitoba, part of a project to do an emblematic watercolour of every township in my province. I still, also, want to reach the highest point in Manitoba—Mount Baldy up in the Duck Mountains. Used to do all my traveling on foot, and then bicycle, but of late (alas for my early poem "Klaxon") have had to learn how to drive a car! Ugh!

In order to deal with increasing theatrical activity in the mid-1960s, I slowly curtailed the typesetting associated with *Alphabet* and swung over to the world I am just sliding out of now—that of countless theatre workshops involving local stories and myths, using students here, special theatre groups of professionals mixed with amateurs, lots of children in schools and out, puppets, and community plays which have involved the populations of whole towns. The literary properties dearest to me are the four children's plays: *Apple Butter* (puppets), aforenamed *Names and Nicknames* whose technique was suggested by an old speller of my father's, *Geography Match,* aimed at our

centennial, and *Ignoramus,* an Aristophanic satire on the educational horrors John Dewey let loose on our schools, first visible to me when the project system hit our country school and my brother and sister learnt to read from the abominable *Dick, Jane and Puff.*

For both adults and children, ultimately, I also mention *Listen to the Wind,* based apparently on my grandmother's copy of Rider Haggard's first novel, *Dawn,* though actually about myself and my cousins as Brontë children; then *Colours in the Dark,* autobiographical fantasia, premiered in 1967 at the Stratford Festival, John Hirsch directing; then *The Donnellys,* a trilogy workshopped in Halifax and premiered at Tarragon in Toronto.

Since *The Donnellys* toured nationally in 1975, the floodgates opened and commissions poured in—my favourite being invited by my old high school to write a play with their students about some Stratford theme. I chose the controversial General Strike of 1933 and spent four months, helped by Jerry Franken, happily moulding 136 kids and citizens into a musical comedy, *King Whistle,* filled with everything from Communist agitators to pickers of chicken

The author manipulating puppets with student Gillian Ferns for Apple Butter, *1964*

feathers at Swift's, paid a penny a bird!, to the life of the first working-class mayor of Stratford, the late Oliver Kerr. Occasionally, it's my luck to get an interviewer who is appalled at my prolificness. I hope you aren't because, to use a Blakean term, the Devourer in these times is very much abroad and we cannot have enough art that seeks to wake up people and get them in touch with their identities through its theatricality.

My two remaining children (son and daughter) are in publishing, impelled there no doubt by a house with a lot of Baskerville type around. Colleen has just published her fifth book—*The Artemisia Book, Poems New and Selected.* Her grandfather's house was built on the townline between Artemisia township and Glenelg township so that the Thibaudeaux dined in Glenelg and slept in Artemisia (all up in Grey County on the Niagara Escarpment):

> Sometimes I wonder whether I am the last person left
>   alive
> Who started school with a slate and slate pencil.

In conclusion, my teacher Northrop Frye died this January after publishing a book called *Words with Power.* My own life is living proof that words are more powerful than swords or guns. Every time one of my plays works on an audience successfully you can see how it is possible to change the world, how you can with strong poetry and theatricality bring children and grown-ups closer to the Paradise we should never have left.

And isn't it odd that my mother was fired from teaching at the Irish School for doing too many plays with the young people, but that her son, at Western at least, actually had his salary raised, basically for doing the same sort of thing?

Monday, June 24, 1991
London, Ontario

BIBLIOGRAPHY

Poetry:

The Red Heart, McClellan & Stewart, 1949.

A Suit of Nettles, Macmillan, 1958.

Twelve Letters to a Small Town, Ryerson, 1962.

The Dance of Death at London, Ontario, Alphabet Press, 1963.

Poems, Germain Warkentin, editor, New Press, 1972.

Selected Shorter Poems, G. Warkentin, editor, Porcepic, 1976.

Selected Longer Poems, G. Warkentin, editor, Porcepic, 1976.

Performance Poems (illustrated by the author), Moonstone Press, 1990.

Plays:

The Killdeer and Other Plays (contains "Night-Blooming Cereus," broadcast as radio play, 1959, first produced in Toronto, 1960; "The Killdeer" [also see below], first produced in Toronto, 1960; "One-Man Masque," first produced in Toronto, 1960; "Sun and Moon," first produced in Winnipeg, 1972), Macmillan, 1962.

Let's Make a Carol: A Play with Music for Children, Waterloo Music Co., 1965.

Colours in the Dark (first produced in Stratford, Ontario, 1967), Talonbooks-Macmillan, 1969.

Masks of Childhood (contains "The Killdeer," revised version, first produced in Vancouver, 1970; "The Easter Egg," first produced in Hamilton, Ontario, 1962; "Three Desks," first produced in Calgary, 1967), edited by Brian Parker, New Press, 1972.

Listen to the Wind (three-act; first produced in London, Ontario, 1965), Talonbooks, 1972.

Apple Butter and Other Plays for Children (contains "Names and Nicknames," first produced in Winnipeg, 1963; "Apple Butter," first produced in London, Ontario, 1965; "Ignoramus"; "Geography Match"), Talonbooks, 1973; all published separately by Talonbooks, 1978.

The Donnellys: A Trilogy, Part I: *Sticks and Stones* (first produced in Toronto, 1973), Porcepic, 1975; Part II: *The Saint Nicholas Hotel* (first produced in Toronto, 1974), Porcepic, 1976; Part III: *Handcuffs* (first produced in Toronto, 1975), Porcepic, 1976; published as *The Donnelly Trilogy,* Porcepic, 1983.

(With John Beckwith) *All the Bees and All the Keys* (for children), Porcepic, 1976.

(With C. H. Gervais) *Baldoon* (two-act), Porcupine's Quill, 1977.

The Dismissal, Porcepic, 1978.

(Librettist) John Beckwith, *Shivaree,* Performing Rights Organization of Canada, 1978.

King Whistle, Brick, 1979.

Wacousta (adapted from a novel by John Richardson), Porcepic, 1980.

Imprecations, Black Moss Press, 1984.

Take the Big Picture, Porcupine's Quill, 1986.

(Librettist) John Beckwith, *Crazy to Kill,* Guelph Spring Festival, 1988.

(Librettist) Harry Somers, *Serinette,* York Pioneer Society, 1990.

A Sleigh Without Bells (puppet play), premiered in London, Ontario, 1991.

Also author of *The Boy with the "R" in His Hand* (juvenile novel, illustrated by Leo Rampen; Macmillan, 1965) and *Fourteen Barrels from Sea to Sea* (travel diary; Porcepic, 1977), and editor and founder of the magazine *Alphabet: the iconography of the imagination*, 1960–71.

Harrison E. Salisbury

1908-

I grew up in an old Victorian house at 107 Royalston Avenue in Minneapolis. It was a curving street, shaded by great elms, in what had been a stylish neighborhood when my grandfather built his house in the early 1880s. By the time I was growing up it had entered a precipitous decline.

Although Queen Victoria had died a few years before my birth it was her influence, not that of her son Edward VII who had waited so long to take the throne, which dominated the life of 107 Royalston Avenue, all wooden gingerbread in the finest tradition of the day, mansard roofs, redbrick chimneys, greenish copper gutters, broad porches, set back on a clipped lawn where my grandfather had planted a hawthorn hedge, a handsome arborvitae tree, and two red cedars which grew more and more spindly each year. A fine oak shaded the rear of the house where my sister, our friends, and myself played summer and winter, morning till nightfall—except when school was in session.

The rooms of 107 Royalston were stacked with books. So was the cranky attic, huddled under the mansards—books in shelves, books in stacks, and books tossed helter-skelter into a great packing box, waiting to be sorted out. They never were.

The downstairs library was trimmed in cherry wood and bookcases were built into the walls. The upper hallway possessed an ashwood bookcase running its length. There was a bookcase in every room except the front parlor where no one ventured except for Christmas or a big family party.

My grandfather was a great reader, particularly in his last three years when he sat in a rocking chair awaiting the heart attack which finally took his life. He was a doctor in the age when country doctors went out on calls at all hours and all seasons with horse and buggy or sleigh in winter. He worked himself to death.

I grew up thinking that books and writing were the most important things in life. This belief was nourished by my mother who was a frustrated writer. She had written essays and poetry all her life. Her literary efforts did not see the light of day but she dreamed that if she could not win recognition her son would.

Harrison E. Salisbury, "In my New York Times office, poster of the Paris exposition of the works of the famous Soviet Russian artist and poet Vladimir Mayakovski on the wall," 1975

Perhaps I would have become a writer without her fierce ambition but perhaps not. When I entered the University of Minnesota at the age of sixteen I had no idea of what I would do with myself. There was a blank on the admission form in which you jotted down your goal. I wrote the word "chemistry" (I had been delighted with an experimental chemistry course in high school) but that was the first and last step of my chemist's career.

Later that day I strolled over to a dark red granite building called Pillsbury Hall and signed up to work on the university newspaper. Within a month I was hooked on writing and reporting. I still am.

Propelled into writing by the incessant propaganda of my mother, I had written bits of impressions in a school copybook and in 1917 or 1918 scribbled out with a stubby pencil what I called a "History of the Great War." I was proud of this achievement. So was my mother. My father was more skeptical. He remained that way. When I finished high school he gently tried to persuade me to enter a vocational school and learn a trade, carpentry, perhaps, or electrical work—something that would enable me to earn a living. He saw no practical future in a writing career. He also thought that I was too young for college and that a couple of years at a carpenter's bench or a metal lathe would serve me in good stead. He was right but my mother was appalled. She was determined that her child prodigy would write the Great American Novel.

I do not know why the Great American Novel loomed so large in the Victorian iconography with which I grew up. It had entered my mother's mind long before my birth and held a dominant place there until she died.

"With sister Janet, in a photo taken by my father, Percy P. Salisbury," about 1912

She had been the youngest child in a large Welsh family with a harsh Wesleyan father and several aggressive, ambitious brothers. Evan D. J. Evans (called "Evan Evans Straightback" to distinguish him from the other Evan Evans in the Welsh community of Oak Hill, Ohio) was a contractor. He had built for himself and his family a castle of redbrick on the outskirts of Minneapolis where he presided in patriarchal style. The castle possessed a tower room entered by a ladder and trapdoor. This room became my mother's sanctuary. She spent hours and days there, ruining her sight with endless reading and writing, safe from intrusion once she had pulled up the ladder.

Here she herself tried to compose the Great American Novel with no success. Now with her son she was determined to achieve her goal vicariously.

I was ignorant of these deep psychological drives. I loved to read. I was a bookworm feeding on the endless volumes at my disposal. My taste ran to blood-and-thunder, pirates, and adventure. I devoured the full shelf of Dumas. I read another shelf of Henty and one of Trowbridge (*Cudjo's Cave*, *The Drummer Boy*, and other delights). Gradually I moved into Mark Twain, Victor Hugo, and Thackeray. I didn't care so much for Dickens. Too much stagey dialogue. But his *Tale of Two Cities* was the first novel I read.

I engaged in writing to go along with the reading—suggested, encouraged, and implemented by my mother. My aunt Sue gave me a subscription to *St. Nicholas,* the children's magazine of the 1890s which persisted into the 1920s. It fostered writing contests and I won a silver medal. A patriotic society sponsored an essay competition. I entered one on Alexander Hamilton and won another medal for a tedious compilation of facts and figures almost entirely written by my mother. In high school I worked on the school paper, writing banal editorials and two or three strained poems. Poetry was not my metier.

All that changed at the University of Minnesota. I fell in love with writing and reporting. I spent every free moment with the university paper and stole hours and days from my studies. I shifted my major studies to literature and writing seminars. I wrote gritty and melodramatic sketches of life in the Jewish ghetto and black slum which had arisen in the once upper-middle-class Oak Lake "Addition" where I grew up.

My gods became Theodore Dreiser, Stephen Crane, Frank Norris, Sherwood Anderson, O. E. Rölvaag and, of course, Hemingway. There was no one like Hemingway. No one. I didn't know one striving writer at the end of the 1920s and early 1930s who did not imitate Hemingway. Our characters became so monosyllabic they hardly spoke. A sentence of more than eight words was suspect.

It never occurred to me that my childhood at 107 Royalston Avenue, the old house with its walnut furniture, its oriental rugs which were my father's delight, the great copper-bottomed sink, endlessly soldered until it looked like a map of the Balkans, the crooked alley with its smell of horse piss, the tide of emigrants from the Jewish Pale of Settlement in Russia which filled up the decaying mansions, the handful of blacks who followed in their footsteps, would become my richest memories and almost my stock in trade as a writer.

I thought, as I was growing up, that a writer must have "experiences" and I dreamed a lot about how to have "experiences" which I could convert, somehow, into the Great American Novel. Not for one minute did I doubt the ambition which had been transferred into my mind by my mother's frustration. To write that novel was my ambition and my goal.

The question was how to do it. My aunt Sue, my father's sister, thought she knew the way. It was to "see the world." She herself was the only member of the family who had "seen the world." She had left 107 Royalston when my father and mother were married in 1906 and gone to work as a business secretary. That does not sound revolutionary but in the early 1900s it was. I can see her now in her trim navy blue skirt, her white shirtwaist, a gold watch pinned to her breast, her dark brown hair put up in a bun, telling about distant cities—Chicago, Cleveland—and ultimately New York.

Sue became a "New York businesswoman," sharing an apartment with another young woman, editor of a long-lost children's magazine called *Everyland,* devoted to inducting children in that age of armchair travel into the customs of the Dutch, the Italians, and the Fiji Islanders.

I never doubted that my aunt Sue was right. If I was to become a real writer and compose the Great American Novel I would have to wrest myself out of the Victorian world of my childhood, turn my back on the house on Royalston Avenue with its back stairs, its hidden closets, the nooks under the eaves, the daunting cellar with its two furnaces—one proved incapable of heating the vast windiness of the drafty structure.

No more the gentle curving avenues, the elms, the set-back houses, the soft brown dust of the avenue before it was paved with blocks of cedar that rose up and floated off with every summer rain, no more the yellow-painted sprinkling wagon that twice a day splashed down the dust as we ran after and shouted in the delight of the splashes.

Certainly there was no material for a great literary career in the enclave of Oak Lake with its two little lakes (soon to dry up), its miniature green parks, its nursemaids and enamelled children's carriages, its fire engines—the horse-drawn hose carts, the belching "steamer" to pump the water, lurching around the curves in splendid array. I was frightened of the noise, the plunging horses, the thought that fire might come to our house.

None of this was the stuff of serious prose. This was everyday existence. Written prose, novelistic fiction was something which was garnered in strange and alien shores. Even as I graduated into the Chicago of Frank Norris, the Nebraska of Willa Cather, the New York of O. Henry (so badly treated by American historians but alive and well in most foreign countries), I saw nothing worth writing about in this narrow world.

To be sure I carved out little pieces of pseudo-exotica which I made the stuff of experiments in college writing seminars. But I had my eyes fixed on the exotica not the boring (as I thought) reality.

This was at least in part the influence of Jules Verne, Alexandre Dumas, Jeffrey Farnol (I adored Farnol for two or three years). Fiction was not here and now. Fiction was *away.* Fiction was romance under palm trees or in great grey castles in the Pyrenees. Not at home at 107 Royalston Avenue.

Fiction was plot. For years I labored under the delusion that before you write a novel you have to invent a plot out of thin air. The reality of life was not a plot. The reality was just reporting, strongly differentiated from *writing.* Writing was something different—gussied up in curlyques and angles, life seen through the looking glass of perfumed senses. I didn't have that imagination. Even after I studied Dreiser and Anderson and Hemingway it did not occur to me that they were taking life as they experienced it, changing it a bit, giving it a little more form, but never inventing it. To invent life was to deny it, to intrude a lie. Life itself was the thing.

This understanding finally pounded its way into my brain under the patient guidance of Anna Von Helmholtz Phelan, the genius of my university days, a six-foot-six Valkyrie maiden out of Wagner who conducted writing seminars at Minnesota. But I felt uncomfortable with it. I made a distinction between reportage (a world in which I was wholly comfortable) and *literary* writing. To write literature you had to smoke a pipe, wear a tweedy jacket, speak with a suspicion of an English accent, go for long strolls with your Irish setter over the Sussex downs, and (possibly) have a sophisticated affair with a long-legged golden-haired woman who walked out of the third act of Michael Arlen's *Green Hat.*

I was a naive middle westerner. I knew that. But I was more naive than I realized.

It took me a long time to get away from Minnesota. Often I wonder whether I really have. The imprint of those Victorian days is strong in my mind and character and it still influences almost every act.

Chance, ambition, and curiosity took me all over the world. I have lived and worked in Russia, in China, and in England, but the map of my travels is not as real to me as the atlas I studied as a child. It had belonged to my father and I turned its pages endlessly sprawled on the library floor, catching cold in the icy drafts that found their way past the poorly finished molding of the bookcases and window boxes.

That atlas contained a double-page map of the world, the British Empire displayed in glorious red. The red lapped over every continent, as grand as Victoria was herself. It made the United States, shrunken by Mercator's projection, look like an insignificant patch of drab green. The British Empire glowed. You *knew* the sun never set on the expanse of Canada, South Africa, Australia, Egypt, New Zealand, India, and a hundred other splotches. This was Empire. I felt ashamed of the tiny United States. I fixed my eyes on Puerto Rico, the Philippines, Hawaii, Alaska. But I knew they would never match England, the proudest country in the world. I longed for empire. If only Teddy Roosevelt had not been so modest. At least we could have had Cuba and who knows what else—maybe Spain itself. I was an unabashed chauvinist. I wanted to see the Stars and Stripes flying over every continent.

Nothing made me prouder than to wake up very early on the Fourth of July, just as the sun was cutting a narrow swath through the elm trees on Royalston Avenue, and go with my father to the creaky attic, shove open the front window and hoist the flag, smelling of moth balls (it was made of heavy wool and had, I am afraid, not a few moth holes) and watch it flutter in the gentle breeze. A bit later, my father supervising carefully, we would go out to the front walk and light some firecrackers. Most of these were long strings of tiny Chinese crackers that went off with a drawn out sputter, punctuated by pauses. Sometimes when you thought the string was done there would be a final flutter as the fuse burned its way to the end. I yearned for the great "Minnesota salutes"—three-inch crackers which could lift a tin can high in the air—but I never had one until I was too old to get the pure joy of the explosion, the big bang, the sense of danger.

"World War II passport photo, wearing war correspondents uniform," 1943

I was a passionate patriot. I loved parades and flags and uniforms. In 1917 and 1918 there were Liberty Loan parades in which we school children marched, holding the edges of a vast flag which spread the width of Nicolet Avenue. People tossed war contributions into the flag, and by the time the parade was over it had begun to sag under the weight of small change and heavy round silver dollars, common currency in those days.

Growing up in Minnesota I never had much feeling of state. But I had a vivid feeling of nationality. That was enhanced by the chauvinism and patriotism of World War I. Nothing was better than America. To be an American was tops. But I harbored some sense of inferiority towards England. England was *the* power, the biggest, strongest in the world. Even as a child I recognized that our culture was English. I read about the Black Prince and King Alfred in the *Child's History of England.* That was *my* history. American history did not have the glamor. English history was real history. English authors were real authors. Our library shelves were filled with English authors. I did not read so widely in the leather-bound sets my grandfather had collected except for Thackeray. Dickens's *A Tale of Two Cities* opened my eyes and my mind. It was my first real step toward a wider world. It led to *Vanity Fair.* I thought there had never been such writing. I got a tiny inkling of how reportage could become a novel. Just a glimpse but it was enticing. Dickens was not on my wavelength. Thackeray was and still is. I place him with Zola and Tolstoy, who I did not read until years later. And Macaulay. I read Macaulay with open mouth. I read Green's *History of the English People.* And the *Illustrated London News.* We possessed bound volumes of the *Illustrated London News* going back into the 1890s; I pored over the pages. Beginning with the start of World War I, we subscribed to it, and it was from its pages that I formed my images of war—the German uhlans with their spiked helmets, ravaging the Belgian villages, the thatched roofs and dog-drawn milk carts, the image of Edith Cavell, tortured by the Huns, the artists' representations of nuns roped and swung as bell clappers, nothing too beastly for the imagination of the English propagandists. Every word, every picture was truth to my mind.

Certainly Minneapolis was a Victorian city in the early years of my life. The truth is that the nineteenth century did not come to an end in 1900. Not in Minnesota and not, I think, in the United States. It ran well into the twentieth century and only after World War I did it gradually die away in the glitter of the Jazz Age, Prohibition, the shimmy, the Charleston, F. Scott Fitzgerald, all of those evocative signs of the New Culture.

Minneapolis was a granite-and-sandstone city, dominated by great castles—the old Public Library, the Lumber Exchange, the Masonic Temple building, the West Hotel, and the gray cutstone buildings like the Pillsbury "A" Mill, the Washburn-Crosby Mills, the Exposition Building, and the massive fortresses of the warehouses belonging to Butler Brothers and others.

If I reserved my boyhood patriotism for my country rather than my state (and in speaking of my country I invariably called it "the United States" and never "America" because the latter seemed not quite *patriotic),* I had a plentiful supply left for my native city which in all things seemed to me not only fairer, but more civilized, more grandiose, more metropolitan, and just plain niftier than its twin, St. Paul, which I understood to be populated, in large part, by politicians (a very low breed indeed), Democrats (even more lowly), Irish (another step down), and drunks. Drunkenness, I believed, was the normal condition of the wretched St. Paulites. What a pity the beautiful state capitol with its golden dome, second in beauty only to that in Washington, should have been located in this sink of iniquity. I thought I could detect the difference as soon as we crossed the

boundary line riding the beautiful golden trolley cars which Tom Lowry so beneficently permitted to serve not only Minneapolis but the lower depths of St. Paul. To my boy's eye, once the magic line between the two cities was crossed, one entered (in St. Paul) a region of dismal slums, alien people, narrow streets, and saloons.

This was a peculiarly twisted and inbred chauvinism. The first page-one newspaper headline I ever got I won for a story in the *Minneapolis Journal* revealing that the St. Paul Municipal Airport was underwater. It had been flooded by the spring Mississippi freshets, and the St. Paul authorities had kept this from becoming known. One of the great shocks of my boyhood was learning that my St. Paul uncle (his St. Paul-ness was made up for by the miraculous fact of his being a locomotive engineer) not only was a Democrat but intended to cast his vote for Woodrow Wilson in 1916. In my Teddy Roosevelt Republican family, Democrats equated with town drunks, and Woodrow Wilson was a "yellow dog."

I had, as I say, little feeling of citizenship in Minnesota. My world was much smaller—my family, including my mother and father and sister, the old uncle who lived with us (my father's uncle), and my aunt and uncle and cousin who shared our house.

I think every detail of that house from the depths of the most cobwebby closet to the dank, dark, windowless room behind the furnace, where my great-uncle year after year with total lack of success tried to grow mushrooms, is etched indelibly in my mind. And well it is. Not a matchstick of the house remains. Gone the Gothic gables. Gone the great front lawn where we tumbled in grass piles in the summer twilights. Gone the old backyard oak tree, the coach house, and the manure pile, gone the thornapple hedge and the arborvitae tree. Gone the gas lamp at the front of the lawn and the lamplighter who I watched with his long pole, setting the soft white mantle aglow. Gone, too, the arc light which replaced the gas lamp with a sizzling and sputtering and the smell of ozone. Gone the heavy sledges with their burdens of coal, of lumber, of hay—and gone, too, the children who followed along picking up the spits and dribbles of coal and taking them home to fire their sputtering round stoves.

Gone not only our house but all the houses. Gone the street—indeed, the whole network of streets. Vanished as though they had never been. As though Oak Lake Addition had never existed. Gone from memories. Gone from maps. And in its place acres of blacktop and concrete. Blocks of buildings, military and rectangular.

Gone the slum that grew year by year with the days of my boyhood. Gone Royalston Avenue, Highland Avenue, Sixth Avenue North. Oak Lake itself—dried up, vanished, drained. I don't know what happened to it. It was gone before I went to Sumner School. Gone Sumner School with its sooty yellow brick and its sweat and floor-polish smells. Gone Rappaport's grocery store with its frost-patterned windows, its hanging banana bunches, its salt-glazed glass jar of pickles, its wooden boxes of salt herring and prunes, its small barrels of soda crackers, its nickel milk and nickel bread, its winter smell of asafetida and rotten potatoes. Gone with the hot-ironed tailor shop next door where cloth always seemed to be scorching and the smell of steam and sweat took your breath away. Gone the old paper-box factory and the small pond beside it. Gone within a few years of my birth—Bassett's Creek, corseted into an underground sewer and compelled to flow in these strict bonds into the Mississippi.

Well, they say, it's progress.

No one in those growing-up days worried about growth. What worried people was the slowing of growth. Minneapolis did not grow as rapidly from 1890 to 1900 as in the previous decade.

More people were jumping over the Midwest and heading straight for the Pacific Coast. That was what was worrying. Maybe Minneapolis was beginning to get *old.* And what could be worse? This was a young country. This was the frontier. Fortunes were made (and sometimes lost). But by the time I was growing up those great fortunes in lumber, in flour, in ore, in railroads, and in land had been made. Jim Hill sat in his great Gothic mansion on Summit Avenue and awaited the end. He had spanned the continent with his railroads, the jewels of the Northwest. The mills stood at St. Anthony Falls in their corona of flour dust like blockhouses guarding the rapids of the river. The grain poured in from Montana, the Dakotas, the Red River Valley. It poured into the Minneapolis mills, and the flour in its cotton sacks and its great jute cloaks filled countless red freight cars. The lumber . . . well, it was gone, or almost gone. But there still stands in my nostrils the fresh smell of pungent pine that hung over north Minneapolis, the acrid smell of the sawdust fires, and the terrifying sight of the lumber drives, when the river from shore to shore was a mass of logs and men with peaveys and spiked boots leaping across the logs like mountain goats. Everyone bragged of the timber barons and their exploits, and I grew up to the raw smell of the forest fires—Moose Lake, Cloquet—the

smoke covering the city at noon so thick the sun was black—and birds and animals fled the smoke and took refuge in the city. An owl, blind and staring, sat in our backyard oak, and deer were seen at the outskirts. The timber was gone—slashed, burned, logged, cut away—and northern Minnesota (and northern Wisconsin and Upper Michigan as well) were left an ugly desert.

All of this was in the great Victorian tradition—go out into the world and make a fortune. Build a mill, erect a city, plow the prairie, dig the riches from the bowels of the earth. This was, as I understood it, man's duty. He was not placed on earth to contemplate nature and its beauties. He was placed on earth to do his duty. To improve his own condition (and that of the world along with it).

And yet. My father told me of going to the Dakotas when he was a boy with his father. In those days the buffalo hunters rode the ranges. The buffalo hides were stacked at the prairie stations of the Great Northern and the Burlington lines like cordwood. Thousands and thousands of them. My father had seen the buffalo on the prairie. There was no sight

"With Russian woodcutter Dedya Petya outside my dacha in Saltikova, twenty miles from Moscow," 1953

like it in the world. The great herds stretched to the horizon. They moved slowly over the rich prairie, grazing as they went. And there was no cloud of dust as they passed because the prairie was so rich, so thick, the turf so heavy that the buffalo passed by and did not tear it. Now they were gone. My father was saddened and puzzled by this. "I don't know how it happened," he said. But the great herds were gone.

The prairie was gone, too, and no one understood that. My mother, who had come to Minneapolis from Ohio at the start of the 1880s, remembered the prairie well. It had begun right outside the house where she first lived on Bloomington Avenue, south of Lake Street. The prairie began there and ran on to infinity. She walked on the prairie as a child and picked pasqueflowers, the first flowers of spring. There was nothing like the prairie, she said. The freshness of its smell, its thousand grasses and thousand flowers, and you could walk on it forever. In summer the grass came up to your waist, and the buffalo seemed to swim through it. The turf was so heavy a plow could hardly cut a furrow.

I was conscious of one natural tragedy as a youngster—the disappearance of the passenger pigeon. The passenger pigeon vanished in the first years of my life. I never saw one, but I heard much of them in school, and I think their extinction was the first natural tragedy to arouse me. For years I hoped that I would see a passenger pigeon. I never did.

It never occurred to me when I was growing up that it might be wrong for a public utility to put up a high dam at St. Croix Falls and change the whole ambiance of the St. Croix rapids. I clung to my father's hand looking at that gigantic structure with a mixture of terror and awe at man's ability to erect so remarkable a creation. And the same with the building of the High Dam on the Mississippi. That this dam turned the river into a stagnant pool of sewage was a simple fact—neither bad nor good. What could one do about it? It never occurred to me that something *should* be. What were rivers for? The Chicago drainage canal to divert water from Lake Michigan to convey Chicago's sewage effluent into the Illinois River struck me as a magical kind of super-engineering.

Minnesota was a hotbed of progressive socialist thought. There was a strong movement in the state against World War I when I was growing up, against American involvement and against the influence of the "big interests," Wall Street, and the eastern financiers. In those years there was raging unrest in the West—violent agrarian movements, the rise of the anarchistic philosophy of the IWW (Industrial

"In Red Square, St. Basil's in the background," about 1954

Workers of the World), and the solid and principled socialism that was brought to Minnesota by Swedish, Norwegian, Danish, and German emigrants from the turbulent Europe of the 1840s.

I knew nothing of this until I reached the University of Minnesota in the last years before the Great Depression. I had heard of the IWWs, probably during World War I, as "I-Won't-Work" because that was the way my good Victorian father referred to them. When I first saw the initials IWW chalked on an alley fence, there ran through me a little thrill of fright—who could have scrawled those dread letters on a fence in the back alley which led from our house through the middle of the block? There was a kind of delicious horror in imagining who might have done it—certainly no schoolboy of my age would have been so daring. Certainly none of the solid burghers whose houses backed up to the alley. It must, I realized, have been done by a stableboy or a coachman. At this time most of the sheds and barns on the alley housed horses.

I grew up on the street cries of Minneapolis, the ragpicker's cry, "Rags, rags, old rags, anyone," and the bell which hung just under his cart and jangled as he progressed up the rough stones of the alley. During World War I everything had a value—old copper sinks; newspapers—twenty-five cents a hundred pounds; magazines—forty cents for fifty pounds (we ripped out and sold all of the advertising sections from the stacks of *Scribner's, Harper's,* and the *Atlantic* in the attic); old bottles, old iron, rubber; tinfoil in great round balls; cotton and wool rags (but not, I think, silk rags). Sometimes, the ragpicker would come right into the basement and offer to buy the whole contents for, let's say, three dollars. He had a small spring scale which he held up in his hand when weighing the paper, and he paid his money out of a purse with a nickel clasp. The purse smelled of money.

The Italian vegetable merchant always had a child or two with him on the wagon. My sister and I loved him and made friends with the kids.

Some street vendors plied their trade on the avenue. The scissors grinders, for instance. One who had his own wagon with a jangling bell came down the curve from Highland Avenue.

The popcorn man came just at dusk with his gas-lighted, glass-enclosed wagon, popcorn heaped up to the window level, constantly shaking his popper over the blue flames of the burner. The popcorn man was splendid—the way he picked up the tin pitcher of liquid butter and the gesture as he spilled it over the corn, and the gleaming white paper bags, butter already oiling their walls, that he handed out for a nickel—but he was as nothing compared to the waffle man. The waffle man came once or twice a year at most. Long before he came around the far bend of the avenue I heard the silver bugle he blew as his wagon slowly proceeded down the street. The bugle hung on a blue cord attached to the ceiling of his wagon so that he need use only one hand to let forth a loud tattoo. No one could mistake it. You heard it three or four times before his wagon made its majestic appearance at the curve and slowly, ever so slowly, moved down the street, the crowd of youngsters steadily growing. The waffle man came to a full stop just before getting to our house. Here he handed out the crisp, pale yellow waffles—not covered with maple syrup, as ours at home were, but steeped in butter and sprinkled with powdered sugar.

I have said enough, I think, to make clear that the world into which I was born was essentially a world of the past. To be sure, change went forward constantly, but as a small child I did not perceive change. The world seemed immutable. I did not go to school until the autumn just before I was seven. I came home from my first day at class and told my mother there were seven "Sullivans" in the first grade. She was gently skeptical. With good reason. The seven Sullivans were, in fact, seven Solomons. The well-to-do, upper-middle-class enclave which we inhabited had changed, as my mother's gentle correc-

tion of the Sullivans into Solomons indicated. But I had no more notion of the meaning of the words Jew and Gentile than my aunt Mary, who a few years earlier had been told by a friend that a young man she was going out with was Jewish. "I don't understand what you mean," she said. "Is that some kind of disease?"

One national group I thought I knew something about was the Germans. There was nothing good about Germans. I could not understand why my father could have studied German in school. It seemed wholly right and proper to me that the teaching of this disgusting language was banned in the Minneapolis schools in 1917. Not until some years later did I realize how shameful it had been that Emil Oberhoffer had been harassed as conductor of the Minneapolis Symphony Orchestra. We no longer ate sauerkraut at our house—it was Liberty cabbage—and when my sister and I got ill, it was with Liberty measles.

Far worse than the Germans were the "pros"—that is, the pro-Germans. And the pros might be anyone. Your next-door neighbor, for instance. The pros could be anywhere. Who could know what they might be up to—destroying the grain crops with bacteria and rot, sabotaging the flour mills, or even planning to blow up the shell factory on University Avenue which was turning out shells for the French and the English. Sometimes the pros betrayed themselves. They didn't always give to the Red Cross (and so you kept an eye out to see who didn't have a Red Cross sticker in the window). Or they refused to subscribe to the Liberty Loans and the Victory Loans, and so you tested them out by asking them to contribute somewhat more than others might give. Or, in school, they might not buy war savings stamps. There were many poor children in Sumner School, but at least they should be able to afford twenty-five cents a week in savings stamps. I was *very* suspicious of one schoolmate who bought no savings stamps. Moreover, when the class chose songs to sing, he never picked "Over There" or "Good-bye, Broadway." He always asked for "The Worst Is Yet to Come."

Perhaps I am overemphasizing the racism of my boyhood. Of course, it didn't seem like racism to me, and I would not have known what racism was if I had been asked. My father was, I believe, the most gentle man I have ever known. He had been taught compassion by his doctor father. He once told me, "Always be kind to women. You do not understand the pain and suffering they endure in life." Only once or twice in his life did he ever raise his voice to me. Yet this gentle, quiet, sensitive man customarily spoke of poor Jews as "sheenies" and made a distinction between

Jews who were sheenies and those whom he called "white men." It was a long time before I knew to whom he was referring as sheenies but I finally got it clear. These were the poor Jews, the peddlers, the proprietors of the small notions stores on Sixth Avenue North, the immigrants who had not yet learned the language. The "white men" were the Jewish businessmen, the white-collar Jews.

My father worked all his life in a firm of Scots who had come from Dundee to Minneapolis in the 1880s. There probably was no nationality which he disliked more. He regarded the Scots as mean, grasping, clannish, unpleasant, hard people. He felt that since he was not a Scot but half English and half Welsh he was always kept outside their confidence. He called blacks "niggers" but inherited from his unionist father and uncles an abolitionist support for Negro rights and the Negro cause. He was half Welsh (as was my mother), but he had no use for the Welsh—he thought them sniveling people, not so much a nationality as a race of beggars and ne'er-do-wells. He was cranky over his rights (a policeman had to save him from being beaten up when he insisted on going to the offices of the *Minneapolis Journal* and purchasing his copy of the newspaper during a newsboys' strike). He was very hostile toward organized religion of all kinds, but especially toward Methodism, the Baptist church, and Christian Science. With childish glee he placed in my hands Tom Paine's atheistic tract when I happened to ask him some question about a Sunday school lesson.

I suppose this is why I grew up with a skeptical attitude toward religion. I faithfully attended Sunday School at the Church of the Redeemer, the First Universalist church, but spent most of my time baiting a long-suffering teacher.

Religion played little role in my growing up. I was brought up to be hostile to Roman Catholicism, but I could not tell you why. I never heard any specific faults attributed to the Catholics. The only Roman Catholic priest I can remember meeting was a wonderful man at St. Bonifacius who kept bees. We often went there to buy honey.

The religion which interested me most was the Jewish faith. Almost all of my schoolmates were Jewish. On Jewish holidays Sumner School stayed open, but there were seldom more than four or five children in a class. I thought it most unfair. My classmates took all the holidays plus their own. But I had to go to school. The bitterness was slightly assuaged when someone would appear from the Orthodox Temple at the corner of Sixth Avenue and Lyndale and ask for two or three youngsters to come to the temple to write down the names and the

financial pledges—since writing was forbidden to the Orthodox on the high holidays. I also enjoyed earning ten cents from two or three old Orthodox ladies who paid me to light their stoves so they could get the meal started before the end of the holiday at sundown. All of my friends went to *keder* (Hebrew school), as soon as we were let out at Sumner School, and I had to wander on home, alone and with nothing to do, until they were released an hour later. I didn't see why I shouldn't go to *keder* too. Finally my mother made inquiries, but it was quite apparent that the presence of *goyim* at the orthodox institution would not be welcome. Later on I came to treasure this experience, for I realized that I had reversed the usual pattern. Ordinarily, it was the Jews who grew up as a minority. But in my childhood I was in the minority, on the outside looking in.

It was from poor Jews, the newest wave of immigrants, that I learned about revolution, Russia, the czar, the Bolsheviks, and Petrograd. I sat in the furniture-jammed kitchen of my friend Ruben's house across the street listening to his father talk, his brown eyes gleaming fiercely as he drank tea from a glass (I had never seen that), and hearing how he had smuggled himself across the frontier under a load of hay in a peasant's cart and made his way into Germany where his wife awaited him and how they had traveled thousands of miles to evade the czar's army only to fall into that of King George. I was not quite certain what revolution was, but I knew that we had had our own revolution in the United States. Obviously, what was good for the United States would be good for Russia. I was automatically on the side of the revolutionaries.

It was these Russian Jewish refugees who began to open a bit wider the narrow doors of my Victorian world. They lived in a milieu of ideas, of culture, of philosophy, of literature, of mores which I did not know existed. They did not eat their meals at regular hours. They did not get up from the table after eating. They sat right at the kitchen table and talked and talked and talked. Everyone took part and my opinion (if I had one) seemed to count as much as that of anyone else. Sometimes I was shocked. I directed the question of a Child of Plenty to a youngster across the street: "What are you having for Christmas dinner?" And she complacently replied, "Cheese sandwiches."

Christmas was *the* day of my childhood—a private day, really. Just the family. My aunt and uncle and cousins. A day of excitement, of joy. Usually either my sister or I got sick. Sometimes both. The climax of the pre-Christmas activity was the visit to Holtzermann's store. I don't know how I managed to square this most wonderful of institutions with my deep-seated Germanophobia. Holtzermann's had been transported direct from the Black Forest. It was crammed from top to bottom with German toys (and there *were* no other toys in the years coming up to World War I). Somehow, possibly through Captain von Boy-Ed and his U-boat, or more likely by prudent advance buying, the stock of German toys, the mechanized animals, the Anchor blocks, the miniature trees, the small chimes which played "Stille Nacht," the lebkuchen, the pfeffernusse, the gilded angels, the shepherds, the golden stars, and the crimson ornaments with German Christmas mottoes did not vanish in 1914. They went on through 1915 and 1916. Only in 1917 did Holtzermann's become a ghost with Japanese trinkets replacing the Black Forest music boxes and cuckoo clocks, although the great basement bins of Dutch wooden shoes were somehow still filled. But no tin soldiers, no Prussian horsemen with their lances, no small leaden cannons, no banners and flags of grenadier regiments, no flaxen-haired dolls with slow-closing blue eyes, no stuffed animals with genuine leather hides.

What I think of as the Minnesota contribution to my growing up is the spirit which I acquired at the University of Minnesota, and this, I think, was not to be found at the other neighboring universities. It was a spirit of independent and even crochety thinking. A heels-dug-in attitude toward the world, not accepting beliefs or doctrines or movements simply on their credentials but subjecting them to skeptical scrutiny. I suppose it was (and is) a kind of "aginism." A little like that I'm-from-Missouri attitude. But in Minnesota it took a more social form. It was not so individualistic. The Minnesota way was more thoughtful—the long hard look, the deliberately provoked argument to see what each side had to say, the determined search not for two sides of a question but a third or even a fourth side; an independence from political clichés, and a determination not to be bound by the past or by a stereotype of the future.

I have been an enrolled member of the Republican party since 1932. This is partly the chance of inheritance and partly, I suppose, a kind of crankiness. But in Minnesota Republicans have always insisted on the right to be what they wanted to be, regardless of national policy or candidates. And, if the party proved too restrictive, no Minnesota Republican thought nothing of breaking the ties and fitting on another label. All of the great American progressive and agrarian movements had their origins in the Republican party, a breeding ground of Bull Moose-ism, mugwumpism, and radical doctrines.

The politics of my childhood was button-oriented and straight-party-line. I wore a Hughes button in 1916 (although my secret passion was for Teddy Roosevelt), a Harding button—God help me!—in

"In Hanoi, December 24, 1966, inspecting damage in center of city inflicted by U.S. bombs"

1920 (although my personal favorite was Blackjack Pershing), and I was all for Coolidge in 1924. My party moorings began to waver in 1928. I wore a button for Hoover, but I was strongly attracted to Al Smith, and in 1932 when I voted for the first time as a registered Republican I voted for FDR for president and Floyd Olson, the Farmer-Labor candidate, for governor. I don't know which Republican I voted for, but I was proud of the fact that I crossed my ballot so completely that I voted for one candidate of almost every party except the Prohibitionist ticket.

When the boom burst in 1929, I was at the university. It did not seem that the Wall Street crash would have much effect on Minnesota. I had been raised in sharp memory of earlier busts. I knew of the crash of 1893 because several Minneapolis banks had failed and most of my grandfather's money had been lost. I knew about the crash of 1907 because it was close to my childhood. And everyone in Minnesota knew of the postwar crash. This was a special crash which didn't affect the rest of the country but affected us very much. In World War I the price of wheat went up to $2.50 a bushel. The boom in wheat meant enormous prosperity. Twice a month my father brought two things to my mother. His pay envelope, a small brown tough-paper packet tied with red string. She would strip it open and topple out a small stream of golden coins—twenty-dollar gold pieces—ten of them, I believe. The second present was a box of chocolates from Ivey's on Nicollet Avenue.

This cosy Victorian affluence of gold and chocolates long since had come to an end. By the time I was ready to go to college, there simply was no money for it although my father carefully and typically concealed this fact. I should—like most of my classmates—have stayed out of school and earned enough to get started at the university. A year or two later I discovered to my horror that my father had sold the small stock of men's jewelry he possessed (most of it his father's)—a few pairs of cuff links, some gold tie-pins—and had pawned his watch. I had sense enough to understand that the worst thing was to let him know that I shared his secret. I made one resolution—to earn as much money as I could in my spare time to pay my own expenses and to help out with the household. I kept that resolution—not brilliantly, but fairly well.

Neither I nor my classmates at the university took the Great Crash seriously. Our crash had come nearly ten years earlier. My class at the university graduated to a world of no jobs. I was the fortunate one. I had a newspaper job, working at the United Press. I had been lucky enough to get it before I finished school. My friends had no jobs. That summer they rode the rods because no one had money to travel and there were no jobs in Minneapolis. Perhaps there would be jobs in Chicago, New York, or Seattle. Or maybe you could ship on a freighter and find something in Shanghai. It was a help if you carried a "red card," an IWW card. The fraternity of the "bos"—the migrant workers—was still strong. A card would get you a place at the slumgullion can in the Hoovervilles that began to spring up near the railroad junction points. A card admitted you to the fraternity of the wandering jobless.

The Victorian era into which I was born had ended, sharply, suddenly, finally.

By the time I left Minneapolis in January of 1931, taking the coach to Chicago, sitting up all night on the plush seat, paying $8.33 from my own pocket to transfer from a job with United Press in St. Paul to one in Chicago, I had acquired almost the full baggage of ideas, habits—good and bad—ideals, and visions which were to carry me through adult life.

I was not much of a writer. I had written rather ponderous glosses about the old Oak Lake neighborhood. Together with three friends we had published a slim volume (bound in black-and-gold wallpaper) which we called "Broken Mirrors," displaying the best of our adolescent talents. I had learned to write a spare, fast-paced kind of newspaperese—crisp sentences Hemingway would approve, I thought, few adverbs, one or two snappy adjectives, accent on active verbs, Anglo-Saxon nouns, swift detail that did not slow the flow. That was UP style. I was good at it. UP gave me another gift—a priceless blessing. We had to write at top speed. Seconds counted in the frantic competition with AP (Associated Press). If you couldn't do it you were out. If you could they would let you have any story in the world—war, presidents, kings, assassinations, catastrophes.

I already had cynicism in my baggage—a bulky portmanteau I had inherited from my adventurous Uncle Scott who travelled the country, a money belt full of gold coins around his middle and a Colt .32 and a bottle of Johnny Walker Black Label in his bag. Like all UP men I was a skeptical romantic. It was a characteristic that sustained me through the Capone era in Chicago, the whiz-bang days of New Deal Washington, sitting up half the night turning out penny-a-liners to sustain a failing marriage and a bright-eyed pair of sons, into World War II and the delight and disillusion of London in the blitz, the froth of Eisenhower in North Africa, an ugly passage through Cairo and Teheran, and into Russia where I learned about real war in Leningrad.

"With Zhou Enlai and my wife Charlotte Young Salisbury in Beijing," 1972

Nothing which I wrote in those times possessed a half-life of more than a few hours. There is nothing quite so fleeting as agency journalism. I look at the yellowed headlines of the Big Stories. Sometimes the headlines are so big and black they fill half the front page with a byline that could go up in Broadway lights. They are monuments of forgotten clichés. Each story is the biggest. Each victory surpassed the defeat of Carthage or the slaughter at Agincourt. Nothing trivial. What had been a lean style sank in the sea of hyperbole.

The free-lance writing—and there were hundreds of articles for long since sunken and forgotten magazines—*Coronet, Ken, Liberty, Collier's,* the *Saturday Evening Post* (still alive as a condominium for senior citizens), *Look, Life, Pageant*—has no saving graces, just grist for the pulp mills. But they had a wondrous quality. They paid the bills. My god, how they paid the bills. Thanks to the UP's deadline-every-minute training in speed writing they poured out of the old Underwood like chaff from a spouting thresher.

War was not a writing experience. War was a living experience. If Minnesota had fixed my charac-

ter, given me guidelines, values, attitudes, war tested them, broadened them, deepened them. Death taught me life. A silly cliché, perhaps, but true. I stood at the bar in El Vino's pub in Fleet Street, drank my pint, and watched and listened; there were few Americans—these were the English, mostly journalists from Fleet Street, the *News of the Week,* the *Daily Express,* the *Mirror,* and the *News-Chronicle,* usually sallow, not red-faced in the rain-and-wind English style, thin—almost clinically undernourished—threadbare, worn with the strain of roofwatching by night for Nazi firebombs and a long day's work. Londoners. Gritty, underspoken, brave. I loved them as I later was to love the people of Leningrad.

Londoners gave me a sense of values. The war had pared them to bone-and-gristle. They did not flinch. If they complained it was just a ritual to show they knew what was right and what was wrong. I trusted their judgments. They cut through cant like laser beams.

I had thought they were soft when I first came, elderly messengers in the City hurrying about in morning clothes as they delivered the day's accounts, law clerks out of Dickens. Why weren't they at war? It took time to understand they were all at war. Everyone. London was the front. There was no rear.

I learned the difference the moment my DC-4 touched down in Marrakesh and went on to Algiers, to Tunis, and to Cairo. North Africa was a war zone. But it was not at war. Not the people of North Africa. It was a place where war was being fought but the people who lived there could care less. Even the English, the Americans, the Italians, and the Germans didn't belong there. It just happened to be the theater of activities of the moment. They had never seen these lands before and once the fighting was over they would never see them again.

London and Leningrad were different. They *were* the war.

I arrived in Leningrad on the frosty morning of February 8, 1944. The nine-hundred-day siege had come to an end a week before. The bus from the railroad station took us down Nevsky Prospekt, its

"Crossing the Luding Bridge over the River Dadu, northwest China, with Charlotte, retracing the six-thousand-mile Long March of Mao Zedong and the Red Army," 1984

windows so frosted the city seemed to exist in a haloid refraction. I gnawed at the frost with my fingernail to catch a glance at the city which had bowed neither to Hitler's will nor that of Stalin.

Through the tiny opening I could see no damage as we bumped down the once-magnificent Prospekt, sides heaped with snow higher than a tall man's head. It was hard to believe. Nor, as it was revealed, was it true. Leningrad had been damaged badly by bombs and German siege guns, but her artists had painted false fronts on canvas and framed them up along the Nevsky so the casual eye would not notice the gaping holes.

I can see today, fifty years later, the bright face of a blonde teenager in the Arctic chill of the Kirov works turning out shell fuses and telling how once a week she and her friend took their children's sleds and went to the unheated apartments where their parents lived and to two or three others, to see if they were still alive and, if someone had died, to lash the corpse to the sled and pull it to the mountains of the dead which towered near the entrance of every cemetery and hospital in Leningrad. The ground was frozen as iron. Not until spring could it be dynamited and the mountains of corpses put into common graves.

Nothing in my lifetime of reporting was to move me more than this city of heroes. To this day I feel the blood flush in my cheeks as I think of the heroism in the city of Peter without food, without heat, without light, without water, without electricity, without telephones, without transport. With nothing on which to live but pride and heroism.

No one who met the heroes of Leningrad escaped the spell they cast of men and women who possessed a spirit superior to that of all other humans. Long afterward in the deepest recesses of Russia, far out in Gulag, I would sometimes see a proud face, a man or woman who held his or her head high and straight. I would ask: "You are from Leningrad?" Always they would smile proudly and say yes. I never made a mistake.

That example was Russia's finest gift to me. I learned how people could live without possessions and almost without food. So long as they had pride and courage. The body might wither away but the soul lived on. Long after they are dead they glow in the minds of all who have known them.

In my life there have been moments of fear and terror—alone thousands of miles east of Moscow deep in KGB country, the prison camps still running full blast, a dozen police agents on my trail, no one in the world knowing where I am, no one in Moscow, no one in New York; behind the lines in Hanoi, American B-52s overhead, the slam of SAM missiles all around, squatting in a shallow shelter not deep enough for a lanky western body, listening to the roar of the bombs and feeling the earth in a seismic seizure; walking the midnight streets of Red Hook, Brooklyn, imagining a teenage gang swooping from the deep shadows; inching on a rocky path along the face of Flame Mountain, wondering whether I will survive the descent to the River of Golden Sands on Mao's six-thousand-mile Long March route in the wilds of western Sichuan.

At these moments and a score of others of despair and danger I thought of the men and women of Leningrad and cursed myself as a whimpering coward. Their dangers, their sacrifices were real. Mine were, for the most part, terrors of the mind.

I learned another recipe for soothing tortured nerves. When I lay on a crude cot somewhere deep in North Vietnam—I didn't even know the name of the place and still don't—awake while the camp of the enemy stirred and bustled with secret sounds in the night, I forced my mind back to the house at 107 Royalston Avenue. I got down from my father's small carriage at the granite stepping stone with my mother and father and small sister and climbed the eight steps to the lawn, then across the lawn and up the porch steps and through the double oak door with its brass fittings and into the entry, past the umbrella stand and through the frosted-pane door into the hall with the elk head and the round oak newel post at the foot of the stairs, and began my walk through each of the thirteen rooms, room by room, stopping to look at each piece of furniture, the old red-velvet upholstered chair where my grandfather had sat reading in the months before his death, the mahogany table my great-grandfather had fashioned himself, the sentimental picture of the *Age of Innocence* which my mother adored and hung in the parlor, the fumed-oak dining room table, the library fireplace roaring in winter. I visited every room, one by one, and my breathing slowed, my nerves relaxed, and soon I was asleep back in the house of my childhood.

Maturity brought me a life of incessant travel, country after country, always seeking and searching, for what I still do not know. From my earliest days I had been fascinated with China, the China of my father's curios, the old opium pipe, the tiny pair of shoes for the bound feet of a Chinese bride, the enamelled chest of many drawers, which my father filled with old Chinese coins. I was sure it possessed a secret compartment but, if so, I could never find it. In our old neighborhood there was a store run by two Chinese. My mother used to take me

there when she went to buy candied ginger and kumquat preserves in rough green earthen jars. I was fascinated and full of fear, seeing the Chinese sitting in the back of the store, smoking long pipes (I was sure it was opium) and playing fan tan.

Out of such thin and childish stirrings arose a fascination and curiosity about China. By my senior year at Minnesota this had become a determination to go to China, to follow the example of my good friend Gordon Roth (and many others), to ride the rods to Seattle, sign on a freighter for the China coast, jump ship in Shanghai or Tientsin, and go to work on an English-language paper in one of the treaty ports. I had no idea then that my friend of the future, Edgar Snow, author of *Red Star over China*, harbored just such an ambition and carried it out the very year I turned my back on China because I had landed a full-time job with UP at thirty dollars a week. Full-time jobs in 1930 were too rare to be lightly given up for romantic impulse. Besides, I told myself, I'll get UP to send me there. They never did.

My China ambitions sank under the weight of covering World War II. Even a wartime assignment to Chungking was lost when my orders were switched to the South Pacific and New York.

I did not make it to China until 1972, soon after Nixon's epochal visit. Not for lack of trying. I had spent much time and effort after completing my assignment with the *New York Times* in Moscow trying to get to China. In fact, I had tried several times to go to China from Moscow. No luck. When I finally saw Premier Zhou Enlai in 1972 he apologized for the long delay. He knew all about my efforts. They had been stymied because, he said, I was too well known an opponent of Moscow. To give me a visa might have interfered with Sino-Soviet relations. A nice diplomatic pat but Sino-Soviet relations were in such a state I knew a visa for me would have hardly ruffled the surface.

That visit of 1972 and a long swing through China was only the first of endless trips and travel and interviews and learning to know something about this land which is, as it has long understood, a world in itself, an experience in adjustment to a society and a culture which has roots that go as far back in time, and possibly further, than those of the Greco-Roman origin of our own civilization.

I finally came to understand that the world has, in fact, two principal cradles—Asia Minor and the eastern Mediterranean, and the Yellow River of China, two deep streams which because of geography and the slow rise of rapid long-distance intercourse and communication are only gradually and painfully converging.

My dedication to study of this global phenomenon was stimulated in 1959 when on a long trip to distant Outer Mongolia I saw clear evidence that the Sino-Soviet alliance on which the division of the world into Communist and Capitalist camps was based had sundered. I did not think it likely that it would be brought back together and I jumped to the conclusion that no process would be more important in the next era than the breach and mounting antagonism of the Communist behemoths. I think I was right. I did not then foresee that internal contradictions would slowly but surely debase and erode the whole world order which had been founded after World War II, much on the order of a Hegelian thesis and antithesis. The two worlds antagonistic to each other but bound into one like the molecules of a giant atom.

My Chinese experience differed from my Russian experience. Russia was where I lived for years, where I travelled, where I knew almost every intimate detail of life. I read and spoke the language. I fell in love with Chekhov, with Stanislavsky's Moscow Art Theater, with the melancholy of the Russian landscape, the endless fields of grain, the deep bogs, and the crystal lakes and forests of Siberia so like those of my native Minnesota.

I did not like Moscow. It always had a fusty, bureaucratic, inbred air. I loved Siberia and the "free Siberians," as they liked to call themselves, so much like the American frontiersmen.

I did not have this experience in China. It was travel, travel, travel, ceaseless seeking for facts. I came to meet and talk, often again and again, with the Chinese leaders. I knew and understood them (I think) as I never could understand the sphinxlike Stalin. It was not possible to know Russian politicians until Stalin died. Then I got to know a few, notably Nikita Khrushchev and Anastas Mikoyan, rather well. I liked them both.

But from the start in China I went right to the top. I knew them all (except for Mao, old and ill by the time I finally made it to Beijing). My friends, my real friends, were the young Chinese, the Chinese students both in China and in America and especially a handful of extraordinarily gifted young people, many of them in the Foreign Ministry, many of them sons and daughters of high Chinese, young people of boundless energy, patriotism, and aspirations for China, extraordinarily perceptive of their country's history and of its struggle to enter the twentieth and twenty-first century.

By sheer chance I was in Beijing at the time of Tiananmen, was in the square until a couple of hours before the shooting, watched the tanks roll by firing as they moved up Chang-an Avenue, saw the people

"In Tiananmen Square a few hours before the shooting," June 1989

mowed down, the hallucinated terror which brought an end to the aspirations of Deng Xiaoping to create a new and better China by the use of profit motivation and foreign entrepreneurism. It was a tragedy I did not wish to see, a curtain raiser for the drama that was to happen a year later when the wall went down in Berlin and two years later when communism broke apart in Russia and ended the era begun by Lenin in 1917.

Many of these events I tried to reinvoke in print, sometimes with more success than at other times. I wrote two novels of Russian life which brought me more pleasure in writing than anything I have ever done and two books of which I am proud—*The 900 Days: The Siege of Leningrad* and *The Long March: The Untold Story*, recounting the classic tale of the rise of Mao Zedong and his Communists and their 6500-mile retreat through China's wilderness, every step of which I retraced with Charlotte and two marvellous Chinese companions, Zhang Yuanyuan of the Foreign Ministry and General Qin Xinghan, director of the Revolutionary Military Museum in Beijing.

"Working in my study at Taconic, Connecticut," 1984

There are two other works of which I am especially proud: *Black Night, White Snow: Russia's Revolutions 1905–1917*, published in 1977, which is almost a handbook to the events of 1991–92, and *The New Emperors: China in the Era of Mao and Deng*, published in January 1992 by Little, Brown.

Now in 1991–92 I am preparing to write again—this time about the new Russia, its hopes and dangers.

BIBLIOGRAPHY

Russia on the Way, Macmillan, 1946.

American in Russia, Harper, 1955 (published in England as *Stalin's Russia and After*, Macmillan [London], 1955).

The Shook-up Generation, Harper, 1958.

To Moscow—and Beyond: A Reporter's Narrative, Harper, 1960.

Moscow Journal: The End of Stalin, University of Chicago Press, 1961.

A New Russia?, Harper, 1962.

The Northern Palmyra Affair (novel), Harper, 1962.

The Key to Moscow, Lippincott, 1963.

Russia, Atheneum, 1965 (published in England as *The Soviet Union*, Encyclopedia Britannica Educational Corp., 1967).

Behind the Lines—Hanoi, December 23, 1966–January 7, 1967, Harper, 1967.

Orbit of China, Harper, 1967.

(Editor and contributor) *The Soviet Union: The First Fifty Years*, Harcourt, 1967 (published in England as *Anatomy of the Soviet Union*, Thomas Nelson, 1967).

(Editor) Andrei Sakharov, *Progress, Coexistence, and Intellectual Freedom*, Norton, 1968.

(Editor) Georgi K. Zhukov, *Marshal Zhukov's Greatest Battles*, Harper, 1969.

The 900 Days: The Siege of Leningrad, Harper, 1969, reprinted with a new introduction, De Capo Press, 1985 (published in England as *The Siege of Leningrad*, Secker & Warburg, 1969).

War between Russia and China, Norton, 1969 (published in England as *The Coming War between Russia and China*, Secker & Warburg, 1969).

The Many Americas Shall Be One, Norton, 1971.

(Author of commentary) Emil Schulthess, *Soviet Union,* Harper, 1971.

(Editor) *The Eloquence of Protest: Voices of the 70's,* Houghton, 1972.

(Editor and contributor, with James A. Keith and Ida Prince Nelson) *Project WERC Resource Book,* Teacher Assist Center, 1972.

(Editor with David Schneiderman) *The Indignant Years: Art and Articles from the Op-Ed Page of the New York Times,* Crown/Arno Press, 1973.

To Peking—and Beyond: A Report on the New Asia, Quadrangle, 1973.

(Editor and author of forward) A. Sakharov, *Sakharov Speaks,* Knopf, 1974.

The Gates of Hell (novel), Random House, 1975.

Travels around America, Walker, 1976.

Black Night, White Snow: Russia's Revolutions, 1905–1917, Doubleday, 1978.

Russia in Revolution, Holt, 1979.

(Editor) *Russian Society since the Revolution,* Ayer Co., 1979.

Without Fear or Favor: The New York Times and Its Times, New York Times, 1980, published as *Without Fear or Favor: An Uncompromising Look at the New York Times,* Ballantine, 1981.

China: 100 Years of Revolution, Holt, 1983.

A Journey of Our Times: A Memoir, Harper, 1983.

(Editor and author of introduction) *Vietnam Reconsidered: Lessons from a War,* Harper, 1984.

The Long March: The Untold Story, Harper, 1985.

A Time of Change: A Reporter's Tale of Our Time, Harper, 1988.

The Great Black Dragon Fire: The Chinese Inferno, Little, Brown, 1989.

Tiananmen Diary: Thirteen Days in June, Little, Brown, 1989.

The New Emperors: China in the Era of Mao and Deng, Little, Brown, 1992.

Noted journalist and editor with United Press, 1930–48, and the *New York Times,* 1949–75.

Thomas Savage

1915-

DILLON, MONTANA: A SOURCE

"The courthouse of Beaverhead County in Dillon, Montana. I listened to the clock strike The Three Ones, the ghostly hours at half past midnight, one, and one-thirty as I worked solving problems in chemistry and physics. . . ."

I don't know much about bells, but I believe bells are sounded by the clapper or tongue, and that most bells are made of brass. Important bells have affectionate names, and the Liberty Bell was cracked either on cooling or when it was first rung. Which, I don't know. Bells are cast by foundries in molds, and I believe that somewhere in the land is a foundry that has but a single mold for those bells that toll away the hours in county courthouses.

For not so long ago and sometime after midnight I drove into Port Angeles, Washington, on my way to see a city that had been described to me as small and exquisite—Victoria, British Columbia. The ferry left at eight in the morning from Port Angeles about which I knew nothing except that it was the county seat of a county whose name escaped me—if it was ever uttered. I hired a room in a sad motel with a winking sign, and prepared for bed. It's a long haul from Seattle.

Suddenly, somewhere in the distance, a clock struck one, marking twelve-thirty, one, or one-thirty, a sequence that I had long ago named The Three Ones. The surrounding darkness of the past hours had swallowed up most of my idea of time. But it was not my temporary confusion that made me stand there rapt, but the timbre of the bell as a mallet struck brass. It struck the same notes and released the same overtones as one other bell I knew; I was hurled back sixty years to a county seat in Montana called Dillon, on a railroad called the Union Pacific, and named after the president of the line.

I was surprised, on leafing through a volume of the most recent *Encyclopaedia Britannica,* Volume 4—Delusion-Fressen—to find Dillon, Montana, a town that figures in half my novels. The material on Dillon, Montana, in the *Encyclopaedia,* hardly rates the listing, that the economy depends on ranching and farming, that dude ranches dot the surrounding countryside, and that the Clark Canyon Reservoir State Recreation Area is twenty miles to the south. That's it. I suspect that an editor of the *Encyclopaedia* by some weird chance knew somebody from Dillon and wanted to please him. Not a word about Kate Kelly, the madam at the Red, White, and Blue Rooms. Not a word about Anne Chapman, or R. W. Boone, who ran the Savings and Loan and whose daughter treated his balding scalp with Listerine and a fine-tooth comb. She was paid twenty-five cents. Her father called her Bug. She looked far too much like her mother.

Not a word about the Hartwig Theater.

Let's say it's a Friday night at the Hartwig Theater, and I'm ten years old.

I recall little now of the action on that silver screen. An actor named Harold Lloyd wore horn-rimmed glasses. Horn-rimmed glasses were thought amusing, what a man wears who reads too many books and is a little precious. Harold Lloyd clutched the hands of a clock in a steeple, way, way up there and appealed to one's morbid fear of height. Scene: an automobile, boxy enough to be an Essex, is about to go over the edge of a cliff, but that was in a serial and you had to wait until next week to find out how many had died. Scene: A woman's mouth is fixed in a soundless scream. I recall little. But I still see the people in that town as clearly as if they themselves were on a film that unwinds and rewinds and unwinds in my head. Nobody in the screen in my head gets old, or wastes away with cancer, or is abandoned, and nobody disappears into California or even into New England, as I did.

In 1925 the Hartwig Theater was grander than many moving-picture theaters: the Hartwig had an organ instead of your regular old piano to mask the uncomfortable silence of the film and to enhance certain scenes with "In a Persian Market," "In a Chinese Temple Garden," and Sousa's "Washington Post March." Persia and all the Far East was about as far as you could get from Dillon and that was worth the price of admission. And who didn't sit straight and feel proud, hearing Sousa? Proud of the United States, proud to be an American, proud of the Woolworth Building in New York City and Niagara Falls. Miss Pegram had a noble repertoire of chase music, both comic chase and serious. She accompanied scenes about fallen women with "The Meditation" from *Thäis.* Fallen women commanded more attention in those days.

Miss Pegram was short and dumpy and not secure on tiny feet. She arrived at the theater on the dot of time—seven-thirty—and, moving down the aisle, she leaned a little backwards to compensate for the marked forward tilt of the floor. As the lights dimmed, she began to shrug off her fur-collared coat a dozen feet from the pit where she presided. She had, apparently, but small life apart from the organ, nor had she married, perhaps because a serious dedication to music left her with little free time. She lived with her mother across the town. She was, it was supposed, thirty or forty years old, and God only knows how old the mother was. The mother was almost never seen, so little seen that some suspected something queer. Some of the older boys, out of knickers and into long pants and into high school who claimed to have done it with girls, called Miss Pegram "Piggy," and within her hearing. Their lack of respect for a professional entertainer and their rude whispers as she passed somewhat off balance down the aisle marked them as ones who had already taken a wrong turn, and it is not likely that much became of them.

Two thousand people lived in Dillon in maybe eight hundred houses. Three eighth-graders, who already knew the value of a dollar, distributed each Saturday afternoon the handbills in many brilliant colors that announced the new bill at the Hartwig. The Hartwig was such a center of attraction it would seem that a single handbill posted out front would have sufficed; everybody paused there to inspect the big stills locked behind glass that promised so much. There was little to do evenings in Dillon apart from the movies if you were a decent sort of person, not much except to make fudge, see how many stations you could find on the radio, the Fada, the Spartan, the Radiola, or the Freed-Eismann, if you had that kind of money, and log the most distant stations, and tell people. Distance counted in those days. You might walk in the summer twilight to the gray stone library with a little tower on the corner and peer at slides of Egypt, especially the Sphinx, through the stereoscope.

But Hartwig had apparently found it profitable to see that a bright handbill was placed flat on the porch of almost every house in town, and he contributed to the building of character in a few eighth-graders. They learned early, as many of us never learn, that money grows otherwise than on trees. They rode, like the paperboys who were a part of the same aggressive crowd, on Schwinn bicycles and carried the colorful handbills in a basket fixed to the handlebars. The boy assigned to South Pacific Street probably had the best of it; it was he who left handbills at the top of several steep stairs in the alley behind the street, there where you could smoke cigarettes and urinate if you had to, stairs leading to whorehouses, the Red, White, and Blue Rooms, to the Crystal Rooms, and to The Stag. Dillon was the center of trade for a sprawling ranching country of sagebrush flats and broad hayfields and streams and distant mountains where wild horses grazed. There were cowboys out there and sheepherders and ranch hands all without women, who needed women. Wives were reserved for settled men, men who hadn't made a mess of their lives. It's not likely that a thirteen-year-old knew precisely what transpired behind the doors at the top of the stairs, but to consider it, especially at night and in bed, made the heart race, the breath to fly into the throat, and the groin to stir. It's not likely he revealed to his mother the extent of his appointed rounds; that would be about the last

thing a mother would want to hear, wouldn't it? But he was questioned closely by friends at Dillon Public School—DPS—as they spoke of it to one another, out there on the vast cinder-covered playground where fights broke out no matter what the principal threatened. Out there, far to one side, the iron handles attached to chains on the Giant Stride tolled against the tall, hollow iron pole. The boy understood that whores would never dream of attending the Hartwig Theater, to do so they'd have to be heavily disguised with false hair and sunglasses, lest they be recognized by customers or decent women in town who sometimes had an exciting glimpse of them as they ate clubhouse sandwiches at dawn when their work was done and they could eat hidden behind green baize curtains in a booth at the Sugar Bowl Cafe. Decent women, catching a glimpse, could not but consider how different their own lives were, how lucky, perhaps, they were. Nevertheless, it isn't so pleasant to spend your entire life starching and ironing shirts and getting dinner on the table.

One of those bad women had spoken to him from the top of the stairs.

"Hello, Sonny," is what she'd said, and he had seen her teeth.

Sonny!

And another kind of outcast had spoken to him.

Just recently the old widow of one of the town's founding fathers had died, not to put too fine a point

"Beaverhead County High School, shortly after it was built, around 1910. By 1928 the vacant lots were gone. Here Miss Schoenborn taught me Spanish so thoroughly I could speak it as well as I spoke English. No longer."

on it, an old woman named Galt who sometimes appeared at her windows in a kind of kimono, for she had long passed the age where modesty counted. Old Galt had struck gold up a creek in 1871 and bought all that rich hay land along the river; he built a fine house for his wife who'd been a cook in a lumber camp, a fine house in town with a tower where she could go up and look down. Who wouldn't occasionally want to do that? There was gingerbread all over the front porch, two stained glass windows with a lot of expensive red you don't see much because it contains gold. To one side of the house was a porte cochere; when it rained she could come out and get into her buggy and not get wet.

She died in a hospital she had financed and named the Anna Galt, for her. One wonders if she felt the irony, going into her own hospital to die. She left half a million. Banks are not supposed to tell people how much money other people have, but sometimes they do. They are not supposed to tell because then people will treat other people differently when they know.

For a long time the old lady had been too fragile to climb into the tower, and her children and grandchildren had long ago shown the town a clean pair of heels. For years she'd been tended to by a Mrs. Lewis, a woman almost as old but livelier, with flat cheeks and sad eyes. Mr. Lewis, while he lived, drank.

"But I could always tell when Mr. Lewis was going to sober up. 'Mary,' he'd say, 'put me on a great big steak.'" Mr. Lewis had been talented with the violin. "He could play 'The Last Rose of Summer' to bring tears to your eyes."

The departure of the Galt children and grandchildren was seen as a judgement of the town, but you noticed they all came back up in the summer from California or wherever they happened to roost in the winter, arriving in their big cars when the fishing was good in the river. They said how little the town had changed.

They put up at the new Andrus Hotel. The high heels of their women were sharp and loud on the white octagonal tiles in the lobby. At dinner they sat together at a big table; they had called ahead. They sat apart like lords of the universe and to see them there made clear the awful power of money. True, they were not so rich as the town's single millionaire, but they felt superior to him and his wife, perhaps for a good reason. Money, then, isn't everything. There wasn't much to say to them, now that they were so little a part of the town. Those who had the courage to speak to them, who took the bull by the horns, could manage not much more than, "How are things in California?"

If they had been living in California, they'd answer, "Just about the same." That isn't much of an answer. If you don't know how things were in California in the first place, "Just about the same" doesn't clear anything up.

When old lady Galt died, people said, "It's the end of an era." People say that when somebody dies, when a building is razed, when a country is laid waste by revolution. The new era in town began when a bootlegger and a woman moved into the Galt house; he garaged his car in the carriage house, a Hudson Super Six, a favorite machine of bootleggers hurtling down back roads from Canada. Neighbors lying awake at night during those little hours when so much seems so hopeless recall the broad flash of headlights moving along the walls and then across the ceiling over their beds. There was a good deal of coming and going out there, and sometimes laughter and profanity.

Many thought it reprehensible of the man to come there. What he did was clearly illegal—had been for six years. Some said his customers were no better than he. Others argued, No. They said that if he didn't have it for sale, nobody would buy it. He was likened to the wicked who tempt children with sweets and promises.

Was the woman his wife? What kind of woman would share a bed with a man so beyond the law? What did she now expect of life—that she would be called on? Considered a part of the town?

And yet, she was a pretty woman, with a way of tilting her head. She wasn't blonde or redheaded as one might expect. No, her hair was dark; she had not yet had it bobbed, but wore it braided and wrapped about her head in a fetching way—artifice, maybe, an attempt to put one off the scent. The illegal are often clever; they live by their wits. It is sometimes hard for those who do not live by their wits to understand those who do live by their wits. And it may have been artifice that she came to the porch that was so heavily covered with trumpet vines just as the thirteen-year-old boy laid flat an orange-colored handbill announcing: Pearl White in *Plunder.* She moved to the porch in a modest housedress, one proper unless guests were expected, and she carried on a plate a wedge of pie. She was smiling. Was she, then, attempting to curry favor, to gain a foothold in town through kindness to somebody's son? To receive an invitation to take a hand at bridge? Had she the Altar Guild in mind?

"How would you like this?" she asked.

What can a boy say but "Hey"? "Hey," the boy said, "Hey, thanks."

"My wife, Elizabeth, and I on my stepfather's ranch in 1941. My wife wrote nine novels for Little, Brown. She was Phi Beta Kappa in her junior year and was salutatorian at Colby College in 1940. I did no more than win the Greek Prize, but I did finish a first draft of my first novel, The Pass, *there."*

Just so, she set herself up as a woman who knows about boys, that they liked to fish, to play marbles, mumblety-peg, pocketknives, steam locomotives, dogs, not cats, BB guns, slingshots, swimming naked, tree houses, a box to put things in. What she did not understand was that eating pie, unlike eating cookies which can be seized and run with, meant sitting on the steps with the plate and pie and fork, a spectacle for passengers of all passing cars. Somehow he knew then that she had no children. But somehow he also knew that he would report none of this at home. He felt this woman was no more likely to appear at the Hartwig than the women at the top of the stairs. There would be no question of her being asked to join a party bound for Dillmont Park to fox-trot to the Baxter-Tonrey Orchestra and to wander along the riverbank and hear the water passing. Alas, each town has its outcasts, and their amusements they must find among themselves, and hope to be as happy with their distractions as their betters are happy with theirs. It may be that there is room somewhere for everybody.

At last I saw the boy lay flat an orange handbill on the porch of a family named Boone. I had a purpose for it. I thought it remarkable that it was so insistently orange, so perfect a complement of the season, of fallen leaves, of autumn's bounty, of Thanksgiving.

I took the handbill, blank on the back, to my room upstairs in the Boone house. The Boones would never miss it. Anyway, my need was greater than theirs. I had just now composed a poem in my head that wanted writing down. For some minutes I looked out at the roof of the shed that sheltered the Boone's Buick touring car. I licked my lips and then the lead at the end of the pencil, and I wrote, "We thank Thee for the corn and wheat / we thank Thee for the pumpkin's meat."

The upper case ecclesiastical pronoun I'd picked up at Sunday school in the musty, low-ceilinged basement of St. James Episcopal Church whose shady grounds when darkness fell were haunted by the Holy Ghost. It was only that day I learned that what you eat of a pumpkin can be called meat. I thought that a miraculous image—it transferred an insentient vegetable into the lively animal kingdom.

There was no school near my stepfather's ranch. Children who lived out there in the country were granted thirty dollars a month by the state, and that covered my room and board at the Boone's in Dillon, forty-five miles north of the ranch. The Boones had rented several different houses in the years I boarded and roomed with them, and each house smelled of good cooking and furniture polish. She had interesting pillows that she placed to look casually arranged on the couch in the living room. They were made of a strange silk that was green if you looked at it one way, and purple if you looked at it another way. Mrs. Boone often prepared a casserole of dried lima beans, garlic, ham, and evaporated milk, and I call her blessed. When I lived in Maine and had already written six or eight novels, a woman wrote me from upstate New York. She wrote that she was collecting the favorite recipes of authors. I sent her Mrs. Boone's lima bean recipe. The trick is a lot of garlic. The beans are served on thick slices of good bread, buttered.

I was told years ago when I passed through the town that the Boones, the old ones, were dead, so I supposed they were, there being no reason to name them dead if they were not. And I heard that the Boone son, Billy, two years older than I, had begun to drink shortly after high school, and soon disappeared. That happens to people.

Sometimes some word of the vanished one drifts back.

"I heard he was over around Butte."

He had been seen in San Francisco.

It is sad to realize that someone once prominent on the high school roster, so good at basketball, is missing or dead or worse.

That left a Boone girl a few years older than I, and a Boone girl just younger than I and who, alas, resembled her mother in shape.

Mrs. Boone was squat.

She had been Lena Johnson, and had once stepped out with a man who later on became wildly successful as a director of movies in Hollywood, but she had ended up with Boone. Surely when she attended the Hartwig Theater, she felt a twinge when the credits were flashed on the screen, for although her once companion may have had nothing at all to do with the moving picture she had paid to watch, she knew that he was in touch with swimming pools, familiar with Pierce-Arrow automobiles, and the all but eternal sunshine down there, and she was not.

The Boone name could not overshadow the fact that she'd been born a Johnson, and of this she was reminded over and over when she met her brother on the street. He walked a good deal on the street. She wished he would not so much. She often crossed to the other side, wondering if this maneuver had been noticed, if someone must think her heartless, a woman who would cross over to the other side to avoid a brother. Or she turned her face away to look into the window of the City Drug Company at rubber goods displayed there, articles to correct or alleviate some common physical difficulty. But surely Sid, that was his name, as he passed would have recognized her by her shape, so familiar he was with that, so his not pausing to speak to her as she looked in at the rubber goods meant that he knew she did not wish to acknowledge his presence on the street, and he'd have to take that thought home to his little house with the one bedroom built long ago by one who like Sid despaired of having children or even a guest. A little house close by that of Miss Pegram in a lost part of town where nothing much ever turned out right.

Sid Johnson wore a three-piece suit that underscored the distinct pearshape of his body. He drank, and from time to time sold small objects from door to door, melon scoops, sewing kits, egg slicers, all little objects that find final haven in thrift shops. Oh, his sister did wish he'd leave town, go to where he was unknown, start all over again. Try someplace else. She winced when she considered how often he must have been rebuffed, and she thought, "If I don't want those things he tries to sell, why would anybody else?" How many times must someone have said, "Sid, what are you trying to sell now?" And Sid, using those words as an opening, a foot in the door, would then show what little trick it was he had to peddle. To peddle! What an awful word! Sid was the only one she knew—man, woman, or child—who managed to be cheerful and sad at the same time. She believed he understood that he stood in her way socially, that it was because of him that she had never set foot in several houses in town, such people as the Galts and the Danzies, say. She cringed to consider that he had stopped at the Galt and the Danzie front doors with his pathetic wares.

Sid did not come to the Boone home unless he called first, and on those occasions she often had an excuse ready, dentist, arrival of people, headache, sick child. She had dreams that he turned up at her bridge afternoons, and in the dreams he spoke, addressed her as Sis, a word she hated with not understanding why. He was, and that is all there was to it—he was the kind of man you're afraid in a few minutes is going to reach out and touch you. And so it had been from the time he was a little boy. It must have been terrible, she thought, for Mother.

Meeting the Boones for the first time you wouldn't think you'd find a grand piano in the Boone living room, but you would. It was not the best, neither Steinway nor Bösendorfer, but it was a grand, all right. Meeting Mr. Boone, a stranger would doubt that music had ever crossed Mr. Boone's mind, and the stranger would be right, except possibly for "Home on the Range," a tune that sometimes crept into Mr. Boone's consciousness. For him, the words and tune seemed to recall a beautiful lost world he'd never known. But there was a persistent streak of music in Mrs. Boone and a downright pronounced streak in the elder Boone daughter. Across the closed back of the piano Mrs. Boone had cast a Spanish shawl, held in place by the Boone wedding portrait taken almost nineteen years before. It had been professionally tinted. Mr. Boone had an eager look, as small men sometimes do; Mrs. Boone, who had so recently been Lena Johnson, looked tense, as if she had just now considered possible and perhaps unpleasant surprises in the marriage bed. Sometimes, moving to adjust the shawl and portrait because the material of the shawl was heavy and slippery and the overhang, thanks to gravity, constantly and little by little shifted the position of the portrait, she wished she had studied Spanish. She liked Spanishy things.

She sat often at the piano on a round stool that had been spiralled up as far as it would go to accommodate her short stature; the difficulty was that high up there she had to reach hard for the pedals; sometimes she simply gave the pedals up. She had read somewhere that the Austrian composer Mozart had not used pedals at all. She sang to her own accompaniment in a high, sweet voice. It may have been her voice that first attracted Mr. Boone. She sang the words to songs by Carrie Jacobs Bond, and especially "When You Come to the End of a Perfect Day."

> *When you come to the end of a perfect day,*
> *And you sit alone with your thoughts . . .*

She could seldom sing the song without thinking how often she had sat alone with her thoughts. She sang "The Rosary" although she was by no means Catholic but Methodist, rather. The Catholic church was by far the largest ecclesiastical structure in town, but the congregation, except for the town's one millionaire and his wife, were largely laborers who spoke foreign languages and the Irish. Mrs. Boone was known within her Methodist church as one to count on to wait tables at the annual Chicken Festival,

"*Where we lived from 1935 until 1985, near Georgetown, Maine. That's the Atlantic Ocean out there. Two years after this picture was taken at ten in the morning on February 8, 1978, in a winter storm the ocean hit the side of this house and knocked it off its foundation and flooded everything inside. . . . This part of the coast was declared a disaster area, but I was able to get the money needed for moving the house and repairs . . .*"

and to supply hot biscuits. Her divinity candy was popular at the Christmas bazaar.

The present minister of the Methodist church had come there a year before in 1924 and a year later there were some, including Mrs. Boone, who wished he had not come because of his perpetual sadness. You could not wish but to avoid him, as one who had a communicable disease. Not that he could help it, possibly. To begin with, his name was Ricketts. It did seem that the Evil Eye was upon him because his daughter, an only child named Dorothy, had rickets. She was about fourteen and walked bent forward with a peculiar shuffling, straddling gait. Pale as a ghost, she somehow resembled a wolf—something about her teeth. Mrs. Boone thought it too bad that Sunday which should be a happy and holy day should make a person uncomfortable because Ricketts and his daughter reminded a person how tragedies are visited at random on the just as well as the unjust. It almost seemed as if she might just as well throw up her hands.

Mr. Boone ran a small building and loan outfit. It was located in what had once been a small bank that had gone under, as banks do. There remained of the failed bank a big walk-in safe, and when in the morning Mr. Boone dialed the correct combination and strained to pull open the enormous door, he did seem a small man in so great a safe as he withdrew for the day's needs rather small money to be protected by so important a door.

He had but one employee, a Mrs. Blynn. She wore a green celluloid eyeshade and sat on a stool at a high desk like Bob Cratchit's, but there the resemblance to Cratchit ended. Mrs. Blynn was by no means under Mr. Boone's thumb; she appeared at the very luncheons where Mrs. Boone appeared, and herself gave luncheons. Mr. Blynn sold coal, and people who sell coal often do pretty well. It had puzzled some why, unless she had more than a passing interest in Boone himself, year after year she toiled away at that high desk on those big ledgers. A relative who sniffed impropriety and had nothing to lose had questioned her.

Mrs. Blynn had then turned from the waist and fixed her eyes on the relative.

"Because I like to work." The relative, who was one of that tribe who cannot imagine such a thing, thought that a strange remark. But in truth Mrs. Blynn, even as a child, was not one to run with the pack.

Mr. Blynn and Mr. Boone, having Mrs. Blynn in common—in quite different ways—played rummy with many other comfortable men at Terry's Place on Saturday and Sunday afternoons. Terry's Place occupied the northeast corner of the first floor of the Andrus Hotel which I've called the Andrews Hotel and made use of in several novels. I experienced a frisson two years ago on seeing in the *New Yorker* an advertisement for an Andrews Hotel in San Francisco. I felt there was an eye upon me; something was afoot. Then soon I came to live in San Francisco. Was that part of the plan? I felt hurled into an unimagined and possibly dangerous future.

The Andrus Hotel or, to make it more important, The Hotel Andrus, occupied most of a city block. Built in 1920, it put to shame the old Metlen Hotel, where the rich old retired ranchers used to hang out, hating change, hating the years that changed them, crippled good men who had been young and lively. Most did not move to the Andrus Hotel. At least they could prevent that change.

The Hotel Andrus was constructed of pale yellow brick, went up four storeys, had a flat roof, the first flat roof in town. Except for the old Metlen, it was the tallest building in Dillon. The Metlen was but two storeys tall, but it had been finished off with a useless tower—a monument, perhaps, to Metlen's dreams. The tower appears in my last published novel, *The Corner of Rife and Pacific,* 1988. The novel was nominated for the PEN/Faulkner Award, and I read a chapter from it in 1989 at the Folger Shakespeare Library in Washington, D.C.

It is surprising how many hotels burn to the ground because of the careless cigarette or deliberate torch. They burn at an early hour when those who manage to escape stand half-naked in the street. The Andrus Hotel was fitted with proper fire escapes that zigzagged down the side. The old Metlen also had fire escapes, but in a certain antique fashion. The Metlen escapes were ropes coiled just under a window in each room, and could have saved no one but the young and the agile; their presence recalled the unpleasant natural law concerning the survival of the fittest.

The Andrus Hotel had the insouciant, cosmopolitan air of a grand hotel. Fairly important people might turn up there, the governor of the state, and his lady and chauffeur; out-of-town mining men come to look into things; provident Easterners about to make their way into the mountains to hunt and to fish. The lobby was an expanse of small, white, octagonal tiles now seen sometimes in bathrooms, and these ran under the door of the men's room, and swept on past the urinals and stalls.

When I first stood in the lobby of the Ritz in Boston, I was surprised there was nowhere to sit except for a single hard, tapestry-covered bench beside the entrance to the coffee shop, but the big chairs in the Andrus Hotel lobby were many and comfortable, of stuffed, dark green leather, often occupied by rich old retired ranchers who had heartlessly deserted the Metlen Hotel they had once called home, and from there, before long, to an ultimate home, to Mountain View Cemetery not half a mile away. They lived from meal to meal. Sometimes they walked to the Hartwig Theater, marvelling; only yesterday there was no such thing as moving pictures. Few walked to the public library across the street. Few had been tutored in reading; what reading they did was in the pages of the *Miner,* thrown off the evening train from Butte.

One big green chair was frequently occupied by a brindle Great Dane. He belonged to Harry Andrus and was therefore at leisure to sit where he pleased. A proud dog, almost human in size, he sat in almost human fashion. My mother, in town and at the Andrus every week or so to shop at Eliel's, "The Store Beautiful," hated him. She didn't think dogs deserved human privilege.

"It drools. Somebody ought to speak to Harry Andrus."

It was known that wild parties were the rule at roadhouses around Dillon—The Green Lantern, The Red Rooster, The Buffalo Lodge—roadhouses hastily constructed of raw lumber and cinderblock following Prohibition. All of them were bleak in the light of day and haunted by the abandon of the early hours before. But Pierce-Arrows and Packards occasionally stopped at the Andrus for wild parties. Adjoining rooms were hired, room service summoned. Wild parties required liquor and the exchange of partners, a more serious matter then. And music on a phonograph. If the Great War did nothing else, it acquainted Americans with exotic place names that turned up, soon after, in popular music: Dardanelles, Hindustan, Valencia, "Roses are blooming in Picardy."

One wild, historic party exploded in the hotel dining room. It was hoped that the functional water-and-steam pipes were adequately concealed by artificial vines and fists of glass grapes. (This wild party was in the midtwenties when I didn't yet understand wild parties, and a dozen years before I attended one. An almost vanished scar on my forehead attests to that one.)

When I was in high school I remember seeing a man on the street who had attended that party. He was one of the principals. He was a judge, now retired, and dressed in a white shirt, black suit, and a black hat whose broad shape recalled the Old South. In his later years he had been seized by Parkinson's disease. There on the corner of Rife and South Pacific streets his hands trembled as with a white handkerchief he wiped at the encrusting spittle from the quivering left side of his poor mouth. Some who took the Bible—well, as gospel—wondered if it were not God's judgement that he'd been struck by disease. For at that wild party, ten years ago, he was said to have allowed his wife to remove her clothing, and to dance on a table in the dining room of the Andrus Hotel.

It was down South Pacific Street that a certain woman used to drive at about nine each morning. She was a beauty. My mother was a beauty; I don't write that out of loyalty. Her picture appears on the dust jacket of my novel *I Heard My Sister Speak My Name.* Besides my mother, I have seen three other beauties; one was in the congregation of the Church of St. John the Evangelist, in Boston; her beauty was such that some of us found it hard to concentrate on the Mass.

"The hotel in Armstead, Montana, twenty-two miles south of Dillon. This hotel I had in mind when I wrote of The Red Mill in The Power of the Dog. *It was upstairs in such a building that Johnny Gordon hanged himself. Armstead is under water now because of a dam, part of which is the hill where my stepfather and I saw the shape of an Indian made out of sagebrush and slide-rock."*

There was a woman who walked out of an apartment building in Cambridge, Massachusetts, in a black dress and a scarf of silver fox. I never saw her again.

But first there was that beauty who drove at about nine o'clock down South Pacific Street. I stood still as she passed. In a novel of mine, *The Corner of Rife and Pacific*, her beauty and the tasteless behavior of the poor judge's wife are combined in a single character, the chief character.

Harry Andrus of the Andrus Hotel was a smiler, a greeter. He walked just ahead, turning to smile and to beckon. Something of mystery hung over his hotel. Where had the money come from? The mystery was compounded by a charming but elusive quality in his wife and two daughters. All three were auburn-haired, his wife probably falsely so; at that time it was thought a little racy if a woman dyed her hair; she so obviously wished to continue to attract men when most women have despaired and tossed in their cards.

Pretty women, they were often together on the street and then suddenly together in the lobby of the hotel, their high heels like castanets on the tiled expanse. They trailed a jasmine scent. Then swift as swallows they were in the elevator and swept up to their mysterious rooms above. I never saw their quarters, but I had heard of fringed silk lampshades, of a Chinese screen, of a Steinway piano. In hotels you don't often hear piano music played above the first floor.

They had such names, the daughters. Faye and Fern. Touched by such names, they might have been conceived in a glen. Fern had appeared some time after the opening of the hotel. Said to have been married. Had her arrival been expected? Was there an extra bedroom in the Andrus suite, sheets and pillowcases? Hard to tell whether she was the younger or the older sister. It was she who wore a hat with a veil when she was in the public eye. Impossible to tell whether a man had beaten her or had simply deserted her. It is sometimes the eyes that let the cat out of the bag.

Faye was settled, in a way. She had married the Terry of Terry's Place, his last name Browning; he lived up above with Faye, perhaps in connecting rooms. Terry Browning had to do with the Browning who had invented automatic rifles, the Browning rifle, and as a Browning he was given his due—that part of the country respected a family who invented guns; out there in the fall when frost lingered on the stubble and thin, ice-coated still waters, thoughts turned to gunning down animals; spirits rose as one thought of a man taking aim, firing, then seeing the prey stagger and fall. You got him! There's to be

game in the larder, a sharing of meat with friends. A man was proud to be a good shot. He was likely to be a good provider.

Possible Browning money was behind the Andrus Hotel, for Harry Andrus with his bowing and scraping didn't strike one as a man capable of accumulating capital. His wide, welcoming gestures resembled those of a man more adept at scattering, rather than collecting, money.

Browning was said to drink, and the brand of his liquor and the amount of it was next to common knowledge. It can't have been comfortable for Faye to live with a man—even a Browning—who consumed each day a quart of Cutty Sark. But I never heard of drunken shouts and shifting furniture in the Andrus quarters, nor of a hopeless voice raised in vain accusation. There was some sort of understanding.

I was not popular. Maybe few wanted the company of a boy who used his rancher stepfather's name and pretended it was his own. Children sniff out frauds. As a child I would have traded whatever else I had for popularity. I had to choose my friends where I could, and one of them was a thin, artistic boy—Roscoe Gordon.

No Gordon father was evident. Mrs. Gordon, whom I remember standing just behind a screen door, had a scar running down the left side of her face and neck; she was said to have attempted suicide by swallowing carbolic acid. The liquid had permanently twisted her lips; she now wore the faint perpetual smile common to antique Greek sculpture.

Roscoe Gordon was fearful on the playground. He stood in the shadows while the others played ball in the sun and their wild, confident cries smashed against the school building. He was said to play with dolls. I wonder how I had the courage to walk with him, whatever my need. Doubtless he was homosexual, but such knowledge, even had I possessed it, would have meant little. At eleven a boy is not much attracted to sex. But five years later Roscoe Gordon was thrashed—I think that's the word used for the punishment that is thought to be deserved—by a boy who complained Roscoe had "gotten funny" with him.

But at eleven years old we were ambling down Pacific Street. I saw our reflections in the window of the Tribune Book Store. I liked seeing myself with somebody. It was just there that Terry Browning stepped out from the store and, smiling, he stood before Roscoe in such a way that Roscoe was blocked unless he wished to be rude and step around. Had that happened, I think Browning would have kept smiling and blocked him again. Browning drew up his

"Some of my family at a restaurant in Las Vegas or Reno about 1950: my grandfather, Thomas Yearian, with the cigar (I was named after him; he lived to be a hundred), then my mother, Beth Yearian Brenner, my stepfather, Charles Brenner, my aunt Helen, her husband, Bill Hanmer, and my aunt Edwina."

smooth, plump stature and spoke to Roscoe as to an adult.

"Just how are things?" he asked. "Just how are things, Clarice?" The name Clarice, deliciously sibilant, was superbly camp in Browning's mouth, and his intent to humiliate couldn't have been lost on Roscoe who by now must have begun to wonder about himself. Why, except for me, he was always alone.

I have often considered Browning's cruelty. Maybe if he hadn't spoken that day on that sunny street Roscoe might have later walked in the sunny world as most men do. But I doubt it. Now it seems clear that homosexuals are born, not made. A gay man can no more be made straight than a straight man can be made gay. The gay man's tragedy is that the world thinks he had a choice. I wonder if Roscoe cried that night; I think he didn't tell his mother; she had enough problems. It was Roscoe Gordon I had in mind when I wrote of Peter in *The Power of the Dog*, and he in mind when I wrote of young Forest in *I Heard My Sister Speak My Name*. He shows up in *The Corner of Rife and Pacific*. For Roscoe, every play-

ground was a Gethsemane. If you read this, Roscoe, I valued your friendship.

Along the back roads that led into Dillon remained the tattered remnants of posters tacked against the sides of barns, allowed there in exchange for a little silver and tickets to the circus on August 24th through the 27th. What year was not specified, for that year was known then. Those who looked there could still see, in but little imagination, the lovely, shapely lady hanging from the trapeze bar. By her teeth, it seemed. Who would not lay out good money to see this in the flesh? Beneath her wild animals snarled and raged, waiting to tear her apart when she fell. Imagine taking such a woman to your bed.

On the last night of the circus, when the tents were folded and animals gathered together and everything rolled away, it was found that two boys of sixteen had disappeared, sick unto death of Dillon, seeing no future there nor even in the entire state of Montana, tired of the sound of familiar voices, tired of the same windows lighted at night, of the bottle of milk on the doorstep, of school where pointless demands were made. How they did long for a life where tomorrow is but casually considered, if at all, where there is laughter and danger and loud music.

One boy returned not a month later and spoke but little. The other seemed to have vanished forever; no one asked any longer if he'd been heard from.

One man who worked for the circus remained behind, in town.

That country was known for sudden, wild thunderstorms. Cattle, huddled against wire fences where they'd been driven by the storm, were sometimes electrocuted every one when the lightning struck the fence somewhere beyond them. The wind had begun early in the afternoon of that last 26th of August. The circus tents swelled and billowed. The audience, afraid to be trapped inside, began to hurry out, recalling that people had suffocated under collapsed canvas, how those who had not suffocated had been trampled by hysterical animals. Those few who carried pocketknives were somewhat comforted, believing that if they were suddenly engulfed in canvas they might cut themselves out of the tough cloth.

A black man had joined the circus down South to escape the word *nigger*. He helped unfurl and set up the tents and was particularly adept at cleaning up after the elephants when they performed in the ring. The black man himself performed with such style, using a flat scoop and a smart little red cart, that he sometimes upstaged the animals. On the afternoon of the 26th of August he was pounding in the tent pegs against the storm when he was struck by a bolt of lightning. From the point of view of physics, wielding a steel-headed sledgehammer, he was a perfect target for huge electricity. He lay prone for some time; he seemed to rest, or to sleep. He regained his senses in the Galt Hospital where he was looked upon as a curiosity. Black men had been seen in the movies singing and dancing away, happy as children with their white folks, but they had not been seen in that town in the flesh.

The black man's unique experience convinced him that the Lord wished him to remain behind in Dillon; otherwise, the Lord would have killed him outright. And now he was alone of his kind in the town. In the men's room of the Andrus Hotel he swabbed the white tiled floor with a spaghetti mop; he cleaned the toilets and cast fragrant crystals into the porcelain urinals. He set up a kind of throne just outside the men's room where a white man might sit in style, one who was disappointed by the look of his feet. Salesmen know the worth of a smile, of a new haircut, and newly shined shoes, but Harry Andrus believed it out of the question to hire a white man to attend to the shoes of other white men; to so attend to the feet or shoes of others is to humble oneself; the act of shining shoes requires one to assume a kneeling, squatting posture, a position of submission.

Along with his work at the hotel, the black man, whom they at once labelled Rastus, attended to the express truck at the Union Pacific depot. He hauled it up to the sliding doors of the baggage car after the six o'clock train rushed in. He sometimes received sour smelling boxes of peeping baby chicks; the boxes had been perforated with many neat holes that the chicks might breathe throughout their passage. Sometimes Rastus took brief possession of a coffin containing somebody whose terminal thoughts may have been Dillon. In the coffin there were no holes.

A broad green lawn stretched to one side of the Union Pacific depot and picked out there in whitewashed stones was the word DILLON. No one was sure whose task it was to keep the stones whitewashed, and few could remember ever having seen it done. Inside the depot, just beside the door, stood a water bubbler too high for a child to slake its thirst. The waiting room was furnished with heavy oak benches wisely screwed to the floor. To steal them would require the heaviest of screwdrivers and the screws were so many that surely before all had been removed, the authorities would arrive. Each bench had a fancy cast-iron armrest on either end; a third armrest had been installed in the center of each bench making it exactly impossible for anyone to lie down and to become a problem.

Inside, to the left, was the ticket window, heavily barred with vertical brass rods that framed an arched space underneath just big enough for a hand to pass through. There was no telling what desperate one might try to crawl through an unbarred window and gather up money and tickets. With enough money and tickets a man might successfully disappear forever and leave behind him only a legend.

At midnight the depot was alive with magic. At midnight the night telegraph operator came on— Tom Carney. He was of Irish background. His parents had wandered to Peru, where he was born; he still spoke Spanish. He unlocked and entered a door outside the building, his own entrance; once inside he turned on a green shaded drop light that hung low over the gleaming brass telegraph key. He ran water into a kettle; he put the kettle on a hot plate. He sat down before the telegraph key.

I was one of two he allowed to visit him, one of two high school boys who longed to show the town a clean pair of heels. Both of us had chosen Spanish as our foreign language in case we happened into Mexico or Spain. We felt halfway there when we talked Spanish with Tom Carney. We drank the strong black coffee as men will who crave the lift of caffeine; damned men, perhaps.

The dots and dashes that fled silently along the telegraph wires entered that little room and came alive, chattering of God knows what ecstasy or loss. A ghostly freight train rushed past; out the window the moon slipped down under the mountains. We talked Spanish, a foreign tongue, and supposed it happened we never had to go home?

One of us, my friend or I, was the high school boy in the final scene of *The Corner of Rife and Pacific*.

Maybe you can feel safer, knowing a millionaire. Not that the millionaire is going to do anything for you. On the other hand, he might. He might speak to people who fear him, and get them off your back. People may not know just how well you know a millionaire. They might think you know him no better than they do, but they can't take the chance.

Dillon had one millionaire; he had a wife, Jessie, and a son, Jack. While I was in high school learning from Miss Schoenborn that there are two different endings for the past subjunctive used in South America, Jack was away at a school said to be only for the sons of millionaires. I wondered if he'd had to fill out and sign a form swearing his father was in fact a millionaire, and not a cheat with only a few hundred thousand, like the Galts. This Jack appears as a spoiled young man in *The Corner of Rife and Pacific*.

Their name was Barrett, and Barrett had a bank. Bob Barrett. His father before him had founded the bank in the eighties when most of the town was still mud and dust and tar shacks. Bob's father came in from his big ranch in the lower valley, founded the bank, and built a house in town, a mansion of the same red brick as the bank. It remained, except for one other, the grandest house in town. Visitors to Dillon were driven past it, often in the middle of the afternoon when time might hang heavy and it has been established that the visitors never nap in the afternoon. If those driving past the house had been inside the house, they might describe the parquet floors, the heavy, cream-colored rugs patterned with enormous roses, the Steinway square piano inlaid with mother-of-pearl, a drinking fountain with a graceful spout set into the wall of the dining room, the brass cage where the old, original Mrs. Barrett had kept a parrot. There was always the possibility, on driving past, that a visitor from out of town might get a glimpse of the young Mrs. Barrett on her way somewhere, and if she realized she was being seen, she might wave or make a similar brief sign that she recognized someone in the cruising automobile. It

was not likely that a visitor would lay eyes on the boy, Jack, since he'd likely be away at his school where they recognized the peculiar problems of young millionaires. Nor would they lay eyes on Mr. "Bob" Barrett. He would be at his bank. It is rather pleasant to consider that the town you live in has produced and nurtured a millionaire, but not at all pleasant to wonder why it was not you who had become one. Old Barrett, Bob's father, was so closemouthed and so cautious it could not be imagined that he, no matter what the circumstance, had announced himself a millionaire, but Bob Barrett was easygoing, for a banker, and had, in fact, made it easy for people to call him Bob instead of Robert or Mr. Barrett. Maybe in some intimate moment—possibly in answer to the direct question, "Tell me, Bob, are you or are you not a millionaire?" And Bob, maybe having had a drink, might have said, "Yes, I am a millionaire." He occasionally took a drink, but not so often nor so much that people feared for their money. Only enough and so often that he seemed to be like other people, and people liked that.

It may have been his wife, Jessie, who let the cat out of the bag, for wouldn't many women want the world to know that her husband was a millionaire, and that she was the one who had enchanted him? And think what money does, socially, what money excuses. And in sober truth, excusing had to be done. And what needed to be excused accounts for the fact that it was not uncommon to see Jessie Barrett's automobile (a big Nash, early on, and later a twelve-cylinder Cadillac) parked before the Boone house and even lesser residences.

Jessie Barrett was a taut, pretty, redheaded woman said to have a terrible temper within her own walls. She was said not to be able to keep any help. Her demands were excessive. It was her physical equipment rather than her temper that had attracted Bob Barrett, and it had seemed to him that she was fair game for a romp in a double bed in a room in the Andrus Hotel. Barrett and Harry Andrus were friends, as a millionaire is often the friend of the owner of a hotel. Andrus instructed the night clerk to look entirely the other way. Because of who he was and because of who she was, Barrett could not imagine that Jessie would expect things to go farther than occasional romps and occasional money.

However.

Her two brothers were horse thieves. At them, turning around in his saddle, my stepfather had once pointed a rifle (they were chasing him) and he pulled the trigger. Fortunately for my stepfather, the rifle was not loaded and his family, who came from the

Maine line in Philadelphia, was not touched with murder, however provoked.

Apparently Barrett believed the brothers would forgive what was going on if handed a little money. And maybe he was right. What he hadn't counted on was their ambition for their sister and, in a way, for themselves. Who does not wish to have the ear of a millionaire? And right in the middle of the third romp in the double bed, the brothers appeared glowering and with loaded six-guns. A locked door meant absolutely nothing to them. It was blackmail, for unless Bob Barrett married Jessie Ferris, his life forever afterwards would be subject to accidents, one of them fatal.

And Jessie was not the only one in the marriage with something slightly irregular to live with. Bob Barrett was no real Barrett, but the adopted son of old Martin Barrett, and had spent the first twelve years of his life at the orphans' home. He knew the sour odor of charity, of meatloaf, cabbage, and disinfectant. At Christmastime the tree was such that only orphans can expect, trimmed with strings of cranberries, strings of popcorn put together by the littlest ones just beginning to use their fingers with a purpose, for it is best if orphans use their fingers purposefully at an early age; there will probably be but little room in the cold world beyond the orphanage walls for idle or frittering fingers. Presents under the tree were from no one, really, and they were chiefly of pasteboard. There were crayons. There was never a bicycle, never a catcher's mitt. And anyway, it wasn't presents Bob had wanted. He had wanted love.

Years passed. He saw younger children taken as sons and daughters, and probably loved. Those who came to adopt a child thought: Too old, too grown-up, too formed now to be shaped into a family; he would always be who he was, and not partly themselves. He thought his mother had waited on tables in Butte; words overheard told him his father's name was Moody. Sometimes when he looked across the field where cars ran along the dirt highway towards Butte and spewed clouds of dust behind that roiled and glowed in the sunlight—sometimes he thought, What if one of those cars slowed down, and drove into the parking lot where the trees were kept green, and a man would get out of the car and he would see the man walk up the steps. Then in a few minutes somebody would come up the stairs and say to him, "You're wanted downstairs." If the word was "wanted" and the word was "downstairs," that meant the office, and anything could happen there.

Downstairs, Mrs. Willis, who was in charge of everything as long as he could remember, would be standing to one side of the bust of George Washing-

"My sister, Patricia, on the Oregon coast. I didn't know she existed until 1969, when I was fifty-four years old. My aunt, in Salmon, Idaho, wrote to me in Maine, 'I've just had a queer telephone call from an attorney in Seattle. He says that his client claims to be your sister. That's nonsense, of course.' That it was not nonsense is the gist of my novel I Heard My Sister Speak My Name."

ton and in line with the American flag. The man would stand beside her.

Mrs. Willis would say, "This man is your father."

This man, this father, would say, "My boy, my boy," and hold out his arms.

Does this ever happen?

Not very often. But something else did.

Mrs. Martin Barrett was barren, and as a barren woman she could never know a mother's fierce love for a helpless child. And needing some kind of responsibility, she bought a parrot.

She grew rigid and cool towards Barrett. There was no possibility of divorce. They were Roman Catholics. They had bought four of the Tiffany stained glass windows and many priestly garments. No, she could not be replaced by a fertile woman. And Barrett's position in the town rendered hanky-panky out of the question.

But Barrett needed an heir. What was the good of all he'd done, all he had, if there was no one to inherit, no one to stand at his coffin, no one to carry out last wishes? What good the acres, the house— what good anything? It was clear to old Barrett that unless there was a meaning to continuation, there was no meaning to life itself.

Barrett believed a twelve-year-old would be about right, especially so since his wife whom he always thought of as Mrs. Barrett knew nothing of diapers and colic.

Therefore old Barrett died in his own room when young Bob was just thirty-five, an ideal age to assume the complicated business of banking, an age when a bit of appropriate gray hair is noticed at the temples and wild oats are comfortably in the past.

Old Mrs. Barrett had so long ago divorced herself from life that her death would come as no surprise to anybody but she continued to linger. The old do so often linger and so tenaciously that it is next to impossible to make plans of one's own. In her great age she had but small affection for anything other than the parrot. The parrot had grown accustomed to the dark silences in the house; what little he heard he repeated.

He cried, "Holy Mary! Mother of God! Fruit of thy womb!" The word womb cannot but have been painful to the old lady, for what good is a woman if her womb has not been occupied?

But one day the parrot, grown old and disagreeable, reached and bit the old lady and she died of that rare disease so difficult to spell and yet so prevalent however rare, as pets, parrots are. Now, now at last there was no reason to carry soft food to the second floor of the big redbrick house, no reason now to shush everybody, to whisper, and the young Barretts overnight became the old Barretts. Their son, who was scarcely known in the town, for whom Bob wanted more than he had had, education at a school far different from an orphanage—their son was killed in a hideous automobile accident on a bad curve on the river road. It was the custom of the highway department to erect wooden crosses just off the road after each fatal accident. The Barrett's son's was the fourth. Those who had not liked the young man felt compunction; some as if they had even contributed to the accident—not caused it, but certainly had not prevented it. There had been something about him, and it is true that the rich are often not loved for themselves.

In the early fifties, when the Barretts were truly getting old, twenty years after I'd left Montana for Boston and Maine, I saw them again. I drove back with my wife and two sons of twelve and ten and a daughter, two. I drove back in a black Rolls-Royce that had been the Rolls-Royce exhibit at the 1939 World's Fair in New York. I owned it at second hand, of course. Moving across the face of the United States, it had caused quite a stir, for although

everybody had heard of Rolls-Royces, few beyond the Mississippi had ever seen one.

I saw the Barretts, Bob and Jessie, sitting in a roadhouse built high over the Beaverhead River quite near where the cross had been erected. The place was called the Pipe Organ Lodge; vertical outcroppings of igneous rocks across the river resembled a bank of pipes. The Lodge attracted tourists seeking local color, and ranchers, rich in those days before it was believed that eating red meat shortens human life. Pants were tight, buckles were of sterling silver, shirts sported pearl buttons and colorful piping. Boots were fashioned of rare leathers, alligator and ostrich. Some women wore many jewels.

The bartender was of a certain kind common to bars and roadhouses in the West. He called himself Tennessee, and doubtless he had some connection with that state. He made broad gestures and moved slowly as if time were eternity, and he drawled, his vaguely Southern accent coloring the too familiar speech patterns of the Mountain states. Customers wooed him, wooed the mystery and sinister in him, the idea of the many women who had showered him with gifts, golden cigarette lighters, money, suits of clothes, the promise of automobiles, women abandoned and left in tears; women to whom he had kindly but firmly explained again and again that he was a lone wolf, a rolling stone, not the marrying kind, and they now wanting only to be promised that sometime in the future they might see him again, if only to say hello. Tennessee was a man indifferent to the future, and diffident towards friends. They must take him as he was, or lose him.

Drinks at the bar were simple, whiskey and water without ice, called "ditch," or whiskey and ginger ale. Rarely, late in the evening, a woman, overwhelmed by her femininity, might order creme de menthe or a sloe gin fizz, but regular customers noted that the exotic liquids in bottles along the back bar remained month after month—even year after year—at about the same level.

The Barretts sat apart at a table in the dark corner of the small dining room; I felt they were apart not because they felt special and apart because they were rich but because they had few friends. Was it the darkness of the corner or the years that made the Barretts just recognizable? Jessie's hair was still red, but now certainly falsely so. They smiled at me. I recall Bob's smile; it seemed to beg forgiveness for a role he had assumed.

Jessie said, "You're Tom Brenner."

I said, "I pretended to be."

I had assumed my true name when my wife was pregnant with our first child. I had then realized how important a name is, how it sets one apart, and how I had no right to deprive an unborn child of his real name. He might make something of it, as I felt I had not.

Jessie said, "Bob was adopted, you know."

I thought, What kind people, to offer me their secret, even if it were not a secret, how kind to let me know that I was not alone in bearing an assumed name. I wondered if Bob Barrett, like me, honestly believed that people believed Barrett was his real name as I honestly believed that people believed Brenner was mine. I recall my shock in chemistry lab in high school when a pale boy named Bobby Irwin— he was often absent from school—leaned close to me and whispered, "I know your name isn't Brenner."

Pretence. The second-hand Rolls out front was pretence, too. I told people (who were bound to ask) that the car satisfied my desire to own perfection, as others might desire a Patek Philippe pocket watch. In truth, I hoped to be taken for a man who could afford a Rolls, or at least a man who deserved one. That car turns up in my fourth novel, *Trust in Chariots,* and it still hovers in my dreams.

My novels are pretence, too. I'd lived a life of pretence, sometimes wanting to escape that life, to come to terms out in the open, as when I said— confessed to Jessie Barrett—"I pretended to be." That was my first oral confession, and by far the least damaging.

Had the Barretts ever done what millionaires might do? Built a great stone house high above the rocky coast of Maine? Toured France in a Hispano-Suiza, stopping to picnic from a wicker hamper on cucumber sandwiches and cold white wine? Rented a penthouse on Park Avenue? Floated down the Nile? At the moment they sat in a tacky roadhouse outside of town where money meant little. What counted was whether Tennessee at the bar would remember your name, if he would grin his slow grin and honor you with speech.

I wondered if Bob Barrett was comfortable with his adopted name, if he had hoped sometimes in the early hours that his real father or his real mother would appear like the genii and claim him. If he had come to terms with himself.

"It's been a long time," I said.

When I knew the Barretts, I was a junior in high school. In my upstairs room at the Boone's, I solved physics problems night after night, anxious for Mr. Ogren's approval and an *A* on my report card. I heard the courthouse clock strike one for the ghostly hours, for half after midnight, for one o'clock, and for one-thirty—The Three Ones, magic hours when I hoped I might amount to something.

To that room, in those hours, came a Miss Snodgrass, who taught in the grammar school. She had but recently come to room at the Boone's. She was thirty or so.

"You don't know what it is to be horribly ugly," she said, and began to cry. Her thin shoulders shook.

She was, I suppose, horribly ugly. She had almost no nose. The school children, with that idiot, atavistic cruelty meant to drive the different from the tribe, had surely mocked her within her hearing. She could not bear her grief alone.

I was sixteen; I didn't know how to handle raw anguish. Never before had anyone so opened a heart to me. I blurted out, "You're not ugly. If you were, it wouldn't matter, or God wouldn't have made you like that."

I already had reason to know that was nonsense. Anyway, one had only to glance at a newspaper to understand that God, if God existed, didn't give a hoot how people look or what happens to them. As when an only child is killed in a frightful automobile accident.

"It's been good to see you again," said Bob Barrett, and he rose and shook my hand. Good to see me? Maybe I was proof that there was a past, when the future might have been otherwise, and their son still lived. They hadn't, I knew, adopted a child like Old Barrett, a child to inherit their rooms and their money and to fulfill their dreams. I think they couldn't bear to replace their son with a stranger.

There is one novel I shall not live to finish. It is unlikely that I shall be carried off shortly after I write the last line. No, there will remain an unfinished manuscript, two pages, maybe fifty pages, and page fifty-one still in this machine. Pages that must be considered by whoever tidies up the room, pages considered perhaps as trash, perhaps as mementos, maybe as part of my "papers" Boston University has requested for its archives. And people will come into this room to take me away, perhaps after dinner, and one may return later on to unplug this machine and offer it to somebody who'd always wanted one.

In 1967 I lived to complete a novel called *The Power of the Dog.* Two characters, a man and a boy, have a special relationship because they both can make out on the face of a distant mountain, because of the erratic distribution of the timber, the shape of a running dog. For one of them, the relationship was fatal.

That there was a dog on the face of the mountain was fiction. But it is not fiction that twenty miles north of my stepfather's ranch is a hill with a flat flank, and high up there, composed of slide-rock

"February 1991. Blind in my right eye, I'm standing in front of the Andrews Hotel in San Francisco where I live now. In my novels I called the Andrus Hotel the Andrews Hotel and was astonished to find an Andrews Hotel in San Francisco and to find that the owner's name is Harry Andrews. Harry Andrus was the owner of the Andrus Hotel in Dillon. My life is cluttered with coincidences."

and sagebrush, was the proud profile of an American Indian in a feathered warbonnet. This trick of nature my stepfather pointed out to me soon after I came to the ranch with my mother. I was six years old. I said, "He's got his fist up under his chin."

I felt my stepfather's eyes on me, and then he said to my mother, "By golly! He saw it right off—he really saw it!" Then I felt the palm of his hand on the top of my head.

I was proud, and he was pleased. My having seen the Indian vindicated his insistence that the Indian was up there to be seen, and that he had not been—as he put it—"talking through my hat."

He was kind to me, and that might have been hard, for a stepchild can be troubling to a man, a

perpetual reminder that his wife has first loved another man. He was a quiet man. I never heard him speak unkindly of anyone. I can't imagine his ever lying or stealing. He was protective of my mother as my father had never been, and generous.

Now sixty years later I drove back to the ranch in my second-hand Rolls-Royce, and I looked up once again at that hill—foolishly, that's true, for the Indian's profile had been composed of tentative stuff—spreading sagebrush and shifting slide-rock subject to sixty years of cloudburst, drought, and gravity.

My stepfather was dead now twenty years. My mother went before him; there wasn't much for him after that. He thought he'd take a little trip to southern Idaho where an old friend still lived, and they would talk. He had a heart attack driving his car on a dusty road not far from a little Mormon town. He crashed into a fence.

So I looked up to the spot where the Indian had brooded over the vast, empty prairie below, his fist curved up under his chin. In the past I'd looked up there each time I passed in a car or on horseback. Now I looked up, in memory, and in thanks.

. . . I felt a chill, as if someone touched me.

I think I'll live to finish a book dedicated "To a good man." You see, the Indian is still up there.

BIBLIOGRAPHY

Fiction:

The Pass, Doubleday, 1944.

Lona Hanson, Simon & Schuster, 1948.

A Bargain with God, Simon & Schuster, 1953.

Trust in Chariots, Random House, 1961.

The Power of the Dog, Little, Brown, 1967.

The Liar, Little, Brown, 1969.

Daddy's Girl, Little, Brown, 1970.

A Strange God, Little, Brown, 1974.

Midnight Line, Little, Brown, 1976.

I Heard My Sister Speak My Name, Little, Brown, 1977.

Her Side of It, Little, Brown, 1981.

For Mary, with Love, Little, Brown, 1983.

The Corner of Rife and Pacific, Morrow, 1988.

Contributor of stories to periodicals.

Francis Sparshott
1926-

Francis Sparshott: "Our daughter, Pumpkin, Kitty, and me," Tobermory, Ontario, 1990

I am in a classroom, in the back row, third from the right. The English teacher—the history teacher, really, but he is teaching us English, anyone can teach English—is taking us through a free-verse poem by Robert Bridges. I like the way the poem moves. Afterwards, we have to write something about it. I say that the poem seems shapeless but is not really. The teacher says I must make up my mind. But my mind *is* made up.

How old was I? Hard to say. All my memories exist for me as visions clear or cloudy, without context. But I must have been ten, in the lower fourth form of the King's School in Rochester, England. I remember the episode because it was then that I first realised that I understood poetry in a way

that my teachers did not. By the time I was fourteen, I knew that poetry was my business and that I was brought into the world to make poems and for no other reason. I am still convinced of that, though it seems that the poems I was born to make were not of an important sort. And I knew that the poetry I existed to make was a sort of music in the meanings of speech.

The man who taught Bridges with so little insight was in fact my father. He had recently been appointed master of the junior boarding house of my school, and my mother became its unpaid housekeeper. Father was good with young children, but he should have never have taken the job on, because Mother lived on the edge of nervous collapse in a nightmare of migraines, and because the housemaster's accommodation had no room for the children. I became a boarder in my father's house. That has shaped my world. Children who go to school normally have a double danger and a double sanctuary. The intimacy of home protects them from the savagery of school, the anonymity of school is a refuge from parental pressures. But in my world there was no place to hide. Home followed me to school, school came home with me. At last, in July 1952, I discovered (in an Indian burial mound on the shore of Rice Lake, near Hastings, Ontario) a young woman who had been to a high school where her father was a teacher; within a year we were married. Who else would have understood us at all? She must speak for herself, but I cannot imagine what would have become of me without her.

How did I as the housemaster's son fare with my rough schoolfellows? Not badly. I became a clown. I can still usually make people laugh on a suitable occasion. Actually it is easy: all one has to do is to tell the exact truth. Nothing is funnier than things as they really are, but I can do puns and stuff as well, and my biggest success in that line is a booklet called *A Book,* which I had printed in 1970 or so under the pseudonym "Cromwell Kent"—if, as experience proves, a philosopher can be called Stuart Hampshire, why not Tudor Cornwall or Cromwell Kent? The booklet was beautifully designed and produced for me by John Meyer, who in the goodness of his heart charged me nothing but a commission on the printing. I put it in for the Leacock Prize for Humor, but got nowhere, though I do have in my possession a big piece of stiff paper recording that I won an Honorable Mention for Humor in the National Magazine Awards some years later (for the poem "A Brief History of the Kalamazoo Kazoo Company, Incorporated," which had appeared in *Saturday Night).* Anyway I sold all five hundred copies of *A Book,* and I am told that in one particular set of tunnels it is an "underground classic."

Clowning averts malice, but has its dangers. People keep reminding me of witty sayings and putdowns they say I made. I am shocked at the cruelty of these sayings and at the meanness of anyone who would say them. "I would never say a thing like that," I tell them. But I suppose I must have.

Father, Frank Brownley Sparshott

So much for the funny stuff. Time to get back to my schooldays, when I was a boarder in my father's house. Eventually a room was divided up and I had a place to sleep at home. Mother told me later that she insisted on it when she realized that even in vacations I was calling her "Mrs. Sparshott"; but more recently my sister told me that it was not like that at all. The King's School (so called because King Henry VIII established it in 1542 to replace the school of a monastery he had just destroyed) was run by the dean and chapter of Rochester Cathedral, but it received public funds and was therefore subject to government inspection. An inspector's report on the housemaster's living conditions was so scathing that it could not be ignored. At the same time my sister told me why Father had taken the job. It was during the Depression. The then headmaster called Father in and offered him the position. Father declined, because of Mother's health. Then the headmaster told him that it was that job or no job at all.

My new sleeping quarters did me little good, because war broke out and the school was evacuated: Rochester had an aircraft factory and an important bridge and was near a naval dockyard, and was expected to be heavily bombed. As war approached in the summer of 1939 the headmaster purchased seventy-four bedsteads and we—our family, the headmaster's family, some junior masters—sat around the school swimming pool and waited. Within days of the declaration of war the school (or what was left of it) was scattered among country houses in and around the village of Lamberhurst, in Kent: Scotney Castle (where my parents were, with the littlest boys), Bayham Abbey (where I was), Finchcocks, Coggers' Hall, others I forget. We got around on bicycles. I remember it as a happy time, though it was a hard winter. On the frozen moat of Scotney Castle I learned to skate, dodging between the lily pads. I formed the habit of taking long, lonely walks through forests, a habit I retain, so that the slowly changing patterns of tree growth are a sort of home for my mind. It is these slow changes above all that I have preserved with my camera, since photography has become a passion for me.

One episode from that year at Lamberhurst stays in my mind. The school cadet corps ("OTC") was commanded by Captain Sparshott—my father. I hadn't joined. One day Captain Sparshott told me to report for duty on the next parade day. I did not know how to ask whether he gave me that order as parent or as officer. So I turned up as ordered, cycling through the new snow. As it happened, the parade was cancelled for that day, the snow being judged too deep. Still, I was now in the OTC, that was

Mother, Gladwys Winifred Sparshott, around 1928

the main thing. I still don't know whether it was Father or the Captain who got me into it.

In June 1940 France fell, and the school was evacuated again, out of the line of the expected invasion. As the world knows, Hitler would never win command of the air and there would be no invasion, but there we were in a fleet of buses, to be billeted on Taunton School, where at first we slept (on the seventy-four bedsteads the headmaster had bought in the last summer of peace) in a covered playground, with a canvas slung between us and the playing field. Beyond the playing field was the nightlong noise of the shunting engines of the Great Western Railway.

World War II, which killed so many and destroyed so much, brought good to some, and I was one. Eventually it paid for my university training, as a war veteran. Meanwhile it brought me to a much better school, where there was good music—listening to music has been a passion of my life, though performing it was declared to be forever beyond my capacity at the age of eight, when the unfortunate Miss Taylor told my parents that after three full years of painful toil it was evident that I could *never* be taught to play the piano—and a library where I found the poems of W. H. Auden, and an English teacher, A. F. Scott, who had studied with I. A. Richards and understood poetry. For the rambling excesses of my verse, which I showed him, A. F. Scott prescribed as a suitable antidote the procedures of William Empson, advice I have always treasured too deeply to use.

Who am I, and who was this father of mine? I don't know much about his family. I tell people we are Jutes, which I mean for a joke, but when I was in Denmark on a poetry-reading tour in 1981 every woman I saw looked like a Sparshott aunt. Anyway, Father's great-grandfather was a craftsman in Winchester, said to have been a cooper, who moved north to Staffordshire in the hard times of the 1830s. One of his sons, William (a harsh-looking man in the only photograph I have seen of him), became a schoolmaster in a village near Tamworth, and William's youngest son, my grandfather, Francis Joseph, came back south to be master of the Endowed School at Whitstable in Kent. He had four children. Mary, the elder daughter, who taught me how racing drivers negotiate turns, married an oil man and went to live in Persia. Christine, the younger daughter, went to be a missionary in Tunis and other Near Eastern places. The baby of the family, Claud, went to Newfoundland to become an Anglican priest and joined a mission in Cartwright, Labrador. The war brought them all back to England, but until then the only one who stayed on native soil was Father. Perhaps he had seen enough of foreign parts on the Western Front in World War I. He was born in November 1897, so he was sixteen when that war broke out and still at school, but he joined up at once. His family tracked him down and got him out, but in 1916 he was old enough to get back in as a private in the Buffs (the East Kent Regiment). Within the year he was wounded, somewhere near Arras, a Blighty one as they used to say, and spent the rest of the war as a corporal teaching musketry at Hythe. By 1919 he was at New College, Oxford, reading history. He specialized in International Relations—a mistake, he told me, it was a new subject and not properly organized, and he got a mediocre degree. Then he took this job at the King's School and stayed there, moving when the school moved, until 1954. It can't have paid well, but it was a job, and he had promised Mother he would marry her before her twenty-fifth birthday, and he did.

Mother must have met Father at Whitstable, so her father must have worked there. He was employed by the post office, and we all thought of him as a man of mystery. He was said to be Welsh, but nothing was known of his family—no doubt they were sheep stealers. We only knew that his name was Albert Charles Head, and he must have fought in the Boer War because Granny had a picture of him in uniform. A few years ago I learned that there was no real mystery. Albert's father was in the building business in London, but had made a second marriage (to his cook) that the family affected to think disgraceful, so that all communications had been severed.

About Mother's mother there was no mystery. She was a Halfacre, her family were farmers near Windsor and always had been. Cousins abounded. Granny was rather a grump, whereas Grandad was lots of fun, full of jokes and stories. But it seems it was Grandad who prevented Mother (and her younger sister) from having a proper education. He packed her off to be trained as a children's nurse, and she worked at that—taking time off for a nervous breakdown—until her marriage. Father was gentle and modest; his lack of fire must have been an exasperation for Mother, a woman of ferocious intelligence and masterful character whose resentments and aimless malice often made life at home uncomfortable.

That leaves Father's mother, who died when I was about eight, a saintly person much given to good works. Descended from a Dr. Mitchell of Ballarat, she came from Australia as children's nurse to a family rich enough to give her a fine silver coffee set when she left them. Australian kin abound but they are strangers to us, and for practical purposes Hannah Elizabeth Brownley is as isolated a phenomenon as Albert Charles Head.

Both pairs of our grandparents had retired to settle at seaside resorts, and we children grew up taking it for granted that most of the long summer holidays would be spent on the beach, in and out of the warm sea. And before and after our parents ran that boarding house we lived in one or another house on the chalk slope of the North Downs beside the Medway estuary, looking down over the factory where Short Brothers built their flying boats. The Stranraer and Sarafand biplanes, and a rare gull-winged monoplane for which I forget the name, would come in for refits, and then there were the new Empire Class craft for Imperial Airways and their military counterparts, the Sunderlands. When the wind was right they would fly right over our house, low enough it seemed they must take the roof off, lined up with the long reach of water to the west where they would come down like ducks. It still seems unnatural to me not to live by a substantial body of water. When I came to Canada and got married it turned out that my wife could not endure Toronto's

"As a new boy at King's School, aged eight," Rochester, England, 1934

summer heat, so we lived in apartments all winter and bought a cottage beside the rocky shore of Lake Huron (a good friend lent me the money when the bank would not), where we have spent July and August since 1957. All my books except the first have mostly been written there—or rather, have been written *here* where I write these words, with nothing to distract me but the sound of the waves on our shore, and the birds in our trees, and our neighbors' chainsaws all around. For the rest of the year we lived within walking distance of the university—or, at worst, within bicycling distance; but one Saturday afternoon in 1966 we happened to drive by a house on a cliff edge in the eastern suburbs, on the famous Scarborough Bluffs, with almost every window looking directly over Lake Ontario, and behold! a sign said it was for sale. We scraped the money together and that is where we live. On a nice day I can still cycle to work, but it takes longer.

Sometimes the water comes too close. In the 1970s Lake Huron rose and swamped many cottages; we were unscathed but many were not, and I dreamed of great waves blinding the cottage windows with solid green. As for the Scarborough Bluffs, they erode steadily at a rate of three feet every five years, and we figured the house would last our time especially since there was a road between us and the edge. But in 1976 an underground stream emerged halfway down the cliff and began to melt it away. By the fall of 1978 we were collecting boxes to pack books in, because the house seemed certain to fall before summer. Our next-door neighbors, with our less strenuous assistance, convened meetings and lobbied politicians. At last the three levels of government involved realised the danger and sprang into action: granular fill was poured, wells were drilled, the shore was lined with boulders. Work continues, but the Bluffs are stable now, though acquaintances who meet us occasionally and can think of nothing better to say still ask us, "Have you fallen over the cliff yet?"

My parents married as soon as Father graduated and found his teaching job, and their first child was a daughter, June Elizabeth. Next came me, Francis Edward, two years later, in May 1926. I was named for my grandfather, and Father's given name was Frank, so nobody (except one life insurance salesman who was a dear soul and for whom allowances had to be made) has ever abbreviated me to Frank. Eight years later there was another daughter, Margaret Mary. When I was six I was sent to Miss Snowden Smith's preparatory school for boys, where I never understood anything that was going on. The first time I played cricket they told me where to stand. I stood there. A few minutes later a red leather ball came rolling past my feet. "That was your ball, Francis," said Miss Snowden Smith. I didn't know what she meant. After two years of this I was ready for the King's School, where things were explained better. But I still had to play cricket. (The last cricket game I played in was in 1952, for Princeton University against Brooklyn Cricket Club—a deeply humiliating experience.)

English schools specialize earlier than American schools do. At the King's School, one had a choice between Latin and German, and later one could stop doing science and do Greek instead. The school rather specialized in "classics," and as a teacher's son I seem to have been expected to follow along, so I did, though I never saw the point of dead languages and was intrigued by what science I had learned. I was good at classics, though, and it was assumed that I would go to university if I could get a scholarship. It was taken for granted that the university would be Oxford, where my father and my classics teacher had both been. I applied to New College, because that is where Father went, but put down Corpus Christi College first, partly because my best friend was going there and partly because they offered more scholarships in classics than anyone else. The College did give me one of those scholarships, so I went there in 1943, though not to join my friend—he was working on a farm, having been found unfit for military service.

The classics course in Oxford is in two parts: first languages and literatures ("Mods"), then philosophy and history ("Greats"). The first part took me a year, after which I had three peaceful years in the army. Before they let me go in 1947 I wrote to the president of Corpus suggesting I might change my subject to English, since that was what I was interested in. His reply was courteously evasive, and somehow there was never a good time to bring the subject up, so philosophy and ancient history was what I did. (By the time I got back to Oxford my friend, who had left his farm work at the war's end, was in his final year, so I didn't see so much of him after all.) I got my degree at Christmas 1949, and I signed on for a B.Phil. This was a newly invented degree, brought into existence because the army would pay for ex-service people (like me) to do graduate work; I signed on because there was nothing else I wanted to do except write poetry, which doesn't pay. I had done about equally well in both subjects (I scraped a first), but philosophy seemed marginally the less futile so I did that. By the summer of 1950, however, it was obvious that I would fail the degree, because I had rashly chosen as my special subject an author (Aristotle) of whose works I could not understand one word. In any case, I was thoroughly tired of being a student.

Meanwhile, in the city of Dublin, a young furniture dealer named Campbell died suddenly, and his brother Charles had to be brought back to run the family business. Charlie was teaching ancient philosophy at the University of Toronto, and his departure sent the head of the department across the Atlantic to find someone who could read Plato in Greek and teach at the bottom of the salary scale. He went to Oxford and got a list of names from Gilbert Ryle, who was my supervisor, and worked down the list. On the 25th of August he reached my name; on Sunday the 27th, in his London hotel bedroom, knee to knee, I on the chair and he on the bed, a dresser filling the bay window and the remains of a bottle of whisky in the bottom drawer of the dresser, he offered me the position of Lecturer in Philosophy, no

questions asked, at a salary of $2800 a year; on the 29th I accepted; on the 5th of October I sailed. And that is how I came to be a philosopher.

I entered Canada on a six-month tourist visa, having had no time for the chest X ray mandatory for immigrants. When lectures ended in April I had my X ray and walked along to Davenport Road and immigrated. And that is how I came to be a Canadian.

Of course, there is more to it than that. Even if I was not meant to be a poet, I was meant to be a writer at any event—novels, philosophical treatises, letters to editors, anything. Prose came naturally to me, colons and all. Observing my academic colleagues shows what a rare blessing this is: after honing their thoughts, they must labor to hammer them into sentences. That is never a problem for me, nor has it ever been a problem to think of something to say, more or less suitable and more or less the right length. True, the outcome strikes me as essentially worthless—but who am I to say? The structure of our civilization certainly calls for universities, and for philosophy teachers to teach and write in them, just as it calls for literature and assigns a place (curiously compounded of reverence and contempt) to poets; I know of no reason to prefer my own judgment to the consensus of the civilized world.

There is yet more to it. Philosophy, of a sort, comes easy to me because I cannot understand things that seem obvious to everyone else. But I keep puzzling away at them. It is my good fortune that all I need to do is worry away at things the way I like to do, and worry away at what sort of worrying I am doing, and I am automatically doing philosophy in a way that other philosophers will accept. Almost no one ever quotes my work or uses my ideas, but I have kept my job and been offered other jobs and never had to apply for a job, so from a practical point of view I must be doing something right.

There is even more than that to it. The fact is, I do find philosophy interesting. That is because, on a good day, I find everything interesting, because everything is strange. Philosophy is no less interesting than other things. Taking the line of least resistance has sufficed to lead me through a career of inexhaustible fascination. And, in the end, philosophical thinking has become a part of me: the shapes of argument and of philosophical dialectic have become a living reality that I feel on my nerves, plastic and malleable.

There is more to my becoming a Canadian, as well. Lots of people cross the ocean, don't like it here, go back to the old country, can't stand it there, come back again. . . . I was glad to arrive and never wanted to return. Throughout North America, I found, the people one deals with mostly assume that people should have as much as possible of what they want, and should be cheerful with each other. The people I left behind in postwar England made a point of being grudging and surly. America, again, is far from being a class-free society, but is even further from the probing malice of the English class system. English coffee, English cabbage, English custard, the three *c*'s that are the curse of English cuisine, are other things I was glad to put behind me forever. And then there were my parents. I have given the wrong idea about them. When they were young they liked games and songs and parties, they loved and cherished us, and we loved them too, and we had wonderful times together; but life bore on them heavily, and ten days of the tensions that radiated from Mother's tormented personality were all I could enjoy. Love was easier from two thousand miles away. But now, when my sisters tell me of family history I never knew, things that were often kept from me at the time, it is like hearing about strangers in a strange land.

I wish I had known my father, but it was not to be. When I left for Canada he was still too much the schoolmaster. We were too constrained, I had too little adult experience to share. Three years later, when I brought my new wife to stay with my parents, she remembers me saying: "There is something wrong with Father, he isn't talking." Next year he had to retire, unable to do more than stand and gaze at the rioting children in his classes. By 1955, when we brought our new daughter to meet her grandparents, conversation was impossible. The name "Alzheimer's" was not yet in use, and it was not so easy to say what was wrong; now I don't need to explain. Five years later he died, in hospital. My mother lived on for nearly thirty years; after a while, whatever demons had tormented her left her alone until nearly the end. But I was in Canada with my own life and my wife and her family and our daughter, and everything before that is like something I know by hearsay, even if it is my own memory I hear it from.

One thing I suppose I got from Mother, along with my brains and my rage, was migraine. "Sick headaches" they were called when I first got them, at the age of seven, when they mostly came at crises like the beginning of term. Before I reached puberty I

The Sergeants' Mess, No. 3 Wireless Regiment, Sarafand el Amar, Palestine, 1946.
"I am standing third from left."

was getting them quite regularly; for the decades before they went away, when I was about fifty, I had one every five days. I almost never had to cancel a class because of them, but I could do little else; since they left off, I haven't known how to organize my life, lacking that enforced sabbath. At my army medical I forgot to mention them—I managed them with aspirin and I don't think anyone noticed. (That is the way things were in the Intelligence Corps. I recall a moment in the canteen when a sergeant patted a corporal on the hand and said, "Never mind, John; we're all neurotics here.") Their most disconcerting feature was the way they affected my temper, shifting my whole view of the world in a way I can't describe or explain so that I would say embarrassing and unpardonable things. But people mostly did pardon them, or forget them; and I picked up the pieces and went on until the next time.

No one in my family or school thought of these headaches as a condition that the medical profession might do something about. I suppose headaches were just things women got and schoolboys had no business getting. I do remember at Taunton School waiting in the school hospital for surgery hour so that I could get an aspirin, and being told impatiently to control myself. Looking back, I find it hard to excuse. But, as many novelists have told, British boarding schools were like that. It is not that they were full of beatings and bullyings. It is rather that nothing could be done about things, it was useless to look for justice or understanding. (Hearing my father talk, I realized how little the masters understood of the lives they meddled with.) One had to learn to live one's life in the interstices, as it were, of an institution that was at best stupid and indifferent. That is a good preparation for the adult world, and is one of the two things school taught me; the other was to get on with whatever I was doing without being put off by other people's racket. For those two lessons it would have been worth while putting up with all the Latin and Greek, even if those languages had not come in handy later; but I sometimes wonder if a humane upbringing would not have made it easier for me to become a good spouse and parent.

It was my wife who made me see a doctor for my migraines, having an informed interest in medicine and in me. Her name had been Kitty ("Kathleen" only on legal documents) Vaughan, elder daughter of a high-school principal whose father had immigrated as a child from Ballyshannon in Donegal. (In 1953 Kitty and I went to Ballyshannon, found the name "Vaughan" over a grocer's shop, introduced ourselves and soon learned which cousin had been the emigrant. The grocer [after showing us the Protes-

tant graveyard where everybody was] took us out to the farm where that family still lived; and now we are all connected up.) Kitty's mother comes from Bothwell, Ontario; her family are scattered all over North America, where they have lived for centuries, and merely to list their names would fill the rest of this essay, so let's leave them out of it, merely remarking that Kitty has more family than any husband needs—there are plentiful cousins on the Vaughan side too, equally widespread but less numerous. Kitty was a whiz at schoolwork (better than I had been) and decided to go in for medicine, got through two premedical years at the University of Toronto before deciding that other things were more her style, finished a general arts degree, did a brilliant M.A. in anthropology and started gearing up for doctoral work somewhere in the States where one could study linguistics.

Of all my writings, the most important to me is a paper on Plotinus (still unpublished) I worked on in my very first years in Toronto. In the spring of 1952 this project led me to investigate some aspects of the coinage of the Roman Empire. To do this, I had to use the library of the Royal Ontario Museum. My studies in that library were alleviated by sessions in the museum cafeteria, where I struck up acquaintance with one of the staff who was organizing an archaeological dig for the coming summer. Would I like to join? No pay, of course, but free meals and lodging and fresh air. So later that summer I and half a dozen other young people were sharing a cottage on Rice Lake. One member of the party was to join later—an M.A. student in anthropology, rounding out her archaeology. Well, we know who *that* turned out to be. Kitty says the first thing she noticed when she came into the cottage was a young man with a beard, sitting in the only comfortable chair, under the only light, reading Aristotle. Everyone on the dig except Kitty and me was either too young or spoken for, so everything went as it should. We were married on February 7, 1953, in the Anglican church in Mimico, with about a dozen guests. The way I remember it, we gave our families a fortnight's notice—it would have been a week, but Kitty's parents had already been invited to a wedding on the preceding Saturday, with a reception in the Oak Room at the Royal York Hotel, and they were damned if they were going to miss that.

I could stop right there, because after that almost nothing happened, which is what fairy tales mean when they say that people lived happily ever after. Our daughter was born in August 1954, and her story is hers to tell. We called her Margaret Elizabeth,

"My parents and sisters: Margaret Mary in the bow, June Elizabeth next to Father amidships, Mother anxiously watching photographer son," Oxford, 1949

but in her teens she decided she was Pumpkin, and was so exasperated by people asking what her *real* name was that she went to court and is now legally Pumpkin Margaret Elizabeth, so that there are extensive circles in Toronto society in which I am known only as Pumpkin's father. She has no siblings, not from our choice but for reasons of blood chemistry which probably help to account for the scarcity of Sparshotts in your local phone book. After five years teaching in the central department at Toronto, I was shunted—by a process and for reasons I have never fully understood—to Victoria College at the same institution, a Methodist foundation, where I stayed. After five years there as an Assistant Professor, with a solid book published and another accepted for publication, there was no sign of promotion, so when a neighbouring university offered me a job as Associate I was ready to accept. My employers panicked, and promised that if I stayed I should be an Associate as soon as I returned from a forthcoming sabbatical and Full Professor two years later. So that was that, and

there was nothing left to happen except academic politics until my enforced but welcome retirement a few weeks ago. But I did keep on writing, and since I am appearing here in the guise of Author the rest of this story will be the narrative of my authorship.

I am riding my bicycle over the Devonshire hills on a misty afternoon in 1943. I am waiting for the results of my Oxford scholarship examination, and taking a few days riding round the country, sleeping where I may sleep, with sweaters and bread and apples in my saddlebag. As I am going down a hill near Newton Abbot, a poem comes into my head, complete, not quite all at once but nearly so, except that it is in two stanzas and the second one comes first—I know it does, and I almost see the arrow pointing it to its place. All I have to do at the end of the day's ride is write it down. One line was wrong and had to be changed about five years later, but apart from that it passed muster and I kept it. It is almost the only poem I have kept from my schooldays; you can find it under the name "Mist Forms" in my first volume. Poems have not often come to me like that, complete and unheralded, but some have. Before it can happen at all, though, many poems must be worked out in full awareness.

I have written poems since I was about twelve, as ideas or images came to me. But at a few times in my life there have been periods of a month or more when I wrote poetry every day, knowing I would do so and had to do so, a curious tumescent certainty that eventually weakened and went away. The earliest of these spells was during my first year at Oxford, from January to March 1944; the last was in 1985, and the poems that came from that were meagre and sour— you can find them in my last book, *Sculling to Byzantium*.

Usually my head is so full of philosophy and of the various obsessional anxieties of teaching and academic busywork that poetry is crowded out; the periods of continual poetizing, when I wait and listen every day for the poetry that I know will come, have almost all occurred in the interstices of my career, at the beginnings of sabbaticals or the ends of research projects. The poetry that comes to me then may be of little consequence, but that is beside the point, this is the poetry that it is given to me to bring into existence. Just one of these periods, in the summer of 1970, was in its way special. I had a dream, in which I read a book of poems, poems I knew I had written but had forgotten so that they were quite strange to me, and were unlike any poems I had ever read, hard, cold, gnarled—there are no good words for it, they were unlike anything I have ever read sleeping or waking. When I woke up I recognized the book. It was a green exercise book I had, and I knew I must fill it with poems. And I did. I went on until there were a hundred of them. I knew from my dream that the name of the book had to be *The Book of Dried Ballads.* The poems in it were simply poems, of course, bits of poetry stuff, not like the poems in my dream at all. Only dreams are like dreams.

Before I went to college I had written a lot of verse, in the concentration of excitement that only adolescence knows. A. F. Scott found nothing more in them than literary reminiscence and incantation, but I felt he was wrong: they were realities I had somehow brought into being without knowing quite what they were. In the course of the next year, before I went into the army, I wrote an elaborate commentary on them, looking into their construction and imagery, to see what it was they were. Scott was right, of course, but I was right too, and my examination proved to be a real self-discovery. When I moved into middle age I finally threw the manuscript away—it would have been dreadful to have it discovered among my posthumous papers; but it got me in the habit, which I have never lost, of giving a hard scrutiny to even those of my poems that feel most inevitable.

By the time I left for Canada in 1950 I had enough poems for a book, and a shape for the book to take. My alphabet poem "Alpha to Omega" is the table of contents of the book, itself to have the same name. For each poem in the alphabet there would be a "theorem": "Theorem A for Ark" was probably the poem "Seasalter," which is about Noah's flood. In some cases there would be one or more additional poems ("corollaries") for the same alphabet word. But for one or two words there was still no poem, and no poem came to me for them—one might think I could have sat down and manufactured one, but the intricate inner law under which I write poetry inhibited me. It was not until 1957 that the last poem was in its place in the book. In the meantime, while learning to be an academic functionary, I had written little poetry and published none. But one day in that year or the next a colleague at Victoria, the poet Jay Macpherson, asked me if I didn't have some poems that I would like to show her. I asked her how she knew, and she replied that I just looked like the kind of person who might. So of course I told her all about it, and she did what I would not have presumed to do, sent poems to the editors of suitably selected journals. Several of them were printed. One of them even got a prize as the "best poem" to appear in a Canadian journal in 1958; unfortunately the prize was sponsored by a local university, and one really can't go around boasting that one has been awarded the

Graduation day, Oxford University, 1950

President's Medal of the University of Western Ontario.

It was time to think seriously of launching *Alpha to Omega.* The publisher I approached turned the book down: they didn't do much poetry, she said, and anyway the "geometrical" framework I had imposed did nothing for the reader. How my first book actually got printed seems to have been as follows. A local magazine, *The Tamarack Review,* brought out a collection from its first five years, including some poems of mine. But careless wielding of a blue pencil resulted in one of my poems being printed with part of a different poem tacked on to the end. Nobody else noticed, but I noticed, and I complained to the publisher—in the nicest possible way. The publisher, Oxford University Press, was abashed, and I think it was this embarrassment that led that distinguished house to publish a selection from my book, called *A Divided Voice,* in 1965. Reviews were variously disparaging, but there were reviews. My name was beginning to be known by the few hundred people who read Canadian poetry.

Oxford didn't do the whole book, and rejected the "theorem" business out of hand—if you want to see what it was like, there is a copy in the Pratt Library of Victoria University, who get my manuscripts and drafts when I have finished with them. My editor, William Toye, pointed out that my poetry was very uneven in quality. I agreed, but I didn't agree that the ones he had chosen were always the best. Those he left out, together with some other poems that hadn't fitted the scheme of *Alpha to Omega,* and some incidental poems I wrote along the way, together with the product of a burst of continual composition in early 1966 (between the end of a term in Toronto and the beginning of a visiting semester at the University of Illinois), gave me enough poems for a new book. I could hardly send it to Oxford, but fortunately the clause in my contract giving them an option on my next book was already fulfilled by a philosophy manuscript. The new book was issued by the old Toronto firm of Clarke, Irwin in 1969. I don't know quite how that came about. Clarke, Irwin had decided to bring out three poetry books at once—one by the New Brunswick poet Alden Nowlan, and a couple of makeweights who turned out to be me and Clifton Whiten. They got an outside editor to arrange the package, but how I came to be chosen I don't recall. Anyway the new book was called *A Cardboard Garage,* the cardboard of course being the covers of the book, its contents divided between "Brittle Bodies" and "Soft Engines" depending on whether or not they rhymed and scanned. The book got at least one usefully good review, but Clarke, Irwin had never been famous for plugging their publications and some years later went decorously bankrupt, the upshot being that if you want a hundred or so copies of *A Cardboard Garage* you have only to ask me.

The "dried ballads" from the green book of 1970, with other more occasional productions, amply replenished my stock of uncollected poems, but it was not until 1979 that I had another book out. And then there were two. Among the "dried ballads" had been many haiku, a form I had practised occasionally since the army taught me the rudiments of Japanese. But about 1970 I read a new translation of Basho's *Journey to the Deep North* and the outcome was scores of haiku, many of them about travel—back and forth, up and down, with the poet's shamanic journey to the depths and return as an underlying theme. Next fall I filled my free hours by making a handwritten transcription of 150 of these, to be called *The Rainy Hills.* I had long thought that it was absurd to expend all the machinery of typesetting and book production on something that would have at most a couple of

hundred grudging readers, and would have to be subsidized at that. And haiku should be handwritten anyway. So I set them down with a calligraphic pen, carefully spaced on the page, with a few drawings placed where I wanted them, and an introduction carefully typewritten with no mistakes and the lines all justified—all ready for the camera.

No one would publish *The Rainy Hills,* and at last I took it to that brilliant printer and poet Tim Inkster of the Porcupine's Quill at Erin, asking him simply to do a facsimile in a tidy binding. Tim saw at once what I wanted, but demurred. Typesetting the introduction wouldn't cost much and would go better with the handwriting. It would be better to use more pages and change the spacing, and . . . "Trust me," he said. Since he was Tim Inkster, I trusted him. When I saw what he had done I could not believe that it wasn't just what I had meant all along. The trouble is, it looked so good that I ordered 500 copies instead of the original 300. I easily sold most of the 300 by direct mail and other subterfuges, but the other 200 sales weren't there—if anyone would like 100 copies of *The Rainy Hills,* they have only to ask. But I did recover my outlay, at a modest price, and without calling on public funds.

Much of the rest of the "dried ballads" was brought out in the same year, 1979, by Marty Gervais at the Black Moss Press in Windsor. Again, I forget how that came about. By this time I was well known in the Canadian poetic community, not so much for my verse as for my bureaucratic involvement. In 1966 a group of senior Canadian poets decided to form a sort of guild or union to maintain the artistic integrity and so forth of poetry in Canada, and in 1968 this group was established as the League of Canadian Poets. I was brought into the administration almost from the start (Raymond Souster, when I asked him why me, said "Because you'll do some work, damn it!"; and, poets being what they are, the explanation suffices.) Mostly I was Toronto representative, but the reason people got to know me was because I took on the job as paymaster for an annual series of poetry readings in Ontario schools, which the League was organizing at the expense of the Province of Ontario Council for the Arts. After a few years I had to give that up, but when I came back to the annual meeting in 1977 I was prevailed on to let myself be nominated for the presidency. I really hate institutions, but somehow I keep getting sucked into them, and on this occasion the excuse was the identity of the only alternative candidate. The argument was cogent, overpowering. I ran. I was elected.

Not all the best poets in Canada belong to the League, and some of the worst do, but on the whole

"Kitty and her mother, Ardath Vaughan, holding our daughter Margaret Elizabeth; Kitty's father, Stewart Vaughan, front; seated at right is Kitty's mother's mother, Berta May Pope. The other three are George, Ethel, and Malcolm Kennedy, who lived next door," at Kitty's parents' home in Mimico, Ontario, 1954

the president of the League does get to know a lot of poets. So I knew Marty anyway, and he knew me; but then I knew other people too, and I don't remember just how Black Moss became my publisher this time. The title *Book of Dried Ballads*, it was decided, would not sell, and *The Naming of the Beasts* is what it came to be called. That didn't sell either.

My next poetry book came about as follows. CBC Radio began sponsoring an annual set of literary prizes, worth good money and (unlike the president of the University of Western Ontario) with good publicity value. The names of the judges were announced in advance. One year the three poetry judges included a poet who I knew liked my style, a CBC man whose mind I found congenial, and I forget who the third one was. I knew at once that if my entry was good enough it would win the prize—usually, it was not worth entering, because the way I do poetry is not the way that wins the best prizes in Canada.

The poem I wrote, the right length for a half-hour radio program, was called "The Cave of Tro-

phonius," and had to do (like the haiku book) with the descent and return of the shaman. It did get the first prize for 1981, but was not broadcast because of a strike—friends told me they heard it later in the year, but I had not been forewarned and when I wrote to ask if a tape was available my letter was not answered. Still, I did get the check. I honestly expected that magazine editors and publishers would ask if the poem was available for publication—silly of me. But the time was ripe for another book, anyway. The poet Jan Zwicky, whom I knew as a budding philosopher, had recently had a book accepted by Brick Books of Ilderton, Ontario, and she suggested I contact them. After an exchange of letters I shipped my whole big bundle of uncollecteds, a baggy monster called *Storms and Screens*, off to Brick, who in 1983 brought out *The Cave of Trophonius*, a small collection consisting of the prize poem plus a handful of leftover haiku and similarly laconic pieces.

That still left me with a mass of unplaced poems to move, and I found that *Childe Thursday*, which lives in Toronto and consists of my old friends David and M. L. Knight, would be happy to oblige. They have done my last three books. The less solemn pieces appeared as *The Hanging Gardens of Etobicoke* in 1983—in fact, they beat Brick to the draw; the more solemn ones came out as *Storms and Screens* in 1986; and *Sculling to Byzantium* (1989) has left my barrel-bottom scraped. Childe Thursday as a publisher has three advantages. First, David and M. L. not only like my work but understand it. Second, David has adorned two of the books with illustrations and decorations which, though they come from a sensibility very different from mine, have a wit that fills me with amazement and delight and respond perfectly to the point of the poems they accompany. And, third, their methods are economically rational, using the most straightforward technology and needing no government subsidy. The defect of these advantages is that, because the books are not opulent, reviewers don't review them and people don't buy them. A book of new Canadian poems is supposed to have a bright-colored glossy cover with an eye-catching picture on the front. What is not gift-wrapped, it

Francis Sparshott reading some of his poems at the St. Lawrence Centre, Toronto, 1970

seems, cannot be worth reading. But this defect has itself a compensating advantage: I can now blame my failure to sell on something other than the poor quality of my work.

I mentioned learning Japanese for the army, but didn't explain. When I finished the first component of my Oxford degree, in July 1944, I was conscripted, like everyone else at that time who had a scholarship to learn dead languages, straight into the army Intelligence Corps to learn enough Japanese to translate intercepted radio messages. Within three months of the end of the course, Japan surrendered and there was no more translating to do. But the authorities couldn't flood the job market and the schools by letting all us conscripts go at once, and it was two years before I got back to Oxford. What they did meanwhile was send me to Palestine in November 1945, still in the radio interception business but doing clerical work. Palestine was peaceful at first but that didn't last, with the remnant of the European Jews desperate to come in and the Arabs who lived there desperate to keep them out. A midnight service in the fields outside Bethlehem on Christmas Eve, meditation in Jerusalem on Easter morning, a visit to the kibbutz at Ein Gev, and many afternoons on the beach at Bat Yam—all very nice, but interceptors of radio signals need security and early in 1947 our unit was moved to Cyprus. Before we left Palestine, though, one could not but be moved by the condition of the country. It was fully inhabited by Arabs whose families had lived there from time immemorial. It was plainly their place. On the other hand, there was nowhere else for the Jews to go and nothing else they could be doing, and they could not be kept out of a country that had been politically constituted to be their "national home." I was moved and am still moved by the unassailability of the arguments on both sides, their irreconcilability, and above all by the refusal of each side to admit that the other side's case was as compelling as its own. It is not surprising, then, that my first writing in philosophy had to do with the ways in which moral cases are framed and supported: *An Enquiry into Goodness and Related Concepts* was published by the University of Toronto Press in 1958. A university professor's job has two parts, advancing some branch of learning and teaching it to others, and the publication that issues from this employment hardly counts as writing and seldom merits reading. But a writer is what I was anyway, and if it hadn't been philosophy it would have been fiction or travel books or something else involving the compulsive emission of prose. My books may not be worth reading, but they are written as if they were.

This first prose book of mine actually started as what would have been a dissertation for the B.Phil. degree, but its mainspring was neither that nor the insight into moral argument that Palestine gave me. It was part of a project to write a theodicy. How can the God of AIDS and the holocaust be good? How can God not be good? Before one could answer that one would have to explain just what is meant by calling *anything* good and really meaning it. So that was what this book was for, though the theodicy never got written.

An Enquiry into Goodness got the whole front page of the London *Times Literary Supplement* to itself, so naturally it sold like hot cakes—UK sales totalled 134 copies, or maybe it was 137. The University of Chicago Press took an edition of 1500 copies and remaindered it within three years, which still seems to me an odd thing to do. However, Northwestern University gave me a visiting position for a year on the strength of it, and the University of Chicago offered me a job. I didn't take the job. One night I was in a Chicago bar with a tableful of people, and I was saying how exaggerated the accounts of street violence seemed to be, but it turned out that every single person at that table had been either burgled or mugged—one of them twice. So Kitty and I preferred to raise our family in Toronto. So obvious was my determination, and so transparent my demeanor, that the principal of Victoria College told me to my face that it was obviously unnecessary to promote me in order to keep me; so he didn't.

While the University of Chicago Press were thinking about publishing me, they were also considering a little collection of essays about the nature of philosophy, to be called *Looking for Philosophy*. Their reader was most enthusiastic; publication seemed assured; but the enthusiasm was not shared in all the necessary quarters, and nothing came of that.

My second book arose from necessity. The University of Toronto did not have enough ancient philosophy to fill my timetable, so at the end of my first year I was told that next year I would be teaching aesthetics as well. Aesthetics!? What on earth was that? At Oxford in my day aesthetics ranked with phrenology and metaphysics among outmoded follies. It seemed that in the New World things were a bit different. Investigation revealed that aesthetics was what was contained in Melvin Rader's anthology *A Modern Book of Esthetics*. So I made that my text. But nothing in that book showed how the different theories it contained fitted together, nor did anything else I could find; so I had to write my own text, which appeared as *The Structure of Aesthetics* from the University of Toronto Press in 1963. It went well

enough, though the Press never put it in paperback, but two things went wrong. First, they declined to use the numbering system that made the schematic arrangement perspicuous, and I, like a fool, kept no copy of the manuscript that contained it, so that even the archives of Victoria University contain no clue to the book's formal architecture. Second, I found I could not use it as a text after all. If one teaches out of one's own book one's students accuse one of vanity and greed, and since one is indeed vain and greedy one cannot gainsay them.

My next book, *The Concept of Criticism,* is the one I used to get me off the hook on which Oxford University Press had impaled me with *A Divided Voice.* They sent it to their British counterparts, who issued it in 1967. The occasion of writing it was a discussion group I attended, consisting mostly of literature teachers who found themselves perplexed in their work of critical exposition by an uncertainty as to exactly what criticism was. I wrote the book to tell them. I have to admit that they were not the least bit grateful. The book sold out quite soon and was not reprinted.

Meanwhile, during a sabbatical, on a croft on the Hebridean island of Harris in the summer of 1962, I added a concluding chapter to *Looking for Philosophy* and sent it off once more to look for a publisher. The University of Toronto Press kept it for eighteen months before deciding it was offensively self-conscious and generally unworthy of them, and eventually McGill-Queen's University Press brought it out in a very handsome format in 1972. I don't know how many they sold (they still have a lot left, and so do I), but it made me for a while a sort of cult figure among feminist philosophers, who are always looking for ways of philosophizing that depart from the male norms of confrontation and domination. My book began and ended with dialogues and didn't try to prove anything, so that was all right.

Shortly after this, the Canadian Philosophical Association made me their president for a year, apparently because of my prolixity—at least, I never heard any better explanation. "Services to Canadian philosophy," grunted the only member of the nominating committee I dared to ask, making his eyebrows as sardonic as he knew how. I cannot remember anything that my labors for the Association accomplished, but they certainly took a lot of time, and are what made me give up my connection with the League of Canadian Poets for a while.

My prolixity, however, had yet to reach its peak. My next book, developed in connection with my graduate seminar in the philosophy of art from 1967 onward, ran to 726 pages; I wrote a shorter version

At a seminar on a Norwegian farm: (from left) Professor Per Seyersted (University of Oslo), Betty Jane Wylie (Canadian playwright), Sparshott, and student, 1981

first, but that did not look at all convincing. It was an explanation of just why the philosophy of art not only is a mess but must continue to be one, so it had to go into detail. McGill-Queen's, my publisher, when warned how big it was likely to be, expressed misgivings but said they would see what could be done. Meanwhile the philosophy editor of Princeton University Press, Sanford G. ("Sandy") Thatcher, had learned that I had been awarded a fellowship by the Killam Foundation to bring this project to fruition, and wrote to ask if it was likely to issue in publication. I told him about the book, and explained about the qualms of the publisher who had the first refusal. He suggested that I send Princeton a copy of the manuscript anyway, just in case. I did so. As it turned out, McGill-Queen's never came to a decision because they temporarily suspended their whole publication program. Princeton brought the book out at a suitably magisterial price in 1982, under the title *The Theory of the Arts*. For the cover, I prepared a collage of Duchamp's "Nude Descending a Staircase" coming down the stairs in one of Piranesi's "Prisons";

Princeton's designer kept the prison but left out the nude, with mystifying but perhaps impressive results.

Meanwhile, yet another organization, the American Society of Aesthetics, had entangled me in its affairs, and in due course it too made me its president—this time, not merely because of my prolixity but because I had done the local arrangements for what turned out to be a successful meeting of the Society at Toronto in 1976. I recall that it was Jerome Stolnitz who persuaded me to let my name go forward, leaning over the back of my seat on a tour bus one rainy Saturday afternoon in Seattle while I was trying to carry on a conversation with Jenefer Robinson of Cincinnati. I remember him as smoking a cigar at the time, but surely one cannot smoke a cigar on a tour bus.

However that may be, it was at the 1981 meeting of the ASA that I was waylaid by Selma Jeanne Cohen outside the Museum of the Cigar at Old Tampa, Florida. She asked me why I had never written about the aesthetics of dance—she had seen me at dance performances, so she knew I could, and would I kindly do so. As the world knows, people who are told to do things by Selma Jeanne Cohen do what they are told. On inspecting the manuscript for my new big book I found that indeed there was little about dance in it, though there had been a great deal in the material I had assembled. Why was this? Is there something about dance that resists aesthetics, or do aestheticians shy away from dance? I wrote a long article about that, which circulated in mimeographed form and an expansion of which eventually appeared in *Dance Research Journal,* and began sketching a book to deal with that and with everything else that ought to go into a book on the philosophy of dance, if there were to be such a thing.

Shortly after this, I was giving a lecture on the philosophy of dance at Princeton, and Sandy Thatcher asked me whether I might not have a book on that topic in me somewhere. I told him that the book was not only in me but already oozing out, so we agreed that when it had finished emerging I should submit it for possible publication. As usually happens, prolixity took over, and the book fell into two parts. We

decided to do the first part separately, and Princeton published it as *Off the Ground* in 1988. Only Jay Macpherson noticed that the title pays homage to the poet Walter de la Mare. A full draft of the second part exists, but Sandy Thatcher has gone off to direct another publishing house and the new regime have different ideas about what Princeton wants to do, so there the matter rests at present.

Early in 1983, between the first sketchy draft of *Off the Ground* and the final version, the world changed for me as it has changed for so many writers. I bought a word processor. Authors who never had to learn that the first rule of authorship is that the shiny side of the carbon faces away from you, cannot imagine how these machines have changed the whole rhythm of composition. Even in poetry, which people still mostly compose in longhand, the process of going through endless revisions has changed. Typewriters rewarded caution with fidelity; word processors encourage a carefree facility, only to betray it with grotesque calamities. I was able to afford this breakthrough into contemporaneity because the University of Toronto had recently bestowed on me the confus-

The author and his wife at home with Susan, their cat, in Scarborough, Ontario, 1991

ing and invidious title of "University Professor." This appellation was entirely empty, except that for the first five years its bearer received an annual expense allowance of $3000. As a senior recipient of this allowance said to me when I met him one morning on the subway, "It is better than to shit in the hollow of your hand."

Let me end as I began, with a schoolroom scene. Again I am in the Lower Fourth, ten years old. This time it is hobbies period. Once a year the boys bring to class the fruits of their pastimes, to be judged. The master this time is Noel Johnston, our Form Master. I have brought a rather large car I have designed and built from Meccano. It is propelled by twisted elastic, like a model plane, and the steering depends on string. "Good Heavens, Sparshott!" says Mr. Johnston; "However long did it take you to make *that?*" But he only gives me 45 percent, not a good mark. True, it had needed more elastic than I expected, but somehow it trundled across the floor. What more can be asked of any of us?

It is only as I write this now, not having thought of the matter for many years, that it occurs to me that children should not be graded for their hobbies.

BIBLIOGRAPHY

Poetry:

A Divided Voice, Oxford University Press, 1965.

A Cardboard Garage, Clarke, Irwin, 1969.

(Contributor) John Robert Colombo, editor, *How Do I Love Thee: Sixty Poets of Canada Select and Introduce Their Favourite Poems from Their Own Work,* Hurtig, 1970.

The Rainy Hills: Verses after a Japanese Fashion, privately printed by Porcupine's Quill, 1979.

The Naming of the Beasts, Black Moss, 1979.

New Fingers for Old Dikes, League of Canadian Poets, 1980.

The Cave of Trophonius and Other Poems, Brick Books, 1983.

The Hanging Gardens of Etobicoke, Childe Thursday, 1983.

Storms and Screens, Childe Thursday, 1986.

Sculling to Byzantium, Childe Thursday, 1989.

Nonfiction:

(Under name F. E. Sparshott) *An Enquiry into Goodness and Related Concepts,* University of Toronto Press, 1958, University of Chicago Press, 1958.

The Structure of Aesthetics, University of Toronto Press, 1963.

(Under name F. E. Sparshott) *The Concept of Criticism,* Clarendon Press, 1967.

(Under name F. E. Sparshott) *Looking for Philosophy,* McGill-Queen's University Press, 1972.

(Author of introduction) John M. Robson, editor, *Essays on Philosophy and the Classics. Collected Works of John Stuart Mill,* Volume XI, University of Toronto Press, 1978.

The Theory of the Arts, Princeton University Press, 1982.

Off the Ground: First Steps to a Philosophical Consideration of the Dance, Princeton University Press, 1988.

Contributor:

Paul Hernadi, editor, *What Is Literature?,* Indiana University Press, 1978.

Stanley G. French, editor, *Philosophers Look at Canadian Confederation,* Canadian Philosophical Association, 1979.

New Grove Dictionary of Music and Musicians, Macmillan, 1980.

Hernadi, editor, *What Is Criticism?,* Indiana University Press, 1981.

Denis Dutton and Michael Krausz, editors, *The Concept of Creativity in Science and Art,* Nijhoff, 1981.

Eleanor Cook and Julian Patrick, editors, *Centre and Labyrinth: Essays in Honour of Northrop Frye,* University of Toronto Press, 1983.

D. Dutton, editor, *The Forger's Art,* University of California Press, 1983.

Philip Alperson, editor, *What Is Music?,* Haven Publications, 1987.

Other:

(Under pseudonym Cromwell Kent) *A Book* (fiction), privately printed, 1970. Contributor of essays to periodicals, including *Ethics, Journal of Aesthetic Education,* and *Philosophy and Literature;* contributor of poetry to periodicals, including *Canadian Forum, Fiddlehead, Literary Review, Nation, Poetry,* and *West Coast Review.*

Lloyd Van Brunt

1936-

I FALL IN LOVE WITH NANCY DREW

My father was a WPA (Works Progress Administration) worker in 1936 when I was born. He worked ten days a month spreading concrete for roads and sidewalks, and took home twenty-seven dollars. On that he and my mother, both teenagers, feasted on franks and beans and hamburgers, and had bacon and eggs for breakfast on Saturdays and Sundays.

My mother, Elva Gladys Johnson (formerly Johanssen, I am sure), was seventeen when I was born and never tired of telling me of the pain and travail my birth had caused her. I was two weeks overdue when the doctor was finally able to drag me, feet-first, from her womb, and I weighed ten-and-a-half pounds. My mother said she went almost out of her mind with pain and fear, and I can only guess the mixed emotions she had when the nurse cradled me in her arms, a red and blue howling mass of protoplasm that eagerly sought her breasts.

I was fed that way for eleven months, until my mother became pregnant again. Some neighbors kept goats, including a nanny, and I was switched to a diet of goat's milk and bits of what my parents ate.

We lived in one side of a rundown duplex house in Sand Springs, Oklahoma, about fifteen miles and a forty-five-minute trolley ride from Tulsa and St. John's hospital, where I had been born. I cried only rarely after I was born, my mother said, and when I did it was only after long suffering a dirty diaper, or not being fed on time—usually when my parents, who were crazy about movies, were away evenings at the "picture show" in Tulsa and I was left alone with a hired girl who paid little or no attention to me. I was, I believe, like someone who had survived a serious illness, grateful to be alive. Like someone who had nearly died, I saw the world with astonished eyes.

I was a large, happy baby, my mother said, probably exaggerating, rolling in goat's milk fat, always smiling, eager to please, to be the center of my teenage parents' attention. My father later told me that he was the one who first thought of taking me to the movies with them, stuffed into a jerry-built pack of flour sacks and cord, content and quiet on his or

Lloyd Van Brunt, 1991

my mother's shoulders, absorbed as they were by the make-believe images of other worlds projected on the magic screen.

Light splotches the Sheetrock wall, blonde plasmic light. The wool blanket feels scratchy and suffused with body heat, my own. Voices rise in the next room, the familiar male tones of Uncle Buddy and my new stepfather Charlie. One has made a fire in the front room stove, the other in the woodburning kitchen range.

The tangy smell of coffee and bacon brings moisture to my mouth and I debate whether to get up

"My father (left), Howell Harold Van Brunt, somewhere in the South Pacific," 1942

now or go back to sleep. I have been three years old for six months now, and this is my first moment of true consciousness, the first thing I'll remember. My mother will relate details of earlier events to me but those memories will be hers, not mine.

For instance, I do not remember the car that skidded around the corner where I played in a sandpile. The car bolted the sidewalk and bore down on me. I must have screamed. Perhaps the impact and a subsequent two-week coma blotted all earlier memories—for I had nearly cut off my tongue, my mother told me, while playing with a butcher knife on the kitchen table, my concentration total and tongue-protruding as I took a tumble. No wonder my parents named me after "the funniest man alive," Harold Lloyd, who was always taking pratfalls, always playing the fool. Howell Lloyd Van Brunt, my birth certificate read. I could have inherited my father's middle name, Harold, but I guess my parents thought Howell Harold Lloyd Van Brunt would be too hard to write. I still swallow sibilants sometimes.

Nor do I remember scarlet fever and a temperature of 105 about six months after the tongue-whack-

ing incident. Was that before my sullen young father stopped coming home altogether, stopped tossing a delight-squealing me high in the air, or after? I remained loyal to his memory, refusing to accept the attentions of the looming older man who tried picking me up. I literally hid behind my mother's skirts, she said. Charles Bryan Reynolds, my stepfather-to-be, was miffed, and quickly turned his attention to the baby, my sister Betsy.

Some strangeness in my character began to assert itself after one of Charlie's late-night visits. My mother said I began to butt my head against the wall of the room where she slept with my sister, and had slept with Charlie earlier. I got up as though sleepwalking and began my abrasive quest to break down that wall.

Later, Charlie would joke that I drank too much goat's milk too early. I knew that was a lie. I knew he knew the true reason, that my mother should have waited for my natural father to come back, that he was the only man who belonged in her bed. I must have had a strong sense of the proprieties even then, and an even stronger urge to correct the course of events headed in the wrong direction. I continued to butt my head against walls, much to the amusement of my stepfather and his beer-drinking cronies. An infant Telemachus, I was waiting for my father to return and throw the rascals out. I think I must have imagined the blood, the gore.

Charlie's nephew, "Uncle" Buddy, was the first man to make contact with me again. Buddy had five daughters, not a son in sight, and had himself "cut" after the birth of his last daughter. He wrestled and tickled me and tossed me nearly to the ceiling, and played cars with me, the accelerator of his tongue far out-decibelling my own bumblebee efforts.

The lights on the wall had shifted now, no longer plasmic and pulsing, turning the rectangular sections of Sheetrock a lighter shade, the vertical and horizontal dotted lines of nail heads evenly spaced, prosaic as geometry, no longer sparkling like sequins in first light. I peed in the rank-smelling outhouse back of the kitchen, then walked barefoot into that warm and vaporous room where my mother and Uncle Buddy and his lank wife Verna and, of course, the scarecrow figure of jug-eared Charlie sat eating bacon and fried eggs and stove-top toast, slurping coffee and making adult jokes about the Great Depression I had no interest in.

I stood by Uncle Buddy who slipped me fragments of bacon, fed me as he would a dog, and patted my head from time to time just as unself-consciously. There was an ache in the bottom of my stomach even then. I wanted my face reflected back at me from the breakfast table. I wanted my young, strong father, the sharp thrill of his morning whiskers against my cheek, my mother curled up close on the other side, kissing both of us.

Mrs. Cooper hauled sinners out of the shower one by one and with energetic strokes laid a sappy switch across the backs and butts of miscreants. The rest of us huddled together, a few of the older boys covered their genitals as best they could with long splayed fingers. The boy being punished inevitably began bawling after the first few welts began to swell across the slightly broken skin.

When the matrons at the Tulsa Children's Home felt really mean they would use a razor "strop" instead of a willow switch. The stiff piece of leather was almost biblical in proportion, and it was used carefully only on our legs and butts so our backs wouldn't be scarred. In her early fifties, Mrs. Cooper, who supervised the boys' dormitory, was stout and strong, her gray hair was done up in a severe bun, and we made secret fun of the dead-white mustache that threatened to engulf her upper lip.

But no one dared to make fun of her in the shower. You never knew who would be next. Cooper kept a daybook of transgressions. She would peer down through grandmotherly reading spectacles at an entry, close the diary book with a snap, and reach her clubby right arm in among us to drag a stiff-legged body towards her.

"*You*, Delbert, you *sinned* today!" The switch whistled and made a kind of thwacking sound as it bit into flesh. Within seconds, the bawling boy would be on his naked knees, bowed in supplication before her. Cooper would close her eyes, lift the switch in her strong right arm toward heaven, and pray earnestly to The Lord for this particular sinner's forgiveness, her left hand clutching the boy's wet hair.

The incongruity of the punishment and the praying, the absurd juxtaposition of brutality and religion, made me want to grin and cry at the same time. Cooper's behavior simply did not make sense to me then, and my reaction to irrational behavior was to laugh at it. Later, when I learned something of Freud and Jung, I classified Mrs. Cooper as a psychopath, a sexual deviant, a power-mad monster.

She was none of these things. She was merely dull, both in mind and body, and was, by her lights, doing right by her charges, many of whom had prisoner fathers, by not sparing the rod. She was, too, usually willing to discuss our transgressions detail by detail in the privacy of her cozy room that abutted the boys' dorm. She would read long passages from the Old Testament to illustrate a point, her slow and grave and nasal voice rising and falling, the granny glasses slipping down her nose, while the now-forgiven boy sat at the foot of her rocking chair, nodding.

Cooper had pale blue watery eyes, her iron-gray hair still had reddish streaks, and her forearms were covered with large splotchy freckles. She was a widow with two sons and numerous grandchildren whose photographs she was proud of. I hated her for weeks after one of those beatings in the shower room, to the point of fantasizing sneaking up behind her with a large rock, but I suppose I also loved her. She was the only mother I had during those long years.

My real mother had caught tuberculosis from a woman who was hired to help with the housework while my mother recuperated from the birth of her fifth child, my sister Merrylyn Kay. My mother was sent to the state tuberculosis sanitarium in the western part of Oklahoma. TB was usually deadly then and it was thought she would die. Charlie wanted no part of us on his own, and we were deposited, newborn baby and all, in the Tulsa Children's Home, a kind of semi-official orphanage on the outskirts of Tulsa.

September 1945. I was nine years old. A city marshal drove us to the home. A large star had been stencilled on the left front door of the Plymouth coupe, which was too small for the five of us and him. I held the baby in my lap. Mother told me to be a little man and to take care of my sisters. They were in tears, of course, and I tried dutifully to shush them. It was embarrassing to me for them to cry in front of this uniformed stranger, whose huge pistol dangled so far down on his thigh I thought it would catch on the gear shift. The baby, at least, slept. I was allowed to see my sisters only on visiting days during the next few years. The girls' dormitory occupied the left wing of the home, the boys' the right, and a forbidden corridor ran between them.

Times were hard. My real father was in the psycho ward of Letterman General Hospital in San Francisco, after two years of fighting in the South Pacific, suffering from "combat fatigue" and malaria. I had never heard from him, nor had my mother since their divorce when I was two. I was alone. After Mrs. Spessard, the superintendent of the home, told us we were lucky to be there, with a place to sleep and something to eat, I handed over the baby to a nurse, my sisters were led off in one direction, and Mrs. Cooper warred down the stairs and clamped a firm hand on my shoulder. My heart beat violently but I was determined not to cry in front of these women, and I didn't. Of course I cried and whimpered and felt awfully sorry for myself for what seemed nearly the whole night. My bunk bed was near a window and

I crept there when everyone else was asleep and watched the dusk turn dark and the dark to dawn, till the tower of a downtown building far in the distance stopped switching colors, from pale green to orange to a kind of cream color.

I had learned to read in nursery school when I was three and four when we still lived in that shaky house by the railroad tracks in North Tulsa. I learned nothing much in the first grade at a Tulsa school and then less in the second from Mr. Tilford, sole teacher, principal, and proprietor of the Wingin' On Country School near the scruffy farm Charlie bought in 1942. Mr. Tilford's specialty was hate—how to hate the dirty Huns (whom he had personally fought in World War I) and even more the "Japs," bandy-legged, slant-eyed devils who raped defenseless white women and impaled babies on bayonets.

Mr. Tilford read Dick and Jane to us and we copied out their stories in Big Chief notebooks. I thought Dick and Jane, their dog Spot, and their parents were stupid, and gorged on the true life stories in old issues of *Reader's Digest,* which Mr. Tilford let me carry home to the farm. The only reading material there was my mother's Bible, a couple of tattered hymn books, and the Sears, Roebuck catalogue.

I hated the work, mostly hoeing weeds in the ten-acre cornfield Charlie planted, but I loved the woods and stayed in them as much as I could, much to the delight of our dogs Trixie, part fox terrier, and Shep, part everything. I took refuge from the constant bickering in the house between my mother and Charlie by literally hiding in the woods. The dogs and I ambushed the neighbor's steers, and, occasionally, by all three of us working carefully together, we managed to bring down a rabbit or a squirrel, Trixie holding the hapless animal down until it was still. I then pried it from her growling jaws and split the prize in two with a hatchet. The dogs gobbled and fought over their half while I washed the blood from mine in the nearby creek.

Charlie had fun making fun of me, as my mother would patiently skin the hind quarters of a rabbit and fry them for me—but I had the inward satisfaction of knowing that the dogs and I killed more game than he did with his lever-action Marlin .22 rifle with the fancy scope mounted on it. I knew also that he was envious of the devotion of "his" dogs to me. He worked as a carpenter, helping to build the Grand River dam during those years and drove down to the farm only on weekends, carrying what we hoped was a week's worth of groceries in a 1932 Dodge that just barely backfired up the steep hill from the creek.

Weekends were too often for Charlie and me to see each other, and I dreaded the two-week vacations he took during the spring and fall to plant and harvest the corn. I hated and avoided him and he knew it, and I did everything I could think of to undermine his influence with my mother. My hate, I later realized, was not for what Charlie had done to me but what I knew he was strong enough to do— almost anything my imagination could conjure. He hardly ever touched me after backhanding me across the mouth when I was six.

He came home early one Friday afternoon from the dam and I ambushed his car with hefty rocks, heaving one through the back windshield. Skidding to a stop he jumped out and chased me down before I could reach the house and the safety of my mother. He was so mad I thought he would punch me with his fists but he caught himself and sent a tremendous bony backhand across my face. I had one of my "seizures" then—I had suffered near-epileptic fits since almost being beheaded by that drunk woman's out-of-control automobile when I was two—twitching on the gravel road where he straddled me, rolling my eyeballs, and almost swallowing my tongue, grunting and moaning, out of my head.

My stepfather must have thought he might have killed me. My mother heard my cries and came screaming down the road and literally flew into him, beating at him with the sides of her fists. She told me she swore to kill him with a butcher knife if he ever touched me again.

Charlie's first wife, Mae, was now confined in the state "insane asylum" for, among other things, confusing Charlie with the Devil. She told the court that she woke up one morning, looked at her husband sleeping beside her, and noticed a set of reddish hairy horns protruding from his head. As she continued to gaze down at him, she saw a red tail with a black horny barb at the end twitching back and forth at the foot of the bed. The cruel-looking black barb bothered her most of all and she tried cutting it off with the biggest knife she could find in the kitchen. Though he told this story often and seemed to relish its details, my stepfather wanted no part of any woman with a knife. Even the threat of one was enough to keep him away from me.

Our psychological warfare, though, was so intense that he began to avoid me as much as I him. We came to a kind of understanding, a kind of truce: Stay out of my way and I'll stay out of yours. "Blockhead" was his favorite epithet for me, and he was never short of insults for my Dutch ancestry—the Dutch according to Charlie were just a bunch of "low Krautheads." He bragged what he would do to my real father if that "drunk" ever showed up around "his" place.

"My father is a hero," I shouted back. "He's fighting the Japs."

"Yeah, yeah," Charlie said, "the Japs are so little anybody could beat them up." I would fly out the door and take off for the woods. I knew my father was a hero, he had won the Bronze Star, my own grandfather told me that.

In 1943 my grandfather and grandmother Van Brunt came to visit my sister and me. My mother had forced Charlie to rent a house in Tulsa, not much of one, again one side of an old duplex, but at least she wasn't stuck down on "that old farm," alone except for her children, the nearest and not especially friendly neighbor two miles away, no telephone, no car, and no way to get anywhere.

"Burning good money," Charlie said, but he reluctantly shelled out for the rent, still coming home only on weekends from the dam. After taking some tests I was promoted to the third grade in a nameless Tulsa elementary school and read everything the school librarian would allow me to read, pestering her for the latest editions of the "adult magazines" reserved for teachers. I was trying to keep up with the war in the South Pacific. I was trying to keep up with my real father.

My grandfather Peter Van Brunt sat in the rocking chair on the front porch, my grandmother hunkered down beside him in a straight kitchen chair, spitting a gob of snuff over the porch railing now and then, until my mother hurriedly fetched her an empty syrup pail. My grandfather fired up his pipe and did most of the talking, shushing his wife when she tried to interrupt. I sat and leaned on the railing, squirming, self-conscious, and embarrassed. My sister Betsy sat in a corner, legs drawn up under her dress, watching our grandparents with large cautious eyes.

"Yes, he's a Van Brunt all right, Esther," said my grandfather, reaching out an enormous paw to examine my profile.

"And a Perkins, too," my grandmother piped in. Born Esther Perkins in south Kentucky of Irish immigrant parents from the Aran Islands, my father's mother at fifty still had mostly red hair, her steely-blue eyes unclouded by the cataracts that would nearly blind her later. My grandfather would die of a stroke within a scant two years but right now he was very much alive, large with a paunch he carried well, dressed neatly in a pair of pressed overalls, a railroader's striped shirt, and sporting a new pair of black high-top brogans. I admired especially his engineer's cap, which he removed from time to time to fan himself. His widow's peaks were pronounced but at

At eleven years of age, Tulsa Children's Home, 1947

sixty he still had what was then called a full head of hair, though it had turned salt-and-pepper gray.

Over the next two hours I learned of the glorious history of the American Van Brundt clan (my grandfather told me to insist on spelling our name with the aristocratic "d"). We had been lords of the Hudson, patroons with mansions and servants, well before the upstart English had taken over the territory of New Amsterdam. Our direct ancestor, "The Colonel," disgruntled at losing a vast inheritance, had drifted south in the late eighteenth century, to Kentucky first, then Tennessee, and finally to the delta land of southeast Arkansas, where it abuts on the Mississippi River, then a wilderness watery and snake-ridden, from which he hewed, with the cooperation of red and black slaves, a plantation that became renowned for the quality of its cotton, and the good manners and hospitality of its proprietor.

My head swelled, my heart turned righteous with indignation at our present state, and my imagination knew no boundaries. I lay close in my grandfather's lap now, my arms around his ample girth. At last I was home, among my own, blood-, bone-, and sinew-connected to this old man and to our common male ancestor, a pioneer, a hero, a man who had helped build this country.

When I turned to look up into my grandfather's visionary blue eyes, I saw my own small features magnified by his, the same broad forehead, straight-as-an-arrow nose, smallish mouth, and dimpled chin. He rose to show me the chocolate birthmark indented on the small of his back, and I showed him mine. I, alone, of all his many grandchildren, had that mark—the birthmark of an aristocrat, he declared. So it had been, so it would be. The mantle of Van Brundt glory had been passed on to me, and I was more than willing to wear it. For years I took refuge in the imaginary land of my ancestors.

The fact was, as one Scots-Irish peasant named Charles Bryan Reynolds made sure I knew, my grandfather was an ex-bootlegger who had made a small fortune on illicit whiskey during the twenties, with which he bought a large farm, only to lose it to the wind during the Dust Bowl and Depression thirties. After losing the big farm, on which he hoped to rebuild a bit of Van Brundt glory, my grandfather and his numerous sons were reduced to doing yard work for the oil-rich families in south Tulsa. He called himself a contractor but was in fact just another hired hand, mowing lawns, topping out trees, and shaping shrubbery.

"Yes, sir! A real nabob," Charlie cackled over supper that evening. "I hope that mole don't turn cancerous on you. There was an old boy at the dam had one of them." Turning to mother, he continued: "He bit the *big* bullet, didn't git out of this world alive." He cackled some more then, displaying that set of stained horse teeth, squarish but long, his whole mouth taken up by his teeth. When Charlie smiled, I thought, he was like a mule laying bare its teeth, getting ready to kick you.

I did not deign to answer, but crossed my fingers under the table, the way Grandmother Van Brundt showed me how to ward off evil spells. I looked blank and shut up bragging about my grandfather. I knew who and what I was, I thought, and no amount of heckling from some lowlife redneck was to dissuade me from my belief that I had been handpicked by destiny to restore the rightful luster to the Van Brundt name. "You wait," I said to myself, "you just wait."

The daily shower ordeal over, boys, eleven and under, filed into the large rectangular dorm and stood by narrow, pillowless, bunk beds while Cooper tallied each boy and bunk in her book. We slept naked during the summer, and in hand-me-down longjohns when it was cold. Friends would later remark on my penchant for pajamas. They, of course, bragged of sleeping nude. Don't know me too soon, I would think. Each of us accords with stereotypes, rebelling against the kind of clothes we were made to wear as children, habits and customs thereof. "You are *so* middle-class," a Vassar graduate told me during the sixties—speaking for herself I thought. I suffered enough from nightmares, without riding naked into them.

Speaking of the middle class, its children quickly learn that compliments and flattery grease the wagon wheels of daily life. Working-class children learn insults, the kind that hurt, about one's mother and father, uncles and cousins, or lack of them. At the children's home we clawed at one another's self-esteem until the only way of not feeling bad was to make someone else feel worse, reduce him to bawling. The best candidates were the new and usually younger boys who had not yet formed a skein of hate and contempt to protect their emotional wounds—a newly dead mother, a convict father who never wrote, blood kin that never visited on the last Sunday of the month, "visiting day." A normal initiation was for an eight-year-old to be pushed and prodded across the playground by a dozen or so older boys, who would chant insanely over and over, "Your mother's dead / Your father's a Red / You wet the bed / You little shithead." Wretched rhyme. Welcome to our world, kid, welcome to our world.

In the late and hot Oklahoma summers we would be loaded on stakeboard trucks and hauled off to work the fields on the farms of "big contributors." For our labor the home received half the harvest of string beans, corn, or melons, and we were treated to "lunches" of pork chops or roast beef and potatoes, with fresh fruit pie and milk for dessert. We would return that evening to our usual diet of Chef Boy-R-Dee canned spaghetti and watery bread pudding at the home.

Brown-bottomed oatmeal alternated at breakfast with scrambled powdered eggs, both agglutinative masses that lay in the stomach like mossy stones. We were not allowed to eat lunch at the John J. Pershing Elementary School cafeteria, but had to walk and half-run to the home and back for the usual burnt macaroni and cheese. One of superintendent Spessard's favorite sayings was there are no free lunches. I thought the implied metaphor banal and mean then and despise those who still use it. David Stockman's tombstone should be a giant ketchup bottle. When we received World War II K-rations that lasted a month, they were a treat, and so were the infrequent peanut-butter-and-jelly sandwiches. My best friend Jack

Pease swiped candy bars from grocery stores and bragged about it but of course the Peases were famous bank robbers, murderers, and thieves, going back to the time of Oklahoma Territory. When Jack would toss me a Milky Way after school, I ate it gratefully and did not reflect on its rightful ownership.

My real home was the Phillips Memorial Library, a spacious room on the first floor across from Mrs. Spessard's office. A marble fireplace, adorned with nymphs and fauns, reflected the refulgent glow of the afternoon sun, and shelf upon shelf of virgin editions of Nancy Drew, the Hardy Boys, the Bobbsey Twins, Tom Swift, and a lavishly illustrated complete Mark Twain gleamed in stiff blue covers with gold lettering on the spines.

Impatiently I would separate the pages of a new book in a series with a special sky-blue-handled knife I placed back in its groove beneath the oil portrait of my benefactor (his widow, really, a chatty lady draped in fur stoles, their attenuated heads jouncing glass-eyed above her swinging hips as she came traipsing down the forbidden hallway from the girls' wing to

"With my sister Betsy and our Choctaw grandmother, Rebecca," Children's Home, 1945

our own, trailing the delicious aroma of French perfume. Mrs. Spessard in her Sunday best on one elbow, the chairman of the fund-raising committee on the other, Mrs. Harrison Phillips II was a splendid personage whose black chauffeur always had his arms full of candy and new plastic toys, a bag of candy and a toy for each boy and girl). Mr. Phillips was himself a large hearty-looking person in a dark blue suit, snowy-white shirt topped with a snazzy bow tie, a long unlit cigar tucked deftly between the knuckles of his right hand. "Uncle," I called him fondly. None of the other kids came into the library so we kept each other company for years.

I fell madly in love with Nancy Drew, whip-smart girl that she was, plucky enough to dare murderers and haunted houses in the dead of night, always outwitting both malefactors and grownups who thought they knew all the answers . . . Tom Sawyer, Tom Swift (boy inventor), and Huck Finn were some of my other favorites. Of course I identified with Huck the most, low-class and yet noble as he was, and Jim, wise and gentle as a genie, and superstitious as my half-Choctaw grandmother Rebecca, who cajoled either Charlie or one of her sons into driving her out to see us on visiting day, bringing nothing but herself, an ample female warmth to which my sisters and I clung as to a raft on a flooding river.

I disdained the usual children's books of the times, most of the ones in the school library, already treacly with false sentiments and little do-gooders that never went to the bathroom or had snotty noses. I admired the violence of authentic emotions. Jack London and Mark Twain were probably the only "literary" authors whose works were collected by Mrs. Phillips or her advisor. I immediately felt the difference between the fascinating characters in their books and the ones in the Hardy Boys and the Bobbsey Twins—although I enjoyed the latter and wished that all parents were as reasonable as theirs.

Next to Huck Finn, my true Penelope, were the animal books, London's *Call of the Wild* and *White Fang* and the Black Stallion series of William Farley. I was not a literary snob and read anything that would allow my imagination off the ground. The characters in good books acted the way people should, dramatically and decisively, and with a purpose. My real-life companions, Jack Pease included, were, by comparison, drab and predictable.

I led half-a-dozen of them in a runaway attempt during the early morning hours of a humid July day (my birthday, I think I decided to give myself at least one present) to the Arkansas River where we would, of course, build or find a raft, drift down the sand-barred Arkansas to the Mississippi where we would have adventures like Huck and Jim all the way down to New Orleans. There, we would catch a freighter to the Orient and have more adventures.

Late that afternoon when we were all bedraggled and hungry and tired, some of the younger boys started whimpering. Even Jack sided with those who wanted to trek back to the home. We had eaten only the Jello packets stolen from basement stores (while Mrs. Cooper snored deliciously overhead) and the remains of a few half-rotten watermelons salvaged from scraggly gardens. I was hungry, thirsty, tired, and disgusted but I had no intention of returning to the good graces of Spessard, Cooper, and Company. I agreed to go with these cowards only as far as the wrought-iron gate of the home, but a police cruiser stopped us as we struggled up the final hill before the entrance to the home. Mrs. Spessard insisted we be taken to the police station, "like common criminals," and there we suffered a long harangue by an over-sized police sergeant, who immediately divined that I was the ringleader and directed his gaze straight into my face. His eyes were like the agates we prized in marble games, cloudy and yet rock hard.

Other human beings were becoming increasingly unreal to me. I allowed into my consciousness only those aristocratic beings (Huck, Tom, Nancy, the stallion, et al.) I thought belonged there. Actually, I hoped the sergeant would use the nightstick he tapped menacingly on the desk as he lectured us. That would have confirmed my low opinion of human nature in general, and authority figures in particular. Later I knew the man was well-meaning and trying to be kind.

He told us we might have been kidnapped by perverts who liked young boys (I puzzled over that), murdered by escaped convicts from the state prison, poisoned by crazy old ladies or, most likely, mutilated by drunk drivers. He said we were lucky there were six of us, one or two wouldn't have stood a chance. I was still mad as hell about not finding a raft, and the defection of trusted lieutenants to the enemy cause. I stood there, sullen and frustrated, in disgrace.

"I don't like you boys much," the sergeant continued. "We been out half the night and all today looking for you all." He glanced around the dog-eared squad room at some other policeman lounging around.

"Instead of apprehending real criminals we been searching for a bunch of raggedy-ass orphan boys that ain't got the God-given sense to stay in a place where they're fed and housed and get to go to school."

"And have a playground and balls to throw around," piped in another officer.

"And have a playground and balls to throw around," repeated the sergeant, and the thought of a playground with balls to throw around seemed to infuriate him. He got up and stood over me at the head of the bench. "You wanna make your own livin', boy, go ahead, git outta here. Go hop a freight train. You'd be cornholed to death in a week." The other three policemen guffawed at this and nodded their heads. I had got the idea of catching a freight train from a Jack London book, mentioning the possibility of it when the others gave up on finding a raft conveniently tied to a tree, by the bank of the river—as Huck Finn had. We found only mud-caked drift-wood, certainly nothing to make a decent raft of. I was disappointed in my imaginary hero, but of course he had lived in better days.

I did not like being made fun of, laughed at. I was now eleven, nearly six feet of gangly arms and legs, and was known as one rough guy in the sixth grade. I could throw a regulation football over fifty yards with fair accuracy and was much in demand as a quarterback in after-school games, even by the junior high guys who sometimes joined us, turning our games of touch into tackle. I loved to bore a bony shoulder into some fat seventh grader's gut and hear him grunt and look surprised. The satisfying thwack of contact gave me a sense of power, the elation of seeing a stranger in pain instead of my own head from butting a wall. These guys didn't know it but I had the advantage of years of practice at gaining my goat-like momentum.

"Nobody's cornholing me," I told the sergeant, not even knowing the real meaning of the word. Though scared enough, I was mad, too, and tried to affect the insouciance of one of the East Side gang whose adventures we cheered at the movies the Junior League ladies escorted us to. I managed only to be squeaky, though, to the sergeant, almost swallowing that mysterious word. I wondered if it was in the big dictionary in the Phillips library.

"Son," the sergeant replied, "Mrs. Spessard said I should whip all you boys." Already a wide black belt with a cruel-looking steel buckle had appeared in his hands. He must have been hiding it behind his back. "But," he continued, "I think I'll just concentrate on you."

The beating I took in an adjacent room was thorough and passionless. The sergeant neither spoke nor prayed. He did help me up from the floor where I lay doubled up and writhing. I had grunted and gritted my teeth, but a fierce and unnatural pride kept me from crying out. Damn! He was a pro with that belt, I thought, unerringly seeking out the fleshy parts of my lank body. I hated him as he led me to a nearby bathroom to clean up, but admired him, too, as one who knew the importance of a job well done. I ached and smarted for weeks but strangely accepted the punishment as my due, as something one real man might do to another, and as a valuable lesson in how far my powers extended. Cooper and even Spessard might be cowed by my size now but this policeman had not been impressed at all. He had shown me just how vulnerable I was, and I was not soon again to confuse the seductive fantasies of books and movies with the cinder-block abrasiveness of everyday life. Good-bye, childhood. I was tough only in my imagination, I decided, and that was where I intended to live.

I arrived in New York City in June 1958, fresh degree in hand, not yet twenty-two, determined and confident that within ten years I would be a world-famous writer. My stories had been praised in class, I still bore the birthmark my long-dead grandfather bragged of, and two tightly folded-together fifty-dollar bills scrunched in the watch pocket of my jeans.

I was soon settled in a seventy-dollar-a-month cold-water flat in Little Italy south of Houston Street, and working at WBAI radio station cataloging records. I worked with ballet dancers (and soon began to date one), a soprano from Texas, a touchy Italian-American tenor, an Abstract Expressionist painter, and a playwright (who had heard all the latest lowdown gossip about Tennessee Williams). Pacifica Radio was just starting up then and we worked in shifts round the clock, typing data from record jackets on three-by-five index cards.

During the first few months in New York I was ecstatic. I knew there was something better than Oklahoma, and here it was. *La Boheme!* Despite past experiences, I was blithe and ignorant and believed the arts were exempt from the general corruption of human nature. I got my ideas of the artist's proper integrity from Hemingway and Faulkner. I would ask for no favors and give none.

I tried to pick up women at the White Horse Tavern, famous then as the favored bar of the late Dylan Thomas, and had a fair success. L., an older Jewish woman, taught me more about sex in two weeks than I had ever learned in Oklahoma. I was a willing student, and she suggested I might become a gigolo. I was complimented and insulted at the same time. I wrote furiously between midnight and dawn, typing out the longhand drafts of my stories and poems on a new Hermes Rocket ("weighs only six pounds, take it with you to Europe") that I spent my first WBAI paycheck on.

"From Brooklyn Bridge," New York, 1968

The fact that my early stories were dull and my poems bathetic (though the poems had *some* good images my White Horse and WBAI friends insisted) did not, of course, seem obvious to me. I brought my dates to poetry readings at coffee shops and wondered why they were bored by the likes of Ginsberg and Corso. I drank with Alfred K. and other relics of the age of Bohemia in Greenwich Village and styled myself as a true bohemian.

After reading one of my stories, an older writer at the White Horse suggested that I study with Mark Van Doren at Columbia. I was allowed to monitor one of his classes on seventeenth-century English literature. I wallowed in the sonorities of Sir Thomas Browne and John Donne, the grave sweetness of Herbert, the neat wit of Andrew Marvell. We read commentaries on these sacred personages, including T. S. Eliot's. Eliot was persuasive and so was Van Doren, but there was something off-putting about these literary aristocrats. I did not feel a sense of kinship with them, as I did with Faulkner and Hemingway, Hart Crane and e.e. cummings.

The first time I spoke up in class, more than a few smiles and headshakes greeted my comments. My classmates were mostly male and mostly prep-school and Ivy League–educated. My Oklahoma drawl was broad and eye-squinching. Almost unconsciously I began aping the patrician accent of our good professor. Always an excellent mimic (I had done my stepfather perfectly for years), I could enunciate a fair copy of a Van Doren lecture by the time that class was over.

Van Doren encouraged me with an unofficial *B* (not a bad grade then, though I was not a matriculated student) and suggested that I should enroll in graduate school. Columbia courses even then were a few hundred dollars each, much more than I could borrow or earn. He was a thoroughly decent man, though, and gave me the good advice that I was a more natural poet than fiction writer. My only acceptance during the first two New York years was of a short poem "Atlas Shrugged" by the venerable old poetry magazine *Poet Lore.*

So I settled down to become a poet. I had brought my worn copy of Brooks' and Warren's *Understanding Poetry* with me from Oklahoma and it was my literary bible. Dutifully I labored over sonnets

Hambidge Center, Rabun Gap, Georgia, 1976

and sestinas. I studied metrics by reading Robert Frost and was intrigued by his tricks of syntax, and impressed by his theory of running natural speech rhythms across various meters in a kind of counterpoint. The rhythms of American speech were fascinating, the permutations inexhaustible.

I sent my poems out to literary magazines and ran literally into a wall of printed impersonal rejection slips, but I was proud of them in a perverse way (at least they proved I was a working writer) and arranged a formal collection of them on a bulletin board salvaged from the Commerce Street gutter. My new digs, a fifth-floor walkup apartment on the corner of Bedford and Commerce, were catercorner from the preposterously narrow house of Edna St. Vincent Millay on Bedford, and I thought that a good omen, since I had early gone to school on Millay's poems, good technician that she was.

I wrote and memorized Crane, Millay, Stevens, Eliot, Williams. I learned to write images from studying C. F. MacIntyre's translations of the early Rilke (I did not then appreciate the odes which I now consider among the greatest poems of this century) and by puzzling over Harold Henderson's great if short book on Japanese poetry. I read some early Robert Bly translations of Neruda and Jimenez, Machado and Lorca, and was impressed enough to fill the margins of those thin books with notes. I did not like Walt Whitman and still do not. I thought there was something phoney about the persona of the caped poet always being poetic. He was a windbag, with a few startling and authentic moments.

I read and reread Walter Jackson Bates's biography of my teenage hero John Keats; I lingered over the exquisite long letters. I loved Keats, the man, the poet, generous spirit. He could, I was sure, have equalled Shakespeare if he had lived longer than the measly twenty-six years of his destiny. A poor boy, mostly an autodidact, he whipped bullies with his fists, and died maligned by upper-class critics, who could not stand the idea that a mere "stable boy" could be blessed by so much talent. I thought of Keats as my spiritual father and still do.

I read and wrote and studied my texts during those early morning hours, until the sky turned mauve and purple over the West Village rooftops, isolated water towers, a campanile, TV aerials, all the way to Sixth Avenue. I felt like Wordsworth on Westminster Bridge: "And all that mighty heart is lying still." I listened to Mozart, Beethoven, Schubert, and Sibelius with Jinx, an orange alley cat I had picked up on the street when he was a kitten. He was the perfect companion, snoring faintly beside me. "My home is in my head," I wrote, and continued to live in my imagination. I wrote and wrote and rewrote and revised, trying in my head-busting, straight-ahead way to compose what I would later call "The Perfect Yvor Winters Poem."

I saw this woman and that one, no one for very long. When drunk beyond a certain point I became paranoid, hostile, "an injustice seeker," as a psychiatrist would later tell me. All the conflicts and confusions of my childhood would come raging up. I called friends and told them what I really thought of them. I had many lovers but I was alone. No one understood me but John Keats and perhaps Hart Crane. I did not write to anyone in Oklahoma. I hated the fact that I had been born there, and I unconsciously despised the orphan boy I had been there. I envied the middle-class childhoods of some of my friends, their advantages, their sense of entitlement. I delighted in turning others as sour and bitter as I was at my worst. In romance I was a one-man wrecking crew. No woman could put up with my rages. I needed psychiatric help but scorned psychiatrists as cranks. Besides, artists needed to be neurotic, didn't they? That was the source of their power. Anyway, in the spirit of the times, I thought anyone adjusted to our sick society insane. I was a mess, but some of the poems I wrote during the early and mid-sixties weren't bad.

By 1966 I was so disgusted with myself and the country I lived in I decided to live in Europe, to become an expatriate. Politically I suppose I was an anarchist-Luddite. I wanted the whole power structure of American society torn down so that childhoods like mine could not be repeated. I was always for the underdog, all right, but mostly that meant me. As for political change, I had tried working with some radicals on the Lower East Side, and found the cadre-leaders insufferable. They were always correcting my opinions. I was the only working-class member of a committee and I felt the others were patronizing me. I was their "Okie." To hell with them, their slogans and group-think. I had always been on my own.

The *Queen Frederika* was an ancient, German-built liner that now flew the blue-and-white flag of Greece. I had sold my furniture, and the rights to my Commerce Street apartment, and some odds and ends for nearly two thousand dollars—after reading and believing an article in one of the writers' magazines: "Greece: Paradise for Writers." I was still a sucker for the written word, and Huck Finn had infected me early on with a taste for adventure.

Of course I couldn't travel second class aboard an ocean liner. I was a pitiful snob so although I could not afford the thousand for first-class passage I did pay six hundred for "Captain's Class," which entitled me to eat and hobnob with a few rich Greek-American families, not the international set I had imagined dancing and dining and fornicating in the sacred precincts of first class. The Greeks there were clannish, spoke only to one another and then usually in Greek. My romantic adventure at sea was turning into a bore. There were no attractive single women in first class so I started hanging out with the regular people when we were about halfway across the Atlantic. One night I was invited to smoke grass with N. and her teenaged companion.

I had been in love before, had left women and had them leave me. I suffered most over O., after she married someone else—because he was a professional man, she told me, could support her and her painting, and because marriage to him meant exchanging her green card for a certificate of citizenship. I went violently crazy for a few weeks after their marriage, crying and moaning to Sibelius's Violin Concerto, so drunk I couldn't get up off the floor, estranging the neighbors by refusing to turn down the volume, picking fistfights in bars, not caring whether I won or lost them so long as I got in some good licks.

I vowed after that never to let anyone get as close to me again. O. and I had read Faulkner's *The Wild Palms* together. We *were* the doomed lovers in that story: she died symbolically and "between grief and nothing" I took grief. O., of course, had a firm layer of Swedish common sense in her romantic mixture. I hated the very thought of limitations, of boundaries—they were for dull peasants, in the gray zones of what Charlie Reynolds called "horse sense." Well, horses had to be led from burning barns, the one we had at the farm would stand on your foot when she got the chance and try to bite you at every opportunity. They were all instinct, with brains the size of walnuts. If that was what common sense was, I wanted no part of its mean mentality. But I thought I might die of grief during those weeks. I had been abandoned again, and it took months if not years for the desolation to leave.

But N. was different. Our romance was shipboard, starlight and ouzo, retsina and spicy Greek food that was reputed to have the effect of an aphrodisiac. We needed no such help. I was twenty-nine, she still nineteen, we ached with love for each other. We danced slow-motion across the Mediterranean, the old Greeks smiled and raised their glasses to us, long streams of phosphorescence trailed from the stern, Europe lay off the port bow, Africa off the right, Italy was dead ahead, and Greece a dip across the Adriatic.

The relationship between N. and me was symbiotic. We were brother and sister, father and daughter, mother and son, dependent on each other as Siamese twins in a new and strange country. Greeks had a disconcerting way of staring at foreigners, the same way young children stare without a trace of self-consciousness at adults. In Oklahoma a stare was hostile—a prelude to combat. A friend explained later that the Greeks were merely intensely curious. I thought they were merely yokels and rude ones.

We found a large room with a balcony in a bright hilltop house, fragrant with pots and planters of flowers and shrubs the French-speaking landlady watered with a long-nose can. She wore a blue silk bathrobe with a yellow dragon emblazoned on the back, Chinese I thought or perhaps Japanese, and shuffled around the veranda where we took breakfast in upturned Turkish house shoes, also blue. We called her Madame and she reminded us of a character in *Zorba the Greek,* the sad but appealing old French tart that Anthony Quinn takes advantage of. Her coffee was delicious, and she served croissants from her own kitchen. We looked down early mornings on the jumbled rooftops of Athens, across to the dew-sparkling slopes of the Acropolis. We did not admit the slightest imperfection in our foreign paradise. To hell with the charcoal haze of exhaust fumes that hung over downtown Athens.

This was our youth, and we would take it here and on the islands, amid the bluest sea in the world, on Spetsai, on Hydra, on Mykonos—when it was still just another Greek island visited by cruise ships—and in the Athens Museum, where I gazed for hours at the magnificent bronze statue of Zeus-Poseidon. If God took the form of a larger-than-life statue, this would surely be him.

We saw *The Sound of Music* with Greek subtitles and walked back to the "Communist Hotel." We had to leave the relatively expensive spaciousness of Madame's house for a dank room we rented for a dollar a night. The proprietor was a Communist and bragged about it, the first such true believer I had met. His rooms stank, though, and we felt cheated and soon left Athens for the islands. The islanders didn't stare as much at us as the Athenians. There was an excellent museum on Mykonos, and its beaches then were unspoiled by tourist hordes. We were, of course, travelers and explorers, not tourists. We nearly got seasick on the small boat to Delos, climbing the waves and sliding down them, but the deserted island was worth the discomfort. We peeked at the decorative tiles of 2,500-year-old houses, rubbed the heads of the Naxian lions, and stood for a long afternoon hour by the altar on top of the island's

"At an upstate New York school," 1987

highest hill, the sea surrounding the island, surrounding us, the wind in the long hay grass washing over it like an invisible surf.

On the ferry to Venice, N. had honeymoon sickness and stayed in our cabin hard by the engine room most of the first day. She felt better by the time we docked at Dubrovnik. We walked up the steep hill to the town and she bought a gorgeous fisherman's sweater to cheer herself up. We drank instant Nescafé, "American coffee," at a hotel restaurant, paid for it in dollars and received Yugoslavian dinars in change. The waiter looked blank when we asked the denominations of the coins. Our Baedeker was *Europe on $5 a Day* and we were trying to watch our expenses. We thought our next stop Corfu was overrated, and were back on board well before the ship sailed for Venice. The Adriatic was glass-smooth, illumined by a full moon. The workingmen Greeks and Turks on board stared hungrily at N. as we strolled around the small deck. She looked at them in disgust, saying she had never felt less sexy.

On that bright May morning in 1966 the wind must have been blowing the wrong way because

Venice, which we had been told was foul, was fragrant with flowers and the pleasant graveyard smell of antiquity. N. bargained in French with the shouting porters on the dock. The winner trundled our suitcases to a small albergo that had a circular staircase in the center and balconies overlooking a canal. N. loved Venice. I thought most of the Italians there were out to scam the tourists, and I was glad when we boarded the southbound train two weeks later for Florence. I liked Florence and so did N. We stayed for nearly two months at the Albergo Speranza e Commercio (The Inn of Hope and Commerce) about a half-mile, after-midnight walk from the old train station, across from a bakery, next door to a cheese shop.

We ate loads of pasta and drank cheap but good Italian red wine; we stood in line with handkerchief-headed Italian housewives to buy warm bread from the bakery when it reopened in the afternoon, and ate it with soft Provolone from the cheese shop. The stone house of the Albergo was so old the tile floors canted, but we loved our large room on the fifth floor, bathroom and running water in the hall, with windows that opened on a courtyard loud with the same voices we heard at the bakery. This was the real Italy, working-class—though our esteemed proprietor was a Contessa, the house having been in the family for centuries, and she would bore her tenants (ten dollars a week) with interminable details of the family tree, though she was slow enough to replace the bed we broke on our first night, but when she did it was enormous and the softest bed I ever slept in. Giacomo the handyman carried up the bed, piece by piece, dwarfed by the huge mattress, and assembled it, then stood back—as a painter from a masterpiece—with his arms open. He was a bandy-legged little man with a gap-toothed smile. He refused the tip I offered him, looking at both of us gravely, bowed and took his leave, having bestowed on us the ancient gift of grace of heart.

We grew museum-weary, even in Florence. We spent days if not weeks at the Ufizzi and Pitti Palace. I liked Donatello's small bronze David better than Michelangelo's giant marble. I didn't think it odd then that the two statues I liked best were of men at war—the Zeus-Poseidon's arm drawn back with a spear or trident, David standing over the head of Goliath.

More, different, somewhere else. How about Barcelona. A couple of weeks there and it was on to hot and dusty Madrid where the Prado was the only thing I found interesting. N. had her eye firmly fixed on Morocco. We took the train to Algeciras and a ferry to Tangier. I was not comfortable there, neither on the beach nor in the Casbah—dirty, loud, with beggars pulling at your sleeves. N. loved the place and spoke French to the Arabs.

Harry Smith's letter inviting us to Austria came just in time. I was determined to leave Morocco, on my own if necessary. Harry, his wife Marian, and their three young children were summering in an archduke's baronial manor that overlooked the water of Unterach-am-Attersee. Marian's parents were rich and a whole extended family of Petchek's were ensconced in "the castle" when we arrived, after a one-week stopover in Paris. We had been so broke in Tangier I hocked my English raincoat to buy food. In the castle one left one's shoes outside the door at night for the butler to polish. The butler's wife was the cook and housekeeper, in charge of numerous maids who knocked on our door at inappropriate times. Social life at the castle was obligatory and boring and we enjoyed ourselves only when driving around the countryside with Harry and Marian, and to Salzburg for a Mozart concert, followed by a beerhall dinner.

The Petchecks were old-world-mannerly and moralistic. When N.'s mother phoned and asked for her by her rightful and maiden name, Marian's mother reckoned we were not properly man and wife. The next morning Harry accompanied us on our walk to the village and told us we would have to leave the castle, as soon as possible. We moved to a desolate room in the back of a villager's house. We were almost broke, it was late August, turning chilly and rainy in the mountains, and we were waiting for money orders from home.

Finally, they arrived. Good-bye, Austria, and we hope we never see you again, with your jack-booted policemen who, we suspected, made anti-Semitic remarks about N.'s long Jewish nose. There was something sinister about the Austrians, so bowingly polite to one's face while they cheated and short-changed tourists at every opportunity.

The last week of August in Paris was windy and cool, spacious along the boulevards on the Left Bank. The Parisians who had not fled the city for the annual holiday seemed more polite now. I wrote well during the next two weeks on the Hermes, revising the twenty-odd poems I had started in Greece, Italy, Spain, Morocco, and France. We took long walks on the gravel paths in the parks, we held hands and made love often. N. would have to leave soon. She had been six months away from home and her parents were worried about her. Who was this "poet" she had been traveling around with? What did he do for a living?

The author at the Virginia Center, 1987

Did he teach at a university? Did he have a job to return to?

Alas, I was a poor poet who did odd office jobs for a living, but I felt myself rich with the poems in manuscript of my first book *Uncertainties,* which Harry Smith would publish under his own imprint of The Smith, Publishers two years later. I saw N. to the airport bus, both of us in tears. I ran alongside the bus, waving and waving. Abandoned again, I walked back to the cheap pension and made myself sleep round-the-clock.

Two months later N.'s parents were not particularly glad to meet me. N. and I had a glorious reunion night in the hotel across West End Avenue from the apartment house where her family lived. I was soon writing "poetic" captions for the photographs in her father's interior design magazine. It was boring work, beneath my talents I thought, but I showed up dutifully at her father's office every morning, saw N. evenings two or three times a week and then more often when her uncle found an apartment for me on West Eighty-second Street.

I applied for a job as a reporter at Fairchild Publications and got one, covering housewares fairs

for *Home Furnishings Daily,* among other duties. I bought N. an engagement ring with a seven-point diamond that did not exactly knock your eyes out. But she was proud of it—for a while. After four months at Fairchild I was fired for sloppy work. I hated checking facts for boring articles and interviews, and would often make them up. My pieces read well whether factually true or not but the managing editor of *Home Furnishings Daily* did not appreciate my literary flair.

N.'s parents gave up on me then and, I believe, urged her to. On a ragged wet day in Central Park she handed back the pitifully thin engagement ring. We could continue to see each other from time to time but she definitely did not want to marry me, or anyone else.

Nearly seventeen years later N. phoned the Lower East Side cafe where I was doing a reading with my old friend Laura Foreman and left a message. I had been living with J., first in Bowie, Maryland, and then on Capitol Hill for six years. Four of my books had been published, the first two by Harry Smith and the third and fourth by Carnegie-

Mellon University Press. A friend, Michael Rutherford, had published a chapbook of my nature poems, *Feral,* in 1975. *For Luck: Poems 1962–1977,* my third book, published by Carnegie-Mellon University Press, had been favorably reviewed in the *New York Times Book Review* by David Ignatow. I got several readings and short-term residencies on the strength of that review and others, and I was doing well enough in 1984 when N. tried to call me in New York—though I was having serious problems trying to switch from a tight lyric style to one more capable of bearing a long narrative. I knew well enough that most of the work I did in the early and mid-eighties was bad, experiments with narrative that simply did not work.

J., a photographer whom I had met at Ragdale, an artists' colony near Chicago in 1979, bore with me through those difficult times. I drank too much, abused her verbally, and her sound and fundamentally cheerful nature turned sour in the wake of my onslaughts. I stayed away longer and more often at colonies. Truthfully, though I enjoyed a certain reputation in the Washington, D.C., area, I was in despair about my life and my work. I was nearly fifty years old and going nowhere working as a poet-in-the-schools and teaching workshops for adults at The Writer's Center. I labored to do a good job both with adults and children, but my heart was not in my teaching. It interfered with my work. I did it merely for the money, which was not very good, and dreaded the actual classroom teaching. I was cheating myself and my students, and I felt more and more helpless about my work.

I tried calling N. back that May night in 1984 but the guy who took the message was drunk and got the number wrong. I could have called information, but did I really want to talk to her? I wasn't sure, but I did send her a postcard from the Ucross Foundation in Wyoming that fall, and we had our reunion dinner in February 1985. I was teaching weekdays at elementary schools on Long Island and Saturdays at The Writer's Center in Washington, over-extending myself, getting up at 4:30 to get to my first class in North Babylon, riding the New York Air shuttle back and forth on weekends.

N. looked mature and beautiful at dinner, no longer the grave, young woman I had known, much more secure now—though we both were suspicious of the other, the conversation halting and guarded. I sweated over the lobster, gave up on it, and chain-smoked cigarettes. We talked a little of old times but studiously avoided mentioning what was in the back of both our minds, the abortion she had in 1967. "Our child," nearly four months in the womb, had been a boy, the doctor told her, and perfectly formed

for his age. She blamed me for not letting her have the abortion sooner. I pleaded with her to have the baby and to marry me, but she was determined to be an actress and had no room in her life for a baby or a husband. So she had the awful abortion, nearly died of its aftermath, had a nose job a few months later, for which her father paid, as well as for a wardrobe of new clothes, and was off to New Haven and Yale with a theater director. I drank too much, bitter and alone, for years after that, and finally, more out of indifference and loneliness than love, ended up in L.'s small apartment on Leroy Street. I didn't love L. and she knew it but she loved me and that was enough for eight years—until I met twenty-two-year-old J. at Ragdale, the love of my life, who thought I was a great poet, who loved and supported me in every way she could think of for the next seven years.

In 1983, when we moved to A Street S.E. in Washington, J. convinced me to see a psychiatrist, a Jungian, Dr. F., at Georgetown University. If she had not, I might not be alive and writing this memoir in 1991. More and more during those years I was drawn to suicide. All my emotional barriers were coming down. I was breaking up.

Dr. F. prescribed Xanax for my depression and acute anxiety attacks. I tried to quit drinking, at least in front of J., who was terrified of me when I changed into a drunken, out-of-control Mr. Hyde. I tried to tell Dr. F. everything I could think of about my past, no matter how shameful, including two episodes of childhood incest. For the first time I told another human being exactly what I thought and felt—or tried to. I had been lying to myself and others for so long, putting on and taking off the masks of false personae, the habit was almost impossible to break. When I confessed to Dr. F. that I had lied to him in a few particulars, he said I needed to tell those lies. He encouraged me to have fantasies but not to drink and try acting them out. I needed to see Dr. F. two or three times a week but I could afford an appointment only every two weeks. I was doing my best though to alleviate a deteriorating condition, and I thought my work started to improve—when I had time for it.

J. was in Africa during the winter of 1985, visiting her older sister who worked for the World Bank in Abijan, the Ivory Coast. I was lonely and called N. and we arranged a date for that first dinner in seventeen years. We took long walks on the Lower East Side, had brunch at the South Street Seaport, and went to movies where we held hands almost shyly. After seeing *Amadeus* about two months after that first dinner, she invited me to the Prince Street apartment.

J. is back at A Street now. I sleep with her on Saturday nights and with N. on Sundays. I teach five and a half days a week, feel exhausted and confused, but also exhilarated. "The Captain's Paradise," Dr. F. tells me. "Every red-blooded American boy's dream, a girl in every port." I had seen the Alec Guinness movie in which he plays a sea captain with two wives. In the picture the situation was funny and sexy, in real life it was turning into one of my usual nightmares.

"Watch out," Dr. F. warned, "you might lose both of them."

I do watch out. I tell J. elaborate lies about why I must return to New York early on Sunday mornings. I rush from the airport to N.'s apartment. It is as if seventeen years had not passed. We love each other again, with the same passion we had in Greece and Italy, Barcelona and Paris. Her father had died, her mother is affable and glad to see me. I feel awful. J. and I have made a commitment to each other for life. I have sundered our old-fashioned pact of fidelity. Never mind that the two women I am sleeping with on weekends are the two great loves of my life. I am not a natural philanderer. But I cannot stand the thought of losing either of them.

That summer I go away to another colony. I must do my work. J. understands. She respects my need for solitude. She loves me, she loves my work. I want mightily to justify her faith in me. N. calls me at the colony, in tears. Her dog has been hit by a truck. Can't I come down for a few days? Yes, of course. The poor dog wears a cast on his right back leg and one of those cones around his neck so he can't bite off the cast. He is miserable, so is N. She misses me, she wants me. Can't I tell J. about her and move in with her? No, I reply. I will not hurt J. She has treated me better than anyone in my whole life. I feel so confused back at the colony I can't work. I leave early and go back home to J. I vow to break it off with N. It's just sentimentality, I tell myself, and more than a little revenge. The woman who spurned you now begs you to live with her. Sometimes I hate her for complicating my life.

Capitol Hill in August is humid, hot, impossible. J. finds a studio for rent a few blocks from our apartment where she can silk-screen her photographs.

"In Moscow," 1991

She sets up a desk and file cabinet for me there. She will share the studio with me. The more she does for me the more I hate myself. I am cold to N.'s imploring calls, but I always call her back.

September. The Feast of San Gennaro blares outside N.'s windows that look out over Mulberry Street, across from old St. Patrick's Cathedral. I am enroute to an upstate school. This is the last time I can see her, I explain. I have to be off early the next morning. Late that night N. answers the phone.

"Yes, he's right here," she says cheerfully. "Would you like to speak to him?" I know it's J. I have carelessly (or perhaps not) left N.'s number on the desk at the studio. J. knows everything. She starts to cry when I say hello. I bluster and try to deny everything, then start to cry myself.

The next winter I have my first appointment with Dr. Bose. N. has arranged this through her shrink. She thinks it's wonderful that I have been seeing a psychiatrist in Washington. New York is full of them, she says. The best ones. I'll soon get over my guilt about J.—who is miserable and depressed on A Street, but who insisted that I move out. J. calls me and tells me that she doesn't know how much longer she can stand the pain I have caused her. "Betrayed" is the word she uses, as if we had been living in a country of our own making and I had defected. I tell her that I hurt, too, that I truly loved her and still do. She says she knows I have feelings, but at least I have N. to comfort me.

I feel trapped in the cramped Prince Street apartment with N. I think I begin to hate her more than I love her. I have no place to work. The apartment, which had seemed charming on visits, is now crammed with my belongings. The dog, still hobbling around, seems confused. Who lives here anyway?

Bose infuriates me during the first session. He tells me that the matrons at the orphans' home have done a number on me. That I really yearn for respectability and middle-class status. That I am not a committed revolutionary at all but merely anti-social and, probably, a psychopath, hence my involvement with confrontational politics during the sixties. I am outraged and vow never to see this rude "Krauthead" (Dr. Bose is a German immigrant) again. It is amazing how I revert to my hated stepfather's prejudices when I am angry.

Two years pass. I leave Bose's office every two weeks disturbed, sometimes in one of my rages, but I always return. He tells me truths about myself that I have been blind to, ugly truths about selfishness and narcissism, and using others, manipulating them. He says the fantasy defenses I built as a child serve me ill

as an adult. I must take full responsibility for myself, for my life. Nobody can replace the relatively carefree childhood I didn't have. He weans me from Xanax. No longer do I convulsively clutch the pill vial in my pocket when I feel a panic attack coming on. I do a deep-breathing exercise instead. I learn, reluctantly, to withstand the terror of these attacks.

And they lessen after one breakthrough nightmare: I am being chased from room to room in a haunted house by a group. I know the house is haunted because it is endless, the hallways never end, and the front door creaks when I open it. I have been told by my mother not to play in this house. Bad people live there. Insane people. And they do. They won't let me join their gang and the leader, dressed in black, wears a full-face black mask. He mocks my every imploring word. A long, blue-handled dagger appears in his hand. I know him, and I know he has no mercy in his heart—that he hates everyone and everything. He chases me down one of the endless halls but I am cunning. I duck into a room and peek at him as he approaches, dagger upraised in the classic murderer's posture, then karate-kick his elbow, and slip a cobra hold on him, a move I practiced for years in karate class. I have the bastard now. Just a little pressure from my left hand will break his neck. He drops the knife, goes limp, and starts to bawl.

I let him go, ripping the mask from his face. The face of doom, my own, stares back at me wearing the smirking grin I get when drunk.

"How do you like it?" he asks. "Neat costume, eh." I stare, shocked by my malicious-face double, the nightmare I've had since I was ten, a masked man chasing me down with a huge dagger upraised. He stabs me again and again. I always woke up screaming from those nightmares but not this time. The only model I have for this confrontation is the plot of an old episode of "Star Trek," in which Captain Kirk is divided into separate ego and id selves. I reasoned with my double the way the Captain did. I will hold and comfort him.

He twists away. "You never let me feel *good*," he screams, "I want to feel good."

I take him, trembling, into my arms. "It's time for us to grow up," I tell him, feeling cornball for saying such a trite thing. My *Doppelganger* would have to be a stereotype!

I wake from this dream in my small room at the Barn, Edward Albee's colony for artists in Montauk, New York. I wonder if I have screamed and woken up my friends Leah and Karl down the hall. Everything is quiet, a few stubborn crickets mixing a perfect blend of stillness in the early morning fog. I try to be quiet, making coffee downstairs in the

The author at Blue Mountain Center, 1991

kitchen. I sit down to write. I have never felt better—
I have never written better poems.

The Stars Like Minstrels Sing to Blake

A wire strung with starlings, all
fluffed and bobbed in a stormy wind
black as their shako tails.
They seem to be squeezing that electric wire.
They seem to be playing it with their feet,
the stops pitched higher than human hearing,
like some kind of music of the hemispheres—
like 24 hands at the same piano.
When they leave together
the way a school of bait-fish jump
from shallows when a shadow
veers into view
the wire that hums volts to this studio
swings like a jump-rope—about to explode
and snap through the window. If you were holding
   me now
a current of fear might light up your bones like mine.

My grandmother said never reach to help
man, woman, or child that's been struck by
        lightning. Leave them there
on the ground, by a tree, or a tractor. The current
   remains

live long after the scorched heart
stills in the blazed body
and if you even touch them
you'll light up once and turn dark forever.

Though the stars like minstrels sing to Blake
I don't woo death any more than those birds
that ignorant of science rest
clef feet on a singing wire.
But it's necessary to touch death sometimes.
It's necessary to reach out for bodies
struck by lightning
slumped on city streets these days—
superstitious bodies
lying there all exposed
blazed with the mark of Cain—
bundles that might explode
and light you up like a Christmas tree.

              (From *Working Firewood for the Night*)

Wanda Pickles

In the talent search you sang *Smoke Gets in Your Eyes*
In such a chanteuse way that Jack Pease and I
Stopped making fun of everything and
Goosing one another and the fat girls whose butts
Stuck out of those metal folding chairs
In the cafeteria-auditorium. Wanda Pikulski,
Touched by a magic wand—I mean smoke *did*

Get in our mean eyes and every boy in the 8th
And 9th grades dropped the drawers of adolescent
Adoration down to his ankles for the cross-eyed girl
Who never said more than an averted hi. Good-
goddamn!
The sweet-strings background music staticked out of
Those old bullhorn speakers, and above it and
through it
And beyond it thrilled that unbelievable contralto
voice,
Assured, controlled, husky in all the right places. And
how
Dressed up you were in that low-cut gown, make-up
and no
Glasses, and the spotlight on you like a rouged Miss
America.
When you repeated "When a lovely flame dies,"
A thousand 13-year-old hearts died right there with
you and
ached
For you never to stop. Wanda "Pickles," the nerdy
duckling,
So sophisticated she could have been a movie star.
And it
Wasn't just the song but the way you hung out over
the edge
Of the melody, pushing it up and over the entire
Lowell
Junior High Assembly, including the teachers in the
back
Row—as if you were the heroine on a precipice
And kept hanging over, teetering there to our oohs
and aahs
And the prayer of Sweet Jesus don't let her fall over.
We knew
in our
Nasty but innocent hearts that in a being so
transformed
Into sweet celebrity, there was hope for us all.

That in the agony of acne and pimples that bled
And all those hormones ballooning in our bodies,
And voices that were adenoidal and sinus-hoarse—
That never repeated anything the way it was
rehearsed
In the fever of imagination, where they were always
suave
As Melvyn Douglas wooing Greta Garbo
At the Orpheum Theater on Saturday night—
Where we never suffered the nerves of bad breath
Or had our voices, strangulated, break—
You were not only speaking but singing for us all,
And you brought the song off with a high crescendo,
Leaving the last sibilant, the last liquid syllable
Like a soap bubble poised in the air,
Trembling with the promise of a rainbow life.

(From *Working Firewood for the Night*)

Untitled

I want the stillness of snow in woods
when big-slow pieces trail down through trees
and the lights have gone out in all the houses
and snow is alone with itself—alone

with that other hush
that only the sick and wounded hear.
I want to close my eyes and imagine snow
drifting down on them—
as if I were a falling tree lying out in a field,
as if I didn't care anymore about the living,
the always-trying of one breath on another,
but settled myself in to breathe like snow
and the planet's slow turning through the starry dark.
I don't want to think of anything ahead
but more and more infinite and infinite spaces
and more and more stillness, more and more dark.
I want to remember when I was falling and dying
late last summer, the ambulance and helicopter,
and how I lay there like a weathered log
being pushed and prodded
busily back toward a loud life.
I want to remember how I turned away—
how I wish they would all just leave me alone—
for I was imagining winter then,
seeing range after range of mountain woods
lit up by dark lamps of snow.
As I sank in cold-sweat lakes of pain,
as I passed out again and again,
I came to enjoy such a sweet relief
I was like a child, the only one awake
in a houseful of strangers,
the one who goes to a balcony
and puts his hands on the snowy railing
and feels his body draw back from the cold
but is so enchanted by the spectacle of snow
in darkness and stillness
he decides to walk out in the woods and sleep there.
And so amid the sharp-cold voices,
        the needles and tubes and lights,
my body swollen and feverish,
I was walking through woods
in the fiery dark,
I was a candle burning,
I was a light in the distance,
I was wind where the wind dies down with a hush,
I was a slender tree,
I was someone who keeps on going the wrong way,
I was one of those small animals
        whose homes are never found,
I was a child trailing through snow
back to its own world.

(From *Working Firewood for the Night*, also appears
        in *The American Poetry Review*)

Rembrandt's Horses

You used to fondle my shirts and jackets,
you said, while I was long away.
You slid open the slatted closet door
and felt the soft forms pinioned there
in the dark,
shoulders, sleeves, the odd loose button,
the Pendletons with torn pockets,
the Donegal tweed
with the broken back.
You toed as if for South Bay clams
the dirty sneakers
piled up like tires.

In that respect you were like my mother
who mourned my father by keeping his clothes
pristine in garment bags. You were like her, too,
in letting me dither, make all the conversation
during the long-sullen silences.

I wish you hadn't liked Rembrandt's horses,
the stallions on the poster taped to the door—
liked them so well you hung six more copies
around the studio like mobiles.
No matter in which direction I turned
those strobe-light eyes revolved to meet me.
I recognized, I knew those eyes,
red as a wolf-pack's in the dark.
I felt those frenzied bodies,
milling, rushing back and forth,
breaking down the barriers.

I would like to open that old closet
now that it's empty,
now that broken-shouldered hangers
stir like homemade wind chimes
everytime one of those moving vans
shifts gears
halfway up the hill to the warehouse-

now that those crazed horses
round far turns known as nightmares,
rolling their eyes like police car sirens
rushing through the night—

now that you fondle another man
and make believe his clothes are him
I would like to sit in that old closet
and hug my knees,
the way I used to when mother locked me
away with a final click, shouting: "I hate your face,
I can't stand your father's goddamn face! Now play in
    there."
I would like to slide open the slatted door
and whisper to the dirty and huddled boy:
"The eyes you see are yours, not your father's,
the hate-stubborn eyes you see are yours."

I might then let go of all the confusion—
the times I imagined hurting mother,
the times my body went slack with love—
and lose, too, the appetite for pride,
the appetite for the feral and unforgiving,
the appetite for sadness—

and, most of all, let go of regret:
that I always thought
of the perfect thing that should have been said
to you, to mother, to all the others—
the words that could have saved my father
the night he drove away, drunk—
a moment, a day, a week or so later.

Our heart's desire is not for love
but to make one moment
match the imagination.

(From the new poems section of *La Traviata in
    Oklahoma, Selected and New Poems, 1961–1991*)

Breakfast in Iraq

Greetings to you from "Mrs. Death,"
Stencilled on the cannon of an American tank
By a crew illiterate of e.e. cummings,
The barrel knobby with instrumentation,
The lipstick-shaped shells poised to "kiss some ass."
Such sleek technology, such genius for destruction,
Such a seamless fusion of function and design
(While at home the homeless drift around
Like crippled vultures,
And more and more of the middle class
Stare wall-eyed at vacant walls),
Such pure American utilitarianism—
Hearkening back to the first repeating rifles
And double-action six-guns that won the West
From "primitives with crooked arrows"—
This triumph of style of over gross content,
So pleasing to the current aesthetic eye,
May in a flash that leaves an afterglow
Like halos fading through the retina
Convert the human eye into jam or jelly
And the body it balanced into burnt toast.

(From the new poems section of *La Traviata in
    Oklahoma, Selected and New Poems, 1961–1991*)

Taken Away

"Don't whip that goddamned saw. Let
the tool do the work." The voice, low,
and guttural, and spent—
without emotion—meaning only what was meant.
This belted one stinks of gasoline.
I have been trimming the old maple all this
    morning,
and letting my thoughts idle like the saw
    in idle moments—
wasting the earth's bile, and raising my own.

"You son-of-a-bitch," I replied, to myself,
"Mother knows you raped my sister.
You're going to jail. You are going to
    jail!"
Yet his rhythm was like a rocking horse's—
steady as the hymn that feathered from his throat
    last Sunday morning
like some huge black bird with its yellow eyes
    blind on a paradise
of thirteen-year-old raven-haired maidens,
    like my sister.
Mother chimed, and took everything in.

In those woods I rocked from cloud to tree
and back to rock. From my pulpit-stump
I converted the heathen animals
(those he had not shot)
to a kind of pagan Christianity:
They were free to worship the old gods of crows,
    bluejays, sunlight,
meadows, clearings, the round of seasons,
    the clouds' tall ghost ships in procession—
only they must not *do* original sin.

They must not sin and yet be natural
as the gander and goose he bought my mother

for agreeing to come back to this "place
   forsaken"
(they collected us from the Children's Home
matrons bragged we might not leave).
The geese had never seen one another before
   but loved the other in watery reflections.
O it was a fairy beginning!
I thought all life must have the dignity,
   the slow devotions of those birds.

This rusty chair honks like a goose,
and I am reminded of their grave eyes
   and winding necks
as they saw my mother, taut as a hatchet.
She was killing all her garbled hopes and dreams—
   the shame of sickness, the shame of her children
in orphanages and foster homes.
She was deriding most the promises of men—
"the providers, the rapers of children."
If she could have managed it alone, she would that
   day
     have laid her own fevered neck across that bloody
      stump.

He arranged the yellow-eyed heads like question
   marks
back on their sockets,
and cupped the still-warm bodies side to side,
then held his own head in his hands,
as if he had been the one decapitated,
whiskery face blotched blue and red,
as an hour-glass flow of red dirt fluted
from the end of my shovel down to the white breasts.

"No need at all, no need at all . . ." He strangled
and stuttered and started in with the saw,
and me, again—as if he found in that rhythm
     a poem or a prayer that said it all.
So we sweated on, working firewood for the night,
waiting for a siren to interrupt the drone
     and rasp of dialogue between us—
waiting till police forced us to abandon
   in mid-stroke steel teeth in bark
(the crosscut saw tilted toward the heavens)
and the guilt our bloody hands held in common.

          (From *Working Firewood for the Night*)

Verdigris

     For Nina, Hanukkah-Christmas, 1989

Swiss powdered soup, Italian water
cold from a courtyard spigot,
splashed into a Boy Scout camp-cook pot,
a tea bag of Tuscan herbs
lowered into this verdigris . . .
flames from a Sterno can
scorching the slick aluminum,
dyeing a ring on the Florentine floor—
tiles so bleached the pairs of long-robed figures
linked across them look like stains.
You, kneeling, brushing hair
back with one hand while the other
trails a spoon that steers the crusts
and bubbles breaking on the soup.

We knew the dog of the concierge
across the street only by its yowling
that went off, wolf-like, with the Catholic bells
on Sunday mornings. Their resonance,
and the lone coyote-calling,
half-clown and half-saint,
disturbed us like half-waking dreams.
We dubbed him "born-again,"
the saint of Sunday mornings,
the wolf that nips the stolid sheep
and herds them out to Elysian pastures
where god, like Moses with flint-rock eyes
pinches the Devil with a witching wand
that makes him spring up straight
and speak in tongues.

We liked our mornings still
on the stone courtyard stairs
cool with condensation,
heavy with trellises
of dewy morning glories,
our milk and coffee aerial,
the wall-shadows evaporating.

Firenze, 1966, Prince Street, 1989—
I think as I watch the blue gas flames
raise the kettle to a soprano pitch
of that albergo and its name,
"Speranza e Commercio,"—
how it was so unthinkable then
to link commerce with hope,
or predict I would move those shadowed mornings
back toward today.
I see your kneeling figure where
you were only 19, the grave-blank face,
a girl's graveness,
a figure I might have seen in Hals,
a late teen-age girl and her grieving—
the loneliness of unbound breasts
tendered to a room of drunken men.

When I bring our coffee to the bed
the spiderwebs on your sleeping face,
the inaudible breath, the tide of dreaming
trembling through a fisted hand,
break in my throat a tuneless song,
and I want to howl like that dumb dog
for the nameless feelings that will not be stilled,
for the charity of women's bodies—
for the veins that climb your thighs
like blue morning glories.

          (From *Working Firewood for the Night*)

BIBLIOGRAPHY

Poetry:

Uncertainties, The Smith, 1968.

Indian Territory and Other Poems, The Smith, 1974.

Feral: Crow Breath and Caw, Conspiracy Press, 1975.

For Luck: Poems 1962–1977, Carnegie-Mellon University Press, 1977.

And the Man Who Was Traveling Never Got Home, Carnegie-Mellon University Press, 1980.

Working Firewood for the Night, The Smith, 1990.

La Traviata in Oklahoma: Selected and New Poems, 1961–1991, The Smith, 1992.

Nonfiction:

I Fall in Love with Nancy Drew (memoir), forthcoming.

Represented in anthologies, including *Men of Our Time: Contemporary Male Poetry in America,* University of Georgia Press, 1992, and *Only Morning in Her Shoes,* Utah State University Press, 1991. Contributor, since 1959, of more than 300 poems to periodicals, including *American Poetry Review, Harper's, Nation, Georgia Review, Ohio Review, New Letters, South Dakota Review* and *The Smith.*

Cumulative Index

CUMULATIVE INDEX

The names of essayists who appear in the series are in boldface type. Subject references are followed by volume and page number(s). When a subject reference appears in more than one essay, names of the essayists are also provided.

INDEX

INDEX

INDEX